D0572023

SECOND EDITION

JUVENILE DELINQUENCY

Historical, Theoretical, and Societal Reactions to Youth

Editors

Paul M. Sharp

Auburn University at Montgomery

Barry W. Hancock

Indiana University/South Bend

Prentice Hall
Upper Saddle River, New Jersey 07458

Library of Congress Cataloging-in-Publication Data

Juvenile delinquency : historical, theoretical, and societal reactions
   to youth / edited by Paul M. Sharp, Barry W. Hancock. —2nd ed.
         p.   cm.
   Includes bibliographical references.
   ISBN 0-13-237272-X (paper)
      1. Juvenile delinquency—United States.   I. Sharp, Paul M.
   II. Hancock, Barry W.
   HV9104.J845   1998
   364.36'0973—dc21   97-35450
                                                                              CIP

Editorial director: Charlyce Jones Owen
Editor in chief: Nancy Roberts
Associate editor: Sharon Chambliss
Editorial/production supervision
   and interior design: Mary Araneo
Buyer: Mary Ann Gloriande
Cover director: Jayne Conte

This book was set in 10/11 New Baskerville by A & A Publishing Services, Inc.,
and was printed and bound by Hamilton Printing Company. The cover
was printed by Phoenix Color Corp.

© 1998, 1995 by Prentice-Hall, Inc.
A Pearson Education Company
Upper Saddle River, New Jersey 07458

Printed in the United States of America

10 9 8 7 6 5 4 3 2 1

ISBN 0-13-237272-X

Prentice-Hall International (UK) Limited, London
Prentice-Hall of Australia Pty. Limited, Sydney
Prentice-Hall Canada Inc., Toronto
Prentice-Hall Hispanoamericana, S.A., Mexico
Prentice-Hall of India Private Limited, New Delhi
Prentice-Hall of Japan, Inc., Tokyo
Pearson Education Asia Pte. Ltd., Singapore
Editoria Prentice-Hall do Brasil, Ltda., Rio De Janeiro

Contents

Preface   xi

PART I: HISTORY OF THE LEGAL AND SOCIAL DEFINITIONS OF JUVENILE DELINQUENCY   1

1 The Child-Saving Movement and the Origins of the Juvenile Justice System, Anthony Platt   3

Questions for Discussion, Applications, and Key Terms   17

2 Attitudes and Policies Toward Juvenile Delinquency in the United States: A Historiographical Review, Robert M. Mennel   19

Questions for Discussion, Applications, and Key Terms   39

3 The Crime of Precocious Sexuality: Female Juvenile Delinquency in the Progressive Era, Steven Schlossman and Stephanie Wallach   41

Questions for Discussion, Applications, and Key Terms   62

4 History Overtakes the Juvenile Justice System, Theodore N. Ferdinand   64

Questions for Discussion, Applications, and Key Terms   77

PART II: THEORIES OF JUVENILE DELINQUENCY 78

5 Social Structure and Anomie,
Robert K. Merton 81

Questions for Discussion, Applications, and Key Terms 88

6 Social Learning and Deviant Behavior: A Specific Test of General Theory,
Ronald L. Akers, Marvin D. Krohn, Lonn Lanza-Kaduce, Marcia Radosevich 90

Questions for Discussion, Applications, and Key Terms 97

7 A Control Theory of Delinquency,
Travis Hirschi 98

Questions for Discussion, Applications, and Key Terms 104

8 Techniques of Neutralization: A Theory of Delinquency,
Gresham M. Sykes, David Matza 105

Questions for Discussion, Applications, and Key Terms 111

9 Social Change and Crime Rate Trends: A Routine Activity Approach,
Lawrence E. Cohen, Marcus Felson 113

Questions for Discussion, Applications, and Key Terms 133

10 Poverty, Income Inequality, and Community Crime Rates,
E. Britt Patterson 135

Questions for Discussion, Applications, and Key Terms 150

11 Toward an Interactional Theory of Delinquency,
Terence P. Thornberry 151

Questions for Discussion, Applications, and Key Terms 168

12 Girls, Crime and Woman's Place: Toward a Feminist Model of Female Delinquency, Meda Chesney-Lind **169**

Questions for Discussion, Applications, and Key Terms **184**

13 Foundation for a General Strain Theory of Crime and Delinquency, Robert Agnew **185**

Questions for Discussion, Applications, and Key Terms **210**

PART III: THE SOCIAL CONTEXT OF JUVENILE DELINQUENCY 212

14 At the Roots of Violence: The Progressive Decline and Desolution of the Family, George B. Palermo, Douglas Simpson **214**

Questions for Discussion, Applications, and Key Terms **222**

15 Delinquency and the Age Structure of Society, David F. Greenburg **223**

Questions for Discussion, Applications, and Key Terms **238**

16 School Bonding, Race, and Delinquency, Stephen A. Cernkovich, Peggy C. Giordano **240**

Questions for Discussion, Applications, and Key Terms **259**

17 The Neophyte Female Delinquent: A Review of the Literature, George Calhoun, Janelle Jurgens, Fengling Chen **260**

Questions for Discussion, Applications, and Key Terms **266**

18 Recent Gang Research: Program and Policy Implications, James C. Howell **268**

Questions for Discussion, Applications, and Key Terms **280**

19 Players and Ho's,
Terry Williams, William Kornblum **282**

Questions for Discussion, Applications, and Key Terms **290**

20 The Saints and the Roughnecks,
William J. Chambliss **291**

Questions for Discussion, Applications, and Key Terms **300**

**PART IV: INSTITUTIONAL RESPONSES TO JUVENILE
DELINQUENCY 302**

21 The Gault Decision: Due Process and the Juvenile Courts,
Alan Neigher **304**

Questions for Discussion, Applications, and Key Terms **316**

22 A Comparative Analysis of Organizational Structure and Inmate
Subcultures in Institutions for Juvenile Offenders, Barry C. Feld **317**

Questions for Discussion, Applications, and Key Terms **333**

23 Juvenile Diversion: A Look at the Record,
Kenneth Polk **335**

Questions for Discussion, Applications, and Key Terms **342**

24 Juvenile Parole Policy in the United States: Determinate versus
Indeterminate Models, Jose B. Ashford, Craig Winston LeCroy **343**

Questions for Discussion, Applications, and Key Terms **354**

25 Females Under the Law: "Protected" but Unequal,
Gail Armstrong **355**

Questions for Discussion, Applications, and Key Terms **364**

26 Restitution and Recidivism Rates of Juvenile Offenders: Results from Four Experimental Studies, Anne L. Schneider **366**

Questions for Discussion, Applications, and Key Terms 379

PART V: JUVENILE DELINQUENCY AND PUBLIC POLICY 380

27 Rethinking the Juvenile Justice System, Travis Hirschi, Michael R. Gottfredson **382**

Questions for Discussion, Applications, and Key Terms 388

28 Juvenile Justice and the Blind Lady, Hunter Hurst, Louis W. McHardy **390**

Questions for Discussion, Applications, and Key Terms 398

29 A Policy Maker's Guide to Controlling Delinquency and Crime through Family Interventions, Karen E. Wright, Kevin N. Wright **399**

Questions for Discussion, Applications, and Key Terms 410

30 Serious and Violent Juvenile Crime: A Comprehensive Strategy, John J. Wilson, James C. Howell **412**

Questions for Discussion, Applications, and Key Terms 423

31 Emerging Trends and Issues in Juvenile Justice, Michael F. Aloisi **424**

Questions for Discussion, Applications, and Key Terms 435

Preface

This collection of readings in juvenile delinquency is aimed at satisfying professors and students in both undergraduate and graduate programs that include courses which focus on the subject of delinquency. We are especially proud that there is no particular ideological agenda followed in this collection. Quite simply, we have created a comprehensive work which contains classics in the field, contemporary research articles, some much-needed historical materials, yet remains nonencyclopedic in presentation.

We began the collection with several goals in mind. First, we wanted an anthology that was more comprehensive, in-depth, and yet more readable than any currently available. We have produced a unique set of readings that can be used alone or used to supplement a text in courses in juvenile delinquency and other crime-related courses. Brought together in one work for the first time are a combination of historical pieces, classic and contemporary theoretical articles, and the inclusion of more materials concerning females, gangs, violence among teens, and societal reactions to youth.

Second, we wanted to create pedagogical materials which would facilitate the student in understanding the articles, aid the professor in the presentation of the subject, and serve as an avenue towards further discussions and applications of the key concepts and ideas. This was achieved by creating three sections at the end of each article which draw materials, ideas, and terms from each article as well as from the larger body of delinquency literature. The questions for discussion, applications, and key terms combine to make the book easy to use as a primary text. Further, these exercises are a unique feature of this anthology.

Third, we wanted more articles and information concerning female delinquency, legal issues in delinquency, and public policy information. The addition of this type of information challenges traditional old-school approaches to the study of delinquency. Deletion of these materials in many texts is indicative of, as we see it, an ideological myopia balanced in favor of the author and not the reader.

Fourth, the measurement and magnitude of delinquency in this collection is not covered in the traditional sense by using the official sources for offenses: court statistics, huge national studies, or data banks. Many of these issues are covered directly or indirectly in several of the articles, and we feel most professors can teach the source materials for official and unofficial delinquency much better in lecture than we could by providing articles which typically argue strengths or weaknesses of collection techniques. The methodological issues of measurement, estimates, and trends in delinquency-related behaviors are complex and create some of the most highly debated issues in the field. We feel that a base for understanding data sources must come from the instructor, with strengths, weaknesses, and possible solutions being parts of the discussion concerning the collection as well as the uses of these data.

Juvenile Delinquency: Historical, Theoretical, and Societal Reactions to Youth is organized into five parts. The first, "History of the Legal and Social Constructions of Juvenile Delinquency," presents four articles that form, as a whole, a solid foundation upon which an understanding of historical definitions of youth statuses and behavioral expectations becomes possible in light of today's juvenile justice system. We selected these articles to serve as a backdrop to understanding the dynamics of the historical definitions and subsequent legal and societal reactions to youth and youth behavior. This historical treatment is a unique feature not found in many anthologies of this kind and rarely presented except in encyclopedic formats.

Part II, "Theories of Juvenile Delinquency," presents classic as well as contemporary theoretical ideas of delinquency. Certainly, one could create a book dedicated exclusively to theory and nothing more. Our goal, however, was to present articles which represent some of the most outstanding theoretical genre dealing with crime and delinquency. These readings, combined with the articles concerning history, challenge the reader to broaden the concept of delinquency and vividly expose the confusion in dealing with youth statuses, behavioral expectations, self-concept, youth culture, and theoretical attempts at explanation.

Part III, "The Social Context of Juvenile Delinquency," presents some of the livelier readings in the collection. Families, schools, subcultural groups, youth culture, the idea of "crime as play," and drug use are addressed in articles that are squarely in the social problems area of the delinquency field. This collection ranges from traditional to contemporary approaches to understanding youth and delinquency issues.

In Part IV, "Institutional Responses to Juvenile Delinquency," we address some of the most important concepts and issues in delinquency research: the legal and formal institutional actions and reactions towards youth and delinquency. The legal processes of restricting rights and then extending rights along with the differential treatment of youths and adults makes this section vitally important. The differential responses of formal organizations based on status rather than behavior is central to understanding delinquency as well as the broader societal reactions to youth.

Finally, Part V, "Juvenile Delinquency and Public Policy," presents five problem-solving arguments which range from social science research to justice system overhaul. Hopefully, these selections will add fuel to the debates as to future directions in delinquency research and social problem solutions. The selections here point out the difficulties experienced in solution-directed research. Public policy debate, after all, is often balanced on a fine line between the rights of individuals and the rights of society.

ACKNOWLEDGMENTS

We would like to extend our appreciation to several people who assisted us in preparing *Juvenile Delinquency: Historical, Theoretical, and Societal Reactions to Youth*. Nancy Roberts, executive editor at Prentice Hall, and her staff and production team were invaluable with assisting in the development and production of this text anthology. It is simply a pleasure to have this sort of professional working relationship. We'd also line to acknowledge the following Prentice Hall reviewers for their input: Eric L. Jensen of the University of Idaho and Barry A. Kinsey of The University of Tulsa. Our sincere thanks go out to all of those individuals concerned with the welfare of our young people, regardless of the scope and depth of their caring and involvement. Finally, to our many students who voiced their opinions that studying original sources added greatly to their learning experiences, we extend our gratitude.

JUVENILE DELINQUENCY

I

HISTORY OF THE LEGAL AND SOCIAL CONSTRUCTIONS OF JUVENILE DELINQUENCY

Understanding juvenile delinquency requires a familiarity with the historical treatments of the legal and social constructions of children and youth. Statuses, and the behavioral expectations related to age, have historically been and are powerful social forces in every society. These expectations have created many ideals of childhood and young adulthood that are in constant conflict with the dynamic changes brought on by the rapidity of modernization over the past two centuries. The age at which an individual acquires the status of adult and what constitutes delinquency are two of the most poignant issues that have shaped the definitions, research, and societal reactions to youth in the modern world. In most respects, societal reactions to youth have had more influence on the current definitions, attitudes, and responses to delinquency than any other single variable. Throughout the world, with few exceptions, children are considered different from adults and thus require special kinds of care and treatment. In fact, our current conceptions of childhood grew out of the fertile philosophical debates in Europe during the enlightenment that forged a new concern for the moral and social welfare of children instead of the exploitation and manipulation considered acceptable practices in previous times.

The reforms that began in Europe gave tremendous momentum to the formalization of a separate system for children and youth. We have selected four articles for Part I of the anthology that represent a superb collection dealing with the many historical and social constructions of youth. The antecedants to the current system of juvenile justice are to be found in the historical developments and ideological issues addressed so eloquently by these authors.

The cornerstone of the historical constructions of juvenile delinquency, in our anthology, begins with Anthony Platt's superb article "The Child-Saving Movement and the Origins of the Juvenile Justice System." Platt argues, as do many others, that the system of juvenile justice achieved success by rationalizing the dependent status of youth. The preoccupation with the control of youth was the prevailing ideological foundation upon which much of the system has evolved. The state as superparent, the emergence of the juvenile court, and the reformatory movement are examples of this powerful rationalizing force regarding youth as a dependent status.

Our second selection, "Attitudes and Policies toward Juvenile Delinquency in the United States: A Historiographical Review" by Robert M. Mennel, is critical of the policy-making processes and historical accounts of juvenile delinquency. Mennel covers a wide array of subject matter from the beginnings of definitions of youthful mis-behavior to the development of the juvenile court. This article provides an excellent set of references for further study with some of the most important and famous works in the history of delinquency cited.

"The Crime of Precocious Sexuality: Female Juvenile Delinquency in the Pro-gressive Era" is a historical essay by Steven Schlossman and Stephenie Wallach that implicitly draws relevant parallels to our contemporary juvenile justice system. These parallels mirror the progressive era practices of discrimination and unequal treat-ment. Most important, it is the societal reactions to the status of youth rather than the behavior that should remind us of the ideology of the past that has, largely, shaped the juvenile justice system of today. The combination of statuses such as gender, delin-quency, and race as they relate to discriminatory practices provides a remarkable foun-dation for further understanding the history of a separate system for juveniles in the United States.

We conclude Part I with a more recent historical piece by Theodore N. Ferdi-nand, "History Overtakes the Juvenile Justice System." Ferdinand eloquently argues that many of the juvenile courts' problems today stem from the ambivalence created by trying to fulfill the *parens patriae* doctrine within the bounds of civil court processes. These processes are difficult, if not impossible, given the custodial or punitive design of the system. The historical shift to a due process/just deserts orientation by which juveniles are treated more like adults in a retributive justice system may have dire consequences for future crime rates and the entire system of criminal justice. Of sig-nificance in much of your reading in the area of delinquency is the continuing debate raised over the issue of treatment as opposed to punishment. Treatment programs for youthful offenders, because of the ideological swing toward retributive justice, are under attack from many sides. While most reformers and scholars realize that selec-tive incapacitation is a reality when dealing with extreme forms of violence among youth, they also realize that most young people are in need of guidance and minor intervention.

1

The Child-Saving Movement and the Origins of the Juvenile Justice System

Anthony Platt

TRADITIONAL PERSPECTIVES ON JUVENILE JUSTICE

The modern system of crime control in the United States has many roots in penal and judicial reforms at the end of the nineteenth century. Contemporary programs which we commonly associate with the "war on poverty" and the "great society" [of the 1960s] can be traced in numerous instances to the programs and ideas of nineteenth century reformers who helped to create and develop probation and parole, the juvenile court, strategies of crime prevention, the need for education and rehabilitative programs in institutions, the indeterminate sentence, the concept of "half-way" houses, and "cottage" systems of penal organization.

The creation of the juvenile court and its accompanying services is generally regarded by scholars as one of the most innovative and idealistic products of the age of reform. It typified the "spirit of social justice," and, according to the National Crime Commission, represented a progressive effort by concerned reformers to alleviate the miseries of urban life and to solve social problems by rational, enlightened and scientific methods.[1] The juvenile justice system was widely heralded as "one of the greatest advances in child welfare that has ever occurred" and "an integral part of total welfare planning."[2] Charles Chute, an enthusiastic supporter of the child-saving movement, claimed that "no single event has contributed more to the welfare of children and their families. It revolutionized the treatment of delinquent and neglected children and led to the passage of similar laws throughout the world."[3] Scholars from a variety of disciplines, such as the American sociologist George Herbert Mead and the German psychiatrist August Aichhorn, agreed that the juvenile court system represented a triumph of progressive liberalism over the forces of reaction and ignorance.[4] More recently, the juvenile court and related reforms have been characterized as a "reflection of the humanitarianism that flowered in the last decades of the 19th century"[5] and an indication of "America's great sense of philanthropy and private concern about the common weal."[6]

Histories and accounts of the child-saving movement tend either to represent an "official" perspective or to imply a gradualist view of social progress.[7] This latter view is typified in Robert Pickett's study of the House of Refuge movement in New York in the middle of the last century:

In the earlier era, it had taken a band of largely religiously motivated humanitarians to see a need and move to meet that need. Although much of their vision eventually would be sup-

"The Child-Saving Movement and the Origins of the Juvenile Justice System," in Richard Quinney (Ed.), *Criminal Justice in America* (Boston: Little Brown, 1974), pp. 362–383. © 1974 by Anthony Platt.

planted by more enlightened policies and techniques and far more elaborate support mechanisms, the main outlines of their program, which included mild discipline, academic and moral education, vocational training, the utilization of surrogate parents, and probationary surveillance, have stood the test of time. The survival of many of the notions of the founders of the House of Refuge testifies, at least in part, to their creative genius in meeting human needs. Their motivations may have been mixed and their oversights many, but their efforts contributed to a considerable advance in the care and treatment of wayward youth.[8]

This view of the nineteenth century reform movement as fundamentally benevolent, humanitarian and gradualist is shared by most historians and criminologists who have written about the Progressive era. They argue that this reform impulse has its roots in the earliest ideals of modern liberalism and that it is part of a continuing struggle to overcome injustice and fulfill the promise of American life.[9] At the same time, these writers recognize that reform movements often degenerate into crusades and suffer from excessive idealism and moral absolutism.[10] The faults and limitations of the child-saving movement, for example, are generally explained in terms of the psychological tendency of its leaders to adopt attitudes of rigidity and moral righteousness. But this form of criticism is misleading because it overlooks larger political issues and depends too much on a subjective critique.

Although the Progressive era was a period of considerable change and reform in all areas of social, legal, political and economic life, its history has been garnished with various myths. Conventional historical analysis, typified by the work of American historians in the 1940s and 1950s, promoted the view that American history consisted of regular confrontations between vested economic interests and various popular reform movements.[11] For Arthur Schlesinger, Jr., "liberalism in America has been ordinarily the movement of the other sections of society to restrain the power of the business community."[12]

. . . Conventional histories of progressivism argue that the reformers, who were for the most part drawn from the urban middle classes, were opposed to big business and felt victimized by the rapid changes in the economy, especially the emergence of the corporation as the dominant form of financial enterprise.[13] Their reform efforts were aimed at curbing the power of big business, eliminating corruption from the urban political machines, and extending the powers of the state through federal regulation of the economy and the development of a vision of "social responsibility" in local government. They were joined in this mission by sectors of the working class who shared their alienation and many of their grievances.

. . . The political and racial crises of the 1960s, however, provoked a reevaluation of this earlier view of the liberal tradition in American politics, a tradition which appeared bankrupt in the face of rising crime rates, ghetto rebellions, and widespread protests against the state and its agencies of criminal justice. In the field of criminology, this reevaluation took place in national commissions such as the Kerner Commission and President Johnson's Commission on Law Enforcement and the Administration of Justice. Johnson's Crime Commission, as it is known, included a lengthy and detailed analysis of the juvenile justice system and its ineffectiveness in dealing with juvenile delinquency.

The Crime Commission's view of the juvenile justice system is cautious and pragmatic, designed to "shore up" institutional deficiencies and modernize the system's efficiency and accountability. Noting the rising rate of juvenile delinquency, increasing disrespect for constituted authority and the failure of reformatories to rehabilitate offenders, the Commission attributes the failures of the juvenile justice system to the "grossly overoptimistic" expectations of nineteenth century reformers and the "community's continuing unwillingness to provide the resources—the people and facilities and concern—necessary to permit [the juvenile courts] to realize their potential. . . ."[14]

. . . In the following pages we will argue that the above views and interpretations of juvenile justice are factually inaccurate and suffer from a serious misconception about the functions of modern liberalism. The prevailing myths about the juvenile justice system can be summarized as follows: (1) The child-saving movement in the late nineteenth century was successful in humanizing the criminal justice system, rescuing children from jails and prisons, developing humanitarian judicial and penal institutions for juveniles, and defending the poor against economic and political exploitation. (2) The child-savers were "disinterested" reformers, representing an enlightened and socially responsible urban middle class, and opposed to big business. (3) The failures of the juvenile justice system are attributable partly to the overoptimism and moral absolutism of earlier reformers and partly to bureaucratic inefficiency and a lack of fiscal resources and trained personnel.

These myths are grounded in a liberal conception of American history which characterizes the child-savers as part of a much larger reform movement directed at restraining the power of political and business elites. In contrast, we will offer evidence that the child-saving movement was a coercive and conservatizing influence, that liberalism in the Progressive era was the conscious product of policies initiated or supported by leaders of major corporations and financial institutions, and that many social reformers wanted to secure existing political and economic arrangements, albeit in an ameliorated and regulated form.

THE CHILD-SAVING MOVEMENT

Although the modern juvenile justice system can be traced in part to the development of various charitable and institutional programs in the early nineteenth century,[15] it was not until the close of the century that the modern system was systematically organized to include juvenile courts, probation, child guidance clinics, truant officers, and reformatories. The child-saving movement—an amalgam of philanthropists, middle-class reformers and professionals—was responsible for the consolidation of these reforms.[16]

The 1890s represented for many middle-class intellectuals and professionals a period of discovery of "dim attics and damp cellars in poverty-stricken sections of populous towns" and "innumerable haunts of misery throughout the land."[17] The city was suddenly discovered to be a place of scarcity, disease, neglect, ignorance, and "dangerous influences." Its slums were the "last resorts of the penniless and the criminal"; here humanity reached the lowest level of degradation and despair.[18] These conditions were not new to American urban life and the working class had been suffering such hardships for many years. Since the Haymarket Riot of 1886, the centers of industrial activity had been continually plagued by strikes, violent disruptions, and widespread business failures.

What distinguished the late 1890s from earlier periods was the recognition by some sectors of the privileged classes that far-reaching economic, political and social reforms were desperately needed to restore order and stability. In the economy, these reforms were achieved through the corporation which extended its influence into all aspects of domestic and foreign policies so that by the 1940s some 139 corporations owned 45 percent of all the manufacturing assets in the country. It was the aim of corporate capitalists to limit traditional laissez-faire business competition and to transform the economy into a rational and interrelated system, characterized by extensive long-range planning and bureaucratic routine.[19] In politics, these reforms were achieved nationally by extending the regulatory powers of the federal government and locally by the development of commission and city manager forms of government as an antidote to corrupt machine politics. In social life, economic and political reforms were paralleled by the construction of new social service bureaucracies which regulated crime, education, health, labor and welfare.

The child-saving movement tried to do for the criminal justice system what industrialists and corporate leaders were trying to do for the economy—that is, achieve order, stability and control while preserving the existing class system and distribution of wealth. While the child-saving movement, like most Progressive reforms, drew its most active and visible supporters from the middle class and professions, it would not have been capable of achieving significant reforms without the financial and political support of the wealthy and powerful. Such support was not without precedent in various philanthropic movements preceding the child-savers. New York's Society for the Reformation of Juvenile Delinquents benefited in the 1820s from the contributions of Stephen Allen, whose many influential positions included Mayor of New York and president of the New York Life Insurance and Trust Company.[20] The first large gift to the New York Children's Aid Society, founded in 1853, was donated by Mrs. William Astor.[21] According to Charles Loring Brace, who helped to found the Children's Aid Society, "a very superior class of young men consented to serve on our Board of Trustees; men who, in their high principles of duty, and in the obligations which they feel are imposed by wealth and position, bid fair hereafter to make the name of New York merchants respected as it was never before throughout the country."[22] Elsewhere, welfare charities similarly benefited from the donations and wills of the upper class.[23] Girard College, one of the first large orphanages in the United States, was built and furnished with funds from the banking fortune of Stephen Girard,[24] and the Catholic bankers and financiers of New York helped to mobilize support and money for various Catholic charities.[25]

The child-saving movement similarly enjoyed the support of propertied and powerful individuals. In Chicago, for example, where the movement had some of its most notable successes, the child-savers included Louise Bowen and Ellen Henrotin who were both married to bankers.[26] Mrs. Potter Palmer, whose husband owned vast amounts of land and property, was an ardent child-saver when not involved in the exclusive Fortnightly Club, the elite Chicago Woman's Club or the Board of Lady Managers of the World's Fair;[27] another child-saver in Chicago, Mrs. Perry Smith, was married to the vice-president of the Chicago and Northwestern Railroad. Even the more radically-minded child-savers came from upper-class backgrounds. The fathers of Jane Addams and Julia Lathrop, for example, were both lawyers and Republican senators in the Illinois legislature. Jane Addams' father was one of the richest men in northern Illinois, and her stepbrother, Harry Haldeman, was a socialite from Baltimore who later amassed a large fortune in Kansas City.[28]

The child-saving movement was not simply a humanistic enterprise on behalf of the lower classes against the established order. On the contrary, its impetus came primarily from the middle and upper classes who were instrumental in devising new forms of social control to protect their privileged positions in American society. The child-saving movement was not an isolated phenomenon but rather reflected massive changes in productive relationships, from laissez-faire to monopoly capitalism, and in strategies of social control, from inefficient repression to welfare state benevolence.[29] This reconstruction of economic and social institutions, which was not achieved without conflict within the ruling class, represented a victory for the more "enlightened" wing of corporate leaders who advocated strategic alliances with urban reformers and support of liberal reforms.[30]

Many large corporations and business leaders, for example, supported federal regulation of the economy in order to protect their own investments and stabilize the marketplace. Business leaders and political spokesmen were often in basic agreement about fundamental economic issues.... "Few reforms were enacted without the tacit approval, if not the guidance, of the large corporate interests." For the corporation executives, liberalism meant "the responsibility of all classes to maintain and increase the efficiency of the existing social order."[31]

Progressivism was in part a businessmen's movement and big business played a central role in the Progressive coalition's support of welfare reforms. Child labor legislation in New York, for example, was supported by several groups, including upper-class industrialists who did not depend on cheap child labor. According to Jeremy Felt's history of that movement, "the abolition of child labor could be viewed as a means of driving out marginal manufacturers and tenement operators, hence increasing the consolidation and efficiency of business."[32] The rise of compulsory education, another welfare state reform, was also closely tied to the changing forms of industrial production and social control. Charles Loring Brace, writing in the mid-nineteenth century, anticipated the use of education as preparation for industrial discipline when, "in the interests of public order, of liberty, of property, for the sake of our own safety and the endurance of free institutions here," he advocated "a strict and careful law, which shall compel every minor to learn and read and write, under severe penalties in case of disobedience."[33] By the end of the century, the working class had imposed upon them a sterile and authoritarian educational system which mirrored the ethos of the corporate workplace and was designed to provide "an increasingly refined training and selection mechanism for the labor force."[34]

While the child-saving movement was supported and financed by corporate liberals, the day-to-day work of lobbying, public education and organizing was undertaken by middle-class urban reformers, professionals and special interest groups. The more moderate and conservative sectors of the feminist movement were especially active in antidelinquency reforms.[35] Their successful participation derived in part from public stereotypes of women as the "natural caretakers" of "wayward children." Women's claim to the public care of children had precedent during the nineteenth century and their role in child rearing was paramount. Women, generally regarded as better teachers than men, were more influential in child-training and discipline at home. The fact that public education also came more under the direction of women teachers in the schools served to legitimize the predominance of women in other areas of "child-saving."[36]

The child-saving movement attracted women from a variety of political and class backgrounds, though it was dominated by the daughters of the old landed gentry and wives of the upper-class nouveau riche. Career women and society philanthropists, elite women's clubs and settlement houses,

and political and civic organizations worked together on the problems of child care, education and juvenile delinquency. Professional and political women's groups regarded child-saving as a problem of women's rights, whereas their opponents seized upon it as an opportunity to keep women in their "proper place." Child-saving became a reputable task for any woman who wanted to extend her "housekeeping" functions into the community without denying anti-feminist stereotypes of woman's nature and place.[37]

For traditionally educated women and daughters of the landed and industrial gentry, the child-saving movement presented an opportunity for pursuing socially acceptable public roles and for restoring some of the authority and spiritual influence which many women felt they had lost through the urbanization of family life. Their traditional functions were dramatically threatened by the weakening of domestic roles and the specialized rearrangement of the family.[38] The child-savers were aware that their championship of social outsiders such as immigrants, the poor and children, was not wholly motivated by disinterested ideals of justice and equality. Philanthropic work filled a void in their own lives, a void which was created in part by the decline of traditional religion, increased leisure and boredom, the rise of public education, and the breakdown of communal life in large, crowded cities. "By simplifying dress and amusements, by cutting off a little here and there from our luxuries," wrote one child-saver, "we may change the whole current of many human lives."[39] Women were exhorted to make their lives useful by participating in welfare programs, by volunteering their time and services, and by getting acquainted with less privileged groups. They were also encouraged to seek work in institutions which were "like family-life with its many-sided development and varied interests and occupations, and where the woman-element shall pervade the house and soften its social atmosphere with motherly tenderness."[40]

While the child-saving movement can be partly understood as a "symbolic crusade"[41] which served ceremonial and status functions for many women, it was by no means a reactionary and romantic movement, nor was it supported only by women and members of the old gentry. Child-saving also had considerable instrumental significance for legitimizing new career openings for women. The new role of social worker combined elements of an old and partly fictitious role—defender of family life—and elements of a new role—social servant. Social work and professional child-saving provided new opportunities for career-minded women who found the traditional professions dominated and controlled by men.[42] These child-savers were members of the emerging bourgeoisie created by the new industrial order.

It is not surprising that the professions also supported the child-saving movement, for they were capable of reaping enormous economic and status rewards from the changes taking place. The clergy had nothing to lose (but more of their rapidly declining constituency) and everything to gain by incorporating social services into traditional religion. Lawyers were needed for their technical expertise and to administer new institutions. And academics discovered a new market which paid them as consultants, elevated them to positions of national prestige and furnished endless materials for books, articles and conferences.

. . . While the rank and file reformers in the child-saving movement worked closely with corporate liberals, it would be inaccurate to simply characterize them as lackeys of big business. Many were principled and genuinely concerned about alleviating human misery and improving the lives of the poor. Moreover, many women who participated in the movement were able to free themselves from male domination and participate more fully in society. But for the most part, the child-savers and other Progressive reformers defended capitalism and rejected socialist alternatives. Most reformers accepted the structure of the new industrial order and sought to moderate its cruder inequities and reduce inharmonies in the existing system.[43] Though many child-savers were "socialists of the heart" and ardent critics of society, their programs were typically reformist and did not alter basic economic inequalities.[44] Rhetoric and righteous indignation were more prevalent than programs of radical action.

IMAGES OF CRIME AND DELINQUENCY

. . . The child-savers viewed the "criminal classes" with a mixture of contempt and benevolence. Crime was portrayed as rising from the "lowest orders" and threatening to engulf "respectable" society like a virulent disease. Charles Loring Brace, a leading child-saver, typified popular and professional views about crime and delinquency:

> As Christian men, we cannot look upon this great multitude of unhappy, deserted, and degraded boys and girls without feeling our responsibility to God for them. The class increases: immigration is pouring in its multitudes of poor foreigners who leave these young outcasts everywhere in our midst. These boys and girls . . . will soon form the great lower class of our city. They will influence elections; they may shape the policy of the city; they will assuredly, if unreclaimed, poison society all around them. They will help to form the great multitude of robbers, thieves, and vagrants, who are now such a burden upon the law-respecting community. . . .[45]

This attitude of contempt derived from a view of criminals as less-than-human, a perspective which was strongly influenced and aggravated by nativist and racist ideologies.[46] The "criminal class" was variously described as "creatures" living in "burrows," "dens," and "slime"; as "little Arabs" and "foreign childhood that floats along the streets and docks of the city—vagabondish, thievish, familiar with the vicious ways and places of the town";[47] and as "ignorant," "shiftless," "indolent," and "dissipated."[48]

The child-savers were alarmed and frightened by the "dangerous classes" whose "very number makes one stand aghast," noted the urban reformer Jacob Riis.[49] Law and order were widely demanded:

> The "dangerous classes" of New York are mainly American-born, but the children of Irish and German immigrants. They are as ignorant as London flashmen or costermongers. They are far more brutal than the peasantry from whom they descend, and they are

much banded together, in associations, such as "Dead Rabbit," "Plug-ugly," and various target companies. They are our *enfant perdus*, grown up to young manhood. . . . They are ready for any offense or crime, however degraded or bloody. . . . Let but Law lift its hand from them for a season, or let the civilizing influences of American life fail to reach them, and, if the opportunity offered, we should see an explosion from this class which might leave this city in ashes and blood.[50]

These views derived considerable legitimacy from prevailing theories of social and reform Darwinism which . . . proposed that criminals were a dangerous and atavistic class, standing outside the boundaries of morally regulated relationships. Herbert Spencer's writings had a major impact on American intellectuals and Cesare Lombroso, perhaps the most significant figure in nineteenth century criminology, looked for recognition in the United States when he felt that his experiments on the "criminal type" had been neglected in Europe.[51]

Although Lombroso's theoretical and experimental studies were not translated into English until 1911, his findings were known by American academics in the early 1890s, and their popularity, like that of Spencer's works, was based on the fact that they confirmed widely-held stereotypes about the biological basis and inferior character of a "criminal class." A typical view was expressed by Nathan Allen in 1878 at the National Conference of Charities and Correction: "If our object is to prevent crime in a large scale, we must direct attention to its main sources—to the materials that make criminals; the springs must be dried up; the supplies must be cut off."[52] This was to be achieved, if necessary, by birth control and eugenics. Similar views were expressed by Hamilton Wey, an influential physician at Elmira Reformatory, who argued before the National Prison Association in 1881 that criminals had to be treated as a "distinct type of human species."[53]

Literature on "social degradation" was extremely popular during the 1870s and 1880s, though most such "studies" were little more than crude and racist polemics, padded with moralistic epithets and preconceived value judgments. Richard Dugdale's series of

papers on the Jukes family, which became a model for the case-study approach to social problems, was distorted almost beyond recognition by anti-intellectual supporters of hereditary theories of crime.[54] Confronted by the evidence of Darwin, Galton, Dugdale, Caldwell and many other disciples of the biological image of behavior, many child-savers were compelled to admit that "a large proportion of the unfortunate children that go to make up the great army of criminals are not born right."[55] Reformers adopted and modified the rhetoric of social Darwinism in order to emphasize the urgent need for confronting the "crime problem" before it got completely out of hand. A popular proposal, for example, was the "methodized registration and training" of potential criminals, "or these failing, their early and entire withdrawal from the community."[56]

Although some child-savers advocated drastic methods of crime control—including birth control through sterilization, cruel punishments, and life-long incarceration—more moderate views prevailed. This victory for moderation was related to the recognition by many Progressive reformers that short-range repression was counter-productive as well as cruel and that long-range planning and amelioration were required to achieve economic and political stability. The rise of more benevolent strategies of social control occurred at about the same time that influential capitalists were realizing that existing economic arrangements could not be successfully maintained only through the use of private police and government troops.[57] While the child-savers justified their reforms as humanitarian, it is clear that this humanitarianism reflected their class background and elitist conceptions of human potentiality. The child-savers shared the view of more conservative professionals that "criminals" were a distinct and dangerous class, indigenous to working-class culture, and a threat to "civilized" society. They differed mainly in the procedures by which the "criminal class" should be controlled or neutralized.

Gradually, a more "enlightened" view about strategies of control prevailed among the leading representatives of professional associations. Correctional workers, for example, did not want to think of themselves merely as the custodians of a pariah class. The self-image of penal reformers as "doctors" rather than "guards," and the medical domination of criminological research in the United States at that time facilitated the acceptance of "therapeutic" strategies in prisons and reformatories.[58] Physicians gradually provided the official rhetoric of penal reform, replacing cruder concepts of social Darwinsim with a new optimism. Admittedly, the criminal was "pathological" and "diseased," but medical science offered the possibility of miraculous cures. Although there was a popular belief in the existence of a "criminal class" separated from the rest of humanity by a "vague boundary line," there was no good reason why this class could not be identified, diagnosed, segregated, changed and incorporated back into society.[59]

By the late 1890s, most child-savers agreed that hereditary theories of crime were overfatalistic. The superintendent of the Kentucky Industrial School of Reform, for example, told delegates to a national conference on corrections that heredity is "unjustifiably made a bugaboo to discourage efforts at rescue. We know that physical heredity tendencies can be neutralized and often nullified by proper counteracting precautions."[60] E. R. L. Gould, a sociologist at the University of Chicago, similarly criticized biological theories of crime as unconvincing and sentimental. "Is it not better," he said, "to postulate freedom of choice than to preach the doctrine of the unfettered will, and so elevate criminality into a propitiary sacrifice?"[61]

Charles Cooley, writing in 1896, was one of the first American sociologists to observe that criminal behavior depended as much upon social and economic circumstances as it did upon the inheritance of biological traits. "The criminal class," he observed, "is largely the result of society's bad workmanship upon fairly good material." In support of this argument, he noted that there was a "large and fairly trustworthy body of evidence" to suggest that many "degenerates" could be converted into "useful citizens by rational treatment."[62]

Although there was a wide difference of opinion among experts as to the precipitating causes of crime, it was generally agreed that criminals were abnormally conditioned by a multitude of biological and environmental forces, some of which were permanent and irreversible. Strictly biological theories of crime were modified to incorporate a developmental view of human behavior. If, as it was believed, criminals are conditioned by biological heritage and brutish living conditions, then prophylactic measures must be taken early in life. "We must get hold of the little waifs that grow up to form the criminal element just as early in life as possible," exhorted an influential child-saver. "Hunt up the children of poverty, of crime, and of brutality, just as soon as they can be reached."[63] Efforts were needed to reach the criminals of future generations. "They are born to crime," wrote the penologist Enoch Wines, "brought up for it. They must be saved."[64] New institutions and new programs were required to meet this challenge.

JUVENILE COURT AND THE REFORMATORY SYSTEM

The essential preoccupation of the child-saving movement was the recognition and control of youthful deviance. It brought attention to, and thus "invented" new categories of youthful misbehavior which had been hitherto unappreciated. The efforts of the child-savers were institutionally expressed in the juvenile court which, despite recent legislative and constitutional reforms, is generally acknowledged as their most significant contribution to progressive penology. There is some dispute about which state first created a special tribunal for children. Massachusetts and New York passed laws, in 1874 and 1892 respectively, providing for the trials of minors apart from adults charged with crimes. Ben Lindsey, a renowned judge and reformer, also claimed this distinction for Colorado where a juvenile court was, in effect, established through an educational law of 1899. However, most authorities agree that the Juvenile Court Act, passed by the Illinois legislature in the same year, was the first official enactment to be recognized as a model statute by other states and countries.[65] By 1917, juvenile court legislation had been passed in all but three states and by 1932 there were over 600 independent juvenile courts throughout the United States.[66]

The juvenile court system was part of a general movement directed towards developing a specialized labor market and industrial discipline under corporate capitalism by creating new programs of adjudication and control for "delinquent," "dependent" and "neglected" youth. This in turn was related to augmenting the family and enforcing compulsory education in order to guarantee the proper reproduction of the labor force. For example, underlying the juvenile court system was the concept of *parens patriae* by which the courts were authorized to handle with wide discretion the problems of "its least fortunate junior citizens."[67] The administration of juvenile justice, which differed in many important respects from the criminal court system, was delegated extensive powers of control over youth. A child was not accused of a crime but offered assistance and guidance; intervention in the lives of "delinquents" was not supposed to carry the stigma of criminal guilt. Judicial records were not generally available to the press or public, and juvenile hearings were typically conducted in private. Court procedures were informal and inquisitorial, not requiring the presence of a defense attorney. Specific criminal safeguards of due process were not applicable because juvenile proceedings were defined by statute as civil in character.[68]

The judges of the new court were empowered to investigate the character and social background of "predelinquent" as well as delinquent children; they concerned themselves with motivation rather than intent, seeking to identify the moral reputation of problematic children. The requirements of preventive penology and child-saving further justified the court's intervention in cases where no offense had actually been committed, but where, for example, a child was posing problems for some person in authority, such as a parent or teacher or social worker.

The role model for juvenile court judges was doctor-counselor rather than lawyer. "Judicial therapists" were expected to establish a one-to-one relationship with "delinquents" in the same way that a country doctor might give his time and attention to a favorite patient. Juvenile courtrooms were often arranged like a clinic and the vocabulary of its participants was largely composed of medical metaphors. "We do not know the child without a thorough examination," wrote Judge Julian Mack. "We must reach into the soul-life of the child."[69] Another judge from Los Angeles suggested that the juvenile court should be a "laboratory of human behavior" and its judges trained as "specialists in the art of human relations." It was the judge's task to "get the whole truth about a child" in the same way that a "physician searches for every detail that bears on the condition of the patient."[70] Similarly, the judges of the Boston juvenile court liked to think of themselves as "physicians in a dispensary."[71]

The unique character of the child-saving movement was its concerns for predelinquent offenders—"children who occupy the debatable ground between criminality and innocence"—and its claim that it could transform potential criminals into respectable citizens by training them in "habits of industry, self-control and obedience to law."[72] This policy justified the diminishing of traditional procedures and allowed police, judges, probation officers and truant officers to work together without legal hindrance. If children were to be rescued, it was important that the rescuers be free to pursue their mission without the interference of defense lawyers and due process. Delinquents had to be saved, transformed and reconstituted. "There is no essential difference," noted a prominent child-saver, "between a criminal and any other sinner. The means and methods of restoration are the same for both."[73]

The juvenile court legislation enabled the state to investigate and control a wide variety of behaviors. As Joel Handler has observed, "the critical philosophical position of the reform movement was that no formal, legal distinctions should be made between the delinquent and the dependent or neglected."[74] Statutory definitions of "delinquency" encompassed (1) acts that would be criminal if committed by adults; (2) acts that violated county, town, or municipal ordinances; and (3) violations of vaguely worded catch-alls—such as "vicious or immoral behavior," "incorrigibility," and "truancy"— which "seem to express the notion that the adolescent, if allowed to continue, will engage in more serious conduct."[75]

The juvenile court movement went far beyond a concern for special treatment of adolescent offenders. It brought within the ambit of government control a set of youthful activities that had been previously ignored or dealt with on an informal basis. It was not by accident that the behavior subject to penalties—drinking, sexual "license," roaming the streets, begging, frequenting dance halls and movies, fighting, and being seen in public late at night—was especially characteristic of the children of working-class and immigrant families. Once arrested and adjudicated, these "delinquents" became wards of the court and eligible for salvation.

It was through the reformatory system that the child-savers hoped to demonstrate that delinquents were capable of being converted into law-abiding citizens. Though the reformatory was initially developed in the United States during the middle of the nineteenth century as a special form of prison discipline for adolescents and young adults, its underlying principles were formulated in Britain by Matthew Davenport Hill, Alexander Maconochie, Walter Crofton and Mary Carpenter. If the United States did not have any great penal theorists, it at least had energetic administrators—like Enoch Wines, Zebulon Brockway and Frank Sanborn—who were prepared to experiment with new programs.

The reformatory was distinguished from the traditional penitentiary in several ways: it adopted a policy of indeterminate sentencing; it emphasized the importance of a countryside location; and it typically was organized on the "cottage" plan as opposed to the traditional congregate housing found in penitentiaries. The ultimate aim of the reformatory was reformation of the criminal, which could only be achieved "by placing the prisoner's fate, as far as possible, in his own hand, by enabling him, through industry and good conduct to raise himself, step by step, to a position of less restraint. . . ."[76]

Based on a crude theory of rewards and punishments, the "new penology" set itself the task of re-socializing the "dangerous classes." The typical resident of a reformatory, according to one child-saver, had been "cradled in infamy, imbibing with its earliest natural nourishment the germs of a depraved appetite, and reared in the midst of people whose lives are an atrocious crime against natural and divine law and the rights of society." In order to correct and reform such a person, the reformatory plan was designed to teach the value of adjustment, private enterprise, thrift and self-reliance. "To make a good boy out of this bundle of perversities, his entire being must be revolutionized. He must be taught self-control, industry, respect for himself and the rights of others."[77] The real test of reformation in a delinquent, as William Letchworth told the National Conference of Charities and Correction in 1886, was his uncomplaining adjustment to his former environment. "If he is truly reformed in the midst of adverse influences," said Letchworth, "he gains that moral strength which makes his reform permanent."[78] Moreover, reformed delinquents were given every opportunity to rise "far above the class from which they sprang," especially if they were "patient" and "self-denying."[79]

Reformation of delinquents was to be achieved in a number of different ways. The trend from congregate housing to group living represented a significant change in the organization of penal institutions. The "cottage" plan was designed to provide more intensive supervision and to reproduce, symbolically at least, an atmosphere of family life conducive to the resocialization of youth. The "new penology" also urged the benefits of a rural location, partly in order to teach agricultural skills, but mainly in order to guarantee a totally controlled environment. This was justified by appealing to the romantic theory that corrupt delinquents would be spiritually regenerated by their contact with unspoiled nature.[80]

Education was stressed as the main form of industrial and moral training in reformatories. According to Michael Katz, in his study on nineteenth-century education, the reformatory provided "the first form of compulsory schooling in the United States."[81] The prominence of education as a technique of reform reflected the widespread emphasis on socialization and assimilation instead of cruder methods of social control. But as Georg Rusche and Otto Kirchheimer observed in their study of the relationship between economic and penal policies, the rise of "rehabilitative" and educational programs was "largely the result of opposition on the part of free workers," for "wherever working-class organizations were powerful enough to influence state politics, they succeeded in obtaining complete abolition of all forms of prison labor (Pennsylvania in 1897, for example), causing much suffering to the prisoners, or at least in obtaining very considerable limitations, such as work without modern machinery, conventional rather than modern types of prison industry, or work for the government instead of for the free market."[82]

Although the reformatory system, as envisioned by urban reformers, suffered in practice from overcrowding, mismanagement, inadequate financing and staff hiring problems, its basic ideology was still tough-minded and uncompromising. As the American Friends Service Committee noted, "if the reformers were naive, the managers of the correctional establishment were not. Under the leadership of Zebulon R. Brockway of the Elmira Reformatory, by the latter part of the nineteenth century they had co-opted the reformers and consolidated their leadership and control of indeterminate sentence reform."[83] The child-savers were not averse to using corporal punishment and other severe disciplinary measures when inmates were recalcitrant. Brockway, for example, regarded his task as "socialization of the anti-social by scientific training while under completest governmental control."[84] To achieve his goal, Brockway's reformatory became "like a garrison of a thousand prisoner soldiers" and "every incipient disintegration was promptly checked and disinclination of individual prisoners to conform was overcome."[85] Child-saving was a job for resolute professionals who realized that "sickly sentimentalism" had no place in their work.[86]

"Criminals shall either be cured," Brockway told the National Prison Congress in 1870, "or kept under such continued restraint as gives guarantee of safety from further depredations."[87] Restraint and discipline were an integral part of the "treatment" program and not merely expediencies of administration. Military drill, "training of the will," and long hours of tedious labor were the essence of the reformatory system and the indeterminate sentencing policy guaranteed its smooth operation. "Nothing can tend more certainly to secure the most hardened and desperate criminals than the present system of short sentences," wrote the reformer Bradford Kinney Peirce in 1869.[88] Several years later, Enoch Wines was able to report that "the sentences of young offenders are wisely regulated for their amendment; they are not absurdly shortened as if they signified only so much endurance of vindictive suffering."[89]

Since the child-savers professed to be seeking the "best interests" of their "wards" on the basis of corporate liberal values, there was no need to formulate legal regulation of the right and duty to "treat" in the same way that the right and duty to punish had been previously regulated. The adversary system, therefore, ceased to exist for youth, even as a legal fiction.[90] The myth of the child-saving movement as a humanitarian enterprise is based partly on a superficial interpretation of the child-savers' rhetoric of rehabilitation and partly on a misconception of how the child-savers viewed punishment. While it is true that the child-savers advocated minimal use of corporal punishment, considerable evidence suggests that this recommendation was based on managerial rather than moral consideration. William Letchworth reported that "corporal punishment is rarely inflicted" at the State Industrial School in Rochester because "most of the boys consider the lowering of their standing the severest punishment that is inflicted."[91] Mrs. Glendower Evans, commenting on the decline of whippings at a reform school in Massachusetts, concluded that "when boys do not feel themselves imprisoned and are treated as responsible moral agents, they can be trusted with their freedom to a surprising degree."[92] Officials at another state industrial school for girls also reported that "hysterics and fits of screaming and of noisy disobedience, have of late years become unknown. . . ."[93]

The decline in the use of corporal punishment was due to the fact that indeterminate sentencing, the "mark" or "stage" system of rewards and punishments, and other techniques of "organized persuasion" were far more effective in maintaining order and compliance than cruder methods of control. The chief virtue of the "stage" system, a graduated system of punishments and privileges, was its capacity to keep prisoners disciplined and submissive.[94] The child-savers had learned from industrialists that persuasive benevolence backed up by force was a far more effective device of social control than arbitrary displays of terrorism. Like an earlier generation of penal reformers in France and Italy, the child-savers stressed the efficacy of new and indirect forms of social control as a "practical measure of defense against social revolution as well as against individual acts."[95]

Although the child-saving movement had far-reaching consequences for the organization and administration of the juvenile justice system, its overall impact was conservative in both spirit and achievement. The child-savers' reforms were generally aimed at imposing sanctions on conduct unbecoming "youth" and disqualifying youth from the benefit of adult privileges. The child-savers were prohibitionists, in a general sense, who believed that social progress depended on efficient law enforcement, strict supervision of children's leisure and recreation, and enforced education. They were primarily concerned with regulating social behavior, eliminating "foreign" and radical ideologies, and preparing youth as a disciplined and devoted work force. The austerity of the criminal law and penal institutions was only of incidental concern; their central interest was in the normative outlook of youth and they were most successful in their efforts to extend governmental control over a whole range of youthful activities which had previously been handled locally and informally. In this sense, their reforms were aimed at defining, rationalizing and regulating the dependent status of youth.[96] Although the child-savers' attitudes to youth were often paternalistic and romantic, their commands

were backed up by force and an abiding faith in the benevolence of government.

The child-saving movement had its most direct impact on the children of the urban poor. The fact that "troublesome" adolescents were depicted as "sick" or "pathological," imprisoned "for their own good," addressed in paternalistic vocabulary, and exempted from criminal law processes, did not alter the subjective experiences of control, restraint and punishment. It is ironic, as Philippe Ariès observed in his historical study of European family life, that the obsessive solicitude of family, church, moralists and administrators for child welfare served to deprive children of the freedoms which they had previously shared with adults and to deny their capacity for initiative, responsibility and autonomy.[97]

NOTES

1. See, for example, The President's Commission on Law Enforcement and Administration of Justice, *Juvenile Delinquency and Youth Crime* (Washington, D.C.: U.S. Government Printing Office, 1967), pp. 2–4.

2. Charles L. Chute, "The Juvenile Court in Retrospect," 13 *Federal Probation* (September, 1949), p. 7; Harrison A. Dobbs, "In Defense of Juvenile Court," *Ibid.*, p. 29.

3. Charles L. Chute, "Fifty Years of the Juvenile Court," *National Probation and Parole Association Yearbook* (1949), p. 1.

4. George H. Mead, "The Psychology of Punitive Justice," 23 *American Journal of Sociology* (March, 1981), pp. 577–602; August Aichhorn, "The Juvenile Court: Is It a Solution?" in *Delinquency and Child Guidance: Selected Papers* (New York: International Universities Press, 1964), pp. 55–79.

5. Murray Levine and Adeline Levine, *A Social History of Helping Services: Clinic, Court, School, and Community* (New York: Appleton-Century-Crofts, 1970), p. 156.

6. Gerhard O. W. Mueller, *History of American Criminal Law Scholarship* (New York: Walter E. Meyer Research Institute of Law, 1962), p. 113.

7. See, for example, Herbert H. Lou, *Juvenile Courts in the United States* (Chapel Hill: University of North Carolina Press, 1927); Negley K. Teeters and John Otto Reinmann, *The Challenge of Delinquency* (New York: Prentice-Hall, 1950); and Ola Nyquist, *Juvenile Justice* (London: Macmillan, 1960).

8. Robert S. Pickett, *House of Refuge: Origins of Juvenile Reform in New York State, 1815–1857* (Syracuse: Syracuse University Press, 1969), p. 188.

9. See, for example, Arthur M. Schlesinger, Jr., *The*

American as Reformer (Cambridge: Harvard University Press, 1950).

10. See, for example, Richard Hofstadter, *The Age of Reform* (New York: Vintage Books, 1955), and Joseph R. Gusfield, *Symbolic Crusade: Status Politics and the American Temperance Movement* (Urbana: University of Illinois Press, 1963).

11. R. Jackson Wilson (Ed.), *Reform, Crisis, and Confusion, 1900–1929* (New York: Random House, 1970), especially pp. 3–6.

12. Arthur M. Schlesinger, Jr., *The Age of Jackson* (Boston: Little, Brown, 1946), p. 505.

13. Hofstadter, *op. cit.*, chapter IV.

14. The President's Commission on Law Enforcement and Administration of Justice, *op. cit.*, pp. 7, 8.

15. For discussions of earlier reform movements, see Pickett, *loc. cit.* and Sanford J. Fox, "Juvenile Justice Reform: An Historical Perspective," 22 *Stanford Law Review,* (June, 1970), pp. 1187–1239.

16. The child-saving movement was broad and diverse, including reformers interested in child welfare, education, reformatories, labor and other related issues. This paper is limited primarily to child-savers involved in anti-delinquency reforms and should not be interpreted as characterizing the child-saving movement in general.

17. William P. Letchworth, "Children of the State," *National Conference of Charities and Correction, Proceedings* (St. Paul, Minnesota, 1886), p. 138.

18. R. W. Hill, "The Children of Shinbone Alley," National Conference of Charities and Correction, *Proceedings* (Omaha, 1887), p. 231.

19. William Appleman Williams, *The Contours of American History* (Chicago: Quadrangle Books, 1966), especially pp. 345–412.

20. Pickett, *op. cit.*, pp. 50–55.

21. Committee on the History of Child-Saving Work, *History of Child-Saving in the United States* (National Conference of Charities and Correction, 1893), p. 5.

22. Charles Loring Brace, *The Dangerous Classes of New York and Twenty Years' Work Among Them* (New York: Wynkoop and Hallenbeck, 1880), pp. 282–83.

23. Committee on the History of Child-Saving Work, *op. cit.*, pp. 70–73.

24. *Ibid.*, pp. 80–81.

25. *Ibid.*, p. 270.

26. For more about these child-savers, see Anthony Platt, *The Child-Savers: The Invention of Delinquency,* (Chicago: University of Chicago Press, 1969), pp. 75–100.

27. Louise C. Wade, *Graham Taylor: Pioneer for Social Justice, 1851–1938* (Chicago: University of Chicago Press, 1964), p. 59.

28. G. William Domhoff, *The Higher Circles: The Governing Class in America* (New York: Random House, 1970), p. 48, and Platt, *op. cit.*, pp. 92–98.

29. "The transformation in penal systems cannot be explained only from changing needs of the war against crime, although this struggle does play a part. Every system of production tends to discover punishments which correspond to its productive relationships. It is thus necessary to investigate the origin and fate of penal systems, the use or avoidance of specific punishments, and the intensity of penal practices as they are determined by social forces, above all by economic and then fiscal forces." Georg Rusche and Otto Kirchheimer, *Punishment and Social Structure* (New York: Russell & Russell, 1968), p. 5.

30. See, for example, Gabriel Kolko, *The Triumph of Conservatism: A Reinterpretation of American History, 1900–1916* (Chicago: Quadrangle Books, 1967); James Weinstein, *The Corporate Ideal in the Liberal State, 1900–1918* (Boson: Beacon Press, 1969); Samuel Haber, *Efficiency and Uplift: Scientific Management in the Progressive Era, 1890–1920* (Chicago: University of Chicago Press, 1964); and Robert H. Wiebe, *Businessmen and Reform: A Study of the Progressive Movement* (Cambridge: Harvard University Press, 1962).

31. Weinstein, *op. cit.*, pp. ix, xi.

32. Jeremy P. Felt, *Hostages of Fortune: Child Labor Reform in New York State* (Syracuse: Syracuse University Press, 1965), p. 45.

33. Brace, *op. cit.*, p. 352.

34. David K. Cohen and Marvin Lazerson, "Education and the Corporate Order," 8 *Socialist Revolution,* (March–April, 1972), p. 50. See also Michael B. Katz, *The Irony of Early School Reform: Educational Innovation in Mid-Nineteenth Century Massachusetts,* (Cambridge: Harvard University Press, 1968), and Lawrence A. Cremin, *The Transformation of the School: Progressivism in American Education, 1876–1957* (New York: Vintage, 1961).

35. It should be emphasized that child-saving reforms were predominantly supported by more privileged sectors of the feminist movement, especially those who had an interest in developing professional careers in education, social work and probation. In recent years, radical feminists have emphasized that "we must include the oppression of children in any program for feminist revolution or we will be subject to the same failing of which we have so often accused men: of not having gone deep enough in our analysis, of having missed an important substratum of oppression merely because it didn't directly concern *us*." Shulamith Firestone, *The Dialectic of Sex: The Case for Feminist Revolution,* (New York: Bantam, 1971), p. 104.

36. Robert Sunley, "Early Nineteenth Century American Literature on Child-Rearing," in Margaret Mead and Martha Wolfenstein (Eds.), *Childhood in Contemporary Cultures* (Chicago: University of Chicago Press, 1955), p. 152; see, also, Orville G. Brim, *Education for Child-Reading* (New York: Free Press, 1965), pp. 321–49.

37. For an extended discussion of this issue, see Platt, *loc. cit.* and Christopher Lasch, *The New Radicalism in America, 1889–1963: The Intellectual as a Social Type* (New York: Alfred A. Knopf, 1965), pp. 3–68.

38. Talcott Parsons and Robert F. Bales, *Family, Socialization and Interaction Process* (Glencoe, Illinois: Free Press, 1955), pp. 3–33.

39. Clara T. Leonard, "Family Homes for Pauper and Dependent Children," Annual Conference of Charities, *Proceedings* (Chicago: 1879), p. 175.

40. W. P. Lynde, "Prevention in Some of Its Aspects," *Ibid.*, pp. 165–66.

41. Joseph R. Gusfield, *Symbolic Crusade, loc. cit.*

42. See, generally, Roy Lubove, *The Professional Altruist: The Emergence of Social Work as a Career, 1880–1930* (Cambridge: Harvard University Press, 1965).

43. Williams, *op. cit.*, p. 373 and Weinstein, *op. cit.*, p. 254.

44. Williams, *op. cit.*, pp. 374, 395–402.

45. Committee on the History of Child-Saving Work, *op. cit.*, p. 3.

46. See, generally, John Higham, *Strangers in the Land: Patterns of American Nativism, 1860–1925* (New York: Atheneum, 1965).

47. Brace, *op. cit.*, pp. 30, 49; Bradford Kinney Peirce, *A Half Century with Juvenile Delinquents* (Montclair, New Jersey: Patterson Smith, 1969, originally published 1869), p. 253.

48. Nathan Allen, "Prevention of Crime and Pauperism," Annual Conference of Charities, *Proceedings* (Cincinnati, 1878), pp. 111–24.

49. Jacob A. Riis, *How the Other Half Lives* (New York: Hill and Wang, 1957, originally published in 1890), p. 134.

50. Brace, *op. cit.*, pp. 27, 29.

51. See, for example, Lombroso's comments in the Introduction to Arthur MacDonald, *Criminology* (New York: Funk and Wagnalls, 1893).

52. Allen, *loc. cit.*

53. Hamilton D. Wey, "A Plea for Physical Training of Youthful Criminals," National Prison Association, *Proceedings* (Boston, 1888), pp. 181–93. For further discussion of this issue, see Platt, *op. cit.*, pp. 18–28 and Arthur E. Fink, *Causes of Crime: Biological Theories in the United States, 1800–1915* (New York: A. S. Barnes, 1962).

54. Richard L. Dugdale, *The Jukes: A Study in Crime, Pauperism, Disease, and Heredity* (New York: G. P. Putnam's Sons, 1877).

55. Sarah B. Cooper, "The Kindergarten as Child-Saving Work," National Conference of Charities and Correction, *Proceedings* (Madison, 1883), pp. 130–38.

56. I. N. Kerlin, "The Moral Imbecile," National Conference of Charities and Correction, *Proceedings* (Baltimore, 1890), pp. 244–50.

57. Williams, *op. cit.*, p. 354.

58. Fink, *op. cit.*, p. 247.

59. See, for example, Illinois Board of State Commissioners of Public Charities, *Second Biennial Report* (Springfield: State Journal Steam Print, 1873), pp. 195–96.

60. Peter Caldwell, "The Duty of the State to Delinquent Children," National Conference of Charities and Correction, *Proceedings* (New York, 1898), pp. 404–10.

61. E. R. L. Gould, "The Statistical Study of Hereditary Criminality," National Conference of Charities and Correction, *Proceedings* (New Haven, 1895), pp. 134–43.

62. Charles H. Cooley, " 'Nature' in the Making of Social Careers," National Conference of Charities and Correction, *Proceedings* (Grand Rapids, 1896), pp. 399–405.

63. Committee on the History of Child-Saving Work, *op. cit.*, p. 90.

64. Enoch C. Wines, *The State of Prisons and of Child-Saving Institutions in the Civilized World* (Cambridge: Harvard University Press, 1880).

65. Helen Page Bates, "Digest of Statutes Relating to Juvenile Courts and Probation Systems," 13 *Charities* (January, 1905), pp. 329–36.

66. Joel F. Handler, "The Juvenile Court and the Adversary System: Problems of Function and Form," 1965 *Wisconsin Law Review* (1965), pp. 7–51.

67. Gustav L. Schramm, "The Juvenile Court Idea," 13 *Federal Probation* (September, 1949), p. 21.

68. Monrad G. Paulsen, "Fairness to the Juvenile Offender," 41 *Minnesota Law Review* (1957), pp. 547–67.

69. Julian W. Mack, "The Chancery Procedure in the Juvenile Court," in Jane Addams (Ed.), *The Child, the Clinic and the Court* (New York: New Republic, 1925), p. 315.

70. Miriam Van Waters, "The Socialization of Juvenile Court Procedure," 21 *Journal of Criminal Law and Criminology* (1922), pp. 61, 69.

71. Harvey H. Baker, "Procedure of the Boston Juvenile Court," 23 *Survey* (February, 1910), p. 646.

72. Illinois Board of State Commissioners of Public Charities, *Sixth Biennial Report* (Springfield: H.W. Rokker, 1880), p. 104.

73. Frederick H. Wines, "Reformation as an End in Prison Discipline," National Conference of Charities and Correction, *Proceedings* (Buffalo, 1888), p. 198.

74. Joel F. Handler, *op. cit.*, p. 9.

75. Joel F. Handler and Margaret K. Rosenheim, "Privacy and Welfare: Public Assistance and Juvenile Justice," 31 *Law and Contemporary Problems* (1966), pp. 377–412.

76. From a report by Enoch Wines and Theodore Dwight to the New York legislature in 1867, quoted by Max Grünhut, *Penal Reform* (Oxford: Clarendon Press, 1948), p. 90.

77. Peter Caldwell, "The Reform School Problem," National Conference of Charities and Correction, *Proceedings* (St. Paul, 1886), pp. 71–76.

78. Letchworth, op. cit., p. 152.

79. Committee on the History of Child-Saving Work, *op. cit.*, p. 20.

80. See Platt, *op. cit.*, pp. 55–66.

81. Katz, *op. cit.*, p. 187.

82. Rusche and Kirchheimer, *op. cit.*, pp. 131–132.

83. American Friends Service Committee, *op. cit.*, p. 28.

84. Zebulon R. Brockway, *Fifty Years of Prison Service* (New York: Charities Publication Committee, 1912), p. 393.

85. *Ibid.*, pp. 310, 421.

86. *Ibid.*, pp. 389–408.

87. *Ibid.*

88. Peirce, *op. cit.*, p. 312.

89. Enoch Wines, *op. cit.*, p. 81.

90. On informal cooperation in the criminal courts, see Jerome H. Skolnick, "Social Control in the Adversary System," 11 *Journal of Conflict Resolution* (March, 1967), pp. 52–70.

91. Committee on the History of Child-Saving Work, *op. cit.*, p. 20.

92. *Ibid.*, p. 237.

93. *Ibid.*, p. 251.

94. Rusche and Kirchheimer, *op. cit.*, pp. 155–156.

95. *Ibid.*, p. 76. For a similar point, see American Friends Service Committee, *op. cit.*, p. 33.

96. See, generally, Frank Musgrove, *Youth and the Social Order* (London: Routlege and Kegan Paul, 1964).

97. Philippe Ariès, *Centuries of Childhood: A Social History of Family Life* (New York: Vintage Books, 1965).

QUESTIONS FOR DISCUSSION

1. According to the author, there are three "prevailing myths" about the juvenile justice system. List these myths and discuss how they developed.

2. In what ways did economics and social class dimensions affect the evolution of the child-saving movement?

3. One of the outcomes of the child-saving movement was the creation of the reformatory. What were the goals of the reformatory? By what specific means did the reformatory attempt to achieve these goals?

APPLICATIONS

1. The child-saving movement in America began in the nineteenth century and has continued, in some respects, to the present day. In contemporary America we speak of "at risk" children and adolescents when describing young people who for various reasons have an enhanced probability of being socially dysfunctional.

   a. How are at risk children similar and/or dissimilar to the children of the nineteenth century.

   b. Discuss several ways in which society has changed since the nineteenth century?

   c. What challenges and difficulties did you face as a child that were significantly different than those faced by children of the nineteenth century?

2. After reading this article, it should be clear that policies about the appropriate handling of children are influenced by several major social institutions in America.

   a. In your opinion, how do the following entities affect the way children are treated today?

   (1) politics

   (2) religion

   (3) schools

   (4) families

KEY TERMS

bureaucracy typically a governmental group characterized by specialization of functions, adherence to fixed rules, and a hierarchy of authority.

constituency a group or geographical area of people who are represented by an elected official.

humanistic an attribute that stresses an individual's dignity, worth, and capacity for self-realization through the use of logic and reason.

laissez–faire a doctrine opposing governmental interference in economic affairs beyond the minimum necessary for the maintenance of peace and property rights.

liberalism a philosophy based on a belief in progress, the essential goodness of the human race, individual autonomy, and the protection of political and civil liberties.

nouveau riche a person with newly ascribed or achieved wealth.

parens patriae a judicial doctrine that allows the court, acting on behalf of the government, to intervene into family relations whenever a child's welfare is threatened.

philanthropic dispensing money or other resources as aid for humanitarian purposes. May include giving food, clothing, and other items to charitable organizations.

progressivism the belief in moderate political change and social improvement by governmental action.

rhetoric a speech or discourse. Often this word is used to indicate insincere or grandiloquent language.

social class a grouping of people based on one or more common characteristics. May include groupings by economic strength, social status, or political power.

2

Attitudes and Policies toward Juvenile Delinquency in the United States: A Historiographical Review

Robert M. Mennel

During the past decade, the history of juvenile delinquency has attracted considerable scholarly attention. This reflects both the recent popularity of social history and the desire of some historians to become involved in the policymaking process. Generally, interpretations have emphasized the social-control motives of the founders of institutions and the juvenile court while portraying the delinquents themselves as victims of social and economic discrimination. Recent research has neglected case studies and the comparative approach. Several recent works have uncovered some popular support for institutions and shown American policies, at least in the nineteenth century, to be less disadvantageous than European formulations. These studies have also stressed the significant differences between programs and institutions in the United States. Future research can profitably examine the post–World War II era, focusing particularly on the influence of legal changes, professional study, and government policy on programs and institutions. Scholars undertaking this work can make their contributions more useful by declining to view themselves as policymakers.

The American juvenile justice system remains a topic of national concern. Peter Prescott's *The Child Savers* (1981), a bleak portrait of the

"Attitudes and Policies toward Delinquency in the United States," *Crime and Justice: An Annual Review of Research,* 4 (Chicago: University of Chicago Press 1982), pp. 191–224. Reprinted by permission of the publisher.

New York City Family Court, is the latest in a long series of indictments. A representative sampling might include Howard James, *Children in Trouble* (1970), Albert Deutsch, *Our Rejected Children* (1952), Clifford Shaw, *The Jack-Roller* (1930), and John Peter Altgeld, *Our Penal Machinery and Its Victims* (1886) and perhaps might begin with Elijah Devoe's 1848 exposé of the New York House of Refuge. Prescott popularizes the principal policy implication of sociological labeling theory, that is, that the more fortunate youths were those who slipped off the official blotter and escaped future treatment. Traditionally, scholars and reformers who have condemned one approach have always had a new institution or mode of treatment on hand. Thus, critics of congregate reform schools promoted cottage and farm schools. Scientists distrustful of the determinism of Lombrosian criminology advocated psychological study. Even today, most of us resist the notion that little can be done or, even worse, that institutions and programs have been created in the knowledge that they will fail. We would rather think of juvenile delinquency as a symptom of larger disjunctions and inequalities in American life, of problems thus far unsolved but not insoluble.

This critical but hopeful spirit has animated the "new" social history that has been the vogue of the profession in the 1960s and 1970s. The fundamental premise, epitomized by Tamara

K. Hareven, ed., *Anonymous Americans: Explorations in Nineteenth-Century Social History* (1971), was that historians had ignored "ordinary" people and vulnerable or disadvantaged groups such as women, children, and minorities. Traditional history was also indicted for minimizing ideological conflict in order to persuade readers of the benevolence and indispensability of existing institutions and power relationships. The novelty of this perspective has been questioned. More than fifty years ago, Charles and Mary Beard's *The Rise of American Civilization* exalted common people and castigated "robber barons," while Mary Beard's collection of documents, *America through Women's Eyes* (1933), helped inaugurate women's history. The Beards, however, were mavericks in a small, genteel profession, whereas contemporary social historians occupy dominant positions in a vastly larger and more complex enterprise. The difference is important and has implications for writing on the history of delinquency and correctional institutions.

The American Historical Association's recent survey of historical writing (Kammen 1980) reveals a specialized and increasingly compartmentalized discipline. One is amazed by the variety of research but sobered by the fact that a growing number of chronological and topical experts communicate more within subgroups than among them. In this context the history of crime and delinquency is but a chapter of social history. I prefer to think of it as a wave—a separate entity yet one that is inextricably connected to other topics such as the history of law, social welfare, education, and the family. Understanding of the origins of the concept of juvenile delinquency, for example, owes much to Bernard Bailyn's *Education in the Forming of American Society* (1960), which linked institutional development of all sorts to the effect of socioeconomic forces upon family government in the late eighteenth century. Thus, historians have been attracted to the topic of delinquency because of its interstitial qualities. As scholars, it challenges them to utilize a wide range of related historical work. As potential reformers, it offers a means of cooperation with presentist and policy-oriented social scientists who share their view that history is a tool to promote change. An illustrative way to date the beginning of the current era may be to note

the simultaneous appearance in 1960 of Cloward and Ohlin's *Delinquency and Opportunity* (1960), a cornerstone of the War on Poverty, and Griffen's *Their Brothers' Keepers: Moral Stewardship in the United States, 1800–1865* (1960), which stressed the social control motives of urban elites responsible for the first wave of asylums, prisons, and reform schools.

This essay examines historical works on juvenile delinquency and juvenile correctional institutions. Since the literature, with several notable exceptions, is not widely known, section I briefly notes the principal scholars and includes a paragraph about my own background. Section II identifies some general characteristics and conceptual problems of contemporary scholarship. For the rest of the essay, I have adopted an approach that is both chronological and analytical. Section III begins with a discussion of interpretations of the origins and treatment of juvenile delinquency in the nineteenth century. The advent of the juvenile court is a natural midpoint (section IV), and challenges to the benevolent purposes of the court in the 1960s and the concomitant deinstitutionalization movement form section V. In crossing this terrain, I hope to offer the reader a summary view of developments, indicate interpretive controversies, and also suggest opportunities and strategies for future research.

I. SCHOLARSHIP

The most prominent American historian focusing upon juvenile delinquency is David Rothman, whose two volumes, *The Discovery of the Asylum* (1971) and *Conscience and Convenience* (1980), relate definitions and institutional expressions of criminal justice, juvenile justice, and mental health to the major changes in American society from the colonial era to the eve of World War II. My own work, *Thorns and Thistles: Juvenile Delinquents in the United States, 1825–1940* (Mennel 1973b), is narrower in scope but attempts a similar transit. Joseph Hawes, *Children in Urban Society: Juvenile Delinquency in Nineteenth Century America* (1971), is yet more confined and episodic, though it does include a chapter on juvenile delinquency in children's literature.

Several studies develop their effect by utilizing the case study approach: Robert Pickett, *House of Refuge: Origins of Juvenile Reform in New York State, 1815–1854* (1969), is self-explanatory. Anthony Platt's *The Child Savers: The Invention of Delinquency* (1977a) studies child-saving philanthropy in late-nineteenth-century Chicago as a preface to an explanation of the beginning of the Illinois juvenile court, the first of its kind; Steven Schlossman, *Love and the American Delinquent: The Theory and Practice of "Progressive" Juvenile Justice, 1825–1920* (1977), follows a general analysis of doctrine with a detailed examination of the Wisconsin system and the early juvenile court in Milwaukee; Jack Holl, *Juvenile Reform in the Progressive Era: William R. George and the Junior Republic Movement* (1971), investigates an important private institution that attempted to reform children by requiring them to participate in a model "free enterprise" system. Miriam Langsam, *Children West: A History of the Placing Out System of the New York Children's Aid Society, 1853–1890* (1964), examines the leading example of anti-institutional reformism. Michael Gordon, *Juvenile Delinquency in the American Novel, 1905–1965* (1971), surveys a variety of scenarios.

Assessment of the juvenile court is an important aspect of the studies cited above and has attracted separate attention as well. Ellen Ryerson, *The Best Laid Plans: America's Juvenile Court Experiment* (1978), is a general study of reformer's attitudes, while Charles Larsen, *The Good Fight* (1972), recounts the life of Ben Lindsey, America's most famous juvenile court judge.

These represent only the major studies. Examples of related works include documentary collections (Abbott 1938; Bremner 1970–74; Sanders 1970), articles (Fox 1970; Mennel 1980a, 1980b; Parker 1976a, 1976b; Teeters 1960; Wohl 1969; Zuckerman 1976), dissertations (Brenzel 1978; Pisciotta 1979; Schupf 1971; Stack 1974; Stewart 1980; Wirkkala 1973); studies with major chapters on delinquency (Katz 1968; Leiby 1967; Levine and Levine 1970); and the principal works of earlier generations (Beaumont and Tocqueville 1835; Brace 1872; Burleigh and Harris 1923; Folks 1902; Healy 1915; Hurley 1907; Reeves 1929; Shaw 1929; Snedden 1907; Thomas 1923; Thrasher 1927; Thurston 1942; Van Waters 1925; Wines and Dwight 1867, 1880).

My research interest developed from participation in the Child and State Project directed by Robert H. Bremner of Ohio State University. This work, funded by the federal government and administered by the American Public Health Association, took its name and inspiration from Grace Abbott's two-volume documentary history (1938) covering most aspects of child-state relations. The new volumes, *Children and Youth in America: A Documentary History* (Bremner 1970–74), represented a thorough restudy and expansion of the original. I edited the juvenile delinquency documents and in the process gathered material for my dissertation (Mennel 1969), which was expanded to *Thorns and Thistles* (Mennel 1973b).

II. HISTORIOGRAPHICAL ISSUES

Michael Ignatieff's thoughtful article (1981) on the historiography of punishment raises basic issues that can help shape consideration of this topic as well. His dialectic begins with Whiggish accounts that portray the creation of systematic law codes and penitentiaries as the enlightened activity of altruistic citizens who eventually triumphed over the foul conditions and "barbaric" punishment characteristic of the medieval period and early modern age. The reformers' accomplishments were described as monuments to their benevolent intent and also harbingers of future and presumable equally reformative programs. In the 1960s, historians joined others in questioning the wisdom of some of these initiatives (psychosurgery and behavior modification, for example) and in reflecting doubts about "the size and intrusiveness of the modern state." Ignatieff notes, "The prison was thus studied not for itself, but for what its rituals of humiliation could reveal about a society's ruling conceptions of power, social obligation and human malleability" (Ignatieff 1981). Of late, however, "antirevisionists" or "counterrevisionists" have appeared on the scene to attack these accounts "for over-schematizing a complex story, and for reducing the intentions behind the new institution to conspiratorial class strategies of divide and rule." Counterrevisionism, charges Ignatieff, "abdicates from the task of historical explanation altogether," since it "merely maintains that historical reality is more complex than the revisionists assumed, that reformers were more humanitarian than revisionists made them out to be, and that there are no such things as classes." The task of future research thus becomes the development of a historiography "which accounts for institutional change without imputing conspiratorial rationality to a ruling class, without reducing institutional development to a formless *ad hoc* adjustment to contingent crisis, and without assuming a hyper-idealist, all triumphant humanitarian crusade."

Ignatieff's essay challenges revisionists including himself ("a former though unrepentant member of the revisionist school") to undertake their future research on the basis of a renewed appreciation for the volitional bases of human activity. Revisionists should question their faith that "the state enjoys a monopoly of the primitive sanction, that its moral authority and practical power are *the* binding sources of social order and that all social relations can be described in the language of power and domination." Ignatieff dismisses "counterrevisionists," generally identified as authors of case studies of French and English institutions, because they minimize the significance of the penitentiary by stressing local resistance to the rationalist ideas that produced it. Future history will be accomplished by revisionists who have seen the light.

The historiography of delinquency runs parallel to Ignatieff's account in some respects. There was a period when historians linked nineteenth-century institution founding and certainly the juvenile court to the march of American progress (Faulkner 1931; Tyler 1944). And certainly the predominant emphasis of 1960s scholarship reflected the egalitarian values and social anger of that era. The coerciveness of the elites who founded the institutions is stressed, and sympathy for the children designated delinquents is widespread. The titles of the monographs convey the message. Who "loves" a delinquent? No one. What happens to the "best laid plans"? They go astray, of course. What did the "child savers" do? They "invented" a pathology. Also like Ignatieff's scholars, historians of juvenile delinquency seldom venture beyond 1940. Whether this stems

from the general tendency of the discipline to relegate the recent past to journalism or from the proliferation and complexity of government programs and professional study is impossible to say. The paucity of work is clear, however, and makes a trenchant analysis such as John Moore's article (1969) on early federal policy all the more valuable.

There have also been substantial disagreements between scholars of delinquency. Rothman's review (1974) of my book and Platt's review (1977b) of Schlossman's illustrate the sharp tone of the debate. Scholarly dialogue has been limited. My study commends certain approaches, particularly the environmentalism of the early children's aid societies and the Chicago sociologists of the 1920s. "Tony" Platt, editor of *Crime and Social Justice*, regards variations between programs expressing the nature or the nurture philosophy as less significant than the controlling inequalities of capitalist society. These are differences between a moderate and a radical, but Platt probably views the gap as unbridgeable.

Platt, Rothman, and others have acted upon their convictions and become involved in preventive work. David and Sheila Rothman, for example, are codirectors of the Project on Community Alternatives for the mentally disabled. These are commendable efforts. But in the dominant ahistoricism of contemporary life, the historian/policymaker faces a dilemma beyond the bureaucratic frustrations and resource problems common to most social programs. To illustrate: Prescott's study (1981) bears the same title as Platt's, originally published in 1969 and revised in 1977. This shows bad manners but is not surprising. The modern world has little time for historians. The point here is that historians can make their most useful contribution by writing better history. How then should this be done?

In contrast to Ignatieff, I suggest that the demanding task is to "merely maintain" the complexity of historical reality. To do so, the historian must be primarily concerned with shaping the data of the past into a plausible representation of reality. The important skills are preciseness in describing events, sensitivity to distinctions, fairness in appraising individuals and groups, and enthusiasm in collecting and relating material. These count more than assertiveness or conviction in propounding a particular view. Such an approach does not require, in the case at hand, the conclusion that reformers were humanitarian or that social classes were illusory. Nor does it pretend to objectivity in the manner of Leopold von Ranke and the German school of the late nineteenth century. We are the products of our own age and will surely reflect it in our writing. But we must protest this fact. For, just as Horace Mann proclaimed himself the lawyer of the next generation, so historians are or should be the lawyers for generations gone by. Theory can be helpful in addressing this work, but it must always be ready to yield to the experiences of people who are now dead.

From this perspective there are two major shortcomings that characterize the historical literature on juvenile delinquency: (1) the failure to utilize the comparative approach, (2) the shortage of comprehensive case studies linking institutions and programs to the society that produced and sustained them. The reasons for these deficiencies are not hard to find. The language skills of American historians, never great, have followed the general downward trend of recent years. Even studies of European subjects written in English are ignored. Although there have been several case studies, they are vulnerable to the objection that they are unrepresentative. For the incipient policymaker, generalizations on the national level are important. Consequently, the preferred method is to gather a few facts and opinions on many programs rather than to accept the inherent contingency of the case study in exchange for the possible reward of an understanding that is both concrete and illustrative.

III. THE NINETEENTH CENTURY

Let us start by summarizing the inception of efforts to define and treat juvenile delinquency. The term itself was almost never used before 1800 because public authorities relied upon family government to correct or at least contain children who misbehaved or committed crimes. Early law codes and commentaries, such as Blackstone's, recognized mitigating circumstances for accused children, but the purpose of these statutes was not to exonerate or to categorize youthful wrongdoing but to sustain the family-based system of discipline. Colonial laws commanded parents to punish their children so that court officials would not have to intervene. By the late eighteenth century, however, the ability of family government to serve as the keystone of social control came to be doubted as villages developed into commercial towns and cities and as work left the home for the shop and factory. Families could no longer absorb vagrant youths as servants and apprentices. The children of poorer families left home, or were cast loose, to seek their way as deprived individuals. They became the source material for new definitions of crime, poverty, and juvenile delinquency.

The initial definers were established male citizens of the major East Coast cities, New York, Philadelphia, and Boston. Their sense of duty as well as their fear of impoverished, unfamiliar faces and anonymously committed crime led them to create a variety of institutions—almshouses, insane asylums, penitentiaries. They hoped these would not only isolate troublesome and indigent individuals but also provide them with the habits necessary to function as law-abiding individuals in a volatile capitalistic society.

Neglected and delinquent children were the objects of special attention because their behavior was more likely to be viewed as the product of environmental stimuli than as a sign of innate depravity. The basic fear was that children who were convicted of crimes suffered corruption by mixing with adult criminals, as did children who were released by sympathetic judges and juries. Thus, special institutions for children proliferated. These were first called houses of refuge, then reform schools, to indicate emphasis upon the growing enthusiasm for common schooling in the mid-nineteenth century. As this occurred, the concept of juvenile delinquency was born and began to come of age. Beyond describing the criminal and vagrant status of certain children, it announced the institutions that would correct, educate, and socialize apart from the ministrations of family government.

A word about the institutions themselves.

The houses of refuge and many of the early reform schools were organized on a congregate basis; that is, the children lived in cells or large dormitories and followed rigid schedules based upon contract labor in central workshops. Surrounded by high walls and characterized by harsh discipline, the refuges resembled the adult penitentiaries of the day. After lengthy incarcerations, the children were considered trained "for usefulness" and were released or apprenticed, the boys to local artisans and farmers, the girls to domestic service. The proliferation of these institutions in the mid-nineteenth century was marked. In 1867, Wines and Dwight noted seven state reform schools outside of New York and local refuges and reform schools in nine eastern and midwestern cities. By 1900 all states and major cities outside the Deep South had boys' reform schools and, in most cases, separate institutions for girls as well.

By this time an alternative strategy for preventing delinquency had developed. Epitomized by the work of Charles Loring Brace and his New York Children's Aid Society (1853), this approach emphasized noninstitutional solutions such as placing out. Brace agreed with reform-school founders that the temptations of the volatile urban environment were the basis for delinquency, but, unlike them, he believed that children were born with a disposition to do good and hence did not require lengthy incarceration. "The best of all asylums for the outcast child is the *farmer's home*," said Brace, and until the agrarian depression of the late 1880s he sent railroad cars full of "street arabs" to the western states.

Brace's ideas found institutional expression with the opening of the Massachusetts Industrial School for Girls (1856) and the Ohio Reform Farm (1857). The cottage or family plan reformatory, with its agrarian location and routine and its "elder brothers," "elder sisters," or surrogate parents supervising youths divided into "families," became the dominant type of reform school in the late nineteenth century. The family organization maintained its popularity even when vocational programs shifted from farm chores to industrial training in the twentieth century.

The end result was hardly a smooth-running

system. Institutionalists and advocates of placing out bickered constantly. Nativist Protestants expressed their preferences, thus hastening the development of Roman Catholic institutions. Delinquent girls did institutional housework and often were sexually abused when placed out. Negro children were initially more fortunate, since few institutions accepted them. Once admitted, they were usually segregated. By the Civil War, several institutions had experienced rioting and incendiarism, which usually began in the workshops where contract labor encouraged exploitation.

But it was a legitimized system. Institution founders and public authorities successfully defended themselves against the claims of parents who regarded reform schools and children's aid societies as usurpers of family government. In the precedent-setting decision *Ex Parte Crouse* (4 Wharton 9, Pennsylvania [1838]), the Pennsylvania Supreme Court denied the attempt of a father to free his daughter on a writ of habeas corpus from the Philadelphia House of Refuge saying, "The right of parental control is a natural, but not an inalienable one. . . . The infant has been snatched from a course which must have ended in confirmed depravity; and, not only is the restraint of her person lawful, but it would be an act of extreme cruelty to release her from it."

Historians' accounts of these developments are deficient in several respects. They gloss over the colonial era, describing the rudimentary state of institutions but relating this mainly to the still-powerful Calvinist ideology that resisted the concept of malleable human nature. They utilize the comparative method, but only to indicate the presence of seemingly similar reform activity in Europe; American institutions are usually presented as indigenous responses to the physical and social mobility of the Jacksonian era.[1] Also, scholars tend to rely upon the social control desires of elites as a sufficient causal explanation, and this blurs the variety of the institutional impulse. Of course these generalizations cannot be uniformly applied. Rothman (1971) and Mennel (1973b), for example, treat the colonial period, but in summary form. Neither gives concrete illustrations of shifting patterns of crime and family life that might have set the stage for institution building. Schlossman (1974, 1977) relates reform schools to emerging instrumentalist definitions of education, law, and even polite advice literature. The general criticisms hold, however, and can be best demonstrated by referring to a variety of studies and sources in addition to the principal monographs.

The colonial period is thinly treated because family history has become, in good measure, the property of colonial scholars, hence "warning out" modernists. Lawrence Stone's recent survey (1981) shows the increasing complexity of the subject and the intensity of its application in the pre-1800 era. He summarizes that, while the family was a key mediator in the change from traditional to modern society, it displayed a variety of types, by class, region, and religious affiliation, substantially limiting efforts to reach general conclusions. The difficulty peculiar to the study of delinquency is that the literary evidence is heavily weighted toward memoirs of genteel family life, thus favoring the definers of social problems and founders of institutions and relegating the inarticulate—that is, the clients and inmates—to demographic accounts.

This barrier may be more apparent than real. A number of studies (Ariès 1965; Bremner 1970–74; Jones 1938; Laslett 1965; Pinchbeck and Hewitt 1969–73) have confirmed important trends such as the decline of household-based apprenticeship and the proportionately increasing number of unattached young wage laborers living in cities, all of which precipitated planning for schools, missions, and houses of refuge. Moreover, the accounts of the elite bear closer reading, since they link the anxieties of affluent parents about their own children to their fears about the children of the poor. Allan Horlick (1975) has used such materials to show how New York businessmen of the 1840s, reflecting both the uncertainties of their own climb to power and the difficulty of limiting the aristocracy of the next generation to young men who endorsed charitable activity, created remedies and screening groups in the form of moralistic literature and the YMCA. The memoirs of the men who founded the first houses of refuge demonstrate that they conceived of the insti-

tutions as serving not only the court system but also a broad range of families who requested or were offered their assistance as patriarchs and neighbors (Pickett 1969; Mennel 1980a). The refuge founders placed substantial authority in the hands of the superintendents, whose conduct they expected would further exemplify their ideal of a society cemented by patriarchal families. The neighborhood orientation and local scope of the institutions (only New York and Philadelphia had refuges), as well as their quasi-public organization (state chartered but privately managed and funded by combinations of donations and public revenues), suggest a limited comparison with English institutions such as the Philanthropic Society's reformatory (1788) in London (Carlebach 1970; Heale 1976; Owen 1964; Pinchbeck and Hewitt 1969–73). The Anglo-American connection, as illuminated by family history, provides an additional way to demarcate the first years of definition and treatment.

In the later nineteenth century, the increasing number and variety of institutions made more apparent, though it did not originate, philosophical differences on the nature and requirements of childhood. Even the management of the refuges alternated between proponents of Benthamite rationalism, who drew their inspiration from the disciplinary routines of the penitentiaries, and advocates of the Swiss pedagogue Johann Pestalozzi, who believed that children were unique individuals who became socialized by appeals to their inherently good sentiments and thoughts (Lewis 1965; Mennel 1973b; Pickett 1969; Schlossman 1977; Slater 1970). The rationalists prevailed in the refuges, but the romantic ideal, fueled by religious evangelicalism, reappeared in the family reform schools and childrens' aid societies and also animated other reform activity such as the urban missions (Banner 1973; Langsam 1964; Rosenberg 1971; Smith 1957; Sutherland 1976; Wohl 1969).

The differences between silent obedience and emotional allegiance to adult values may appear moot to some contemporary observers, but they mattered greatly to nineteenth-century people and thus appeared in related facets of American life. The trend toward instrumentalism in law, for example, reflected the rationalist faith that human conduct could be improved by public policy (Horwitz 1971; Schlossman 1974). The growing genre of children's literature increasingly portrayed the young as disposed toward the path of virtue and receptive to confirmation through adult kindness and personal attention (Kiefer 1948; Wishy 1968). Education, like juvenile reform, stood at the crossroads. Many urban schools, with their hierarchical monitorial systems and emphasis upon rote learning and compulsory attendance, displayed the social control philosophy (Kaestle 1973; Kaestle and Vinovskis 1980; Katz 1968; Lazerson 1971). But in other schools the influence of Horace Mann's ideas liberated students and teachers alike from the narrow curriculum and harsh discipline of the colonial past, and they responded eagerly to the possibilities of learning (Cremin 1961; Messerli 1973). Reform school founders conceived of their institutions as midpoints between the common school and the penitentiary. They rejected serious offenders and utilized both rationalist and romantic approaches in their attempt to change young people (Fox 1970; Mennel 1973b).

The significance of early reform schools is best revealed in a comparative setting. Pedagogues such as Horace Mann and Henry Barnard publicized the development of European institutions, giving special prominence to two family schools: Johann H. Wichern's Rauhe Haus, founded in Hamburg in 1833, and Frederic A. DeMetz's "La Colonie Agricole" in Mettray, France (1839). American institution founders visited to study their agricultural routines and the cottage organization where "elder brothers" utilized various combinations of merit badges, military drill, singing, and close personal supervision to seek the allegiance of the *colóns* to the values of their keepers. The transfer of techniques is interesting, but the comparative approach is most informative in noting differences and omissions. In the 1850s, for example, western states often ignored European innovations and copied the congregate institutions of the East, while even those who undertook pilgrimages to Mettray or Hamburg did so with only hazy knowledge of Mann's or Barnard's work (Foucault 1978;

May 1973; Mennel 1980a, 1980b; Thavenet 1976).[2]

I used the comparative perspective in a case study of the Ohio Reform School for Boys (1857), one of the first cottage and farm institutions. The "Farm" was organized with reference to Mettray and other European schools, but differed from them in operation and reformatory goals. In Ohio, literacy and individual attainment were encouraged; nearly all of the entering boys could read, and half could write and cipher. Most could do all three upon release. They also had the opportunity to participate in dramatics and both solo and group singing. Education at Mettray was limited to thirty minutes a day and spent mostly on reading the catechism. Dramatics were not performed, and the boys were allowed to sing only as a group. Released *colóns* were often illiterate or could only read. Former Mettray inmates were carefully placed, usually in the army or in menial farm labor with families other than their own. They were then kept in these positions by the supervision of local notables or the military. Ohio boys were usually released to the care of parents or friends or left to their own devices; farm labor apprenticeships were regarded as confining. The parents of American delinquents were treated permissively in another respect. Local committing jurisdictions did not pursue them to pay individual maintenance costs despite administrative and legislative injunctions to do so. European, especially English, institutions forced parents to contribute to institutional income (Carlebach 1970; Mennel 1980a, 1980b; Pinchbeck and Hewitt 1969–73).

Institutional hierarchies and sociopolitical allegiances also present striking contrasts. At Mettray, all officers were trained, with a classical education, at the institution's Ecole Préparatoire. *Colóns* could serve as monitors (*frères aînés*) but could not aspire to higher positions. Ohio "elder brothers" were not required to have special training. Inmates could and did achieve these positions, and a few even became superintendents of other institutions. The chief obstacle to such advances was the disposition of superintendents and trustees to hire their own friends and relatives. European institutions underwrote hereditary power and privilege.

Wichern consistently supported the German monarchy, while DeMetz demonstrated his loyalty by sending a contingent of *colóns* to help the national guard crush the republican forces in the revolution of 1848. On the other hand, boys and officers from the Ohio Reform Farm joined the Union army in large numbers, in part because they opposed slave-owning (Mennel 1980a, 1980b; Muller 1976; Shanahan 1954).

The comparative method helps to show some of the salient characteristics of American institutions. Americans took selective readings of European schools, purposefully or unintentionally ignoring their hierarchical characteristics and lauding their agricultural routine and small-group organization. But this is what one should expect from a country where social relations were dynamic, where urbanism was a growing but disagreeable trend, and where racism and nativism coexisted with dedication to the ideal of equal opportunity.

The further significance of American reform schools is that they were broadly publicized and, at least at first, popularly supported. Ohio Farm annual reports were printed in German and English and summarized in local newspapers. Didactic children's literature and journals of education spoke well of the institutions but also used them to caution their juvenile audience. There was only minor political opposition to the founding of the schools; in the sea of turmoil that was Ohio politics in the 1850s, the reform school was an island of consensus. During the first two decades of operation there was a waiting list, and large numbers of parents and guardians committed their own children. Boys who were released, and even some who escaped, wrote letters on their own volition praising the institutions. Discharge papers were valued because they "proved character." In the early 1870s there was even an alumni association that returned for an annual picnic (Mennel 1980a, 1980b).

What this suggests is not that reform schools were idyllic retreats, but that they may have met the needs of a variety of people, not all of whom were founders of institutions. Other scholars have contended the same thing about the juvenile court, and John Hagan has noted that truly unpopular social control movements, such as Prohibition, are repealed (Hagan 1980;

Schlossman 1977; Schultz 1973). Paul Boyer's recent study (1978) has urged us to be sensitive to nineteenth-century reformers who sought to defuse broad-based fears of disorder that gained their lethal force from combining with equally popular suspicion of institutional solutions. The reform school's opponents were not academicians but country people ("Jacksonians") who regarded them as "soft" boarding schools. Labor groups complained about the contract system, while agricultural organizations such as the Patrons of Husbandry refused to cooperate with the farm reform schools because they were afraid that the status of farming would be degraded (Mennel 1980a, 1980b; Pickett 1969).

Eventually, of course, the institutions lost whatever value they had as redemptive agencies. The reasons are various. Gradual though grudging popular acceptance of industrialization secured the workshop as an organizational form and limited the development of farm schools. Workshops had been sore points from the beginning, especially when outside contractors were used. But even though the institution staff ran the shops by the 1880s, the rate of work-related death and injury continued to increase, and most fires were set there (Mennel 1973b; Pickett 1969; Rothman 1971). Thomas Bender has related the changing character of charity societies to the passing of the generation of founders who had daily contact with the presumed objects of their beneficence. Their successors, perhaps because they tended to accept more easily the prevalent social divisions, relied upon paid subordinates to organize the daily work (Bender 1975). The same trend was evident in reform schools, where the demands for routinized operation were even greater. Superintendents and staff increasingly functioned as buffers, which meant keeping the children in, since the outside world no longer viewed the institutions as novelties (National Conference of Charities and Correction 1893). Serious politicians and distinguished foreign visitors like Alexis de Tocqueville and Charles Dickens no longer came to call. However, the schools did serve occasionally as party spots for sporting trustees and state legislators. Reform school officials, emulating their superiors, began to insulate themselves from their inmates. Attendance at summer schools and charity conferences came to count more for advancement than time spent with the children. The Ohio superintendent visited the Rauhe Haus and proclaimed his allegiance to its warm personal style and humble cottages. To implement this ideal, he requested an appropriation to build large Gothic residence halls and an administration building, thus permitting the demolition of the original farm cottages.[3]

Conflict continued, but the institutions endured. And why not? Their rise had occurred in a society where economic and social change had rendered ambiguous the scope and authority of existing institutions, particularly the patriarchal family. In their early careers, the schools had accomplishments to be proud of, and even in decline they served as conveniences that society was unwilling to abandon. But they were blatant advertisements for social control, inappropriate for a society that increasingly valued elaborate though unspecific warnings, particularly to the young. Thus the opposition that began to form came less from the inmates and their parents than from the young middle-class men and women who promoted a more decentralized system, one that promised broader though less intense surveillance as well as the opportunity to apply social and psychological therapies. This interpretation has stressed popular acceptance of the institutions and of gradual efforts to change them and suggests that recent studies have overemphasized the power and coerciveness of those who founded and managed the schools.

Before discussing the juvenile court and its influence, special mention should be made of two research areas: local studies on crime, order, and police and works on female delinquency. Recent crime and police studies have excelled in analyzing the ecology and etiology of lawbreaking and disorder (Johnson 1973, 1979; Lane 1967; Laurie 1973; Monkkonen 1975; Richardson 1970; Schneider 1980). Boys and young men appear here as gang members and fire laddies, some of whom were surely sent to institutions. But examination of reform school records reveals that only a minority of inmates arrived via local criminal courts. County common pleas and probate courts were more likely venues, and disputes within families were often precipitating factors (Mennel 1980b). Local court studies could clarify the extent to which courts and institutions served families seeking to commit their children or citizens fearing crime and disorder. The implication is that gangs, particularly when they were affiliated with local political organizations, may have been able to protect their members from classification as delinquents, while young people who conflicted with their parents and had no peer groups to support them were prime candidates for reform school.

The relative scarcity of recent studies on the history of female delinquency (Manton 1976; Brenzel 1975, 1978; Schlossman and Wallach 1978) may be explained in part by the challenges they pose on perplexing and controversial issues in the writing of women's history. On the one hand, to the degree that institutions confined women and girls on morals charges, they require censure, since these were unpunished male offenses. But criticism must be tempered for several reasons. First, as Barbara Brenzel has shown (1978, 1980), the schools did provide a degree of care and protection for homeless and abused girls. Second, and more important, women administrators took charge of female institutions in the late nineteenth century, which may be interpreted as a sign of progress in the narrative of women's history.

A complicating factor, raised though certainly not encompassed by female reform schools, is the meaning of sexual behavior. Homosexuality and lesbianism were regular features of life in juvenile institutions. After 1900, a few adult female reformatories had permissive attitudes toward lesbian relationships (Freedman 1981). In general, however, extraordinary efforts were made to suppress sexual activity, of which there was plenty. The matron at the Western House of Refuge (New York) complained that she could not prevent black and white girls from "[getting] together in bed." An 1891 investigation of the Ohio Reform School discovered many boys with venereal sores on the mouth and noted the superintendent's practice of personally applying a blistering fluid to the sexual organs of boys who were caught masturbating (Mennel 1973b, 1980b). Historians might profitably relate adult attitudes to the imperatives of the economy, which condoned gluttony and overdressing while frowning upon sex and desire. The trick is to convey the ways contemporary mores encouraged as well as dampened libidinal drives and to do so without succumbing to the vogue of intimate self-revelation and imposing one's own preferences upon the reader.

IV. THE JUVENILE COURT

The first juvenile court opened in Illinois in 1899, and the idea spread rapidly to other states; by 1912 twenty-two states had passed juvenile court legislation, and all but two had done so by 1932. In one sense the court represented the culmination of efforts to reform children without committing them to reform school or sending them to jail. The Illinois law combined the concept of probation, first developed in Massachusetts (1869), where children's aid societies supervised children who were awaiting trial or who had been sentenced, with several New York laws providing for separate trial sessions and detention facilities. As courts developed their own probation staffs, detention homes, and investigative services, the reform schools were relegated to places of "dernier resort," in the words of one superintendent (Mennel 1972).

The juvenile court was more than a systematic alternative to incarceration, however; Jane Addams claimed that it signified "almost a change in mores." She referred not only to the legal innovations but also to the fact that the court's leverage—that is, its administrative power to gather case histories and its generally urban location—made it a key weapon in the Progressive campaign to get government to assume a greater responsibility for social welfare (Flexner and Baldwin 1912; Lou 1927). The social and psychological facts about the children appearing before the court offered the most compelling evidence for the adoption of child labor laws, mothers' pensions, municipal playgrounds, compulsory school attendance, public health care for children, and rigorous regulation of tenement-building. Thus the popularity of the juvenile court derived in some measure from the fact that it served as a laboratory for the professional study of delinquency. Theoretical works based on empirical research flourished, with the ecological

approach of the University of Chicago sociologists and the psychological studies of William Healy becoming ancestors of the type. In the daily operation of the court, this trend was manifested in the eclipse of voluntary probation officers by civil service professionals trained in the "art" of gathering desired information and supervising a client population (Levine and Levine 1970; Lubove 1965; Mennel 1973b).

An important result of this activity was to rescue the *parens patriae* doctrine from the reform schools, where its credibility was being seriously undermined. By expressing a preference for diagnosis and probation, the court implicitly downgraded incarceration, yet retained it as a judicial option. Court decisions soon ratified the new arrangement. *Commonwealth v. Fisher* (213 Pennsylvania 48 [1905]), a decision upholding the parental character of the Pennsylvania juvenile court, became the most often cited precedent, concluding, "the legislature surely may provide for the salvation of . . . a child, if its parents or guardians be unable or unwilling to do so, by bringing it into one of the courts of the state without any process at all, for the purpose of subjecting it to the state's guardianship and protection."

The court did not lack criticism even in its early days (Eliot 1914). This stemmed mostly from its imprecise, encompassing jurisdiction, a situation that was addressed by the development of family and domestic relations courts. Occasional studies such as Sheldon and Eleanor Glueck's *One Thousand Delinquents* (1934) faulted the effectiveness of the court and its agencies but did not question the institution's benevolent intent. After World War II, however, a number of investigations accused local and state governments of not providing entitled services to wards of the court. In time, legal decisions ratified this disillusion by according children who appeared in court most of the rights of adults accused of crimes (Bremner 1970–74; Mennel 1973b).

Research on the modern era is complicated by a new obstacle but characterized by traditional defects. Confidentiality of records poses the additional problem. Archivists and institution officials are understandably edgy about providing access to the records of living persons. Of course they must also take into account the possibility of objections from descendants of nineteenth-century delinquents. In either case, the scholar's promise to use pseudonyms or initials can sometimes allay official doubts. As noted earlier, however, the importance of the issue is deflated because few historians are interested in the case study approach, which makes the heaviest demands upon archival holdings where confidentiality is likely to be a consideration. Rather, they are content to sample published works from a variety of locations and generalize therefrom. These points can be illustrated by referring to the literature.

We begin with the exception that proves the case. Stephen Schlossman's *Love and the American Delinquent* (1977) is the most useful study because of its case study orientation. Schlossman uses court and institution records to systematically link the failures of the Wisconsin reform school to the later flounderings of the Milwaukee Juvenile Court and to put both into the context of the larger reform movements of their times. Thus the cottage school was connected to the domestic advice literature of Lydia Maria Child and Catharine Beecher, which sanctified the family as a refuge against social and economic disorder. And the juvenile court, like the playground movement, mothers' pensions, and home economics programs, reflected the greater optimism of the Progressive era. All of the latter were designed to strengthen and discipline the families of the poor with minimal reference to institutional sanctions. Yet, as Schlossman notes, the court no less than the institution set aside "affectional discipline" in favor of a more expeditious approach. The detention center became a jail, and judges browbeat children and punished them for offenses unrelated to those that brought them into court. Reformatory and court authorities showed little interest in establishing personal relationships with the children but eagerly counted as successes those who dropped out of sight. These officials, Schlossman emphasizes, were not members of a status-conscious local elite but rather shared the disadvantaged origins of their clients (Schlossman 1977).

The only incongruous note is Schlossman's conclusion that a child-centered approach, epitomized to him by Ben Lindsey's Denver Juvenile Court, is possible. Schlossman's evidence,

however, sketches fundamentally shallow and manipulative adult personalities clearly incapable of effecting such a transformation. The contradiction may not be that serious. Lindsey was a master of public relations, as much absorbed in the creation of his own image as a crusader as in spending time talking to children. Like "Daddy" George, founder of the George Junior Republic ("nothing without labor"), he gave affection to people of all ages in the course of a life filled with many interests. What set Lindsey apart was his insatiable curiosity and encompassing humanity, rare traits in any field of endeavor. But he did share some of the less attractive characteristics of Schlossman's little-known court authorities (Holl 1971; Larsen 1972; Mennel 1973b).

Like Schlossman, David Rothman is concerned with the rift between humanitarian rhetoric and neglectful practice. He utilizes conscience and convenience to describe the division in order to emphasize the pridefulness of early twentieth century reformers, particularly their faith that the new social and behavioral sciences would provide a theory of treatment based upon "individual justice." Convenience signifies the ease with which political and bureaucratic interests frustrated these ideals. Rothman shares with Schlossman (and with the reform school and juvenile court founders themselves) a belief that the downward direction of historical change is not inevitable, though neither is specific about desirable therapies or about strategies for institutionalizing them. Ryerson, reflecting the more limited view of the juvenile court implicit in the *Gault* decision (*In Re Gault*, 387 U.S. 1[1967]), is more cautious but, like Rothman and Schlossman, believes that somewhere in the vast array of delinquency prevention programs is one that not only works but can be generally applied (Rothman 1980; Ryerson 1978; Schlossman 1977).

This faith is commendable in that it encourages at least the mention of various programs extant in given periods. It resists the determinism characteristic of other accounts such as Anthony Platt's *The Child Savers* (1977a) and Christopher Lasch's *Haven in a Heartless World* (1977). Platt's analysis of child-saving philanthropy in late nineteenth century Illinois caricatures the role of middle-class women from

Hull House who helped to create the first juvenile court, presenting them as agents of corporate capitalism primarily intent on diminishing the civil liberties and privacy of lower-class and immigrant youth. Lasch portrays social workers and psychologists as absorbed in creating therapeutic jargon in order to secure themselves as professional groups by making their audiences expert-dependent. Both of these works deny altruism as a cause of welfare activity. Lasch's, however, is more interesting, since it documents a strain of intolerance among professional groups advocating egalitarian social policies (Lasch 1973, 1977). De Tocqueville first made this connection after observing Jacksonian democracy. Lasch is intrigued by the hostility of most social scientists to the suggestion that their work, even when publicly supported, may contribute little to the diminution of crime, delinquency, and mental illness.[4]

Rothman's work deserves separate treatment here since it is the best known. *Conscience and Convenience* has a moderate appearance, being neither as harshly skeptical as Lasch and Platt nor as partial to early social workers and juvenile court proponents as a number of studies (Chambers 1963, 1971; Davis 1967; Leiby 1967; Trattner 1968). But Rothman is unpersuasive, at least insofar as his treatment of delinquency is concerned, because he does not utilize the relevant work of other scholars or respect the complexity of his subjects' thoughts and actions.[5] For example, Rothman presents the psychologist G. Stanley Hall as a key influence in the development of the juvenile court because of his supposed enthusiasm for individual case study and environmental causation. But a reading of Dorothy Ross's excellent though difficult study (1972) shows Hall's greatest interest to be the development of a neo-Darwinist philosophy of human development in which youthful misbehavior was a "stage" that could be little influenced by institutions. And Miriam Van Waters, the foremost figure in female corrections from 1920 to 1950, walked out of Hall's seminar after disputing his contention that a prostitute was a "type" (Mennel 1973b).

Rothman's discussion of Dr. William Healy, founder of the first mental hygiene clinic for juvenile court children, best illustrates the problem. To Rothman, the essence of Healy's representativeness was his aimless experimentalism. Supposedly, Healy dabbled with Freud but propounded no particular psychological theory in amassing *The Individual Delinquent* (1915), the book for which he is best known. This may be a proper charge to level against someone who was styling himself as a social psychologist, but Rothman has an obligation to discuss the term. Healy was clearly influenced by the studies of George Mead and Charles Cooley, who rejected the determinisms of Freud and John B. Watson and described the self as originating both in the social process and in the images that the individual constructed of other persons and objects. The premise of *The Individual Delinquent* was that human behavior was shaped largely by the self-concept the individual acquired from society. Moreover, as John Burnham has shown (1961), Healy's work marked the beginning of a more open-ended approach to the scientific study of delinquency by repudiating the monocausism of eugenicists and Lombrosian criminologists. Healy himself had first studied delinquents by taking anatomical measurements to see whether youthful offenders conformed to Lombroso's description of the born criminal. Finally, Healy's lukewarm Freudianism developed later, after the Glueck's study (1934) reported a high rate of recidivism among children treated at the Judge Baker Center (Boston) where Healy was director. This cast general doubt upon the usefulness of community mental health clinics, a movement popularized by Healy in the 1920s, and thus encouraged him to stress the familial causes of delinquency (Mennel 1973b).

Rothman's incomplete analysis of Healy's ideas is matched by his failure to probe the broader significance of the Judge Baker Center's mediocre record. No thorough study of the subject exists, but it is not difficult to speculate on the quality of the relationship that existed between the Protestant psychologists from the center and the Roman Catholic judges, politicians, and social workers in the Boston Juvenile Court.[6] How were they supposed to react to the demand of Augusta Bronner, Healy's lifelong collaborator and second wife, for greater authority to remove delinquent children from their homes in order "to make over unworthy or stupid parents, to teach them the principles of child psychology, to alter in very fundamental ways a considerable share of mankind"? In Rothman's narrative, Catholic aid societies exist mainly to play cooperative roles (as they did in the Chicago Juvenile Court) in the emergence of the powerful secular state. His disinclination to discuss the recrudescent character of religious and cultural conflict is ironic, since his own style resembles the jeremiad of the Puritan preacher. For the mid-twentieth century believer, therapy replaces religion to sustain the faithful in an error-prone world and nurtures the possibility that they may inherit the earth. Nothing dates Rothman's work more than the contemporary revival of interest in the religiocultural bases of life.

Rothman makes some interesting points but generally does not follow through with sustained analysis. He notes, for example, that district attorneys favored the juvenile court because it uncluttered their calendars. To what degree was this so? Rothman does not pursue this issue or related questions such as the role of local bar associations in the formation and operation of the court. On another subject, he establishes that reformatory superintendents favored military drill over psychiatric treatment as the prime agent of reform. Rothman sees this preference as a reflection of their army careers but also as a necessity, given low staff wages that attracted purportedly unskilled applicants. A complete discussion, however, would probe the connection between reform schools and military enlistment and note the high esteem that military forces then enjoyed. Doubtless some of the reform school staff were former enlisted men and therefore skilled in teaching calisthenics and drill. Morris Janowitz (1978) has noted that war and peacetime drafts were important integrators of American society in the fifty years before Vietnam. Reformatory institutions complemented this development in a minor way. The point here is not to praise reform school militarism but to explain it in the context of earlier twentieth century history instead of judging it from the inclinations of the age of therapy.

The strangest thing about Rothman's book is that is contains no analysis at all of the crime and delinquency studies of the Chicago school of sociology. Clifford Shaw's Chicago Area Pro-

ject (1934) stressed the inevitability of delinquency in slum areas and the need to channel the energies of delinquent gangs into legitimate community and neighborhood groups that could apply pressure for better services on municipal and state welfare bureaucracies (Shaw and McKay 1942). This approach influenced a later generation of planners, especially those organizing the Community Action Programs in the War on Poverty (Marris and Rein 1973). One would think that Rothman might want to search out other anti-institutional enthusiasts even though his own interests focus upon mental patients rather than delinquent gangs.

Chicago sociologists were also great believers in the importance of the delinquent youth's own account of his life and troubles, with Shaw's *The Jack-Roller* (1930) being the model of the type. Contemporary social scientists and historians, by contrast, are interested mainly in clinical case histories, which is a pity since the major autobiographies of delinquents are among the more revealing documents of modern times. Brendan Behan's *Borstal Boy* (1959), an acid portrayal of the class hatreds embedded in British reformatory policy, can profitably be compared with the endorsement of Borstals by Healy and Bendict Alper (1941), which shows how Americans, who refused to acknowledge the existence of social classes, expressed opinions about them. The account of Josiah Flynt Willard (1908) and Jean Genêt (1966) are equally shattering in their effect because they put society rather than the individual youth under the microscope.

To conclude, the reader interested in gaining a comprehensive understanding of the origins of modern delinquency programs ought to supplement the accounts mentioned above with more general histories of social welfare activity. Trattner's biography (1968) of the social-work executive Homer Folks and Chambers's biography (1971) of Paul Kellogg, editor of the *Survey*, show reformers with broad interests, reflective attitudes toward their own policies, and distrust of panaceas, such as eugenics, that minimized human capacity to change. Allen Davis's study (1967) of the settlement house movement presents young men and women, often with sheltered upbringings, motivated by their compassion for the trials of recent immigrants and their confidence that the new biological and statistical sciences could improve urban life for everyone. The juvenile court was but one part of this hope, and, like related causes (child labor and consumer protection laws, etc.), it suffered from the general disillusion with social explanation that flowed from World War I and its aftermath. Roy Lubove (1965) traces this shift within social work as early practitioners defined the profession on the basis of social diagnostic skills, but later created an internal hierarchy enshrining psychoanalytic case work as "queen" in the 1920s. In all of these studies we see life through the eyes of decades other than our own and can easily imagine that some delinquents fared better than others.

V. RECENT STUDY

Several histories touch one aspect or another of delinquency policy in the era since World War II, but there has been no interest comparable to earlier periods. The Bremner documents provide summary coverage to the early 1970s, and two political studies perceptively analyze the tangled underbrush of congressional study and Great Society policy (Bremner 1970–74; Marris and Rein 1973; Moore 1969). Some works discuss various social and psychological theories but suffer from limited knowledge of the range of therapies and of the particular reasons for the popularity of any one approach (Finestone 1976; Levine and Levine 1970; Ryerson 1978). As I noted earlier, the lack of interest may be attributed in part to disciplinary inhibitions and to the overwhelming volume and variety of programs encouraged by a welfare state that continued to expand until 1980.

There may be another, more significant reason for the lack of scholarly activity. In recent years the definition and treatment of delinquency has been most influenced by the alteration of the juvenile court following the *Gault* decision and by the growth of diversion programs predicated upon broad professional distrust of institutions. By conveying to juveniles most of the standards and safeguards of criminal law, *Gault* and related decisions undercut the court's reputation, which was both valid and hyperbolic, as a humanitarian agency. This reduction in authority was accelerated by the

prevalent assumption of many community-based programs that delinquents were not guilty of crimes but were victims of social and economic deprivation (U.S. President's Commission on Law Enforcement and Administration of Justice 1967). The relevant point is that both developments accorded with the transcendental mood of historical scholarship in the late 1960s and 1970s. Current reticence, therefore, may derive from the fact that one generation's panaceas have not worked.

Why not? A standard reply is that they were never tried. The antipoverty initiatives of the Great Society were buried in Vietnam and the Middle East, and a series of conservative administrations ensured that there would be no resurrection. Such an explanation exemplifies what Charles Sanders Peirce called the method of tenacity, that is, settling doubt by adhering without reflection to original premises. A more flexible method of inquiry hints at uncomfortable truths. For example, the United States Comptroller General's Report (1975), detailing the failures and corruption of federal antidelinquency programs, would not surprise the student of early federal policy. Miriam Van Waters's report for the National Commission on Law Observance and Enforcement (1931) outlined the cruelty and neglect suffered by youthful violators of federal law. Moreover, any appraisal of recent federal programs, particularly in the area of children's rights, ought to recognize that their libertarian character left a mixed legacy. Formal rights were conveyed, but alternative policies based upon economic redistribution were frustrated.

The fundamental premise of libertarian reform was that families, group homes, and peer groups would provide suitable alternatives to the discredited courts and institutions. In fact, the family became libertarianism's most prominent victim, since the philosophy's basic expression was the quest for individual authenticity in the marketplace. In the study of social problems, this meant the atomistic proliferation of "fields" of study. The subjects were serious enough—child abuse, "parenting," and so forth—but the investigative results were often either obvious or wrong. Additionally, to the degree that study was animated by the desire to make professional status a universal social goal, it put heavy pressure on families who dissented from it. The historians' culpability here is compounded because they gave deinstitutionalization a glamorous gloss by idealizing the colonial period because of its reliance upon family government.

Disillusion, deceit, and now political opposition have flowed inexorably from the contradictions of Great Society programs. Thus Margaret Rosenheim's *Justice for the Child* (1962) became *Pursuing Justice for the Child* (1976), expressing the increasing tentativeness of veteran social investigators. Malcolm W. Klein has noted (1979) that evaluations of programs designed to keep children out of institutions have shown that the programs develop strategies ("net widening" is the operative term) to maintain their client populations, presumably at the level necessary to secure continued funding. And surely, the Reagan administration's proposed policy of block-granting many social programs is based in part upon belief that sociological study may exacerbate rather than solve life's problems. The bet is that state and local governments agree and will fund programs whose constituent demands (day care and centers for the elderly, for examples) are more pressing than those of the advice-giving industry.

There is no cause for celebration here. We currently lack only the assurance of a high government official that the administration is not "antiyouth" to know for certain that valuable programs as well as dubious research will be eliminated. Indeed, the new age arrived before the 1980 election, with many states passing laws lowering the age and increasing the number of offenses for which juveniles could be sent to criminal court. The new conservatism appears harsher than that of Potter Stewart and Warren Burger, whose dissenting opinions in the *Gault* era were based upon the belief that conveying constitutional safeguards to youthful lawbreakers was less important than providing the juvenile court more resources to fulfill its mandate.

Popular reaction to forthcoming reductions in government services is still uncertain, but there is agreement that a half-century of growth in federal and state programs has ended. Historians may or may not be apprehensive about future developments, but they generally welcome watersheds because these help to organize and explain significant blocks of time.

Some scholars regard periods mainly as conveniences, but others take seriously Hegel's injunction that the importance of things becomes apparent at the moment of their disappearance—or, as he put it, the Owl of Minerva flies only at dusk. The fact of flight should encourage historians to explore the recent past. Why did psychological study enjoy such a vogue in the 1940s and 1950s? To what extent did institutions incorporate psychoanalytic techniques? Did the revival of social theory in the 1960s make a similar impact? How did the two approaches interact at various levels of government and within particular institutions? In answering these and related questions, historians should utilize case studies, biographies, and the comparative approach.

As they conduct these investigations, historians should remind themselves of the essentials of their calling. Charles Rosenberg (1979) comments, "It is no more than a truism to observe that social scientists are trained to discern and formulate patterns that can be expressed in general terms, while the historian is tied by sensibility and socialization to the particular." If so, it bears repeating, because historians embarrass themselves when they forget. History succeeds when the author addresses readers in a suggestive rather than a didactic tone in order to vivify forces and lives beyond the audience's immediate experiences. Social investigators may enhance their own studies by appreciating the difference.

NOTES

1. "Jacksonian reform" is one of those phrases that historians casually accept and shouldn't. Few of the individuals who built reformatory institutions supported Jackson; many more viewed his vigorous individualism as a prime cause of social disorder (Mennel 1973b). Furthermore, scholars do not use presidents' names to characterize reform in later periods. "Lincolnian" sounds awkward, as does "Rooseveltian," which is confusing as well. "Jacksonian" is euphonious, elastic (from the Battle of New Orleans to the Mexican War), but not very helpful to the matter at hand.

2. The low rate of emigration from France to the United States contributed to the fact that Mettray was never well understood. The Rauhe Haus fared better because it was known in the Lutheran settlements where Wichern's umbrella organization, die Innere Mission, was active. However, these communities were themselves fairly well insulated from the non-German-speaking community.

3. European institutions such as Red Hill (the Philanthropic Society's home), Mettray, and the Rauhe Haus have retained or replicated their original buildings. At Mettray the church occupies the central place reserved for the administration building in American reform schools.

4. See also Henrika Kuklick's review of a related work, Burton J. Bledstein, *The Culture of Professionalism* (1976), *Journal of American History* 68 (1981):152–53. Richard Sennett, *Families against the City* (1970), a study of one middle-class Chicago neighborhood's reaction to the Haymarket Massacre (1886), illustrates yet another determinism. On the basis of extremely limited evidence, Sennett contends that demands for more police protection came mainly from nuclear families who had isolated themselves from the diversity of the city as extended families had not.

5. The same has also been said about his discussion of mental health. See Gerald Grob's review of *Conscience and Convenience* in *Commentary* 70 (1980):75–77. See also Gerald N. Grob, "Abuse in American Mental Hospitals in Historical Perspective: Myth and Reality," *International Journal of Law and Psychiatry* 3 (1980):295–310.

6. Morris J. Vogel, *The Invention of the Modern Hospital: Boston, 1870–1930* (Chicago: University of Chicago Press, 1980), discusses the conflict between Protestant trustees of Boston City Hospital and Irish ward politicians.

REFERENCES

ABBOTT, GRACE, ED.
1938   *The Child and the State.* 2 vols. Chicago: University of Chicago Press.

ALTGELD, JOHN P.
1886   *Our Penal Machinery and Its Victims.* Chicago: A. C. McClurg.

ARIÈS, PHILLIPE
1965   *Centuries of Childhood: A Social History of Family Life.* New York: Vintage Books.

BAILYN, BERNARD
1960   *Education in the Forming of American Society.* Chapel Hill: University of North Carolina Press.

BANNER, LOIS
1973   "Religious Benevolence as Social Control: A Critique of an Interpretation," *Journal of American History* 60:23–41.

BARNARD, HENRY
1854   *National Education in Europe.* Hartford: F. C. Brownell.

BEARD, CHARLES, AND MARY BEARD
1927   *The Rise of American Civilization.* New York: Macmillan.

BEARD, MARY, ED.
1933   *America through Women's Eyes.* New York: Macmillan.

BEAUMONT, GUSTAYE DE, AND ALEXIS DE TOCQUEVILLE
1835   *On the Penitentiary System of the United States.* Carbondale: Southern Illinois University: 1964 reprint edition.

BEHAN, BRENDAN
1959   *Borstal Boy.* New York: Alfred A. Knopf.

BENDER, THOMAS
1975   *Toward an Urban Vision: Ideas and Institutions in Nineteenth Century America.* Lexington: University Press of Kentucky.

BLEDSTEIN, BURTON J.
1976   *The Culture of Professionalism: The Middle Class and the Development of Higher Education in America.* New York: Norton.

BOYER, PAUL
1978   *Urban Masses and the Moral Order in America, 1820–1920.* Cambridge: Harvard University Press.

BRACE, CHARLES LORING
1872   *The Dangerous Classes of New York, and Twenty Years' Work among Them.* New York: Wynkoop and Hallenbeck.

BREMNER, ROBERT H.
1956   *From the Depths: The Discovery of Poverty in the United States.* New York: New York University Press.
1970–74 *Children and Youth in America: A Documentary History.* 3 vols. Cambridge: Harvard University Press.

BRENZEL, BARBARA M.
1975   "Lancaster Industrial School for Girls: A Social Portrait of a Nineteenth Century Reform School," *Feminist Studies* 3:40–53.
1978   "The Girls at Lancaster: A Social Portrait of the First Reform School for Girls in North America, 1856–1905." Ed.D. dissertation, Harvard University.
1980   "Domestication as Reform: A Study of the Socialization of Wayward Girls, 1856–1905," *Harvard Educational Review* 50:196–213.

BURLEIGH, EDITH N., AND FRANCES K. HARRIS
1923   *The Delinquent Girl.* New York: New York School of Social Work.

BURNHAM, JOHN C.
1961   "Oral History Interviews of William Healy and Augusta Bronner." Houghton Library, Harvard University.

CARLEBACH, JULIUS
1970   *Caring for Children in Trouble.* New York: Humanities Press.

CHAMBERS, CLARKE A.
1963   *Seedtime of Reform: American Social Service and Social Action, 1918–1933.* Minneapolis: University of Minnesota Press.
1971   *Paul U. Kellogg and the "Survey": Voices for Social Welfare and Social Justice.* Minneapolis: University of Minnesota Press.

CLOWARD, RICHARD, AND LLOYD OHLIN
1960   *Delinquency and Opportunity: A Theory of Delinquent Gangs.* New York: Free Press.

CREMIN, LAWRENCE
1961   *The Transformation of the School: Progressivism in*

American Education, 1876–1957. New York: Alfred A. Knopf.

DAVIS, ALLEN F.
1967   *Spearheads for Reform: The Social Settlements and the Progressive Movement, 1890–1914.* New York: Oxford.

DEUTSCH, ALBERT
1952   *Our Rejected Children.* Boston: Little, Brown.

ELIOT, THOMAS D.
1914   *The Juvenile Court and the Community.* New York: Macmillan.

FAULKNER, HAROLD U.
1931   *The Question for Social Justice, 1898–1914.* New York: Macmillan.

FINESTONE, HAROLD
1976   *Victims of Change: Juvenile Delinquents in American Society.* Westport, Conn.: Greenwood Press.

FLEXNER, BERNARD, AND ROGER N. BALDWIN
1912   *Juvenile Courts and Probation.* New York: Century.

FLYNN, FRANK T.
1954   "Judge Merritt W. Pinckney and the Early Days of the Juvenile Court in Chicago," *Social Service Review* 28:20–30.

FOLKS, HOMER
1902   *The Care of Destitute, Neglected and Delinquent Children.* New York: Macmillan.

FOUCAULT, MICHEL
1978   *Discipline and Punish.* New York: Pantheon.

FOX, SANFORD J.
1970   "Juvenile Justice Reform: An Historical Perspective," *Stanford Law Review* 22:1187–1239.

FREEDMAN, ESTELLE B.
1981   *Their Sisters' Keepers: Women's Prison Reform in America, 1830–1930.* Ann Arbor: University of Michigan Press.

GENÊT, JEAN
1966   *Miracle of the Rose.* New York: Grove Press.

GLUECK, SHELDON, AND ELEANOR GLUECK
1934   *One Thousand Juvenile Delinquents.* Cambridge: Harvard University Press.

GORDON, MICHAEL
1971   *Juvenile Delinquency in the American Novel, 1905–1965: A Study in the Sociology of Literature.* Bowling Green, Ohio: Bowling Green University Popular Press.

GRIFFEN, CLIFFORD S.
1960   *Their Brothers' Keepers: Moral Stewardship in the United States, 1800–1865.* New Brunswick, N.J.: Rutgers University Press.

HAGAN, JOHN
1980   "The Legislation of Crime and Delinquency: A Review of Theory, Method and Research," *Law and Society Review* 14:603–28.

HAREVEN, TAMARA K., ED.
1971   *Anonymous Americans: Explorations in Nineteenth-Century Social History.* Englewood Cliffs, N.J.: Prentice-Hall.

HAWES, JOSEPH M.
1971   *Children in Urban Society: Juvenile Delinquency in Nineteenth Century America.* New York: Oxford.

HEALE, MICHAEL J.
1976   "From City Fathers to Social Critics: Humanitarianism and Government in New York, 1790–1860," *Journal of American History* 43:21–41.

HEALY, WILLIAM
1915   *The Individual Delinquent.* Boston: Little, Brown.

HEALY, WILLIAM, AND BENEDICT S. ALPER
1941   *Criminal Youth and the Borstal System.* New York: Commonwealth Fund.

HOLL, JACK M.
1971   *Juvenile Reform in the Progressive Era: William R. George and the Junior Republic Movement.* Ithaca: Cornell University Press.

HORLICK, ALLAN STANLEY
1975   *Country Boys and Merchant Princes: The Social Control of Young Men in New York.* Lewisburg: Bucknell University Press.

HORWITZ, MORTON J.
1971   "The Emergence of an Instrumental Conception of American Law," *Perspectives in American History* 5:287–328.

HURLEY, TIMOTHY D.
1907   *The Origin of the Juvenile Court Law.* Chicago: Visitation and Aid Society.

IGNATIEFF, MICHAEL
1978   *A Just Measure of Pain: The Penitentiary in the Industrial Revolution, 1750–1850.* New York: Pantheon.

1981   "State, Civil Society and Total Institution: A Critique of Recent Social Histories of Punishment." In *Crime and Justice: An Annual Review of Research,* vol. 3, ed. Michael Tonry and Norval Morris. Chicago: University of Chicago Press.

JAMES, HOWARD
1970   *Children in Trouble: A National Scandal.* New York: David McKay.

JANOWITZ, MORRIS
1978   *The Last Half-Century: Societal Change and Politics in America.* Chicago: University of Chicago Press.

JOHNSON, DAVID R.
1973   "Crime Patterns in Philadelphia, 1840–70." In *The Peoples of Philadelphia: A History of Ethnic Groups and Lower-Class Life, 1790–1940,* ed. Allen F. Davis and Mark H. Haller. Philadelphia: Temple University Press.

1979   *Policing the Urban Underworld: The Impact of Crime on the Development of the American Police, 1800–1887.* Philadelphia: Temple University Press.

JONES, MARY G.
1938   *The Charity School Movement: A Study of Eighteenth Century Puritanism in Action.* Cambridge: Cambridge University Press.

KAESTLE, CARL F.
1973.   *The Evolution of an Urban School System: New York City, 1750–1850.* Cambridge: Harvard University Press.

KAESTLE, CARL F., AND MARIS A. VINOVSKIS.
1980   *Education and Social Change in Nineteenth-Century Massachusetts.* Cambridge: Cambridge University Press.

KAMMEN, MICHAEL, ED.
1980   *The Past before Us: Contemporary Historical Writing in the United States.* Ithaca: Cornell University Press.

KATZ, MICHAEL B.
1968   *The Irony of Early School Reform: Educational Innovation in Mid-Nineteenth Century Massachusetts.* Cambridge: Harvard University Press.

KIEFER, MONICA
1948   *American Children through Their Books.* Philadelphia: University of Pennsylvania Press.

KLEIN, MALCOLM W.
1979   "Deinstitutionalization and Diversion of Juvenile Offenders: A Litany of Impediments." In *Crime and Justice: An Annual Review of Research,* vol. 1, ed. Norval Morris and Michael Tonry. Chicago: University of Chicago Press.

LANE, ROGER
1967   *Policing the City: Boston, 1822–1885.* Cambridge: Harvard University Press.

LANGSAM, MIRIAM Z.
1964   *Children West: A History of the Placing out System of the New York Children's Aid Society, 1853–1890.* Madison: State Historical Society of Wisconsin.

LARSEN, CHARLES
1972   *The Good Fight: The Life and Times of Ben B. Lindsey.* Chicago: Quadrangle.

LASCH, CHRISTOPHER
1973   "Origins of the Asylum." In *The World of Nations: Reflections on American History, Politics, and Culture,* ed. Christopher Lasch. New York: Alfred A. Knopf.
1977   *Haven in a Heartless World: The Family Besieged.* New York: Basic Books.

LASLETT, PETER
1965   *The World We Have Lost: England before the Industrial Age.* New York: Charles Scribner's Sons.

LAURIE, BRUCE
1973   "Fire Companies and Gangs in Southwark: The 1840's." In *The Peoples of Philadelphia: A History of Ethnic Groups and Lower-Class Life, 1790–1940,* ed. Allen F. Davis and Mark M. Haller. Philadelphia: Temple University Press.

LAZERSON, MARVIN
1971   *The Origins of the Urban School.* Cambridge: Harvard University Press.

LEIBY, JAMES
1967   *Charity and Correction in New Jersey: A History of State Welfare Institutions.* New Brunswick, N.J.: Rutgers University Press.
1978   *A History of Social Welfare and Social Work in the United States.* New York: Columbia University Press.

LEVINE, MURRAY, AND ADELINE LEVINE
1970   *A Social History of Helping Services.* New York: Appleton-Century-Crofts.

LEWIS, W. DAVID
1965   *From Newgate to Dannemora: The Rise of the Penitentiary in New York, 1746–1848.* Ithaca: Cornell University Press.

LOU, HERBERT H.
1927   *Juvenile Courts in the United States.* Chapel Hill: University of North Carolina Press.

LUBOVE, ROY
1965   *The Professional Altruist: The Emergence of Social Work as a Career, 1880–1930.* Cambridge: Harvard University Press.

MANTON, JO
1976   *Mary Carpenter and the Children of the Streets.* Exeter, N.H.: Heinemann.

MARRIS, PETER, AND MARTIN REIN
1973   *Dilemmas of Social Reform: Poverty and Community Action in the United States.* Rev. ed. Chicago: Aldine.

MAY, MARGARET
1973   "Innocence and Experience: The Evolution of the Concept of Juvenile Delinquency in the Mid-Nineteenth Century," *Victorian Studies* 18:7–29.

MENNEL, ROBERT
1972   "Origins of the Juvenile Court: Changing Perspectives on the Legal Rights of Juvenile Delinquents." *Crime and Delinquency* 18:68–78.
1973a   "Juvenile Delinquency in Perspective," *History of Education Quarterly* 13:275–81.
1973b   *Thorns and Thistles: Juvenile Delinquents in the United States, 1825–1940.* Hanover: University Press of New England.
1980a   "The Family System of Common Farmers: The Early Years of Ohio's Reform Farm, 1858–1884," *Ohio History* 89:279–322.
1980b   "The Family System of Common Farmers: The Origins of Ohio's Reform Farm, 1840–1858," *Ohio History* 89:125–56.

MESSERLI, JONATHAN
1973   *Horace Mann: A Biography.* New York: Alfred A. Knopf.

MOHL, RAYMOND
1970   *Poverty in New York, 1783–1823.* New York: Oxford.

MONKKONEN, ERIC H.
1975   *The Dangerous Class: Crime and Poverty in Columbus, Ohio, 1860–1885.* Cambridge: Harvard University Press.

MOORE, JOHN
1969   "Controlling Delinquency: Executive, Congressional and Juvenile, 1961–64." In *Congress and Urban Problems,* ed. Frederic N. Cleaveland. Washington, D.C.: Brookings Institution.

MULLER, NORBERT
1976   "La Colonie Agricole Pénitentiare de Mettray." Memoire, Université de Tours.

NATIONAL COMMISSION ON LAW OBSERVANCE AND ENFORCEMENT
1931   *The Child Offender in the Federal System of Justice.* Washington, D.C.: U.S. Government Printing Office.

NATIONAL CONFERENCE OF CHARITIES AND CORRECTION
1893   *History of Child Saving in the United States.* Boston: n.p.

OWEN, DAVID
1964   *English Philanthropy, 1660–1960.* London: Oxford.

PARKER, GRAHAM
1976a   "The Juvenile Court Movement." *University of Toronto Law Journal* 26:140–72.
1976b   "The Juvenile Court: The Illinois Experience." *University of Toronto Law Journal* 26:253–306.

PICKETT, ROBERT S.
1969   *House of Refuge: Origins of Juvenile Reform in New York State, 1815–1857.* Syracuse: Syracuse University Press.

PINCHBECK, IVY, AND MARGARET HEWITT
1969–73 *Children in English Society.* 2 vols. London: Routledge and Kegan Paul.

PISCIOTTA, ALEXANDER W.
1979   "The Theory and Practice of the New York House of Refuge, 1857–1935." Ph.D. dissertation, Florida State University.

PLATT, ANTHONY M.
1974   "The Triumph of Benevolence: The Origins of the Juvenile Justice System in the United States." In *Criminal Justice in America,* ed. Richard Quinney. Boston: Little, Brown.
1977a   *The Child Savers: The Invention of Delinquency.* 2d ed. Chicago: University of Chicago Press.
1977b   Review of Schlossman, *Love and the American Delinquent, Crime and Social Justice* 8:80–83.

PRESCOTT, PETER S.
1981   *The Child Savers.* New York: Alfred A. Knopf.

REEVES, MARGARET
1929   *Training Schools for Delinquent Girls.* New York: Russell Sage.

RICHARDSON, JAMES F.
1970   *The New York Police: Colonial Times to 1901.* New York: Oxford.

ROSENBERG, CARROLL SMITH
1971   *Religion and the Rise of the American City: The New York City Mission Movement, 1812–1870.* Ithaca: Cornell University Press.

ROSENBERG, CHARLES
1979   "Toward an Ecology of Knowledge: On Discipline, Context and History." In *The Organization of Knowledge in Modern America, 1860–1920,* ed. Alexandra Oleson and John Voss. Baltimore: Johns Hopkins University Press.

ROSENHEIM, MARGARET K., ED.
1962   *Justice for the Child: The Juvenile Court in Transition.* New York: Free Press.
1976   *Pursuing Justice for the Child.* Chicago: University of Chicago Press.

ROSS, DOROTHY
1972   *G. Stanley Hall: The Psychologist as Prophet.* Chicago: University of Chicago Press.

ROTHMAN, DAVID J.
1971   *The Discovery of the Asylum: Social Order and Disorder in the New Republic.* Boston: Little, Brown.
1974   Review of Mennel, *Thorns and Thistles, American Historical Review* 79:244–45.
1980   *Conscience and Convenience: The Asylum and Its Alternatives in Progressive America.* Boston: Little, Brown.

RYERSON, ELLEN
1978   *The Best Laid Plans: America's Juvenile Court Experiment.* New York: Hill and Wang.

SANDERS, WILEY B., ED.
1970   *Juvenile Offenders for a Thousand Years: Selected Readings from Anglo-Saxon Times to 1900.* Chapel Hill: University of North Carolina Press.

SCHLOSSMAN, STEVEN L.
1974   "Juvenile Justice in the Age of Jackson," *Teachers College Record* 46:119–33.
1977   *Love and the American Delinquent: The Theory and Practice of "Progressive" Juvenile Justice, 1825–1920.* Chicago: University of Chicago Press.

SCHLOSSMAN, STEVEN L., AND STEPHANIE WALLACH
1978   "The Crime of Precocious Sexuality: Female Juvenile Delinquency in the Progressive Era," *Harvard Educational Review* 48:65–94.

SCHNEIDER, JOHN
1980.   *Detroit and the Problem of Order, 1830–1880.* Lincoln: University of Nebraska Press.

SCHULTZ, J. LAWRENCE
1973   "The Cycle of Juvenile Court History," *Crime and Delinquency* 19:457–76.

SCHUPF, HARRIET W.
1971   "The Perishing and Dangerous Classes: Efforts to Deal with the Neglected, Vagrant and Delinquent Juvenile in England, 1840–1872." Ph.D. dissertation, Columbia University.

SENNETT, RICHARD
1970   *Families against the City.* Cambridge: Harvard University Press.

SHANAHAN, WILLIAM O.
1954   *German Protestants Face the Social Question.* South Bend: University of Notre Dame Press.

SHAW, CLIFFORD R.
1929   *Delinquency Areas.* Chicago: University of Chicago Press.
1930   *The Jack-Roller: A Delinquent Boy's Own Story.* Chicago: University of Chicago Press.

SHAW, CLIFFORD R., AND HENRY D. MCKAY
1942   *Juvenile Delinquency in Urban Areas.* Chicago: University of Chicago Press.

SLATER, PETER G.
1970   "Views of Children and of Child Rearing during the Early National Period: A Study in the New England Intellect." Ph.D. dissertation, University of California, Berkeley.

SMITH, TIMOTHY
1957   *Revivalism and Social Reform in Mid-Nineteenth Century America.* New York: Abingdon Press.

SNEDDEN, DAVID
1907   *Administrative and Educational Work of the American Reform School.* New York: Columbia University Press.

STACK, JOHN
1974   "Social Policy and Juvenile Delinquency in England and Wales, 1815–75." Ph.D. dissertation, University of Iowa.

STEWART, JOSEPH M.
1980   "A Comparative History of Juvenile Correctional Institutions in Ohio." Ph.D. dissertation, Ohio State University.

STONE, LAWRENCE
1981   "Family History in the 1980's," *Journal of Interdisciplinary History* 12:51–87.

SUTHERLAND, NEIL
1976   *Children in English-Canadian Society, 1880–1920.* Toronto: University of Toronto Press.

TEETERS, NEGLEY K.
1960   "The Early Days of the Philadelphia House of Refuge," *Pennsylvania History* 27:165–87.

THAVENET, DENNIS
1976   "'Wild Young "Uns" in Their Midst': The Beginning of Reformatory Education in Michigan." *Michigan History* 60:240–59.

THOMAS, WILLIAM I.
1923   *The Unadjusted Girl.* Boston: Little, Brown.

THRASHER, FREDERIC M.
1927   *The Gang: A Study of 1,313 Gangs in Chicago.* Chicago: University of Chicago Press.

THURSTON, HENRY W.
1942   *Concerning Juvenile Delinquency: Progressive Changes in Our Perspective.* New York: Columbia University Press.

TRATTNER, WALTER I.
1968   *Homer Folks: Pioneer in Social Welfare.* New York: Columbia University Press.

TYLER, ALICE FELT
1944   *Freedom's Ferment: Phases of American Social History to 1860.* Minneapolis: University of Minnesota Press.

U.S. COMPTROLLER GENERAL
1975   *Report to Congress: How Federal Efforts to Coordinate Programs to Mitigate Juvenile Delinquency Proved Ineffective.* Washington, D.C.: Government Printing Office.

U.S. PRESIDENT'S COMMISSION ON LAW ENFORCEMENT AND ADMINISTRATION OF JUSTICE
1968   *The Challenge of Crime in a Free Society.* Washington, D.C.: U.S. Government Printing Office.

VAN WATERS, MIRIAM
1925   *Youth in Conflict.* New York: New Republic.

VOGEL, MORRIS J.
1980   *The Invention of the Modern Hospital: Boston 1870–1930.* Chicago: University of Chicago Press.

WILLARD, JOSIAH FLINT [JOSIAH FLYNT]
1908   *My Life.* New York: Outing.

WINES, ENOCH C., AND THEODORE W. DWIGHT
1867   *Report on the Prisons and Reformatories of the United States and Canada.* Albany: Van Benthuysen.
1880   *The State Prisons and Child Saving Institutions in the Civilized World.* Cambridge, Mass.: J. Wilson.

WIRKKALA, JOHN
1973   "Juvenile Delinquency and Reform in Nineteenth Century Massachusetts." Ph.D. dissertation, Clark University, Worcester, Mass.

WISHY, BERNARD
1968   *The Child and the Republic.* Philadelphia: University of Pennsylvania Press.

WOHL, R. RICHARD
1969   "The 'Country Boy' Myth and Its Place in American Urban Culture," *Perspectives in American History* 3:77–158.

ZUCKERMAN, MICHAEL.
1976   "Children's Rights: The Failure of Reform," *Policy Analysis* 2:371–85.

QUESTIONS FOR DISCUSSION

1. The author is generally critical of the historical accounts of juvenile delinquency. What are his criticisms? Do you think these criticisms are valid?

2. What social changes of the late 1800s severely hampered the family unit's ability to govern and control youth?

3. Discuss the major differences between the juvenile delinquency policies of the 1960s and those of the 1980s. Name several reasons these changes occurred.

APPLICATIONS

1. Identify an individual who is over the age of forty. This could be a parent, a friend, a teacher, or another acquaintance. Using a tape recorder or a note pad, ask that person about his or her experiences as a youth. Ask specific questions such as the following:
   a. How has the world changed since you were a teenager? Are the social pressures any different?
   b. How are teenagers different now?
   c. Are today's teenagers more prone to break the law?

2. Let us assume that you are in charge of reviewing and making recommendations about policies that will decrease juvenile delinquency and improve the juvenile justice system. What would you recommend?

KEY TERMS

almshouse a privately financed home for the poor.

altruism unselfish regard for or devotion to the welfare of others.

determinism the theory or doctrine which maintains that acts of will, occurrences in nature, or social and/or psychological phenomena are caused by preceding events or natural law.

egalitarian a belief in human equality with respect to social, political, and economic rights and privileges.

eugenics a science that deals with improving a race or breed by controlling mating habits, genetic engineering, and hereditary qualities.

hierarchy a grouping of people by rank, according to economic, social, or professional standing.

historiography the writing of history based on the critical examination of sources.

ideology a systematic body of concepts about human life or culture.

mores the fixed, morally binding customs of a particular group; habits or mannerisms.

penitentiary an institution in which offenders of the law are confined for detention or punishment. Historically, offenders were to feel regret and sorrow for their deeds; repenting from their sins.

reformatory a penal institution to which young and first-time offenders are committed for training and reformation.

revisionism a movement in revolutionary Marxian socialism favoring evolutionary rather than revolutionary change.

3

The Crime of Precocious Sexuality: Female Juvenile Delinquency in the Progressive Era

Steven Schlossman
Radcliffe Institute, Harvard University

Stephanie Wallach
Simmons College

The juvenile justice system's discrimination against poor and minority children has been well documented, but the system's discrimination on the basis of gender has been less widely recognized. Drawing on neglected court records and secondary sources, Steven Schlossman and Stephanie Wallach show how girls bore a disproportionate share of the burden of juvenile justice in the Progressive era. The authors note that during the Progressive era female juvenile delinquents often received more severe punishments than males, even though boys usually were charged with more serious crimes. Schlossman and Wallach conclude that the discriminatory treatment of female delinquents in the early twentieth century resulted from racial prejudice, new theories of adolescence, and Progressive-era movements to purify society.

This essay is an historical inquiry into the practice of sexual discrimination against female juvenile delinquents. Although American public policy toward girl offenders first took shape in the middle decades of the nineteenth century—the Victorian era—we have decided to focus on the Progressive era of the early twentieth century. During this latter period scientific and popular literature on female delinquency expanded enormously, and most states

"The Crime of Precocious Sexuality: Female Juvenile Delinquency in the Progressive Era," *Harvard Educational Review,* 48:1, pp. 65–94. Copyright © 1978 by the President and Fellows of Harvard College. All rights reserved.

adopted the main components of modern correctional machinery. Our essay spotlights the differences between stated intentions, revealed preferences, and actual outcomes.[1] Although we attempt to develop a broad interpretation, we must emphasize the selectivity of our historical research. We do not pretend to have exhausted available sources, to have explored all possible interpretations of our evidence, or, certainly, to have written the definitive account. Instead, we offer a preliminary synthesis of untapped sources in an effort to call attention to a neglected subject, to encourage additional research on it, and to suggest ways of integrating the topic of female delinquency into the rapidly growing fields of women's history and the history of corrections.

Our essay speaks only indirectly to modern-day issues in juvenile justice. Continuities between past and present will often be apparent, to be sure, but we dare not draw them too explicitly for the simple reason that social scientists know very little about the theory and practice of female juvenile justice between the 1920s and the 1960s.[2] Nonetheless, we do believe it is possible to use history as a force for social change by laying bare the roots and assumptions of anachronistic policies—policies, in this instance, that lag behind our current attitudes toward female sexuality and equal justice for women. Given our reformist goals, it may be useful to explain in advance why we focus on sexual discrimination as opposed to other equally blatant injustices in the correctional system.

Like other critics of American juvenile justice, we decry practices that lead to unwarranted labeling and incarceration of children and that discriminate against poor, minority youth, regardless of sex.[3] We consider it indisputable that, from the early nineteenth century to the present, the juvenile justice system has systematically singled out lower-class children for punishment and ignored middle- and upper-class youth.[4] In this essay, however, our main concern is not with class, ethnic, racial, or age bias, for we believe those themes have been adequately treated elsewhere. Rather, what most interests us now is how, in a correctional system that discriminates consistently against poor, minority children as a whole, females carry a disproportionate share of the burden of injustice.

Discussion of female delinquency is conspicuously absent from most scholarly writing on criminal justice. Despite a persistent hue and cry during the last decade about spiraling rates of delinquency, despite mounting evidence demonstrating the ineffectiveness of correctional programs, and despite the women's rights movement, girl offenders are largely ignored. Even as the number of females processed through the juvenile courts climbs steadily, an implicit consensus remains that the male teenager defines the delinquency problem in modern America and suffers most egregiously from correctional injustices.[5]

We suggest two main reasons why girl delinquents receive so little attention. First, girls are accused primarily of so-called victimless crimes, that is, offenses that do not involve clear-cut damage to persons or property. If committed by adults, these actions would not be legally punishable; if committed by boys, the same acts would be interpreted less seriously and punished less severely. Thus, rather ironically, the plight of female delinquents receives little scrutiny because they are accused of committing less flagrant violations of legal codes. Second, traditional stereotypes of women as the weaker and more dependent sex rationalize, indeed even legitimate, discriminatory correctional practices in the name of humanitarian-

ism. As the half-century struggle to enact the Equal Rights Amendment makes abundantly clear, one of the most tenacious beliefs in our society is that women require more comprehensive legal protection than do men. Society justifies "preventive" intervention into the lives of antisocial girls under the rationale that they are especially vulnerable to evil forces and temptations. This so-called chivalrous attitude leads to earlier intervention and longer periods of supervision for delinquent girls than delinquent boys.

The sparse historical writing about female delinquency concentrates on reformatories, especially the pioneering nineteenth-century institutions, rather than on the juvenile justice system as a whole.[6] Furthermore, several of the studies are uncritical and Whiggish in their interpretations, seeing a benign humanitarian spirit behind early twentieth-century correctional innovations for girls. Margaret Reeves, for example, conducted an exhaustive survey of girls' reformatory programs in the 1920s and concluded, with few reservations, that they embodied the triumph of social conscience in America and the onward march of correctional science.[7] Recently, Robert Mennel, in his ambitious survey of juvenile correctional history, described Progressive-era policies as "the first sign of a more sympathetic attitude toward female delinquents."[8]

On the basis of our research, we consider the traditional interpretation to be lacking in four principal respects: it offers little empirical evidence of benign or effective treatment of girl offenders; it generally blurs the distinction between the stated intentions of correctional reformers and the actual outcomes of their efforts; it deals inadequately with the fears and prejudices underlying benevolent programs for poor, immigrant children; and it does little to illuminate, even obliquely, the practice of sexual discrimination in the juvenile justice system today. We do not quarrel with historians who emphasize the humanitarian spirit that guided such famous juvenile reformers as Jane Addams, Sophonisba Breckinridge, and Edith Abbott, or such lesser figures as Augusta Bronner, Mabel Elliott, Emma Lundberg, and Edith Burleigh.[9] But we do believe that the humanitarian schemes were often quite repressive in design and even more so in outcome.

Our main arguments can be sketched as follows. Although public response to female delinquency emerged in the Victorian era, not until the Progressive period was female delinquency widely perceived as a social problem requiring extensive governmental intervention. In the Progressive period the abundant literature on delinquency was riddled with stereotypical assumptions about women and, in particular, about immigrant women. These stereotypes laid a basis for more punitive treatment of delinquent girls than delinquent boys. Girls were prosecuted almost exclusively for "immoral" conduct, a very broad category that defined all sexual exploration as fundamentally perverse and predictive of future promiscuity, perhaps even prostitution. But while girls, unlike boys, were almost never accused of violating criminal statutes, they received stiffer legal penalties.

Discriminatory treatment of female delinquents was consistent with racial prejudices in the Progressive period. Ethnic girls—immigrants or daughters of immigrants—were seen as inherently more predisposed to immoral conduct than Yankee girls—daughters of native-born parents. Discriminatory correctional practices also embodied the new wisdom of the behavioral sciences, particulary the theories of adolescence generated by such pioneer psychologists as G. Stanley Hall. Finally, the practice of female juvenile justice reflected the quasi-utopian, but ultimately repressive, pursuit of Progressive-era reformers for a more "pure" society, as revealed in the eugenics, antiprostitution, and sex-education campaigns.

FEMALE DELINQUENCY: THE EMERGENCE OF A SOCIAL PROBLEM

Public response to female delinquency can be traced at least as far back as the Jacksonian period, although the traditional date of origin is 1856, when Massachusetts opened the nation's first reform school for girls. Well known in the latter half of the century, the Massachusetts example inspired emulation by diverse philanthropic organizations in the East and Midwest. Several state governments responded to the wishes of these organizations and built reformatories for girls. Compared to the huge reformatories for boys erected in the nineteenth century—by the 1850s the New York House of Refuge held over one thousand inmates—the institutions for girls were generally small and makeshift, often consisting of two or three converted farmhouses. Several of the girls' facilities were little more than receiving stations; their primary purpose was to facilitate the smooth operation of boys' reformatories after attempts to house both sexes in the same buildings had proved embarrassing failures.[10]

The female reformatories incorporated the evangelical spirit of Victorian religious revivalism. Until the end of the nineteenth century the image of the female delinquent remained mainly that of the individual "fallen woman."[11] This image contrasted sharply with that of the male delinquent, who was described less as a sinner than as a carefully nurtured young criminal.[12] To be sure, boys' delinquencies were routinely condemned but were rarely, as was often the case with girls', regarded as indications of innate moral perversity.

Nineteenth-century authors of crime literature wrote endlessly about delinquency—the classic presentation being Charles Loring Brace's *The Dangerous Classes of New York and Twenty Years' Work Among Them*[13]—but they paid very little attention to female delinquents. The "dangerous classes" against whom the reformers warned and about whom newspapers printed sensational stories were overwhelmingly male.[14] When the girl offender did appear in the literature, she was treated mainly as a footnote to the problem of boy delinquency. But early in the twentieth century—especially in the decade preceding the First World War—female delinquency began to attract increasing attention as a separate and pressing social problem.

The heightened public awareness of and growing governmental response to female delinquency in the Progressive era are well documented. Articles on girl offenders appeared in a wide range of popular and scholarly journals. The prestigious philanthropic organization, the National Conference of Charities and Correction, began to discuss female delinquency regularly for the first time since the organization's founding in the early 1870s. Several books were devoted in whole or in part to female criminality. While the mass media continued to emphasize the "boy problem," many civic groups began giving equal attention to the "girl problem." Local organizations such as PTAs, juvenile protective associations, women's clubs, and settlement houses sponsored lectures and discussions on the causes and cures of girls' delinquency; they also led campaigns to garner funds for such innovations as girls' clubs, YWCA summer camps, and, to a lesser extent, Girl Scouts.[15]

Governmental investment in the custody and treatment of female delinquents increased dramatically in the Progressive era. The decade between 1910 and 1920 was an especially prolific period for the creation of publicly sponsored reformatories for girls. Whereas between 1850 and 1910 an average of fewer than five new reformatories were created per decade, twenty-three new facilities opened between 1910 and 1920. Furthermore, older nineteenth-century reformatories were expanded in size, staff, and clientele in this decade. Equally important, a number of states took over private girls' reformatories.[16] In short, the involvement of government with female delinquency grew sharply in the Progressive period, reflecting the expanded discussion of the subject in the literature on juvenile crime.

THE PRACTICE OF SEXUAL DISCRIMINATION

Before trying to explain the rising interest in female delinquency in the Progressive era, it is necessary to demonstrate that girls received discriminatory treatment in juvenile courts and reformatories. The historical sources for such an empirical study are vast but have never been tapped. We have examined the sources selectively and have chosen for close analysis those we believe are representative of three bodies of evidence.

First, we briefly analyze scattered statistical data to demonstrate that juvenile courts treated female delinquents more harshly than male delinquents. Second, we present an overview of cases in a single juvenile court to evoke the actual decision-making process and thereby show that sentimental notions of the "good girl" and conventional ideals of domesticity prefigured punitive treatment for girl delinquents. Third, we look synoptically at the rehabilitative goals and methods of female reformatories to illuminate further the discriminatory nature of treatment. Our goal is to provide empirical evidence for the contention, developed later in this essay, that the practice of female juvenile justice coincided with the ideology of treatment. Discrimination on the basis of sex was no accident, we believe, but rather was integral to both the theory and practice of Progressive-era juvenile justice.

The first body of evidence was derived from court records in Chicago, San Francisco, Milwaukee, and New Haven. Several points stand out most prominently from these data: the vast majority of delinquents, boy and girls alike, were poor, ghetto-dwelling children of recent immigrants; however, unlike males, females were brought to court almost exclusively for alleged early sexual exploration; and female offenders were treated more punitively than males.

The ethnic origins of both boy and girl delinquents are revealing. In Milwaukee, for example, more than 90 percent of the children brought into court were the offspring of European immigrants. Of these, three out of four were either German or Polish. In Chicago, San Francisco, and New Haven the ethnic background of delinquents was similar, although southeastern European countries were more frequently represented, reflecting the different patterns of immigrant settlement in these cities.[17]

That the delinquents were predominantly poor is evident in a number of ways. Although it is impossible to compare the incomes of families of delinquent and nondelinquent children or to assess the contributions of different family members to total income, we do have periodic salary data for the fathers of delinquent youth in Milwaukee. These data suggest the truth of the popular impression that delinquents were primarily from the working class. Their fathers' salaries were low, generally reported to be less than ten dollars per week. Moreover, the salaries were highly irregular: many fathers moved frequently from job to job; many were unemployed for long periods because of seasonal hiring, debilitating illnesses (particularly tuberculosis), and drinking bouts. In addition, an analysis of the occupations of delinquents' fathers, using city directories and addresses supplied in court to distinguish individuals with the same names, indicates that the majority were working class or lower on the economic scale, the single largest category being that of "laborer."[18] A further indication that delinquents came mainly from poor, ghetto families is their residence patterns. The majority of Milwaukee delinquents lived in the poorest immigrant neighborhoods surrounding the city's scattered railway network.

Although similar in their social and cultural backgrounds, girl and boy delinquents were treated very differently in court. Consider the types of crimes for which boys and girls made their first courtroom appearances. The majority of boys were charged with offenses that fell under the adult criminal code. In Chicago, for example, stealing accounted for more than half of the reported crimes.[19] The charges against girls were of an entirely different nature. The majority were charged under the loose heading of "immorality";[20] however, a charge of "immorality" did not mean that a girl had had intercourse or performed some other mature sexual act. Rather, a girl only had to show "signs" in her appearance, conversation, and bearing that she had probably had intercourse in the past or might do so in the near future. These criteria naturally opened the way to invidious judgments, especially because the delinquents were mainly daughters of immigrants, who were, according to contemporary racial mythology, instinctively emotional and lacking in self-restraint. Thus judges and probation officers would see precocious sexual activity where it did not exist, would prematurely regard unfamiliar cultural patterns of behavior and expression as signs of advanced sexual experience, and would be more pessimistic about the implications of sexual exploration by ethnic than by Yankee girls.

In practice, an extraordinarily wide range of conduct was included under the label of immorality: staying away from home, associating with persons of dubious character, going to dance houses, fornicating, coming home late at night, masturbating, using obscene lan-

guage, riding at night in automobiles without a chaperone, strutting about in a lascivious manner, and so forth. To the courts, being "on the road to ruin" was but one short step from being "ruined"; hence, so-called predelinquents were treated much like those who actually engaged in mature sexual relations. The ostensible purposes behind such a loose definition of crime were to root out the underlying causes of misconduct as soon as they became evident and to instruct ethnic girls that their Yankee counterparts upheld higher standards of sexual propriety than their own parents practiced or condoned.[21]

The different treatment of boy and girl delinquents was even more apparent in the disposition of cases. Far more frequently than girls, boys received the relatively noncoercive sanction of probation—supervision in the child's own home or in a surrogate home approved by the court. In Chicago, for instance, 59 percent of the boys who appeared in court between 1899 and 1909 were placed on probation, as compared to only 37 percent of the girls. Conversely, significantly higher proportions of girls than boys were incarcerated in reformatories for sentences that could last several years. In Milwaukee twice as many girls as boys were committed, and in Chicago one-half of the girl delinquents, as contrasted with one-fifth of the boy delinquents, were sent to reformatories.[22] In sum, girls appeared in juvenile court on noncriminal charges far more frequently than boys; nonetheless, girls received more punitive dispositions.[23]

We turn now to another body of evidence: the day-to-day experiences of girls in juvenile court. From the archival records of the Milwaukee Children's Court we have chosen several cases from between 1901 and 1920 for examination. Transcripts from actual hearings, we believe, provide the most vivid and dramatic demonstration of the assumptions that shaped the definition and treatment of female delinquency in the Progressive era.[24]

Alleged girl delinquents in Milwaukee had their private lives probed in fine detail so that judges and probation officers could assess the underlying causes of misbehavior. Whenever it could be demonstrated that a girl had used vile language, masturbated, or indulged in lascivious thoughts, the court freely employed some type of intervention, usually probation. Consider the case of Annagret Schmitt. Neither the hearing transcript nor the accompanying records provides a precise reason why Annagret was brought into court—a common occurrence, since it was assumed that some form of aberrant sexual expression was behind any specific accusation. Thus Annagret, like every girl who appeared in court, was subjected to a vaginal examination. The only proof of virginity was an intact hymen. To his own surprise the examining doctor concluded that Annagret was still a virgin, but he informed the court that irritation in her clitoral area indicated she was a regular masturbator. The probation officer, a woman, analyzed the situation as follows: "She masturbates, and she has somewhat injured herself in that way, and probably this is the cause of her conduct at home, and says things [sic] that are not true . . . . [Annagret] most likely is trying to imagine things, and then believes everything is true." Thus, according to the court, Annagret's masturbatory habits explained her penchant for fantasy and justified labeling her a delinquent and placing her under supervision.

In cases of advanced sexual misconduct, the court usually explored the circumstances in excruciating detail. The ostensible goals were to procure evidence against the male or males involved and to evaluate the girls' attitudes toward men and sex. At times, though, the immediate goal seemed to be nothing other than sheer titillation, much like the famous vice reports in this period. Such reports offered, in the names of science and social reform, pornographic scenes that would have been censored in the commercial media. In court, girls were required to recount, with some attempt to re-create the atmosphere, the steps that led to their sexual encounters, their physical experiences ("How far did he go into you; what did you feel; did you bleed?"), and their later subjective reactions. In pursuing this line of questioning the court's assumptions were transparent; it presumed that a girl's moral condition and potential for rehabilitation depended on just how much of her biological purity had been preserved and on how morally revolted she was by her experiences.

At the same time that the court avidly investigated the girls' sex lives, it preached a conventional code of Victorian morality, highlighting especially the virtues of chastity and the joys of marriage. With all good intentions the court lectured sexually precocious girls on how their behavior was endangering their later salability as wives. Without doubt many of the sexually active girls who appeared in juvenile court were immature and would have benefited from intelligent advice about sex. But the advice the court proffered must have struck these girls as naive and irrelevant to their current needs and past experiences. Consider, for example, one judge's advice to a girl who had contracted venereal disease:

> By and by, three or four years from now, some nice fellow will come along, and you love him, and he will love you, and you will get married, and live right. That ought to be the aim of a girl like you, to look forward to the time you have a good home and a good man.

Quaint moral admonitions like these were the court's main antidote to sexual precocity among girls and, if nothing else, reveal the cultural stereotypes that shaped the legal processing of female delinquents.

As observed earlier, juvenile courts did not distinguish between actual delinquency and predelinquency because they saw their mission as the treatment of underlying causes. The courts aimed to "save" girls once it became apparent they were "on the road to ruin." Consider the case of Sara Wadrewski. Sara's father had brought her into court on a charge of disobedience, alleging that she had refused to work, stayed out late, and gone to parties where the girls dressed like boys. As often happened, a probation officer was on hand to supplement the parents' charges by relating neighborhood gossip. Sara, he intimated, probably had had intercourse with several boys because she was seen lying on the grass with them in a local park. A group of neighbors made similar accusations. To the judge's question, "In what way is she a bad girl?" one neighbor responded, "Why, for the reason that she bums around and doesn't work, and doesn't bring no money home, and runs to parties, and then calls names, calls her brother names, he is a cripple." Sara roundly denied most of the allegations, particularly the charges that she had had group sex, or indeed, that she had ever had "connection." But her protestations of virginity were to no avail; shortly after the initial hearing she was committed to the local Catholic reformatory.

Juvenile court sessions were often like scenes from a Kafka novel. One could never be sure that the disposition of a case would be on the basis of the accusations or on the quality of evidence. Despite these uncertainties it was almost guaranteed that a girl would be sent to a reformatory if either she or her parents, especially her mother, were not blushingly contrite about the girl's sexual adventures. A classic case is that of fifteen-year-old Deborah Horwitz, who freely admitted staying out late at night with many boys and who casually flaunted her sexual desires. In addition to Deborah's self-incriminating testimony, efficient snooping by a probation officer into Deborah's bedroom bureau turned up even more incriminating evidence: five self-photos that the court considered racy (although Deborah got no more racy than opening the top button of her high-necked blouse and removing her hat); and a remarkably candid series of letters to a sailor friend that left no doubt about her initiation into the joys of sex.

In such cases the court's custom was to blame the mother for her daughter's actions. Mrs. Horwitz, however, would not stand for it: "I got lots of trouble with the other girl, she needs an operation, and I got lots of trouble with the other children." Nor would Deborah accept the court's harsh evaluation of her behavior. Thus the judge intoned:

> Well, Deborah, this is a very serious matter. If you would live a good life you would be a good woman, and be useful to society, but you have started out very bad. There is only one way to reform you and this is to send you to an institution. I cannot let you go home to your parents. . . . How is it, can't you stop?

Deborah responded, "I can stop, of course I can." "Why don't you behave yourself, then?" the judge rejoined. "These boys tell me that

you just coax them." "I never coaxed anybody," Deborah maintained. But to no effect. Precocious sexuality in a girl who would not at least feign repentance and whose parents would not at least feign shock was intolerable to the court. Deborah was committed forthwith to the state reformatory for girls.

As these excerpts reveal, the court defined female delinquency wholly in sexual terms and responded to girls on the basis of Victorian views of women's social role and sexuality. We shall have more to say later about the persistence of these Victorian assumptions in the Progressive period. For the present we will extend our study of actual treatment by examining the female reformatories, which, as noted earlier, expanded rapidly in the early twentieth century. Like the juvenile courts, the reformatories operationalized prevailing cultural stereotypes about women and transformed these stereotypes into tools for punishment and rehabilitation.

Female reformatories in the Progressive era had four principal goals. The basic one was the isolation from males of sexually precocious females, preferably in bucolic settings. Elaborate efforts were made to keep all men away from the institutions or, indeed, from anywhere near the girls. In California, for example, sponsors of the female reformatory concluded that the mile separating the male from the female institution was inadequate. A new facility far removed from males was essential to eliminate "the influences that mysteriously emanate from the proximity of the sexes."[25] The mere act of isolating delinquent girls came to be seen as a rehabilitative tool. As such, it served an important, latent economic function by rationalizing a minimal public investment in other, more positive, methods of treatment.

Not only were the institutions situated so as to eliminate sexual temptation, but they were also designed to serve a second long-range function. Safe custody was considered a spur to later marriage. By incarcerating delinquent girls the reformatories removed them from the unregulated sexual marketplace of ghetto streets and forced them to save their sexual favors, moral reputations, and health until they were of marriageable age. Most inmates of female reformatories were fifteen or sixteen years old, too young to marry in most states. A minimal stay of two to three years was therefore considered essential; upon release the girls would be of marriageable age and could seek legitimate gratification for their pent-up sexual energies. The institutions further promoted marriageability by placing the girls, after release, in new social settings where their moral improprieties were not common knowledge and where they could search anew for companionship.[26] Like the isolation of inmates from all contacts with men, the assumption that custodial care could have long-term therapeutic value underlay the marital goals of the reformatories. Thus, it could seriously be argued that custody in female reformatories was itself a form of treatment.[27]

Female reformatories did employ nominally rehabilitative programs, if only to give the girls something to do while their virtue was being protected. These programs embodied traditional stereotypes about women. The institutions attempted to instill in inmates the ideology of domesticity and the minimal skills necessary for its practice. According to correctional administrators, a girl's delinquency alone revealed that she had not learned to revere domestic pursuits. Instruction in domesticity was allied with the reformatories' marital goals: inmates would become so devoted to and skillful at domestic chores that they would easily attract husbands. It was as if, in the moral calculus of the juvenile reformers, a rigorous pursuit of domesticity would compensate for the girls' previous immoralities. Moreover, even if the girls failed to find mates shortly after release, they would at least be trained as domestics and so could support themselves while working in upright, middle-class households.[28]

Inmates were expected to take care of their reformatory cottages with the same pride that middle-class women lavished on their homes. Ideally, the girls would assimilate middle-class domestic values and lower-class domestic skills.[29] In each reformatory cottage, the matron served as the domestic educator, teaching girls both proper attitudes and skills. To increase public regard for the vocational-training programs, reformatory superintendents described them as if they were part of the larger home-economics movement that swept the country in the Progressive era.[30] Actually, the training rarely went beyond the chores necessary for

personal hygiene and cottage upkeep, with a cooking class or two added for good measure. As one superintendent blithely argued,

> We never have taught typewriting and stenography. I find that in our community you can get about a dozen girls, who want to use a typewriter to one that wants to use a scrubbing brush. It seems to me that if you can get girls to understand that to be a homemaker is about the best thing that can come into the life of a woman, this is almost the best education they can have at the present time.[31]

Another superintendent was candid enough to admit what must often have been true in other reformatories that boasted "scientific" courses in home economics: "We teach the girls in practical cooking, as few are mentally capable of appreciating food values as taught in regular domestic science courses."[32]

The fourth and final goal of the female reformatories, surely their most ambitious, is implicit in the previous remark on inmates' mental limitations. The female reformatories were expected to play a central role in fulfilling the objectives of the eugenics movement, which achieved its greatest popularity at precisely the same time that governmental investment in female corrections significantly expanded.[33]

Eugenicists in the Progressive era sought to improve the "genetic fund" of the American population by discouraging and, if possible, forcibly preventing propagation by individuals considered innately inferior in culture and intellect. Almost by definition, the eugenicists identified recent immigrants from southeastern Europe as inferior. Relying on the rediscovery of Mendelian genetic theory in 1900, the eugenicists presented several key arguments: social conditions, such as poverty, and personality traits, such as laziness and courage, were discrete "unit characters" transmitted through heredity; unit characters were immutable; race was the primary determinant of human capacities; in some races socially undesirable unit characters predominated; and social legislation was necessary to encourage breeding of the racially fit and discourage breeding of the unfit. According to the eugenicists, persistent immorality among children was a sign of their genetic inferiority or racial degeneracy. To keep these degenerates from further diluting the nation's "genetic fund" and to prevent the nation from committing "race suicide," eugenicists insisted that permanent institutionalization and, if possible, sterilization were essential. The hereditarily degenerate threatened the eugenicists' vision of a more perfect and efficient world devoid of crime, poverty, and disease—a world quite consistent with the vision of many well-known reformers who outwardly were not eugenicists themselves.

Male and female reformatories were to play a special role in the larger eugenics campaign, as early detectors of innate criminality. In this role, however, the reformatories faced a unique problem: from a clientele composed mainly of children of racially inferior immigrants, how were they to identify those whose inheritance was so inferior as to warrant permanent incarceration or sterilization? By the 1910s the principal method of detection became mental testing, which rapidly evolved through a bewildering variety of forms, culminating in the 1916 Stanford revision of the Binet test—the intelligence quotient (IQ) test. With a seemingly precise instrument like the Stanford-Binet test in hand, psychologists and their helpers administered mental tests with virtual abandon to captive inmate populations. The tests were purported to identify those delinquents whose innate intelligence was so low that, in the judgment of the psychologists, they could never learn to control their instincts and become civilized members of society. These defective delinquents, as they were commonly called, were to be transferred from the reformatories and incarcerated, if facilities permitted, in homes for feeble-minded children—institutions that proliferated in the Progressive era. In sum, the newly devised mental test legitimated eugenic goals by providing a scientific instrument for weeding out from the delinquent population those children whose antisocial behavior was inbred.[34]

Eugenic goals, as we noted, applied equally to male and female reformatories, and IQ and other mental tests were freely administered in both. But the literature on delinquency discussed feeble-mindedness among girls with a special urgency. In part this was because delinquent girls appeared at first to test at somewhat lower levels than delinquent boys.[35] More important, though, were the two widely held beliefs that women bore the primary moral responsibility for determining whether to have children and that women lacked the sexual drives of men. From this perspective, sexually precocious girls were morally and biologically perverse. When this view was joined with the belief that delinquent girls' intelligence was so far below normal that they could never learn to control their instincts, it becomes clear why the specter of female delinquency haunted the eugenics movement and why delinquent girls were more frequently incarcerated than delinquent boys.

SEXUAL PRECOCITY AND THE SOCIAL ORDER IN THE PROGRESSIVE ERA

Having sketched the main elements of female juvenile justice in the Progressive era, we return to our earlier questions: why did public interest and investment in female delinquency burgeon so noticeably in this period, and why were girls treated more punitively than boys?

Perhaps the most obvious explanation of the rising interest in female delinquency in the Progressive period would be that the incidence of female delinquency grew until it simply could not be ignored. Much evidence could be marshaled to sustain this argument. One could turn, for example, to the remarkable data on family breakdown, cultural disintegration, and crime in urban immigrant communities documented in Thomas and Znaniecki's 1927 classic, *The Polish Peasant in America*.[36] Equally familiar are Jane Addams's poignant commentaries on the tensions and communication gulfs between mothers and daughters in *Democracy and Social Ethics* and *The Spirit of Youth and the City Streets*.[37] Similarly, one could assess the moral consequences of growing female participation in the work force. Did the increasingly familiar, "promiscuous" social relations of young men and women at work, mainly in the factory, encourage early sexual experimentation, as many contemporaries feared?[38] Finally, one could point to the pervasive image of the white-slave trade, as embodied in the work of the Chicago Vice Commission or Jane Addams's *A*

New Conscience and an Ancient Evil.[39] The image of the white-slave trader fueled the era's antiprostitution campaigns and expressed metaphorically the common view that impoverished women were vulnerable to unscrupulous entrepreneurs. In short, the rising public investment in and sensitivity to female delinquency could be seen as a pragmatic response to a real and growing social problem.

Although this argument is appealing, two serious limitations, one methodological and the other conceptual, persuade us, while not ignoring or denying it, to focus our attention elsewhere. First, the argument encounters the methodological difficulties common to all attempts to calculate the actual incidence of crime, whether in the present or, especially, in the past. We agree with modern-day sociologists and criminologists that official crime data and popular impressions of crime waves are unreliable indices of illegal activity in any period.[40] Second, as Edwin Schur and others have argued, the traditional foci in criminological research on the incidence of crime and the personal characteristics of offenders have often obscured the fact that crime is a social and legal artifact.[41] Crime does not exist in the abstract; certain activities become illegal only when so labeled. This holds true particularly for juvenile delinquency because, as we have seen, its legal definition is extremely broad and imprecise.

To reiterate, we do not deny the possibility that rates of female delinquency were actually on the rise in the Progressive era, although it would be nearly impossible, given the broad definition of delinquency, to determine how to measure its incidence. Rather, our point is simply that the public agencies responsible for defining, prosecuting, and punishing antisocial behavior invariably shape a society's awareness of criminal conduct at any moment. Therefore, whatever the actual incidence of delinquency, it is essential to examine the cultural context in which delinquency was defined and the legal and penal context in which codes were enforced.[42]

We believe the heightened sensitivity to female delinquency and the growing governmental investment in correctional institutions can be best understood in relation to three developments that directly and indirectly affected social policies—eugenic solutions to social problems, increasing popularity of theories of adolescence, and the movement for "social purity." We have already dealt with the first development, the pervasive appeal of eugenics,[43] and so will proceed to the second development, the growing popularity of theories of adolescence.

Differential treatment of boy and girl delinquents did not represent a failure in implementation, we believe, but rather was an inevitable outcome of the sexually biased social-science theories of adolescence that matured in the Progressive era.[44] These theories gave the imprimatur of science to traditional Victorian views of women as weak, impressionable, emotional, and yet erotically impassive.[45] Moreover, these theories helped shape juvenile justice in two major ways: they invalidated the most optimistic features of the juvenile court movement as applied to girls, and they legitimated the creation of new reformatories for girls just when institutional care for boys was being widely challenged.

The central role of Clark University president G. Stanley Hall in developing and popularizing new ideas about adolescence has been well documented.[46] Following Hall's lead, reformers of various hues portrayed adolescence as at once the most malleable and the most problematic time of development. Adolescence represented a new stage of life: anything was possible, for better or for worse. Most important, during adolescence a child's permanent character took shape. Jane Addams captured the common viewpoint most poignantly in her paean to the "spirit of youth": in adolescence the human spirit bursts forth anew in unsuspecting children, enthralling them with the enchantment of life, confusing them with the rush of passion and idealism.[47] During this stage of life, the reformers admonished, children required especially solicitous parental care and creative social planning to help them cope safely with the potentials of adolescence.

Not surprisingly, most commentators believed that the female youngsters of poor immigrant families were particularly vulnerable. They grew up in slums, came from inferior racial stock, and were scarred by cultural norms that sanctioned the open display of male sexual interest. However, this concern for the vulnerability of ethnic girls did not lead to extensive social programs for them. The many organizations developed for children in the Progressive era, such as day and evening clubs, scouts, and summer camps, were promoted much less vigorously for girls than for boys.[48] This resulted, in part, because boys were a much more immediate social threat: their delinquencies posed a clear and present danger, whereas girls' delinquencies engendered more long-term fears. But the best explanation, we believe, lies in the fact that adolescent girls were considered much less malleable than adolescent boys. Institutions like girls' clubs and Girl Scouts received less support than their male counterparts because adolescence in girls, as a life stage, was regarded as a much less promising period for reshaping character. Rather than a new beginning, adolescence in girls was the time when character traits instilled earlier were put to the test. Most writers assumed that by the time girls reached puberty the most promising time for shaping their character had long since passed.[49] Thus, while the psychological theories of adolescence provided a new source of "scientific" optimism for preventing delinquency among boys, they gave no such hope for aiding girls.[50]

For similar reasons, we believe, the promise of the juvenile court movement was less widely acclaimed for girls than for boys. As Schlossman argues in his history of "progressive" juvenile corrections, the main rehabilitative tool of the court movement was probation.[51] Ideally, probation was to be a means of family education. Probation officers were to function less as agents of law enforcement than as visiting teachers who would instruct parents and children on how to eliminate family stress and how to use community resources to increase economic security and recreational enjoyment. The theory of probation was built firmly on the assumptions that most children became delinquent during their adolescent years, that adolescents were especially malleable, and that the successful rechanneling of youthful energies into lawful pursuits would motivate parents to modify their behavior toward their children

and eliminate delinquency-producing conditions in the home. Probation epitomized the belief that adolescents merited several chances to become upright citizens.

Not so—or at least markedly less so—with erring adolescent girls.[52] Writers on female delinquency argued that, while a female's delinquencies were less criminally culpable, they were also less amenable to change through a relatively informal means of supervision like probation. Girls also received probation less frequently than boys because of the greater tendency to blame parents of delinquent girls. Unlike boys, it was argued, girls did not have places other than their homes in which to spend free time safely. Although writers on delinquency recognized that immigrant mothers and youth entered the work force because of poverty, they nonetheless held that rearing a girl imposed special moral responsibilities. Thus all mothers, regardless of economic circumstances, were obliged to keep their girls at home, when not in school or church, and to transform homes into refuges for protecting female virtue. This tendency to hold mothers more directly responsible for the behavior of girl delinquents than of boy delinquents further diminished the likelihood of probation for girls. If the female delinquent was considered less redeemable than her male counterpart, so too was her mother.

As probation was devalued for girl offenders, incarceration was judged more suitable. Earlier we examined the main rationales for female reformatories; here we will present additional justifications that illuminate why girl and boy delinquents were treated differently. One was the belief that girl delinquents, unlike boys, were not at all childlike in their behavior. By usurping the ultimate adult prerogative—sexual intercourse—female delinquents forfeited their right to be regarded merely as innocent, curious children. Moreover, precocious sexual exploration by girls threatened society's attempt to keep children innocent, chaste, and dependent until marriageable age. Female delinquents thereby subverted family government and had to be removed from their natural homes for the protection of neighborhood youth. Finally, imprisonment was seen as a boon to rehabilitation because of the speed with which neighborhood grapevines disseminated the reputations of "bad girls." One writer summed up these diverse rationales for more frequent incarceration of delinquent girls:

And suppose a boy does bolt? He can try again. Suppose he "goes bad" a second or a third time, either through animal spirits or bad companions? He can begin all over again. Suppose he even stays out nights, and goes into lower forms of degradation? Even then if he can pull himself together physically and morally, he has not lost the chance for a decent manhood and a square deal. But is it so with any delinquent girl? No, a thousand times no! By the publicity of even the appearance in Court her reputation is tarnished, and with her reputation in question, her chance to retrieve herself in the same environment is very small. And in that eighty percent of crimes against the person, does my girl get a fair chance to "try again?" No, the world is against her, evil men are ready to tempt her further, the industrial situation helps to put her at their mercy, and even nature herself gives her a last push towards the downward path when she physically handicaps herself. No! My girl who has once become delinquent finds it a 1000 times more difficult to straighten herself than the boy. The delinquent girl must be preserved against the *opportunities* of temptation which are inevitably more fatal to her than to the boy.[53]

Clearly, then, the juvenile reformatory was the best possible place to treat delinquent girls—to protect society from them and them from society.

The third and final development behind growing awareness of female delinquency in the Progressive era was the movement for "social purity." More particularly, we want to analyze the relation of the purity ideal to what several historians have described as the "sexual revolution" of the Progressive era or the beginnings of "the modernization of sex." We believe that changes in sexual mores provided the cultural foundation for the burgeoning interest in female delinquency, the expansion of female reformatories, and the differential treatment of boy and girl delinquents. To explicate our position, we will first examine changing sexual mores in the Progressive era and then point up how they shaped new policies toward female delinquents.[54]

Increasing investment in reformatories for sexually precocious girls reflected a widespread revulsion against the growing frequency and legitimacy of sex as an everyday topic of discussion.[55] The expansion of the government's capacity to punish sexual promiscuity formed one phase of what we term a "sexual counterrevolution." The men and women who led this counterrevolution were, by and large, the same types of middle-class, nonethnic individuals who participated in the better-known political and social reforms of the period. For these men and women, the sexual counterrevolution represented a moral analogue to the cleansing of corruption in the political and economic arenas.[56]

To the counterrevolutionists the public's fascination with sex was inherently dangerous because it threatened the maintenance of conventional family life. They were particularly troubled by many recent changes: the flagrant commercialization of sex in the press; the demystification of sex by doctors, psychologists, and intellectuals; the increasingly open propaganda for dissemination of birth-control devices; and the moral dangers inherent in the discovery of new medical remedies for venereal disease. The counterrevolutionists urged that new strategies were essential to revitalize older sexual ideals, neutralize overstimulated sexual appetites, and purify social discourse on sex. If reticence was no longer possible, purity was.[57]

The counterrevolutionists engaged in three major "reform" campaigns: the wholesale destruction of prostitution; the widespread dissemination of sex education; and, our main subject, the punishment of sexually precocious girls. Each campaign had a number of concrete, functional goals, but each needs to be seen symbolically as well. Together, the campaigns represented a ritualistic protest against cultural changes, a spirited reaffirmation of older moral ideals, and an urgent call for creative new strategies to realize them.

The campaign against prostitution was, ironically, both a contribution to and a sharp reaction against what one author wittily called the arrival of "sex o'clock" in America.[58] Prostitution had been a widespread and fairly well-accepted part of American urban life. To be sure, moralists of many kinds had periodically demonstrated against the easy acceptance of prostitution and were probably responsible for insuring that only one brief effort was made, in St. Louis, to experiment with European methods of regulation.[59] By and large, though, prostitutes sold their services with little interference, and, all evidence indicates, remarkably large percentages of American males used them.[60]

In the Victorian years prostitution was silently tolerated for three principal reasons. For one, prostitutes thrived mainly in the poorer, immigrant neighborhoods, and the feeling was, then as now, that as long as prostitutes remained in the slums, more respectable communities need not worry unduly about them. Second, nineteenth-century popular opinion sanctioned the view that men possessed superabundant sexual energies that required frequent release for mental and physical health. We must be careful not to exaggerate here; for opposite beliefs on male sexuality were also held in the Victorian period. Several reformers argued, for example, that sexual indulgence destroyed men's bodies and minds and that men should be continent in their sexual expression.[61] In retrospect, though, what is remarkable is how easily these contradictory sentiments coexisted—the latter as ideology for public consumption, the former as an "underground" precept guiding actual behavior.[62]

The third reason for toleration of prostitution was the Victorian sentimentalization of womanhood.[63] "Respectable" women—the only kind men dared marry—were placed gingerly upon a pedestal and viewed as rarefied creatures without sexual motivation. By nature they were so innocent and gentle that it would have been cruel for husbands to impose their sexual lusts upon them. This viewpoint obviously facilitated public acceptance of prostitution: the practice was rationalized as a protection of the home and domestic life through the absorption of men's excess sexual energies.

In the reform campaigns of the Progressive era, the ambivalences and contradictions of Victorian sexual thinking gave way to the unyielding pursuit of purity and innocence. Under the leadership of the counterrevolu-

tionists, city after city conducted elaborate studies of prostitution, revealing how openly prostitution flourished. Estimates varied, but it was conservatively calculated that well over half of American males from all social classes used or had used prostitutes and that many had contracted some form of venereal disease. Using these facts to support their position, the counterrevolutionists attacked regulation or even the toleration of prostitution as blasphemy. The wholesale destruction of prostitution became their goal, and, to a remarkable extent, they succeeded in wiping out many of the nation's most famous red-light districts in the years before the First World War.[64]

The metaphor of the white-slave trade fueled the antiprostitution campaign, but the extent to which prostitution was centrally organized was always uncertain.[65] Two other well-publicized arguments, though, helped sustain the fight against prostitution. The first resulted from several major scientific advances in detection and treatment of venereal disease. The counterrevolutionists drew grave moral implications from these scientific developments. On the one hand, they insisted, the physical devastation and easy communicability of venereal disease demanded rapid elimination of prostitution to safeguard family health. On the other hand, they asserted, the discovery of effective cures for venereal disease required quick destruction of prostitution, lest men be tempted to greater vice by the knowledge that they need not fear infection.[66]

The second rationale for destroying prostitution also drew upon medical opinion, although in this instance it was more a medical assertion than a demonstrable advance in scientific knowledge. The counterrevolutionists contended that a single standard of sexual behavior—that of continence—should prevail for men and women.[67] This ideal, as we observed, also had its supporters in the Victorian era. The twentieth-century proponents of continence did little to challenge the underground Victorian view that men's sexual appetites were ravenous. Instead, they emphatically urged continence as part of the larger Progressive-era moral revival, which included such other popular displays of conscience as the prohibition movement and the campaigns against child labor, dime novels, cheap movies, and the easy availability of narcotic drugs. Furthermore, the counterrevolutionists now gained the concerted support of powerful medical organizations against the underground doctrine of "sexual necessity." Three hundred of the nation's leading physicians, for example, issued a much-publicized manifesto in favor of male continence, which declared in part:

> In view of the individual and social dangers which spring from the widespread belief that continence may be detrimental to health, and of the fact that municipal toleration of prostitution is sometimes defended on the ground that sexual indulgence is necessary, we, the undersigned, members of the medical profession, testify to our belief that continence has not been shown to be detrimental to health or virility; that there is no evidence of its being inconsistent with the highest physical, mental, and moral efficiency; and that it offers the only sure reliance for sexual health outside of marriage.[68]

In sum, the counterrevolutionists, who led the antiprostitution campaign, relied heavily on medical opinion to persuade the American public that Victorian sexual liberties were sinful and unhealthy and that continence was possible through moral exertion and the removal of temptation. Paradoxically, then, at the very time when sex was becoming an accepted part of social discourse, a surprisingly effective campaign was led to eliminate one of the most common figures of nineteenth-century society, the prostitute.

Like the antiprostitution crusade, the sex-education movement drew heavily on medical science. Proponents of sex education saw themselves as progressive, fearlessly attacking the Victorian "conspiracy of silence" about sex. On closer inspection, though, sex education appears to have been anything but a modernizing influence. The sex educators fought mainly against imaginary adversaries, for sex was already an everyday topic of conversation. Moreover, the movement's rhetoric was largely puritanical, revealing deep fears about the moral impact of cultural change.[69]

The main goals of sex education were to purify discourse on sex, particularly in the pop-ular press and among children, and to instill moral inhibitions against sexual gratification now that effective birth control and cures for venereal disease were becoming widely available. The sex educators were moral crusaders marching under the banners of medical and pedagogical science. They sought to develop instructional techniques for innocently conveying new medical knowledge abut sex to children and, at the same time, imbuing sex with older spiritual meanings. Sex education was a means of pedagogical warfare against the purveyors of sexual titillation. Far from encouraging freer discussion of sex, the sex educators wanted to discipline lust and channel it to conventional moral ends.[70]

While the sex educators claimed to bring discussion of sex into the open, their pedagogical approach was so indirect as to be obscurantist. About the only form of open sexual discussion they could tolerate, in fact, involved the mating of plants. The copulation of pistils and stamens served as a model for teaching children acceptable sexual emotion and was much preferred to analogies between human and animal sexuality.[71] To the extent that sex educators actually discussed human sex, it was always as a form of spiritual communion; intercourse was mainly a melding of chaste minds. The sex-education movement, then, is best conceived as part of a new strategy for realizing Victorian moral ideals in an era growing increasingly comfortable with sex. If adults in the Progressive period had become unduly attracted to sex, their children need not be.[72]

How is the sexual counterrevolution related to our main subject—female juvenile justice in the Progressive era? We believe the sentiments that motivated the antiprostitution and sex-education campaigns also inspired punitive treatment of female delinquents. The expansion of female reformatories was especially significant, for they played important instrumental and symbolic roles in the sexual counterrevolution. First, and most pragmatically, the female reformatories assisted in the medical effort to eliminate venereal disease. They isolated those girls who were assumed most likely to become disease carriers. If the girls were already carriers, the reformatories prevented them from spreading disease and made treatment possible. Second, and most presumptuously, the incarceration of sexually promiscuous girls was thought to facilitate the moral ideal of male continence. By removing from view a prime source of sexual temptation, the reformatories, it was earnestly hoped, would also eliminate a stimulant of sexual desire in ghetto communities, especially for teenage boys. Third, and most urgently, the reformatories took sexually active girls off the street during the age range when prostitutes were most commonly recruited.[73] Hence reformatories, aided by the juvenile courts' punitive attitude toward sexual precocity among girls, would contribute to the attack on prostitution by cutting off a likely supply of new recruits.

Finally, and most idealistically, the reformatories assumed a special symbolic role in the sexual counterrevolution. In an era becoming increasingly fascinated by all things sexual, reformatories offered a warning that society would still not tolerate girls who showed the same interest in sex as boys and reinforced the traditional belief that "normal" girls were sexually impassive. These sentiments seem to us to have represented, to a large extent, a rearguard defense against emerging modern views on the reality of female sexual desire. But if, in fact, the counterrevolutionists lost the war, they were a powerful enough force in the Progressive era to win important battles. We should not gauge their significance in the early twentieth century by their long-term defeat in the battle for sexual liberation.

In sum, we believe that female juvenile justice in the Progressive era was closely tied to the evolution of sexual mores. In an era of shifting cultural norms, new social policies emerged to defend older moral ideals. As we noted earlier, we do not deny the possibility that there may have been a real increase in female delinquency in the early twentieth century. But we insist that, whether the increase was real or imagined, the public response to female delinquency formed part of a larger cultural reaction, an attempt to revitalize Victorian morality and to punish women—prostitutes and sexually precocious girls alike—who impeded attainment of that goal.

CONCLUSION

We promised earlier not to draw glib comparisons between past and present because of the incomplete nature of our historical research. But our research unequivocally demonstrates that the roots of sexual discrimination in juvenile justice are indeed deep. Despite radically different attitudes today toward the social role and sexual desires of women, our correctional polices share many of the assumptions common in the nineteenth and early twentieth centuries.[74] Perhaps mainstream ideas about the proper role of women and of female sexuality have not changed as much as some may think;[75] perhaps correctional policies always lag behind changes in cultural perception; perhaps we as a society are trying unconsciously to relieve guilt about the passing of older moral standards by continuing to punish the most vulnerable group of females—poor, minority children who today, as in the past, predominate among incarcerated girls. We do not have a ready answer, but we do believe that there is an intimate relation between a society's correctional system and its deepest values and beliefs. And without doubt the values and beliefs that shaped a discriminatory system of juvenile justice in the Victorian and Progressive eras still dominate the administration of female juvenile justice today.

NOTES

1. See Lawrence Cremin, "Foreword," in *American Education and Vocationalism,* eds. Marvin Lazerson and W. Norton Grubb (New York: Teachers College Press, 1974), p. ix.

2. One reason for the lack of scholarly attention to girl offenders in this period was the emphasis on gang delinquency, in which girls participated very little. There is, however, Paul Tappan's classic *Delinquent Girls in Court* (Montclair, N.J.: Patterson Smith, 1969), originally published in 1947.

3. See, for example, Lois Forer, *"No One Will Lissen"* (New York: Grosset and Dunlap, 1970); Patrick Murphy, *Our Kindly Parent . . . The State* (New York: Viking, 1974); Lisa Richette, *The Throwaway Children* (New York: Dell, 1969); and Ken Wooden, *Weeping in the Playtime of Others* (New York: McGraw-Hill, 1976).

4. See, for example, Michael Katz, *The Irony of Early School Reform* (Cambridge, Mass.: Harvard University

Press, 1968); Anthony Platt, *The Child Savers* (Chicago: University of Chicago Press, 1969); Alexander Liazos, "Class Oppression: The Functions of Juvenile Justice," *The Insurgent Sociologist*, Fall 1974, **1**, 2–24; and Steven Schlossman, *Love and the American Delinquent* (Chicago: University of Chicago Press, 1977).

5. For exceptions see Don Gibbons, *Delinquent Behavior* (Englewood Cliffs, N.J.: Prentice-Hall, 1976), 2nd ed., pp. 169–189; William Sanders, *Juvenile Delinquency* (New York: Praeger, 1976), pp. 64–83; Rose Giallombardo, *The Social World of Delinquent Girls* (New York: Wiley, 1974); Meda Chesney-Lind, "Juvenile Delinquency: The Sexualization of Female Crime," *Psychology Today*, July 1974, **8**, 43–46; Meda Chesney-Lind, "Judicial Enforcement of the Female Sex Role: The Family Court and the Female Delinquent," *Issues in Criminology*, Fall 1973, **8**, 51–69; Kristine Rogers, " 'For Her Own Protec-tion . . .': Conditions of Incarceration for Female Juvenile Offenders in the State of Connecticut," *Law and Society Review*, 1972, **7**, 223–246; Sarah Gold, "Equal Protection for Juvenile Girls in Need of Supervision in New York State," *New York Law Forum*, 1971, **17**, 570–598; Robert Terry, "Discrimination in the Handling of Juvenile Offenders by Social Control Agencies," in *Becoming Delinquent*, eds. Peter Garabedian and Don Gibbons (Chicago: Aldine, 1970), pp. 78–92; Freda Adler, *Sisters in Crime* (New York: McGraw-Hill, 1975), chap. 4; *Crime and Delinquency*, 1977, **23** (issue theme: "Criminal Justice to Women: Not Fair!"); and Paul Katzeff, "Equal Crime," *Boston Magazine*, December 1977, 107–108, 206, 208–210. For an estimate that girls now form nearly one-quarter of the juvenile court clientele, see Rosemary Sarri and Robert Vintner, "Justice for Whom? Varieties of Correctional Approaches," in *The Juvenile Justice System*, ed. Malcolm Klein, **v** (New York: Russell Sage, 1975), p. 171.

6. See the pioneering studies by Barbara Brenzel, "Lancaster Industrial School for Girls: A Social Portrait of a Nineteenth Century Reform School for Girls," *Feminist Studies*, Fall 1975, **3**, 40–53; and by Estelle Freedman, "Their Sisters' Keepers: The Origins of Female Corrections in America," Dissertation, Columbia University, 1976.

7. Margaret Reeves, *Training Schools for Delinquent Girls* (New York: Russell Sage, 1929).

8. Robert Mennel, *Thorns and Thistles* (Hanover, N.H.: University Press of New England, 1973), p. 172.

9. See especially Robert Bremner, *From the Depths* (New York: New York University Press, 1956); and Walter Trattner, *Crusade for the Children* (Chicago: Quadrangle, 1970).

10. Brenzel, "Lancaster"; Mennel, *Thorns and Thistles*, chap. 4; Freedman, "Their Sisters' Keepers," chaps. 3 and 4.

11. On the image of the "fallen woman," see Freedman, "Their Sisters' Keepers," chap. 2; for the emphasis on environmental causes behind male criminality, see David Rothman, *The Discovery of the Asylum* (Boston: Little, Brown, 1971).

12. Schlossman, *Love*, chaps. 2, 3, and 5.

13. Charles Loring Brace, *The Dangerous Classes of New York and Twenty Years' Work among Them* (New York: Wynkoop and Hallenbeck, 1872).

14. Miriam Langsam, *Children West* (Madison, Wis.: State Historical Society of Wisconsin, 1964); Thomas Bender, *Toward an Urban Vision* (Lexington, Ky.: University Press of Kentucky, 1975); and Steven Schlossman, "The 'Culture of Poverty' in Ante-Bellum Social Thought," *Science and Society*, 1974, **38**, 150–166.

15. These observations draw upon Schlossman's study of social-reform groups in Milwaukee and of parent-education organizations throughout the country. See Schlossman, *Love*, chap. 7, and "Before Home Start: Notes Toward a History of Parent Education in America. 1897–1929," *Harvard Educational Review*, 1976, **46**, 436–467. Also useful is David McLeod, "Good Boys Made Better: The Boy Scouts of America, Boys' Brigades, and YMCA Boys' Work, 1880–1920," Dissertation, University of Wisconsin, 1973.

16. Reeves, *Training Schools*, pp. 39ff; and Mennel, *Thorns and Thistles*, pp. 171–179.

17. For data on Milwaukee see Schlossman, *Love*, appendix 2, table 6. Our main source for Chicago is Sophonisba Breckinridge and Edith Abbott, *The Delinquent Child and the Home* (New York: Russell Sage, 1912); for San Francisco, Emily Huntington, Leona Jones, Donna Moses, and Ruth Turner, "The Juvenile Court," Bachelor of Arts Thesis, University of California at Berkeley, 1917; and for New Haven, Mabel Wiley, *A Study of the Problem of Girl Delinquency in New Haven* (New Haven, Conn.: Civic Federation of New Haven, 1915).

18. Schlossman, *Love*, pp. 143–144.

19. Breckinridge and Abbott, *The Delinquent Child*, pp. 28–35. See also Huntington et al., "The Juvenile Court," appendix.

20. Breckinridge and Abbott, *The Delinquent Child*, pp. 38–40; Huntington et al., "The Juvenile Court," appendix; Alida Bowler, "A Study of Seventy-Five Delinquent Girls," *Journal of Delinquency*, 1917, **2**, 157; Mabel Elliott, *Correctional Education and the Delinquent Girl* (Harrisburg, Pa.: Commonwealth of Pennsylvania Department of Welfare, 1928), pp. 34–35; Louise Ordahl and George Ordahl, "A Study of Delinquent and Dependent Girls," *Journal of Delinquency*, 1918, **3**, 34–35; and Wiley, *A Study of the Problem*, p. 11.

21. Bowler, "A Study of Seventy-Five Delinquent Girls," p. 159; Breckinridge and Abbott, *The Delinquent Child*, pp. 35–39; Elliott, *Correctional Education*, pp. 34–35; Ordahl and Ordahl, "A Study of Delinquent and Dependent Girls," pp. 55–59; and Wiley, *A Study of the Problem*, p. 9.

22. Breckinridge and Abbott, *The Delinquent Child*, p. 41; and Schlossman, *Love*, appendix 2, table 3.

23. In arguing that girls received more punitive treatment, we assume that incarceration is, by its very nature, a harsher form of punishment than probation. We are *not* saying, however, that the treatment of

girls in reformatories was harsher than that of boys in reformatories.

24. These cases derive from Schlossman's sample of 1,200 cases in Milwaukee (10 percent of the total heard in this period). To the best of our knowledge, the Milwaukee court is the only one to have opened its early records for historical investigation; it is consequently impossible to say whether they are strictly representative of experiences in courts elsewhere. Although selected with an eye toward the exemplary and archetypal, each case was necessarily idiosyncratic because, obviously, no two children or their parents were exactly alike. The cases that follow should be appreciated much like opera highlights, as suggestive of a larger drama and of characteristic patterns of interaction among protagonists. To protect client anonymity we have changed the names of children and parents who appeared in court, although we have tried to retain their particular ethnic origins. For the same reason we have not cited the specific dates or docket numbers of individual cases.

25. Adina Mitchell, *Special Report on the Whittier State School* (Sacramento, Calif.: State Printing Office, 1896), p. 11. See also Mary Berry, "The State's Duty to the Delinquent Girl," National Conference on the Education of Truant, Backward, Dependent and Delinquent Children, *Proceedings* (1918), pp. 82–83; Mrs. Jennie Griffith, "The Training of Delinquent Girls," Conference of the National Committee on Prisons and Prison Labor, *Proceedings* (1919), pp. 15, 17; Miriam Van Waters, "Where Girls Go Right," *Survey Graphic*, 1922, **1**, 365; and Maine Industrial School for Girls, *Annual Report* (Waterville, Me.: Sentinel Publishing Co., 1909), pp. 7–8.

26. Breckinridge and Abbott, *The Delinquent Child*, p. 8; Huntington et al., "The Juvenile Court," appendix; Olga Bridgman, "An Experimental Study of Abnormal Children, with Special Reference to the Problems of Dependency and Delinquency," University of California, *Publications in Psychology*, 1918, **3**, 8; Berry, "The State's Duty," p. 87; Edith Burleigh and Frances Harris, *The Delinquent Girl* (New York: New York School of Social Work, 1923), pp. 32, 38–43; Mary Dewson, "Probation and Institutional Care of Girls," in *The Child in the City*, ed. Sophonisba Breckinridge (Chicago: Chicago School of Civics and Philanthropy, 1912), pp. 360–362; Martha Falconer, "Work of the Girls' Department, House of Refuge, Philadelphia," National Conference of Charities and Correction, *Proceedings* (1908), p. 393; and National Conference of Charities and Correction, *Proceedings* (1903), p. 517. Elliott's *Correctional Education*, a follow-up study of ex-inmates from the Sleighton Farms reformatory in Pennsylvania, left no doubt that marriage was the most important variable in explaining post-release behavior.

27. This argument was rarely advanced about the boys' reformatories. In fact, although historians have yet to provide adequate documentation, male reformatories apparently experimented with a variety of new correctional ideas in the Progressive era and participated tangentially in the "progressive education" movement. Elaborate vocational-training programs at a few of the larger reformatories became the envy of "progressive" educators such as David Snedden. In addition, many public reformatories experimented with self-government programs designed loosely along the lines suggested by William George in his famous Junior Republics; many adopted new forms of recreational and military training to improve health and discipline and upgraded their academic offerings for older inmates. Of course we do not believe that these newer correctional programs necessarily rehabilitated inmates. Our point is simply that levels of interest and public investment in rehabilitative programs were greater in boys' than girls' reformatories. For background on the relation between "progressive education" and juvenile corrections, see Walter Drost, *David Snedden* (Madison, Wis.: University of Wisconsin Press, 1967); and Jack Holl, *Juvenile Reform in the Progressive Era* (Ithaca, N.Y.: Cornell University Press, 1971).

28. A widely discussed social "problem" in the Progressive era was the declining availability of trained domestic help; hence it can be argued that the reformatories' emphasis on domestic training was economically functional for the girls. It was also recognized, though, that domestics received wages so low that some were tempted to turn to prostitution for supplementary income.

29. Mary Berry, "Co-Ordination of Industrial and Vocational Work with Parole Administration," National Conference on the Education of Truant, Backward, Dependent and Delinquent Children, *Proceedings* (1902), pp. 52–60; Bowler, "A Study of Seventy-Five Delinquent Girls," pp. 156–157; Burleigh and Harris, *The Delinquent Child*, pp. 8–9; William Fairbanks, "Girls' Reformatories and Their Inherent Characteristics," National Conference of Charities and Correction, *Proceedings* (1901), pp. 254–262; Miss Mary Hinkley, "Problems of Administration: The Responsibilities of a School Toward its Girls," National Conference on the Education of Truant, Backward, Dependent and Delinquent Children, *Proceedings* (1920), pp. 20–23; Maine Industrial School for Girls, *Annual Report* (1909), p. 15; Griffith, "The Training of Delinquent Girls," p. 17; and Miss Elizabeth Mansell, "An Institution Program for Delinquent Girls," National Conference on the Education of Truant, Backward, Dependent and Delinquent Children, *Proceedings* (1917), p. 35.

30. See Emma Weigley, "It Might Have Been Euthenics: The Lake Placid Conference and the Home Economics Movement," *American Quarterly*, 1974, **26**, 79–96; and Barbara Ehrenreich and Deidre English, "The Manufacture of Housework," *Socialist Revolution*, October–December, 1975, **5**, 5–40.

31. National Conference of Charities and Correction, *Proceedings* (1901), p. 258.

32. California School for Girls, *Biennial Report* (Sacramento, Calif.: State Printing Office, 1918), p. 9.

33. For background on the eugenics movement we have relied especially on Mark Haller, *Eugenics* (New

Brunswick, N.J.: Rutgers University Press, 1963); Donald Pickens, *Eugenics and the Progressive Era* (Nashville, Tenn.: Vanderbilt University Press, 1968); Rudolph Vecoli, "Sterilization: A Progressive Measure?" *Wisconsin Magazine of History*, 1960, **48**, 190–203; Peter Tyor, "Segregation or Surgery: The Mentally Retarded in America, 1850–1920," Dissertation, Northwestern University, 1972; and Allan Chase, *The Legacy of Malthus* (New York: Knopf, 1976).

34. *The Journal of Delinquency*, published in California, provided the principal forum for discussing this use of mental tests. Its articles were written mainly by psychologists, physicians, psychiatrists, and correctional workers. The *Journal* came especially under the influence of Lewis Terman and several of his students at Stanford, although other prominent members of its editorial board included William Healy, founder of the Juvenile Psychopathic Clinic in Chicago, and Arnold Gesell, the developmental psychologist from Yale.

35. See, for example, C. S. Bluemel, "Binet Tests on Two Hundred Juvenile Delinquents," *Training School Bulletin*, 1915, **12**, 191. Of all the drawbacks of the early IQ tests administered to delinquents, the most basic one was the leeway given to the examiner. The tests left much room for interpretation; often there was no clear-cut right or wrong answer. In such instances the examiners frequently came to dubious conclusions about inmates' mental ages. Consider the following example from Bluemel (p. 187), in which the examiner asked:

> "What is the difference between pride and pretension?" The first replies: "If you have too much pride, you go to certain places— cafes and dance halls. Some pretend to be proud but are poor." The second replies: "Pride means to be proud, and pretension means to pretend to be something that you are not." The third replies: "Pride is something in you that makes you—if you have enough of it—hold yourself a little above people that are without pride. Pretension is false pride." Obviously, these answers indicate that the three girls are at different mental levels. This fact is also attested by their answers to the other questions; and the answers in their totality permit one to make a fair estimate of their mental ages.

See also Ordahl and Ordahl, "A Study of Delinquent and Dependent Girls," pp. 41–73; and Jean Walker, "Factors Contributing to the Delinquency of Defective Girls," University of California, *Publications in Psychology*, 1925, **3**, 147–207.

36. William Thomas and Florian Znaniecki, *The Polish Peasant in America*, 2 vols. (New York: Knopf, 1927).

37. Jane Addams, *Democracy and Social Ethics* (New York: Macmillan, 1902); and *The Spirit of Youth and the City Streets* (New York: Macmillan, 1909).

38. For example, see "Are Low Wages Responsible for Women's Immorality?," *Current Opinion*, May 1913, **54**, 402.

39. Jane Addams, *A New Conscience and an Ancient Evil* (New York: Macmillan, 1913).

40. The previously cited texts of Gibbons and Sanders (see footnote 5) are especially sensitive to this difficulty. See also the essays collected under the heading, "The Data of Delinquency: Problems of Definition and Measurement," in *Juvenile Delinquency*, ed. Rose Giallombardo (New York: Wiley, 1966).

41. Edwin Schur, *Radical Non-Intervention* (Englewood Cliffs, N.J.: Prentice-Hall, 1973).

42. See especially Platt, *The Child Savers*; and Leon Radzinowicz, *Ideology and Crime* (New York: Columbia University Press, 1966).

43. The theories and policies proposed in the eugenics movement drew upon several long-term preoccupations of American social reformers. Hereditarian thinking and racial mythologies were staples of American social thought throughout the nineteenth century, existing before the influence of Social Darwinism. Similarly, anti-immigrant hostility was common from the early nineteenth century onward, particularly in the large cities of the Northeast. We believe, nonetheless, that racial mythologies and anti-immigrant prejudice attained, in tandem, a new degree of legitimacy after the rediscovery in 1900 of Mendel's ideas, especially after these were popularized, and distorted, by social scientists whose influence on social policy grew enormously in the Progressive period. For example, Henry Goddard, one of the leading applied social scientists in the country and the first person to translate and adapt the Binet-Simon intelligence tests to American needs, wrote the best-selling bible of the eugenics movement, *The Kallikak Family* (New York: Macmillan, 1912) and led campaigns for literacy tests, restrictive marriage covenants, sterilization laws, and immigration restrictions. Even Jane Addams, a quintessential environmentalist, could endorse "the new science of eugenics" and "its recently appointed university professors" (*A New Conscience*, pp. 130–131). See Charles Rosenberg, "The Bitter Fruit: Heredity, Disease, and Social Thought," *Perspectives in American History*, 1974, **8**, 189–235; Ray Billington, *The Protestant Crusade, 1800–1860* (New York: Macmillan, 1938); and Oscar Handlin, *Boston's Immigrants* (Cambridge, Mass.: Harvard University Press, 1941). On the growing role of social scientists, see Julius Weinberg, *Edward Alsworth Ross and the Sociology of Progressivism* (Madison, Wis.: State Historical Society of Wisconsin, 1972); Barry Karl, *Charles E. Merriam and the Study of Politics* (Chicago: University of Chicago Press, 1974); Julia and Herman Schwendinger, *Sociologists of the Chair* (New York: Basic Books, 1974); and Chase, *The Legacy of Malthus*, pt. 2.

44. Although such theories were not nearly as new as their proponents claimed, they did exert considerable influence on Progressive-era social reformers. See Joseph Kett, *Rites of Passage* (New York: Basic Books, 1977), chap. 8; and Steven Schlossman, "G. Stanley Hall and the Boys' Club: Conservative Applications of the Recapitulation Theory," *Journal of the History of the Behavioral Sciences*, 1973, **9**, 140–147.

45. Two articles that advance the same argument as it applies to formal criminological theory are Doris Klein, "The Etiology of Female Crime: A Review of the Literature," *Issues in Criminology*, Fall 1973, **8**, 3–30; and Dale Hoffman-Bustamante, "The Nature of Female Criminality," *Issues in Criminology*, Fall 1973, **8**, 117–136.

46. See Dorothy Ross, *G. Stanley Hall* (Chicago: University of Chicago Press, 1972); Kett, *Rites of Passage*, chap. 8; and Schlossman, "G. Stanley Hall and the Boys' Club."

47. Addams, *The Spirit of Youth*.

48. On boys' clubs, see Schlossman, "G. Stanley Hall and the Boys' Club"; on camps, see McLeod, "Good Boys Made Better"; on Boy Scouts, see Jeffrey Hantover, "Sex Role, Sexuality, and Social Status: The Early Years of the Boy Scouts of America," Dissertation, University of Chicago, 1976; and Peter Schmitt, *Back to Nature* (New York: Oxford University Press, 1969), chap. 10. For a more comprehensive synthesis of these and other organizations aimed at youth, see Kett, *Rites of Passage*, chaps. 7 and 8.

49. In reaching this conclusion we have relied especially upon: Augusta Bronner, "Effect of Adolescent Instability on Conduct," *Psychological Clinic*, 1915, **7**, 249–265; Burleigh and Harris, *The Delinquent Girl*; Mary Paddon, "A Study of Fifty Feeble-Minded Prostitutes," *Journal of Delinquency*, 1918, **3**, 1–11; Maude Miner, "The Woman Delinquent," New York City Conference of Charities and Correction, *Proceedings*, (1911), pp. 152–165; Rheta Dorr, "Reclaiming the Wayward Girl," *Hampton's Magazine*, January 1911, **26**, 67–78; Bridgman, "An Experimental Study of Abnormal Children"; Mary Moxcey, *Girlhood and Character* (New York: Abingdon, 1916); Winifred Richmond, *The Adolescent Girl* (New York: Macmillan, 1926); Ruth True, "The Neglected Girl," in *West Side Studies*, ed. Pauline Goldmark (New York: Survey Associates, 1914), pp. 1–134; Emily Lamb, "A Study of Thirty-Five Delinquent Girls," *Journal of Delinquency*, 1919, **4**, 75–85; Ordahl and Ordahl, "A Study of Delinquent and Dependent Girls"; Merritt Pinkney, "The Delinquent Girl and the Juvenile Court," in *The Child in the City*, ed. Breckinridge, pp. 349–354; Breckinridge and Abbott, *The Delinquent Child*; Wiley, *A Study of the Problem*; William Thomas, *The Unadjusted Girl* (Boston: Little, Brown, 1923): Miriam Van Waters, "Causes and Cure" and "The True Value of Correctional Education," in the Miriam Van Waters Papers, Box 11, Schlesinger Library, Radcliffe College; Falconer, "Work of the Girls' Department"; Elliott, *Correctional Education*; Huntington et al., "The Juvenile Court"; Walrek, "Factors Contributing to the Delinquency of Defective Girls"; Miss Vida Francis, "The Delinquent Girl," National Conference of Charities and Correction, *Proceedings* (1906), pp. 138–145; and Jane Rippin, "Social Readjustment as the Function of the Judge," Conference of the National Committee on Prisons and Prison Labor, *Proceedings* (1919), pp. 25–31.

50. We quote from Kett, *Rites of Passage*, p. 224; "Hall, moreover, had written very little about girls, a bias fully reflected in both the literature on boys-work after 1900 and in the masculine orientation and sexual segregation of scouting. . . . It was a boy's world, not a girl's and not a man's, a fact which prompted H. W. Gibson, a YMCA tractarian and boys-worker, to reduce all of adolescent psychology to something called 'boyology.' " A very useful compendium which nicely captures the differences in the theories is *Boy Training*, ed. John Alexander (New York: Association Press, 1915).

51. Schlossman, *Love*, chap. 4.

52. The citations in note 49 are all relevant here, especially Breckinridge and Abbott, *The Delinquent Child* pp. 35–38, 72–73, 169; Ordahl and Ordahl, "A Study of Delinquent and Dependent Girls," pp. 60–61; Van Waters, "Causes and Cure," p. 5; Paddon, "A Study of Fifty Feeble-Minded Prostitutes," p. 10; and True, "The Neglected Girl," p. 19.

53. Francis, "The Delinquent Girl," p. 140.

54. In the 1950s and 1960s the most common historical approach to the subject of morals and sex in the Progressive era was to emphasize its puritanical features. This approach flowed from the interpretation of social-reform movements epitomized by the work of Richard Hofstadter, especially *The Age of Reform* (New York: Knopf, 1955). In the past few years a different historical interpretation has emerged that stresses the loosening grip of Victorian morality on sexual attitudes and hold that "modern" attitudes toward sex first emerged in the Progressive era rather than, as is more commonly thought, in the 1920s. This view rests on several sources of evidence: the work of historical demographers, who argue that rates of premarital pregnancy rose markedly in this period; self-report studies, which indicate that dramatic increases in premarital intercourse occurred; and reexamination of literary sources, which suggests that social discourse in the Progressive era was a good deal less prudish than had been thought. As examples, see Linda Gordon, *Woman's Body, Woman's Right* (New York: Grossman, 1976), pt. 2; Paul Robinson, *The Modernization of Sex* (New York: Harper & Row, 1976); John Burnham, "The Progressive-Era Revolution in American Attitudes Toward Sex," *Journal of American History*, 1973, **59**, 885–908; James McGovern, "The American Woman's Pre-World War I Freedom in Manners and Morals," *Journal of American History*, 1968, **55**, 315–333; and Carl Degler, "What Ought to Be and What Was: Women's Sexuality in the Nineteenth Century," *American Historical Review*, 1974, **79**, 1467–1490. While we agree with the historians who argue that the early twentieth century witnessed a marked increase in the public's willingness to discuss sex openly, we are uneasy about the tendency to locate the origins of sexual modernity in the Progressive era. This approach, we feel, exaggerates indications of the new morality and plays down evidence of older Victorian thinking. Most important for the history of female juvenile justice, this interpretation shifts attention away from major efforts in this period to reaf-

firm Victorian moral and sexual standards as well as to recast older religious commands into new secular, scientific language. Thus we both agree and disagree with the new interpretation.

55. On the scholarly side, the psychologist Helen Thompson Woolley noted that between 1910 and 1914 "the number of experimental investigations in the field [psychology of sex] has increased to such an extent that whereas it was difficult at that time [1910] to find anything to review, it is now impossible to review all that I could find" ("The Psychology of Sex," *The Psychological Bulletin*, 1914, **11**, 353). If scholars were having a field day with sex, so was the American public: "A wave of sex hysteria seems to have invaded this country," wrote the anonymous author of a piece which has since become an historical classic. "Our former reticence on matters of sex is giving way to a frankness that would even startle Paris." ("Sex O'Clock in America," *Current Opinion*, August 1913, **55**, 113).

56. This is our impression from reading the literature; we have not conducted empirical research on the social origins of the counterrevolutionists. Certainly Theodore Roosevelt was the most prominent of the individuals who engaged as fervidly in moral as in political reform. Roosevelt popularized the notion of "race suicide" and boasted that one of his greatest achievements was to have exercised enough will power to remain a virgin until marriage (William Harbaugh, *The Life and Times of Theodore Roosevelt* [New York: Oxford University Press, 1975], p. 15).

57. For general background see David Pivar, *Purity Crusade* (Westport, Conn.: Greenwood, 1973); and David Kennedy, *Birth Control in America* (New Haven, Conn.: Yale University Press, 1970).

58. "Sex O'Clock in America."

59. John Burnham, "Medical Inspection of Prostitutes in Nineteenth Century America—The St. Louis Experiment and Its Sequel," *Bulletin of the History of Medicine*, 1971, **45**, 203–218.

60. See Roy Lubove, "The Progressives and the Prostitute," *Historian*, 1962, **24**, 308–330; Robert Riegel, "Changing American Attitudes toward Prostitution (1800–1920)," *Journal of the History of Ideas*, 1968, **29**, 437–452; Keith Thomas, "The Double Standard," *Journal of the History of Ideas*, 1959, **20**, 195–216; Egal Feldman, "Prostitution, the Alien Woman and the Progressive Imagination, 1910–1915," *American Quarterly*, 1967, **19**, 192–206; Eric Anderson, "Prostitution and Social Justice: Chicago, 1910–15," *Social Service Review*, 1974, **48**, 203–228; Claudia Johnson, "That Guilty Third Tier: Prostitution in Nineteenth-Century American Theatres," in *Victorian America*, ed. Daniel Howe (Philadelphia: University of Pennsylvania Press, 1976), pp. 111–120; and James Wunsch, "Prostitution and Public Policy: From Regulation to Suppression, 1858–1920," Dissertation, University of Chicago, 1976.

61. A very useful introduction to the ideals and practices of sex in the Victorian period is *Primers for Prudery*, ed. Ronald Walters (Englewood Cliffs, N.J.: Prentice-Hall, 1974). See also Gordon, *Woman's Body*, chaps.

4 and 8; and Patricia Vertinsky, "Education for Sexual Morality: Moral Reform and the Regulation of American Sexual Behavior in the Nineteenth Century," Dissertation, University of British Columbia, 1974, sect. 2.

62. We borrow the term "underground" from Bryan Strong, who writes of the attempt in the early twentieth century "to counteract the underground belief in what was called the 'sexual necessity,' which declared that men must exercise their sexual power lest their organs weaken or atrophy for want of use. Belief in a 'sexual necessity,' of course, was inconsistent with the ideal of chastity and continence" ("Ideas of the Early Sex Education Movement in America, 1890–1920," *History of Education Quarterly*, 1972, **12**, 145).

63. See, for example, Anne Scott, *The Southern Lady* (Chicago: University of Chicago Press, 1970); and Barbara Welter, "The Cult of True Womanhood: 1820–1860," *American Quarterly*, 1966, **18**, 151–174.

64. See Gordon, *Woman's Body*, p. 204. While we find her argument intriguing, we do not believe there is sufficient evidence to support Gordon's cause-effect contention that "the basis for the weakening of prostitution between 1910 and 1920 was not the conversion of men to purity; it was the conversion of women to 'indulgence'" (p. 192).

65. For example, see Clifford Roe, *The Prodigal Daughter: The White Slave Evil and the Remedy* (Chicago: L. W. Walter, 1911); and *War on the White Slave Trade*, ed. Ernest Bell (Chicago: Charles C. Thompson, 1909).

66. The principal medical spokesperson and organizational leader of the counterrevolutionists was Dr. Prince Morrow, whose activities are well treated in Burnham, "The Progressive Era Revolution."

67. See especially Thomas, *The Unadjusted Girl*; and Strong, "Ideas of the Early Sex Education Movement."

68. Quoted in Maurice Bigelow, *Sex-Education* (New York: Macmillan, 1918), p. 161.

69. We are especially indebted to the works of Pivar, Strong, and Vertinsky, "Education for Sexual Morality." The best primary sources, in our estimation, are *The Social Emergency*, ed. William Foster (Boston: Houghton-Mifflin, 1914); Bigelow, *Sex-Education*; and National Society for the Scientific Study of Education, *Education with Reference to Sex* (Chicago: University of Chicago Press, 1909).

70. Although the sex educators, by and large, wanted nothing to do with Freud, they were advocating a form of creative repression akin to the goals of the early conservative champions of Freud in America. See Nathan Hale, *Freud and the Americans* (New York: Oxford University Press, 1971).

71. For example, Bigelow writes in *Sex-Education*: "Like eating [sex] is a necessary function inherited from animals; but there has been an evolution of greater significance. In the animal world, sexual activity has only one function, reproduction; but human life at its highest has superadded psychical and social meaning to sexual relationships, and the result has been affection and the human

family. If we reject this higher view of the double significance of sexuality in human life, and insist that only the necessary propagate function is worthy of recognition, it is almost inevitable that most people will continue to accept the hopeless view that human sexuality is on the same vulgar plane as that of the animals; in short, that it is only an animal function. This, I insist, is a depressing interpretation that will never help overcome the prevailing vulgar attitude toward sex" (p. 74).

72. For assessments of the influence of the sex-education movement, see Strong, "Ideas of the Early Sex Education Movement," pp. 152–153; and Vertinsky, "Education for Sexual Morality," chap. 9.

73. According to Jane Addams, "it has been estimated that at any given moment the majority of girls utilized by the trade are under twenty years of age and that most of them were procured when younger. . . . the average age of recruits to prostitution is between sixteen and eighteen years. . . . All the recent investigations have certainly made clear that the bulk of the entire traffic is conducted with the youth of the community, and that the social evil, ancient though it may be, must be renewed in our generation through its younger members. The knowledge of the youth of its victims doubtless in a measure accounts for the new sense of compunction which fills the community." *A New Conscience*, pp. 52, 142.

74. Richard Flaste, "Is Juvenile Justice Tougher on Girls Than on Boys?" *New York Times*, 6 September 1977, p. 48, cols. 1–4.

75. The classic argument, of course, is presented in Betty Friedan, *The Feminine Mystique* (New York: Norton, 1963). In addition to previously cited books and articles, the following historical works shed much light on continuities between past and present: Charles Rosenberg, "Sexuality, Class, and Role," *American Quarterly*, 1973, **25**, 131–153; Charles Rosenberg and Carroll Smith-Rosenberg, "The Female Animal: Medical and Biological Views of Women," *Journal of American History*, 1973, **60**, 332–356; Rosalind Rosenberg, "The Dissent from Darwin, 1890–1930: The New View of Woman among American Social Scientists," Dissertation, Stanford University, 1974; and Paula Fass, *The Damned and the Beautiful* (New York: Oxford University Press, 1977).

A GUIDE TO ADDITIONAL PRIMARY-SOURCE MATERIALS ON FEMALE JUVENILE DELINQUENCY IN THE EARLY TWENTIETH CENTURY

BOWEN, MRS. JOSEPH "The Delinquent Child of Immigrant Parents." National Conference of Charities and Correction, *Proceedings* (1909), pp. 255–261.

BRIDGMAN, OLGA "An Experimental Study of Abnormal Children with Special Reference to the Problems of Dependency and Delinquency." University of California, *Publications in Psychology*, 1918, **3**, 2–59.

BRONNER, AUGUSTA *A Comparative Study of the Intelligence of Girls*. New York: Teachers College Press, 1914.

BURLEIGH, EDITH "The Advantage of Parole Under a Separate Superintendent." National Conference on the Education of Truant, Backward, Dependent and Delinquent Children, *Proceedings* (1916), pp. 80–83.

BURLEIGH, EDITH "Some Principles for Parole for Girls." National Conference of Charities and Correction, *Proceedings* (1918), pp. 147–154.

DEBOLT, MRS. L. N. "Industrial Employment as a Factor in the Reformation of Girls." National Conference of Charities and Correction, *Proceedings* (1900), pp. 214–220.

DUMMER, MRS. W. F. "Introduction to Roundtable Discussion on the Delinquent Girl." The American Sociological Society, *Publications*, 1921, **16**, 185–186.

DYE, CHARLOTTE "The Defective Delinquent." National Conference on the Education of Truant, Backward, Dependent and Delinquent Children, *Proceedings* (1917), pp. 78–82.

FALCONER, MARTHA "The Culture of Family Life Versus Reformatory Treatment." National Conference of Charities and Correction, *Proceedings* (1914), pp. 108–110.

FALCONER, MARTHA "Reformatory Treatment for Women." National Conference of Charities and Correction, *Proceedings* (1914), pp. 253–256.

GODDARD, HENRY "The Treatment of the Mental Defective Who Is Also Delinquent." National Conference of Charities and Correction, *Proceedings* (1911), pp. 64–65.

HAMILTON, DR. ALICE "Venereal Disease in Institutions for Women and Girls." National Conference of Charities and Correction, *Proceedings* (1910), pp. 53–56.

HARRIS, DR. MARY "Preparing Delinquent Women for the New Citizenship." Conference of the National Committee on Prisons and Prison Labor, *Proceedings* (1919), pp. 6–14.

HARRIS, DR. MARY *I Knew Them in Prison*. New York: Viking, 1936.

HOAG, DR. ERNEST, AND DR. EDWARD WILLIAMS *Crime, Abnormal Minds and the Law*. Indianapolis, Ind.: Bobbs-Merrill, 1923.

HODDER, JESSIE "The Next Step in the Treatment of Girls and Women Offenders." National Conference of Charities and Correction, *Proceedings* (1918), pp. 117–121.

HOLSOPPLE, FRANCIS "Social Non-Conformity: An Analysis of 420 Delinquent Girls and Women." Dissertation, University of Pennsylvania, 1919.

KAUFFMAN, REGINALD *The Girl That Goes Wrong*. New York: Macaulay, 1911.

KENWORTHY, DR. MARION "The Logic of Delinquency." The American Sociological Society, *Publications*, 1921, **16**, 197–204.

LUNDBERG, EMMA "The Child-Mother as a Delinquency Problem." National Conference of Charities and Correction, *Proceedings* (1920), pp. 167–168.

MINER, MAUDE　*Slavery of Prostitution.* New York: Macmillan, 1916.

MINER, MAUDE　"The Individual Method of Dealing with Girls and Women Awaiting Court Action." Congress of the American Prison Association, *Proceedings* (1921), pp. 8–12.

MONTGOMERY, MISS SARAH　"Discipline and Training of Girls in Industrial Schools." National Conference of Charities and Correction, *Proceedings* (1908), pp. 198–201.

MORROW, DR. LOUIS, AND DR. OLGA BRIDGMAN　"Delinquent Girls Tested by the Binet Scale." *Training School Bulletin*, 1912, **9**, 33–36.

MORSE, MRS. FRANNIE　"The Methods Most Helpful to Girls." National Conference of Charities and Correction, *Proceedings* (1904), pp. 306–311.

MURRAY, VIRGINIA　"The Runaway Girl and the Stranded Girl." National Conference of Charities and Correction, *Proceedings* (1920), pp. 175–180.

NATIONAL CONFERENCE ON THE EDUCATION OF TRUANT, BACKWARD, DEPENDENT AND DELINQUENT CHILDREN, *Proceedings* (1915), pp. 49–53, and (1917), pp. 36–41, 82–90.

RENZ, EMILE　"The Intelligence of Delinquents and the Eugenic Significance of Mental Defect." *Training School Bulletin*, 1914, 11, 37–39.

RIPPIN, JANE　"Municipal Detention for Women." National Conference of Charities and Correction, *Proceedings* (1918), pp. 132–139.

SESSIONS, DR. KENOSHA　"Some Deductions from the Wasserman Test." National Conference on the Education of Truant, Backward, Dependent and Delinquent Children, *Proceedings* (1915), pp. 47–49.

SESSIONS, DR. KENOSHA　"The Delinquent Girls as a Community Problem." National Conference on the Education of Truant, Backward, Dependent and Delinquent Children, *Proceedings* (1918), pp. 76–78.

SMITH, DR. CARRIE　"The Unadjusted Girl." National Conference of Charities and Correction, *Proceedings* (1920), pp. 180–183.

TAFT, JESSIE　"Some Problems in Delinquency—Where Do They Belong?" The American Sociological Society, *Publications*, 1921, **16**, 186–196.

VAN WATERS, MIRIAM　"Juvenile Court Procedure as a Factory in Diagnosis." The American Sociological Society, *Publications*, 1921, **16**, 209–217.

WALD, MRS. LILLIAN　"The Immigrant Young Girl." National Conference of Charities and Correction, *Proceedings* (1909), pp. 261–266.

WILSON, OTTO　*Fifty Years' Work with Girls, 1883–1933.* Alexandria, Va.: National Florence Crittendon Mission, 1933.

WORTHINGTON, GEORGE, AND RUTH TOPPING　*Specialized Courts Dealing with Sex Delinquency.* New York: Frederick H. Hitchcock, 1925.

QUESTIONS FOR DISCUSSION

1. Compared to delinquent boys, delinquent girls have received far less attention in historical literature and research studies. What two main reasons do the authors give for this?

2. The authors cite four principal reasons why the traditional interpretations of Progressive era policies regarding delinquent girls are lacking. List these reasons. Do you think the authors make a convincing argument? Why?

3. Discuss the four principal goals of female reformatories in the Progressive era. How and why did male reformatories differ from female reformatories?

APPLICATIONS

1. Set up an appointment with a member of the local judiciary, preferably a juvenile judge or probation officer. Ask this official about the differences in offenses committed by females and by males. Next, ask about the differences in the court sentences or treatment of these juveniles. Are there any disparities?

2. Do you believe that females and males should be treated differently for similar offenses? Why?

KEY TERMS

anachronistic a person or thing that is out of place chronologically; a concept or theory from a former era that is incongruous or inapplicable to the present.

bucolic refers to rural settings; relating to typical rural life.

chivalrous marked by honor, generosity, and courtesy; tradionally high-minded consideration for women.

disposition to deal with conclusively; to make a final decision or arrangement.

immutable not capable of or susceptible to change.

legal artifact an object that is created or results from a legal institution or activity (e.g., legal precedence, documents).

pragmatism relating to matters in a practical way as opposed to an idealistic, intellectual, or artistic manner.

precocious exhibiting unusually mature qualities at an early age.

Progressive era that period from approximately 1900 to 1930 characterized by beliefs and attitudes of moderate social and economic reform by the government.

revivalism a new presentation or publication of something old; a reviving or restoring of a past belief, attitude, or ideology. Typically a religious notion but can be applied to governmental philosophies.

Victorian era that period from approximately 1870 to 1900 characterized by rigid moral standards, attitudes, and conduct; considered to be an especially repressive period with regard to dress and behavior; also characterized by stuffiness and hypocrisy.

4

History Overtakes
the Juvenile Justice System

Theodore N. Ferdinand

Justice systems have a way of shaping their parts to the needs of the whole, and the juvenile justice system is no exception. Many of the juvenile court's problems can be understood in terms of how the court adjusted over the years to the custodial institutions, clientele, and treatment facilities it served. Its deficiencies today stem largely from its roots in the civil courts and the difficulties it encountered in fulfilling *parens patriae* in a system of juvenile institutions already dominated by a custodial if not a punitive viewpoint. The juvenile justice system has acted very much as a loose but dynamic system over the last 165 years, and to understand its difficulties we need to look to the historical contradictions that were built into the juvenile justice system during its early years.

Of particular interest are several questions that have been raised repeatedly over the years. First, what purposes did the juvenile justice system serve when it was introduced in eastern cities during the early nineteenth century, and what role did the juvenile court play in that system when it was introduced in the early part of the twentieth century? Second, why has treat-

ment been such an uneven enterprise in juvenile justice? Is the process of treating delinquents fraught with such obstacles that consistent success is impossible, or are less formidable reasons responsible for this inconsistency? Finally, why has juvenile justice been unable to maintain a *parens patriae* focus within its custodial institutions? Is there an inherent flaw in such institutions that ultimately vetoes any long term effort to improve juveniles in institutions?

Many have addressed these and similar questions, and along these lines Cohen (1985) has identified four distinct approaches to the problems of the justice system. The "conventional" view asserts that flaws in the justice system derive basically from the limitations of its pioneers. If their vision is partly cloudy, or their commitment falters, their reforms ultimately founder on inertia and indifference. But different leaders inject new enthusiasms, and the overall result is gradual progress in the justice system through the cumulated efforts of its visionaries over generations.

The second approach, "we blew it," as represented by David Rothman (1980) in his work, *Conscience and Convenience,* is less optimistic. It sees the sources of ineffectiveness in the justice system in the inevitable triumph of mindless routine and parochial interest over moral purpose. The possibility of lasting progress in

Theodore N. Ferdinand, "History Overtakes the Juvenile Justice System," *Crime and Delinquency* 37 (2) (April 1991): 204–24. Reprinted by permission of Sage Publications, Inc.

the justice system is compromised by custodial inertia and trivial, convenient routine.

Cohen (1985) describes in addition two other approaches: "It's all a con" and, most recently, "destructuring." Foucault (1979) represents the first with his suggestion in *Discipline and Punish* that the justice system before all else buttresses order in civil society by its threat of punishment, however ineffective it may be in rehabilitating offenders. It is indispensable as a reinforcement of responsibility, no matter how dismal its treatment record or brutish its methods. We must forgive its ineffectiveness for the sake of its crucial symbolic value. The "destructuralists," today's visionaries, are less programmatic and more idealistic. They claim that order overwhelms and stultifies humanity, and to reawaken moral ideals in society, order must be sacrificed.

My approach to this issue concedes the importance of juvenile justice as a symbol of responsibility, but I locate the failures of juvenile justice not simply in compromise with routine, nor in the fallibilities of its pioneers, but in the conflicts that different approaches have built into juvenile justice over the years. We must probe the sources of juvenile justice's ailments in the nineteenth century, if we ever hope to understand their essential nature and correct them.

THE NINETEENTH CENTURY ORIGINS OF JUVENILE JUSTICE

During the Jacksonian era industrialization took firm root in several American cities. As trade with Europe, the Caribbean and other American cities flourished, as new factories for spinning yarn and weaving cloth were built, and as new schools opened, employment grew more plentiful. The slow drift of population to centers of commerce and industry grew very quickly to sizable proportions in the northeast, and several American cities began to encounter adolescent misbehavior and waywardness in a variety of forms (see, for example, Ferdinand 1989: 94–97). Not only were wayward children nuisances on the city's streets, but when convicted of crimes in the criminal courts, they were sometimes sent to adult prisons where they mixed with hardened convicts and became career criminals.

But unless wayward children were criminals, the criminal courts had no jurisdiction over them. A convenient doctrine—*parens patriae*—however, enabled the civil courts to step in and take custody of these wayward or dependent children. The criminal law served for those children who had violated the criminal code, but for those who were merely beyond control, or whose parents were negligent, *parents patriae* sufficed. The child's first responsibility was to obey his or her parents, and the nascent juvenile justice system awaited those few who steadfastly rejected parental authority.

Furthermore, in many eastern cities bold plans for compulsory education were underway (see Schultz 1973). On the eve of the industrial revolution in 1789 Boston authorities established a system of free grammar schools, and in 1821 the city opened its first public high school, Boston English High. By 1826 Boston's school system enrolled a majority of its school-aged children (Kaestle and Vinovskis 1980).

These new schools represented a second arena wherein many children were held accountable. Just as children who were beyond parental control and roamed the city at night could not be ignored, so too children who disrupted school or truanted needed to be held in check. *Parens patriae* was applicable here as well, because the children were in school for their own well being. The schools' problem children became a second concern for the nascent juvenile justice system.

In short as compulsory education and industrialization swept America's cities in the nineteenth century, they produced a growing troop of wayward, incorrigible children who resisted in one fashion or another the efforts of society to shape them for adulthood. Something like a juvenile justice system was needed to bolster the authority of the family and the school in industrializing America so that both could be more effective in socializing young people. The juvenile justice system, as it emerged, represented the community's attempt to come to grips with a new social status: the juvenile.

At first the effort was limited to the major cities where education and economic development were centered, but soon it spread to entire states as whole regions were developed. The juvenile was expected to be obedient to both parents and teachers, and if he refused, he was held liable by the courts. The juvenile justice system was basically a sociological institution for holding juveniles accountable and for strengthening both the family and the school as they adapted to the changing social order.[1]

Recently John Sutton (1988) uncovered evidence that strongly confirms this view of the relationship between emerging school systems and juvenile justice. He investigated the impact of growing school enrollments on the introduction of juvenile reformatories in the latter half of the nineteenth century and found it more powerful than either industrialization or the growth of government. According to Sutton (1988:114), "from 1850 to 1880, a 1 percent increase in school attendance is associated with a 13 percent increase in adoption rates (of juvenile reformatories)."

As a concept of the juvenile emerged, the juveniles' parents and teachers were responsible for them, and they were expected to obey both. *Parens patriae* was the relevant legal doctrine, because it allowed the state to intervene when either the family or the school was deficient. Because *parens patriae* was available only in the civil courts, juvenile delinquency was lodged in that jurisdiction. It covered all but the major criminal offenses by juveniles, which were still handled in the criminal courts.

Under *parens patriae* the civil courts acted in behalf of the child against ineffective parents or the child himself and provided dispositions that a responsible parent would. If the parents could control the child, the courts accepted them as the proper guardian. For the most part, state appellate courts endorsed this mission for the court (see, for example, *Ex parte Crouse* 1838; *In re* Ferrier 1882; *Commonwealth v. Fisher* 1905; Garlock 1979:399).

The civil courts still could not deal with juveniles who violated the criminal law, and many communities continued to send serious juvenile offenders to the criminal courts. Although most were sent to juvenile facilities upon conviction, some were still sent to adult institutions (see Garlock 1979, Appendix).

Several facts stand out regarding the juvenile justice system up to 1899. First, it consisted of a very diverse collection of private and public institutions and community programs including probation for minor delinquents and status offenders, all served by the civil court and its doctrine of *parens patriae*. A survey (see Mennel 1973:49) of juvenile reform schools conducted in 1880, for example, found an extraordinary heterogeneity. Six accepted children convicted of crimes punishable by imprisonment, and fourteen took children who had committed minor offenses. Thirteen schools specialized in children rebelling against parental authority; seven accepted mainly neglected or deserted children; and five dealt with children committed by their parents for various reasons.[2] Coordination among such a diverse group of custodial institutions and the civil courts must have been difficult, indeed.

Second, the civil court with its doctrine of *parens patriae* provided moral leadership within the system. But its authority was at best exhortatory and informal. It had little control over the staffing, budgets, practices, or objectives of the far flung juvenile programs it served.

Third, this system was kept largely separate from the criminal justice system. Juvenile miscreants who warranted a criminal court hearing by virtue of serious offending were handled as adults. The rest were handled by the civil court and sent to juvenile facilities. In the nineteenth century a bifurcated justice system handled a bifurcated population of juvenile offenders. The early juvenile justice system neatly avoided today's complexity in which serious offenders are handled along with minor offenders in a single, *parens patriae* system.

This system was the result of separate initiatives at several different levels of government over the better part of a century. Even though most juvenile facilities were guided at first by a *parens patriae* philosophy, the system had no central authority that could impose a focus or common mission on the whole. Without a central organizing authority, however, the system was left to respond as local conditions dictated. And it continues today to embrace a growing variety of public and private facilities (Sutton 1990:1369–70).

Moreover, as the nineteenth century drew

to a close, it was becoming clear that the civil courts could not handle the sheer volume of juvenile cases coming into the system. As early as the Civil War, for example, the mass of juveniles arrested in Boston was already large, and the same was true of other eastern cities as well.

During the 1820s and early 1830s very few juveniles were charged with serious offenses in Boston's felony court—the municipal court. But by 1850 indictments had grown in the municipal court to 220 per 10,000 juveniles (Ferdinand 1989, fig. 2) and were the fastest growing component in Boston's crime problem. Furthermore, between 1849 to 1850 and 1861 to 1862 the arrest rate for juveniles rose 479% from 506 to 2,932 per 10,000 juveniles (Ferdinand 1989, fig. 3).[3] After the Civil War, juvenile arrests in Boston receded somewhat from the high rates of the Civil War period (Ferdinand 1989, fig. 3). Still, from 1870 to 1900 they ranged between 7,900 and 11,200 arrests annually.

This sizable flow of juvenile cases no doubt strengthened the argument that juveniles needed a specialized court—a court that was attuned to their special needs. First, they needed a judge who was familiar with the social psychological nuances of family conflict as well as the legal complexities of family/child problems. They needed a legal doctrine that took into account their social deficits as well as their misbehavior. Juveniles also needed a court whose officers were closely familiar with the range of facilities available for troubled children and could assign each to a program that was geared to his or her own needs.

The older civil court served the legal needs of juveniles, but it was devoted foremost to other issues. It dealt with divorces, torts, contracts, and wills—all adult issues. The civil law was narrow and intricate, and few probate judges or lawyers had a strong interest in the psychology of juveniles or their facilities and potential. They were largely amateurs in those areas most relevant to juveniles and their problems.

Frederick Wines, a noted criminologist, commented in Chicago in 1898 that "an entirely separate system of courts [was needed] for children . . . who commit offenses which would be criminal in adults. We ought to have a 'chil-

dren's court' in Chicago, and we ought to have a 'children's judge,' who should attend to no other business" (quoted in Mennel 1973:131).

THE NEW JUVENILE COURT

In 1899 the Illinois legislature enacted the first juvenile code and established, in Chicago, the first juvenile court. Its jurisdiction extended to virtually all juveniles—serious criminal offenders, status offenders, and neglected and dependent children. It embraced a much wider jurisdiction than the nineteenth century juvenile justice system ever had. Nevertheless, its mandate was to deal with all of them by means of *parens patriae.*

Several contemporary observers commented on the new court's usefulness. The new court gave custodial institutions "the legal status and powers that they have most stood in need of" and "in large cities juvenile courts are little more than clearing houses to get together the boy or girl that needs help and the agencies that will do the most good" (Sutton 1988:143). It gave authority to social services, it provided intelligent assessments of juveniles, and it assigned them to programs that were closely related to their needs. It offered a specialized knowledge of and commitment to juveniles and their needs that the old civil courts could never provide.

In their enthusiasm, however, the reformers failed to ask whether serious offenders with criminal intent were appropriate subjects for a *parens patriae* court.[4] Furthermore, the new court did little to unify the juvenile justice system. It was still a very loose collection of programs and facilities with no central direction.

Despite these defects the remaining states quickly followed Illinois' example, and thirty states had established juvenile courts by 1920. By 1945 all had. The juvenile justice system was separate from the adult system. *Parens patriae* was the philosophic foundation of the court, and many if not most of its facilities and programs subscribed to that perspective.

These programs, as we have seen, had emerged in haphazard fashion during the preceding eighty years and most were organized by state or city governments. Because the juvenile court was generally lodged at the county level, juvenile programs both public and private were still largely free to follow their own mandate.

The new court was hailed as a visionary institution that would bring clarity, order, and humanity to the emerging juvenile justice system. In addition, the new court provided a podium for the *parens patriae* approach in the justice system, and its early judges were outspoken in advocating treatment and humane care for offenders.

Judge Benjamin Lindsey of Denver, for example, was one of the first to argue in behalf of juveniles, and in 1904 he wrote, "The Juvenile Court rests upon the principle of love. Of course there is firmness and justice, for without this [sic] there would be danger in leniency. But there is no justice without love" (quoted in Mennel 1973:138). Many of the early judges felt the same way, although many were critical of Lindsey's flamboyance.

The juvenile court maintained an informal atmosphere and gave the judges ample room to carry out their rehabilitative philosophy. The early courts were fortunate in that many judges showed a deep sympathy for young delinquents. Judge Richard Tuthill, the first judge of Chicago's juvenile court, proclaimed, "I talk with the boy, give him a good talk, just as I would my own boy, and find myself as much interested in these boys as I would if they were my own" (quoted in Mennel 1973:135). Judge George W. Stubbs of Indianapolis said, "It is the personal touch that does it. I have often observed that if . . . I could get close enough to [the boy] to put my hand on his head or shoulder, or my arm around him, in nearly every such case I could get his confidence" (quoted in Mennel 1973:135). With the appearance of the juvenile court in many communities, vigorous and often eloquent spokesmen for a *parens patriae* handling of juveniles got, and kept, the public's attention.

As the juvenile court spread through the states during the first two decades of the twentieth century, however, commitments to juvenile institutions went down (Sutton 1990:1392). A growing number of judges were becoming uncomfortable with custodial institutions for children.

Parens Patriae and Fairness

Shortly after World War II the critique of the juvenile court got underway with Paul Tappan's (1946) keen analysis of the court's due process failures. Tappan, a legally trained criminologist, pointed out that many constitutional rights of juveniles were ignored in the *parens patriae* juvenile court.

Others took up the same complaint (see Allen 1964 and Caldwell 1961). They noted that the court's therapeutic measures, even when sincerely applied, often turned out to be worse than routine punishments. It was not unusual in the 1960s to find that status offenders were punished more severely than all but the most serious delinquents (see Creekmore 1976; Cohn 1963; and Terry 1967), and racial discrimination in the juvenile court, though not found in some courts, was all too common (see Thornberry 1973 and Fagan, Slaughter, and Hartstone 1987; but see also Rubin 1985:203–5; Cohen, 1976:51–54; and Dungworth 1977).[5] Such flagrant violations of equal protection under the law were intolerable especially in the charged atmosphere of the 1960s and 1970s.

A Growing Demand for Reform

In addition to Tappan's early criticism of the court's due process lapses and the discovery of racial and gender biases, steady reports of scandalous conditions in state training schools began to surface (see Rothman 1980:268–86; Deutsch 1950). The need for reform in juvenile justice was inescapable, and the response took several forms.

First, the states attempted to cope with difficulties inherent in combining serious and minor offenders in the same system by separating status offenders from delinquents in confinement and later, by removing most of them (status offenders) from the juvenile court's jurisdiction. California differentiated delinquents and status offenders in its original juvenile statute, and in 1962 New York passed a Family Court Act, which among other things distinguished status offenders (renamed PINS) from delinquents. In 1973 the New York Court of Appeals ruled in *In re* Ellery (1973) that the policy of confining PINS with delinquents in an institution was unconstitutional, although in 1974 in *In re* Lavette (1974) the same court ruled that PINS could be confined in facilities organized for PINS.

In the decades that followed many states enacted similar statutes, separating status offenders and delinquents both in definition and treatment, and by the late 1970s many had gone even further by making court-ordered treatment plans for status offenders voluntary. Such children had committed no criminal offense and legally did not deserve custodial confinement.

Juvenile justice in the United States seemed to be following a path charted in Scandinavia in which problem juveniles under twenty-two years of age are treated voluntarily in social agencies, and serious offenders after fifteen years of age are handled in the criminal courts (see Sarnecki 1988). Such a plan often fails, however, in that it permits status offenders to respond with either a "political" compliance to treatment suggestions or an impulsive rejection of them.

The Failures of Treatment

At the same time ambiguities surrounding the rehabilitative approach spurred the federal government to sponsor a host of delinquency prevention projects. In the mid-1960s under the impetus of President Lyndon Johnson's War on Poverty, a major effort to prevent delinquency and rehabilitate delinquents was undertaken by the Office of Economic Opportunity. As a centerpiece the War on Poverty mounted a massive preventive program on the Lower East Side of Manhattan—Mobilization for Youth. It was modeled after the Chicago Area Projects and addressed the problems of preschool children, juveniles, gangs, schools, and community adults. But it was too broad and complex to evaluate, and we will never know as with the Chicago Area Projects whether this community approach to delinquency prevention was effective.[6]

More specialized programs dealing with distinctive facets of delinquency were also fielded

in Boston, Chicago, and elsewhere. Studies of innovative juvenile programs were funded in Michigan, Massachusetts, and Utah, and community-based treatment programs in California were generously supported. The federal government in conjunction with the Ford Foundation and other private groups sought to determine whether juvenile justice could remedy its ills.

Sentiment for reform of the juvenile justice system was strong, but the direction of reform was still hotly debated. Should it focus on pre-delinquents with the idea of keeping them out of the juvenile justice system, should it reform the court itself, or should it concentrate on juvenile institutions? Much hinged on the outcome of the War on Poverty programs, and millions of dollars were spent to insure that sound methods and skilled researchers were used. But to nearly everyone's dismay, few if any initiatives were effective. In the 1960s the detached worker program investigated by Walter Miller (1962) in Boston and later in Los Angeles by Malcolm Klein (1971) were worse than ineffective. Klein found that in Los Angeles detached workers actually made delinquency worse. Gerald Robin (1969) evaluated the Neighborhood Youth Corps and its attempts to provide counseling, remedial education, and supervised work for juveniles in both Cincinnati and Detroit. He found no positive effect in either program.

In Provo, Utah, Empey and Erickson (1972) designed a community program for delinquents in which they participated in group therapy sessions for five or six months. Empey and Erickson compared the delinquents with a comparison group of boys who had simply been placed on community probation and a second comparison group that had been sent to the state training school. Although the boys in the community treatment program averaged about half as many arrests as the boys who were sent to a training school, the difference between them and the boys placed on probation was small. Moreover, when a similar program was repeated at Silverlake in Los Angeles, boys in the community treatment program showed only slightly lower delinquency rates than boys who were sent to an open institution for delinquents (Empey and Lubeck 1971). In effect the failure of these several delinquency treatment programs discredited treatment as a method for reforming delinquents or predelinquents.

To be sure successes were also found among the treatment projects. Probation, for example, has been thoroughly studied in terms of the degree of supervision afforded juveniles and its success rate (see Diana 1955; Scarpitti and Stephenson 1968). The results indicate that despite haphazard supervisory practices a large majority of juveniles complete probation without further incident and go on to crime-free adult lives as well.

Further, Warren (1976) and Palmer (1974) reported strong results in treating specific types of delinquents in the community when compared with similar youngsters sent to custodial institutions in California. In addition the studies of Street, Vinter, and Perrow (1966) in Michigan discovered that benign institutions with supportive staffs were much more effective in molding positive attitudes in children than custodial institutions and punitive staff. The former were especially successful in instilling a prosocial climate among the bulk of their children. Finally, Kobrin and Klein (1983, chapters 5, 6) found that the level of coordination of diversion programs with established juvenile justice agencies strongly influenced their success. Where diversion programs were implemented in close cooperation with existing agencies, they were usually effective, but where the two worked at cross-purposes, diversion was ineffective.

Nearly all of these studies have been rigorously scrutinized, and serious reservations have been lodged against several (see, for example, Lerman 1975). However, the critics have not been able to defeat the obvious conclusion that significant numbers of juveniles respond to sound treatment programs, especially when these juveniles are assigned to program and treatment staff according to their need (see Lipsey 1991; Andrews et al. 1990). Despite these results, the view took hold that treatment, whether in an institution or in the community, is ineffective in reducing delinquency (Martinson 1974).

THE CRISIS IN JUVENILE JUSTICE

The conclusion that treatment does not work seemed to strike a chord in the nation at large, and the advantage swung quickly to those who favored a retributive approach to delinquency. Criminologists had been arguing for decades as to the causes of delinquency and the best methods of treatment. This quarrel was more basic and more serious.

The evidence was by no means unequivocal, but the fact that a retributive response was so widely endorsed suggests that something much deeper was responsible. No doubt a general disillusionment with professionalism and government was a factor as well as the conservative views of the Nixon and Reagan administrations.

If the juvenile court could not provide wholesome treatment for juveniles under its care, it seemed to imply that the *parens patriae* court was discredited. *Parens patriae* was a noble idea, but if the juvenile court could not act effectively as a parent, the least it could do was act effectively as a court by finding guilt justly and by administering punishments fairly. In effect the juvenile court and *parens patriae* were held hostage to the ineffectiveness of community and institutional treatment programs in rehabilitating delinquents!

Why Do Treatment Programs Fail?

As we have seen, the juvenile court has never had much influence over treatment programs, whether in custodial institutions or in the community, because both were almost always organized by independent agencies. The one program the court did control, probation, has been effective in helping delinquents regain their social composure. In effect the juvenile court and *parens patriae* have been evaluated not only in terms of their relevance to the needs of juveniles, but in terms of their ability to guide the rest of the juvenile justice system along the path of treatment.

The critics of the *parens patriae* court expected it to impose its rehabilitative mission on the rest of juvenile justice despite its very limited ability to shape therapeutic programs whether in the community or in custodial institutions. It was doomed from the start by the contradiction between its mission and its limited authority.

The *parens patriae* court did not fail. The state failed, because it enacted a *parens patriae* court without providing solid support for community and institutional treatment programs. True, state programs, first as individual juvenile institutions and then more recently as systems of state juvenile facilities, have been established, some even predating the juvenile court. But these programs had as their first objective the confinement of juveniles in large institutions where custodial policies and attitudes soon dominated (see Schlossman 1977; Brenzel 1983; Pisciotta 1985). Rehabilitation, though used effectively as a public relations device, was almost always a secondary consideration with these state-based programs. Rarely has a state agency had any responsibility for funding and directing treatment programs in the community for delinquents.

Many treatment institutions and community programs were established over the years with the help of private philanthropy, religious groups, social welfare agencies, and even the federal government. But these were either underfunded or short term, or both. These nonstate programs were hobbled by uncertainty. Because state correctional agencies were committed basically to providing secure facilities and nonstate rehabilitative programs were uncertain both as to funding and to endurance, inevitably the *parens patriae* effort fell short.

No state agency had primary responsibility for the treatment of delinquents, and no state agency developed the necessary skills in creating and administering programs for delinquents. However, without cumulative experience in staffing and administering treatment programs, no one gained the necessary skills to guide such programs. Ironically, in most states the only state agency serving delinquent youth was the department handling juvenile corrections. States became skilled in developing custodial facilities for juveniles, but no state agency had lengthy experience in providing effective treatment programs for juvenile delinquents.

A PROPOSAL

It would seem that the solution to the problem of effective treatment programs is straightforward. A continuing public authority is needed with responsibility for treatment programs both in the community and in juvenile institutions.[7] Where it should be situated in the hierarchy of state services to juveniles, or the scope and details of its responsibilities to delinquents need not concern us here. Whether it should be an independent department, part of the Department of Social Services, or the Department of Juvenile Corrections and Parole is not at issue at this point. Its mission should be treatment, and it should be in effect the court's rehabilitative arm, just as juvenile corrections is the court's custodial arm.[8]

Treatment programs for juveniles with psychological or social needs are as essential in civil society as unemployment insurance is for adults. Many juveniles need wise, skilled help in making a sound adjustment in adolescence, but unfortunately many cannot get such help from their families or anyone else, and to deny them by abandoning treatment programs is in effect cruel and socially destructive.

Treatment has worked only haphazardly because it has not been championed consistently by experienced agencies with roots in local communities. Where such agencies have emerged, as in Massachusetts during 1972 in the Department of Youth Services and in Utah during 1981 in the Division of Youth Corrections, the results have been generally humane and effective.[9]

Massachusetts under the Department of Youth Services has been using a system of community-based treatment programs for its delinquents since 1972 with solid results (see Loughran 1987). On any given day its youthful clients number about 1,700. Some 1,000 youths live at home and participate in a wide variety of treatment and educational community programs. The remaining children, 700, are divided between foster homes (30), nonsecure residential programs (500), and secure facilities (170). Serious offenders are dealt with via careful screening for violent tendencies, emotional stability, threat to the community, and social needs and are given programming specially designed for their situation.

The results in Massachusetts have been noteworthy (Miller and Ohlin 1985; Krisberg, Austin, and Steele 1989). In the beginning budgetary costs of caring for children via a system of community-based treatment programs were slightly more than for the old network of custodial institutions (Coates, Miller, and Ohlin 1976, chapters 7, 8). However, the two systems were compared as of 1974, after only two years experience under the new system. More recently the system has become more effective, and today the annual cost per child in the Department of Youth Services (DYS) is about $23,000 compared with $35,000–40,000 reported by many other states (Krisberg, Austin, and Steele, 1989:32–37).

Since 1974 DYS has strengthened its program, and by 1986 delinquency arraignments in Massachusetts had dropped by 24% from their 1980 level (Massachusetts Department of Youth Services 1987: 10).[10] Further, delinquency arraignments for all released offenders compared with their level before admission to DYS is about one half, and arraignments for chronic or violent offenders decreased by slightly more than half (Krisberg, Austin, and Steele 1989:19). In addition, the number of adult inmates in Massachusetts who had also been clients of the juvenile justice system in that state dropped from 35% in 1972 to 15% in 1985 (Loughran 1987). Since 1974 recidivism rates measured in terms of delinquency arraignments among DYS youth have dropped sharply, from 74% in 1974 (see Coates, Miller, and Ohlin 1976) to about 51% in 1985 (Krisberg, Austin, and Steele 1989:24–25). In comparison with other states where recidivism has been measured comparably, DYS discharges have equalled or bettered the recidivism rates of all other state systems (Krisberg, Austin, and Steele 1989:26–32). These results suggest that many serious juvenile offenders within the Department of Youth Services have been helped by their experiences in the system.

In Utah, a new Division of Youth Corrections modeled after the Massachusetts Department of Youth Services was inaugurated in 1981 with full responsibility for secure and community-based treatment programs for delinquents in the state. Although the system is still too new to offer firm evidence of its effectiveness, its architects are delighted with results so far.

First, the shift to community-based programming required a budget $250,000 less than the old custodial-oriented system (Simon and Fagan 1987). The number of beds in secure facilities in Utah dropped from 450 in 1976 to 70 in 1986, while beds in community facilities increased from under 50 to 157 during the same period. Children in jails dropped from more than 700 in 1976 to 26 in 1986, and status offenders in detention declined from 3,324 to only 162 between 1976 and 1986. The shift was on to nonsecure facilities in Utah under the new treatment-oriented system.

Proof of its results is in the system's effects on delinquents. Preliminary data indicate that, as in Massachusetts, the community-based system is probably less criminogenic than the custodial system it replaced. A study by the Utah Division of Youth Corrections (1986) found that 73% of the youths who had received community placements remained free of criminal convictions for twelve months following their release, although fully 76% of the youths confined in secure facilities were reconvicted during their first year after release. Even here their offenses were much less serious. Before commitment these youths had averaged twenty-four convictions, including many serious violent and property offenses. After their term in Youth Corrections they were convicted primarily of minor offenses.

The twin goals of rehabilitation and justice can be blended effectively in the juvenile justice system. If dependable diagnostic and treatment programs can be made available to juvenile judges via a state treatment authority, justice in adjudication can be balanced with humane, effective treatment in dispositions.

Bifurcation: A Stumbling Block?

A difficult problem still remains. The history of juvenile justice confirms that secure facilities tend to become more punitive with age. Since the time of the houses of refuge, custodial institutions have shown a clear custodial drift with time (Ferdinand 1989:87–93).

According to Cohen (1985:218–35), institutions tend to differentiate themselves into custodial, punitive, exclusionary programs and rehabilitative, community-based, inclusionary programs. Cohen saw this bifurcation as paralleling a bifurcation of the system's clientele. On one hand, we have a small stream of stigmatized, antisocial offenders committed to a criminal way of life. On the other, we have a large stream of tractable but problem-bound offenders who want to become contributing citizens. Punitive, exclusionary programs serve the former and transform them into hardened, predatory criminals who are feared and shunned by the community. Inclusionary programs serve constructive offenders who are still looking for a rewarding life in mainstream society. Many of them, however, become agency-dependent and socially peripheral (see Ferdinand 1989).

According to Cohen (1985, chapter 7) inclusionary programs themselves become punitive and stigmatizing and are transformed thereby into exclusionary programs by virtue of the fact that newly established programs draw off the best clientele from older programs, leaving them to deal mainly with intractable inmates. As older programs adapt to a deteriorating population mix, they change slowly into punitive centers. Inclusionary programs gradually become exclusionary programs, and a long term pattern of institutional decay is established as the system repeatedly attempts to reform itself by reaching out to more responsive populations and relegating the rest to older, established programs.

Although Cohen was interested primarily in the adult system, he describes almost exactly the century-long development of juvenile justice in the United States (Ferdinand 1989). The houses of refuge were greeted enthusiastically by reform-minded progressives, only to see them transformed into punitive, stigmatizing institutions over the years (Brenzel 1983; Pisciotta 1982). The same was true of the state juvenile reformatories established in the last half of the nineteenth century (Rothman 1980; Schlossman 1977).

Ultimately, the juvenile correctional system in many states came to resemble a hierarchical system (see Steele and Jacobs 1975, 1977) of punitive, exclusionary institutions at the deep end (the maximum-security level) serving predatory, antisocial inmates, coupled with inclusionary, community-based programs at the shallow end serving a social tractable clientele with more focused problems. As each new program came on stream, it attracted the most promising clientele and the most progressive staff, and the rest were forced to adapt as best they could in the ensuing realignment.

An answer to this repetitive pattern of reform and decay, however, is not difficult to imagine. New programs need not focus on just the more tractable, responsive clientele. They could focus also on the other end—on the more serious, predatory offenders. After all, these are the offenders that spell the most trouble for society in the long run, and any advances in dealing with their problems would certainly be helpful. In this case the older programs would be asked to give up some of their *least* responsive inmates; their inmate mix would improve with each reform at the deep end; and one source of custodial drift, at least, would be arrested.

Such a policy would avoid drawing off the more promising clientele from the older, more experienced centers, but it would also foster small, specialized treatment settings—exactly the kind of centers that foster personal relationships among staff and children and thereby offer a chance for the staff to influence youth in positive ways (Street, Vinter, and Perrow 1966). Such centers are also easier to manage and supervise, with the result that treatment policies can be implemented more consistently over the long term.

This policy has been followed by Massachusetts since 1972—small, treatment oriented centers for virtually all juveniles in the Department of Youth Services (the largest is only thirty-six beds)—and no doubt some of the success of the DYS can be attributed to the positive attitudinal climate that small centers usually generate (see Krisberg, Austin, and Steele 1989:4). But if this analysis is correct, this policy will also help to inhibit the souring of the custodial centers as their programs become routine.

A system of small treatment facilities must still be closely monitored lest some of them stray from their assigned mission. There is always the possibility that a center will develop punitive policies for other reasons. To avoid such missteps it is essential that each center be held closely accountable to clear standards of performance. Each center should be required to justify its policies with verifiable research.

CONCLUSION

Few maintain that juvenile justice has lived up to its promise in the United States, and many assert that its future lies basically with a due process/just deserts orientation. If treatment and rehabilitation are abandoned, however, in favor of a just deserts policy whereby serious delinquents are punished in large, custodial institutions, several untoward consequences would probably result.

First, delinquency would deepen in seriousness and expand its sway, laying the foundation for a worsening problem among adult predatory criminals in the years ahead. Second, an important voice for humane programs in the justice system would be stilled with the result that a monolithic retributive system and its programs would prevail not only in delinquency but in criminal justice as a whole.

The difficulties of treating juveniles in residential centers are, however, soluble. Differentiated systems of small, community-based treatment facilities in both Massachusetts and Utah have shown themselves as more humane, comparable in cost, and more effective than the traditional network of juvenile custodial institutions. A permanent state agency committed to delinquency treatment programs would be a more responsible manager over the long term than the haphazard collection of private philanthropy, correctional departments, and federal agencies that have spearheaded most treatment reforms in the states up to now.

State departments of treatment services for delinquents also need research arms that can evaluate their programs with an eye to weeding out those programs that are ineffective. They need detailed information on their programs to represent the rehabilitation philosophy to state government and the mass media. The people of a state must ultimately choose the direction that is best for them, but they must be fully informed of the alternatives.

If such departments were available at the state level, it would give an immense lift to the juvenile court. This court has long pursued *parens patriae* in the community but with uncertain success and lately with waning confidence. A department of treatment services could provide both the variety in community programming and political support that the court needs to carry out its mission effectively.

The juvenile court cannot be both classification agent and programs agent for the rehabilitative process. It was never given a mandate to sponsor community-based treatment programs. The court is reasonably effective as a juvenile classification and assignment agency, but it needs an effective right arm to create and evaluate treatment programs throughout the state geared to local needs. Local juvenile courts working hand in glove with a state department of treatment services could finally realize the full potential of *parens patriae*.

To improve the juvenile court it is important to strengthen its links with the rest of the system, especially with those agencies that sponsor treatment programs. Up to now responsibility for these programs has been left mainly to custodial or private initiatives. Without a concept of the system as a whole, reform of the court inevitably focuses on inappropriate remedies, and the situation of delinquents only deteriorates. If the failure to rehabilitate juveniles lies with juvenile custodial facilities, reform should focus there and not solely on the *parens patriae* mandate of the court. Historical analysis can pinpoint the sources of the court's difficulties and thereby suggest appropriate lines of reform. Without such analyses our efforts will remain limited by ideological blinders and our reforms will decay as usual into tomorrow's problems.

NOTES

1. It is interesting that as the juvenile court's jurisdiction over status offending has eroded in the last 30 years, runaways and school misbehavior have grown dramatically (see Gough 1977:283–87; Shane 1989). Although other factors have been active in this arena, the court's abandonment of status offenders may have contributed to the reemergence of these problems in the modern era.
2. Overlap among these schools accounts for the fact that their sum is much more than 30.

3. These figures were computed from statistics issued by the Boston Police Department and the U.S. Bureau of the Census. The population data for 1860 were gathered during an especially turbulent period, and may have missed a substantial portion of the transient population including juveniles. Thus delinquency arrest rates for that period may be over estimated.

4. In this sense the new court was a step back from the old civil court, because it handled the most hardened, serious offenders in the same way as minor status offenders.

5. There is no room in juvenile justice for racial or gender bias, but most studies of bias have ignored an important fact that throws new light on the problem. Because the community (parents, school officials, and neighbors) enjoys wide discretion in defining juvenile offending, an officer's decision to make an arrest, or a court's decision to detain a juvenile depends heavily on the biases of the complainant (see Hazard 1976; Black and Reiss 1970). Where a biased victim demands action against a minority juvenile, chances are good that the police or the court will comply. A dismissal is difficult, if a complainant seeking punishment is close at hand. Thomas and Cage (1977) found in a study of more than 1,500 juveniles that their sanctioning in court was more severe if someone close to the case was pushing it.

6. Earlier the renowned Chicago Area Projects initiated by Henry Shaw and Clifford McKay in the 1930s probably had been successful, even though a failure to use an experimental design rendered a definitive statement as to their success impossible (see also Schlossman and Sedlak 1983).

7. We might call this authority the Department of Youth Services. Many states have a Department of Family Services that serves nondelinquent children, and the Department of Youth Services would offer many of the same programs for delinquents and children at risk of delinquency. It would coordinate its efforts with the juvenile courts, just as juvenile corrections does. Three state agencies, therefore, would provide social services to adolescents: Juvenile Corrections, which manages custodial institutions for juveniles; the Department of Youth Services, which manages the treatment effort for juvenile delinquents; and the Department of Family Services, which manages the treatment function for nondelinquent youth. Further consolidation of these three agencies need not be ruled out.

8. Some will say, "The state has already proven its ineptness in programs for youth. It does not deserve a second chance." My response is, if that is true, then the *only* alternative is the status quo, that is, a due process court and punitive juvenile institutions. Rehabilitating delinquents is too important to abandon simply because the state has stumbled in its efforts to fulfill *parens patriae*. If we can understand some of the reasons behind the state's ineptness, for example, a primary commitment to security in facilities, we can correct them.

9. Youth Services Bureaus, an offspring of Lyndon Johnson's 1960s campaign against delinquency, represented a similar effort to bring treatment programs together under a single community agency. They were locally financed and suffered budget problems in many small cities, and they often differed with judges as to what delinquents needed.

10. Certainly, other factors, for example, the downside of the baby boom and the cooling of the drugs epidemic among high schoolers, have contributed to this decline. But the size of the decline—24%—is consistent with a positive effect from juvenile justice.

REFERENCES

ALLEN, FRANCIS A. 1964. *The Borderland of Criminal Justice.* Chicago: University of Chicago Press.

ANDRES, D. A., IVAN ZINGER, ROBERT D. HODGE, JAMES BONTA, PAUL GENDREAU, AND FRANCIS T. CULLEN. 1990. "Does Correctional Treatment Work? A Clinically Relevant and Psychologically Informed Meta-Analysis." *Criminology* 28:369–404.

BLACK, DONALD J. AND ALBERT J. REISS, JR. 1970, "Police Control of Juveniles." *American Sociological Review* 15(February):63–77.

BREAZEL, BARBARA M. 1983. *Daughters of the State.* Cambridge: MIT Press.

CALDWELL, R. G. 1961. "The Juvenile Court: Its Development and Some Major Problems." *Journal of Criminal Law, Criminology, and Police Science* 51:493–511.

COATES, ROBERT B., ALDEN D. MILLER, AND LLOYD E. OHLIN. 1976. *Diversity in a Youth Correctional System.* Cambridge: Ballinger.

COHEN, LAWRENCE E. 1976. *Delinquency Dispositions: An Empirical Analysis of Processing of Decisions in Three Juvenile Courts.* National Criminal Justice Information and Statistics Service, Law Enforcement Assistance Administration. Washington. DC: U.S. Government Printing Office.

COHEN, STANLEY. 1985. *Visions of Social Control.* Cambridge: Polity Press.

COHN, YONA. 1963. "Criteria for Probation Officers' Recommendations to the Juvenile Court." *Crime & Delinquency* 1:267–75.

COMMONWEALTH V. FISHER 213 Pa. 48, 1905.

CREEKMORE, MARK. 1976. "Case Processing: Intake, Adjudication, and Disposition." Pp. 119–51 in *Brought to Justice? Juveniles, the Courts, and the Law,* edited by Rosemary Sarri and Yeheskel Hasenfeld. Ann Arbor: University of Michigan.

DEUTSCH, ALBERT. 1950. *Our Rejected Children.* Boston: Little, Brown.

DIANA, LEWIS. 1955. "Is Casework in Probation Necessary?" *Focus* 34(January): 1–8.

DUNGWORTH, TERRENCE. 1977. "Discretion in the Juvenile Justice System: The Impact of Case Characteristics on Prehearing Detention." Pp. 19–43 in *Little Brother Grows Up,* edited by Theodore N. Ferdinand. Beverly Hills, CA: Sage.

EMPEY, LAMAR AND STEVEN G. LUBECK. 1971. *Silverlake Experiment: Testing Delinquency Theory and Community Intervention.* Chicago: Aldine Press.

EMPEY, LAMAR AND MAYNARD ERICKSON. 1972. *The Provo Experiment: Evaluating Community Control of Delinquency.* Lexington, MA: Lexington Books.

Ex parte Crouse, 4 Whart. 9, Pa. 1838.

FAGAN, JEFFERY, ELLEN SLAUGHTER, AND ELLIOT HARTSTONE. 1987. "Blind Justice? The Impact of Race on the Juvenile Justice Process." *Crime & Delinquency* 33:224–58.

FERDINAND, THEODORE N. 1989. "Juvenile Delinquency or Juvenile Justice: Which Came First?" *Criminology* 27:79–106.

FOUCAULT, MICHEL. 1979. *Discipline and Punish.* New York: Vintage Books.

GARLOCK, PETER D. 1979. "'Wayward' Children and the Law, 1820–1900: The Genesis of the Status Offense Jurisdiction of the Juvenile Court." *Georgia Law Review* 13:341–448.

GOUGH, AIDAN R. 1977. "Beyond Control Youth in the Juvenile Court—the Climate for Change." Pp. 271–96 in *Beyond Control: Status Offenders in the Juvenile Court,* edited by Lee E. Teitelbaum and Aidan R. Gough, Cambridge, MA: Ballinger.

HAZARD, GEOFFREY C., JR. 1976. "The Jurisprudence of Juvenile Deviance." Pp. 3–19 in *Pursuing Justice for the Child,* edited by Margaret K. Rosenheim. Chicago: University of Chicago Press.

In re Ellery C., 347 N.Y.2d 51 1973.

In re Ferrier, 103 Ill. 367, 1882.

In re Lavette M., 359 N.Y.2d 201, 1974.

KAESTLE, CARL F. AND MARIS A. VINOVSKIS. 1980. *Education and Change.* London: Cambridge University Press.

KLEIN, MALCOLM. 1971. *Street Gangs and Street Workers.* Englewood Cliffs, NJ: Prentice-Hall.

KOBRIN, SOLOMON AND MALCOLM KLEIN. 1983. *Community Treatment of Juvenile Offenders.* Beverly Hills, CA: Sage.

KRISBERG, BARRY, JAMES AUSTIN, AND PATRICIA A. STEELE. 1989. *Unlocking Juvenile Corrections: Evaluating the Massachusetts Department of Youth Services.* San Francisco: National Council on Crime and Delinquency.

LERMAN, PAUL. 1975. *Community Treatment and Control.* Chicago: University of Chicago Press.

LIPSEY, MARK W. 1991. "Juvenile Delinquency Treatment: A Meta-Analytic Inquiry into the Variability of Effects." *Meta-Analysis for Explanation: A Casebook.* New York: Russell Sage Foundation.

LOUGHRAN, EDWARD J. 1987. "Juvenile Corrections: The Massachusetts Experience." Pp. 7–18 in *Reinvesting in Youth Corrections Resources: A Tale of Three States,* edited by Lee Eddison. Ann Arbor; School of Social Work, University of Michigan.

MARTINSON, ROBERT. 1974. "What Works—Questions and Answers About Prison Reform." *Public Interest* 32:22–54.

MASSACHUSETTS DEPARTMENT OF YOUTH SERVICES. 1987. "Annual Report 1986," pp. 1–16. Boston: Author.

MENNEL, ROBERT M. 1973. *Thorns & Thistles.* Hanover, NH: University Press of New England.

MILLER, ALDEN D. AND LLOYD E. OHLIN. 1985. *Delinquency and Community.* Beverly Hills, CA: Sage.

MILLER, WALTER. 1962. "The Impact of a 'Total-Community' Delinquency Control Project." *Social Problems* 10: 168–91.

PALMER, TED. 1974. "The Youth Authority Community Treatment Project." *Federal Probation* 38:3–14.

PISCIOTTA, ALEXANDER W. 1982. "Saving the Children: The Promise and Practice of Parens Patriae, 1838–1898." *Crime & Delinquency* 28:410–25.

———. 1985. "Treatment on Trial: The Rhetoric and Reality of the New York House of Refuge, 1857–1935." *American Journal of Legal History* 29:151–81.

ROBIN, GERALD N. 1969. "Anti-Poverty Programs and Delinquency." *Journal of Criminal Law, Criminology, and Police Science* 60:327.

ROTHMAN, DAVID J. 1980. *Conscience and Convenience.* Boston: Little, Brown.

RUBIN, H. TED. 1985. *Juvenile Justice,* 2nd ed. New York: Random House.

SARNECKI, JERZY. 1988. *Juvenile Delinquency in Sweden.* Stockholm: National Council for Crime Prevention, Information Division.

SCARPITTI, FRANK R. AND RICHARD M. STEPHENSON. 1968. "A Study of Probation Effectiveness." *Journal of Criminal Law, Criminology, and Police Science* 3:361–69.

SCHLOSSMAN, STEVEN L. 1977. *Love and the American Delinquent.* Chicago: University of Chicago Press.

SCHLOSSMAN, STEVEN L. AND MICHAEL SEDLAK. 1983. "The Chicago Area Project Revisited." *Crime & Delinquency* 29:398–462.

SCHULTZ, STANLEY K. 1973. *The Culture Factory: Boston Public Schools, 1789–1860.* New York: Oxford University Press.

SHANE, PAUL G. 1989. "Changing Patterns of Homelessness and Runaway Youth." *American Journal of Orthopsychiatry* 59:208–14.

SIMON, CINDY AND JULIE FAGAN. 1987. "Youth Corrections in Utah: Remaking a System." *National Conference of State Legislatures* 12:1–12.

STEELE, ERIC H. AND JAMES B. JACOBS. 1975. "A Theory of Prison Systems." Crime & Delinquency 21:149–62.

———. 1977. "Untangling Minimum Security: Concepts, Realities, and Implications for Correctional Systems." *Journal of Research in Crime and Delinquency* 14:68–83.

STREET, DAVID, ROBERT D. VINTER, AND CHARLES PERROW. 1966. *Organization for Treatment.* New York: Free Press.

SUTTON, JOHN R. 1988. *Stubborn Children.* Berkeley: University of California Press.

———. 1990. "Bureaucrats and Entrepreneurs: Institutional Responses to Deviant Children, 1890–1920s." *American Journal of Sociology* 95:1367–1400.

TAPPAN, PAUL. 1946. "Treatment Without Trial?" *Social Problems* 24:306–11.

TERRY, ROBERT. 1967. "Discrimination in the Police Handling of Juvenile Offenders by Social Control Agencies." *Journal of Research in Crime and Delinquency* 4:212–20.

THOMAS, CHARLES W. AND ROBIN J. CAGE. 1977. "The Effects of Social Characteristics on Juvenile Court Dispositions." *Sociological Quarterly* 18:237–52.

THORNBERRY, TERENCE P. 1973. "Race, Socieconomic Status and Sentencing in the Juvenile Justice System." *Journal of Criminal Law and Criminology* 64:90–98.

UTAH STATE DIVISION OF YOUTH CORRECTIONS. 1986. "Planning Task Force Final Report." Salt Lake City, December.

WARREN, MARGUERITE. 1976. "Intervention with Juvenile Delinquents." Pp. 176–204 in *Pursuing Justice for the Child,* edited by Margaret K. Rosenheim. Chicago: University of Chicago Press.

QUESTIONS FOR DISCUSSION

1. Discuss the juvenile justice system up to 1899. What were the differences in society's view of juveniles during this period as compared to the early 1900s?

2. List and discuss several juvenile treatment programs that failed. Can you identify any common reasons as to why these programs might have failed?

3. Explain what the author of this article means when he says, "It would seem that the problem of effective treatment programs is straightforward." What is the author proposing?

4. If treatment and rehabilitation are abandoned in favor of more punishment and custody what, according to the author, may be the consequences?

APPLICATIONS

1. Identify several individuals in your community who work in the juvenile justice system (e.g., a judge, probation officer, corrections officer). Interview each person and ask him or her what he or she believes the future of juvenile justice may be. Will the trend be toward harsher punishment, more treatment, or a combination of both? Compare their responses.

2. Visit the local police department and speak to the officers in the juvenile division. Ask how juvenile crime has changed over the past ten years. What do the juvenile officers recommend with respect to juvenile justice?

KEY TERMS

bifurcated   refers to anything that is split into branches or divisions.

disposition   a decision or arrangement by a judge as to what consequences an offender must undergo based on the severity of the offense.

intractable   refers to something with which it is difficult to deal; unmanageable.

miscreant   a criminal or a villain.

nuances   refers to slight differences in certain situations, meaning, or emotion.

retributive   refers to a meting out of rewards or punishments according to what one deserves.

stultifies   to render futile or useless.

therapeutic   refers to something that cures or corrects.

II

THEORIES OF JUVENILE DELINQUENCY

Many theoretical formulations concerning juvenile delinquency are also found in criminology, criminal justice, police science, public safety, and deviance courses. Without exception, all theories of delinquency deal with human behavior and therefore are often found in related courses and fields. Theory is speculation as to the causes of an event or the nature of something. Although somewhat abstract, theory is an attempt to provide an explanation. One of the essential elements involved in the study of delinquency is a solid grasp of the classic as well as the more contemporary theories of delinquency. Understanding how others have conceptualized delinquency and how they have created theoretical explanations for delinquency will be of assistance in installing a critical element in your thinking about the subject. The student of delinquency research should remember that no theory is completely correct or accepted. There is always room for revision, expansion, and if needed, a complete rejection of a particular theory. This rejection has occurred often in the area of crime-related research in which a major paradigmatic shift changes the fundamental approach taken by certain disciplines. Some theories presented here are carefully structured in terms of causal statements and hypothetical derivations, while others are eloquently simple. Part II is a collection consisting of nine articles that represent some of the most important theoretical explanations in delinquency research. Each of these works was selected as a representative of an important and major theoretical genre and for the historical importance of the article itself. Some of these works have been pivotal in deciding the future direction of entire disciplines and the larger investigation of crime and deviance.

We begin with one of the more influential structural theories, Robert K. Merton's "Social Structure and Anomie," which questions the biological explanations of deviance and instead offers a sociological alternative that is still affecting the deviance and criminological researchers of today. This theory is known as a strain theory because Merton argues that lower-class individuals in particular experience frustration due to an inability to achieve cultural goals that have been blocked by differential opportunities. This frustration, or "anomie," leads some individuals to achieve goals through deviant or criminal opportunities.

Akers et al. present another remarkably important sociological theory that attempts to explain crime. Their social learning theory claims that we learn crime just as we learn most everything else; through interaction in association with significant others. This learning includes crime techniques as well as attitudes, rationalizations, and beliefs about these behaviors. Two of the most important ways in which we learn throughout our lives are through imitation and by moving from discomfort toward comfort. The real power of this theory is demonstrated by its channeling much of the thinking about crime and delinquency away from the biological toward the environmental explanations. One need not be a high-powered criminologist to apply these ideas to peer or reference groups. The research here is testament to the powerful influences of learning and social environment regarding delinquency.

Our third selection reverses the question of why individuals deviate and asks instead, "Why do people conform?" Travis Hirschi offers us "A Control Theory of Delinquency," in which he answers that the stronger the "bond to society" the less likely one is to deviate. The stronger our attachments to our parents, schools, and conventional society, the less likely we are to violate the rules of society. When the bonds are weak or broken we are more likely to violate rules.

In "Techniques of Neutralization," Gresham M. Sykes and David Matza combine some of the elements of both the learning and control theories. These "techniques" serve as defenses to delinquency-related behaviors and provide a rationale which allows the person to "drift" into nonconformity and yet not transform their nondelinquent identity. These defenses allow the person to vacillate from conformity to delinquency and back again. All of us can easily recall some clever rationalizations we have used to justify our behavior and can therefore more easily understand this theory.

Lawrence E. Cohen and Marcus Felson offer a "routine activities approach" to the theoretical genre of delinquency. The convergence in time and space of three elements (motivated offenders, suitable targets, and the absence of capable guardians) is the major focus of this approach. The factors that increase the opportunities to enjoy freedom may also increase the opportunities for predatory victimizations. Illegal activities expand as legal activities expand away from the households and families into the larger society. The "routine activities approach" has become a very important theoretical strain in research focusing on delinquency over the past two decades. It is based, in part, on the earlier works of the ecological approach to social problems popularized in the first half of the century.

E. Britt Patterson asks, "What is the relationship between crime rates and the economic conditions of social areas?" His research "Poverty, Income Inequality, and Community Crime Rates" attempts to answer this age-old question. The relationship between poverty and crime have been addressed by scholars for centuries with mixed results. Poverty, in and of itself, is not the major focus, but instead it is the related community organization or disorganization produced by poverty rates and lack of opportunities. This research is a superb example of the structural approach to crime.

"Towards an Interactional Theory of Delinquency," by Terence P. Thornberry presents a blend of many of the previous theories and yet places delinquency in the larger causal network of social factors which he claims is dynamic rather than static and that develops over the lifetime of the individual. The fact that female delinquency has all but been ignored and that salient explanations of female deviance are next to nil is presented with clarity by Meda Chesney-Lind in "Girls' Crime and Woman's Place: Toward a Feminist Model of Female Delinquency." The societal reactions to female deviance or delinquency have too often been based on a patriarchal ideology rather than being viewed within the larger social context. She makes many suggestions as to the directions of future theoretical formulations of delinquency.

Our final selection, "Foundation for a General Strain Theory of Crime and Delinquency," by Robert Agnew is an excellent example of the more contemporary attempts at theoretical revisions based on new and updated thinking and knowledge. He argues that the revisions in the older strain models can make strain theories viable again as major explanations rather than as minor elements in some of the learning or control theories. Rather than blending several theories together, Agnew concentrates on elaborating strain theory as a general one and accepts that it cannot be used as a full replacement of the earlier strain models.

5

Social Structure and Anomie

Robert K. Merton

There persists a notable tendency in sociological theory to attribute the malfunctioning of social structure primarily to those of man's imperious biological drives which are not adequately restrained by social control. In this view, the social order is solely a device for "impulse management" and the "social processing" of tensions. These impulses which break through social control, be it noted, are held to be biologically derived. Nonconformity is assumed to be rooted in original nature.[1] Conformity is by implication the result of an utilitarian calculus or unreasoned conditioning. This point of view, whatever its other deficiencies, clearly begs one question. It provides no basis for determining the nonbiological conditions which induce deviations from prescribed patterns of conduct. In this paper, it will be suggested that certain phases of social structure generate the circumstances in which infringement of social codes constitutes a "normal" response.[2]

The conceptual scheme to be outlined is designed to provide a coherent, systematic approach to the study of sociocultural sources of deviant behavior. Our primary aim lies in discovering how some social structures *exert a definite pressure* upon certain persons in the society to engage in nonconformist rather than

"Social Structure and Anomie," *American Sociological Review,* 3 (October 1938), pp. 672–682.

conformist conduct. The many ramifications of the scheme cannot all be discussed; the problems mentioned outnumber those explicitly treated.

Among the elements of social and cultural structure, two are important for our purposes. These are analytically separable although they merge imperceptibly in concrete situations. The first consists of culturally defined goals, purposes, and interests. It comprises a frame of aspirational reference. These goals are more or less integrated and involve varying degrees of prestige and sentiment. They constitute a basic, but not the exclusive, component of what Linton aptly has called "designs for group living." Some of these cultural aspirations are related to the original drives of man, but they are not determined by them. The second phase of the social structure defines, regulates, and controls the acceptable modes of achieving these goals. Every social group invariably couples its scale of desired ends with moral or institutional regulation of permissible and required procedures for attaining these ends. These regulatory norms and moral imperatives do not necessarily coincide with technical or efficiency norms. Many procedures which from the standpoint of *particular individuals* would be most efficient in securing desired values, for example, illicit oil-stock schemes, theft, fraud, are ruled out of the institutional area of permitted conduct. The choice of expedients is limited by the institutional norms.

To say that these two elements, culture goals and institutional norms, operate jointly is not to say that the ranges of alternative behaviors and aims bear some constant relation to one another. The emphasis upon certain goals may vary independently of the degree of emphasis upon institutional means. There may develop a disproportionate, at times, a virtually exclusive, stress upon the value of specific goals, involving relatively slight concern with the institutionally appropriate modes of attaining these goals. The limiting case in this direction is reached when the range of alternative procedures is limited only by technical rather than institutional considerations. Any and all devices which promise attainment of the all important goal would be permitted in this hypothetical polar case.[3] This constitutes one type of cultural malintegration. A second polar type is found in groups where activities originally conceived as instrumental are transmuted into ends in themselves. The original purposes are forgotten, and ritualistic adherence to institutionally prescribed conduct becomes virtually obsessive.[4] Stability is largely ensured while change is flouted. The range of alternative behaviors is severely limited. There develops a tradition-bound, sacred society characterized by neophobia. The occupational psychosis of the bureaucrat may be cited as a case in point. Finally, there are the intermediate types of groups where a balance between culture goals and institutional means is maintained. These are the significantly integrated and relatively stable, though changing, groups.

An effective equilibrium between the two phases of the social structure is maintained as long as satisfactions accrue to individuals who conform to both constraints, viz., satisfactions from the achievement of the goals and satisfactions emerging directly from the institutionally canalized modes of striving to attain these ends. Success, in such equilibrated cases, is twofold. Success is reckoned in terms of the product and in terms of the process, in terms of the outcome and in terms of activities. Continuing satisfactions must derive from sheer *participation* in a competitive order as well as from eclipsing one's competitors if the order

itself is to be sustained. The occasional sacrifices involved in institutionalized conduct must be compensated by socialized rewards. The distribution of statuses and roles through competition must be so organized that positive incentives for conformity to roles and adherence to status obligations are provided *for every position* within the distributive order. Aberrant conduct, therefore, may be viewed as a symptom of dissociation between culturally defined aspirations and socially structured means.

Of the types of groups which result from the independent variation of the two phases of the social structure, we shall be primarily concerned with the first, namely, that involving a disproportionate accent on goals. This statement must be recast in a proper perspective. In no group is there an absence of regulatory codes governing conduct, yet groups do vary in the degree to which these folkways, mores, and institutional controls are effectively integrated with the more diffuse goals which are part of the cultural matrix. Emotional convictions may cluster about the complex of socially acclaimed ends, meanwhile shifting their support from the culturally defined implementation of these ends. As we shall see, certain aspects of the social structure may generate countermores and antisocial behavior precisely because of differential emphases on goals and regulations. In the extreme case, the latter may be so vitiated by the goal emphasis that the range of behavior is limited only by considerations of technical expediency. The sole significant question then becomes, which available means is most efficient in netting the socially approved value?[5] The technically most feasible procedure, whether legitimate or not, is preferred to the institutionally prescribed conduct. As this process continues, the integration of the society becomes tenuous and anomie ensues.

Thus, in competitive athletics, when the aim of victory is shorn of its institutional trappings and success in contests becomes construed as "winning the game" rather than "winning through circumscribed modes of activity," a premium is implicitly set upon the use of illegitimate but technically efficient means. The star of the opposing football team is surreptitiously slugged; the wrestler furtively incapacitates his opponent through ingenious but illicit techniques; university alumni covertly subsidize "students" whose talents are largely confined to the athletic field. The emphasis on the goal has so attenuated the satisfactions deriving from sheer participation in the competitive activity that these satisfactions are virtually confined to a successful outcome. Through the same process, tension generated by the desire to win in a poker game is relieved by successfully dealing oneself four aces, or, when the cult of success has become completely dominant, by sagaciously shuffling the cards in a game of solitaire. The faint twinge of uneasiness in the last instance and the surreptitious nature of public delicts indicate clearly that the institutional rules of the game *are known* to those who evade them, but that the emotional supports of these rules are largely vitiated by cultural exaggeration of the success-goal.[6] They are microcosmic images of the social macrocosm.

Of course, this process is not restricted to the realm of sport. The process whereby exaltation of the end generates a *literal demoralization*, i.e., a deinstitutionalization, of the means is one which characterizes many[7] groups in which the two phases of the social structure are not highly integrated. The extreme emphasis upon the accumulation of wealth as a symbol of success[8] in our own society militates against the completely effective control of institutionally regulated modes of acquiring a fortune.[9] Fraud, corruption, vice, crime, in short, the entire catalogue of proscribed behavior, becomes increasingly common when the emphasis on the *culturally induced* success-goal becomes divorced from a coordinated institutional emphasis. This observation is of crucial theoretical importance in examining the doctrine that antisocial behavior most frequently derives from biological drives breaking through the restraints imposed by society. The difference is one between a strictly utilitarian interpretation which conceives man's ends as random and an analysis which finds these ends deriving from the basic values of the culture.[10]

Our analysis can scarcely stop at this juncture. We must turn to other aspects of the social structure if we are to deal with the social genesis of the varying rates and types of deviate behavior characteristic of different societies. Thus

far, we have sketched three ideal types of social orders constituted by distinctive patterns of relations between culture ends and means. Turning from these types of *culture patterning*, we find five logically possible, alternative modes of adjustment or adaptation *by individuals* within the culture-bearing society or group.[11] These are schematically presented in the following table, where (+) signifies "acceptance," (−) signifies "elimination," and (±) signifies "rejection and substitution of new goals and standards."

		Culture Goals	Institutionalized Means
I.	Conformity	+	+
II.	Innovation	+	−
III.	Ritualism	−	+
IV.	Retreatism	−	−
V.	Rebellion[12]	±	±

Our discussion on the relation between these alternative responses and other phases of the social structure must be prefaced by the observation that persons may shift from one alternative to another as they engage in different social activities. These categories refer to role adjustments in specific situations, not to personality *in toto*. To treat the development of this process in various spheres of conduct would introduce a complexity unmanageable within the confines of this paper. For this reason, we shall be concerned primarily with economic activity in the broad sense, "the production, exchange, distribution, and consumption of goods and services" in our competitive society, wherein wealth has taken on a highly symbolic cast. Our task is to search out some of the factors which exert pressure upon individuals to engage in certain of these logically possible alternative responses. This choice, as we shall see, is far from random.

In every society, Adaptation I (conformity to both culture goals and means) is the most common and widely diffused. Were this not so, the stability and continuity of the society could not be maintained. The mesh of expectancies which constitutes every social order is sustained by the model behavior of its members falling within the first category. Conventional role behavior oriented toward the basic values of the group is the rule rather than the exception. It is this fact alone which permits us to speak of a human aggregate as comprising a group or society.

Conversely, Adaptation IV (rejection of goals and means) is the least common. Persons who "adjust" (or maladjust) in this fashion are, strictly speaking, *in* the society but not *of* it. Sociologically, these constitute the true "aliens." Not sharing the common frame of orientation, they can be included within the societal population merely in a fictional sense. In this category are *some* of the activities of psychotics, psychoneurotics, chronic autists, pariahs, outcasts, vagrants, vagabonds, tramps, chronic drunkards, and drug addicts.[13] These have relinquished, in certain spheres of activity, the culturally defined goals, involving complete aim-inhibition in the polar case, and their adjustments are not in accord with institutional norms. This is not to say that in some cases the source of their behavioral adjustments is not in part the very social structure which they have in effect repudiated nor that their very existence within a social area does not constitute a problem for the socialized population.

This mode of "adjustment" occurs, as far as structural sources are concerned, when both the culture goals and institutionalized procedures have been assimilated thoroughly by the individual and imbued with affect and high positive value, but where those institutionalized procedures which promise a measure of successful attainment of the goals are not available to the individual. In such instances, there results a two-fold mental conflict insofar as the moral obligation for adopting institutional means conflicts with the pressure to resort to illegitimate means (which may attain the goal) and inasmuch as the individual is shut off from means which are both legitimate *and* effective. The competitive order is maintained, but the frustrated and handicapped individual who cannot cope with this order drops out. Defeatism, quietism, and resignation are manifested in escape mechanisms which ultimately lead the individual to "escape" from the requirements of the society. It is an expedient which arises from continued failure to attain the goal by legitimate measures and from an inability to adopt the illegitimate route because of internalized prohibitions and institutional-

ized compulsives, *during which process the supreme value of the success-goal has as yet not been renounced.* The conflict is resolved by eliminating *both* precipitating elements, the goals and means. The escape is complete, the conflict is eliminated, and the individual is associalized.

Be it noted that where frustration derives from the inaccessibility of effective institutional means for attaining economic or any other type of highly valued "success," that Adaptation II, III, and V (innovation, ritualism, and rebellion) are also possible. The result will be determined by the *particular* cultural background, involved. Inadequate socialization will result in the innovation response whereby the conflict and frustration are eliminated by relinquishing the institutional means and retaining the success-aspiration; an extreme assimilation of institutional demands will lead to ritualism wherein the goal is dropped as beyond one's reach but conformity to the mores persists; and rebellion occurs when emancipation from the reigning standards, due to frustration or to marginalist perspectives, leads to the attempt to introduce a "new social order."

Our major concern is with the illegitimacy adjustment. This involves the use of conventionally proscribed but frequently effective means of attaining at least the simulacrum of culturally defined success—wealth, power, and the like. As we have seen, this adjustment occurs when the individual has assimilated the cultural emphasis on success without equally internalizing the morally prescribed norms governing means for its attainment. The question arises, Which phases of our social structure predispose toward this mode of adjustment? We may examine a concrete instance, effectively analyzed by Lohman,[14] which provides a clue to the answer. Lohman has shown that specialized areas of vice in the near north side of Chicago constitute a "normal" response to a situation where the cultural emphasis upon pecuniary success has been absorbed, but where there is little access to conventional and legitimate means for attaining such success. The conventional occupational opportunities of persons in this area are almost completely limited to manual labor. Given our cultural stigmatization of manual labor, and its correlate, the prestige of white collar work, it is clear that the result is a strain toward innovational practices. The limitation of opportunity to unskilled labor and the resultant low income cannot compete *in terms of conventional standards of achievement* with the high income from organized vice.

For our purposes, this situation involves two important features. First, such antisocial behavior is in a sense "called forth" by certain conventional values of the culture *and* by the class structure involving differential access to the approved opportunities for legitimate, prestige-bearing pursuit of the culture goals. The lack of high integration between the means-and-end elements of the cultural pattern and the particular class structure combine to favor a heightened frequency of antisocial conduct in such groups. The second consideration is of equal significance. Recourse to the first of the alternative responses, legitimate effort, is limited by the fact that actual advance toward desired success symbols through conventional channels is, despite our persisting open-class ideology,[15] relatively rare and difficult for those handicapped by little formal education and few economic resources. The dominant pressure of group standards of success is, therefore, on the gradual attenuation of legitimate, but by and large ineffective, striving and the increasing use of illegitimate, but more or less effective, expedients of vice and crime. The cultural demands made on persons in this situation are incompatible. On the one hand, they are asked to orient their conduct toward the prospect of accumulating wealth and on the other, they are largely denied effective opportunities to do so institutionally. The consequences of such structural inconsistency are psychopathological personality, and/or antisocial conduct, and/or revolutionary activities. The equilibrium between culturally designated means and ends becomes highly unstable with the progressive emphasis on attaining the prestige-laden ends by any means whatsoever. Within this context, Capone represents the triumph of amoral intelligence over morally prescribed "failure," when the channels of vertical mobility are closed or narrowed[16] *in a society which places a high premium on economic affluence and social ascent for all its members.*[17]

This last qualification is of primary impor-tance. It suggests that other phases of the social structure besides the extreme emphasis on pecuniary success must be considered if we are to understand the social sources of antisocial behavior. A high frequency of deviate behavior is not generated simply by "lack of opportunity" or by this exaggerated pecuniary emphasis. A comparatively rigidified class structure, a feudalistic or caste order, may limit such opportunities far beyond the point which obtains in our society today. It is only when a system of cultural values extols, virtually above all else, certain *common* symbols of success *for the population at large* while its social structure rigorously restricts or completely eliminates access to approved modes of acquiring these symbols *for a considerable part of the same population* that antisocial behavior ensues on a considerable scale. In other words, our egalitarian ideology denies by implication the existence of noncompeting groups and individuals in the pursuit of pecuniary success. The same body of success symbols is held to be desirable for all. These goals are held to *transcend class lines*, not to be bounded by them, yet the actual social organization is such that there exist class differentials in the accessibility of these *common* success symbols. Frustration and thwarted aspiration lead to the search for avenues of escape from a culturally induced intolerable situation; or unrelieved ambition may eventuate in illicit attempts to acquire the dominant values.[18] The American stress on pecuniary success and ambitiousness for all thus invites exaggerated anxieties, hostilities, neuroses, and antisocial behavior.

This theoretical analysis may go far toward explaining the varying correlations between crime and poverty.[19] Poverty is not an isolated variable. It is one in a complex of interdependent social and cultural variables. When viewed in such a context, it represents quite different states of affairs. Poverty as such, and consequent limitation of opportunity, are not sufficient to induce a conspicuously high rate of criminal behavior. Even the often mentioned "poverty in the midst of plenty" will not necessarily lead to this result. Only insofar as poverty and associated disadvantages in competition for the culture values approved for *all* members of the society are linked with the assimilation of a cultural emphasis on monetary accumulation as a symbol of success is antisocial conduct a "normal" outcome. Thus, poverty is less highly correlated with crime in southeastern Europe than in the United States. The possibilities of vertical mobility in these European areas would seem to be fewer than in this country, so that neither poverty *per se* nor its association with limited opportunity is sufficient to account for the varying correlations. It is only when the full configuration is considered, poverty, limited opportunity, and a commonly shared system of success symbols, that we can explain the higher association between poverty and crime in our society than in others where rigidified class structure is coupled with *differential class symbols of achievement.*

In societies such as our own, then, the pressure of prestige-bearing success tends to eliminate the effective social constraint over means employed to this end. "The-end-justifies-the-means" doctrine becomes a guiding tenet for action when the cultural structure unduly exalts the end and the social organization unduly limits possible recourse to approved means. Otherwise put, this notion and associated behavior reflect a lack of cultural coordination. In international relations, the effects of this lack of integration are notoriously apparent. An emphasis upon national power is not readily coordinated with an inept organization of legitimate, i.e., internationally defined and accepted, means for attaining this goal. The result is a tendency toward the abrogation of international law, treaties become scraps of paper. "Undeclared warfare" serves as a technical evasion, the bombing of civilian populations is rationalized,[20] just as the same societal situation induces the same sway of illegitimacy among individuals.

The social order we have described necessarily produces this "strain toward dissolution." The pressure of such an order is upon outdoing one's competitors. The choice of means within the ambit of institutional control will persist as long as the sentiments sporting a competitive system, i.e., deriving from the possibility of outranking competitors and hence enjoying the favorable response of others, are distributed throughout the entire system of activities and are not confined merely to the

final result. A stable social structure demands a balanced distribution of affect among its various segments. When there occurs a shift of emphasis from the satisfactions deriving from competition itself to almost exclusive concern with successful competition, the resultant stress leads to the breakdown of the regulatory structures.[21] With the resulting attenuation of the institutional imperatives, there occurs an approximation of the situation erroneously held by utilitarians to be typical of society generally wherein calculations of advantage and fear of punishment are the sole regulating agencies. In such situations, as Hobbes observed, force and fraud come to constitute the sole virtues in view of their relative efficiency in attaining goals—which were for him of course, not culturally derived.

It should be apparent that the foregoing discussion is not pitched on a moralistic plane. Whatever the sentiments of the writer or reader concerning the ethical desirability of coordinating the means-and-goals phases of the social structure, one must agree that lack of such coordination leads to anomie. Insofar as one of the most general functions of social organization is to provide a basis for calculability and regularity of behavior, it is increasingly limited in effectiveness as these elements of the structure become dissociated. At the extreme, predictability virtually disappears and what may be properly termed cultural chaos or anomie intervenes.

This statement, being brief, is also incomplete. It has not included an exhaustive treatment of the various structural elements which predispose toward one rather than another of the alternative responses open to individuals; it has neglected, but not denied the relevance on the factors determining the specific incidence of these responses; it has not enumerated the various concrete responses which are constituted by combination of specific values of the analytical variables; it has omitted, or included only by implication, any consideration of the social functions performed by illicit responses; it has not tested the full explanatory power of the analytical scheme by examining a large number of group variations in the frequency of deviate and conformist behavior; it has not adequately dealt with rebellious conduct which seeks to refashion the social framework radically; it has not examined the relevance of cultural conflict for an analysis of culture-goal and institutional-means malintegration. It is suggested that these and related problems may be profitably analyzed by this scheme.

NOTES

1. E.g., Ernest Jones, *Social Aspects of Psychoanalysis*, 28, London, 1924. If the Freudian notion is a variety of the "original sin" dogma, then the interpretation advanced in this paper may be called the doctrine of "socially derived sin."

2. "Normal" in the sense of a culturally oriented, if not approved, response. This statement does not deny the relevance of biological and personality differences which may be significantly involved in the *incidence* of deviate conduct. Our focus of interest is the social and cultural matrix; hence we abstract from other factors. It is in this sense, I take it, that James S. Plant speaks of the "normal reaction of normal people to abnormal conditions." See his *Personality and the Cultural Pattern*, 248, New York, 1937.

3. Contemporary American culture has been said to tend in this direction. See André Siegfried, *America Comes of Age*, 26–37, New York, 1927. The alleged extreme(?) emphasis on the goals of monetary success and material prosperity leads to dominant concern with technological and social instruments designed to produce the desired result, inasmuch as institutional controls become of secondary importance. In such a situation, innovation flourishes as the *range of means* employed is broadened. In a sense, then, there occurs the paradoxical emergence of "materialists" from an "idealistic" orientation. Cf. Durkheim's analysis of the cultural conditions which predispose toward crime and innovation, both of which are aimed toward efficiency, not moral norms. Durkheim was one of the first to see that "contrairment aux idées courantes le criminal n'apparait plus comme un être radicalement insociable, comme une sorte d'élément parasitaire, de corps étranger et inassimilable, introduit au sein de la société; c'est un agent régulier de la vie sociale." See *les Régles de la Méthode Sociologique*, 86–89, Paris, 1927.

4. Such ritualism may be associated with a mythology which rationalizes these actions so that they appear to retain their status as means, but the dominant pressure is in the direction of strict ritualistic conformity, irrespective of such rationalizations. In this sense, ritual has proceeded farthest when such rationalizations are not even called forth.

5. In this connection, one may see the relevance of Elton Mayo's paraphrase of the title of Tawney's well-known book. "Actually the problem is *not that of the sickness of an acquisitive society; it is that of the acquisitiveness of a sick society.*" *Human Problems of an Industrial Civilization*, 153, New York, 1933. Mayo deals with the process

through which wealth comes to be a symbol of social achievement. He sees this as arising from a state of anomie. We are considering the unintegrated monetary-success goal as an element in producing anomie. A complete analysis would involve both phases of this system of interdependent variables.

6. It is unlikely that interiorized norms are completely eliminated. Whatever residuum persists will induce personality tensions and conflict. The process involves a certain degree of ambivalence. A manifest rejection of the institutional norms is coupled with some latent retention of their emotional correlates. "Guilt feelings," "sense of sin," "pangs of conscience" are obvious manifestations of this unrelieved tension; symbolic adherence to the nominally repudiated values or rationalizations constitute a more subtle variety of tensional release.

7. "Many," and not all, unintegrated groups, for the reason already mentioned. In groups where the primary emphasis shifts to institutional means, i.e., when the range of alternatives is very limited, the outcome is a type of ritualism rather than anomie.

8. Money has several peculiarities which render it particularly apt to become a symbol of prestige divorced from institutional controls. As Simmel emphasized, money is highly abstract and impersonal. However acquired, through fraud or institutionally, it can be used to purchase the same goods and services. The anonymity of metropolitan culture, in conjunction with this peculiarity of money, permits wealth, the sources of which may be unknown to the community in which the plutocrat lives, to serve as a symbol of status.

9. The emphasis upon wealth as a success symbol is possibly reflected in the use of the term "fortune" to refer to a stock of accumulated wealth. This meaning becomes common in the late sixteenth century (Spenser and Shakespeare). A similar usage of the Latin *fortuna* comes into prominence during the first century B.C. Both these periods were marked by the rise to prestige and power of the "bourgeoisie."

10. See Kinglsey Davis, "Mental Hygiene and the Class Structure," *Psychiatry*, 1928, 1:esp.62–63; Talcott Parsons, *The Structure of Social Action*, 59–60, New York, 1937.

11. This is a level intermediate between the two planes distinguished by Edward Sapir; mainly, culture patterns and personal habits systems. See his "Contribution of Psychiatry to an Understanding of Behavior in Society," *Amer. J. Sociol.*, 1937, 42:862–870.

12. This fifth alternative is on a plane clearly different from that of the others. It represents a *transitional* response which seeks to *institutionalize* new procedures oriented toward revamped cultural goals shared by the members of the society. It thus involves efforts to *change* the existing structure rather than to perform accommodative actions *within* this structure, and introduces additional problems with which we are not at the moment concerned.

13. Obviously, this is an elliptical statement. These indi-

viduals may maintain some orientation to the values of their particular differentiated groupings within the larger society or, in part, of the conventional society itself. Insofar as they do so, their conduct cannot be classified in the "passive rejection" category (IV). Nels Anderson's description of the behavior and attitudes of the bum, for example, can readily be recast in terms of our analytical scheme. See *The Hobo*, 93–98, *et passim*, Chicago, 1923.

14. Joseph D. Lohman, "The Participant Observer in Community Studies," *Amer. Sociol. Rev.*, 1937, 2:890–898.

15. The shifting historical role of this ideology is a profitable subject for exploration. The "office-boy-to-president" stereotype was once in approximate accord with the facts. Such vertical mobility was probably more common then than now, when the class structure is more rigid. (See the following note.) The ideology largely persists, however, possibly because it still performs a useful function for maintaining the *status quo*. For insofar as it is accepted by the "masses," it constitutes a useful sop for those who might rebel against the entire structure, were this consoling hope removed. This ideology now serves to lessen the probability of Adaptation V. In short, the role of this notion has changed from that of an ideology, in Mannheim's sense.

16. There is a growing body of evidence, though none of it is clearly conclusive, to the effect that our class structure is becoming rigidified and that vertical mobility is declining. Taussig and Joslyn found that American business leaders are being *increasingly* recruited from the upper ranks of our society. The Lynds have also found a "diminished chance to get ahead" for the working classes in Middletown. Manifestly, these objective changes are not alone significant; the individual's subjective evaluation of the situation is a major determinant of the response. The extent to which this change in opportunity for social mobility has been recognized by the least advantaged classes is still conjectural, although the Lynds present some suggestive materials. The writer suggests that a case in point is the increasing frequency of cartoons which observe in a tragi-comic vein that "my old man says everybody can't be President. He says if ya can get three days a week steady on W.P.A. work ya ain't doin' so bad either." See F. W. Taussig and C. S. Joslyn,

American Business Leaders, New York, 1932; R. S. and H. M. Lynd, *Middletown in Transition*, 67 ff., chap. 12, New York, 1937.

17. The role of the Negro in this respect is of considerable theoretical interest. Certain elements of the Negro population have assimilated the dominant caste's values of pecuniary success and social advancement, but they also recognize that social ascent is at present restricted to their own caste almost exclusively. The pressures upon the Negro which would otherwise derive from the structural inconsistencies we have noticed are hence not identical with those upon lower class whites. See Kinglsey Davis, *op. cit.*, 63; John Dollard, *Caste and Class in a Southern Town*, 66ff., New Haven, 1936; Donald Young, *American Minority Peoples*, 581, New York, 1932.

18. The psychical coordinates of these processes have been partly established by the experimental evidence concerning *Anspruchsniveaus* and levels of performance. See Kurt Lewin, *Vorsatz, Willie und Bedurfnis*, Berlin, 1926; N. F. Hoppe, "Erfolg und Misserfolg," *Psychol. Forschung.* 1930, 14:1–63; Jerome D. Frank, "Individual Differences in Certain Aspects of the Level of Aspiration," *Amer. J. Psychol.*, 1935, 47:119–128.

19. Standard criminology texts summarize the data in this field. Our scheme of analysis may serve to resolve some of the theoretical contradictions which P. A. Sorkin indicates. For example, "not everywhere nor always do the poor show a greater proportion of crime . . . many poorer countries have had less crime than the richer countries. . . . The [economic] improvement in the second half of the nineteenth century, and the beginning of the twentieth, has not been followed by a decrease of crime." See his *Contemporary Sociological Theories*, 560–561, New York, 1928. The crucial point is, however, that poverty has varying social significance in different social structures, as we shall see. Hence, one would not expect a linear correlation between crime and poverty.

20. See M. W. Royse, *Aerial Bombardment and the International Regulation of War*, New York, 1928.

21. Since our primary concern is with the socio-cultural aspects of this problem, the psychological correlates have been only implicitly considered. See Karen Horney, *The Neurotic Personality of Our Time*, New York, 1937, for a psychological discussion of this process.

QUESTIONS FOR DISCUSSION

1. Why does Merton object to attributing problems in society to "biological drives" that have not been adequately restrained?

2. What assumptions are made about cultural goals and institutionalized means in Merton's five-pattern scheme for adaptation?

3. In which of the five patterns do you think we might categorize most juvenile delinquents?

4. Can you think of any individuals or groups that may not fit into Merton's patterns?

5. In what way is the pattern of rebellion different from the other four patterns?

APPLICATIONS

1. On a sheet of paper make two columns. In column 1 list what you believe are the goals of our culture. In column 2 list what you believe are the institutionally approved means for achieving these cultural goals. Compare your responses to other classmates'.

   a. On what goals and means do your classmates agree? How do they disagree?

   b. Utilizing group discussion, attempt to arrive at a full consensus on what should be included as goals and means.

   c. In which of Merton's five patterns would you categorize yourself? Do you think a person could change from pattern to pattern depending on the social situation?

2. When an individual cannot achieve culturally approved goals and/or is denied institutional means for goal obtainment, a condition occurs which Emile Durkheim called *anomie* or normlessness. When an individual loses the attachment to social norms, the sources of social and self-restraint are dissolved. Social disorder is the result. Among individuals and groups, regard for normative and legal prescriptions is lacking or altered.

   a. When the Los Angeles police officers were first acquitted for the alleged beating of Rodney King, there was subsequent looting and arson. This is an example of social disorder. How might the concept of anomie be used to explain this phenomena?

   b. How might we apply Merton's five-pattern scheme in order understand this event?

   c. From your perspective, what changes should be invoked immediately and over the long term to maintain social order in urban areas?

KEY TERMS

anomie a state of normlessness in which the social control of individual behavior has become ineffective.

conceptual scheme a tool or model utilized for describing a particular phenomena.

culture the totality of socially transmitted behavior patterns, arts, beliefs, institutions, and all other products of human work and thought characteristic of a community or population.

folkways patterns of behavior common in and typical to a group.

macrocosm a universal system regarded as an entity containing subsystems or subgroups.

microcosm a system more or less analogous to a much larger system in constitution, configuration, or development.

ritualistic prescribing to any detailed method or procedure faithfully or regularly followed.

role the characteristics and expected social behavior of an individual.

social conflict the absence of harmony, equilibrium, order, or consensus. Disconsensual in terms of values, meanings, or resources.

status a position based on prestige and lifestyle.

6

Social Learning and Deviant Behavior: A Specific Test of General Theory

Ronald L. Akers
Marvin D. Krohn
Lonn Lanza-Kaduce
Marcia Radosevich

INTRODUCTION

In the last decade we have seen a dramatic shift away from sociological explanations of deviant behavior toward developing theoretical perspectives on societal reactions to and definitions of deviance and crime. Labelling and conflict formulations have become major foci of sociological theorizing as well as the sounding boards for most of the controversy and discourse in the field of deviance. This shift in focus was deemed necessary to redress the previous imbalance of attention to the deviant behavior itself (Akers, 1968), and it clearly has had that effect. Unfortunately, it also has led to the neglect of theoretical developments in the etiology of deviant behavior. Neither labelling nor conflict perspectives has offered a general explanation of deviant behavior, although some conflict theorists have offered preliminary but incomplete efforts in that direction (Taylor, et al., 1973; Spitzer, 1975). There have been other efforts directed toward explaining deviant behavior, but these have been fairly narrow in scope; they have usually been limited either to a specific type of deviant behavior or to a restricted range of substantive variables. For example, a good

From *American Sociological Review*, Volume 44 (August 1979), pp. 636–655. Copyright © 1979 by the American Sociological Association. Reprinted by permission.

deal of attention has been paid to the modern resurrection of deterrence theory (Gibbs, 1975; 1977; Waldo and Chiricos, 1972; Tittle, 1975; Silberman, 1976; Erickson et al., 1977; Meier and Johnson, 1977; Geerken and Gove, 1977). The scope of deterrence theory has been changed little, however, since its statement by the classical criminologists two centuries ago and is limited to the actual or perceived certainty, severity, and celerity of formally administered legal sanctions for violations of the criminal law. Another example is Travis Hirschi's (1969) control (social bonding) theory which is a more general explanation of deviance than deterrence theory, but which is, in turn, primarily restricted to informal social control which comes from individuals being bonded to groups and institutions.

The most notable exception to the diminished attention to general explanation of deviant behavior is a form of social learning theory developed first by Robert L. Burgess and Ronald L. Akers as differential association-reinforcement theory (Burgess and Akers, 1966; Akers et al., 1968) and elaborated on later by Akers (1973; 1977). As the name which Burgess and Akers originally chose to apply to this theoretical perspective makes clear, it was constructed as a revision of Edwin H. Sutherland's differential association theory (Sutherland, 1947; Sutherland and Cressey, 1974) in terms of general behavioral reinforcement theory (Skinner, 1953; 1959; Bandura and Walters, 1963; Bandura, 1969; 1977; Staats, 1975). Social learning theory as a general perspective in deviance is part of a larger move toward incorporation of modern behaviorism into sociological theory (Homans, 1961; Burgess' and Bushell, 1969; Kunkel, 1975; Hamblin et al., 1971; Emerson, 1969; 1972; Kunkel and Nagasawa, 1973; Burgess and Nielsen, 1974; Chadwick-Jones, 1976; for reviews of the relevance of behavioral theory for sociology see Friedrichs, 1974; Tarter, 1973). As such it is a theoretical perspective which is compatible with the more specific forays into the explanation of deviant behavior. Indeed, the major features of such theories as deterrence and control theories (Hirschi, 1969) can be subsumed under the principles of social learning theory (Akers, 1977; Conger, 1976; 1977; Feldman, 1977). However, all too often the relevance for social learning theory of some of the deviance research has been ignored or unrecognized even when the authors employ central learning concepts such as reinforcement (Harris, 1975; 1977; Eaton, 1974; Meier and Johnson, 1977; Hirschi and Hindelang, 1977). This inattention is regrettable for, while other theories delineate the structural variables (class, race, anomic conditions, breakdown in social control, etc.) that yield differential rates of deviance, social learning stresses the behavioral mechanisms by which these variables produce the behavior comprising the rates. As such, social learning is complementary to other sociological theories and could be used to integrate extant formulations to achieve more comprehensive explanations of deviance (in this regard see Akers, 1977:63–8).

The basic learning principles on which this theory is based have received empirical support under laboratory and applied experimental conditions (see Skinner, 1953; Honig, 1966; Ullmann and Krasner, 1969; Bandura, 1969; 1977; McLaughlin, 1971; Staats, 197 5). Also, prior research has been supportive of differential association theory (J. Ball, 1957; Short, 1957; Voss, 1964; R. Ball, 1968; Krohn, 1974; Jensen, 1972; Burkett and Jensen, 1975). However, there has been little direct research on learning principles as applied to deviant behavior in

natural settings. Akers (1977) has organized a large body of existing research and theory on a wide range of deviant behavior supportive of or consistent with social learning, but his effort is a post hoc application of theoretical principles for he does not present research designed explicitly to test propositions from the theory (in this regard see also Feldman, 1977). The results of other studies are consistent with Akers's social learning approach (Jessor and Jessor, 1975; Thomas et al., 1975), and a couple of studies explicitly testing social learning using secondary data analysis have found support for it (Anderson, 1973; Conger, 1976). However, more crucial and conclusive tests await collecting the relevant primary data in the community. The present study does that. Our purpose here is to report a specific test of social learning theory using standard sociological techniques of data collection and data analysis.

STATEMENT OF SOCIAL LEARNING THEORY

The social learning theory tested here is summarized from Akers (1977:39–68). The primary learning mechanism in social behavior is operant (instrumental) conditioning in which behavior is shaped by the stimuli which follow, or are consequences of the behavior. Social behavior is acquired both through direct conditioning and through *imitation* or modelling of others' behavior. Behavior is strengthened through reward (positive reinforcement) and avoidance of punishment (negative reinforcement) or weakened by aversive stimuli (positive punishment) and loss of reward: (negative punishment). Whether deviant or conforming behavior is acquired and persists depends on past and present rewards or punishments for the behavior and the rewards and punishments attached to altenative behavior—*differential reinforcement*. In addition, people learn in interaction with significant groups in their lives evaluative *definitions* (norms, attitudes, orientations) of the behavior as good or bad. These definitions are themselves verbal and cognitive behavior which can be directly reinforced and also act as cue (discriminative) stimuli for other behavior. The more individuals define the behavior as good (positive definition) or at least justified (neutralizing definition) rather than as undesirable (negative definition), the more likely they are to engage in it.

The reinforcers can be nonsocial (as in the direct physiological effects of drugs) as well as social, but the theory posits that the principal behavioral effects come from interaction in or under the influence of those *groups which control individuals' mayor sources of reinforcement and punishment and expose them to behavioral models and normative definitions*. The most important of these groups with which one is in *differential association* are the *peer-friendship* groups and the *family* but they also include schools, churches, and other groups. Behavior (whether deviant or conforming) results from greater reinforcement, on balance, over punishing contingencies for the same behavior and the reinforcing-punishing contingencies on alternative behavior. The definitions are conducive to deviant behavior when, on balance, the positive and neutralizing definitions of the behavior offset negative definitions of it. Therefore, deviant behavior can be expected to the extent that it has been differentially reinforced over alternative behavior (conforming or other deviant behavior) and is defined as desirable or justified. Progression into more frequent or sustained use and into abuse is also determined by the extent to which a given pattern is sustained by the combination of the reinforcing effects of the substance with social reinforcement, exposure to models, definitions through association with using peers, and by the degree to which it is not deterred through bad effects of the substance and/or the negative sanctions from peers, parents, and the law.

The social learning theory proposes a process which orders and specifies the interrelationships among these variables. Differential association, which refers to interaction and identity with different groups, occurs first. These groups provide the social environments in which exposure to definitions, imitation of models, and social reinforcement for use of or abstinence from any particular substance take place. The definitions are learned through imitation, and social reinforcement of them by members of the groups with whom one is associated, and once learned, these definitions

serve as discriminative stimuli for use or abstinence. The definitions in interaction with imitation of using or abstinent models and the anticipated balance of reinforcement produces the initial use or continued abstinence. After the initial use, imitation becomes less important while the effects of definitions should continue (themselves affected by the experience of use). It is at this point in the process that the actual consequences (social and nonsocial reinforcers and punishers) of the specific behavior come into play to determine the probability that use will be continued and at what level. These consequences include the actual effects of the substance at first and subsequent use (the perception of which may, of course, be modified by what effects the person has previously learned to expect) and the actual reactions of others present at the time or who find out about it later, as well as the anticipated reactions of others not present or knowing about the use.

From this depiction of them as aspects of the same learning process, we expect the independent variables to be positively interrelated, and we examine the zero-order relationships among them. Nonetheless, the major variables are conceptually distinct and our measures are empirically distinct enough that we do not expect their inter-relationships to preclude separate independent effects. Thus, we also empirically order the independent variables in terms of how much variance is explained in the dependent variables. We test the general hypothesis from the theory that adolescent marijuana and alcohol use and abuse are related to each of the major sets of variables and to all of them combined.

Specifically, we expect that for both alcohol and drugs, the probability of abstinence decreases and the frequency of use increases when there is greater exposure to using rather than to abstinent models, when there is more association with using than with abstinent peers and adults, when use is differentially reinforced (more rewards, fewer punishers) over abstinence, and when there are more positive or neutralizing than negative definitions of use. Similarly, among users the probability of abuse increases with more exposure to abusing rather than moderate or abstinent models, more association with high frequency users or abusers, greater differential reinforcement for abuse over more moderate use, and with more positive and neutralizing rather than negative definitions of use. . . .

METHODOLOGY

Sample and Procedure

Data were collected by administering a self-report questionnaire to 3,065 male and female adolescents attending grades 7 through 12 in seven communities in three midwestern states. A two-stage sample design was followed. First, we selected schools from within each participating school district which were representative in terms of school size and location within the district. In smaller districts this meant selecting all or most of the junior and senior high schools in the district. Secondly, we sampled two to three classrooms (depending on school and average class size) per grade level from among the required or general enrollment classes. Thus, although classrooms were sampled, each student has an approximately equal chance of being included in the sample. The questionnaire (which was pretested in a district not included in the final sample) was administered to all students in attendance in the selected classes on the day of the survey who had obtained written parental permission. The attrition from this parental permission procedure combined with absenteeism on the day of the survey was not great and 67% of the total number of students enrolled (95% of those with parental permission) in the sampled classes completed the questionnaire. . . .

Measurement of Variables

Dependent variables. Abstinence-use of alcohol and marijuana is measured by a six-point frequency-of-use scale ranging from nearly every day to never. A quantity frequency (Q-F) scale was also computed but since there is a near perfect correlation between the Q-F scale and the frequency-of use scale, the analysis here includes only the latter measures. Abuse among users is measured by combining responses to the frequency questions with responses to the

question asking the respondents to check whether or not they had experienced on more than one occasion any of a list of problems while or soon after using alcohol or marijuana. This combination produced a four-point abuse scale ranging from heavy abuse to no abuse.

Independent variables. From the summary of social learning theory presented above it can be seen that the main concepts to be measured are *imitation, differential association, definitions,* and *differential reinforcement.* For the present analysis, we distinguish between differential reinforcement comprised of social reinforcement combined with non-social reinforcement (experienced or anticipated drug or alcohol effects) and that comprised only of social reinforcement. Each of the resulting five concepts are operationalized by a set of items measuring different aspects of each concept. . . .

FINDINGS

. . . The results of the regression analyses show strong support for the social learning theory of adolescent alcohol and drug behavior. When all the independent variables are incorporated into the full regression equation, the model explains 55% of the variance in drinking behavior (abstinence-frequency of use . . . and 68% of the variance in marijuana behavior (abstinence-frequency of use). . . .

. . . [T]he analyses also plainly show that some subsets of variables specified by the theory are more important than others. They are ranked in terms of relative effectiveness in explaining variance in alcohol and marijuana use as follows: (1) differential association, (2) definitions, (3) combined social/nonsocial differential reinforcement, (4) differential social reinforcement, and (5) imitation. Not only does the differential association subset explain the highest proportion of variance, but the differential peer association variable is the most important single variable. The definitions subset accounts for the second highest proportion of variance, and one's positive/negative definitions of the substances is the second most predictive single variable, while one's law-abiding/violating definitions rank third among the single variables. The differential reinforcement variables are next, followed by imitation variables which explain the least amount of variance in the dependent variables.

The fact of peer group influence on substance use comes as no surprise; it is documented by several previous studies. But, previous studies have not shown what the mechanisms are by which peer influence is exerted, and why, therefore, peer group association is so important. Our data show, as predicted by social learning theory, what these mechanisms are—friends provide social reinforcement or punishment for abstinence or use, provide normative definitions of use and abstinence. and, to a lesser extent, serve as admired models to imitate. This is indicated by the fact that these other variables, on their own, explain a substantial amount of the variance in marijuana and alcohol behavior when the effect of the differential peer association variable is removed. . . .

It is evident that social learning theory has been shown to be a powerful explanation of whether youngsters abstain from or are users of alcohol and marijuana. As predicted by the theory, the adolescents in our sample use drugs or alcohol to the extent that the behavior has been differentially reinforced through association in primary groups and defined as more desirable than, or at least as justified as, refraining from use. . . .

The variable of parental reaction appears to be related to abuse in the direction opposite to that found in the analysis of use. For the latter a lower probability of use is found for those reporting the strongest or harshest parental punishment while for the former a lower probability of abuse is found for those reporting lesser punishment or no parental response. . . . [Higher frequency of use and abuse is found with parental response (actual or anticipated) at both the most lenient (encourage or do nothing) and the harshest end of the scale (take some drastic action such as kick the youngsters out of the house or turn them over to the police). The highest probability of abstinence and the lowest levels of use and abuse are found among adolescents who report that their parents have responded or would respond to their use with a moderate negative reaction such as a scolding. Our post hoc interpretation

of these relationships is that anticipated parental punishment is a deterrent to use and sustains abstinence. Even after use has begun a reasonable amount of parental punishment holds down the chances of increasing frequency of use or moving into abuse. However, once adolescents have gotten into heavy use or abuse, parental reaction has lost its effect and the increasing abuse of the substances by their children may produce ever harsher reactions by parents increasingly desperate attempts to do something about it. . . .

SUMMARY AND CONCLUSIONS

. . . All of the dependent variables are strongly related to the social learning variables of differential association, definitions, differential reinforcement, and imitation. The most powerful of these independent variables is differential association. The other variables stand on their own, however, and explain substantial portions of variance even without the differential association measures. . . .

The strength of empirical support for the theory suggests that the theory will have utility in explaining the use and abuse of other substances by adolescents. These findings also indicate that social learning theory will do well when tested with other forms of deviant behavior in future research. . . .

REFERENCES

ABELSON, H. I., R. COHEN, D. SHRAYER, AND M. RAPPEPORT. 1973. "Drug experience, attitudes and related behavior among adolescents and adults." Pp. 488–867 in *Drug use in America: Problem in Perspective*, Vol. 1. Report prepared by the National Commission on Marijuana and Drug Abuse.

AKERS, RONALD L. 1968. "Problems in the sociology of deviance: social definitions and behavior." *Social Forces* 46:455–65.

———. 1973. *Deviant Behavior: A Social Learning Approach.* Belmont: Wadsworth.

———. 1977. *Deviant Behavior: A Social learning Approach.* 2nd ed. Belmont: Wadsworth.

AKERS, RONALD L., ROBERT L. BURGESS AND WELDON JOHNSON. 1968. "Opiate use, addiction, and relapse." *Social Problems* 15:459–69.

ANDERSON, LINDA S. 1973. "The impact of formal and informal sanctions on marijuana use: a test of social learning and deterrence." Master's thesis: Florida State University.

BALL, JOHN C. 1957. "Delinquent and non-delinquent attitudes toward the prevalence of stealing." *Journal of Criminal Law, Criminology and Police Science* 48:259–57.

BALL, RICHARD A. 1968. "An empirical exploration of neutralization theory." Pp. 255–65 in Mark Lefton, James K Sipper and Charles H. McCaghy (eds.), *Approach to Deviance.* New York: Appleton-Century-Crofts.

BANDURA, ALBERT. 1969. *Principles of Behavior Modification.* New York. Holt, Rinehart and Winston.

———. 1977. *Social Learning Theory.* Englewood Cliffs: Prentice-Hall.

BANDURA, ALBERT AND RICHARD H. WALTERS. 1963. *Social Learning and Personality Development.* New York. Holt, Rinehart and Winston.

BLOCK, J. R., N. GOODMAN, F. AMBELLAN AND J. REVENSON. 1974. "A self-administered high school study of drugs." Hempstead: Institute for Research and Evaluation.

BURGESS, ROBERT L. AND RONALD L. AKERS. 1966. "A differential association-reinforcement theory, of criminal behavior." *Social Problems* 14:128–47.

BURGESS, ROBERT L. AND DON BUSHELL (EDS.). 1969. *Behavioral Sociology* New York: Columbia University Press.

BURGESS, ROBERT L. AND JOYCE MCCARL NIELSEN. 1974. "An experimental analysis of some structural determinants of equitable and inequitable exchange relations." *American Sociological Review* 39:427–43.

BURKETT, STEVEN AND ERIC L. JENSEN. 1975. "Conventional ties, peer influence, and the fear of apprehension: a study of adolescent marijuana use." *Sociological Quarterly* 16:522–33.

CALHOUN, J. R. 1974. "Attitudes toward the sale and use of drugs: a cross-sectional analysis of those who use drugs." *Journal of Youth and Adolescence* 3:31–47.

CHADWICK-JONES, J. F. 1976. *Social Exchange Theory: Its Structure and Influence in Social Psychology.* New York: Academic Press.

CONGER, RAND D. 1976. "Social control and social learning b\models of delinquent behavior—a synthesis." *Criminology* 14:17–40.

———. 1977. Rejoinder. *Criminology* 15:117–26.

DRUG ABUSE COUNCIL, INC. 1975. *A Report of the Drug Abuse Council* (by Yankelovich, Skelly, and White, Inc.) Washington, D. C.: Drug Abuse Council.

EATON, WILLIAM W. 1974. "Mental hospitalization as a reinforcement process." *American Sociological Review* 39:252–60.

EMERSON, RICHARD M. 1969. "Operant psychology and exchange theory." Pp. 379–405 in Robert L. Burgess and Don Bushell, Jr. (eds.), *Behavioral Sociology.* New York. Columbia University Press.

———. 1972. "Exchange theory." Pp. 38–87 in Joseph Berger, Morris Zeldifch, Jr. and Bo Anderson (eds.), *Sociological Theories in Progress,* Vol. 2. Boston: Houghton-Mifflin.

ERICKSON, MAYNARD L., JACK P. GIBBS AND GARY F. JENSEN. 1977. "The deterrence doctrine and the perceived certainty

of legal punishment." *American Sociological Review* 42:305–17.

FEJER, DIANNE AND REGINALD G. SMART. 1973. "The knowledge about drugs, attitudes toward them and drug use rates of high school students." *Journal of Drug Education* 3:377–88.

FELDMAN, M. P. 1977. *Criminal Behavior: A Psychological Analysis.* London: Wiley.

FRIEDRICHS, ROBERT W. 1974. "The potential impact of B. F. Skinner upon American sociology." *The American Sociologist* 9:3–8.

GEERKEN, MICHAEL AND WALTER R. GOVE. 1977. "Deterrence, overload, and incapacitation: an empirical evaluation." *Social Forces* 56:424–47.

GIBBS, JACK R. 1975. *Crime, Punishment and Deterrence.* New York: Elsevier.

———. 1977. "Social control, deterrence, and perspectives on social order." *Social Forces* 56:408–23.

GROVES, W. EUGENE. 1974. "Patterns of college student use and lifestyles." Pp. 241–75 in Eric Josephson and Eleanor E. Carrol (eds.), *Drug Use: Epidemiological and Sociological Approaches.* New York: Wiley.

HAMBLIN, ROBERT L. DAVID BUCKHOLDT, DANIEL FERRITOR, MARTIN KOZLOFF AND LOIS BLACKWELL. 1971. *The Humanization Process: A Social Behavioral Analysis of Children's Problems.* New York: Wiley.

HARDT, ROBERT H. AND SANDRA PETERSON-HARDT. 1977. "On determining the quality of the delinquency self-report method." *Journal of Research in Crime and Delinquency* 14:247–61.

HARRIS, ANTHONY R. 1975. "Imprisonment and the expected value of criminal choice: a specification and test of aspects of the labeling perspective." *American Sociological Review* 40:71–87.

———. 1977. "Sex and theories of deviance: toward a functional theory of deviant typescripts." *American Sociological Review* 42:3–16.

HIRSCHI, TRAVIS. 1969. *Causes of Delinquency.* Berkeley and Los Angeles: University of California Press.

HIRSCHI, TRAVIS AND MICHAEL J. HINDELANG. 1977. "Intelligence and delinquency; a revisionist review." *American Sociological Review* 42:571–87.

HOMANS, GEORGE C. 1961. *Social Behavior. Its Elementary Forms.* New York: Harcourt Brace Jovanovich.

HONIG, WERNER. 1966. *Operant Behavior: Areas of Research and Application.* New York: Appleton-Century-Crofts.

JENSEN, GARY F. 1972. "Parents, peers and delinquent action: a test of the differential association perspective." *American Journal of Sociology* 78:63–72.

JESSOR, RICHARD. 1976. "Predicting time of onset of marijuana use: a developmental study of high school youth." *Journal of Consulting and Clinical Psychology* 44:125–34.

JESSOR, R., M. I. COLLINS AND S. L. JESSOR. 1972. "On becoming a drinker: social-psychological aspects of an adolescent transition." *Annals of the New York Academy of Science* 197:199–213.

JESSOR, R., T. D. GRAVES, R. C. HANSON AND S. L JESSOR. 1968.

Society, Personality and Deviant Behavior. A Study of a Tri-Ethnic Community. New York: Holt, Rinehart and Winston.

JESSOR, R. AND S. L. JESSOR. 1975. "Adolescent development and the onset of drinking: a longitudinal study." *Journal of Studies on Alcohol* 36:27–51.

———. 1977. *Problem Behavior and Psychosocial Development: A Longitudinal Study of Youth.* New York: Academic Press.

JESSOR, RICHARD, SHIRLEY L. JESSOR AND JOHN FINNEY. 1973. "A social psychology of marijuana use: longitudinal studies of high school and college youth." *Journal of Personality and Social Psychology* 26:1–5.

JESSOR, R., H. B. YOUNG, E. B. YOUNG AND G. TESI. 1970. "Perceived opportunity, alienation, and drinking behavior among Italian and American youth." *Journal of Personality and Social Psychology* 15:215–22.

JOHNSTON, L. 1973. *Drugs and American Youth.* Ann Arbor: Institute for Social Research.

KANDEL, DENISE. 1973. "Adolescent marijuana use: role of parents and peers." *Science* 181:1067–70.

———. 1974. "Interpersonal influences on adolescent illegal drug use." Pp. 207–40 in Eric Josephson and Eleanor E. Carrol (eds.), *Drug Use: Epidemiological and Sociological Approaches.* New York. Wiley.

———. 1978. *Longitudinal Research on Drug Use.* Ed. by D. Kandel. New York: Halsted.

KENDALL, RICHARD FENWICK. 1976. *The Context and Implications of Drinking and Drug Use among High School and College Students.* Ph.D. dissertation, Department of Psychology, New York University.

KIM, JAE-ON. 1975. "Multivariate analysis of ordinal variables." *American Journal of Sociology* 81:261–98.

KROHN, MARVIN D. 1974. "An investigation of the effect of parental and peer associations on marijuana use: an empirical test of differential association theory." Pp. 75–89 in Marc Reidel and Terrence P. Thornberry (eds.), *Crime and Delinquency: Dimensions of Deviance.* New York: Praeger.

KUNKEL, JOHN H. AND RICHARD H. NAGASAWA. 1973. "A behavioral model of man: propositions and implications." *American Sociological Review* 38:530–43.

KUNKEL, JOHN R. 1975. *Behavior, Social Problems, and Change: A Social Learning Approach.* Englewood Cliffs: Prentice-Hall.

LABOVITZ, SANFORD. 1970. "The assignment of numbers to rank order categories." *American Sociological Review* 35:515–24.

———. 1971. "In defense of assigning numbers to ranks." *American Sociological Review* 36:521–22.

LAWRENCE, T. S. AND J. O. VELLEMAN. 1974. "Correlates of student drug use in a suburban high school." *Psychiatry* 37:129–36.

MCLAUGHLIN, BARRY. 1971. *Learning and Social Behavior.* New York: Free Press.

MEIER, ROBERT F. AND WELDON T. JOHNSON. 1977. "Deterrence as social control: the legal and extralegal production of conformity." *American Sociological Review* 42:292–304.

NATIONAL COMMISSION ON MARIJUANA AND DRUG ABUSE. 1972. *Marijuana: A Signal of Misunderstanding.* New York: New American Library.

O'DONNELL, JOHN, HARWIN L. VOSS, RICHARD R. CLAYTON, AND ROBIN G. W. ROOM. 1976. *Young Men and Drugs—A Nationwide Survey.* Rockville: National Institute on Drug Abuse.

PEARCE, J. AND D. H. GARRETT. 1970. "A comparison of the drinking behavior of delinquent youth versus non-delinquent youth in the states of Idaho and Utah." *Journal of School Health* 40:131–5.

RACHAL, J. V, J. R. WILLIAMS, M. L. BREHM, B. CAVANAUGH, R. P. MOORE, AND W. C. ECKERMAN. 1975. *Adolescent Drinking Behavior, Attitudes and Correlates.* National Institute on Alcohol Abuse and Alcoholism: U. S. Department of Health, Education and Welfare, Contract No. HSM 42-73-80 (NIA).

RADOSEVICH, MARCIA, LONN LANZA-KADUCE, RONALD L. AKERS AND MARVIN D. KROHN. Forthcoming. "The sociology of adolescent drug and drinking behavior: a review of the state of the field: part 1, 2." *Deviant Behavior. An Interdisciplinary Journal.*

ROTTER, JULIAN. 1954. *Social Learning and Clinical Psychology.* Englewood Cliffs: Prentice-Hall.

SHORT, JAMES F. 1957. "Differential association and delinquency." *Social Problems* 4:233–9.

SILBERMAN, MATTHEW. 1976. "Toward a theory of criminal deterrence." *American Sociological Review* 41:442–61.

SINGLE, ERIC, DENISE KANDEL AND BRUCE D. JOHNSON. 1975. "The reliability and validity of drug use responses in a large scale longitudinal survey." *Journal of Drug Issues* 5:426–43.

SKINNER, B. F. 1953. *Science and Human Behavior.* New York. Macmillan.

———. 1959. *Cumulative Record.* New York: Appleton-Century-Crofts.

SPRITZER, STEVEN. 1975. "Toward a Marxian theory of deviance." *Social Problems* 22:638–51.

STAATS, ARTHUR. 1975. *Social Behaviorism.* Homewood: Dorsey Press.

SUTHERLAND, EDWIN H. 1947. *Principles of Criminology* 4th ed. Philadelphia: Lippincott.

SUTHERLAND, EDWIN H. AND DONALD R. CRESSEY. 1974. *Criminology.* 9th ed. Philadelphia: Lippincott.

TARTER, DONALD E. 1973. "Heeding Skinner's call: toward the development of a social technology." *The American Sociologist* 8:153–8.

TAYLOR, IAN, PAUL WALTON AND JACK YOUNG. 1973. *The New Criminology: For a Social Theory of Deviance.* New York: Harper and Row.

TEC, NECHAMA. 1974a. *Grass is Green in Suburbia: A Sociological Study of Adolescent Usage of Illicit Drugs.* Roslyn Heights: Libra.

———. 1974b. "Parent-child drug abuse: generational continuity of adolescent deviancy?" *Adolescence* 9:351–64.

THOMAS, CHARLES W., DAVID M. PETERSEN AND MATTHEW T. ZINGRAFF. 1975. "Student drug use: a re-examination of the hang-loose ethic hypothesis." *Journal of Health and Social Behavior* 16:63–73.

TITTLE, CHARLES R. 1975. "Deterrents or labeling?" *Social Forces* 53:399–410.

ULLMANN, LEONARD P. AND LEONARD KRASNER. 1969. *A Psychological Approach to Abnormal Behavior* Englewood Cliffs: Prentice-Hall.

VOSS, HARWIN. 1964. "Differential association and reported delinquent behavior: a replication." *Social Problems* 12:78–85.

WALDO, GORDON P. AND THEODORE CHIRICOS. 1972. "Perceived penal sanction and self-reported criminality: a neglected approach to deterrence research." *Social Problems* 19:522–40.

WECHSLER, HENRY AND DENISE THUM. 1973. "Teenage drinking, drug use, and social correlates." *Quarterly Journal of Studies on Alcohol* 34:1220–7.

WHITEHEAD, P. C. AND R. G. SMART. 1972. "Validity and reliability of self-reported drug use." *Canadian Journal of Criminology and Corrections* 14:1–8.

QUESTIONS FOR DISCUSSION

1. Provide a brief explanation of each of the following and give an example:

   differential association

   definitions

   differential reinforcement

   incitation

2. What groups, according to the authors, are most influential when one is in differential association? Why?

3. What conclusions were drawn from this study about social learning theory?

APPLICATIONS

1. What does it mean to be a conformer? Write down 10 or 15 attributes that characterize a conforming person. In small groups or as a class have each person read his or her list. See if the class can come to a consensus about 15 attributes of a social conformer.

2. What does it mean to be deviant? As in the previous application, write down 10 to 15 attributes that characterize a deviant person. Can the class come to a consensus about 15 attributes of a social deviant?

KEY TERMS

attrition   a normal reduction in number (e.g., relocation, graduation, death, retirement).

deterrence   a discouragement from some action by making the consequences severe or harsh. In the area of criminal sanctions it is thought that if the punishment is certain, swift, and severe for an offender, other would-be offenders will be discouraged from committing similar acts.

forays   refers to predatory raids for the purpose of obtaining food or stealing by force.

post hoc   after the fact.

subsumed   included in a larger schema or class.

variables   some items that may change independently or in reaction to other surrounding conditions.

7

A Control Theory
of Delinquency

Travis Hirschi

Control theories assume that delinquent acts result when an individual's bond to society is weak or broken. Since these theories embrace two highly complex concepts, the *bond* of the individual to *society*, it is not surprising that they have at one time or another formed the basis of explanations of most forms of aberrant or unusual behavior. It is also not surprising that control theories have described the elements of the bond to society in many ways, and that they have focused on a variety of units as the point of control. . . .

ELEMENTS OF THE BOND

Attachment

In explaining conforming behavior, sociologists justly emphasize sensitivity to the opinion of others.[1] Unfortunately, . . . they tend to suggest that man *is* sensitive to the opinion of others and thus exclude sensitivity from their explanations of deviant behavior. In explaining deviant behavior, psychologists, in contrast, emphasize insensitivity to the opinion of others.[2] Unfortunately, they too tend to ignore vari-

ation, and, in addition, they tend to tie sensitivity inextricably to other variables, to make it part of a syndrome or "type," and thus seriously to reduce its value as an explanatory concept. The psychopath is characterized only in part by "deficient attachment to or affection for others, a failure to respond to the ordinary motivations founded in respect or regard for one's fellow";[3] he is also characterized by such things as "excessive aggressiveness," "lack of superego control," and "an infantile level of response."[4] Unfortunately, too, the behavior that psychopathy is used to explain often becomes part of the *definition* of psychopathy. As a result, in Barbara Wootton's words: "[The psychopath] is . . . *par excellence*, and without shame or qualification, the model of the circular process by which mental abnormality is inferred from anti-social behavior while anti-social behavior is explained by mental abnormality."[5]

The problems of diagnosis, tautology, and name-calling are avoided if the dimensions of psychopathy are treated as causally and therefore problematically interrelated, rather than as logically and therefore necessarily bound to each other. In fact, it can be argued that all of the characteristics attributed to the psychopath follow from, are effects of, his lack of attachment to others. To say that to lack attachment to others is to be free from moral restraints is to use lack of attachment to explain the guiltlessness of the psychopath, the fact that he apparently has no conscience or superego. In this view, lack of attachment to others is not merely a symptom of psychopathy, it *is* psychopathy; lack of conscience is just another way of saying the same thing; and the violation of norms is (or may be) a consequence.

For that matter, given that man is an animal, "impulsivity" and "aggressiveness" can also be seen as natural consequences of freedom from moral restraints. However, since the view of man as endowed with natural propensities and capacities like other animals is peculiarly unpalatable to sociologists, we need not fall back on such a view to explain the amoral man's aggressiveness.[6] The process of becoming alienated from others often involves or is based on active interpersonal conflict. Such conflict could easily supply a reservoir of *socially derived* hostility sufficient to account for the aggressiveness of those whose attachments to others have been weakened.

Durkheim said it many years ago: "We are moral beings to the extent that we are social beings."[7] This may be interpreted to mean that we are moral beings to the extent that we have "internalized the norms" of society. But what does it mean to say that a person has internalized the norms of society? The norms of society are by definition shared by the members of society. To violate a norm is, therefore, to act contrary to the wishes and expectations of other people. If a person does not care about the wishes and expectation of other people—that is, if he is insensitive to the opinion of others—then he is to that extent not bound by the norms. He is free to deviate.

The essence of internalization of norms, conscience, or superego thus lies in the attachment of the individual to others.[8] This view has several advantages over the concept of internalization. For one, explanations of deviant behavior based on attachment do not beg the question, since the extent to which a person is attached to others can be measured independently of his deviant behavior. Furthermore, change or variation in behavior is explainable in a way that it is not when notions of internalization or superego are used. For example, the divorced man is more likely after divorce to commit a number

of deviant acts, such as suicide or forgery. If we explain these acts by reference to the superego (or internal control), we are forced to say that the man "lost his conscience" when he got a divorce; and, of course, if he remarries, we have to conclude that he gets his conscience back.

This dimension of the bond to conventional society is encountered in most social control-oriented research and theory. F. Ivan Nye's "internal control" and "indirect control" refer to the same element, although we avoid the problem of explaining changes over time by locating the "conscience" in the bond to others rather than making it part of the personality.[9] Attachment to others is just one aspect of Albert J. Reiss's "personal controls"; we avoid his problems of tautological empirical *observations* by making the relationship between attachment and delinquency problematic rather than definitional.[10] Finally, Scott Briar and Irving Piliavin's "commitment" or "stake in conformity" subsumes attachment, as their discussion illustrates, although the terms they use are more closely associated with the next element to be discussed.[11]

Commitment

"Of all passions, that which inclineth men least to break the laws, is fear. Nay, excepting some generous natures, it is the only thing, when there is the appearance of profit or pleasure by breaking the laws, that makes men keep them."[12] Few would deny that men on occasion obey the rules simply from fear of the consequences. This rational component in conformity we label commitment. What does it mean to say that a person is committed to conformity? In Howard S. Becker's formulation it means the following:

> First, the individual is in a position in which his decision with regard to some particular line of action has consequences for other interests and activities not necessarily [directly] related to it. Second, he has placed himself in that position by his own prior actions. A third element is present though so obvious as not to be apparent; the committed person must be aware [of these other interests] and must recognize that his decision in this case will have ramifications beyond it.[13]

The idea, then, is that the person invests time, energy, himself, in a certain line of activity—say, getting an education, building up a business, acquiring a reputation for virtue. When or whenever he considers deviant behavior, he must consider the costs of this deviant behavior, the risk he runs of losing the investment he has made in conventional behavior.

If attachment to others is the sociological counterpart of the superego or conscience, commitment is the counterpart of the ego or common sense. To the person committed to conventional lines of action, risking one to ten years in prison for a ten-dollar holdup is stupidity, because to the committed person the costs and risks obviously exceed ten dollars in value. (To the psychoanalyst, such an act exhibits failure to be governed by the "reality-principle.") In the sociological control theory, it can be and is generally assumed that the decision to commit a criminal act may well be rationally determined—that the actor's decision was not irrational given the risks and costs he faces. Of course, as Becker point out, if the actor is capable of in some sense calculating the costs of a line of action, he is also capable of calculational errors: ignorance and error return, in the control theory, as possible explanations of deviant behavior.

The concept of commitment assumes that the organization of society is such that the interest of most persons would be endangered if they were to engage in criminal acts. Most people, simply by the process of living in an organized society, acquire goods, reputations, prospects that they do not want to risk losing. These accumulations are society's insurance that they will abide by the rules. Many hypotheses about the antecedents of delinquent behavior are based on this premise. For example, Arthur L. Stinchcombe's hypothesis that "high school rebellion . . . occurs when future status is not clearly related to present performance"[14] suggests that one is committed to conformity not only by what one has but also by what one hopes to obtain. Thus "ambition" and/or "aspiration" play an important role in producing conformity. The person becomes committed to a conventional line of action, and he is therefore committed to conformity.

Most lines of action in a society are of course conventional. The clearest examples are educational and occupational careers. Actions thought to jeopardize one's chances in these areas are presumably avoided. Interestingly enough, even nonconventional commitments may operate to produce conventional conformity. We are told, at least, that boys aspiring to careers in the rackets of professional thievery are judged by their "honesty" and "reliability"—traits traditionally in demand among seekers of office boys.[15]

Involvement

Many persons undoubtedly owe a life of virtue to a lack of opportunity to do otherwise. Time and energy are inherently limited: "Not that I would not, if I could, be both handsome and fat and well dressed, and a great athlete, and make a million a year, be a wit, a bon vivant, and a lady killer, as well as a philosopher, a philanthropist, a statesman, warrior, and African explorer, as well as a 'tone-poet' and saint. But the thing is simply impossible."[16] The things that William James here says he would like to be or do are all, I suppose, within the realm of conventionality, but if he were to include illicit actions he would still have to eliminate some of them as simply impossible.

Involvement or engrossment in conventional activities is thus often part of a control theory. The assumption, widely shared, is that a person may be simply too busy doing conventional things to find time to engage in deviant behavior. The person involved in conventional activities is tied to appointments, deadlines, working hours, plans, and the like, so the opportunity to commit deviant acts rarely arises. To the extent that he is engrossed in conventional activities, he cannot even think about deviant acts, let alone act out his inclinations.[17]

This line of reasoning is responsible for the stress placed on recreational facilities in many programs to reduce delinquency, for much of the concern with the high school dropout, and for the idea that boys should be drafted into the army to keep them out of trouble. So obvious and persuasive is the idea that involvement in conventional activities is a major deterrent to delinquency that it was accepted even by Sutherland: "In the general area of juvenile delinquency it is probable that the most significant difference between juveniles who engage in delinquency and those who do not is that the latter are provided abundant opportunities of a conventional type for satisfying their recreational interests, while the former lack those opportunities or facilities."[18]

The view that "idle hands are the devil's workshop" has received more sophisticated treatment in recent sociological writings on delinquency. David Matza and Gresham M. Sykes, for example, suggest that delinquents have the values of a leisure class, the same values ascribed by Veblen to *the* leisure class: a search for kicks, disdain of work, a desire for the big score, and acceptance of aggressive toughness as proof of masculinity.[19] Matza and Sykes explain delinquency by reference to this system of values, but they note that adolescents at all class levels are "to some extent" members of a leisure class, that they "move in a limbo between earlier parental domination and future integration with the social structure through the bonds of work and marriage."[20] In the end, then, the leisure of the adolescent produces a set of values, which, in turn, leads to delinquency.

Belief

Unlike the cultural deviance theory, the control theory assumes the existence of a common value system within the society or group whose norms are being violated. If the deviant is committed to a value system different from that of conventional society, there is, within the context of the theory, nothing to explain. The question is, "Why does a man violate the rules in which he believes?" It is not, "Why do men differ in their beliefs about what constitutes good and desirable conduct?" The person is assumed to have been socialized (perhaps imperfectly) into the group whose rules he is violating; deviance is not a question of one group imposing its rules on the members of another group. In other words, we not only assume the deviant *has* believed the rules, we assume he believes the rules even as he violates them.

How can a person believe it is wrong to steal at the same time he is stealing? In the strain theory, this is not a difficult problem. (In fact,

... the strain theory was devised specifically to deal with this question.) The motivation to deviance adduced by the strain theorist is so strong that we can well understand the deviant act even assuming the deviator believes strongly that it is wrong.[21] However, given the control theory's assumptions about motivation, if both the deviant and the nondeviant believe the deviant act is wrong, how do we account for the fact that one commits it and the other does not?

Control theories have taken two approaches to this problem. In one approach, beliefs are treated as mere words that mean little or nothing if the other forms of control are missing. "Semantic dementia," the dissociation between rational faculties and emotional control which is said to be characteristic of the psychopath, illustrates this way of handling the problem.[22] In short, beliefs, at least insofar as they are expressed in words, drop out of the picture; since they do not differentiate between deviants and nondeviants, they are in the same class as "language" or any other characteristic common to all members of the group. Since they represent no real obstacle to the commission of delinquent acts, nothing need be said about how they are handled by those committing such acts. The control theories that do not mention beliefs (or values), and many do not, may be assumed to take this approach to the problem.

The second approach argues that the deviant rationalizes his behavior so that he can at once violate the rule and maintain his belief in it. Donald R. Cressey had advanced this argument with respect to embezzlement,[23] and Sykes and Matza have advanced it with respect to delinquency.[24] In both Cressey's and Sykes and Matza's treatments, these rationalizations (Cressey calls them "verbalizations," Sykes and Matza term them "techniques of neutralization") occur prior to the commission of the deviant act. If the neutralization is successful, the person is free to commit the act(s) in question. Both in Cressey and in Sykes and Matza, the strain that prompts the effort at neutralization also provides the motive force that results in the subsequent deviant act. Their theories are thus, in this sense, strain theories. Neutralization is difficult to handle within the context of a theory that adheres closely to control theory assumptions, because in the control theory there is no special motivational force to account for the neutralization. This difficulty is especially noticeable in Matza's later treatment of this topic, where the motivational component, the "will to delinquency," appears *after* the moral vacuum has been created by the techniques of neutralization.[25] The question thus becomes: Why neutralize?

In attempting to solve a strain-theory problem with control-theory tools, the control theorist is thus led into a trap. He cannot answer the crucial question. The concept of neutralization assumes the existence of moral obstacles to the commission of deviant acts. In order plausibly to account for a deviant act, it is necessary to generate motivation to deviance that is at least equivalent in force to the resistance provided by these moral obstacles. However, if the moral obstacles are removed, neutralization and special motivation are no longer required. We therefore follow the implicit logic of control theory and remove these moral obstacles by hypothesis. Many persons do not have an attitude of respect toward the rules of society; many persons feel no moral obligation to conform regardless of personal advantage. Insofar as the values and beliefs of these persons are consistent with their feelings, and there should be a tendency toward consistency, neutralization is unnecessary; it has already occurred.

Does this merely push the question back a step and at the same time produce conflict with the assumption of a common value system? I think not. In the first place, we do not assume, as does Cressey, that neutralization occurs in order to make a specific criminal act possible.[26] We do not assume, as do Sykes and Matza, that neutralization occurs to make many delinquent acts possible. We do not assume, in other words, that the person constructs a system of rationalizations in order to justify commission of acts he *wants* to commit. We assume, in contrast, that the beliefs that free a man to commit deviant acts are *unmotivated* in the sense that he does not construct or adopt them in order to facilitate the attainment of illicit ends. In the second place, we do not assume, as does Matza, that "delinquents concur in the con-

ventional assessment of delinquency."[27] We assume, in contrast, that there is *variation* in the extent to which people believe they should obey the rules of society, and, furthermore, that the less a person believes he should obey the rules, the more likely he is to violate them.[28]

In chronological order, then, a person's beliefs in the moral validity or norms are, for no teleological reason, weakened. The probability that he will commit delinquent acts is therefore increased. When and if he commits a delinquent act, we may justifiably use the weakness of his beliefs in explaining it, but no special motivation is required to explain either the weakness of his beliefs or, perhaps, his delinquent act.

The keystone of this argument is of course the assumption that there is variation in belief in the moral validity of social rules. This assumption is amenable to direct empirical test and can thus survive at least until its first confrontation with data. For the present, we must return to the idea of a common value system with which this section was begun.

The idea of a common (or perhaps better, a single) value system is consistent with the fact, or presumption, of variation in the strength of moral beliefs. We have not suggested that delinquency is based on beliefs counter to conventional morality; we have not suggested that delinquents do not believe delinquent acts are wrong. They may well believe these acts are wrong, but the meaning and efficacy of such beliefs are contingent on other beliefs and, indeed, on the strength of other ties to the conventional order.[29]

NOTES

1. Books have been written on the increasing importance of interpersonal sensitivity in modern life. According to this view, controls from within have become less important than controls from without in *producing* conformity. Whether or not this observation is true as a description of historical trends, it is true that interpersonal sensitivity has become more important in *explaining* conformity. Although logically it should also have become more important in explaining nonconformity, the opposite has been the case, once again showing that Cohen's observation that an explanation of conformity should be an explanation of deviance cannot be translated as "an expla-

nation of conformity has to be an explanation of deviance." For the view that interpersonal sensitivity currently plays a greater role than formerly in producing conformity, see William J. Goode, "Norm Commitment and Conformity to Role-Status Obligations," *American Journal of Sociology*, LXVI (1960), 246–258. And, of course, also see David Riesman, Nathan Glazer, and Rouel Denney, *The Lonely Crowd* (Garden City, New York: Doubleday, 1950), especially Part I.

2. The literature on psychopathy is voluminous. See William and Joan McCord, *The Psychopath* (Princeton: D. Van Nostrand, 1964).

3. John M. Martin and Joseph P. Fitzpatrick, *Delinquent Behavior* (New York: Random House, 1964), p. 130.

4. *Ibid.* For additional properties of the psychopath, see McCord and McCord, *The Psychopath*, pp. 1–22.

5. Barbara Wootton, *Social Science and Social Pathology* (New York: Macmillan, 1959), p. 250.

6. "The logical untenability [of the position that there are forces in man 'resistant to socialization'] was ably demonstrated by Parsons over 30 years ago, and it is widely recognized that the position is empirically unsound because it assumes [!] some universal biological drive system distinctly separate from socialization and social context—a basic and intransigent human nature" (Judith Blake and Kingsley Davis, "Norms, Values, and Sanctions," *Handbook of Modern Sociology*, ed. Robert E. L. Faris [Chicago: Rand McNally, 1964], p. 471).

7. Emile Durkheim, *Moral Education*, trans. Everett K. Wilson and Herman Schnurer (New York: The Free Press, 1961), p. 64.

8. Although attachment alone does not exhaust the meaning of internalization, attachments and beliefs combined would appear to leave only a small residue of "internal control" not susceptible in principle to direct measurement.

9. F. Ivan Nye, *Family Relationships and Delinquent Behavior* (New York: Wiley, 1958), pp. 5–7.

10. Albert J. Reiss, Jr., "Delinquency as the Failure of Personal and Social Controls," *American Sociological Review*, XVI (1951), 196–207. For example, "Our observations show . . . that delinquent recidivists are less often persons with mature ego ideals or nondelinquent social roles" (p. 204).

11. Scott Briar and Irving Piliavin, "Delinquency, Situational Inducements, and Commitment to Conformity," *Social Problems*, XIII (1965), 41–42. The concept "stake in conformity" was introduced by Jackson Toby in his "Social Disorganization and Stake in Conformity: Complementary Factors in the Predatory Behavior of Hoodlums," *Journal of Criminal Law, Criminology and Police Science*, XLVIII (1957), 12–17. See also his "Hoodlum or Business Man: An American Dilemma," *The Jews*, ed. Marshall Sklare (New York: The Free Press, 1958), pp. 542–550. Throughout the text, I occasionally use "stake in conformity" in speaking in general of the strength of the bond to conventional society. So used, the concept is somewhat

broader than is true for either Toby or Briar and Piliavin, where the concept is roughly equivalent to what is here called "commitment."

12. Thomas Hobbes. *Leviathan* (Oxford: Basil Blackwell, 1957), p. 195.

13. Howard S. Becker, "Notes on the Concept of Commitment," *American Journal of Sociology*, LXVI (1960), 35–36.

14. Arthur L. Stinchcombe, *Rebellion in a High School* (Chicago: Quadrangle, 1964), p. 5.

15. Richard A. Cloward and Lloyd E. Ohlin, *Delinquency and Opportunity* (New York: The Free Press, 1960), p. 147, quoting Edwin H. Sutherland, ed., *The Professional Thief* (Chicago: University of Chicago Press, 1937), pp. 211–213.

16. William James, *Psychology* (Cleveland: World Publishing Co., 1948), p. 186.

17. Few activities appear to be so engrossing that they rule out contemplation of alternative lines of behavior, at least if estimates of the amount of time men spend plotting sexual deviations have any validity.

18. *The Sutherland Papers*, ed. Albert K. Cohen et al. (Bloomington: Indiana University Press, 1956), p. 37.

19. David Matza and Gresham M. Sykes, "Juvenile Delinquency and Subterranean Values," *American Sociological Review*, XXVI (1961), 712–719.

20. *Ibid.*, p. 718.

21. The starving man stealing the loaf of bread is the image evoked by most strain theories. In this image, the starving man's belief in the wrongness of his act is clearly not something that must be explained away. It can be assumed to be present without causing embarrassment to the explanation.

22. McCord and McCord, *The Psychopath*, pp. 12–15.

23. Donald R. Cressey, *Other People's Money* (New York: The Free Press, 1953).

24. Gresham M. Sykes and David Matza, "Techniques of Neutralization: A Theory of Delinquency," *American Sociological Review*, XXII (1957), 664–670.

25. David Matza, *Delinquency and Drift* (New York: Wiley, 1964), pp. 181–191.

26. In asserting that Cressey's assumption is invalid with respect to delinquency, I do not wish to suggest that it is invalid for the question of embezzlement, where the problem faced by the deviator is fairly specific and he can reasonably be assumed to be an upstanding citizen. (Although even here the fact that the embezzler's nonsharable financial problem often results from some sort of hanky-panky suggests that "verbalizations" may be less necessary than might otherwise be assumed.)

27. *Delinquency and Drift*, p. 43.

28. This assumption is not, I think, contradicted by the evidence presented by Matza against the existence of a delinquent subculture. In comparing the attitudes and actions of delinquents with the picture painted by delinquent subculture theorists, Matza emphasizes— and perhaps exaggerates—the extent to which delin-

quents are tied to the conventional order. In implicitly comparing delinquents with a supermoral man, I emphasize—and perhaps exaggerate—the extent to which they are not tied to the conventional order.

29. The position taken here is therefore somewhere between the "semantic dementia" and the "neutralization" positions. Assuming variation, the delinquent is, at the extremes, freer than the neutralization argument assumes. Although the possibility of wide discrepancy between what the delinquent professes and what he practices still exists, it is presumably much rarer than is suggested by studies of articulate "psychopaths."

QUESTIONS FOR DISCUSSION

1. List the major components of *control theory*. Discuss how these elements of the social bond explain delinquency or deviance.

2. Why is Hirschi critical of explanations of delinquency that focus on psychopathology and sociocultural definitions? Provide specific examples of Hirschi's criticisms.

3. According to Hirschi, whether or not a person commits delinquent acts is dependent on the relative strength or weakness of that person's ties to the conventional order. What is the "conventional order"? In a culturally diverse society, are there any problems with the definition of *conventional order*?

APPLICATIONS

1. Make a list of the people to whom you have a social bond. Why are you attached and committed to these people? Does this social bond affect the way you think and behave? Why?

2. Let us assume you are an expert in counseling delinquent youth. How might you use the concepts of control theory to augment behavioral changes?

KEY TERMS

conscience a sense of one's own blameworthiness with regard to conduct, intents, or character; produces a feeling of obligation to do right or be good. Also, that part of the superego which transmits commands and admonitions to the ego.

ego one of three divisions of the psyche (the others are the id and the superego), which serves as the conscious mediator between individual perception and social reality, according to psychoanalytic theory.

internalization the conscious or subconscious incorporation of particular values or patterns of culture as future guiding principles for thought and action.

neutralization refers to rationalizing delinquent behavior; A set of defense mechanisms that releases a youth from the constraints of moral norms (refer to the next article for an in-depth explanation of neutralization techniques).

superego one of three divisions of the psyche (the others are the id and the ego), which represents the internalization of parental conscience and the rules of society, according to psychoanalytic theory; functions to reward and punish through a system of moral attitudes.

syndrome a group of symptoms that occur together and characterize a particular abnormality; in psychology and the medical field the word *syndrome* is generally used to label a group of symptoms when the cause or pathology of the abnormality is unknown.

tautology refers to a needless repetition of an idea or statement; circular reasoning where the cause and effect of a phenomenon are interchangeable; we refer to tautologies as "pretzel logic" because of their circularity.

8

Techniques of Neutralization: A Theory of Delinquency

Gresham M. Sykes
David Matza

In attempting to uncover the roots of juvenile delinquency, the social scientist has long since ceased to search for devils in the mind or stigma of the body. It is now largely agreed that delinquent behavior, like most social behavior, is learned and that it is learned in the process of social interaction.

The classic statement of this position is found in Sutherland's theory of differential association, which asserts that criminal or delinquent behavior involves the learning of (a) techniques of committing crimes and (b) motives, drives, rationalizations, and attitudes favorable to the violation of law.[1] Unfortunately, the specific content of what is learned—as opposed to the process by which it is learned—has received relatively little attention in either theory or research. Perhaps the single strongest school of thought on the nature of this content has centered on the idea of a delinquent sub-culture. The basic characteristic of the delinquent sub-culture, it is argued, is a system of values that represents an inversion of the values held by respectable, law-abiding society. The world of the delinquent is the world of the law-abiding turned upside down and its norms constitute a countervailing force directed against the conforming social order. Cohen[2] sees the process of developing a delinquent sub-culture as a matter of building, maintaining, and reinforcing a code for behavior which exists by opposition, which stands in point by point contradiction to dominant values, particularly those of the middle class. Cohen's portrayal of delinquency is executed with a good deal of sophistication, and he carefully avoids overly simple explanations such as those based on the principle of "follow the leader" or easy generalizations about "emotional disturbances." Furthermore, he does not accept the delinquent sub-culture as something given, but instead systematically examines the function of delinquent values as a viable solution to the lower-class, male child's problems in the area of social status. Yet in spite of its virtues, this image of juvenile delinquency as a form of behavior based on competing or countervailing values and norms appears to suffer from a number of serious defects. It is the nature of these defects and a possible alternative or modified explanation for a large portion of juvenile delinquency with which this paper is concerned.

The difficulties in viewing delinquent behavior as springing from a set of deviant values and norms—as arising, that is to say, from a situation in which the delinquent defines his delinquency as "right"—are both empirical and

"Techniques of Neutralization: A Theory of Delinquency," *American Sociological Review*, 22 (December, 1957), pp. 664–670.

theoretical. In the first place, if there existed in fact a delinquent sub-culture such that the delinquent viewed his illegal behavior as morally correct, we could reasonably suppose that he would exhibit no feelings of guilt or shame at detection or confinement. Instead, the major reaction would tend in the direction of indignation or a sense of martyrdom.[3] It is true that some delinquents do react in the latter fashion, although the sense of martyrdom often seems to be based on the fact that others "get away with it" and indignation appears to be directed against the chance events or lack of skill that led to apprehension. More important, however, is the fact that there is a good deal of evidence suggesting that many delinquents *do* experience a sense of guilt or shame, and its outward expression is not to be dismissed as a purely manipulative gesture to appease those in authority. Much of this evidence is, to be sure, of a clinical nature or in the form of impressionistic judgments of those who must deal first hand with the youthful offender. Assigning a weight to such evidence calls for caution but it cannot be ignored if we are to avoid the gross stereotype of the juvenile delinquent as a hardened gangster in miniature.

In the second place, observers have noted that the juvenile delinquent frequently accords admiration and respect to law-abiding persons. The "really honest" person is often revered, and if the delinquent is sometimes overly keen to detect hypocrisy in those who conform, unquestioned probity is likely to win his approval. A fierce attachment to a humble, pious mother or a forgiving, upright priest (the former, according to many observers, is often encountered in both juvenile delinquents and adult criminals) might be dismissed as rank sentimentality, but at least it is clear that the delinquent does not necessarily regard those who abide by the legal rules as immoral. In a similar vein, it can be noted that the juvenile delinquent may exhibit great resentment if illegal behavior is imputed to "significant others" in his immediate social environment or to heroes in the world of sport and entertainment. In other words, if the delinquent does hold to a set of values and norms that stand in complete opposition to those of respectable society, his norm-holding is of a peculiar sort. While supposedly thoroughly committed to the deviant system of the delinquent sub-culture, he would appear to recognize the moral validity of the dominant normative system in many instances.[4]

In the third place, there is much evidence that juvenile delinquents often draw a sharp line between those who can be victimized and those who cannot. Certain social groups are not to be viewed as "fair game" in the performance of supposedly approved delinquent acts while others warrant a variety of attacks. In general, the potentiality for victimization would seem to be a function of the social distance between the juvenile delinquent and others and thus we find implicit maxims in the world of the delinquent such as "don't steal from friends" or "don't commit vandalism against a church of your own faith."[5] This is all rather obvious, but the implications have not received sufficient attention. The fact that supposedly valued behavior tends to be directed against disvalued social groups hints that the "wrongfulness" of such delinquent behavior is more widely recognized by delinquents than the literature has indicated. When the pool of victims is limited by considerations of kinship, friendship, ethnic group, social class, age, sex, etc., we have reason to suspect that the virtue of delinquency is far from unquestioned.

In the fourth place, it is doubtful if many juvenile delinquents are totally immune from the demands for conformity made by the dominant social order. There is a strong likelihood that the family of the delinquent will agree with respectable society that delinquency is wrong, even though the family may be engaged in a variety of illegal activities. That is, the parental posture conducive to delinquency is not apt to be a positive prodding. Whatever may be the influence of parental example, what might be called the "Fagin" pattern of socialization into delinquency is probably rare. Furthermore, as Redl has indicated, the idea that certain neighborhoods are completely delinquent, offering the child a model for delinquent behavior without reservations, is simply not supported by the data.[6]

The fact that a child is punished by parents, school officials, and agencies of the legal system for his delinquency may, as a number of observers have cynically noted, suggest to the child that he should be more careful not to get caught. There is an equal or greater probability, however, that the child will internalize the demands for conformity. This is not to say that demands for conformity cannot be counteracted. In fact, as we shall see shortly, an understanding of how internal and external demands for conformity are neutralized may be crucial for understanding delinquent behavior. But it is to say that a complete denial of the validity of demands for conformity and the substitution of a new normative system is improbable, in light of the child's or adolescent's dependency on adults and encirclement by adults inherent in his status in the social structure. No matter how deeply enmeshed in patterns of delinquency he may be and no matter how much this involvement may outweigh his associations with the law-abiding, he cannot escape the condemnation of his deviance. Somehow the demands for conformity must be met and answered; they cannot be ignored as part of an alien system of values and norms.

In short, the theoretical viewpoint that sees juvenile delinquency as a form of behavior based on the values and norms of a deviant subculture in precisely the same way as law-abiding behavior is based on the values and norms of the larger society is open to serious doubt. The fact that the world of the delinquent is embedded in the larger world of those who conform cannot be overlooked nor can the delinquent be equated with an adult thoroughly socialized into an alternative way of life. Instead, the juvenile delinquent would appear to be at least partially committed to the dominant social order in that he frequently exhibits guilt or shame when he violates its proscriptions, accords approval to certain conforming figures, and distinguishes between appropriate and inappropriate targets for his deviance. It is to an explanation for the apparently paradoxical fact of his delinquency that we now turn.

As Morris Cohen once said, one of the most fascinating problems about human behavior is why men violate the laws in which they believe. This is the problem that confronts us when we attempt to explain why delinquency occurs despite a greater or lesser commitment to the usages of conformity. A basic clue is offered by the fact that social rules or norms calling for valued behavior seldom if ever take the form of categorical imperatives. Rather, values or norms appear as *qualified* guides for action, limited in their applicability in terms of time, place, persons, and social circumstances. The moral injunction against killing, for example, does not apply to the enemy during combat in time of war, although a captured enemy comes once again under the prohibition. Similarly, the taking and distributing of scarce goods in a time of acute social need is felt by many to be right, although under other circumstances private property is held inviolable. The normative system of a society, then, is marked by what Williams has termed *flexibility*; it does not consist of a body of rules held to be binding under all conditions.[7]

This flexibility is, in fact, an integral part of the criminal law in that measures for "defenses to crimes" are provided in pleas such as nonage, necessity, insanity, drunkenness, compulsion, self-defense, and so on. The individual can avoid moral culpability for his criminal action—and thus avoid the negative sanctions of society—if he can prove that criminal intent was lacking. *It is our argument that much delinquency is based on what is essentially an unrecognized extension of defenses to crimes, in the form of justifications for deviance that are seen as valid by the delinquent but not by the legal system or society at large.*

These justifications are commonly described as rationalizations. They are viewed as following deviant behavior and as protecting the individual from self-blame and the blame of others after the act. But there is also reason to believe that they precede deviant behavior and make deviant behavior possible. It is this possibility that Sutherland mentioned only in passing and that other writers have failed to exploit from the viewpoint of sociological theory. Disapproval flowing from internalized norms and conforming others in the social environment is neutralized, turned back, or deflected in advance. Social controls that serve to check or inhibit deviant motivational patterns are rendered inoperative, and the individual is freed to engage in delinquency without serious damage to his self image. In this sense, the delinquent both has his cake and eats it too, for he remains committed to the dominant normative system and yet so qualifies its imperatives that violations are "acceptable" if not "right." Thus the delinquent represents not a radical opposition to law-abiding society but something more like an apologetic failure, often more sinned against than sinning in his own eyes. We call these justifications of deviant behavior techniques of neutralization; and we believe these techniques make up a crucial component of Sutherland's "definitions favorable to the violation of law." It is by learning these techniques that the juvenile becomes delinquent, rather than by learning moral imperatives, values or attitudes standing in direct contradiction to those of the dominant society. In analyzing these techniques, we have found it convenient to divide them into five major types.

The Denial of Responsibility. In so far as the delinquent can define himself as lacking responsibility for his deviant actions, the disapproval of self or others is sharply reduced in effectiveness as a restraining influence. As Justice Holmes has said, even a dog distinguishes between being stumbled over and being kicked, and modern society is no less careful to draw a line between injuries that are unintentional, i.e., where responsibility is lacking, and those that are intentional. As a technique of neutralization, however, the denial of responsibility extends much further than the claim that deviant acts are an "accident" or some similar negation of personal accountability. It may also be asserted that delinquent acts are due to forces outside of the individual and beyond his control such as unloving parents, bad companions, or a slum neighborhood. In effect, the delinquent approaches a "billiard ball" conception of himself in which he sees himself as helplessly propelled into new situations. From a psychodynamic viewpoint, this orientation toward one's own actions may represent a profound alienation from self, but it is important to stress the fact that interpretations of responsibility are cultural constructs and not merely idiosyncratic beliefs. The similarity between this mode of justifying illegal behavior assumed by the delinquent and the implications of a "soci-

ological" frame of reference or a "humane" jurisprudence is readily apparent.[8] It is not the validity of this orientation that concerns us here, but its function of deflecting blame attached to violations of social norms and its relative independence of a particular personality structure.[9] By learning to view himself as more acted upon than acting, the delinquent prepares the way for deviance from the dominant normative system without the necessity of a frontal assault on the norms themselves.

The Denial of Injury. A second major technique of neutralization centers on the injury or harm involved in the delinquent act. The criminal law has long made a distinction between crimes which are *mala in se* and *mala prohibita*—that is between acts that are wrong in themselves and acts that are illegal but not immoral—and the delinquent can make the same kind of distinction in evaluating the wrongfulness of his behavior. For the delinquent, however, wrongfulness may turn on the question of whether or not anyone has clearly been hurt by his deviance, and this matter is open to a variety of interpretations. Vandalism, for example, may be defined by the delinquent simply as "mischief"—after all, it may be claimed, the persons whose property has been destroyed can well afford it. Similarly, auto theft may be viewed as "borrowing," and gang fighting may be seen as a private quarrel, an agreed upon duel between two willing parties, and thus of no concern to the community at large. We are not suggesting that this technique of neutralization, labelled the denial of injury, involves an explicit dialectic. Rather, we are arguing that the delinquent frequently, and in a hazy fashion, feels that his behavior does not really cause any great harm despite the fact that it runs counter to law. Just as the link between the individual and his acts may be broken by the denial of responsibility, so may the link between acts and their consequences be broken by the denial of injury. Since society sometimes agrees with the delinquent, e.g., in matters such as truancy, "pranks," and so on, it merely reaffirms the idea that the delinquent's neutralization of social controls by means of qualifying the norms is an extension of common practice rather than a gesture of complete opposition.

The Denial of the Victim. Even if the delinquent accepts the responsibility for his deviant actions and is willing to admit that his deviant actions involve an injury or hurt, the moral indignation of self and others may be neutralized by an insistence that the injury is not wrong in light of the circumstances. The injury, it may be claimed, is not really an injury; rather, it is a form of rightful retaliation or punishment. By a subtle alchemy the delinquent moves himself into the position of an avenger and the victim is transformed into a wrong-doer. Assaults on homosexuals or suspected homosexuals, attacks on members of minority groups who are said to have gotten "out of place," vandalism as revenge on an unfair teacher or school official, thefts from a "crooked" store owner—all may be hurts inflicted on a transgressor, in the eyes of the delinquent. As Orwell has pointed out, the type of criminal admired by the general public has probably changed over the course of years and Raffles no longer serves as a hero;[10] but Robin Hood, and his latter day derivatives such as the tough detective seeking justice outside the law, still capture the popular imagination, and the delinquent may view his acts as part of a similar role.

To deny the existence of the victim, then, by transforming him into a person deserving injury is an extreme form of a phenomenon we have mentioned before, namely, the delinquent's recognition of appropriate and inappropriate targets for his delinquent acts. In addition, however, the existence of the victim may be denied for the delinquent, in a somewhat different sense, by the circumstances of the delinquent act itself. Insofar as the victim is physically absent, unknown, or a vague abstraction (as is often the case in delinquent acts committed against property), the awareness of the victim's existence is weakened. Internalized norms and anticipations of the reactions of others must somehow be activated, if they are to serve as guides for behavior; and it is possible that a diminished awareness of the victim plays an important part in determining whether or not this process is set in motion.

The Condemnation of the Condemners. A fourth technique of neutralization would appear to involve a condemnation of the condemners or,

as McCorkle and Korn have phrased it, a rejection of the rejectors.[11] The delinquent shifts the focus of attention from his own deviant acts to the motives and behavior of those who disapprove of his violations. His condemners, he may claim, are hypocrites, deviants in disguise, or impelled by personal spite. This orientation toward the conforming world may be of particular importance when it hardens into a bitter cynicism directed against those assigned the task of enforcing or expressing the norms of dominant society. Police, it may be said, are corrupt, stupid, and brutal. Teachers always show favoritism and parents always "take it out" on their children. By a slight extension, the rewards of conformity—such as material success—become a matter of pull or luck, thus decreasing still further the stature of those who stand on the side of the law-abiding. The validity of this jaundiced viewpoint is not so important as its function in turning back or deflecting the negative sanctions attached to violations of the norms. The delinquent, in effect, has changed the subject of the conversation in the dialogue between his own deviant impulses and the reactions of others; and by attacking others, the wrongfulness of his own behavior is more easily repressed or lost to view.

The Appeal to Higher Loyalties. Fifth, and last, internal and external social controls may be neutralized by sacrificing the demands of the larger society for the demands of the smaller social groups to which the delinquent belongs such as the sibling pair, the gang, or the friendship clique. It is important to note that the delinquent does not necessarily repudiate the imperatives of the dominant normative system, despite his failure to follow them. Rather, the delinquent may see himself as caught up in a dilemma that must be resolved, unfortunately, at the cost of violating the law. One aspect of this situation has been studied by Stouffer and Toby in their research on the conflict between particularistic and universalistic demands, between the claims of friendship and general social obligations, and their results suggest that "it is possible to classify people according to a predisposition to select one or the other horn of a dilemma in role conflict."[12] For our purposes, however, the most important point is that deviation from certain norms may occur not because the norms are rejected but because other norms, held to be more pressing or involving a higher loyalty, are accorded precedence. Indeed, it is the fact that both sets of norms are believed in that gives meaning to our concepts of dilemma and role conflict.

The conflict between the claims of friendship and the claims of law, or a similar dilemma, has of course long been recognized by the social scientist (and the novelist) as a common human problem. If the juvenile delinquent frequently resolves his dilemma by insisting that he must "always help a buddy" or "never squeal on a friend," even when it throws him into serious difficulties with the dominant social order, his choice remains familiar to the supposedly law-abiding. The delinquent is unusual, perhaps, in the extent to which he is able to see the fact that he acts in behalf of the smaller social groups to which he belongs as a justification for violations of society's norms, but it is a matter of degree rather than of kind.

"I didn't mean it." "I didn't really hurt anybody." "They had it coming to them." "Everybody's picking on me." "I didn't do it for myself." These slogans or their variants, we hypothesize, prepare the juvenile for delinquent acts. These "definitions of the situation" represent tangential or glancing blows at the dominant normative system rather than the creation of an opposing ideology; and they are extensions of patterns of thought prevalent in society rather than something created *de novo*.

Techniques of neutralization may not be powerful enough to fully shield the individual from the force of his own internalized values and the reactions of conforming others, for as we have pointed out, juvenile delinquents often appear to suffer from feelings of guilt and shame when called into account for their deviant behavior. And some delinquents may be so isolated from the world of conformity that techniques of neutralization need not be called into play. Nonetheless, we would argue that techniques of neutralization are critical in lessening the effectiveness of social controls and that they lie behind a large share of delinquent behavior. Empirical research in this area is scattered and fragmentary at the present time, but the work of Redl,[13] Cressy,[14] and oth-

ers has supplied a body of significant data that has done much to clarify the theoretical issues and enlarge the fund of supporting evidence. Two lines of investigation seem to be critical at this stage. First, then is need for more knowledge concerning the differential distribution of techniques of neutralization, as operative patterns of thought, by age, sex, social class, ethnic group, etc. On *a priori* grounds it might be assumed that these justifications for deviance will be more readily seized by segments of society for whom a discrepancy between common social ideals and social practice is most apparent. It is also possible however, that the habit of "bending" the dominant normative system— if not "breaking" it—cuts across our cruder social categories and is to be traced primarily to patterns of social interaction within the familial circle. Second, there is need for a greater understanding of the internal structure of techniques of neutralization, as a system of beliefs and attitudes, and its relationship to various types of delinquent behavior. Certain techniques of neutralization would appear to be better adapted to particular deviant acts than to others, as we have suggested, for example, in the case of offenses against property and the denial of the victim. But the issue remains far from clear and stands in need of more information.

In any case, techniques of neutralization appear to offer a promising line of research in enlarging and systematizing the theoretical grasp of juvenile delinquency. As more information is uncovered concerning techniques of neutralization, their origins, and their consequences, both juvenile delinquency in particular, and deviation from normative systems in general may be illuminated.

NOTES

1. E. H. Sutherland, *Principles of Criminology*, revised by D. R. Cressey, Chicago: Lippincott, 1955, pp. 77–80.

2. Albert K. Cohen, *Delinquent Boys*, Glencoe, Ill.: The Free Press, 1955.

3. This form of reaction among the adherents of a deviant subculture who fully believe in the "rightfulness" of their behavior and who are captured and punished by the agencies of the dominant social order can be illustrated, perhaps, by groups such as Jehovah's Witnesses, early Christian sects, nationalist move-

ments in colonial areas, and conscientious objectors, during World War I and II.

4. As Weber has pointed out, a thief may recognize the legitimacy of legal rules without accepting their moral validity. Cf. Max Weber, *The Theory of Social and Economic Organization* (translated by A. M. Henderson and Talcott Parsons), New York: Oxford University Press, 1947, p. 125. We are arguing here, however, that the juvenile delinquent frequently recognizes *both* the legitimacy of the dominant social order and its moral "rightness."

5. Thrasher's account of the "Itschkies"—a juvenile gang composed of Jewish boys—and the immunity from "rolling" enjoyed by Jewish drunkards is a good illustration. Cf. F. Thrasher, *The Gang,* Chicago: The University of Chicago Press, 1947, p. 315.

6. Cf. Solomon Kobrin, "The Conflict of Values in Delinquency Areas," *American Sociological Review,* 16, (October, 1951), pp. 653 – 661.

7. Cf. Robin Williams, Jr., *American Society,* New York: Knopf, 1951, p. 28.

8. A number of observers have wryly noted that many delinquents seem to show a surprising awareness of sociological and psychological explanations for their behavior and are quick to point out the causal role of their poor environment.

9. It is possible, of course, that certain personality structures can accept some techniques of neutralization more readily than others, but this question remains largely unexplored.

10. George Orwell, *Dickens, Dali, and Others,* New York: Reynal, 1946.

11. Lloyd W. McCorkle and Richard Korn, "Resocialization Within Walls," The Annals of the American Academy of Political and Social Science, 293, (May, 1954), pp. 88–98.

12. See Samuel A. Stouffer and Jackson Toby, "Role Conflict and Personality," in *Toward a General Theory of Action,* edited by Talcott Parsons and Edward A. Shils, Cambridge: Harvard University Press, 1951, p. 494.

13. See Fritz Redl and David Wineman, *Children Who Hate,* Glencoe: The Free Press, 1956.

14. See D.R. Cressey, *Other People's Money,* Glencoe: The Free Press, 1953.

QUESTIONS FOR DISCUSSION

1. List and explain the four reasons why the authors do not believe that delinquent behavior arises "from a situation in which the delinquent defines his delinquency as 'right'."

2. What are the five major techniques of neutralization? In your own words, discuss each of them.

3. The authors suggest there are two pressing areas of research that need to be conducted to improve the understanding of neutralization techniques. What are they?

APPLICATIONS

1. Consider the five major techniques of neutralization. Which of these rationalizations have you used to justify your behavior? Do you think these rationalizations are used by all people at one time or another? Do these rationalizations help distinguish the delinquent from the nondelinquent? Why?

2. Think about a young person spray painting his or her name on a bridge or on the face of a building. Upon being apprehended, the police ask the youth why he or she spray painted the building. The youth replies, "Because it was fun!" How would a rationalization like this be explained by the theory of neutralization?

KEY TERMS

a priori refers to a condition or event that previously existed or occurred.

alchemy a power or process of transforming something common into something special.

countervailing refers to compensating or counteracting; offering an opposing opinion.

cynical being contemptuously distrustful of human nature or motives; disbelief in sincerity or integrity.

de novo refers to something new; creating anew.

imperatives actions or ideas that must not be avoided; necessary or obligatory.

indignation anger aroused by something unjust, mean, or that is perceived to be unfair.

jurisprudence the science or philosophy of law.

mala in se behaviors, based on natural law, that are considered wrong in and of themselves; generally includes murder, rape, theft, arson, and other violent crimes.

mala prohibita criminal behaviors that are considered wrong only because they are prohibited by law.

martyrdom suffering or death that occurs because of adherence to a principle, a cause, or a belief.

paradoxical characteristic of something that is seemingly contradictory or opposed to common sense and yet is perhaps true.

significant others those other people who are most important for an individual in determining his or her behavior.

stigma a mark of shame or discredit; an outcast by prevailing social standards.

9

Social Change
and Crime Rate Trends:
A Routine Activity Approach*

Lawrence E. Cohen
Marcus Felson
University of Illinois, Urbana

In this paper we present a "routine activity approach" for analyzing crime rate trends and cycles. Rather than emphasizing the characteristics of offenders, with this approach we concentrate upon the circumstances in which they carry out predatory criminal acts. Most criminal acts require convergence in space and time of likely offenders, suitable targets *and the* absence of capable guardians *against crime. Human ecological theory facilitates an investigation into the way in which social structure produces this convergence, hence allowing illegal activities to feed upon the legal activities of everyday life. In particular, we hypothesize that the dispersion of activities away from households and families increases the opportunity for crime and thus generates higher crime rates. A variety of data is presented in support of the hypothesis, which helps explain crime rate trends in the United States 1947–1974 as a byproduct of changes in such variables as labor force participation and single-adult households.*

INTRODUCTION

In its summary report the National Commission on the Causes and Prevention of Violence (1969: xxxvii) presents an important sociological paradox:

American Sociological Review 1979, Vol. 44 (August):588–608.
Copyright © 1979 by the American Sociological Association. Reprinted by Permission.

Why, we must ask, have urban violent crime rates increased substantially during the past decade when the conditions that are supposed to cause violent crime have not worsened—have, indeed, generally improved?

The Bureau of the Census, in its latest report on trends in social and economic conditions in metropolitan areas, states that most "indicators of well-being point toward progress in the cities since 1960." Thus, for example, the proportion of blacks in cities who completed high school rose from 43 percent in 1960 to 61 percent in 1968; unemployment rates dropped significantly between 1959 and 1967 and the median family income of blacks in cities increased from 61 percent to 68 percent of the median white family income during the same period. Also during the same period the number of persons living below the legally-defined poverty level in cities declined from 11.3 million to 8.3 million.

Despite the general continuation of these trends in social and economic conditions in the United States, the *Uniform Crime Report* (FBI, 1975:49) indicates that between 1960 and 1975 reported rates of robbery, aggravated assault, forcible rape and homicide increased by 263%, 164%, 174%, and 188%, respectively. Similar property crime rate increases reported during this same period[1] (e.g., 200% for burglary rate) suggest that the paradox noted by the Violence Commission applies to nonviolent offenses as well.

In the present paper we consider these paradoxical trends in crime rates in terms of changes in the "routine activities" of everyday life. We believe the structure of such activities influences criminal opportunity and therefore affects trends in a class of crimes we refer to as *direct-contact predatory violations*. Predatory violations are defined here as illegal acts in which "someone definitely and intentionally takes or damages the person or property of another" (Glaser, 1971:4). Further, this analysis is confined to those predatory violations involving direct physical contact between at least one offender and at least one person or object which that offender attempts to take or damage.

We argue that structural changes in routine activity patterns can influence crime rates by affecting the convergence in space and time of the three minimal elements of direct-contact predatory violations: (1) motivated offenders, (2) suitable targets, and (3) the absence of capable guardians against a violation. We further argue that the lack of any one of these elements is sufficient to prevent the successful completion of a direct-contact predatory crime, and that the convergence in time and space of suitable targets and the absence of capable guardians may even lead to large increases in crime rates without necessarily requiring any increase in the structural conditions that motivate individuals to engage in crime. That is, if the proportion of motivated offenders or even suitable targets were to remain stable in a community, changes in routine activities could nonetheless alter the likelihood of their convergence in space and time, thereby creating more opportunities for crimes to occur. Control therefore becomes critical. If controls through routine activities were to decrease, illegal predatory activities could then be likely to increase. In the process of developing this explanation and evaluating its consistency with existing data, we relate our approach to classical human ecological concepts and to several earlier studies.

The Structure of Criminal Activity

Sociological knowledge of how community structure generates illegal acts has made little progress since Shaw and McKay and their colleagues (1929) published their pathbreaking work, *Delinquency Areas*. Variations in crime rates over space long have been recognized (e.g., see Guerry, 1833; Quêtelet, 1842), and current evidence indicates that the pattern of these relationships within metropolitan communities has persisted (Reiss, 1976). Although most spatial research is quite useful for describing crime rate patterns and providing post hoc explanations, these works seldom consider—conceptually or empirically—the fundamental human ecological character of illegal acts as *events* which occur at specific locations in *space* and *time*. involving specific persons and/or objects. These and related concepts can help us to develop an extension of the human ecological analysis to the problem of explaining changes in crime rates over time. Unlike many criminological inquiries, we do not examine why individuals or groups are inclined criminally but rather we take criminal inclination as given and examine the manner in which the spatio-temporal organization of social activities helps people to translate their criminal inclinations into action. Criminal violations are treated here as routine activities which share many attributes of, and are interdependent with, other routine activities. This interdependence between the structure of illegal activities and the organization of everyday sustenance activities leads us to consider certain concepts from human ecological literature.

Selected Concepts from Hawley's Human Ecological Theory

While criminologists traditionally have concentrated on the *spatial* analysis of crime rates within metropolitan communities, they seldom have considered the *temporal* interdependence of these acts. In his classic theory of human ecology, Amos Hawley (1950) treats the community not simply as a unit of territory but rather as an organization of symbiotic and commensalistic relationships as human activities are performed over both space and time.

Hawley identified three important temporal components of community structure: (1) *rhythm*, the regular periodicity with which events occur, as with the rhythm of travel activity; (2) *tempo*, the number of events per unit of time, such as the number of criminal violations per day on a given street; and (3) *timing* the coordination among different activities which are more or less interdependent, such as the coordination of an offender's rhythms with those of a victim (Hawley, 1950:289, the examples are ours). These components of temporal organization, often neglected in criminological research, prove useful in analyzing how illegal tasks are performed—a utility which becomes more apparent after noting the spatio-temporal requirements of illegal activities.

The Minimal Elements of Direct-Contact Predatory Violations

As we previously stated, despite their great diversity, direct-contact predatory violations share some important requirements which facilitate analysis of their structure. Each successfully completed violation minimally requires an *offender* with both criminal inclinations and the ability to carry out those inclinations, a person or object providing a *suitable target* for the offender, and *absence of guardians* capable of preventing violations. We emphasize that the lack of any one of these elements normally is sufficient to prevent such violations from occurring.[2] Though guardianship is implicit in everyday life, it usually is marked by the absence of violations; hence it is easy to overlook. While police action is analyzed widely, guardianship by ordinary citizens of one another and of property as they go about routine activities may be one of the most neglected elements in sociological research on crime, especially since it links seemingly unrelated social roles and relationships to the occurrence or absence of illegal acts.

The conjunction of these minimal elements can be used to assess how social structure may affect the tempo of each type of violation. That is, the probability that a violation will occur at any specific time and place might be taken as a function of the convergence of likely offenders and suitable targets in, the absence of capable guardians. Through consideration of how trends and fluctuations in social conditions affect the frequency of this convergence of criminogenic circumstances, an explanation of temporal trends in crime rates can be constructed.

The Ecological Nature of Illegal Acts

This ecological analysis of direct-contact predatory violations is intended to be more than metaphorical. In the context of such violations, people, gaining and losing sustenance, struggle among themselves for property, safety, territorial hegemony, sexual outlet, physical control, and sometimes for survival itself. The interdependence between offenders and victims can be viewed as a predatory relationship between functionally dissimilar individuals or groups. Since predatory violations fail to yield any net gain in sustenance for the larger community, they can only be sustained by feeding upon other activities. As offenders cooperate to increase their efficiency at predatory violations and as potential victims organize their resistance to these violations, both groups apply the symbiotic principle to improve their sustenance position. On the other hand, potential victims of predatory crime may take evasive actions which encourage offenders to pursue targets other than their own. Since illegal activities must feed upon other activities, the spatial and temporal structure of routine legal activities should play an important role in determining the location, type and quantity of illegal acts occurring in a given community or society. Moreover, one can analyze how the structure of community organization as well as the level of technology in a society provide the circumstances under which crime can thrive. For example, technology and organization affect the capacity of persons with criminal inclinations to overcome their targets, as well as affecting the ability of guardians to contend with potential offenders by using whatever protective tools, weapons and skills they have at their disposal. Many technological advances designed for legitimate purposes—including the automobile, small power tools, hunting weapons, highways, telephones, etc.—may enable offenders to carry out their own work more effectively or may assist people in protecting their own or someone else's person or property.

Not only do routine legitimate activities often provide the wherewithal to commit offenses or to guard against others who do so, but they also provide offenders with suitable targets. Target suitability is likely to reflect such things as value (i.e., the material or symbolic desirability of a personal or property target for offenders), physical visibility, access, and the inertia of a target against illegal treatment by offenders (including the weight, size, and attached or locked features of property inhibiting its illegal removal and the physical capacity of personal victims to resist attackers with or without weapons). Routine production activities probably affect the suitability of consumer goods for illegal removal by determining their value and weight. Daily activities may affect the location of property and personal targets in visible and accessible places at particular times. These activities also may cause people to have on hand objects that can be used as weapons for criminal acts or self protection or to be preoccupied with tasks which reduce their capacity to discourage or resist offenders.

While little is known about conditions that affect the convergence of potential offenders, targets and guardians, this is a potentially rich source of propositions about crime rates. For example, daily work activities separate many people from those they trust and the property they value. Routine activities also bring together at various times of day or night Persons of different background, sometimes in the presence of facilities, tools or weapons which influence the commission or avoidance of illegal acts. Hence, the timing of work, schooling and leisure may be of central importance for explaining crime rates.

The ideas presented so far are not new, but they frequently are overlooked in the theoretical literature on crime. Although an investigation of the literature uncovers significant examples of descriptive and practical data related to the routine activities upon which illegal behavior feeds, these data seldom are treated within an analytical framework. The next section reviews some of this literature.

RELATION OF THE ROUTINE ACTIVITY APPROACH TO EXTANT STUDIES

A major advantage of the routine activity approach presented here is that it helps assemble some diverse and previously unconnected criminological analyses into a single substantive framework. This framework also serves to link illegal and legal activities, as illustrated by a few examples of descriptive accounts of criminal activity.

Descriptive Analyses

There are several descriptive analyses of criminal acts in criminological literature. For example. Thomas Reppetto's (1974) study, *Residential Crime*, considers how residents supervise their neighborhoods and streets and limit access of possible offenders. He also considers how distance of households from the central city reduces risks of criminal victimization. Reppetto's evidence—consisting of criminal justice records, observations of comparative features of geographic areas, victimization survey data and offender interviews—indicates that offenders are very likely to use burglary tools and to have at least minimal technical skills, that physical characteristics of dwellings affect their victimization rates, that the rhythms of residential crime rate patterns are marked (often related to travel and work patterns of residents), and that visibility of potential sites of crime affects the risk that crimes will occur there. Similar findings are reported by Pope's (1977a, 1977b) study of burglary in California and by Scarr's (1972) study of burglary in and around the District of Columbia. In addition, many studies report that architectural and environmental design as well as community crime programs serve to decrease target suitability and increase capable guardianship (see, for example, Newman, 1973; Jeffery, 1971; Washnis, 1976), while many biographical or autobiographical descriptions of illegal activities note that lawbreakers take into account the nature of property and/or the structure of human activities as they go about their illegal work (see, e.g., Chambliss, 1972; Klockars, 1974; Sutherland, 1937; Letkemann, 1973; Jackson, 1969; Martin, 1952; Maurer, 1964; Cameron, 1964: Williamson, 1968).

Evidence that the spatio-temporal organization of society affects patterns of crime can be found in several sources. Strong variations in specific predatory crime rates from hour to hour, day to day, and month to month are reported often (e.g., Wolfgang, 1958; Amir,

1971; Reppetto, 1974; Scarr, 1972; FBI, 1975; 1976), and these variations appear to correspond to the various tempos of the related legitimate activities upon which they feed. Also at a microsocioiogical level, Short and Strodtbeck (1965: chaps. 5 and 11) describe opportunities for violent confrontations of gang boys and other community residents which arise in the context of community leisure patterns, such as "quarter parties" in black communities, and the importance, in the calculus of decision making employed by participants in such episodes, of low probabilities of legal intervention. In addition, a wealth of empirical evidence indicates strong spatial variations over community areas in crime and delinquency rates[3] (for an excellent discussion and review of the literature on ecological studies of crimes, see Wilks, 1967). Recently, Albert Reiss (1976) has argued convincingly that these spatial variations (despite some claims to the contrary) have been supported consistently by both official and unofficial sources of data. Reiss further cites victimization studies which indicate that offenders are very likely to select targets not far from their own residence (see USDJ, 1974a; 1974b; 1974c).

Macrolevel Analyses of Crime Trends and Cycles

Although details about how crime occurs are intrinsically interesting, the important analytical task is to learn from these details how illegal activities carve their niche within the larger system of activities. This task is not an easy one. For example, attempts by Bonger (1916), Durkheim (1951; 1966), Henry and Short (1954), and Fleisher (1966) to link the rate of illegal activities to the economic condition of a society have not been completely successful. Empirical tests of the relationships postulated in the above studies have produced inconsistent results which some observers view as an indication that the level of crime is not related systematically to the economic conditions of a society (Mansfield et al., 1974: 463, Cohen and Felson, 1979).

It is possible that the wrong economic and social factors have been employed in these macro studies of crime. Other researchers have provided stimulating alternative descriptions of how social change affects the criminal opportunity structure, thereby influencing crime rates in particular societies. For example, at the beginning of the nineteenth century, Patrick Colquhoun (1800) presented a detailed, lucid description and analysis of crime in the London metropolitan area and suggestions for its control. He assembled substantial evidence that London was experiencing a massive crime wave attributable to a great increment in the assemblage and movement of valuable goods through its ports and terminals.

A similar examination of crime in the period of the English industrial expansion was carried out by a modem historian, J. J. Tobias (1967), whose work on the history of crime in nineteenth century England is perhaps the most comprehensive effort to isolate those elements of social change affecting crime in an expanding industrial nation. Tobias details how far-reaching changes in transportation, currency, technology, commerce, merchandising, poverty, housing, and the like, had tremendous repercussions on the amount and type of illegal activities committed in the nineteenth century. His thesis is that structural transformations either facilitated or impeded the opportunities to engage in illegal activities. In one of the few empirical studies of how recent social change affects the opportunity structure for crime in the United States, Leroy Gould (1969) demonstrated that the increase in the circulation of money and the availability of automobiles between 1921 and 1965 apparently led to an increase in the rate of bank robberies and auto thefts, respectively. Gould's data suggest that these relationships are due more to the abundance of opportunities to perpetrate the crimes than to short-term fluctuations in economic activities.

Although the sociological and historical studies cited in this section have provided some useful *empirical* generalizations and important insights into the incidence of crime, it is fair to say that they have not articulated systematically the *theoretical* linkages between routine legal activities and illegal endeavors. Thus, these studies cannot explain how changes in the larger social structure generate changes in the opportunity to engage in predatory crime and hence account for crime rate trends.[4] To do so requires a conceptual framework such as that sketched in the preceding section. Before attempting to demonstrate the feasibility of this approach with macrolevel data, we examine available microlevel data for its consistency with the major assumptions of this approach.

Microlevel Assumptions of the Routine Activity Approach

The theoretical approach taken here specifies that crime rate trends in the Post-World War II United States are related to patterns of what we have called routine activities. We define these as any recurrent and prevalent activities which provide for basic population and individual needs, whatever their biological or cultural origins. Thus routine activities would include formalized work, as well as the provision of standard food, shelter, sexual outlet, leisure. social interaction, learning and childrearing. These activities may go well beyond the minimal levels needed to prevent a population's extinction, so long as their prevalence and recurrence makes them a part of everyday life.

Routine activities may occur (1) at home, (2) in jobs away from home, and (3) in other activities away from home. The latter may involve primarily household members or others. We shall argue that, since World War II, the United States has experienced a major shift of routine activities away from the first category into the remaining ones, especially those nonhousehold activities involving nonhousehold members. In particular, we shall argue that this shift in the structure of routine activities increases the probability that motivated offenders will converge in space and time with suitable targets in the absence of capable guardians, hence contributing to significant increases in the direct-contact predatory crime rates over these years.

If the routine activity approach is valid, then we should expect to find evidence for a number of empirical relationships regarding the nature and distribution of predatory violations. For example, we would expect routine activities performed within or near the home and among family or other primary groups to entail lower risk of criminal victimization because they enhance guardianship capabilities. We should also expect that routine daily activities affect the location of property and personal targets in visible and accessible places at particular times, thereby influencing their risk of victimization. Furthermore, by determining their size and height and in some cases their value, routine production activities should affect the suitability of consumer goods for illegal removal. Finally, if the routine activity approach is useful for explaining the paradox presented earlier, we should find that the circulation of people and property, the size and weight of consumer items etc., will parallel changes in crime rate trends for the post-World War II United States.

The veracity of the routine activity approach can be assessed by analyses of both microlevel and macrolevel interdependencies of human activities. While consistencey at the former level may appear noncontroversial, or even obvious, one nonetheless needs to show that the approach does not contradict existing data before proceeding to investigate the latter level.

EMPIRICAL ASSESSMENT

Circumstances and Location of Offenses

The routine activity approach specifies that household and family activities entail lower risk of criminal victimization than nonhousehold-nonfamily activities, despite the, problems in measuring the former.[5]

National estimates from large-scale government victimization surveys in 1973 and 1974 support this generalization (see methodological information in Hindelang et al., 1976: Appendix 6). Table 1 presents several incident-victimization rates per 100,000 population ages 12 and older. Clearly, the rates in Panels A and B are far lower at or near home than elsewhere and far lower among relatives than others. The data indicate that risk of victimization varies directly with social distance between offender and victim. Panel C of this table indicates, furthermore, that risk of lone victimization far exceeds the risk of victimization for groups. These relationships are strengthened by considering time budget evidence that, on the aver-

TABLE 1 Incident-Specific Risk Rates for Rape, Robbery, Assault and Personal Larceny with Contact, United States, 1974

		Rape	Robbery	Assault	Personal Larceny with Contact	Total
A.* PLACE OF RESIDENCE	In or near home	63	129	572	75	839
	Elsewhere	119	584	1,897	1,010	3,610
B. VICTIM-OFFENDER RELATIONSHIP	(Lone Offender)					
	Relative	7	13	158	5	183
	Well Known	23	30	333	30	416
	Casual Acquaintance	11	26	308	25	370
	Don't Know/Sight Only	106	227	888	616	1,837
	(Multiple Offender)					
	Any known	10***	68	252	43	373
	All strangers	25***	349	530	366	1,270
C.* NUMBER OF VICTIMS	One	179	647	2,116	1,062	4,004
	Two	3	47	257	19	326
	Three	0	13	53	3	09
	Four Plus	0	6	43	1	50
D.** LOCATION AND RELATIONSHIP (sole offender only)	Home, Stranger	61	147	345	103	654
	Home, Nonstranger	45	74	620	22	761
	Street, Stranger	1,370	7,743	15,684	7,802	32,460
	Street, Nonstranger	179	735	5,777	496	7,167
	Elsewhere, Stranger	129	513	1,934	2,455	4,988
	Elsewhere, Nonstranger	47	155	1,544	99	1,874

* Calculated from Hindelang et al., 1977: Tables 3.16. 3.18. 3.27, 3.28. Rates are per 100.000 persons ages 12 and over.
** See fn. 6 for source. Rates are per billion person-hours in stated locations.
*** Based on white data only due to lack of suitable sample size for nonwhites as victims of rape with multiple offenders.

age, Americans spend 16.26 hours per day at home, 1.38 hours on streets, in parks, etc., and 6.36 hours in other places (Szalai, 197:795). Panel D of Table 1 presents our estimates of victimization per billion person-hours spent in such locations.[6] For example, personal larceny rates (with contact) are 350 times higher at the hands of strangers in streets than at the hands of nonstrangers at home. Separate computations from 1973 victimization data (USDJ, 1976: Table 48) indicate that there were two motor vehicle thefts per million vehicle-hours parked at or near home, 55 per million vehicle-hours in streets, parks, playgrounds, school grounds or parking lots, and 12 per million vehicle-hours elsewhere. While the direction of these relationships is not surprising, their magnitudes should be noted. It appears that risk of criminal

victimization varies dramatically among the circumstances and locations in which people place themselves and their property.

Target Suitability

Another assumption of the routine activity approach is that target suitability influences the occurrence of direct-contact predatory violations. Though we lack data to disaggregate all major components of target suitability (i.e., value, visibility, accessibility and inertia), together they imply that expensive and movable durables, such as vehicles and electronic appliances, have the highest risk of illegal removal.

As a specific case in point, we compared the 1975 composition of stolen property reported in the Uniform Crime Report (FBI, 1976: Tables 26–7) with national data on personal consumer expenditures for goods (CEA, 1976: Tables 13–16) and to appliance industry estimates of the value of shipments the same year (*Merchandising Week*, 1976). We calculated that $26.44 in motor vehicles and parts were stolen for each $100 of these goods consumed in 1975, while $6.82 worth of electronic appliances were stolen per $100 consumed. Though these estimates are subject to error in citizen and police estimation, what is important here is their size relative to other rates. For example, only 8¢ worth of nondurables and 12¢ worth of furniture and nonelectronic household durables were stolen per $100 of each category consumed, the motor vehicle risk being, respectively, 330 and 220 times as great. Though we lack data on the "stocks" of goods subject to risk, these "flow" data clearly support our assumption that vehicles and electronic appliances are greatly overrepresented in thefts.

The 1976 Buying Guide issue of *Consumer Reports* (1975) indicates why electronic appliances are an excellent retail value for a thief. For example, a Panasonic car tape player is worth $30 per lb., and a Phillips phonograph cartridge is valued at over $5,000 per lb., while large appliances such as refrigerators and washing machines are only worth $1 to $3 per lb. Not surprisingly, burglary data for the District of Columbia in 1969 (Scarr, 1972: Table 9) indicate that home entertainment items alone constituted nearly four times as many stolen items as clothing, food, drugs, liquor, and tobacco combined and nearly eight times as many stolen items as office supplies and equipment. In addition, 69% of national thefts classified in 1975 (FBI, 1976: Tables 1, 26) involve automobiles, their parts or accessories, and thefts from automobiles or thefts of bicycles. Yet radio and television sets plus electronic components and accessories totaled only 0.10% of the total truckload tonnage terminated in 1973 by intercity motor carriers, while passenger cars, motor vehicle parts and accessories, motorcycles, bicycles, and their parts, totaled only 5.5% of the 410 million truckload tons terminated (ICC, 1974). Clearly, portable and movable durables are reported stolen in great disproportion to

their share of the value and weight of goods circulating in the United States.

Family Activities and Crime Rates

One would expect that persons living in single-adult households and those employed outside the home are less obligated to confine their time to family activities within households. From a routine activity perspective, these persons and their households should have higher rates of predatory criminal victimization. We also expect that adolescents and young adults who are perhaps more likely to engage in peer group activities rather than family activities will have higher rates of criminal victimization. Finally, married persons should have lower rates than others. Tables 2 and 3 largely confirm these expectations (with the exception of personal larceny with contact). Examining these tables, we note that victimization rates appear to be related inversely to age and are lower for persons in "less active" statuses (e.g., keeping house, unable to work, retired) and persons in intact marriages. A notable exception is indicated in Table 2, where persons unable to work appear more likely to be victimized by rape, robbery and personal larceny with contact than are other "inactive persons." Unemployed persons also have unusually high rates of victimization. However, these rates are consistent with the routine activity approach offered here: the high rates of victimization suffered by the unemployed may reflect their residential proximity to high concentrations of potential offenders as well as their age and racial composition, while handicapped persons have high risk of personal victimization because they are less able to resist motivated offenders. Nonetheless, persons who keep house have noticeably lower rates of victimization than those who are employed, unemployed, in school or in the armed forces.

As Table 3 indicates, burglary and robbery victimization rates are about twice as high for persons living in single-adult households as for other persons in each age group examined. Other victimization data (USDJ, 1976: Table 21) indicate that, while household victimization rates tend to vary directly with household size, larger households have lower rates per

TABLE 2 Selected Status-Specific Personal Victimization Rates for the United States (per 100,000 Persons in Each Category)

Variables and Sources	Victim Category	Rape	Robbery	Assault	Personal Larceny with Contact	Larceny without Contact
A. AGE	12–15	147	1,267	3,848	311	16,355
(Source:	16–19	248	1,127	5,411	370	15,606
Hindelang, et al., 1977:	20–24	209	1,072	4,829	337	14,295
Table 310, 1974	25–34	135	703	3,023	263	10,354
rates)	35–49	21	547	1,515	256	7,667
	50–64	33	411	731	347	4,588
	65+	20	388	492	344	1,845
B. MAJOR	(Male 16+)					
ACTIVITY OF	Armed Forces	—	1,388	4,153	118	16,274
VICTIM	Employed	—	807	3,285	252	10,318
(Source:	Unemployed	—	2,179	7,984	594	15,905
Hindelang, et al., 1977:	Keep house	—	0	2,475	463	3,998
Table 313, 1974	In school	—	1,362	5,984	493	17,133
rates)	Unable to work	—	1,520	2,556	623	3,648
	Retired	—	578	662	205	2,080
	(Female 16+)					
	Keep house	116	271	978	285	4,433
	Employed	156	529	1,576	355	9,419
	Unemployed	798	772	5,065	461	12,338
	In School	417	430	2,035	298	12,810
	Unable to work	287	842	741	326	1,003
	Retired	120	172	438	831	1,571
C. MARITAL STATUS	(Male 12+)					
(Source:USDJ:	Never Married	—	1,800	5,870	450	16,450
1977, Table 5,	Married	—	550	2,170	170	7,660
1973 rates)	Separated/Divorced	—	2,270	5,640	1,0.40	12,960
	Widowed	—	1,150	1,500	—	4,120
	(Female 12+)					
	Never Married	360	580	2,560	400	12,880
	Married	70	270	910	220	6,570
	Separated/Divorced	540	1,090	4,560	640	9,130
	Widowed	—	450	590	480	2,460

Line indicates too few offenses for accurate estimates of rate. However, rates in these cells are usually small.

person. For example, the total household victimization rates (including burglary, household larceny, and motor vehicle theft) per 1,000 households were 168 for single-person households and 326 for households containing six or more persons. Hence, six people distributed over six single-person households experience an average of 1,008 household victimizations, more than three times as many as one six-person household. Moreover, age of household head has a strong relationship to a household's victimization rate for these crimes. For households headed by persons under 20, the motor vehicle theft rate is nine times as high, and the burglary and household larceny rates four times as high as those for households headed by persons 65 and over (USDJ, 1976: Table 9).

While the data presented in this section were not collected originally for the purpose of testing the routine activity approach, our efforts to rework them for these purposes have proven fruitful. The routine activity approach is consistent with the data examined and, in addition, helps to accommodate within a rather simple and coherent analytical framework certain findings which, though not necessarily new,

TABLE 3   Robbery-Burglary Victimization Rates by Ages and Number of Adults in Household, 1974 and 1976 General Social Survey

Age	Number of Adults in Household One		Two or More		Ratio
18–35	0.200	(140)	0.095	(985)	2.11
36–55	0.161	(112)	0.079	(826)	2.04
56 and over	0.107	(262)	0.061	(640)	1.76
All Ages	0.144	(514)	0.081	(2451)	1.78

(Numbers in parentheses are the base for computing risk rates.)
Source: Calculated from 1974 and 1976 General Social Survey, National Opinion Research Center, University of Chicago.

might otherwise be attributed only "descriptive" significance. In the next section, we examine macrosocial trends as they relate to trends in crime rates.

CHANGING TRENDS IN ROUTINE ACTIVITY STRUCTURE AND PARALLEL TRENDS IN CRIME RATES

The main thesis presented here is that the dramatic increase in the reported crime rates in the U.S. since 1960 is linked to changes in the routine activity structure of American society and to a corresponding increase in target suitability and decrease in guardian presence. If such a thesis has validity, then we should be able to identify these social trends and show how they relate to predatory criminal victimization rates.

Trends in Human Activity Patterns

The decade 1960–1970 experienced noteworthy trends in the activities of the American population. For example, the percent of the population consisting of female college students increased 118% (USBC, 1975: Table 225). Married female labor force participant rates increased 31% (USBC, 1975: Table 563), while the percent of the population living as primary individuals increased by 34% (USBC, 1975: Table 51; see also Kobrin, 1976). We gain some further insight into changing routine activity patterns by comparing hourly data for 1960 and 1971 on households *unattended* by persons ages 14 or over when U.S. census interviewers first called (see Table 4). These data suggest that the proportion of households unattended at 8 A.M. increased by almost half between 1960 and 1971. One also finds increases in rates of out-of-town travel, which provides greater opportunity for both daytime and nighttime burglary of residences. Between 1960 and 1970, there was a 72% increase in state and national park visits per capita (USBC, 1975), an 144% increase in the percent of plant workers eligible for three weeks vacation (BLS, 1975: Table 116), and an 184% increase in overseas travelers per 100,000 population (USBC, 1975: Table 366). The National Travel Survey, conducted as part of the U.S. Census Bureau's Census of Transportation, confirms the general trends, tallying an 81% increase in the number of vacations taken by Americans from 1967 to 1972, a five-year period (USBC, 1973a: Introduction).

The dispersion of activities away from households appears to be a major recent social change. Although this decade also experienced an important 31% increase in the percent of the population ages 15–24, age structure change was only one of many social trends occurring during the period, especially trends in the circulation of people and property in American society.[7]

TABLE 4   Proportion of Households Unattended by Anyone 14 Years Old or Over by Time of Day during First Visit by Census Bureau Interviewer, 1960 and 1971

Time of day	1960 Census	November, 1971 Current Pop. Survey	Percent Change
8:00–8:59 a.m.	29%	43	+48.9%
9:00–9:59 a.m.	29	44	+58
10:00–10:59 a.m.	31	42	+36
11:00–11:59 a.m.	32	41	+28
12:00–12:59 p.m.	32	41	+28
1:00–1:59 p.m.	31	43	+39
2:00–2:59 p.m.	33	43	+30
3:00–3:59 p.m.	30	33	+10
4:00–4:59 p.m.	28	30	+ 7
5:00–5:59 p.m.	22	26	+18
6:00–6:59 p.m.	22	25	+14
7:00–7:59 p.m.	20	29	+45
8:00–8:59 p.m.	24	22	− 8

Source: Calculated from USBC (1973b: Table A).

The importance of the changing activity structure is underscored by taking a brief look at demographic changes between the years 1970 and 1975, a period of continuing crime rate increments. Most of the recent changes in age structure relevant to crime rates already had occurred by 1970; indeed, the proportion of the population ages 15–24 increased by only 6% between 1970 and 1975, compared with a 15% increase during the five years 1965 to 1970. On the other hand, major changes in the structure of routine activities continued during these years. For example, in only five years, the estimated proportion of the population consisting of husband-present, married women in the labor force households increased by 11%, while the estimated number of non-husband-wife households per 100,000 population increased from 9,150 to 11,420, a 25% increase (USBC, 1976: Tables 50, 276; USBC, 1970-1975). At the same time, the percent of population enrolled in higher education increased 16% between 1970 and 1975.

Related Property Trends and Their Relation to Human Activity Patterns

Many of the activity trends mentioned above normally involve significant investments in durable goods. For example, the dispersion of population across relatively more households (especially non-husband-wife households) enlarges the market for durable goods such as television sets and automobiles. Women participating in the labor force and both men and women enrolled in college provide a market for automobiles. Both work and travel often involve the purchase of major movable or portable durables and their use away from home.

Considerable data are available which indicate that sales of consumer goods changed dramatically between 1960 and 1970 (as did their size and weight), hence providing more suitable property available for theft. For example, during this decade, constant-dollar personal consumer expenditures in the United States for motor vehicles and parts increased by 71%, while constant-dollar expenditures for other durables increased by 105% (calculated from CEA, 1976: Table B-16). In addition, electronic

household appliances and small houseware shipments increased from 56.2 to 119.7 million units (*Electrical Merchandising Week*, 1964; *Merchandising Week*, 1973). During the same decade, appliance imports increased in value by 681% (USBC, 1975: Table 1368).

This same period appears to have spawned a revolution in small durable product design which further feeds the opportunity for crime to occur. Relevant data from the 1960 and 1970 Sears catalogs on the weight of many consumer durable goods were examined. Sears is the nation's largest retailer and its policy of purchasing and relabeling standard manufactured goods makes its catalogs a good source of data on widely merchandised consumer goods. The lightest television listed for sale in 1960 weighed 38 lbs., compared with 15 lbs. for 1970. Thus, the lightest televisions were 2½ times as heavy in 1960 as 1970. Similar trends are observed for dozens of other goods listed in the Sears catalog. Data from *Consumer Reports Buying Guide* published in December of 1959 and 1969, show similar changes for radios, record players, slide projectors, tape recorders, televisions, toasters and many other goods. Hence, major declines in weight between 1960 and 1970 were quite significant for these and other goods, which suggests that the consumer goods market may be producing many more targets suitable for theft. In general, one finds rapid growth in property suitable for illegal removal and in household and individual exposure to attack during the years 1960–1975.

Related Trends in Business Establishments

Of course, as households and individuals increased their ownership of small durables, businesses also increased the value of the merchandise which they transport and sell as well as the money involved in these transactions. Yet the Census of Business conducted in 1958, 1963, 1967, and 1972 indicate that the number of wholesale, retail, service, and public warehouse establishments (including establishments owned by large organizations) was a nearly constant ratio of one for every 16 persons in the United States. Since more goods and money were distributed over a relatively fixed number of business establishments, the tempo of business activity per establishment apparently was increasing. At the same time, the percent of the population employed as sales clerks or salesmen in retail trade declined from 1.48% to 1.27%, between 1960 and 1970, a 14.7% decline (USBC, 1975: Table 589).

Though both business and personal property increased, the changing pace of activities appears to have exposed the latter to greater relative risk of attack whether at home or elsewhere, due to the dispersion of goods among many more households, while concentrating goods in business establishments. However, merchandise in retail establishments with heavy volume and few employees to guard it probably is exposed to major increments in risk of illegal removal than is most other business property.

Composition of Crime Trends

If these changes in the circulation of people and property are in fact related to crime trends, the *composition* of the latter should reflect this.

We expect relatively greater increases in personal and household victimization as compared with most business victimizations, while shoplifting should increase more rapidly than other types of thefts from businesses. We expect personal offenses at the hands of strangers to manifest greater increases than such offenses at the hands of nonstrangers. Finally, residential burglary rates should increase more in daytime than nighttime.

The available time series on the composition of offenses confirm these expectations. For example, Table 5 shows that commercial burglaries declined from 60% to 36% of the total, while daytime residential burglaries increased from 16% to 33%. Unlike the other crimes against business, shoplifting increased its share. Though we lack trend data on the circumstances of other violent offenses, murder data confirm our expectations. Between 1963 and 1975, felon-type murders increased from 17% to 32% of the total. Compared with a 47% increase in the rate of relative killings in this

TABLE 5 Offense Analysis Trends for Robbery, Burglary, Larceny and Murder; United States, 1960–1975

A. ROBBERIES[a]	1960	1965	1970	
Highway Robbery	52.6	57.0	59.8	
Residential Robbery	8.0	10.1	13.1	
Commercial Robbery	39.4	32.9	27.1	
Totals	100.0	100.0	100.0	

B. BURGLARIES	1960	1965	1970	1975
Residential	15.6	24.5	31.7	33.2
Residential Nightime	24.4	25.2	25.8	30.5
Commercial	60.0	50.2	42.5	36.3
Totals	100.0	99.9	100.0	100.0

C. LARCENIES	1960	1965	1970	1975
Shoplifting	6.0	7.8	9.2	11.3
Other	94.0	92.2	90.8	88.7
Totals	100.0	100.0	100.0	100.0

D. MURDERS	1963	1965	1970	1975
Relative Killings	31.0	31.0	23.3	22.4
Romance, Arguments[b]	51.0	48.0	47.9	45.2
Felon Types[c]	17.0	21.0	28.8	32.4
Totals	100.0	100.0	100.0	100.0

Source: Offense Analysis from UCR, various years.
[a]Excluding miscellaneous robberies. The 1975 distribution omitted due to apparent instability of post-1970 data.
[b]Includes romantic triangles, lovers' quarrels and arguments.
[c]Includes both known and suspected felon types.

period, we calculated a 294% increase in the murder rate at the hands of known or suspected felon types.

Thus the trends in the composition of recorded crime rates appear to be highly consistent with the activity structure trends noted earlier. In the next section we apply the routine activity approach in order to model crime rate trends and social change in the post-World War II United States.

THE RELATIONSHIP OF THE HOUSEHOLD ACTIVITY RATIO TO FIVE ANNUAL OFFICIAL INDEX CRIME RATES IN THE UNITED STATES, 1947–1974

In this section, we test the hypothesis that aggregate official crime rate trends in the United States vary directly over time with the dispersion of activities away from family and household. The limitations of annual time series data do not allow construction of direct measures of changes in hourly activity patterns, or quantities, qualities and movements of exact stocks of household durable goods, but the Current Population Survey does provide related time series on labor force and household structure. From these data, we calculate annually (beginning in 1947) a household activity ratio by adding the number of married, husband-present female labor force participants (source: BLS, 1975: Table 5) to the number of non-husband-wife households (source: USBC, 1947-1976), dividing this sum by the total number of households in the U.S. (source: USBC, 1947-1976). This calculation provides an estimate of the proportion of American households in year t expected to be most highly exposed to risk of personal and property victimization due to the dispersion of their activities away from family and household and/or their likelihood of owning extra sets of durables subject to high risk of attack. Hence, the household activity ratio should vary directly with official index crime rates.

Our empirical goal in this section is to test this relationship, with controls for those variables which other researchers have linked empirically to crime rate trends in the United States. Since various researchers have found such trends to increase with the proportion of

the population in teen and young adult years (Fox, 1976, Land and Felson, 1976; Sagi and Wellford, 1968; Wellford, 1973), we include the population ages 15–24 per 100,000 resident population in year t as our first control variable (source: USBC, various years). Others (e.g., Brenner, 1976a; 1976b) have found unemployment rates to vary directly with official crime rates over time, although this relationship elsewhere has been shown to be empirically questionable (see Mansfield et al., 1974: 463; Cohen and Felson, 1979). Thus, as our second, control variable, we take the standard annual unemployment rate (per 100 persons ages 16 and over) as a measure of the business cycle (source: BLS, 1975).

Four of the five crime rates that we utilize here (forcible rape, aggravated assault, robbery and burglary) are taken from FBI estimates of offenses per 100,000 U.S. population (as revised and reported in OMB, 1973). We exclude larceny-theft due to a major definitional change in 1960 and auto theft due to excessive multicollinearity in the analysis.[8] For our homicide indicator we employ the homicide mortality rate taken from the vital statistics data collected by the Bureau of the Census (various years). The latter rate has the advantage of being collected separately from the standard crime reporting system and is thought to contain less measurement error (see Bowers and Pierce, 1975). Hence, this analysis of official index crime rates includes three violent offenses (homicide, forcible rape, and aggravated assault), one property offense (burglary), and one offense which involves both the removal of property and the threat of violence (robbery). The analysis thus includes one offense thought to have relatively low reporting reliability (forcible rape), one thought to have relatively high reliability (homicide), and three others having relatively intermediate levels of reporting quality (Ennis. 1967).

Since official crime rates in year t are likely to reflect some accumulation of criminal opportunity and inclinations over several years, one should not expect these rates to respond solely to the level of the independent variables for year t. A useful model of cumulative social change in circumstances such as this is the difference equation, which can be estimated in two forms (see Goldberg, 1958). One form takes the first difference $(y_t - y_{t-1})$ as the dependent variable—in this case, the change in the official crime rate per 100,000 population between year t – 1 and year t. Alternatively, one can estimate the difference equation in autoregressive form by taking the official crime rate in year t as a function of the exogenous predictors plus the official crime rate in year t – 1 on the right-hand side of the equation. (See Land. 1978, for a review of these and other methods and for references to related literature.) Both forms are estimable with ordinary least squares methods, which we employ for the years 1947 through 1974. The N is 28 years for all but the homicide rate, for which publication lags reduce our N to 26.

Even if a positive relationship between the household activity ratio and the official crime rates is observed, with controls for age and unemployment, we are open to the charge that this may be a spurious consequence of autocorrelation of disturbances, that is, the possibility that residuals are systematically related for nearby time points. While spurious relationships are a risk one also takes in cross-sectional regression analysis, time-series analysts have devised a variety of methods for monitoring and adjusting for spuriousness due to this autocorrelation, including the Durbin and Watson (1951) statistic, Durbin's h statistic (Durbin, 1970), the Griliches (1967) criterion, as well as Cochrane and Orcutt (1949) corrections. We employ (but do not report in detail) these methods to check for the likelihood that the observed relationship is spurious. (See Land, 1978, for a review of such tests and the related literature on their applicability and robustness; see Theil, 1971, for a methodological review.)

Findings

Our time-series analysis for the years 1947–1974 consistently revealed positive and statistically significant relationships between the household activity ratio and each official crime rate change. Whichever official crime rate is employed, this finding occurs—whether we take the first difference for each crime rate as exogenous or estimate the equation in autoregressive form (with the lagged dependent variable on the right-hand side of the equation); whether we include or exclude the unemployment variable, whether we take the current scales of variables or convert them to natural log values; whether we employ the age structure variable as described or alter the ages examined (e.g., 14–24, 15–19, etc.). In short, the relationship is positive and significant in each case.

Before calculating the difference equations, we regressed each crime rate in year t on the three independent variables for year t. This ordinary structural equation also produced consistent positive and significant coefficients for the routine activity coefficient, the total variance explained ranges from 84% to 97%. However, the Durbin-Watson statistics for these equations indicated high risk of autocorrelation, which is hardly surprising since they ignore lagged effects. Reestimated equations taking first differences as endogenous reduced the risk of autocorrelation significantly (and also reduced variance explained to between 35% and 77%). These equations also consistently produce significant positive coefficients for the household activity variable. When unemployment is included in these equations, its coefficients are all negative and near zero.

The top panel of Table 6 presents regression estimates of first differences for five official crime rates, with the age structure and household activity variables in year t as the only predictors. Again, the household activity coefficients are consistently positive, with t ratios always significant with a one-tailed test. Except for the aggravated assault equation, the household activity variable has a t ratio and standardized coefficient greater than that of the age structure variable. The standardized coefficients for the household activity variable range from .42 to .72, while the age structure coefficients are consistently positive. In general, the household activity variable is a stronger predictor of official crime rate trends than the age structure.

The equations in the top panel of Table 6 generally have lower variance explained but also lower risk of autocorrelation of disturbances than those reported above. For all five equations, the Durbin-Watson statistic allows accep-

TABLE 6   Regression Equations for First Differences in Five Index Crime Rates and Sensitivity Analyses, the United States, 1947–1974

FIRST DIFFERENCE FORM	(1) Nonnegligent Homicide	(2) Forcible Rape	(3) Aggravated Assault	(4) Robbery	(5) Burglary
Constant	−2.3632	−4.8591	−32.0507	−43.8838	−221.2303
t ratio	.3502	5.3679	7.6567	3.4497	3.7229
Proportion 15–24 (t)					
Standardized	.1667	.1425	.4941	.2320	.1952
Unstandardized	3.2190	6.4685	132.1072	116.7742	486.0806
t ratio	1.0695	.7505	3.3147	.9642	.8591
Household Actively Ratio (t)					
Standardized	.7162	.6713	.4377	.4242	.5106
Unstandardized	4.0676	8.9743	34.4658	62.8834	374.4746
t ratio	4.5959	3.5356	2.9364	1.7629	2.2474
Multiple R^2 Adjusted	.6791	.5850	.7442	.3335	.4058
Degrees of Freedom	23	25	25	25	25
Durbin-Watson Value	2.5455	2.3388	2.3446	1.4548	1.7641
1% test	Accept	Accept	Accept	Accept	Accept
5% test	Uncertain	Accept	Accept	Uncertain	Accept
AUTOREGRESSIVE FORM					
Multiple R^2 Adjusted	.9823	.9888	.9961	.9768	.9859
Durbin's h	−1.3751	−.7487	.9709	1.5490	1.1445
−1% test	Accept	Accept	Accept	Accept	Accept
−5% test	Accept	Accept	Accept	Accept	Accept
Griliches Criterion	Accept	Accept	Accept	Accept	Accept
Cochrane-Orcutt Correction, Effect upon Household Activity	Minimal	Minimal	Minimal	Minimal	Minimal
Unemployment Rate as Control, Effect upon Household Activity	Minimal	Minimal	Minimal	Minimal	Minimal

tance of the null hypothesis that autocorrelation is absent at the 1% level. A 5% level (which *increases* the likelihood of proving the statistic nonzero) allows us neither to accept nor reject the null hypothesis that autocorrelation is absent in the homicide and robbery equations.

Though autocorrelation has not been proven to exist in these five equations, its risk may be sufficient in two to motivate further efforts at equation estimation (see bottom panel of Table 6). We estimated the equations in autoregressive form to see if the risk abates. Since the Durbin-Watson statistic was not designed for evaluating autocorrelation in these equations, we calculated Durbin's h, a statistic specifically designed for equations estimated with a lagged dependent variable (Durbin, 1970), and recently found to be robust for small samples (Maddala and Rao, 1973). This statistic allows acceptance of the null hypothesis (at both 1% and 5% levels) that autocorrelation is absent for all five equations. Application of the Griliches (1967) criterion further allows acceptance of each equation as manifesting distributing lags rather than serial correlation. We also employed the Cochrane-Orcutt (1949) iterative procedure to calculate a correction estimate for any autocorrelation present. The resulting correction for the household activity coefficient proves minimal in all five cases. Finally, we calculated each of the above equations for natural log values of the relevant variables, finding again that the household activity coefficient was consistently positive and statistically significant and the risk of autocorrelation reduced still further.

The positive and significant relationship between the household activity variable and the official crime rates is robust and appears to hold for both macro- and microlevel data; it explains five crime rate trends, as well as the changing composition of official crime rates reported in Table 5. These results suggest that routine activities may indeed provide the opportunity for many illegal activities to occur.

DISCUSSION

In our judgment many conventional theories of crime (the adequacy of which usually is evaluated by cross-sectional data, or no data at all) have difficulty accounting for the annual changes in crime rate trends in the post-World War II United States. These theories may prove useful in explaining crime trends during other periods, within specific communities, or in particular subgroups of the population. Longitudinal aggregate data for the United States, however, indicate that the trends for many of the presumed causal variables in these theoretical structures are in a direction opposite to those hypothesized to be the causes of crime. For example, during the decade 1960–1970, the percent of the population below the low-income level declined 44% and the unemployment rate declined 186%. Central city population as a share of the whole population declined slightly, while the percent of foreign stock declined 0.1%, etc. (see USBC, 1975: 654, 19, 39).

On the other hand, the convergence in time and space of three elements (motivated offenders, suitable targets, and the absence of capable guardians) appears useful for understanding crime rate trends. The lack of any of these elements is sufficient to prevent the occurrence of a successful direct-contact predatory crime. The convergence in time and space of suitable targets and the absence of capable guardians can lead to large increases in crime rates without any increase or change in the structural conditions that motivate individuals to engage in crime. Presumably, had the social indicators of the variables hypothesized to be the causes of crime in conventional theories changed in the direction of favoring increased crime in the post-World War II United States, the increases in crime rates likely would have been even more staggering than those which were observed. In any event, it is our belief that criminologists have underemphasized the importance of the convergence of suitable targets and the absence of capable guardians in explaining recent increases in the crime rate. Furthermore, the effects of the convergence in time and space of these elements may be multiplicative rather than additive. That is, their convergence by a fixed percentage may produce increases in crime rates far greater than that fixed percentage, demonstrating how some relatively modest social trends can contribute to some relatively large changes in crime rate trends. The fact that logged variables improved our equations (moving Durbin-Watson values closer to "ideal" levels)]ends support to the argument that such an interaction occurs.

Those few investigations of cross-sectional data which include household indicators produce results similar to ours. For example, Roncek (1975) and Choldin and Roncek (1976) report on block-level data for San Diego, Cleveland and Peoria and indicate that the proportion of a block's households which are primary individual households consistently offers the best or nearly the best predictor of a block's crime rate. This relationship persisted after they controlled for numerous social variables, including race, density, age and poverty. Thus the association between household structure and risk of criminal victimization has been observed in individual-level and block-level cross-sectional data, as well as aggregate national time-series data.

Without denying the importance of factors motivating offenders to engage in crime, we have focused specific attention upon violations themselves and the prerequisites for their occurrence. However, the routine activity approach might in the future be applied to the analysis of offenders and their inclinations as well. For example, the structure of primary group activity may affect the likelihood that cultural transmission or social control of criminal inclinations will occur, while the structure of the community may affect the tempo of criminogenic peer group activity. We also may expect that circumstances favorable for carrying out violations contribute to criminal inclinations in the long run by rewarding these inclinations.

We further suggest that the routine activity framework may prove useful in explaining why the criminal justice system, the community and the family have appeared so ineffective in exerting social control since 1960. Substantial increases in the opportunity to carry out predatory violations may have undermined society's mechanisms for social control. For example, it may be difficult for institutions seeking to increase the certainty, celerity and severity of punishment to compete with structural changes resulting in vast increases in the certainty, celer-

ity and value of rewards to be gained from illegal predatory acts.

It is ironic that the very factors which increase the opportunity to enjoy the benefits of life also may increase the opportunity for predatory violations. For example, automobiles provide freedom of movement to offenders as well as average citizens and offer vulnerable targets for theft. College enrollment, female labor force participation, urbanization, suburbanization, vacations and new electronic durables provide various opportunities to escape the confines of the household while they increase the risk of predatory victimization. Indeed, the opportunity for predatory crime appears to be enmeshed in the opportunity structure for legitimate activities to such an extent that it might be very difficult to root out substantial amounts of crime without modifying much of our way of life. Rather than assuming that predatory crime is simply an indicator of social breakdown, one might take it as a byproduct of freedom and prosperity as they manifest themselves in the routine activities of everyday life.

NOTES

* Address all communications to: Lawrence E. Cohen; Department of Sociology; University of Illinois; Urbana, IL 61801.

For their comments, we thank David J. Bordua, Ross M. Stolzenberg, Christopher S. Dunn, Kenneth C. Land, Robert Schoen, Amos Hawley, and an anonymous reviewer. Funding for this study was provided by these United States Government grants: National Institute for Mental Health 1-RO1-MH31117-01; National Science Foundation, SOC77-13261; and United States Army RI/DAHC 19-76-G-0016. The authors' name order is purely alphabetical.

1. Though official data severely underestimate crime, they at least provide a rough indicator of trends over time in the volume of several major felonies. The possibility that these data also reflect trends in rates at which offenses are reported to the police has motivated extensive victimology research (see Nettler, 1974; and Hindelang, 1976, for a review). This work consistently finds that seriousness of offense is the strongest determinant of citizen reporting to law enforcement officials (Skogan, 1976: 145; Hindelang, 1976: 401). Hence the upward trend in official crime rates since 1960 in the U.S. may reflect increases in *both* the volume and seriousness of offenses. Though disaggregating these two components may not be fea-

sible, one may wish to interpret observed trends as generated largely by both.

2. The analytical distinction between target and guardian is not important in those cases where a personal target engages in self-protection from direct-contact predatory violations. We leave open for the present the question of whether a guardian is effective or ineffective in all situations. We also allow that various, guardians may primarily supervise offenders, targets or both. These are questions for future examination.

3. One such ecological study by Sarah Boggs (1965) presents some similar ideas in distinguishing *familiarity* of offenders with their targets and *profitability* of targets as two elements of crime occurrence. Boggs's work stands apart from much research on the ecology of crime in its consideration of crime occurrence rates separately from offender rates. The former consist of the number of offenses committed in a given area per number of suitable targets within that area (as estimated by various indicators). The latter considers the residence of offenders in computing the number of offenders per unit of population. Boggs examines the correlations between crime occurrence rates and offender rates for several offenses in St. Louis and shows that the two are often independent. It appears from her analysis that *both* target and offender characteristics play a central role in the location of illegal activity.

4. The concept of the opportunity for crime contained in the above research and in this study differs considerably from the traditional sociological usage of the *differential opportunity* concept. For example, Cloward and Ohlin (1960) employed this term in discussing how legitimate and illegitimate opportunities affect the resolution of adjustment problems leading to gang delinquency. From their viewpoint, this resolution depends upon the kind of social support for one or another type of illegitimate activity that is given at different points in the social structure (Cloward and Ohlin, 1960: 151). Rather than circumstantial determinants of crime, they use differential opportunity to emphasize structural features which motivate offenders to perpetrate certain types of crimes. Cloward and Ohlin are largely silent on the interaction of this motivation with target suitability

5. Recent research indicates the existence of substantial quantities of family violence which remains outside of UCR data (see annotated bibliography of family violence in Lystad, 1974). While we cannot rule out the likelihood that much family violence is concealed from victimization surveys, the latter capture information absent from police data and still indicate that nonfamily members are usually much more dangerous than family members are to each other (see text). Also, when family violence leads to death, its suppression becomes quite difficult. The murder circumstances data indicate that about two-thirds of killings involve nonrelatives. Without denying the evidence that the level of family violence is far greater

than police reports would indicate, available data also suggest that time spent in family activities within households incurs less risk of victimization than many alternative activities in other places. In addition, many of the most *common* offenses (such as robbery and burglary) always have been recognized as usually involving nonfamily members.

6. Billion person-hours can easily be conceptualized as 1,000,000 persons spending 1,000 hours each (or about 42 days) in a given location (Szalai, 1972:795). Fox obtained these data from a 1966 time budget study in 44 American cities. The study was carried out by the Survey Research Center, the University of Michigan. We combined four subsamples in computing our figures. We combined activities into three locations, as follows: (1) at or just outside home; (2) at another's home, restaurants or bars, or indoor leisure; (3) in streets, parks, or outdoor leisure. Our computing formula was

$$Q = [(R \times 10^5) \div (A \times 365)] \times 10^9,$$

where Q is the risk per billion person-hours; R is the victimization rate, reported per 105 pesons in Hindelang et al. (1976: Table 318): A is the hours spent per location calculated from Szalai (1971: 795); 365 is the multiplier to cover a year's exposure to risk; and 109 converts risk per person-hour to billion personhours.

7. While the more sophisticated treatments of the topic have varied somewhat in their findings, most recent studies attempting to link crime rate increases to the changing age structure of the American population have found that the latter account for a relatively limited proportion of the general crime trend (see, for example, Sagi and Wellford, 1968; Ferdinand, 1970; and Wellford, 1973).

8. The auto theft rate lagged one year correlated quite strongly with the predictor variables. This multicollinearity impaired our difference equation analysis, although we again found consistently positive coefficients for the household activity ratio. We were able to remove autocorrelation by logging all variables and including the unemployment as a control, but do not report these equations.

REFERENCES

AMIR, MENACHEM
1971   Patterns of Forcible Rape. Chicago: University of Chicago Press.

BOGGS, SARAH
1965   "Urban crime patterns." American Sociological Review 30:899–905.

BONGER, W. A.
1916   Criminality and Economic Conditions. Boston: Little, Brown.

BOWERS, W. J. AND GLEN L. PIERCE
1975   "The illusion of deterrence of Isaac Ehrlich's

research on capital punishment." Yale Law Journal 85:187–208.

BRENNER, HARVEY
1976a Estimating the Social Costs of National Economic Policy: Implications for Mental and Physical Health and Criminal Aggression. Paper no. 5, Joint Economic Committee. Congress of the United States. Washington. D.C.: U.S. Government Printing Office.
1976b Effects of the National Economy on Criminal Aggression II. Final Report to National Institute of Mental Health. Contract #28276-0355FS.

BUREAU OF LABOR STATISTICS (BLS)
1975 Handbook of Labor Statistics 1975—Reference Edition. Washington, D.C.: U.S. Government Printing Office.

CAMERON, MARY OWEN
1964 The Booster and the Snitch. New York: Free Press.

CHAMBLISS. WILLIAM J.
1972 Boxman: A Professional Thief's Journey. New York: Harper and Row.

CHOLDIN, HARVEY M. AND DENNIS W. ROINCEK
1976 "Density, population potential and pathology: a block-level analysis." Public Data Use 4:19–30.

CLOWARD, RICHARD AND LLOYD OHLIN
1960 Delinquency and Opportunity, New York: Free Press.

COCHRANE. D., AND G. H. ORCUTT
1949 "Application of least squares regression to relationships containing autocorrelated error terms." Journal of the American Statistical Association 44:32–61.

COHEN, LAWRENCE E. AND MARCUS FELSON
1979 "On estimating the social costs of national economic policy: a critical examination of the Brenner study." Social Indicators Research. In press.

COLQUHOUN, PATRICK
1800 Treatise on the Police of the Metropolis. London: Baldwin.

CONSUMER REPORTS BUYING GUIDE
1959 Consumer Reports (December). Mt. Vernon: Consumers Union.
1969 Consumer Reports (December). Mt. Vernon: Consumers Union.
1975 Consumer Reports (December). Mt. Vernon: Consumers Union.

COUNCIL OF ECONOMIC ADVISORS (CEA)
1976 The Economic Report of the President. Washington, D.C.: U.S. Government Printing Office.

DURBIN, J.
1970 "Testing for serial correlation when least squares regressors are tagged dependent variables." Econometrica 38:410–21.

DURBIN, J., AND G. S. WATSON
1951 "Testing for serial correlation in least squares regression, II." Biometrika 38:159–78

DURKHEIM, EMILE
1951 Suicide: A Study in Sociology. New York: Free Press.

1966 The Division of Labor in Society. New York: Free Press.

ELECTRICAL MERCHANDISING WEEK
1964 Statistical and Marketing Report (January). New York: Billboard Publications.

ENNIS, PHILIP H.
1967 "Criminal victimization in the U.S.: a report of a national survey, field surveys II." The President's Commission on Law Enforcement and the Administration of Justice. Washington, D.C.: U.S. Government Printing Office.

FEDERAL BUREAU OF INVESTIGATION (FBI)
1975 Crime in the U.S.: Uniform Crime Report. Washington, D.C.: U.S. Government Printing Office.
1976 Crime in the U.S.: Uniform Crime Report. Washington, D.C.: U.S. Government Printing Office.

FERDINAND, THEODORE N.
1970 "Demographic shifts and criminality." British Journal of Criminology 110:169–75.

FLEISHER, BELTON M.
1966 The Economics of Delinquency. Chicago: Quadrangle.

FOX, JAMES A.
1976 An Econometric Analysis of Crime Data. Ph.D. dissertation, Department of Sociology, University of Pennsylvania. Ann Arbor: University Microfilms.

GLASER, DANIEL
1971 Social Deviance. Chicago: Markham.

GOLDBERG, SAMUEL
1958 Introduction to Difference Equations. New York: Wiley.

GOULD, LEROY
1969 "The changing structure of property crime in an affluent society." Social Forces 48:50–9.

GRILICHES, Z.
1967 "Distributed lags: a survey." Econometrica 35:16–

GUERRY, A. M.
1833 "Essai sur la statistique morale de la France." Westminster Review 18:357.

HAWLEY, AMOS
1950 Human Ecology: A Theory of Community Structure. New York: Ronald.

HENRY, A. F., AND J. F. SHORT
1954 Suicide and Homicide. New York: Free Press.

HINDELANG, MICHAEL J.
1976 Criminal Victimization in Eight American Cities: A Descriptive Analysis of Common Theft and Assault. Cambridge: Ballinger.

HINDELANG, MICHAEL J., CHRISTOPHER S. DUNN, PAUL SUTTON AND ALISON L. AUMICK
1976 Sourcebook of Criminal Justice Statistics—1975. U.S. Dept. of Justice, Law Enforcement Assistance Administration. Washington, D.C.: U.S. Government Printing Office.
1977 Sourcebook of Criminal Justice Statistics—1976. U.S. Dept. of Justice,, Law Enforcement Assistance Administration. Washington, D.C.: U.S. Government Printing Office.

INTERSTATE COMMERCE COMMISSION (ICC)
1974 Annual Report: Freight Commodity Statistics of Class I Motor Carriers of Property Operative in Intercity Service. Washington, D.C.: U.S. Government Printing Office.

JACKSON, BRUCE
1969 A Thief's Primer. New York: Macmillan.

JEFFERY, C. R.
1971 Crime Prevention Through Environmental Design. Beverly Hills: Sage.

KLOCKARS, CARL B.
1974 The Professional Fence. New York: Free Press.

KOBRIN, FRANCES E.
1976 "The primary individual and the family: changes in living arrangements in the U.S. since 1940." Journal of Marriage and the Family 38:233–9.

LAND, KENNETH C.
1978 "Modelling macro social change." Paper presented at annual meeting of the American Sociological Association, San Francisco.

LAND, KENNETH C. AND MARCUS FELSON
1976 "A general framework for building dynamic macro social indicator models: including an analysis of changes in crime rates and police expenditures." American Journal of Sociology 82:565–604.

LETKEMANN, PETER
1973 Crime As Work. Englewood Cliffs: Prentice-Hall.

LYSTAD, MARY
1974 An Annotated Bibliography: Violence at Home. DHEW Publication No. (ADM 75–136). Washington, D.C.: U.S. Government Printing Office.

MADDALA, G. S., AND A. S. RAO
1973 "Tests for serial correlation in regression models with lagged dependent variables and serially correlated errors." Econometrica 41:761–74.

MANSFIELD, ROGER, LEROY GOULD, AND J. ZVI NAMENWIRTH
1974 "A socioeconomic model for the prediction of societal rates of property theft." Social Forces 52:462–72.

MARTIN, JOHN BOWER
1952 My Life in Crime. New York: Harper.

MAURER, DAVID W.
1964 Whiz Mob. New Haven: College and University Press.

MERCHANDISING WEEK
1973 Statistical and Marketing Report (February). New York: Billboard Publications.
1976 Statistical and Marketing Report (March). New York: Billboard Publications.

NATIONAL COMMISSION ON THE CAUSES AND PREVENTION OF VIOLENCE
1969 Crimes of Violence. Vol. 13. Washington, D.C.: U.S. Government Printing Office.

NETTLER, GWYNN
1974 Explaining Crime. New York: McGraw-Hill.

NEWMAN, OSCAR
1973 Defensible Space: Crime Prevention Through Urban Design. New York: Macmillan,

OFFICE OF MANAGEMENT AND THE BUDGET (OMB)
1973 Social Indicators 1973. Washington, D.C.: U.S. Government Printing Office.

POPE, CARL E.
1977a Crime-Specific Analysis: The Characteristics of Burglary Incidents. U.S. Dept. of Justice, Law Enforcement Assistance Administration. Analytic Report 10. Washington, D.C.: U.S. Government Printing Office.

1977b Crime-Specific Analysis: An Empirical Examination of Burglary Offense and Offender Characteristics. U.S. Dept. of Justice, Law Enforcement Assistance Administration. Analytical Report 12. Washington, D.C.: U.S. Government Printing Office.

QUÈTELET, ADOLPHE
1842 A Treatise on Man. Edinburgh: Chambers.

REISS, ALBERT J.
1976 "Settling the frontiers of a pioneer in American criminology: Henry McKay." Pp. 64–88 in James F. Short, Jr. (ed.), Delinquency, Crime, and Society. Chicago: University of Chicago Press.

REPPETTO, THOMAS J.
1974 Residential Crime. Cambridge: Ballinger.

RONCEK, DONNIS
1975 Crime Rates and Residential Densities in Two Large Cities. Ph.D. dissertation, Department of Sociology, University of Illinois, Urbana.

SAGI, PHILLIP C. AND CHARLES E. WELLFORD
1968 "Age composition and patterns of change in criminal statistics." Journal of Criminal Law, Criminology and Police Science 59:29–36.

SCARR, HARRY A.
1972 Patterns of Burglary. U.S. Dept. of Justice, Law Enforcement Assistance Administration, Washington, D.C.: U.S. Government Printing Office.

SEARS CATALOGUE
1960 Chicago: Sears.
1970 Chicago: Sears.

SHAW, CLIFFORD R., HENRY D. MCKAY, FREDERICK ZORBAUGH AND LEONARD S. COTTRELL
1929 Delinquency Areas. Chicago: University of Chicago Press.

SHORT, JAMES F., AND FRED STRODTBECK
1965 Group Process and Gang Delinquency Chicago: University of Chicago Press.

SKOGAN, WESLEY G.
1976 "The victims of crime: some material findings." Pp. 131–48 in Anthony L. Guenther (ed.), Criminal Behavior in Social Systems. Chicago: Rand McNally.

SUTHERLAND, EDWIN H.
1937 The Professional Thief. Chicago: University of Chicago Press.

SZALAI, ALEXANDER (ED.)
1972 The Use of Time: Daily Activities of Urban and Suburban Populations in Twelve Countries. The Hague: Mouton.

THEIL, HENRI
1971   Principles of Econometrics. New York: Wiley.

TOBIAS, J. J.
1967   Crime and Industrial Society in the Nineteenth Century. New York: Schocken Books.

U.S. BUREAU OF THE CENSUS (USBC)
1973a   Census of Transportation, 1972. U.S Summary. Washington, D.C.: U.S. Government Printing Office.

1973b   Who's Home When. Working Paper 37. Washington, D.C.: U.S. Government Printing Office.

1975–   Statistical Abstract of the U.S. Washington, D.C.:
1976   U.S. Government Printing Office.

1947–   Current Population Studies, P-25 Ser. Washing-
1976   ton, D.C.: U.S. Government Printing Office.

U.S. DEPARTMENT OF JUSTICE (USDJ)
1974a   Preliminary Report of the Impact Cities, Crime Survey Results. Washington, D.C.: Law Enforcement Assistance Administration (NCJISS).

1974b   Crime in the Nation's Five Largest Cities: Advance Report. Washington, D.C.: Law Enforcement Assistance Administration (NCJISS).

1974c   Crimes and Victims: A Report on the Dayton-San Jose Pilot Survey of Victimization. Washington, D.C.: Law Enforcement Assistance Administration.

1976   Criminal Victimizations in the U.S., 1973. Washington, D.C.: Law Enforcement Assistance Administration (NCJISS).

1977   Criminal Victimizations in the U.S.: A Comparison of 1974 and 1975 Findings. Washington. D.C.: Law Enforcement Assistance Administration (NCJISS).

WASHNIS, GEORGE J.
1976   Citizen Involvement in Crime Prevention. Lexington: Heath.

WELLFORD, CHARLES F.
1973   "Age composition and the increase in recorded crime." Criminology 11:61–70.

WILKS, JUDITH A.
1967   "Ecological correlates of crime and delinquency." Pp. 138–56 in President's Commission on Law Enforcement and the Administration of Justice Task Force Report: Crime and Its Impact—An Assessment. Appendix A. Washington, D.C.: U.S. Government Printing Office.

WILLIAMSON, HENRY
1968   Hustler! New York: Doubleday.

WOLFGANG, MARVIN E.
1958   Patterns of Criminal Homicide. Philadelphia: University of Pennsylvania Press.

QUESTIONS FOR DISCUSSION

1. List and discuss the three elements of direct-contact predatory violations. Provide examples to support your discussion.

2. Explain Hawley's Human Ecological Theory.

3. Provide a discussion and examples of Routine Activities Theory. What are the advantages of considering crime from this perspective?

4. Explain the relationship of family activities and crime rates.

5. The authors state, "it is ironic that the very factors which increase the opportunity to enjoy the benefits of life also may increase the opportunity for predatory violations." Discuss and give examples.

APPLICATIONS

1. One of the tenets of routine activities theory is that the dispersion away from households and families increases the opportunity for crime and thus generates crime. Assuming this to be the case, what social changes over the past twenty or thirty years have contributed to this dispersion? Can this trend be reversed? Discuss these trends with members of your class.

2. What kinds of personal routine changes might an individual make to discourage predatory violence?

KEY TERMS

celerity   rapidity or swiftness.

commensalistic   refers to a relationship between two organisms where benefits are derived without harm or benefit to the other organism.

conceptual framework   a model for considering ideas about events or occurrences.

criminogenic   refers to the root causes of criminal behavior.

empirical   refers to something that is based on experience, trial and error, or experiments.

exogenous   originating outside the organism or person.

iterative   repetitious.

spurious   having the appearance of being real or genuine, but without being so.

symbiotic   refers to the intimate association of two dissimilar organisms or people in which each benefits.

10

Poverty, Income Inequality, and Community Crime Rates

E. Britt Patterson
Florida State University

This paper examines the relationship between crime rates and aggregate economic conditions for 57 small social areas. The principal analyses address a continuing controversy—are community crime rates associated with absolute poverty, relative poverty (i.e., income inequality), or both. Using victimization data from 57 small residential neighborhoods, the analyses examine the association between absolute and relative poverty and rates of violent crime and burglary. The findings indicate that absolute poverty is more strongly associated with neighborhood crime rates, although the relationship is conditional on the type of crime considered. The implications of the findings are discussed within a perspective of community social control.

What is the relationship between crime rates and the economic conditions of social areas? After more than a century and a half of empirical and theoretical investigations (beginning with Guerry, 1833, and Quetelet, 1835), this question remains controversial. Recent research on the social ecology of criminal activity has renewed attention to this question and contributed to the controversy (e.g., Blau and Blau, 1982; Messner, 1982; O'Brien, 1983; Sampson, 1985; Williams, 1984). This paper identifies some issues in the debate and empirically exam-

Criminology, Volume 29, Number 4, 1991. Reprinted by Permission of the American Society of Criminology.

ines the association between crime rates and economic conditions in 57 small residential areas.

CRIME RATES AND ECONOMIC CONDITIONS

Poverty and Crime

The relationship between economic environment and crime has been considered in conflict theories (Bonger, 1916; Taylor et al. 1973), subcultural theories (Cloward and Ohlin, 1960; Wolfgang and Ferracuti, 1967), strain theory (Merton, 1949), opportunity theories (Cantor and Land, 1985; Cohen et al., 1980), and social disorganization theory (Kornhauser, 1978; Shaw and McKay, 1942). Common to many of these perspectives is the position that variation in the spatial distribution of crime are associated with the degree of poverty characterizing an area. In summarizing this orientation, Vold and Bernard (1986:138) pointed out that it is "the lack of some fixed level of material goods necessary for survival and minimum well-being" that causes criminal activity (personal as well as property) to flourish in an area.

As summarized in Table 1, research reveals contradictory support for the poverty/crime thesis.[1] For example, some studies show that poorer areas have higher levels of certain types of violent offending, such as homicide (Bailey,

TABLE 1 Summary of Studies of Poverty and Crime

Study	Location/Year	Sample Size	Variables		Findings
			Dependent	Independent	
Harries (1976)	Cities over 25,000 (1970)	726	Serious crime index: robbery, aggravated assault, burglary, auto theft per 100,000	% of families below low-income level (1969)	Positive correlation with assault*
Mladenka & Hill (1976)	Houston (1973)	20 police districts	Official: total, person, property per 1,000	% of families below poverty level	Total $r = .75$ Property $r = .66$ Person $r = .93$* Strong positive effect in regression**

Decker (1980)	Cities (1972–73)	26	Official: index, violent, property
			Survey: index, violent, property
				(1) No. of persons below poverty level per 100,000;
				(2) No. of families below poverty level per 100,000
					Positive with:
					  survey violent
					  official violent
					  official violent (excluding robbery)
					  official property
					  official property (including robbery)
					  official index
					Negative with:
					  survey violent (excluding robbery)**

Watts & Watts (1981)	All U.S. cities 100,000+ (1970)	152	No. of major crimes reported to police per 1,000	% of families below poverty line	Zero-order correlation: $r = .30$ Negative effect in regression**
Blau & Blau (1982)	SMSAs, Largest (1970)	125	Official: murder, forcible rape, robbery, aggravated assault, total (log base 10)	% poor using poverty index developed by Social Security Admin. (SSA)	In general not related to all rates but is negatively associated with robbery rates** Zero-order correlation: $r = .05$*
Crutchfield et al. (1982)	SMSAs 600,000+ (1970)	65	Official: index, violent, property (average 1969–71)	% of pop. below poverty line	Negative effect with robbery positive effect with assault & burglary**

136

TABLE 1 Summary of Studies of Poverty and Crime (con't.)

Study	Location/Year	Sample Size	Dependent	Independent	Findings
			Variables		
Messner (1982)	SMSAs (1970)	204	Official: murder & nonnegligent homicide per 100,000	% of pop below poverty line (SSA index)	Zero-order correlation: $r = .29$* Poverty inversely related to homicide rate**
Sampson & Castellano (1982)	NCS (1973–78)	Unknown	Theft & violent victimizations per 100,000	Proportion of families with < $5000 income	Low economic status in urban areas exhibits higher rates of personal victimizations**
Messner (1983)	SMSAs (1969–71)	204	Official homicide rates per 100,000 (3-year average)	Income < $1000; Used in index	Zero-order correlation: $r = .77$* Significant positive effect in regression**
Williams (1984)	SMSAs 250,000+ (1970)	125	Official rates of murder and nonnegligent manslaughter (log 10)	% of families below SSA poverty line (log 10)	Significant positive effect**
Loftin & Parker (1985)	Largest U.S. cities (1973)	49	Total, family, other primary, other felony homicides rates	% of families below poverty line	Significant positive effect for all types of homicide (exception: other primary)**
Messner & Tardiff (1986)	Manhattan neighborhoods (1981)	26	Official homicide rates	% pop. with incomes below 75% of poverty line	Significant positive effect**
Sampson (1986)	NCS (1973–78)	Unknown	Theft & violent personal criminal victimizations	% of families < of families < $5000 family income	"For both theft and violent crimes, predicted victimizations are higher in the low category than in the high category" (p. 6).

*Bivariate association.
**Multivariate association.

1984; Loftin and Parker, 1985; Messner, 1983; Smith and Parker, 1980) or assault (Crutchfield et al., 1982; Harries, 1976). Others claim that such relationships are spurious and that once other characteristics of social areas are taken into account, poverty has little if any relationship with homicide, forcible rape, or aggravated assault rates (Blau and Blau, 1982). Still other studies, such as Messner (1983), report that standard metropolitan statistical areas (SMSAS) with high poverty levels have lower homicide rates. Such contradictory evidence also emerges in studies using victimization-based measures of violent crime rates. For example, Sampson and Castellano (1982) and Sampson (1986) report that personal victimizations are significantly higher in poverty-stricken areas, but Decker (1980) found poverty to be negatively related to violent victimizations when robbery was excluded from a violent victimization index.

Fewer studies have examined the relationship between poverty and property crime rates, but the evidence shows a more consistent pattern. Both Mladenka and Hill (1976) and Crutchfield et al. (1982) report that official rates of burglary are positively associated with the percentage of the population living below the poverty level, and research using aggregated victimization data supports this relationship (Sampson, 1986). However, these studies as a rule have examined the relationship between areal crime rates and poverty while controlling for only a few other characteristics of social areas.

Economic Inequality and Crime

Complicating the picture of how economic conditions are related to areal crime rates is a debate regarding the most appropriate way to measure poverty. Some argue that poverty is a subjective concept: "Poverty is always in part a subjective condition, relative to what others have, rather than any simple objective fact of the presence or absence of a certain amount of property or other measure of wealth" (Vold and Bernard, 1986:138). Similarly, the Social Science Council (1968:227–228) concluded that "people are 'poor' because they are deprived of opportunities, comforts, and self-

respect regarded *as normal in the community* to which they belong" (italics added). Consequently, some argue that "relative" poverty (or economic inequality), not absolute poverty, is a more relevant variable for explaining areal variation in criminal activity. From this perspective, the percentage of community members who are poor in absolute terms may not be the most significant correlate of criminal activity. Instead, rates of criminal activity should vary with the degree of inequity in the distribution of wealth or income.

Empirical studies of the income inequality/crime relationship have also produced mixed results. As summarized in Table 2, some studies have found that both income inequality and poverty are significantly associated with homicide rates (Loftin and Hill, 1974). Others report that economic inequality but not poverty is significantly associated with areal variation in this form of violent criminal activity (Blau, 1977; Blau and Blau, 1982). Still other studies find no significant association between income inequality and homicide (Messner, 1982, 1983; Messner and Tardiff, 1986; Williams 1984).

When consideration is given to other forms of criminal activity, inconsistencies persist. For example, Danzinger (1976) reported that income inequality had a significant, positive relationship with rates of robbery in 222 SMSAs, but Rosenfeld (1986) reported a nonsignificant association between income inequality and robbery rates using a different sample of 125 SMSAs. The few studies that have simultaneously examined the effects of poverty and economic inequality on rates of property offending also yielded divergent findings. Some studies found a positive effect of both poverty and income-inequality on property offending rates (Danzinger, 1976), but others concluded that only economic inequality is significantly related to property offending rates (Jacobs, 1981).

Some research goes beyond the question of whether poverty or income inequality has independent effects on crime rates and focuses on contingencies in the relationship between inequality and crime. Blau and Blau (1982), for example, argue that where *ascribed inequality* is present *violent* behavior will be high. Specifically, they suggest (p. 119) that ascriptive socioeconomic inequalities undermines the social integration of a community by creating multiple parallel social differences which widen the separation between social classes, and it creates a situation characterized by much social disorganization and prevalent latent animosities.

Consistent with their hypothesis, Blau and Blau report that areas characterized by extreme racial economic inequality are also areas with high rates of violent crime. However, a subsequent study by Rosenfeld disagrees. According to Rosenfeld (1986:127), "the dollar gap between blacks and whites has no independent influence on crime rates." (See Golden and Messner, 1987, for a discussion of the sources of inconsistency in research examining the racial inequality-violent crime association.)

To summarize, the relationship between aggregate economic conditions and rates of criminal activity remains unclear. Diverse empirical findings have contributed to theoretical ambiguity. The central question persists: Are rates of differing types of criminal activity associated with levels of poverty, economic heterogeneity, or both? Moreover, what are the contingencies of association in the relationship between material well-being and aggregate crime rates? This paper examines these issues with data that include measures of several other theoretically relevant variables.

Issues of Aggregation and Measurement

Two additional issues are pertinent to the specification of the economic conditions-crime relationship. The first involves the correspondence between the empirical and theoretical "unit of analysis" (see Nettler, 1984). The research summarized in Tables 1 and 2 shows the wide range of aggregation in prior studies (e.g., SMSAs over 100,000; nonsouthern cities over 50,000, and police districts). Early theoretical works (e.g., Cloward and Ohlin, 1960; Shaw and McKay, 1942) argued that the most meaningful unit of analysis for examining aggregate variations in delinquency or criminal activity is the social community or neighborhood. The notion of community poses severe operational problems, however, because of the difficulty of defining community boundaries. Most eco-

logical units for which data are available correspond to administrative units of convenience and may not represent communities in the original spirit of the early theoretical works.

As Williams (1984) and Messner and Tardiff (1986) (also see Bailey, 1984) suggest, however, smaller units of aggregation may provide a more meaningful frame of reference for many concepts used in macro theories of criminal activity. For example, the degree of income inequality may represent something completely different at the state level than at the level of police districts or census tracts. Individuals are most aware of the social context to which they are most frequently exposed. Thus, smaller units of aggregation provide measures of income inequality, racial heterogeneity, and residential mobility that are more consistent with the theoretical spirit of most aggregate models of criminal activity. As Williams (1984:285) pointed out in regard to SMSAs and cities: "Regular patterns of interpersonal interaction between people who live in central cities and residents of the suburbs are unlikely. Therefore, it is difficult to imagine how SMSA residents can become aware of income inequality within the SMSA."[2]

Smaller units of aggregation may also provide more meaningful measures of the dependent variable—crime rates. In general, the larger the aggregate, the greater the within-group variation in the measure being aggregated and the smaller the between-group variation (Burstein, 1975). Consider two units of aggregation, neighborhoods and cities. Cities are made up of several neighborhoods, and the measured crime rates of cities may not provide a good approximation of the crime rate in each of the city's neighborhoods. Some areas within a city may be places of little or no criminal activity, and other neighborhoods may be places where crime flourishes. The position taken here is that conceptual arguments relating crime rates and areal attributes are most applicable to smaller geographic units, such as neighborhoods. Thus, the analyses reported in this paper are based on 57 residential areas, which cover, on average, 1.5 square miles. Although it is not possible to assess whether they are "communities" in the sense of Shaw and McKay, these social areas do provide a meaningful

TABLE 2 Summary of Studies of Economic Inequality and Crime

Study	Location/Year	Sample Size	Variables		Findings
			Dependent	Independent	
Watts & Watts (1981)	All U.S. cities 100,000+ (1970)	152	# of major crimes reported to police per 1,000	Dummy variable: 1 = cities with above-average proportion of both poor and wealthy families	Significant positive effect** $r = .26$*
Blau & Blau (1982)	SMSAs, largest (1970)	125	Official: murder, forcible rape, robbery aggravated assault, total (log base 10)	(1) Gini index; (2) Difference in average SES between nonwhites and whites based on Duncan SEI scores	(1) Gini positively related to murder and aggravated assault; (2) SES inequality in race positively related to all dependent except rape**
Messner (1982)	SMSAs (1970)	204	Official: murder & nonnegligent homicide per 100,000	Gini index	Not significant in multivariate**
Messner (1983)	SMSAs (1969–71)	204	Official homicide rates per 100,000 (3-year average)	Gini index	Not significant in multivariate**
Carroll & Jackson (1983)	Nonsouthern cities < 50,000 (1970)	93	Official rates of burglary, robbery, and crimes against person	(1) Gini index; (2) Dollar difference between median white & black family income divided by total median	Strong positive effect on rates of burglary in cities where blacks are closer to whites in terms of family income**
Williams (1984)	SMSAs 250,000+ (1970)	125	Official rates of murder and nonnegligent manslaughter (log 10)	Gini index	Statistically insignificant**
Sampson (1985)	NCS (1973–75)	Unknown	Theft and violent personal criminal victimization	Gini index	Small positive effect**
Rosenfeld (1986)	SMSAs (1970)	125	Official rates of murder, rape, robbery, assault, burglary, larceny, motor vehicle theft	Product of: (1) Difference between mean income of families below poverty level and mean income of all families in SMSA; (2) % of families with income below the federal poverty level in 1969; (3) Ratio of median years of school completed by heads of poverty families to median years of school completed by all family heads	Significant positive effect on all rates except robbery**
Messner & Tardiff (1986)	Manhattan neighborhoods (1981)	26	Official homicide rates	Gini index	No significant effect**

*Bivariate association.
**Multivariate association.

frame of reference for examining the relationship between economic conditions and the crime rates of social areas.

A second concern is how to measure criminal activity across social areas in such a way that comparisons across aggregate units are meaningful (O'Brien, 1983). Most previous research uses official crime data to make comparisons across aggregate units, and some empirical evidence cautions that such comparisons are, with few exceptions, unwise (McCleary et al., 1982; O'Brien, 1985; Skogan, 1976). One increasingly available means of overcoming jurisdictional variations in the recording and reporting of official crime is to use crime rates constructed from victimization survey data. Although not a panacea, victimization-based crime rates do avoid many problems associated with comparing official crime rates across aggregate units (for a list of potential problems involved in comparing official crime rates across jurisdictions, see Beattie, 1960; Maxfield et al., 1980; Seidman and Couzens, 1974; Skogan, 1976; Wilson, 1978). Thus, victimization data may provide a more accurate reflection of differences in rates of criminal activity across social areas by reducing the confounding effects of police agency response (see Smith, 1986). Further, some research indicates that residential proximity to criminal activity is directly related to victimization (Fagan et al., 1987; Garofalo, 1987), which implies that offenders commit crimes in "their own backyards" (Brantingham and Brantingham, 1978; Pyle, 1974). Consequently, this paper uses victimization survey data to operationalize crime rates across social areas.

Crime Rates and Other Attributes of Social Areas

Assessments of the relationship between a neighborhood's economic situation and its rates of criminal activity must also consider a number of other variables that may be associated with the spatial distribution of crime. Among those considered in this study are (1) residential mobility, (2) racial heterogeneity, (3) neighborhood integration, (4) household composition and family disorganization, and (5) population density. Theoretical rationales for how these variables are associated with crime rates vary. However, many of the variables are viewed as important because of their potential association with levels of community social control. For example, rapid population turnover may disrupt primary relationships as well as institutional development. In transient areas, community integration and social control may be weak (Shaw and McKay, 1942), and empirical studies generally show a positive relationship between levels of residential mobility and crime rates (Chilton, 1964; Crutchfield et a]., 1982; Sampson, 1985).

The racial heterogeneity of an area may also impede the establishment of common values (Shaw and McKay, 1942). The close proximity of ethnically diverse groups can engender cultural conflict (Sellin, 1938). Each group may have unique institutions and roles, which may impede the development of shared meaning among members of heterogeneous areas. The lack of common interests and shared meaning may undermine the possibility of social integration and increase the potential for delinquency. Lander (1954) and Smith and Jarjoura (1988), for example, found that delinquency rates were highest in racially mixed areas.

Efforts to measure the degree of informal control of youths across communities have used aggregate measures of household composition and family disorganization. The argument for this approach is that areas characterized by high levels of family disorganization and nonfamily households are less able to maintain "scrutiny, supervision and surveillance designed to preclude, deter or detect deviance" (Kornhauser, 1978:24). Thus, communities characterized by high percentages of single-person households (Roncek, 1981) or female-headed households (Sampson, 1985) are more likely to experience high rates of criminal offending than other communities. The extant empirical evidence is consistent with this expectation (e.g., Cohen and Felson, 1979; Smith and Jarjoura, 1988).

Finally, two other community characteristics (urbanization and percentage of nonwhite population) have been examined in the literature on areal variation in rates of criminal activity. Scholars since Wirth (1938) have argued that more densely populated areas are places of greater criminal activity. Specifically, increasing population density makes social experiences impersonal and transitory. Thus, more urbanized areas are less integrated areas, and effective mechanisms of informal social control are less likely to develop. Extant empirical evidence consistently shows that crime rates are higher in more densely populated areas (Blau and Blau, 1982; Danzinger, 1976).

The final control variable considered in this analysis is the percentage of minority population in an area. In earlier studies, the rationale for expecting certain types of crimes to vary with an area's racial composition was the "subculture of violence" thesis and the argument that social values supportive of violence have arisen among blacks from historical circumstances (see, e.g., Curtis, 1974). The proposed positive association between the percentage of minorities and crime rates of communities has received mixed empirical support. Some studies (e.g., Bordua, 1958; Chilton, 1964; Sampson, 1985; Smith and Jarjoura, 1988) found no association between percentage nonwhite and crime rates, but others reported a positive association between these variables (e.g., Carroll and Jackson, 1983; Messner, 1982; Roncek, 1981). The percent nonwhite variable is included in this analysis because of its frequent use in prior studies.

DATA AND MEASURES

Data used in this study were originally collected in 1977 as part of a larger study of police behavior.[3] Interviews were conducted in 57 residential areas with members of 11,419 randomly selected households. The 57 areas are within three SMSAs (Rochester, New York; St. Louis, Missouri; and Tampa-St. Petersburg, Florida). Data from the interviews were aggregated within neighborhoods to create neighborhood measures. When a resident did report a victimization, he or she was asked to identify where the victimization occurred. Only those acts that occurred within the boundaries of the study neighborhood were used when calculating neighborhood victimization rates. (See Smith, 1986, and Smith and Jarjoura, 1988, for a more detailed discussion of these data.)

Two victimization-based crime rates are used in this study. Rates of burglary per 1,000 households and serious violent crimes (robberies, rapes, and aggravated assaults) per 1,000 residents were calculated from the victimization data. Across the neighborhoods in the study, burglary rates ranged from 32.7 to 235.1 per 1,000 households and serious violent crime rates ranged from 0 to 21.49 per 1,000 persons. No serious violent victimizations were reported in 15 of the 57 residential areas.

Several measures of neighborhood characteristics were constructed by aggregating information from the interviews with residents. A correlation matrix for these variables, along with some descriptive statistics, is presented in Table 3. *Residential instability* is measured as the percentage of households that have been in the area for less than three years. *Racial heterogeneity* is the probability that two randomly selected individuals from a neighborhood would be members of different racial groups. *Neighborhood integration* was measured by asking residents how often they or members of their family got together socially with other residents in the area. Higher values on this variable indicate areas of greater social interaction among residents. *Population density* is the number of persons per square mile of land area. *Percent aged* 12 to 20 is the percentage of the population in that age group. The variable *percent single parent* is the percentage of single-parent households with children in the age range of 12 to 20 years. *Percent nonwhite* and *percent living alone* are self-explanatory variables.

Two measures of the economic status of social areas are considered in this analysis. The first is the percentage of households with an annual household income of less than $5,000. There is substantial variation in this variable in these data. At the one extreme are neighborhoods that contained no households below this income level, and at the other end of the distribution, 58.4% of the households had annual incomes of less than $5,000. This variable is used to measure the absolute poverty level of neighborhoods. The second measure is the gini coefficient of income concentration. This measure is used because it was used in a number of prior studies that examined the association between income inequality and crime rates.[4]

TABLE 3 Correlation Coefficients and Descriptive Statistics for Variables Used in the Analysis ($N = 57$)

	(x1)	(x2)	(x3)	(x4)	(x5)	(x6)	(x7)	(x8)	(x9)	(x10)	(x11)	(x12)	Mean	Range
(x1)Burglary*	1.00												4.53	3.49 – 5.46
(x2)Violent Crime	.64	1.00											5.68	.00 – 21.49
(x3)Residential Mobility	.05	.12	1.00										19.31	6.72 – 34.22
(x4)Racial Heterogeneity	.52	.39	-.13	1.00									.19	.00 –
(x5)Neighborhood Integration	-.44	-.42	.21	-.44	1.00								3.48	2.93 – 3.88
(x6)Population Density*	.52	.67	-.22	.40	-.44	1.00							8.67	7.42 – 9.84
(x7)Percent Aged 12–20	.54	.39	-.17	.31	-.34	.15	1.00						18.97	9.13 – 26.95
(x8)Percent Single Parent	.66	.62	-.13	.46	-.18	.52	.54	1.00					5.17	.53 – 12.86
(x9)Percent Nonwhite	.53	.59	-.31	.58	-.40	.50	.52	.74	1.00				30.89	.50 – 99.50
(xl0)Percent Living Alone	.29	.32	-.03	.26	-.02	.31	-.04	.36	.29	1.00			6.31	.51 – 12.84
(x11)Percent below $5,000 annual income	.37	.51	-.23	.31	.04	.41	.18	.63	.68	.55	1.00		22.13	.00 – 58.40
(x12)Gini Coefficient	.07	.10	-.25	.11	.04	.15	-.20	.08	.05	.37	.30	1.00	.31	.24 – .37
	(x1)	(x2)	(x3)	(x4)	(x5)	(x6)	(x7)	(x8)	(x9)	(x10)	(x11)	(x12)		

*Natural log.

FINDINGS

This analysis is concerned with estimating the association between crime rates and measures of a neighborhood's economic condition. The results shown in Table 4 address the relationship between household burglary rates and economic conditions of communities. Two equations are presented. Equation 1 shows the relationship between burglary rates and other attributes of the social areas. Few surprises emerge from the findings. Higher burglary rates are significantly associated with greater residential instability, higher percentages of youths, and more single-parent households. In more socially integrated areas, burglary rates are significantly lower.

The main concern here is whether an independent statistical association exists between measures of neighborhood economic status and crime rates. Data that address this issue are reported in equation 2 in Table 4.[5] These results show that once the relationship between burglary rates and other neighborhood characteristics is taken into account, measures of a community's economic condition are not significantly associated with rates of burglary. At the same time, both poverty and income

inequality are associated with burglary rates in the expected direction. Additional analyses (not reported) that included only one of the economic measures at a time revealed the same results as when both poverty and income inequality were simultaneously added to the model.

Although there is no evidence that burglary rates are significantly higher in poorer areas or in places where income inequality is greater, it is still possible that the association between crime rates and other neighborhood characteristics may vary with the economic conditions of an area. For example, Blau and Blau (1982) suggested that it may be the combination of racial and income inequality that is most strongly associated with increased crime rates. To address this question, a series of interaction terms were created by multiplying poverty and income inequality by the other attributes of the social areas. Equation 2 in Table 4 was then estimated several more times adding one of these interaction terms each time the equation was reestimated. This process was repeated once for each tested interaction. Results from this process indicated that no interaction term was significantly associated with area burglary rates.[6] Thus, evidence from this analysis indicates that

TABLE 4 Regression Models of Household Burglary Rates on Neighborhood Characteristics (N = 57)

Independent Variables	Equation 1			Equation 2		
Residential Instability	.018[a]	(2.74)[b]	.21[c]	.020	(3.56)	.24
Racial Heterogeneity	.438	(1.66)	.13	.450	(1.69)	.14
Neighborhood Integration	−.701	(−2.43)	−.33	−.888	(−2.64)	−.41
Population Density	.210	(1.67)	.24	.172	(1.34)	.19
Percent Aged 12–20	.049	(3.70)	.35	.054	(4.72)	.39
Percent Single-Parent Households	.067	(2.%)	.38	.064	(3.17)	.36
Percent Nonwhite	−.003	(−1.78)	−.18	−.004	(−2.54)	−.30
Percent Living Alone	.021	(1.13)	.11	.003	(0.17)	.01
Rochester SMSA	.190	(1.09)	.14	.195	(1.40)	.18
Tampa SMSA	.194	(1.39)	.18	.246	(1.34)	.18
Percent Households < $5,000				.007	(1.45)	.19
Gini coefficient				1.574	(1.11)	.09
Constant	3.299			3.659		
Adjusted R^2	.612			.617		
Log Likelihood	−12.830			−11.210		

[a]OLS metric coefficient.
[b]T ratio.
[c]Standardized coefficient.

burglary rates are somewhat higher in poorer neighborhoods and in areas characterized by greater income inequality, but the relationships are not statistically significant nor conditional on other attributes of communities.

In Table 5, attention turns to the relationship between neighborhood characteristics and rates of serious violent crime. In 15 of the 57 neighborhoods, no interviewee reported that he or she or any member of the household had been the victim of a violent crime in the past year. Thus, the distribution of violent crime rates is truncated. Because of this, the relationship between violent crime rates and neighborhood characteristics was estimated using a tobit model (see Amemiya, 1985; Maddala, 1983). One drawback of standard tobit models is that if the disturbance terms are heteroscedastic, the estimated coefficients are not consistent (see Maddala, 1983:178–182). In this analysis, a correction was made for one form of heteroscedasticity.[7]

Table 5 reports estimated coefficients from two tobit models of neighborhood violent crime rates. Equation 1 excludes measures of neighborhood economic conditions, and the results show that higher rates of violent crime are associated with residential instability, population density, age composition, and the percentage of nonwhite residents. When economic variables are added to the model (equation 2), crime rates are significantly associated with the percentage of households in an area with annual incomes below $5,000. No evidence emerges of a meaningful association between violent crime rates and economic inequality.

The addition of poverty to the model also specifies the relationship between violent crime rates and other neighborhood attributes. The percentage of nonwhite population and the percentage of the population in the age range of 12 to 20 years, for example, are not significantly associated with rates of violent crime once the percentage of low-income households is added to the model. Conversely, controlling for the proportion of low-income households reveals that violent crime rates are significantly lower in areas that are more socially integrated. Finally, violent crime rates are higher in areas

TABLE 5   Heteroscedastic Tobit Models of Violent Crime Rates and Neighborhood Characteristics (N = 57)

Independent Variables	Equation 1		Equation 2	
Residential Instability	.551[a]	(4.69)[b]	.286	(3.17)
Racial Heterogeneity	−5.109	(−1.20)	1.568	(.36)
Neighborhood Integration	−.444	(− .12)	−10.761	(−2.47)
Population Density	7.853	(4.39)	4.379	(3.63)
Percent Aged 12–20	.377	(2.08)	.198	(.96)
Percent Single-Parent Households	.080	(.25)	.600	(1.64)
Percent Nonwhite	.078	(2.60)	−.046	(−1.45)
Percent Living Alone	.039	(.15)	−.315	(−1.08)
Rochester SMSA	−3.260	(−1.14)	2.587	(1.54)
Tampa SMSA	−2.310	(−1.02)	1.806	(1.22)
Percent Households < S5,000			.224	(3.91)
Gini coefficient			−.936	(− .05)
Constant	−80.780		−10.520	
Sigma[c]	5.170		2.100	
Alpha[d]	−.180	(−2.37)	.257	(2.12)
Pseudo R^2	.771		.806	
Log Likelihood	−124.650		−121.870	

[a] Maximum likelihood tobit coefficient.
[b] T ratio.
[c] Standardized error of equation.
[d] This coefficient is defined in footnote 7.

that are more densely populated or characterized by greater residential instability.

The analysis also considered whether any significant interactions exist between measures of neighborhood economic status and other attributes of the areas. Following the procedure described in relation to burglary revealed one significant interaction effect. Specifically, in the model that included all the variables in equation 2 in Table 5 plus the product of the percentage of low-income households multiplied by the percentage of single-parent households, the coefficient for the interaction term was negative and significantly different from zero. Because the two components of this interaction term are highly correlated (.63), the robustness of this effect is suspect. After plotting the expected crime rates over different levels of these two variables, it appears that this interaction term may identify threshold effects. Specifically, in neighborhoods where poverty is less prevalent, increasing percentages of single-parent households are associated with higher rates of violent crime. However, in neighborhoods with a substantial percentage of low-income households, changes in the percentage of single-parent households have little effect on already high rates of violent crime.[8]

To summarize, the relationship between economic conditions of social areas and crime rates varies by type of crime and the measure of economic conditions. Measures of household income inequality have no significant direct or conditional association with burglary or violent crime rates in these data. However, the percentage of low-income households in an area is significantly associated with violent crime rates.

DISCUSSION

This research examined the relative importance of poverty and income inequality in explaining criminal activity across social areas. The results indicate that levels of absolute poverty, measured by the percentage of households with annual incomes below $5,000, are significantly associated with higher rates of serious violent crime. Little evidence emerged from this analysis, however, to support the thesis that relative poverty, or income inequality,

is significantly related to rates of violent criminal activity. These findings lend support to the thesis that severe conditions of material disadvantage (absolute poverty) raise levels of community violence by eroding a community's capacity for social control and self regulation. Perhaps the sheer lack of adequate resources precludes the development of effective community-based mechanisms of social control. Where social control is weak, restraints on individual behavior are more tentative. But whatever process is at work, the data show that violence is more prevalent in social areas characterized by greater levels of absolute poverty and that this association is independent of several other attributes of the areas.

Neither the level of absolute poverty in an area nor the degree of inequality in the distribution of household income was significantly related to rates of household burglary. These results do not support claims that extreme differences in the distribution of income among individuals lead to rising rates of property crime (Jacobs, 1981), at least at this level of analysis.

Perhaps the strongest evidence to emerge from this analysis is that variation in community crime rates is most strongly associated with several noneconomic attributes of communities. Areas with transient populations were characterized by higher rates of violent crime and burglary. More socially integrated communities had significantly lower rates of both types of crime. Both of these neighborhood characteristics provide a window on a community's capacity to provide and maintain personal networks of common interests. The results of this analysis suggest that where these networks exist, criminal activity is less prevalent. Other findings from this analysis are also consistent with a social control perspective. Burglary rates were significantly higher in areas with larger youthful populations and higher levels of family disorganization. Rates of serious violent crime varied with population density and absolute poverty.

The issue of specification, coupled with other issues addressed by this research, may account for the particular findings of the study. Specifically, the inconsistencies evident in the extant literature on economic conditions and rates of offending may, at least in part, be a function of the lack of specification in regard to factors of informal community social control and integration. Although controls for such factors are evident in some studies (e.g., Blau and Blau, 1982; Williams, 1984: percent divorced), in general the potential contribution of these factors to more correctly specified models has been attenuated or completely ignored. The findings emerging from this research point to the importance of such factors in the conceptualization and analysis of areal variation in rates of criminal offending.

Collectively, findings from this analysis suggest that the meaning and theoretical utility of aggregate measures of social areas may depend on the level of aggregation. For small social areas, such as those considered in this paper, the concept of community social control makes sense, and several empirical relationships are consistent with a social control framework, including the relationship between absolute poverty and violent crime rates. What is less clear is whether the concept of relative poverty (income inequality) is theoretically meaningful for small units of aggregation. Specifically, one element that gives meaning to economic inequality is the notion of a reference group. It may well be that in a mass media society, reference groups that define standards of success or material advantage transcend neighborhood boundaries. It seems more likely that one compares his or her material position in life, not with that of neighbors but instead with generalized images of success in larger frames of reference, such as advertising media. From this viewpoint, the theoretical utility of income inequality seems more appropriate for larger units of aggregation, such as regions of a country or nations themselves. To the extent this is true, further controversy concerning whether absolute poverty or income inequality is more strongly related to rates of criminal activity may miss the point that the two measures may be applicable at different levels of aggregation. In this analysis, which used small units of aggregation, absolute poverty is clearly more relevant to explaining variation in some forms of criminal activity than the degree of inequality in the distribution of income.

NOTES

1. The concept *absolute poverty* has been measured in many different ways. The following are several of the most common operationalizations: unemployment/occupational distribution (Bates, 1962; Boggs, 1965; Chilton, 1964; Crutchfield et al., 1982; Decker, 1980; Harries, 1976; Polk, 1957, 1967; Quinney, 1964; Schmid, 1960a, 1960b; Schuessler and Slatin, 1964; Watts and Watts, 1981; Wellford, 1974; Willie, 1967); median income/median family income (Beasley and Antunes, 1974; Bordua, 1958; Chilton, 1964; Decker, 1980; Harries, 1976; Mladenka and Hill, 1976; Schmid, 1960a, 1960b; Schuessler and Slatin, 1964); and education distribution (Bates, 1962; Bordua, 1958; Bursik, 1984; Chilton, 1964; Crutchfield et al., 1982; Harries, 1976; Lander, 1954; Messner, 1983; Mladenka and Hill, 1976; Polk, 1957; Quinney, 1964; Schmid, 1960a, 1960b; Willie, 1967).

2. However, Messner and Tardiff (1986) also discuss the possibility that "the salient frames of reference for social comparisons" might be meaningful at higher levels of aggregation. Specifically, "given the widespread exposure to the mass media, and to television in particular, individuals in American society may very well assess economic standing in terms of a style of living that is deemed culturally appropriate for all Americans" (p. 311).

3. Because these data were originally collected to study variation in police behavior, the neighborhood boundaries rely heavily on police department definitions of neighborhoods.

4. For reasons given in Atkinson (1970) and Newbery (1970), the gini coefficient is not considered a particularly good measure of income inequality. However, because several prior studies of income inequality and crime rates used this measure, it is used here to maintain comparability with prior research. Computation of gini coefficients follows the method outlined in Shryrock and Siegel (1973:178–183). Seven income groupings were used, and Blau and Blau's (1982:121) procedure of incrementing the open-ended highest category by 50%, as described in their footnote 9, was followed.

5. The estimated coefficients reported in Table 4 are from a regression analysis using the natural log of burglary rates as the dependent variable. Reported t ratios are based on White's (1980) general correction for heteroscedasticity.

6. These results are available from the author on request.

7. Unlike ordinary least squares equations, in which estimated coefficients are consistent but not efficient when the disturbance terms are heteroscedastic, the coefficients in tobit models are inconsistent if the disturbance terms have unequal variance. In this analysis, a tobit model in which the disturbance term ε_i is a function of the estimated value of the underlying index, βX, is estimated. Specifically, the estimated

coefficients are obtained by minimizing the likelihood:

$$\Phi \left(-\beta X/\sigma_i\right) \qquad \phi((Y_i - \beta X/\sigma_i)/\sigma_{i9}$$

where $\sigma_i = / \sigma + (\alpha(\beta X)$. Thus, the variance of the disturbance term is a linear function of the estimated index (βX) and a constant variance (σ). My thanks go to Bill Rhodes for pointing me in this direction. Coefficients reported in this paper were estimated using Gauss.

8. These results are available from the author on request.

REFERENCES

AMEMIYA, T.
1985   Advanced Econometrics. Cambridge. Mass.: Harvard University Press.

ATKINSON, A.B.
1970   On the measurement of inequality. Journal of Economic Theory 2:244–263.

BAILEY, W.C.
1984   Poverty, inequality and city homicide rates: Some not so unexpected findings. Criminology 22:531–550.

BATES, W.
1962   Caste, class, and vandalism. Social Problems 9:349–358.

BEASLEY. R.W. AND G. ANTUNES
1974   The etiology of urban crime: An ecological analysis. Criminology 11:439–461.

BEATTIE, R.H.
1960   Criminal statistics in the United States—1960. Journal of Criminal Law, Criminology and Police Science 51:49–65.

BLAU, J. AND P.M. BLAU
1982   The cost of inequality: Metropolitan structure and violent crime. American Sociological Review 47:114–129.

BOGGS, S.L.
1965   Urban crime patterns. American Sociological Review 30:899–908.

BONGER, W.A.
1916   Criminality and Economic Conditions. Boston: Little, Brown.

BORDUA, D.J.
1958   Juvenile delinquency and "anomie": An attempt at replication. Social Problems 6:230–238.

BRANTINGHAM, P.J. AND P.L. BRANTINGHAM
1978   A theoretical model of crime site selection. In M.D. Krohn and R.L. (eds.), Crime, Law and Sanctions. Newbury Park, Calif.: Sage.

BURSIK, R.J.
1984   Urban dynamics and ecological studies of delinquency. Social Forces 63:392–413.

BURSTEIN, L.
1975   The use of data from groups for inference about

individuals in educational research. Ph.D. dissertation, Stanford University, Calif.

CANTOR, D. AND K.C. LAND
1985   Unemployment and crime rates in the post-World War II United States: A theoretical and empirical analysis. American Sociological Review 50:317–332.

CARROLL, L. AND P. JACKSON
1983   Inequality, opportunity and crime rates in central cities. Criminology 21:178–194.

CHILTON, R.J.
1964   Continuities in delinquency area research: A comparison of studies for Baltimore, Detroit, and Indianapolis. American Sociological Review 29:71–83.

CLOWARD, R.A. AND L.E. OHLIN
1960   Delinquency and Opportunity: A Theory of Delinquency and Gangs. New York: Free Press.

COHEN, L.E. AND M. FELSON
1979   Social change and crime rate trends: A routine activity approach. American Sociological Review 44:588–608.

COHEN, L.E., M. FELSON, AND K.C. LAND
1980   Property crime rates in the United States: A macrodynamic analysis, 1947–1977; with ex ante forecasts for the mid-1980s. American Journal of Sociology 86:90–118.

CRUTCHFIELD, R., M. GEERKEN, AND W. GOVE
1982   Crime rates and social integration: the impact of metropolitan mobility. Criminology 20:467–478.

CURTIS, L.A.
1974   Criminal Violence. Lexington, Mass.: D.C. Heath.

DANZINGER, S.
1976   Explaining urban crime rates. Criminology 14:291–295.

DECKER, S.H.
1980   Criminalization, Victimization and Structural Correlates of Twenty Six American Cities. Saratoga: Century Twenty One Publishing.

FAGAN, J., E. PIPER, AND Y. CHENG
1987   Contributions of victimization to delinquency in inner cities. Journal of Criminal Law and Criminology 78:505–24.

GAROFALO, J.
1987   Reassessing the lifestyle model of criminal victimization. In M. Gottfredson and T. Hirschi (eds.), Positive Criminology. Newbury Park, Calif.: Sage.

GOLDEN, R.M. AND S.F. MESSNER
1987   Dimensions of racial inequality and rates of violent crime. Criminology 25:525–541.

GUERRY, A.
1833   Essai sur la statistique Morale de la France. Paris: Crochard.

HARRIES, K.D.
1976   Cities and crime. Criminology 14:369–386.

JACOBS, D.
1981   Inequality and economic crime. Sociology and Social Research 66:12–28.

KORNHAUSER, R.R.
1978   Social Sources of Delinquency. Chicago: University of Chicago Press.

LANDER, B.
1954   Toward an Understanding of Juvenile Delinquency. New York: Columbia University Press.

LOFTIN, C. AND R.H. HILL
1974   Regional subcultures and homicide. American Sociological Review 39:714–24.

LOFTIN, C. AND R.N. PARKER
1985   An error-in-variable model of the effect of poverty on urban homicide rates. Criminology 23:269–285.

MADDALA, G.S.
1983   Limited-dependent and qualitative variables in econometrics. New York: Cambridge University Press.

MAXFIELD, M.G., D.A. LEWIS, AND R. SZOC
1980   Producing official crimes: Verified crime reports as measures of police output. Social Science Quarterly 61:221–236.

MCCLEARY, R., B.C. NEINSTEDT, AND J.M. ERVEN
1982   Uniform Crime Reports as organizational outcomes: three time series experiments. Social Problems 29;361–372.

MERTON, R.K.
1949   Social Theory and Social Structure. New York: Free Press.

MESSNER, S.F.
1982   Poverty, inequality and the urban homicide rate. Criminology 20:103–114.

1983   Regional and racial effect on the urban homicide rate: The subculture of violence revisited. American Journal of Sociology 88:997–1007.

MESSNER, S.F. AND K. TARDIFF
1986   Economic inequality and levels of homicide: Am analysis of urban neighborhoods. Criminology 24:297–317.

MLADENKA, K.R. AND K.Q. HILL
1976   A re-examination of the etiology of urban crime. Criminology 13:491–506.

NETTLER, G.
1984   Explaining Crime. New York: McGraw-Hill.

NEWBERY, D.
1970   A theorem on the measurement of inequality. Journal of Economic Theory 2:264–266.

O'BRIEN, R.M.
1983   Metropolitan structure and violent crime: Which measure of crime? American Sociological Review 48:434–437.

1985   Crime and Victimization Data. Beverly Hills, Calif.: Sage.

POLK, K.
1957   The juvenile delinquent and social areas. Social Problems 5:214–217.

1967   Urban social areas and delinquency. Social Problems 14:320–325.

PYLE, G.
1974   The Spatial Dynamics of Crime. Chicago: University of Chicago Press.

QUETELET, A.
1835   Research on the Propensity for Crime at Different Ages, trans. S.F. Sylvester. Cincinnati: Anderson (1984).

QUINNEY, R.
1964   Crime, delinquency and social areas. Journal of Research in Crime and Delinquency 1:149–154.

RONCEK, D.W.
1981   Dangerous places: Crime and residential environment. Social Forces 60:74–96.

ROSENFELD, R.
1986   Urban crime rates: Effects of inequality, welfare dependency, region, and race. In J.M. Byrne and R.J. Sampson (eds.), The Social Ecology of Crime. New York: Springer-Verlag.

SAMPSON, R.J.
1985   Neighborhood and crime: The structural determinants of personal victimization. Journal of Research in Crime and Delinquency 22:7–40.

1986   The effects of urbanization and neighborhood characteristics in criminal victimization. In R. M. Figlio, S. Hakim, and G.F. Rengert (eds.), Metropolitan Crime Patterns. Monsey, N.Y.. Criminal Justice Press.

SAMPSON, R.J. AND T.C. CASTELLANO
1982   Economic inequality and personal victimization. British Journal of Criminology 22:363–385.

SCHMID, C.F.
1960a   Urban crime areas: Part I. American Sociological Review 25:527–443.

1960b   Urban crime areas: Part II. American Sociological Review 25:655–678.

SCHUESSLER, K. AND G. SLATIN
1964   Sources of variation in U.S. city crime, 1950 and 1960. Journal of Research in Crime and Delinquency 1:127–148.

SEIDMAN, D. AND M. COUZENS
1974   Getting the crime rate down: Political pressure and crime reporting. Law and Society Review 8;457–493.

SELLIN, T.
1938   Culture Conflict and Crime. New York: Social Science Research Council.

SHAW, C.R. AND H. MCKAY
1942   Juvenile Delinquency and Urban Areas. Chicago: University of Chicago Press.

SHRYOCK, H.S. AND J.S. SIEGEL
1973   The Methods and Materials of Demography. Social and Economic Statistic Administration. Washington, D.C.: U.S. Department of Commerce.

SKOGAN, W.G.
1976   Crime and crime rates. In W.G. Skogan (ed.) Sample Surveys of Victims of Crime. Cambridge, Mass.: Ballinger.

SMITH, D.A.
1986 The neighborhood context of police behavior. In A.J. Reiss and M. Tonry, Communities and Crime. Chicago: University of Chicago Press.

SMITH, D.A. AND G.R. JARJOURA
1988 Social structure and criminal victimization. Journal of Research in Crime and Delinquency 25:27–52.

SMITH, M.D. AND R.N. PARKER
1980 Types of Homicide and Variation in Regional Rates. Social Forces 59:137–147.

SOCIAL SCIENCE COUNCIL
1968 Research on Poverty. London: Heinemann.

TAYLOR, I., P. WALTON, AND J. YOUNG
1973 The new criminology: For a social theory of deviance. London: Routledge & Kegan Paul.

VOLD, G.B. AND T.J. BERNARD
1986 Theoretical Criminology. New York: Oxford University Press.

WATTS, A.D. AND T.W. WATTS
1981 Minorities and urban crime. Urban Affairs Quarterly 16:423–436.

WELLFORD, C.F.
1974 Crime and the police. Criminology 12:195–213.

WHITE, H.
1980 A heteroscedastic-consistent covariance matrix estimator and a direct test for heteroscedasticity. *Econometrica* 48:817–838.

WILLIAMS, K.
1984 Economic sources of homicide: Reestimating the effects of poverty and inequality. American Sociological Review 49:283–289.

WILLIE, C.Y.
1967 The relative contribution of family status and economic status to juvenile delinquency. Social Problems 14:326–335.

WILSON, J.Q.
1978 Varieties of Police Behavior: The Management of Law and Order in Eight Communities. Cambridge, Mass.: Harvard University Press.

WIRTH, L.
1938 Urbanism as a way of life. American Journal Sociology 44:1–24.

WOLFGANG, M.E. AND F. FERRACUTI
1967 The Subculture of Violence. London: Tavistock.

QUESTIONS FOR DISCUSSION

1. Discuss how poverty and crime are related. Provide examples to support your response.
2. Discuss how the following are related to crime:
   —residential mobility
   —racial heterogeneity
   —neighborhood integration
   —household composition
   —population density
3. Explain why "absolute" poverty is more related to variations in some forms of crime than is the "degree of inequality in the distribution of income."

APPLICATIONS

1. This article makes the case for the relationship between poverty and crime. How might you explain those people living in poverty that do not commit crime?
2. There are many crimes that are committed by individuals who have high incomes. How would you explain those individuals who commit white-collar crime (e.g., fraud, embezzlement, computer crime)?

KEY TERMS

aggregation   to gather into a mass or collection.

ascriptive   refers to something that is assigned; present by virtue of one's birth.

attenuated   refers to something thin or weak.

heterogeneity   the quality of dissimilar or diverse.

panacea   a cure for all ills.

11

Toward an Interactional Theory of Delinquency

Terence P. Thornberry

Contemporary theories of delinquency are seen as limited in three respects: they tend to rely on unidirectional causal structures that represent delinquency in a static rather than dynamic fashion, they do not examine developmental progressions, and they do not adequately link processual concepts to the person's position in the social structure. The present article develops an interactional theory of delinquency that addresses each of these issues. It views delinquency as resulting from the freedom afforded by the weakening of the person's bonds to conventional society and from an interactional setting in which delinquent behavior is learned and reinforced. Moreover, the control, learning, and delinquency variables are seen as reciprocally interrelated, mutually affecting one another over the person's life. Thus, delinquency is viewed as part of a larger causal network, affected by social factors but also affecting the development of those social factors over time.

A variety of sociological theories have been developed to explain the onset and maintenance of delinquent behavior. Currently, three are of primary importance: social control theory (Hirschi, 1969), social learning theory (Akers, 1977), and integrated models that combine them into a broader body of explanatory

"Toward an Interactional Theory of Delinquency," *Criminology*, 25:4 (1987), pp. 863–891. Reprinted by permission of The American Society of Criminology.

principals (Elliott, Ageton, and Canter, 1979; Elliott, Huizinga, and Ageton, 1985).

Control theory argues that delinquency emerges whenever the social and cultural constraints over human conduct are substantially attenuated. As Hirschi states in his classic presentation (1969), control theory assumes that we would all be deviant if only we dared. Learning theory, on the other hand, posits that there is no natural impulse toward delinquency. Indeed, delinquent behavior must be learned through the same processes and mechanisms as conforming behavior. Because of these different starting points, control and learning models give causal priority to somewhat different concepts, and integrated models capitalize on these complementary approaches. Muting the assumptive differences, integrated theories meld together propositions from these (and sometimes other theories—for example, strain) to explain delinquent behavior.

Although these approaches have substantially informed our understanding of the causes of delinquency, they and other contemporary theories suffer from three fundamental limitations. First, they rely on unidirectional rather than reciprocal causal structures. By and large, current theories ignore reciprocal effects in which delinquent behavior is viewed as part of a more general social nexus, affected by, but also affecting, other social factors. Second, current theories tend to be nondevelopmental, specifying causal models for only a narrow age range, usually midadolescence. As a result, they fail to capitalize on developmental patterns to explain the initiation, maintenance, and desistance of delinquency. Finally, contemporary theories tend to assume uniform causal effects throughout the social structure. By ignoring the person's structural position, they fail to provide an understanding of the sources of initial variation in both delinquency and its presumed causes. In combination, these three limitations have led to theories that are narrowly conceived and which provide incomplete and, at times, misleading models of the causes of delinquency.

The present article develops an interactional theory of delinquency that addresses and attempts to respond to each of these limitations. The model proposed here pays particular attention to the first issue, recursive versus reciprocal causal structures, since the development of dynamic models is seen as essential to represent accurately the interactional settings in which delinquency develops.

ORIGINS AND ASSUMPTIONS

The basic premise of the model proposed here is that human behavior occurs in social interaction and can therefore best be explained by models that focus on interactive processes. Rather than viewing adolescents as propelled along a unidirectional pathway to one or another outcome—that is, delinquency or conformity—it argues that adolescents interact with other people and institutions and that behavioral outcomes are formed by that interactive process. For example, the delinquent behavior of an adolescent is formed in part by how he and his parents *interact* over time, not simply by the child's perceived, and presumably invariant, *level* of attachment to parents. Moreover, since it is an interactive system, the behaviors of others—for example, parents and school officials—are influenced both by each other and by the adolescent, including his or her delinquent behavior. If this view is correct, then interactional effects have to be modelled explicitly if we are to understand the social and psycho-logical processes involved with initiation into delinquency, the maintenance of such behavior, and its eventual reduction.

Interactional theory develops from the same intellectual tradition as the theories mentioned above, especially the Durkheimian tradition of social control. It asserts that the fundamental cause of delinquency lies in the weakening of social constraints over the conduct of the individual. Unlike classical control theory, however, it does not assume that the attenuation of controls leads directly to delinquency. The weakening of controls simply allows for a much wider array of behavior, including continued conventional action, failure as indicated by school dropout and sporadic employment histories, alcoholism, mental illness, delinquent and criminal careers, or some combination of these outcomes. For the freedom resulting from weakened bonds to be channeled to delinquency, especially serious prolonged delinquency, requires an interactive setting in which delinquency is learned, performed, and reinforced. This view is similar to Cullen's structuring perspective, which draws attention to the indeterminacy of deviant behavior. "It can thus be argued that there is an *indeterminate* and not a determinate or etiologically specific relationship between motivational variables on the one hand and any particular form of deviant behavior on the other hand" (Cullen, 1984: 5).

Although heavily influenced by control and learning theories, and to a lesser extent by strain and culture conflict theories, this is not an effort at theoretical integration as that term is usually used (Elliott, 1985). Rather, this paper is guided by what we have elsewhere called theoretical elaboration (Thornberry, 1987). In this instance, a basic control theory is extended, or elaborated upon, using available theoretical perspectives and empirical findings to provide a more accurate model of the causes of delinquency. In the process of elaboration, there is no requirement to resolve disputes among other theories—for example, their different assumptions about the origins of deviance (Thornberry, 1987:15-18); all that is required is that the propositions of the model developed here be consistent with one another and with the assumptions about deviance stated above.

ORGANIZATION

The presentation of the interactional model begins by identifying the central concepts to be included in the model. Next, the underlying theoretical structure of the proposed model is examined and the rationale for moving from unidirectional to reciprocal causal models is developed. The reciprocal model is then extended to include a developmental perspective, examining the theoretical saliency of different variables at different developmental stages. Finally, the influence of the person's position in the social structure is explored. Although in some senses the last issue is logically prior to the others, since it is concerned with sources of initial variation in the causal variables, it is discussed last so that the reciprocal relationships among the concepts—the heart of an interactional perspective—can be more fully developed.

Theoretical Concepts

Given these basic premises, an interactional model must respond to two overriding issues. First, how are traditional social constraints over behavior weakened and, second, once weakened, how is the resulting freedom channelled into delinquent patterns? To address these issues, the present article presents an initial version of an interactional model, focusing on the interrelationships among six concepts: attachment to parents, commitment to school, belief in conventional values, associations with delinquent peers, adopting delinquent values, and engaging in delinquent behavior. These concepts form the core of the theoretical model since they are central to social psychological theories of delinquency and since they have been shown in numerous studies to be strongly related to subsequent delinquent behavior (see Elliott et al., 1985, Chs. 1–3, for an excellent review of this literature).

The first three derive from Hirschi's version of control theory (1969) and represents the primary mechanisms by which adolescents are bonded to conventional middle-class society. When those elements of the bond are weakened, behavioral freedom increases considerably. For that freedom to lead to delinquent behavior, however, interactive settings that reinforce delinquency are required. In the model, those settings are represented by two concepts—associations with delinquent peers and the formation of delinquent values—which derive primarily from social learning theory.

For the purpose of explicating the overall theoretical perspective, each of these concepts is defined quite broadly. Attachment to parents includes the affective relationship between parent and child, communication patterns, parenting skills such as monitoring and discipline, parent-child conflict, and the like. Commitment to school refers to the stake in conformity the adolescent has developed and includes such factors as success in school, perceived importance of education, attachment to teachers, and involvement in school activities. Belief in conventional values represents the granting of legitimacy to such middle-class values as education, personal industry, financial success, deferral of gratification, and the like.

Three delinquency variables are included in the model. Association with delinquent peers includes the level of attachment to peers, the delinquent behavior and values of peers, and their reinforcing reactions to the adolescent's own delinquent or conforming behavior. It is a continuous measure that can vary from groups that are heavily delinquent to those that are almost entirely nondelinquent. Delinquent values refer to the granting of legitimacy to delinquent activities as acceptable modes of behavior as well as a general willingness to violate the law to achieve other ends.

Delinquent behavior, the primary outcome variable, refers to acts that place the youth at risk for adjudication; it ranges from status offenses to serious violent activities. Since the present model is an interactional one, interested not only in explaining delinquency but in explaining the effects of delinquency on other variables, particular attention is paid to prolonged involvement in serious delinquency.

Theoretical Structure

The present section develops the reciprocal structure of the interactional model by examining the interplay of the concepts just defined. It begins by describing (Figure 1) the way in which these variables are typically represented in predominately recursive theories of delinquency (see, for example, Johnson, 1979: Weis and Sederstrom, 1981; Elliott et al., 1985).

In these models, all the variables are temporally ordered; earlier ones affect later ones, but there is no provision for feedback or reciprocal causal paths. The unidirectional specification can be illustrated by examining the relationship between attachment to parents and associations with delinquent peers. According to the model, attachment to parents reduces the extent to which the child associates with delinquent peers, an assertion consistent with common observation and empirical research (for example, Poole and Regoli, 1979). Yet, by implication, the model also states that associations with delinquent peers exerts no causal influence on the extent to which the child is attached to parents. If peer associations were thought to influence attachment to parents, then this effect would have to be specified and estimated. As seen in Figure 1, reciprocal effects of this type are excluded by design.

The second feature to note about this model is that it treats delinquency entirely as an outcome of a social process rather than as an integral part of that process. Models such as this assert that various social factors cause delinquent behavior but ignore the possibility that delinquency and its presumed causes are part of a reciprocal causal structure, mutually influencing one another over the person's life span. For example, these models state that associations with delinquent peers increase the likelihood of delinquent conduct, an obviously reasonable assertion, but ignore the possibility that delinquent conduct affects the likelihood and intensity of associations with delinquent peers. Similar statements can be made for the other relationships in which delinquency is embedded.

It should be noted at the outset that there is nothing inherently incorrect with recursive models; if the causal processes are unidirectional, recursive models offer a correct specification and should be used. It is only when the causal processes are in fact reciprocal that models such as these lead to problems of misspecification and incorrect interpretations of causal effects. The remainder of this section develops the argument that unidirectional models are inadequate and that reciprocal models are required to understand the causes of delinquency, precisely because delinquency is embedded in an interactive social process, affected by and affecting other variables. As a starting point, the findings of three recent panel studies that examine both unidirectional and reciprocal models of delinquent conduct are considered.

EMPIRICAL FINDINGS

Thornberry and Christenson (1984) estimated a reciprocal causal structure for unemployment and criminal involvement, both measured at the individual level, for a sample of young adult males. They found that unidirectional models, either from unemployment to crime or from crime to unemployment, were inade-

FIGURE 1   A Typical Recursive Causal Model of Delinquency

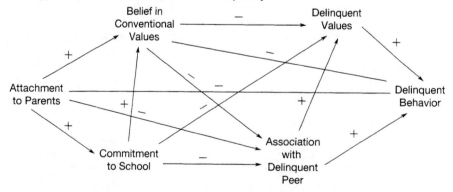

quate to model the causal process. Overall, their findings:

offer strong support for a reciprocal model of crime causation. Consistent with our theoretical specification, unemployment has significant instantaneous effects on crime and crime has significant effects, primarily lagged effects, on unemployment (1984:408).

Liska and Reed (1985) studied the relationship among three control theory variables, attachment to parents, success in school, and delinquency. Although their results differed somewhat for blacks and whites, these variables appear to be embedded in a reciprocal causal loop. Overall, "the analysis suggests that parental attachment affects delinquency, that delinquency affects school attachment, and that school attachment affects parental attachment" (Liska and Reed, 1985:556–557).

Finally, Burkett and Warren (1987) estimate a panel model for four variables: religious commitment, belief in the sinfulness of marijuana use, associations with peers who use marijuana, and self-reported marijuana use. Their basic finding suggests that religious commitment and belief affect marijuana use indirectly, through association with delinquent peers. They also present consistent evidence that these four variables are reciprocally related over time. Marijuana use increases associations with delinquent peers, and associations with delinquent peers reduce religious commitments. In addition, marijuana use at time one significantly affects both religious commitment and beliefs at later times and "this, in turn, contributes to deeper involvement with marijuana-using peers and subsequent continued use in response to direct peer pressure" (1987:123).

All three of these studies derive primarily from a social control framework, but use different data sets, variables, and analytic techniques. Nevertheless, all provide empirical support for the improved explanatory power of reciprocal models. The pattern of relationships observed in these studies strongly suggests that reciprocal causal models are necessary to model adequately the social settings in which delinquent behavior emerges and develops.

These findings also suggest that previous tests of delinquency theories based on recursive causal structures are both incomplete and misleading. As Thornberry and Christenson (1984:399) point out, such tests:

are incomplete since estimates for reciprocal paths simply cannot be obtained. More importantly, recursive tests can produce misleading results since estimates of unidirectional effects obtained from them may be in substantial error. Conceivably, recursive tests could indicate a unidirectional effect between two variables, i.e., X→Y, when the actual relationship (as estimated from a nonrecursive model) could indicate either that the variables are reciprocally related, i.e., X↔Y, or that the direction of the causality is actually reversed, i.e., X←Y (see Heise, 1975:191–93; Hanushek and Jackson, 1977:79–86).

If any or all of these errors exist, and results of recent research suggest they do, then current theories of delinquency, which have been strongly influenced by the results of recursive studies, are inadequate to describe the actual processes in which delinquency is embedded. Because of this, it is important to develop and test interactional models that allow for reciprocal effects.

Model Specification

A causal model allowing for reciprocal relationships among the six concepts of interest—attachment to parents, commitment to school, belief in conventional values, association with delinquent peers, delinquent values, and delinquent behavior—is presented in Figure 2. This model refers to the period of early adolescence, from about ages 11 to 13, when delinquent careers are beginning, but prior to the period at which delinquency reaches its apex in terms of seriousness and frequency. In the following sections the model is extended to later ages.

The specification of causal effects begins by examining the three concepts that form the heart of social learning theories of delinquency—delinquent peers, delinquent values, and delinquent behavior. For now we focus on the reciprocal nature of the relationships, ignoring until later variations in the strength of the relationships.

Traditional social learning theory specifies

FIGURE 2   A Reciprocal Model of Delinquent Involvement at Early Adolescence[a]

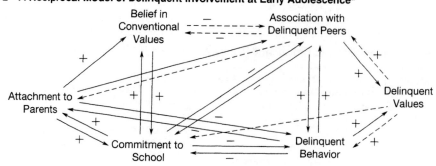

[a]Solid lines represent stronger effects; dashed lines represent weaker effects.

a causal order among these variables in which delinquent associations affect delinquent values and, in turn, both produce delinquent behavior (Akers, Krohn, Lanza-Kaduce, and Radosevich, 1979; Matsueda, 1982). Yet, for each of the dyadic relationships involving these variables, other theoretical perspectives and much empirical evidence suggest the appropriateness of reversing this causal order. For example, social learning theory proposes that associating with delinquents, or more precisely, people who hold and reinforce delinquent values, increases the chances of delinquent behavior (Akers, 1977). Yet, as far back as the work of the Gluecks (1950) this specification has been challenged. Arguing that "birds of a feather flock together," the Gluecks propose that youths who are delinquent seek out and associate with others who share those tendencies. From this perspective, rather than being a cause of delinquency, associations are the result of delinquents seeking out and associating with like-minded peers.

An attempt to resolve the somewhat tedious argument over the temporal priority of associations and behavior is less productive theoretically than capitalizing on the interactive nature of human behavior and treating the relationship as it probably is; a reciprocal one. People often take on the behavioral repertoire of their associates but, at the same time, they often seek out associates who share their behavioral interests. Individuals clearly behave this way in conventional settings, and there is no reason to

assume that deviant activities, such as delinquency, are substantially different in this regard.

Similar arguments can be made for the other two relationships among the delinquency variables. Most recent theories of delinquency, following the lead of social learning theory, posit that delinquent associations lead to the formation of delinquent values. Subcultural theories, however, especially those that derive from a cultural deviance perspective (Miller, 1958) suggest that values precede the formation of peer groups. Indeed, it is the socialization of adolescents into the "lower-class culture" and its particular value system that leads them to associate with delinquent peers in the first place. This specification can also be derived from a social control perspective as demonstrated in Weis and Sederstrom's social development model (1981) and Burkett and Warren's social selection model (1987).

Finally, the link between delinquent values and delinquent behavior restates, in many ways, the basic social psychological question of the relationship between attitudes and behavior. Do attitudes form patterns or does behavior lead to attitude formation? Social psychological research, especially in cognitive psychology and balance models (for example, Festinger, 1957; Brehm and Cohen, 1962) points to the reciprocal nature of this relationship. It suggests that people indeed behave in a manner consistent with their attitudes, but also that behavior is one of the most persuasive forces in the formation and maintenance of attitudes.

Such a view of the relationship between delinquent values and behavior is consistent with Hindelang's findings:

> This general pattern of results indicates that one can "predict" a respondent's self approval [of illegal behaviors] from knowledge of that respondent's involvement/non-involvement [in delinquency] with fewer errors than vice-versa (1974:382).

It is also consistent with recent deterrence research which demonstrates that the "experiential effect," in which behavior affects attitudes, is much stronger than the deterrent effect, in which attitudes affect behavior (Paternoster, Saltzman, Waldo, and Chiricos, 1982; Paternoster, Saltzman, Chiricos, and Waldo 1983).

Although each of these relationships appears to be reciprocal, the predicted strengths of the associations are not of equal strength during the early adolescent period (see Figure 2). Beliefs that delinquent conduct is acceptable and positively valued may be emerging, but such beliefs are not fully articulated for 11- to 13-year-olds. Because of their emerging quality, they are viewed as more effect than cause, produced by delinquent behavior and associations with delinquent peers. As these values emerge, however, they have feedback effects, albeit relatively weak ones at these ages, on behavior and associations. That is, as the values become more fully articulated and delinquency becomes positively valued, it increases the likelihood of such behavior and further reinforces associations with like-minded peers.

Summary: When attention is focused on the interrelationships among associations with delinquent peers, delinquent values, and delinquent behavior, it appears that they are, in fact, reciprocally related. The world of human behavior is far more complex than a simple recursive one in which a temporal order can be imposed on interactional variables of this nature. Interactional theory sees these three concepts as embedded in a causal loop, each reinforcing the others over time. Regardless of where the individual enters the loop, the following obtains: delinquency increases associations with delinquent peers and delinquent values; delinquent values increase delinquent behavior and associations with delinquent peers; and associations with delinquent peers increases delinquent behavior and delinquent values. The question now concerns the identification of factors that lead some youth, but not others, into this spiral of increasing delinquency.

SOCIAL CONTROL EFFECTS

As indicated at the outset of this essay, the premise of interactional theory is that the fundamental cause of delinquency is the attenuation of social controls over the person's conduct. Whenever bonds to the conventional world are substantially weakened, the individual is freed from moral constraints and is at risk for a wide array of deviant activities, including delinquency. The primary mechanisms that bind adolescents to the conventional world are attachment to parents, commitment to school, and belief in conventional values, and their role in the model can now be examined.

During the early adolescent years, the family is the most salient arena for social interaction and involvement and, because of this, attachment to parents has a stronger influence on other aspects of the youth's life at this stage than it does at later stages of development. With this in mind, attachment to parents[1] is predicted to affect four other variables. Since youths who are attached to their parents are sensitive to their wishes (Hirschi, 1969:16–19), and, since parents are almost universally supportive of the conventional world, these children are likely to be strongly committed to school and to espouse conventional values. In addition, youths who are attached to their parents, again because of their sensitivity to parental wishes, are unlikely to associate with delinquent peers or to engage in delinquent behavior.

In brief, parental influence is seen as central to controlling the behavior of youths at these relatively early ages. Parents who have a strong affective bond with their children, who communicate with them, who exercise appropriate parenting skills, and so forth, are likely to lead their children towards conventional actions and beliefs and away from delinquent friends and actions.

On the other hand, attachment to parents is not seen as an immutable trait, impervious to the effects of other variables. Indeed, associating with delinquent peers, not being committed to school, and engaging in delinquent behavior are so contradictory to parental expectations that they tend to diminish the level of attachment between parent and child. Adolescents who fail at school, who associate with delinquent peers, and who engage in delinquent conduct are, as a consequence, likely to jeopardize their affective bond with their parents, precisely because these behaviors suggest that the "person does not care about the wishes and expectations of other people . . ." (Hirschi, 1969:18), in this instance, his or her parents.

Turning next to belief in conventional values, this concept is involved in two different causal loops. First, it strongly affects commitment to school and in turn is affected by commitment to school. In essence, this loop posits a behavioral and attitudinal consistency in the conventional realm. Second, a weaker loop is posited between belief in conventional values and associations with delinquent peers. Youths who do not grant legitimacy to conventional values are more apt to associate with delinquent friends who share those views, and those friendships are likely to attenuate further their beliefs in conventional values. This reciprocal specification is supported by Burkett and Warren's findings concerning religious beliefs and peer associations (1987). Finally, youths who believe in conventional values are seen as somewhat less likely to engage in delinquent behavior.

Although belief in conventional values plays some role in the genesis of delinquency, its impact is not particularly strong. For example, it is not affected by delinquent behavior, nor is it related to delinquent values. This is primarily because belief in conventional values appears to be quite invariant; regardless of class of origin or delinquency status, for example, most people strongly assert conventional values (Short and Strodtbeck, 1965: Ch. 3). Nevertheless, these beliefs do exert some influence

in the model, especially with respect to reinforcing commitment to school.

Finally, the impact of commitment to school is considered. This variable is involved in reciprocal loops with both of the other bonding variables. Youngsters who are attached to their parents are likely to be committed to and succeed in school, and that success is likely to reinforce the close ties to their parents. Similarly, youths who believe in conventional values are likely to be committed to school, the primary arena in which they can act in accordance with those values, and, in turn, success in that arena is likely to reinforce the beliefs.

In addition to its relationships with the other control variables, commitment to school also has direct effects on two of the delinquency variables. Students who are committed to succeeding in school are unlikely to associate with delinquents or to engage in substantial amounts of serious, repetitive delinquent behavior. These youths have built up a stake in conformity and should be unwilling to jeopardize that investment by either engaging in delinquent behavior or by associating with those who do.

Low commitment to school is not seen, however, as leading directly to the formation of delinquent values. Its primary effect on delinquent values is indirect, via associations with delinquent peers and delinquent behavior (Conger, 1980:137). While school failure may lead to a reduced commitment to conventional values, it does not follow that it directly increases the acceptance of values that support delinquency.

Commitment to school, on the other hand, is affected by each of the delinquency variables in the model. Youths who accept values that are consistent with delinquent behavior, who associate with other delinquents, and who engage in delinquent behavior are simply unlikely candidates to maintain an active commitment to school and the conventional world that school symbolizes.

Summary: Attachment to parents, commitment to school, and belief in conventional values reduce delinquency by cementing the person to conventional institutions and people. When these elements of the bond to conventional society are strong, delinquency is unlikely, but when they are weak the individual is placed at much greater risk for delinquency. When viewed from an interactional perspective, two additional qualities of these concepts become increasingly evident.

First, attachment to parents, commitment to school, and belief in conventional values are not static attributes of the person, invariant over time. These concepts interact with one another during the developmental process. For some youths the levels of attachment, commitment, and belief increase as these elements reinforce one another, while for other youths the interlocking nature of these relationships suggests a greater and greater attenuation of the bond will develop over time.

Second, the bonding variables appear to be reciprocally linked to delinquency, exerting a causal impact on associations with delinquent peers and delinquent behavior; they also are causally effected by these variables. As the youth engages in more and more delinquent conduct and increasingly associates with delinquent peers, the level of his bond to the conventional world is further weakened. Thus, while the weakening of the bond to conventional society may be an initial cause of delinquency, delinquency eventually becomes its own indirect cause precisely because of its ability to weaken further the person's bonds to family, school, and conventional beliefs. The implications of this amplifying causal structure is examined below. First, however, the available support for reciprocal models is reviewed and the basic model is extended to later developmental stages.

SUPPORT FOR RECIPROCAL STRUCTURES

The previous section developed a theoretical rationale for moving from recursive to reciprocal causal structures of delinquency. Using an interactional perspective, delinquent behavior, especially sustained involvement with serious delinquent behavior, was viewed as part of an ongoing social process rather than simply a product of other social variables. The present section reviews sources of theoretical and empirical support for this perspective.

First, this model is logically consistent with the approaches of many other theoretical models; see, for example, those proposed by Hirschi (1969), Akers (1977), Elliott et al. (1979, 1985), Weis and Sedestrom (1981), and Snyder and Patterson (in press). Indeed, the present model can be viewed as a logical extension of those theories since it explicitly specifies reciprocal effects that have, until recently, remained largely implicit in criminological theory and research.

Second, as indicated above, recent panel studies that estimate reciprocal effects produce consistent support for this perspective. Whether concerned with unemployment and crime (Thornberry and Christenson, 1984), attachment to parents, commitment to school and delinquency (Liska and Reed, 1985), or religion, peers, and marijuana use (Burkett and Warren, 1987), each of these analyses suggest that there are substantial feedback effects involving delinquency and its presumed causes.

Third, using data from the National Youth Survey, Huizinga and Elliott (1986) report a number of significant reciprocal effects. Although they did not observe feedback effects from delinquent behavior to the conventional bonding variables posited by interactional theory, they do report reciprocal effects among the elements of the bond. They also report that delinquent behavior and associations with delinquent peers are mutually reinforcing (Huizinga and Elliott, 1986:12). Finally, they report that exposure to delinquent friends has significant feedback effects on a wide range of variables, including "internal deviant bonds, perceived sanctions, normlessness, prosocial aspirations, and involvement in prosocial roles" (Huizinga and Elliott, 1986:14).

Fourth, a large number of studies have found that delinquent behavior (including drug use) measured at one time has significant effects on the presumed "causes" of delinquency measured at a later time. Among the variables found to be affected by prior delinquency are educational and occupational attainment (Bachman, O'Malley, and Johnston, 1978: Kandel and Logan, 1984); dropping out of high school (Elliott and Voss, 1974; Bachman et al., 1978; Polk et al., 1981; Thornberry,

Moore, and Christenson, 1985); unemployment (Bachman et al., 1978; Thornberry and Christenson, 1984); attachment to parents (Paternoster et al., 1983); commitment to school (Paternoster et al., 1983; Liska and Reed, 1985; Agnew, 1985); and belief in conventional values (Hindelang, 1974; Paternoster et al., 1983; Agnew, 1985). These empirical findings are quite consistent with theory that posits that delinquent behavior is not only produced by other social variables, but also exerts a significant causal influence on those variables.

Developmental Extensions

The previous section developed a strategy for addressing one of the three major limitations of delinquency theories mentioned in the introduction—namely, their unidirectional causal structure. A second limitation is the nondevelopmental posture of most theories which tend to provide a cross-sectional picture of the factors associated with delinquency at one age, but which do not provide a rationale for understanding how delinquent behavior develops over time. The present section offers a developmental extension of the basic model.

MIDDLE ADOLESCENCE

First, a model for middle adolescence, when the youths are approximately 15 or 16 years of age is presented (Figure 3). This period represents the highest rates of involvement in delinquency and is the reference period, either implicitly or explicitly, for most theories of delinquent involvement. Since the models for the early and middle adolescent periods have essentially the same structure and causal relationships (Figure 2 and 3), discussion focuses on the differences between them and does not repeat the rationale for individual causal effects.

Perhaps the most important difference concerns attachment to parents which is involved in relatively few strong relationships. By this point in the life cycle, the most salient variables involved in the production of delinquency are likely to be external to the home, associated with the youth's activities in school and peer networks. This specification is consistent with empirical results for subjects in this age range (Johnson, 1979:105; and Schoenberg, 1975, quoted in Johnson). Indeed, Johnson concludes that "an adolescent's public life has as much or more to do with his or her deviance or conformity than do 'under-the-roof' experiences" (1979:116).

This is not to say that attachment to parents is irrelevant; such attachments are involved in enhancing commitment to school and belief in conventional values, and in preventing associations with delinquent peers. It is just that the overall strength of parental effects are weaker than at earlier ages when the salience of the family as a locus of interaction and control was greater.

The second major change concerns the increased importance of delinquent values as a causal factor. It is still embedded in the causal loop with the other two delinquency variables,

FIGURE 3   A Reciprocal Model of Delinquent Involvement at Middle Adolescence[a]

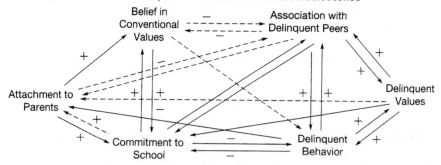

[a]Solid lines represent stronger effects; dashed lines represent weaker effects.

but now it is as much cause as effect. Recall that at the younger ages delinquent values were seen as emerging, produced by associations with delinquent peers and delinquent behavior. Given their emergent nature, they were not seen as primary causes of other variables. At midadolescence, however, when delinquency is at its apex, these values are more fully articulated and have stronger effects on other variables. First, delinquent values are seen as major reinforcers of both delinquent associations and delinquent behavior. In general, espousing values supportive of delinquency tends to increase the potency of this causal loop. Second, since delinquent values are antithetical to the conventional settings of school and family, youths who espouse them are less likely to be committed to school and attached to parents. Consistent with the reduced saliency of family at these ages, the feedback effect to school is seen as stronger than the feedback effect to parents.

By and large, the other concepts in the model play the same role at these ages as they do at the earlier ones. Thus, the major change from early to middle adolescence concerns the changing saliency of some of the theoretical concepts. The family declines in relative importance while the adolescent's own world of school and peers takes on increasing significance. While these changes occur, the overall structure of the theory remains constant. These interactive variables are still seen as mutually reinforcing over time.

LATER ADOLESCENCE

Finally, the causes of delinquency during the transition from adolescence to adulthood, about ages 18 to 20, can be examined (Figure 4). At these ages one should more properly speak of crime than delinquency, but for consistency we will continue to use the term delinquency in the causal diagrams and employ the terms delinquency and crime interchangeably in the text.

Two new variables are added to the model to reflect the changing life circumstances at this stage of development. The more important of these is commitment to conventional activities which includes employment, attending college, and military service. Along with the transition to the world of work, there is a parallel transition from the family of origin to one's own family. Although this transition does not peak until the early 20s, for many people its influence is beginning at this stage. Included in this concept are marriage, plans for marriage, and plans for childrearing. These new variables largely replace attachment to parents and commitment to school in the theoretical

FIGURE 4   A Reciprocal Model of Delinquent Involvement at Later Adolescence[a]

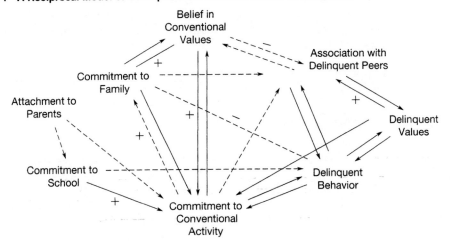

[a]Solid lines represent stronger effects; dashed lines represent weaker effects.

scheme; they represent the major sources of bonds to conventional society for young adults.

Both attachment to parents and commitment to school remain in the model but take on the cast of exogenous variables. Attachment to parents has only a minor effect on commitment to school, and commitment to school is proposed to affect only commitment to conventional activities and, more weakly, delinquent behavior.

The other three variables considered in the previous models—association with delinquent peers, delinquent values, and delinquent behavior—are still hypothesized to be embedded in an amplifying causal loop. As indicated above, this loop is most likely to occur among adolescents who, at earlier ages, were freed from the controlling influence of parents and school. Moreover, via the feedback paths delinquent peers, delinquent values, and delinquent behavior further alienate the youth from parents and diminish commitment to school. Once this spiral begins, the probability of sustained delinquency increases.

This situation, if it continued uninterrupted, would yield higher and higher rates of crime as the subjects matured. Such an outcome is inconsistent with the desistance that has been observed during this age period (Wolfgang, Thornberry, and Figlio, 1987). Rates of delinquency and crime begin to subside by the late teenage years, a phenomenon often attributed to "maturational reform." Such an explanation, however, is tautological since it claims that crime stops when adolescents get older, because they get older. It is also uninformative since the concept of maturational reform is theoretically undefined.

A developmental approach, however, offers an explanation for desistance. As the developmental process unfolds, life circumstances change, developmental milestones are met (or, for some, missed), new social roles are created, and new networks of attachments and commitments emerge. The effects of these changes enter the processual model to explain new and often dramatically different behavioral patterns. In the present model, these changes are represented by commitment to conventional activity and commitment to family.

Commitment to conventional activity is influenced by a number of variables, including earlier attachment to parents, commitment to school, and belief in conventional values. And once the transition to the world of work is made, tremendous opportunities are afforded for new and different effects in the delinquency model. Becoming committed to conventional activities—work, college, military service, and so on—reduces the likelihood of delinquent behavior and associations with delinquent peers because it builds up a stake in conformity that is antithetical to delinquency.

Moreover, since the delinquency variables are still embedded in a causal loop, the effect of commitment to conventional activities tends to resonate throughout the system. But, because of the increased saliency of a new variable, commitment to conventional activities, the reinforcing loop is now set in motion to *reduce* rather than increase delinquent and criminal involvement.

The variable of commitment to family has similar, albeit weaker, effects since the transition to the family is only beginning at these ages. Nevertheless, commitment to family is proposed to reduce both delinquent associations and delinquent values and to increase commitment to conventional activity. In general, as the individual takes on the responsibilities of family, the bond to conventional society increases, placing additional constraints on behavior and precluding further delinquency.

These changes do not occur in all cases, however, nor should they be expected to since many delinquents continue on to careers in adult crime. In the Philadelphia cohort of 1945, 51% of the juvenile delinquents were also adult offenders, and the more serious and prolonged the delinquent careers were, the greater the odds of an adult career (Wolfgang et al., 1987; Ch. 4).

The continuation of criminal careers can also be explained by the nature of the reciprocal effects included in this model. In general, extensive involvement in delinquency at earlier ages feeds back upon and weakens attachment to parents and commitment to school (see Figures 2 and 3). These variables, as well as involvement in delinquency itself,

weaken later commitment to family and to conventional activities (Figure 4). Thus, these new variables, commitment to conventional activities and to family, are affected by the person's situation at earlier stages and do not "automatically" alter the probability of continued criminal involvement. If the initial bonds are extremely weak, the chances of new bonding variables being established to break the cycle towards criminal careers are low and it is likely that criminal behavior will continue.

BEHAVIORAL TRAJECTORIES

The manner in which reciprocal effects and developmental changes are interwoven in the interactional model can be explicated by the concept of behavioral trajectories. At early adolescence, some youths are very weakly attached to their parents, very weakly committed to school, and do not grant legitimacy to conventional values. As indicated above, they are the most likely youngsters for high delinquency involvement. (The term delinquency involvement summarizes the causal loop containing delinquent behavior, delinquent values, and association with delinquent peers.) In turn, high delinquency involvement further attenuates the bonding to parent and to school. This early adolescent situation continues during middle adolescence and substantially reduces the chances of the person reestablishing (or perhaps establishing) bonds to conventional society during late adolescence.

In brief, a behavioral trajectory is established that predicts increasing involvement in delinquency and crime. The initially weak bonds lead to high delinquency involvement, the high delinquency involvement further weakens the conventional bonds, and in combination both of these effects make it extremely difficult to reestablish bonds to conventional society at later ages. As a result, all of the factors tend to reinforce one another over time to produce an extremely high probability of continued deviance.

On the other hand, one can imagine many young adolescents who, at the outset, are strongly attached to their parents, highly committed to school, and believe in conventional

values. The theoretical model predicts that this high level of bonding buffers them from the world of delinquency. Moreover, the reciprocal character of this loop establishes a behavioral trajectory for these youths that tends towards increasing conformity. Their initial strong conventional bonds reduce the chances of involvement in delinquency and thereby increase the chances of commitment to conventional activities and the like at later ages.

Thus, we can conceive of at least two types of adolescents with differing and diverging behavioral trajectories. In one trajectory, social bonds become progressively weaker and delinquent behavior progressively more likely, while in the other commitment to conformity becomes progressively stronger and delinquent behavior progressively less likely.

Of course, if there are these extremes, there are also intermediate cases. In many ways they are the most interesting since their eventual outcome is much more in doubt. For example, there are some youths who have a relatively high level of attachment to parents but low commitment to school (or vice versa). These adolescents are more likely candidates for delinquency involvement than are youths with both high attachment and commitment. But, should the delinquent involvement occur, its feedback effect on the bonding variables is less certain. While the delinquency may further reduce the already weak commitment to school, the strong attachment to parents may serve as a buffer to offset some of the negative feedback. Such a situation, in which the initial bonding variables are neither extremely high nor extremely low, allows for rather varied patterns of interactive effects as the developmental process unfolds. Moreover, the prediction of the eventual outcome for such youths awaits more direct empirical evidence establishing the relative strength of these competing effects.

The concept of behavioral trajectories raises an important theoretical issue. It suggests that the initial values of the process variables play a central role in the entire process since they set the basic path of the behavioral trajectories. Because of this, it is theoretically important to account for variation in those initial values. In the present paper the role of one general class of variables, position in the social structure, is used to illustrate this issue.

Structural Effects

Structural variables, including race, class, sex, and community of residence, refer to the person's location in the structure of social roles and statuses. The manner in which they are incorporated in the interactional model is illustrated here by examining only one of them, social class of origin.

Although social class is often measured continuously, a categorical approach is more consistent with the present model and with most theories of delinquency that incorporate class as a major explanatory variable—for example, strain and social disorganization theories. For our purposes, the most important categories are the lower class, the working lower class, and the middle class.

The lower class is composed of those who are chronically or sporadically unemployed, receive welfare, and subsist at or below the poverty level. They are similar to Johnson's "underclass" (1979). The working lower class is composed of those with more stable work patterns, training for semiskilled jobs, and incomes that allow for some economic stability. For these families, however, the hold on even a marginal level of occupational and economic security is always tenuous. Finally, the middle class refers to all families above these lower levels. Middle-class families have achieved some degree of economic success and stability and can reasonably expect to remain at that level or improve their standing over time.

The manner in which the social class of origin affects the interactional variables and the behavioral trajectories can be demonstrated by comparing the life expectancies of children from lower- and middle-class families. As compared to children from a middle-class background, children from a lower-class background are more apt to have (1) disrupted family processes and environments (Conger, McCarty, Wang, Lahey, and Kroop, 1984; Wahler, 1980); (2) poorer preparation for school (Cloward and Ohlin, 1960); (3) belief structures influenced by the traditions of the American lower class (Miller, 1958; Anderson,

1976); and (4) greater exposure to neighborhoods with high rates of crime (Shaw and McKay, 1942; Braithwaite, 1981). The direction of all these effects is such that we would expect children from lower-class families to be *initially* less bonded to conventional society and more exposed to delinquent values, friends, and behaviors.

As one moves towards the working lower class, both the likelihood and the potency of the factors just listed decrease. As a result, the initial values of the interactional variables improve but, because of the tenuous nature of economic and social stability for these families, both the bonding variables and delinquency variables are still apt to lead to considerable amounts of delinquent conduct. Finally, youths from middle-class families, given their greater stability and economic security, are likely to start with a stronger family structure, greater stakes in conformity, and higher chances of success, and all of these factors are likely to reduce the likelihood of initial delinquent involvement.

In brief, the initial values of the interactional variables are systematically related to the social class of origin. Moreover, since these variables are reciprocally related, it follows logically that social class is systematically related to the behavioral trajectories described above. Youngsters from the lowest classes have the highest probability of moving forward on a trajectory of increasing delinquency. Starting from a position of low bonding to conventional institutions and a high delinquency environment, the reciprocal nature of the interrelationships leads inexorably towards extremely high rates of delinquent and criminal involvement. Such a view is consistent with prevalence data which show that by age 18, 50%, and by age 30, 70% of low SES minority males have an official police record (Wolfgang et al., 1987).

On the other hand, the expected trajectory of middle-class youths suggests that they will move toward an essentially conforming lifestyle, in which their stakes in conformity increase and more and more preclude serious and prolonged involvement in delinquency. Finally, because the initial values of the interactional variables are mixed and indecisive for children from lower-working-class homes, their behavioral trajectories are much more volatile and the outcome much less certain.

Summary: Interactional theory asserts that both the initial values of the process variables and their development over time are systematically related to the social class of origin. Moreover, parallel arguments can be made for other structural variables, especially those associated with class, such as race, ethnicity, and the social disorganization of the neighborhood. Like class of origin, these variables are systematically related to variables such as commitment to school and involvement in delinquent behavior, and therefore, as a group, these structural variables set the stage on which the reciprocal effects develop across the life cycle.

Conclusion

The present article has developed an interactional theory of delinquent behavior. Unlike traditional theories of delinquency, interactional theory does not view delinquency merely as an outcome or consequence of a social process. On the contrary, it views delinquent behavior as an active part of the developmental process, interacting with other social factors over time to determine the person's ultimate behavioral repertoire.

The initial impetus towards delinquency comes from a weakening of the person's bond to conventional society, represented, during adolescence, by attachment to parents, commitment to school, and belief in conventional values. Whenever these three links to conformity are attenuated, there is a substantially increased potential for delinquent behavior.

For that potential to be converted to delinquency, especially prolonged serious delinquency, however, a social setting in which delinquency is learned and reinforced is required. This setting is represented by associations with delinquent peers and delinquent values. These two variables, along with delinquent behavior itself, form a mutually reinforcing causal loop that leads towards increasing delinquency involvement over time.

Moreover, this interactive process develops over the person's life cycle, and the saliency of the theoretical concepts vary as the person ages. During early adolescence, the family is the most influential factor in bonding the youth to conventional society and reducing delinquency. As the youth matures and moves through middle adolescence, the world of friends, school, and youth culture becomes the dominant influence over behavior. Finally, as the person enters adulthood, new variables, especially commitment to conventional activities and to family, offer a number of new avenues to reshape the person's bond to society and involvement with delinquency.

Finally, interactional theory posits that these process variables are systematically related to the person's position in the social structure. Class, minority-group status, and the social disorganization of the neighborhood of residence all affect the initial values of the interactive variables as well as the behavioral trajectories. Youths from the most socially disadvantaged backgrounds begin the process least bonded to conventional society and most exposed to the world of delinquency. Furthermore, the reciprocal nature of the process increases the chances that they will continue on to a career of serious criminal involvement. On the other hand, youths from middle-class families enter a trajectory which is strongly oriented toward conformity and away from delinquency.

But, regardless of the initial starting points or the eventual outcome, the essential point of an interactional theory is that the causal process is a dynamic one that develops over the person's life. And delinquent behavior is a vital part of that process; it is clearly affected by, but it also affects, the bonding and learning variables that have always played a prominent role in sociological explanations of delinquency.

Epilogue

The version of interactional theory presented here is an initial statement of this perspective and does not represent a complete model of all the factors that are associated with delinquency. For example, the role of other structural variables, especially race and sex, which are so strongly correlated with delinquency, has to be fully explicated to better understand the sources of both the delinquency and bonding variables. Similarly, greater attention needs to be paid to the influence of early childhood behaviors and family processes since it is increasingly clear that delinquency is part of a progressive sequence that begins at much earlier ages (Patterson and Dishion, 1985; Loeber and Stouthamer-Loeber, 1986).

In addition, other process variables similar to those incorporated in Figures 2 through 4 need to be considered. For example, the general issue of gang membership and co-offending should be examined in an interactional setting as should concepts such as self-concept and self-efficacy. Finally, developmental stages have been represented here by rough age categories, and they require more careful and precise definition in terms of physical maturation and psychological growth.

Despite these, and no doubt other, limitations, this article accurately represents the basic structure of an interactional theory of delinquency. It has identified the theory's core concepts and described the manner in which they are reciprocally related to account for the initiation of delinquency and its development over time. In the coming years, the theory described here will be developed theoretically and tested empirically.[2]

NOTES

1. The term "attachment to parents" is used throughout the text, but it is clear that parent surrogates—for example foster parents or guardians—can also perform this function.

2. The Rochester Youth Development Study, supported by the Office of Juvenile Justice and Delinquency Prevention and directed with my colleagues Alan Lizotte, Margaret Farnworth, and Susan Stern, is designed to examine the basic causes and correlates of delinquency from this perspective.

REFERENCES

AGNEW, ROBERT
1985   Social control theory and delinquency: A longitudinal test. Criminology 23:47–62.

AKERS, RONALD
1977   Deviant Behavior: A Social Learning Perspective. Belmont: Wadsworth.

AKERS, RONALD L., MARVIN D. KROHN, LONN LANZA-KADUCE, AND MARCIA RADOSEVICH
1979   Social learning theory and deviant behavior. American Sociological Review 44:635–655.

ANDERSON, ELIJAH
1976   A Place on the Corner. Chicago: University of Chicago Press.

BACHMAN, JERALD G., PATRICK M. O'MALLEY, AND JOHN JOHNSTON
1987   Youth in Transition: Adolescence to Adulthood—Change and Stability in the Lives of Young Men. Ann Arbor: Institute for Social Research.

BRAITHWAITE, JOHN
1981   The myth of social class and criminality reconsidered. American Sociological Review 46:36–58.

BREHM, J.W. AND ARTHUR R. COHEN
1962   Explorations in Cognitive Dissonance. New York: Wiley.

BURKETT, STEVEN R. AND BRUCE O. WARREN
1987   Religiosity, peer influence, and adolescent marijuana use: A panel study of underlying causal structures. Criminology 25:109–131.

CLOWARD, RICHARD A. AND LLOYD E. OHLIN
1960   Delinquency and Opportunity: A Theory of Delinquent Gangs. Glencoe: Free Press.

CONGER, RAND D.
1980   Juvenile delinquency: Behavior restraint or behavior facilitation? In Travis Hirschi and Michael Gottfredson (eds.), Understanding Crime. Beverly Hills: Sage.

CONGER, RAND D., JOHN A. MCCARTY, RAYMOND K. WANG, BENJAMIN B. LAHEY, AND JOSEPH P. KROOP
1984   Perception of child, child-rearing values, and emotional distress as mediating links between environmental stressors and observed maternal behavior. Child Development 55:2,234–2,247.

CULLEN, FRANCIS T.
1984   Rethinking Crime and Deviance Theory: The Emergence of a Structuring Tradition, Totowa, NJ: Rowman and Allanheld.

ELLIOTT, DELBERT S.
1985   The assumption that theories can be combined with increased explanatory power: Theoretical integrations. In Robert F. Meier (ed.). Theoretical Methods in Criminology. Beverly Hills: Sage.

ELLIOTT, DELBERT S., SUZANNE S. AGETON, AND RACHELLE J. CANTER
1979   An integrated theoretical perspective on delinquent behavior. Journal of Research on Crime and Delinquency 16:3–27.

ELLIOTT, DELBERT S., DAVID HUIZINGA, AND SUZANNE S. AGETON
1985   Explaining Delinquency and Drug Use. Beverly Hills: Sage.

ELLIOTT, DELBERT S. AND HARWIN L. VOSS
1974   Delinquency and Dropout. Lexington: Lexington Books.

FESTINGER, LEON
1957   A Theory of Cognitive Dissonance. Stanford: Stanford University Press.

GLUECK, SHELDON AND ELEANOR GLUECK
1950   Unraveling Juvenile Delinquency. Cambridge: Harvard University Press.

HANUSHEK, ERIC A. AND JOHN E. JACKSON
1977   Statistical Methods for Social Scientists. New York: Academic Press.

HEISE, DAVID R.
1975   Causal Analysis. New York: Wiley.

HINDELANG, MICHAEL J.
1974   Moral evaluations of illegal behaviors. Social Problems 21:370–384.

HINDELANG, MICHAEL J., TRAVIS HIRSCHI, AND JOSEPH G. WEIS
1981   Measuring Delinquency. Beverly Hills: Sage.

HIRSCHI, TRAVIS
1969   Causes of Delinquency. Berkeley: University of California Press.

HUIZINGA, DAVID AND DELBERT S. ELLIOTT
1986   The Denver High-Risk Delinquency Project. Proposal Submitted to the Office of Juvenile Justice and Delinquency Prevention.

JOHNSON, RICHARD E.
1979   Juvenile Delinquency and Its Origins. Cambridge: Cambridge University Press.

KANDEL, DENISE B. AND JOHN A. LOGAN
1984   Patterns of drug use from adolescence to young adulthood I. Periods of risk for initiation, continued risk and discontinuation. American Journal of Public Health 74:660–667.

KROHN, MARVIN D. AND JAMES MASSEY
1980   Social and delinquent behavior: An examination of the elements of the social bond. Sociological Quarterly 21, 529–543.

LAGRANGE, RANDY L. AND HELENE RASKIN WHITE
1985   Age differences in delinquency: A test of theory. Criminology 23:19–46.

LISKA, ALLEN AND MARK REED
1985   Ties to conventional institutions and delinquency. American Sociological Review 50:547–560.

LOEBER, ROLF AND MAGDA STOUTHAMER-LOEBER
1986   Family factors as correlates and predictors of juvenile conduct problems and delinquency. In Norval Morris and Michael Tonry (eds.). Crime and Justice: An Annual Review of Research Chicago: University of Chicago Press.

MATSUEDA, ROSS
1982   Testing social control theory and differential association. American Sociological Review 47:489–504.

MILLER, WALTER B.
1958   Lower class culture as a generating milieu of gang delinquency. Journal of Social Issues 14:5–19.

PATERNOSTER, RAYMOND, LINDA E. SALTZMAN, GORDON P. WALDO, AND THEODORE G. CHIRICOS
1982   Perceived risk and deterrence: Methodological artifacts in perceptual deterrence research. Journal of Criminal Law and Criminology 73:1,238–1,258.

PATERNOSTER, RAYMOND, LINDA E. SALTZMAN, THEODORE G. CHIRICOS, AND GORDON P. WALDO
1983   Perceived risk and social control: Do sanctions really deter? Law and Society Review 17:457–479.

PATTERSON, GERALD R. AND THOMAS S. DISHION
1985   Contributions of families and peers to delinquency. Criminology 23:63–80.

POLK, KENNETH, CHRISTINE ADLER, GORDON BAZEMORE, GERALD BLAKE, SHEILA CORDRAY, GARRY COVENTRY, JAMES GALVIN, AND MARK TEMPLE
1981   Becoming Adult: An Analysis of Maturational Development from Age 16 to 30 of a Cohort of Young Men. Final Report of the Marion County Youth Study. Eugene: University of Oregon.

POOLE, ERIC D. AND ROBERT M. REGOLI
1979   Parental Support, delinquent friends and delinquency: A test of interactional effects. Journal of Criminal Law and Criminology 70:188–193.

SCHOENBERG, RONALD J.
1975   A Structural Model of Delinquency. Unpublished doctoral dissertation. Seattle: University of Washington.

SHAW, CLIFFORD R. AND HENRY D. MCKAY
1942   Juvenile Delinquency and Urban Areas. Chicago: University of Chicago Press.

SHORT, JAMES F. JR., AND FRED L. STRODTBECK
1965   Group Processes and Gang Delinquency. Chicago: University of Chicago Press.

SNYDER, J. AND GERALD PATTERSON
In Press Family interactions and delinquent behavior. Child Development.

THORNBERRY, TERENCE P.
1987   Reflections on the advantages and disadvantages of theoretical integration. Presented at the Albany Conference on Theoretical Integration in the Study of Crime and Deviance.

THORNBERRY, TERENCE P. AND R.L. CHRISTENSON
1984   Unemployment and criminal involvement: An investigation of reciprocal causal structures. American Sociological Review 49:398–411.

THORNBERRY, TERENCE P., MARGARET FARNWORTH, AND ALAN LIZOTTE
1986   A Panel Study of Reciprocal Causal Model of Delinquency. Proposal submitted to the Office of Juvenile Justice and Delinquency Prevention.

THORNBERRY, TERENCE P., MELANIE MOORE, AND R.L. CHRISTENSON
1985   The effect of dropping out of high school on subsequent delinquent behavior. Criminology 23:3–18.

WAHLER, R.
1980   The insular mother: Her problems in parent-child treatment. Journal of Applied Behavior Analysis 13:207–219.

WEIS, JOSEPH G. AND JOHN SEDERSTROM
1981   The Prevention of Serious Delinquency: What to Do? Washington, D.C., U.S. Department of Justice.

WOLFGANG, MARVIN E., TERENCE P. THORNBERRY, AND ROBERT M. FIGLIO
1987   From Boy to Man—From Delinquency to Crime: Followup to the Philadelphia Birth Cohort of 1945. Chicago: University of Chicago Press.

QUESTIONS FOR DISCUSSION

1. Thornberry, in attempting to create an interactional theory of juvenile delinquency, suggests that there are three limitations of existing approaches that have sought to explain delinquency. Discuss these limitations.

2. Discuss the differences between recursive models of delinquency and reciprocal models of delinquency.

3. What are the major differences between the theoretical models for early, middle, and late adolescence? Which of these differences do you think are most important?

APPLICATIONS

1. According to Thornberry's model do you think the family or the school is more important in affecting a young person's propensity to become delinquent?

2. As an expert on juvenile delinquency, you have been asked to provide recommendations about how the family and schools could better involve themselves in the lives of young people and consequently reduce the delinquency problem. What would your recommendations be? Why?

KEY TERMS

affective relating to or influencing feelings or emotions.

antithetical being in direct or diametric opposition.

attenuation lessening the amount of something or weakening it in relationship to something else.

causal loop an act or event which is antecedently responsible for a subsequent effect, which then continues over time to reproduce the same or similar effect.

exogenous variables those variables introduced or produced from outside a theoretical model that has already attempted to explain a phenomena.

impetus a driving force; stimulation or encouragement resulting in increased activity.

reciprocal effects when two or more variables are not mutually exclusive, but perpetually and mutually reinforce each other over time.

salient something that projects outward and away from its surroundings; something that stands out or is striking.

social nexus a social phenomena that has causal links or connections to other social phenomenon.

tenuous having little substance or strength; as when a theory or assumption about human behavior is thought to be on "shaky ground."

12

Girls' Crime and Woman's Place: Toward a Feminist Model of Female Delinquency

Meda Chesney-Lind

*Associate Professor of Women's Studies,
Center for Youth Research at the University of Hawaii, Manoa*

This article argues that existing delinquency theories are fundamentally inadequate to the task of explaining female delinquency and official reactions to girls' deviance. To establish this, the article first reviews the degree of the androcentric bias in the major theories of delinquent behavior. Then the need for a feminist model of female delinquency is explored by reviewing the available evidence on girls' offending. This review shows that the extensive focus on disadvantaged males in public settings has meant that girls' victimization and the relationship between that experience and girls' crime has been systematically ignored. Also missed has been the central role played by the juvenile justice system in the sexualization of female delinquency and the criminalization of girls' survival strategies. Finally, it will be suggested that the official actions of the juvenile justice system should be understood as major forces in women's oppression as they have historically served to reinforce the obedience of all young women to the demands of patriarchal authority no matter how abusive and arbitrary.

I ran away so many times. I tried anything man, and they wouldn't believe me. . . . As far as they are concerned they think I'm the problem. You know, runaway, bad label. (Statement of a 16-year-

"Girls' Crime and Woman's Place: Toward a Feminist Model of Female Delinquency," *Crime and Delinquency*, 35:1 (January 1989), pp. 5–29. Reprinted by permission of the publisher, Sage Publications. Inc.

old girl who, after having been physically and sexually assaulted, started running away from home and was arrested as a "runaway" in Hawaii.)

You know, one of these days I'm going to have to kill myself before you guys are gonna listen to me. I can't stay at home. (Statement of a 16-year-old Tucson runaway with a long history of physical abuse [Davidson, 1982, p. 26].)

Who is the typical female delinquent? What causes her to get into trouble? What happens to her if she is caught? These are questions that few members of the general public could answer quickly. By contrast, almost every citizen can talk about "delinquency," by which they generally mean male delinquency, and can even generate some fairly specific complaints about, for example, the failure of the juvenile justice system to deal with such problems as "the alarming increase in the rate of serious juvenile crime" and the fact that the juvenile courts are too lenient on juveniles found guilty of these offenses (Opinion Research Corporation, 1982).

This situation should come as no surprise since even the academic study of delinquent behavior has, for all intents and purposes, been the study of male delinquency. "The delinquent is a rogue male" declared Albert Cohen (1955, p. 140) in his influential book on gang delinquency. More than a decade later, Travis

Hirschi, in his equally important book entitled *The Causes of Delinquency*, relegated women to a footnote that suggested, somewhat apologetically, that "in the analysis that follows, the 'non-Negro' becomes 'white,' and the girls disappear."

This pattern of neglect is not all that unusual. All areas of social inquiry have been notoriously gender blind. What is perhaps less well understood is that theories developed to describe the misbehavior of working- or lower-class male youth fail to capture the full nature of delinquency in America; and, more to the point, are woefully inadequate when it comes to explaining female misbehavior and official reactions to girls' deviance.

To be specific, delinquent behavior involves a range of activities far broader than those committed by the stereotypical street gang. Moreover, many more young people than the small visible group of "troublemakers" that exist on every intermediate and high school campus commit some sort of juvenile offense and many of these youth have brushes with the law. One study revealed, for example, that 33% of all the boys and 14% of the girls born in 1958 had at least one contact with the police before reaching their eighteenth birthday (Tracy, Wolfgang, and Figlio, 1985, p. 5). Indeed, some forms of serious delinquent behavior, such as drug and alcohol abuse, are far more frequent than the stereotypical delinquent behavior of gang fighting and vandalism and appear to cut across class and gender lines.

Studies that solicit from youth themselves the volume of their delinquent behavior consistently confirm that large numbers of adolescents engage in at least some form of misbehavior that could result in their arrest. As a consequence, it is largely trivial misconduct, rather than the commission of serious crime, that shapes the actual nature of juvenile delinquency. One national study of youth aged 15–21, for example, noted that only 5% reported involvement in a serious assault, and only 6% reported having participated in a gang fight. In contrast, 81% admitted to having used alcohol, 44% admitted to having used marijuana, 37% admitted to having been publicly drunk, 42% admitted to having skipped classes (truancy), 44% admitted having had sexual intercourse, and 15% admitted to having stolen from the family (McGarrell and Flanagan, 1985, p. 363). Clearly, not all of these activities are as serious as the others. It is important to remember that young people can be arrested for all of these behaviors.

Indeed, one of the most important points to understand about the nature of delinquency, and particularly female delinquency, is that youth can be taken into custody for both criminal acts and a wide variety of what are often called "status offenses." These offenses, in contrast to criminal violations, permit the arrest of youth for a wide range of behaviors that are violations of parental authority: "running away from home," "being a person in need of supervision," "minor in need of supervision," being "incorrigible," "beyond control," truant, in need of "care and protection," and so on. Juvenile delinquents, then, are youths arrested for either criminal or noncriminal status offenses; and, as this discussion will establish, the role played by uniquely juvenile offenses is by no means insignificant, particularly when considering the character of female delinquency.

Examining the types of offenses for which youth are actually arrested, it is clear that again most are arrested for the less serious criminal acts and status offenses. Of the one and a half million youth arrested in 1983, for example, only 4.5% of these arrests were for such serious violent offenses as murder, rape, robbery, or aggravated assault (McGarrell and Flanagan, 1985, p. 479). In contrast, 21% were arrested for a single offense (larceny, theft) much of which, particularly for girls, is shoplifting (Sheldon and Horvath, 1986).

Table 1 presents the five most frequent offenses for which male and female youth are arrested and from this it can be seen that while trivial offenses dominate both male and female delinquency, trivial offenses, particularly status offenses, are more significant in the case of girls' arrests; for example the five offenses listed in Table 1 account for nearly three-quarters of female offenses and only slightly more than half of male offenses.

More to the point, it is clear that, though routinely neglected in most delinquency research, status offenses play a significant role in girls' official delinquency. Status offenses

TABLE 1 Rank Order of Adolescent Male and Female Arrests for Specific Offenses, 1977 and 1986

	Male				Female			
1977	% of Total Arrests	1986	% of Total Arrests	1977	% of Total Arrests	1986	% of Total Arrests
(1) Larceny-theft	18.4	(1) Larceny-theft	20.4	(1) Larceny-theft	27.0	(1) Larceny-theft	25.7
(2) Other offenses	14.5	(2) Other offenses	16.5	(2) Runaway	22.9	(2) Runaway	20.5
(3) Burglary	13.0	(3) Burglary	9.1	(3) Other offenses	14.2	(3) Other offenses	14.8
(4) Drug abuse		(4) Vandalism	7.0	(4) Liquor laws	5.5	(4) Liquor laws	8.4
violations	6.5	(5) Vandalism	6.3	(5) Curfew & loitering		(5) Curfew & loitering	
(5) Vandalism	6.4			violations	4.0	violations	4.7

	1977	1986	% N change		1977	1986	% N change
Arrests for serious violent offenses[a]	4.2%	4.7%	2.3	Arrests for serious violent offenses	1.8%	2.0%	+1.7
Arrests of all violent offenses[b]	7.6%	9.6%	+10.3	Arrests of all violent offenses	5.1%	7.1%	+26.0
Arrests for status offenses[c]	8.8%	8.3%	−17.8	Arrests for status offenses	26.9%	25.2%	−14.7

SOURCE: Compiled from Federal Bureau of Investigation (1987, p. 169).

a. Arrests for murder and nonnegligent manslaughter, robbery, forcible rape, and aggravated assault.
b. Also includes arrests for other assaults.
c. Arrests for curfew and loitering law violation and runaway.

accounted for about 25.2% of all girls' arrests in 1986 (as compared to 26.9% in 1977) and only about 8.3% of boys' arrests (compared to 8.8% in 1977). These figures are somewhat surprising since dramatic declines in arrests of youth for these offenses might have been expected as a result of the passage of the Juvenile Justice and Delinquency Prevention Act in 1974, which, among other things, encouraged jurisdictions to divert and deinstitutionalize youth charged with noncriminal offenses. While the figures in Table 1 do show a decline in these arrests, virtually all of this decline occurred in the 1970s. Between 1982 and 1986 girls' curfew arrests increased by 5.1% and runaway arrests increased by a striking 24.5%. And the upward trend continues; arrests of girls for running away increased by 3% between 1985 and 1986 and arrests of girls for curfew violations increased by 12.4% (Federal Bureau of Investigation, 1987, p. 171).

Looking at girls who find their way into juvenile court populations, it is apparent that status offenses continue to play an important role in the character of girls' official delinquency. In total, 34% of the girls, but only 12% of the boys, were referred to court in 1983 for these offenses (Snyder and Finnegan, 1987, pp. 6–20). Stating these figures differently, they mean that while males constituted about 81% of all delinquency referrals, females constituted 46% of all status offenders in courts (Snyder and Finnegan, 1987, p. 20). Similar figures were reported for 1977 by Black and Smith (1981). Fifteen years earlier, about half of the girls and about 20% of the boys were referred to court for these offenses (Children's Bureau, 1965). These data do seem to signal a drop in female status offense referrals, though not as dramatic a decline as might have been expected.

For many years statistics showing large numbers of girls arrested and referred for status offenses were taken to be representative of the different types of male and female delinquency. However, self-report studies of male and female delinquency do not reflect the dramatic differences in misbehavior found in official statistics. Specifically, it appears that girls charged with these noncriminal status offenses have been and continue to be significantly over-represented in court populations.

Teilmann and Landry (1981) compared girls' contribution to arrests for runaway and incorrigibility with girls' self-reports of these two activities, and found a 10.4% overrepresentation of females among those arrested for runaway and a 30.9% overrepresentation in arrests for incorrigibility. From these data they concluded that girls are "arrested for status offenses at a higher rate than boys, when contrasted to their self-reported delinquency rates" (Teilmann and Landry, 1981, pp. 74–75). These findings were confirmed in another recent self-report study. Figueira-McDonough (1985, p. 277) analyzed the delinquent conduct of 2,000 youths and found "no evidence of greater involvement of females in status offenses." Similarly, Canter (1982) found in the National Youth Survey that there was no evidence of greater female involvement, compared to males, in any category of delinquent behavior. Indeed, in this sample, males were significantly more likely than females to report status offenses.

Utilizing Canter's national data on the exten-siveness of girls self-reported delinquency and comparing these figures to official arrests of girls (see Table 2) reveals that girls are underrepresented in every arrest category with the exception of status offenses and larceny theft. These figures strongly suggest that official practices tend to exaggerate the role played by status offenses in girls' delinquency.

Delinquency theory, because it has virtually ignored female delinquency, failed to pursue anomalies such as these found in the few early studies examining gender differences in delinquent behavior. Indeed, most delinquency theories have ignored status offenses. As a consequence, there is considerable question as to whether existing theories that were admittedly developed to explain male delinquency can adequately explain female delinquency. Clearly, these theories were much influenced by the notion that class and protest masculinity were at the core of delinquency. Will the "add women and stir approach" be sufficient? Are these really theories of delinquent behavior as some (Simons, Miller, and Aigner, 1980) have argued?

This article will suggest that they are not. The extensive focus on male delinquency and

TABLE 2 Comparison of Sex Differences In Self-Reported and Official Delinquency for Selected Offenses

	Self-Report[a] M/F Ratios (1976)	Official Statistics[b] M/F Arrest Ratio	
		1976	1986
Theft	3.5:1 (Felony Theft) 3.4:1 (Minor Theft)	2.5:1	2.7:1
Drug Violation	1:1 (Hard Drug Use)	5.1:1	6.0:1 (Drug Abuse Violation)
Vandalism	5.1:1	12.3:1	10.0:1
Disorderly Conduct	2.8:1	4.5:1	4.4:1
Serious Assault	3.5:1 (Felony Assault)	5.6:1	5.5:1 (Aggravated Assault)
Minor Assault	3.4:1	3.8:1	3.4:1
Status Offense	1.6:1	1.3:1	1.1:1 (Runaway, Curfew)

[a] Extracted from Rachelle Canter (1982, p. 383).
[b] Compiled from Federal Bureau of Investigation (1986, p. 173).

the inattention the role played by patriarchal arrangements in the generation of adolescent delinquency and conformity has rendered the major delinquency theories fundamentally inadequate to the task of explaining female behavior. There is, in short, an urgent need to rethink current models in light of girls' situation in patriarchal society.

To understand why such work must occur, it is first necessary to explore briefly the dimensions of the androcentric bias found in the dominant and influential delinquency theories. Then the need for a feminist model of female delinquency will be explored by reviewing the available evidence on girls' offending. This discussion will also establish that the proposed overhaul of delinquency theory is not, as some might think, solely an academic exercise. Specifically, it is incorrect to assume that because girls are charged with less serious offenses, they actually have few problems and are treated gently when they are drawn into the juvenile justice system. Indeed, the extensive focus on disadvantaged males in public settings has meant that girls' victimization and the relationship between that experience and girls' crime has been systematically ignored. Also missed has been the central role played by the juvenile justice system in the sexualization of girls' delinquency and the criminalization of girls' survival strategies. Finally, it will be suggested that the official actions of the juvenile justice system should be understood as major forces in girls' oppression as they have historically served to reinforce the obedience of all young women to demands of patriarchal authority no matter how abusive and arbitrary.

THE ROMANCE OF THE GANG
OR THE *WEST SIDE STORY* SYNDROME

From the start, the field of delinquency research focused on visible lower-class male delinquency, often justifying the neglect of girls in the most cavalier of terms. Take, for example, the extremely important and influential work of Clifford R. Shaw and Henry D. McKay who beginning in 1929, utilized an ecological approach to the study of juvenile delinquency. Their impressive work, particularly *Juvenile Delinquency in Urban Areas* (1942) and intensive

biographical case studies such as Shaw's *Brothers in Crime* (1938) and *The Jackroller* (1930), set the stage for much of the subcultural research on gang delinquency. In their ecological work, however, Shaw and McKay analyzed only the official arrest data on male delinquents in Chicago and repeatedly referred to these rates as "delinquency rates" (though they occasionally made parenthetical reference to data on female delinquency) (see Shaw and McKay, 1942, p. 356). Similarly, their biographical work traced only male experiences with the law; in *Brothers in Crime*, for example, the delinquent and criminal careers of five brothers were followed for fifteen years. In none of these works was any justification given for the equation of male delinquency with delinquency.

Early fieldwork on delinquent gangs in Chicago set the stage for another style of delinquency research. Yet here too researchers were interested only in talking to and following the boys. Thrasher studied over a thousand juvenile gangs in Chicago during roughly the same period as Shaw and McKay's more quantitative work was being done. He spent approximately one page out of 600 on the five of six female gangs he encountered in his field observation of juvenile gangs. Thrasher (1927, p. 228) did mention, in passing, two factors he felt accounted for the lower number of girl gangs: "First, the social patterns for the behavior of girls, powerfully backed by the great weight of tradition and custom, are contrary to the gang and its activities; and secondly, girls, even in urban disorganized areas, are much more closely supervised and guarded than boys and usually well incorporated into the family groups or some other social structure."

Another major theoretical approach to delinquency focuses on the subculture of lower-class communities as a generating milieu for delinquent behavior. Here again, noted delinquency researchers concentrated either exclusively or nearly exclusively on male lower-class culture. For example, Cohen's work on the subculture of delinquent gangs, which was written nearly twenty years after Thrasher's, deliberately considers only boys' delinquency. His justification for the exclusion of the girls is quite illuminating:

My skin has nothing of the quality of down or silk, there is nothing limpid or flute-like about my voice, I am a total loss with needle and thread, my posture and carriage are wholly lacking in grace. These imperfections cause me no distress—if anything, they are gratifying—because I conceive myself to be a man and want people to recognize me as a full-fledged, unequivocal representative of my sex. My wife, on the other hand, is not greatly embarrassed by her inability to tinker with or talk about the internal organs of a car, by her modest attainments in arithmetic or by her inability to lift heavy objects. Indeed, I am reliably informed that many women—I do not suggest that my wife is among them—often affect ignorance, frailty and emotional instability because to do otherwise would be out of keeping with a reputation for indubitable femininity. In short, people do not simply want to excel; they want to excel as a man or as a woman [Cohen, 1955, p. 138.]

From this Cohen (1955, p. 140) concludes that the delinquent response "however it may be condemned by others on moral grounds has least one virtue; it incontestably confirms, in the eyes of all concerned, his essential masculinity." Much the same line of argument appears in Miller's influential paper on the "focal concerns" of lower-class life with its emphasis on importance of trouble, toughness, excitement, and so on. These, the author concludes, predispose poor youth (particularly male youth) to criminal misconduct. However, Cohen's comments are notable in their candor and probably capture both the allure that male delinquency has had for at least some male theorists as well as the fact that sexism has rendered the female delinquent as irrelevant to their work.

Emphasis on blocked opportunities (sometimes the "strain" theories) emerged out of the work of Robert K. Merton (1938) who stressed the need to consider how some social structures exert a definite pressure upon certain persons in the society to engage in nonconformist rather than conformist conduct. His work influenced research largely through the efforts of Cloward and Ohlin who discussed access to "legitimate" and "illegitimate" opportunities for male youth. No mention of female delinquency can be found in their *Delinquency and Opportunity* except that women are blamed

for male delinquency. Here, the familiar notion is that boys, "engulfed by a feminine world and uncertain of their own identification . . . tend to 'protest' against femininity" (Cloward and Ohlin, 1960, p. 49). Early efforts by Ruth Morris to test this hypothesis utilizing different definitions of success based on the gender of respondents met with mixed success. Attempting to assess boys' perceptions about access to economic power status while for girls the variable concerned itself with the ability or inability of girls to maintain effective relationships, Morris was unable to find a clear relationship between "female" goals and delinquency (Morris, 1964).

The work of Edwin Sutherland emphasized the fact that criminal behavior was learned in intimate personal groups. His work, particularly the notion of differential association, which also influenced Cloward and Ohlin's work, was similarly male oriented as much of his work was affected by case studies he conducted of male criminals. Indeed, in describing his notion of how differential association works, he utilized male examples (e.g., "In an area where the delinquency rate is high a boy who is sociable, gregarious, active, and athletic is very likely to come in contact with the other boys, in the neighborhood, learn delinquent behavior from them, and become a gangster" [Sutherland, 1978, p. 131]). Finally, the work of Travis Hirschi on the social bonds that control delinquency ("social control theory") was, as was stated earlier, derived out of research on male delinquents (though he, at least, studied delinquent behavior as reported by youth themselves rather than studying only those who were arrested).

Such a persistent focus on social class and such an absence of interest in gender in delinquency is ironic for two reasons. As even the work of Hirschi demonstrated, and as later studies would validate, a clear relationship between social class position and delinquency is problematic, while it is clear that gender has a dramatic and consistent effect on delinquency causation (Hagan, Gillis, and Simpson, 1985). The second irony, and one that consistently eludes even contemporary delinquency theorists, is the fact that while the academics had little interest in female delinquents, the same could not be said for the juvenile justice system. Indeed, work on the early history of the separate system for youth, reveals that concerns about girls' immoral conduct were really at the center of what some have called the "childsaving movement" (Platt, 1969) that set up the juvenile justice system.

"THE BEST PLACE TO CONQUER GIRLS"

The movement to establish separate institutions for youthful offenders was part of the larger Progressive movement, which among other things was keenly concerned about prostitution and other "social evils" (white slavery and the like) (Schlossman and Wallach, 1978; Rafter, 1985, p. 54). Childsaving was also a celebration of women's domesticity, though ironically women were influential in the movement (Platt, 1969; Rafter, 1985). In a sense, privileged women found, in the moral purity crusades and the establishment of family courts, a safe outlet for their energies. As the legitimate guardians of the moral sphere, women were seen as uniquely suited to patrol the normative boundaries of the social order. Embracing rather than challenging these stereotypes, women carved out for themselves a role in the policing of women and girls (Feinman, 1980; Freedman, 1981; Messerschmidt, 1987). Ultimately, many of the early childsavers' activities revolved around the monitoring of young girls', particularly immigrant girls', behavior to prevent their straying from the path.

This state of affairs was the direct consequence of a disturbing coalition between some feminists and the more conservative social purity movement. Concerned about female victimization and distrustful of male (and to some degree female) sexuality, notable women leaders, including Susan B. Anthony, found common cause with the social purists around such issues as opposing the regulation of prostitution and raising the age of consent (see Messerschmidt, 1987). The consequences of such a partnership are an important lesson for contemporary feminist movements that are, to some extent, faced with the same possible coalitions.

Girls were the clear losers in this reform effort. Studies of early family court activity reveal that virtually all the girls who appeared in these courts were charged for immorality or waywardness (Chesney-Lind, 1971; Schlossman and Wallach, 1978; Shelden, 1981). More to the point, the sanctions for such misbehavior were extremely severe. For example, in Chicago (where the first family court was founded), one-half of the girl delinquents, but only one-fifth of the boy delinquents, were sent to reformatories between 1899–1909. In Milwaukee, twice as many girls as boys were committed to training schools (Schlossman and Wallach, 1978, p. 72); and in Memphis females were twice as likely as males to be committed to training schools (Shelden, 1981, p. 70).

In Honolulu, during the period 1929–1930, over half of the girls referred to court were charged with "immorality," which meant evidence of sexual intercourse. In addition, another 30% were charged with "waywardness." Evidence of immorality was vigorously pursued by both arresting officers and social workers through lengthy questioning of the girl and, if possible, males with whom she was suspected of having sex. Other evidence of "exposure" was provided by gynecological examinations that were routinely ordered in virtually all girls' cases. Doctors, who understood the purpose of such examinations, would routinely note the condition of the hymen: "admits intercourse hymen rupture," "no laceration," "hymen ruptured" are typical of the notations on the forms. Girls during this period were also twice as likely as males to be detained where they spent five times as long on the average as their male counterparts. They were also nearly three times more likely to be sentenced to the training school (Chesney-Lind, 1971). Indeed, girls were half of those committed to training schools in Honolulu well into the 1950s (Chesney-Lind, 1973).

Not surprisingly, large numbers of girls' reformatories and training schools were established during this period as well as places of "rescue and reform." For example, Schlossman and Wallach note that 23 facilities for girls were opened during the 1910–1920 decade (in contrast to the 1850–1910 period where the average was 5 reformatories per decade [Schlossman and Wallach, 1985, p. 70]), and these institutions did much to set the tone of official response to female delinquency. Obsessed with precocious female sexuality, the institutions set about to isolate the females from all contact with males while housing them in bucolic settings. The intention was to hold the girls until marriageable age and to occupy them in domestic pursuits during their sometimes lengthy incarceration.

The links between these attitudes and those of juvenile courts some decades later are, of course, arguable; but an examination of the record of the court does not inspire confidence. A few examples of the persistence of what might be called a double standard of juvenile justice will suffice here.

A study conducted in the early 1970s in a Connecticut training school revealed large numbers of girls incarcerated "for their own protection." Explaining this pattern, one judge explained, "Why most of the girls I commit are for status offenses, I figure if a girl is about to get pregnant, we'll keep her until she's sixteen and then ADC (Aid to Dependent Children) will pick her up" (Rogers, 1972). For more evidence of official concern with adolescent sexual misconduct, consider Linda Hancock's (1981) content analysis of police referrals in Australia. She noted that 40% of the referrals of girls to court made specific mention of sexual and moral conduct compared to only 5% of the referrals of boys. These sorts of results suggest that all youthful female misbehavior has traditionally been subject to surveillance for evidence of sexual misconduct.

Gelsthorpe's (1986) field research on an English police station also revealed how everyday police decision making resulted in disregard of complaints about male problem behavior in contrast to active concern about the "problem behavior" of girls. Notable, here, was the concern about the girls' sexual behavior. In one case, she describes police persistence in pursuing a "moral danger" order for a 14-year-old picked up in a truancy run. Over the objections of both the girl's parents and the Social Services Department and in the face of a written confirmation from a surgeon that the girl was still premenstrual, the officers pursued the application because, in one officer's words, "I know her sort . . . free and easy. I'm still sus-

picious that she might be pregnant. Anyway, if the doctor can't provide evidence we'll do her for being beyond the care and control of her parents, no one can dispute that. Running away is proof" (Gelsthorpe, 1986, p. 136). This sexualization of female deviance is highly significant and explains why criminal activities by girls (particularly in past years) were overlooked so long as they did not appear to signal defiance of parental control (see Smith, 1978).

In their historic obsession about precocious female sexuality, juvenile justice workers rarely reflected on the broader nature of female misbehavior or on the sources of this misbehavior. It was enough for them that girls' parents reported them out of control. Indeed, court personnel tended to "sexualize" virtually all female defiance that lent itself to that construction and ignore other misbehavior (Chesney-Lind, 1973, 1977; Smith, 1978). For their part, academic students of delinquency were so entranced with the notion of the delinquent as a romantic rogue male challenging a rigid and unequal class structure, that they spent little time on middle-class delinquency, trivial offenders, or status offenders. Yet it is clear that the vast bulk of delinquent behavior is of this type.

Some have argued that such an imbalance in theoretical work is appropriate as minor misconduct, while troublesome, is not a threat to the safety and well-being of the community. This argument might be persuasive if two additional points could be established. One, that some small number of youth "specialize" in serious criminal behavior while the rest commit only minor acts, and, two, that the juvenile court rapidly releases those youth that come into its purview for these minor offenses, thus reserving resources for the most serious youthful offenders.

The evidence is mixed on both of these points. Determined efforts to locate the "serious juvenile offender" have failed to locate a group of offenders who specialize only in serious violent offenses. For example, in a recent analysis of a national self-report data set, Elliott and his associates noted "there is little evidence for specialization in serious violent offending; to the contrary, serious violent offending appears to be embedded in a more general involvement in a wide range of serious and non-serious offenses" (Elliott, Huizinga, and Morse, 1987). Indeed, they went so far as to speculate that arrest histories that tend to highlight particular types of offenders reflect variations in police policy, practices, and processes of uncovering crime as well as underlying offending patterns.

More to the point, police and court personnel are, it turns out, far more interested in youth they charge with trivial or status offenses than anyone imagined. Efforts to deinstitutionalize "status offenders," for example, ran afoul of juvenile justice personnel who had little interest in releasing youth guilty of noncriminal offenses (Chesney-Lind, 1988). As has been established, much of this is a product of the system's history that encouraged court officers to involve themselves in the noncriminal behavior of youth in order to "save" them from a variety of social ills.

Indeed, parallels can be found between the earlier Progressive period and current national efforts to challenge the deinstitutionalization components of the Juvenile Justice and Delinquency Prevention Act of 1974. These come complete with their celebration of family values and concerns about youthful independence. One of the arguments against the act has been that it allegedly gave children the "freedom to run away" (Office of Juvenile Justice and Delinquency Prevention, 1985) and that it has hampered "reunions" of "missing" children with their parents (Office of Juvenile Justice, 1986). Suspicions about teen sexuality are reflected in excessive concern about the control of teen prostitution and child pornography.

Opponents have also attempted to justify continued intervention into the lives of status offenders by suggesting that without such intervention, the youth would "escalate" to criminal behavior. Yet there is little evidence that status offenders escalate to criminal offenses, and the evidence is particularly weak when considering female delinquents (particularly white female delinquents) (Datesman and Aickin, 1984). Finally, if escalation is occurring, it is likely the product of the justice system's insistence on enforcing status offense laws, thereby forcing youth in crisis to live lives of escaped criminals.

The most influential delinquency theories, however, have largely ducked the issue of status and trivial offenses and, as a consequence, neglected the role played by the agencies of official control (police, probation officers, juvenile court judges, detention home workers, and training school personnel) in the shaping of the "delinquency problem." When confronting the less than distinct picture that emerges from the actual distribution of delinquent behavior, however, the conclusion that agents of social control have considerable discretion in labeling or choosing not to label particular behavior as "delinquent" is inescapable. This symbiotic relationship between delinquent behavior and the official response to that behavior is particularly critical when the question of female delinquency is considered.

TOWARD A FEMINIST THEORY OF DELINQUENCY

To sketch out completely a feminist theory of delinquency is a task beyond the scope of this article. It may be sufficient, at this point, simply to identify a few of the most obvious problems with attempts to adapt male-oriented theory to explain female conformity and deviance. Most significant of these is the fact that all existing theories were developed with no concern about gender stratification.

Note that this is not simply an observation about the power of gender roles (though this power is undeniable). It is increasingly clear that gender stratification in patriarchal society is as powerful a system as is class. A feminist approach to delinquency means construction of explanations of female behavior that are sensitive to its patriarchal context. Feminist analysis of delinquency would also examine ways in which agencies of social control—the police, the courts, and the prisons—act in ways to reinforce woman's place in male society (Harris, 1977; Chesney-Lind, 1986). Efforts to construct a feminist model of delinquency must first and foremost be sensitive to the situations of girls. Failure to consider the existing empirical evidence on girls' lives and behavior can quickly lead to stereotypical thinking and theoretical dead ends.

An example of this sort of flawed theory building was the early fascination with the notion that the women's movement was causing an increase in women's crime; a notion that is now more or less discredited (Steffensmeier, 1980; Gora, 1982). A more recent example of the same sort of thinking can be found in recent work on the "power-control" model of delinquency (Hagan, Simpson, and Gillis, 1987). Here, the authors speculate that girls commit less delinquency in part because their behavior is more closely controlled by the patriarchal family. The authors' promising beginning quickly gets bogged down in a very limited definition of patriarchal control (focusing on parental supervision and variations in power within the family). Ultimately, the authors' narrow formulation of patriarchal control results in their arguing that mother's work force participation (particularly in high status occupations) leads to increases in daughters' delinquency since these girls find themselves in more "egalitarian families."

This is essentially a not-too-subtle variation on the earlier "liberation" hypothesis. Now, mother's liberation causes daughter's crime. Aside from the methodological problems with the study (e.g., the authors argue that female-headed households are equivalent to upper-status "egalitarian" families where both parents work, and they measure delinquency using a six-term scale that contains no status offense items), there is a more fundamental problem with the hypothesis. There is no evidence to suggest that as women's labor force participation accelerated and the number of female-headed households soared, aggregate female delinquency measured both by self-report and official statistics either declined or remained stable (Ageton, 1983; Chilton and Datesman, 1987; Federal Bureau of Investigation, 1987).

By contrast, a feminist model of delinquency would focus more extensively on the few pieces of information about girls' actual lives and the role played by girls' problems, including those caused by racism and poverty, in their delinquency behavior. Fortunately, a considerable literature is now developing on girls' lives and much of it bears directly on girls' crime.

CRIMINALIZING GIRLS' SURVIVAL

It has long been understood that a major reason for girls' presence in juvenile courts was the fact that their parents insisted on their arrest. In the early years, conflicts with parents were by far the most significant referral source; in Honolulu 44% of the girls who appeared in court in 1929 through 1930 were referred by parents.

Recent national data, while slightly less explicit, also show that girls are more likely to be referred to court by "sources other than law enforcement agencies" (which would include parents). In 1983, nearly a quarter (23%) of all girls but only 16% of boys charged with delinquent offenses were referred to court by non-law enforcement agencies. The pattern among youth referred for status offenses (for which girls are overrepresented) was even more pronounced. Well over half (56%) of the girls charged with these offenses and 45% of the boys were referred by sources other than law enforcement (Snyder and Finnegan, 1987, p. 21; see also Pope and Feyerherm, 1982).

The fact that parents are often committed to two standards of adolescent behavior is one explanation for such a disparity—and one that should not be discounted as a major source of tension even in modern families. Despite expectations to the contrary, gender-specific socialization patterns have not changed very much and this is especially true for parents' relationships with their daughters (Katz, 1979). It appears that even parents who oppose sexism in general feel "uncomfortable tampering with existing traditions" and "do not want to risk their children becoming misfits" (Katz, 1979, p. 24). Clearly, parental attempts to adhere to and enforce these traditional notions will continue to be a source of conflict between girls and their elders. Another important explanation for girls' problems with their parents, which has received attention only in more recent years, is the problem of physical and sexual abuse. Looking specifically at the problem of childhood sexual abuse, it is increasingly clear that this form of abuse is a particular problem for girls.

Girls are, for example, much more likely to be the victims of child sexual abuse than are boys. Finkelhor and Baron estimate from a review of community studies that roughly 70% of the victims of sexual abuse are female (Finkelhor and Baron, 1986, p. 45). Girls' sexual abuse also tends to start earlier than boys (Finkelhor and Baron, 1986, p. 48); they are more likely than boys to be assaulted by a family member (often a stepfather) (DeJong, Hervada, and Emmett, 1983; Russell, 1986), and as a consequence, their abuse tends to last longer than male sexual abuse (DeJong, Hervada, and Emmett, 1983). All of these factors are associated with more severe trauma—causing dramatic short- and long-term effects in victims (Adams-Tucker, 1982). The effects noted by researchers in this area move from the more well known "fear, anxiety, depression, anger and hostility, and inappropriate sexual behavior" (Browne and Finkelhor, 1986, p. 69) to behaviors of greater familiarity to criminologists, including running away from home, difficulties in school, truancy, and early marriage (Browne and Finkelhor, 1986).

Herman's study of incest survivors in therapy found that they were more likely to have run away from home than a matched sample of women whose fathers were "seductive" (33% compared to 5%). Another study of women patients found that 50% of the victims of child sexual abuse, but only 20% of the nonvictim group, had left home before the age of 19 (Meiselman, 1978).

Not surprisingly, then, studies of girls on the streets or in court populations are showing high rates of both physical and sexual abuse. Silbert and Pines (1981, p. 409) found, for example, that 60% of the street prostitutes they interviewed had been sexually abused as juveniles. Girls at an Arkansas diagnostic unit and school who had been adjudicated for either status or delinquent offenses reported similarly high levels of sexual abuse as well as high levels of physical abuse; 53% indicated they had been sexually abused, 25% recalled scars, 38% recalled bleeding from abuse, and 51% recalled bruises (Mouzakitas, 1981).

A sample survey of girls in the juvenile justice system in Wisconsin (Phelps et al., 1982) revealed that 79% had been subjected to physical abuse that resulted in some form of injury, and 32% had been sexually abused by parents or other persons who were closely connected to their families. Moreover, 50% had been sexually assaulted ("raped" or forced to participate in sexual acts) (Phelps et al., 1982, p. 66). Even higher figures were reported by McCormack and her associates (McCormack, Janus, and Burgess, 1986) in their study of youth in a runaway shelter in Toronto. They found that 73% of the females and 38% of the males had been sexually abused. Finally, a study of youth charged with running away, truancy, or listed as missing persons in Arizona found that 55% were incest victims (Reich and Gutierres, 1979).

Many young women, then, are running away from profound sexual victimization at home, and once on the streets they are forced further into crime in order to survive. Interviews with girls who have run away from home show, very clearly, that they do not have a lot of attachment to their delinquent activities. In fact, they are angry about being labeled as delinquent, yet all engaged in illegal acts (Koroki and Chesney-Lind, 1985). The Wisconsin study found that 54% of the girls who ran away found it necessary to steal money, food, and clothing in order to survive. A few exchanged sexual contact for money, food, and/or shelter (Phelps et al., 1982, p. 67). In their study of runaway youth, McCormack, Janus, and Burgess (1986, pp. 392–393) found that sexually abused female runaways were significantly more likely than their nonabused counterparts to engage in delinquent or criminal activities such as substance abuse, petty theft, and prostitution. No such pattern was found among male runaways.

Research (Chesney-Lind and Rodriquez, 1983) on the backgrounds of adult women in prison underscores the important links between women's childhood victimizations and their later criminal careers. The interviews revealed that virtually all of this sample were the victims of physical and/or sexual abuse as youngsters; over 60% had been sexually abused and about half had been raped as young women. This situation prompted these women to run away from home (three-quarters had been arrested for status offenses) where once on the streets they began engaging in prostitution and other forms of petty property crime. They also begin what becomes a lifetime problem with drugs. As adults, the women continue in these activities since they possess truncated educational backgrounds and virtually no marketable occupational skills (see also Miller, 1986).

Confirmation of the consequences of childhood sexual and physical abuse on adult female criminal behavior has also recently come from a large quantitative study of 908 individuals with substantiated and validated histories of these victimizations. Widom (1988) found that abused or neglected females were twice as likely as a matched group of controls to have an adult record (16% compared to 7.5). The difference was also found among men, but it was not as dramatic (42% compared to 33%). Men with abuse backgrounds were also more likely to contribute to the "cycle of violence" with more arrests for violent offenses as adult offenders than the control group. In contrast, when women with abuse backgrounds did become involved with the criminal justice system, their arrests tended to involve property and order offenses (such as disorderly conduct, curfew, and loitering violations)(Widon, 1988, p. 17).

Given this information, a brief example of how a feminist perspective on the causes of female delinquency might look seems appropriate. First, like young men, girls are frequently the recipients of violence and sexual abuse. But unlike boys, girls' victimization and their response to that victimization is specifically shaped by their status as young women. Perhaps because of the gender and sexual scripts found in patriarchal families, girls are much more likely than boys to be victims of family-related sexual abuse. Men, particularly men with traditional attitudes toward women, are likely to define their daughters or stepdaughters as their sexual property (Finkelhor, 1982). In a society that idealizes inequality in male/female relationships and venerates youth in women, girls are easily defined as sexually attractive by older men (Bell, 1984). In addition, girls' vulnerability to both physical and sexual abuse is heightened by norms that require that they stay at home where their victimizers have access to them.

Moreover, their victimizers (usually males) have the ability to invoke official agencies of social control in their efforts to keep young women at home and vulnerable. That is to say, abusers have traditionally been able to utilize

the uncritical commitment of the juvenile justice system toward parental authority to force girls to obey them. Girls' complaints about abuse were, until recently, routinely ignored. For this reason, statutes that were originally placed in law to "protect" young people have, in the case of girls' delinquency, criminalized their survival strategies. As they run away from abusive homes, parents have been able to employ agencies to enforce their return. If they persisted in their refusal to stay in that home, however intolerable, they were incarcerated.

Young women, a large number of whom are on the run from homes characterized by sexual abuse and parental neglect, are forced by the very statutes designed to protect them into the lives of escaped convicts. Unable to enroll in school or take a job to support themselves because they fear detection, young female runaways are forced into the streets. Here they engage in panhandling, petty theft, and occasional prostitution in order to survive. Young women in conflict with their parents (often for very legitimate reasons) may actually be forced by present laws into petty criminal activity, prostitution, and drug use.

In addition, the fact that young girls (but not necessarily young boys) are defined as sexually desirable and, in fact, more desirable than their older sisters due to the double standard of aging, means that their lives on the streets (and their survival strategies) take on unique shape— one again shaped by patriarchal values. It is no accident that girls on the run from abusive homes, or on the streets because of profound poverty, get involved in criminal activities that exploit their sexual object status. American society has defined as desirable youthful, physically perfect women. This means that girls on the streets, who have little else of value to trade, are encouraged to utilize this "resource" (Campagna and Poffenberger, 1988). It also means that the criminal subculture views them from this perspective (Miller, 1986).

FEMALE DELINQUENCY, PATRIARCHAL AUTHORITY, AND FAMILY COURTS

The early insights into male delinquency were largely gleaned by intensive field observation of delinquent boys. Very little of this sort of work has been done in the case of girls' delinquency, though it is vital to an understanding of girls' definitions of their own situations, choices, and behavior (for exceptions to this see Campbell, 1984; Peacock, 1981; Miller, 1986; Rosenberg and Zimmerman, 1977). Time must be spent listening to girls. Fuller research on the settings, such as families and schools, that girls find themselves in and the impact of variations in those settings should also be undertaken (see Figueira-McDonough, 1986). A more complete understanding of how poverty and racism shape girls' lives is also vital (see Messerschmidt, 1986; Campbell, 1984). Finally, current qualitative research on the reaction of official agencies to girls' delinquency must be conducted. This latter task, admittedly more difficult, is particularly critical to the development of delinquency theory that is as sensitive to gender as it is to race and class.

It is clear that throughout most of the court's history, virtually all female delinquency has been placed within the larger context of girls' sexual behavior. One explanation for this pattern is that familial control over girls' sexual capital has historically been central to the maintenance of patriarchy (Lerner, 1986). The fact that young women have relatively more of this capital has been one reason for the excessive concern that both families and official agencies of social control have expressed about youthful female defiance (otherwise much of the behavior of criminal justice personnel makes virtually no sense). Only if one considers the role of women's control over their sexuality at the point in their lives that their value to patriarchal society is so pronounced, does the historic pattern of jailing of huge numbers of girls guilty of minor misconduct make sense.

This framework also explains the enormous resistance that the movement to curb the juvenile justice system's authority over status offenders encountered. Supporters of the change were not really prepared for the political significance of giving youth the freedom to run. Horror stories told by the opponents of deinstitutionalization about victimized youth, youthful prostitution, and youthful involvement in pornography (Office of Juvenile Justice and Delinquency Prevention, 1985) all neglect the unpleasant reality that most of these behaviors were often in direct response to earlier victimization, frequently by parents, that officials had, for years, routinely ignored. What may be at stake in efforts to roll back deinstitutionalization efforts is not so much "protection" of youth as it is curbing the right of young women to defy patriarchy.

In sum, research in both the dynamics of girls' delinquency and official reactions to that behavior is essential to the developmental of theories of delinquency that are sensitive to its patriarchal as well as class and racial context.

REFERENCES

ADAMS-TUCKER, CHRISTINE
1982   "Proximate Effects of Sexual Abuse in Childhood." *American Journal of Psychiatry* 193: 1252–1256.

AGETON, SUZANNE S.
1983   "The Dynamics of Female Delinquency, 1976–1980.," *Criminology* 21:555–584.

BELL, INGE POWELL
1984   "The Double Standard: Age." in *Women: A Feminist Perspective*, edited by Jo Freeman. Palo Alto, CA: Mayfield.

BLACK, T. EDWIN AND CHARLES P. SMITH
1981   *A Preliminary National Assessment of the Number and Characteristics of Juveniles Processed in the Juvenile Justice System.* Washington, DC: Government Printing Office.

BROWNE, ANGELA AND DAVID FINKELHOR
1986   "Impact of Child Sexual Abuse: A Review of Research," *Psychological Bulletin* 99:66–77.

CAMPAGNA, DANIEL S. AND DONALD I. POFFENBERGER
1988   *The Sexual Trafficking in Children*, Dover, DE; Auburn House.

CAMPBELL, ANN
1984   *The Girls in the Gang.* Oxford: Basil Blackwell.

CANTER, RACHELLE J.
1982   "Sex Differences in Self-Report Delinquency," *Criminology* 20:373–393.

CHESNEY-LIND, MEDA
1971   *Female Juvenile Delinquency in Hawaii*, Master's thesis, University of Hawaii.
——— 1973. "Judicial Enforcement of the Female Sex Role," *Issues in Criminology* 3:51–71.
——— 1978. "Young Women in the Arms of the Law," In *Women, Crime and the Criminal Justice System*, edited by Lee H. Bowker, Boston: Lexington.
——— 1986. "Women and Crime: the Female Offender," *Signs* 12:78–96.
——— 1988. "Girls and Deinstitutionalization: Is Juvenile Justice Still Sexist?" *Journal of Criminal Justice Abstracts* 20:144–165.

——— and Noelie Rodriquez 1983. "Women Under Lock and Key," *Prison Journal* 63:47–65.

CHILDREN'S BUREAU, DEPARTMENT OF HEALTH, EDUCATION AND WELFARE
1965   *1964 Statistics on Public Institutions for Delinquent Children.* Washington, DC; Government Printing Office.

CHILTON, ROLAND AND SUSAN K. DATESMAN
1987   "Gender, Race and Crime: An Analysis of Urban Arrest Trends, 1960–1980," *Gender and Society* 1:152–171.

CLOWARD, RICHARD A. AND LLOYD E. OHLIN
1960   *Delinquency and Opportunity,* New York: Free Press.

COHEN, ALBERT K.
1955   *Delinquent Boys: The Culture of the Gang,* New York: Free Press.

DATESMAN, SUSAN AND MIKEL AICKIN
1984   "Offense Specialization and Escalation Among Status Offenders," *Journal of Criminal Law and Criminology,* 75:1246–1275.

DAVIDSON, SUE, ED
1982   *Justice for Young Women.* Tucson, AZ; New Directions for Young Women.

DEJONG, ALLAN R., ARTURO R. HERVADA, AND GARY A. EMMETT
1983   "Epidemiologic Variations in Childhood Sexual Abuse," *Child Abuse and Neglect* 7:155–162.

ELLIOTT, DELBERT, DAVID HUIZINGA, AND BARBARA MORSE
1987   "A Career Analysis of Serious Violent Offenders," In *Violent Juvenile Crime: What Can We Do About It?* edited by Ira Schwartz, Minneapolis, MN: Hubert Humphrey Institute.

FEDERAL BUREAU OF INVESTIGATION
1987   *Crime in the United States 1986,* Washington DC; Government Printing Office.

FEINMAN, CLARICE
1980   *Women in the Criminal Justice System,* New York: Praeger.

FIGUEIRA-MCDONOUGH, JOSEFINA
1985   "Are Girls Different? Gender Discrepancies Between Delinquent Behavior and Control," *Child Welfare* 64:273–289.

———   1986 "School Context, Gender, and Delinquency," *Journal of Youth and Adolescence* 15:79–98.

FINKELHOR, DAVID
1982   "Sexual Abuse: A Sociological Perspective," *Child Abuse and Neglect* 6:95–102.

———   and Larry Baron. 1986. "Risk Factors for Child Sexual Abuse," *Journal of Interpersonal Violence* 1:43–71.

FREEDMAN, ESTELLE
1981   *Their Sisters' Keepers,* Ann Arbor; University of Michigan Press.

GELTSHORPE, LORAINE
1986   "Towards a Skeptical Look at Sexism," *International Journal of the Sociology of Law* 14:125–152.

GORA, JOANN
1982   *The New Female Criminal: Empirical Reality or Social Myth,* New York: Praeger.

HAGAN, JOHN, A. R. GILLIS, AND JOHN SIMPSON
1985   "The Class Structure of Gender and Delinquency: Toward a Power-Control Theory of Common Delinquent Behavior," *American Journal of Sociology* 90:1151–1178.

HAGAN, JOHN, JOHN SIMPSON, AND A. R. GILLIS
1987   "Class in the Household: A Power-Control Theory of Gender and Delinquency," *American Journal of Sociology* 92:788–816.

HANCOCK, LINDA
1981   "The Myth that Females are Treated More Leniently than Males in the Juvenile Justice System." *Australian and New Zealand Journal of Criminology* 16:4–14.

HARRIS, ANTHONY
1977   "Sex and Theories of Deviance," *American Sociological Review* 42:3–16.

HERMAN, JULIA L.
1981   *Father-Daughter Incest.* Cambridge, MA; Harvard University Press.

KATZ, PHYLLIS A.
1979   "The Development of Female Identity," In *Becoming Female: Perspectives on Development,* edited by Claire B. Kopp, New York: Plenum.

KOROKI, JAN AND MEDA CHESNEY-LIND
1985   *Everything Just Going Down the Drain.* Hawaii; Youth Development and Research Center.

LERNER, GERDA
1986   *The Creation of Patriarchy.* New York: Oxford.

MCCORMACK, ARLENE, MARK-DAVID JANUS, AND ANN WOLBERT BURGESS
1986   "Runaway Youths and Sexual Victimization: Gender Differences n an Adolescent Runaway Population," *Child Abuse and Neglect* 10:387–395.

MCGARRELL, EDMUND F. AND TIMOTHY J. FLANAGAN
1985   *Sourcebook of Criminal Justice Statistics–1984.* Washington, DC; Government Printing Office.

MEISELMAN, KAREN
1978   *Incest.* San Francisco: Jossey-Bass.

MERTON, ROBERT K.
1938   "Social Structure and Anomie." *American Sociological Review* 3(October):672–782.

MESSERSCHMIDT, JAMES
1986   *Capitalism, Patriarchy, and Crime: Toward a Socialist Feminist Criminology,* Totowa, NJ: Rowman & Littlefield.

———   1987. "Feminism, Criminology, and the Rise of the Female Sex Delinquent, 1880–1930," *Contemporary Crises* 11:243–263.

MILLER, ELEANOR
1986   *Street Woman,* Philadelphia: Temple University Press.

MILLER, WALTER B.
1958   "Lower Class Culture as the Generating Milieu of Gang Delinquency," *Journal of Social Issues* 14:5–19.

MORRIS, RUTH
1964   "Female Delinquency and Relational Problems," *Social Forces* 43:82–89.

MOUZAKITAS, C. M.
1981   "An Inquiry into the Problem of Child Abuse and Juvenile Delinquency," In *Exploring the Relationship Between Child Abuse and Delinquency,* edited by R. J. Hunner and Y. E. Walkers, Montclair, NJ: Allanheld, Osmun.

NATIONAL FEMALE ADVOCACY PROJECT
1981   *Young Women and the Justice System: Basic Facts and Issues.* Tucson, AZ; New Directions for Young Women.

OFFICE OF JUVENILE JUSTICE AND DELINQUENCY PREVENTION
1985   *Runaway Children and the Juvenile Justice and Delinquency Prevention Act: What is the Impact?* Washington, DC; Government Printing Office.

OPINION RESEARCH CORPORATION
1982   "Public Attitudes Toward Youth Crime: National Public Opinion Poll." Mimeographed. Minnesota; Hubert Humphrey Institute of Public Affairs, University of Minnesota.

PEACOCK, CAROL
1981   *Hand Me Down Dreams.* New York: Shocken.

PHELPS, R. J. ET AL.
1982   *Wisconsin Female Juvenile Offender Study Project Summary Report,* Wisconsin: Youth Policy and Law Center, Wisconsin Council of Juvenile Justice.

PLATT, ANTHONY M.
1969   *The Childsavers,* Chicago: University of Chicago Press.

POPE, CARL AND WILLIAM H. FEYERHERM
1982   "Gender Bias in Juvenile Court Dispositions," *Social Service Review* 6:1–17.

RAFTER, NICOLE HAHN
1985   *Partial Justice.* Boston: Northeastern University Press.

REICH, J. W. AND S. E. GUTIERRES
1979   "Escape/Aggression Incidence in Sexually Abused Juvenile Delinquents," *Criminal Justice and Behavior* 6:239–243.

ROGERS, KRISTINE
1972   "For Her Own Protection. . . . Conditions of Incarceration for Female Juvenile Offenders in the State of Connecticut," *Law and Society Review* (Winter):223–246.

ROSENBERG, DEBBY AND CAROLE ZIMMERMAN
1977   *Are My Dreams Too Much to Ask For?* Tucson, AZ.: New Directions for Young Women.

RUSSELL, DIANE E.
1986   *The Secret Trauma: Incest in the Lives of Girls and Women,* New York: Basic Books.

SCHLOSSMAN, STEVEN AND STEPHANIE WALLACH
1978   "The Crime of Precocious Sexuality: Female Juvenile Delinquency in the Progressive Era," *Harvard Educational Review* 48:65–94.

SHAW, CLIFFORD R.
1930   *The Jack-Roller,* Chicago: University of Chicago Press.
———   1938. *Brothers in Crime,* Chicago: University of Chicago Press.
———   and Henry D. McKay, 1942. *Juvenile Delinquency in Urban Areas,* Chicago: University of Chicago Press.

SHELDEN, RANDALL
1981   "Sex Discrimination in the Juvenile Justice System: Memphis, Tennessee, 1900–1917." *In Comparing Female and Male Offenders,* edited by Marguerite Q. Warren. Beverly Hills, CA: Sage.
———   and John Horvath, 1986. "Processing Offenders in a Juvenile Court: A Comparison of Males and Females." Paper presented at the annual meeting of the Western Society of Criminology, Newport Beach, CA, February 27–March 2.

SILBERT, MIMI AND AYALA M. PINES
1981   "Sexual Child Abuse as an Antecedent to Prostitution," *Child Abuse and Neglect* 5:407–411.

SIMONS, RONALD L., MARTIN G. MILLER, AND STEPHEN M. AIGNER
1980   "Contemporary Theories of Deviance and Female Delinquency: An Empirical Test," *Journal of Research in Crime and Delinquency* 17:42–57.

SMITH, LESLEY SHACKLADY
1978   "Sexist Assumptions and Female Delinquency," In *Women, Sexuality and Social Control,* edited by Carol Smart and Barry Smart, London: Routledge & Kegan Paul.

SNYDER, HOWARD N. AND TERRENCE A. FINNEGAN
1987   *Delinquency in the Untied States.* Washington, DC: Department of Justice.

STEFFENSMEIER, DARRELL J.
1980   "Sex Differences in Patterns of Adult Crime, 1965–1977," *Social Forces* 58:1080–1109.

SUTHERLAND, EDWIN
1978   "Differential Association." In *Children of Ishmael: Critical Perspectives on Juvenile Justice,* edited by Barry Krisberg and James Austin. Palo Alto, CA: Mayfield.

TEILMANN, KATHERINE S. AND PIERRE H. LANDRY, JR.
1981   "Gender Bias in Juvenile Justice." *Journal of Research in Crime and Delinquency* 18:47–80.

THRASHER, FREDERIC M.
1927   *The Gang.* Chicago: University of Chicago Press.

TRACY, PAUL E., MARVIN E. WOLFGANG, AND ROBERT M. FIGLIO
1985   *Delinquency in Two Birth Cohorts: Executive Summary.* Washington, DC: Department of Justice.

WIDOM, CATHY SPATZ
1988   "Child Abuse, Neglect, and Violent Criminal Behavior." Unpublished manuscript.

QUESTIONS FOR DISCUSSION

1. How does a feminist perspective on female delinquency differ from the traditional perspectives that typically focus on males? Why have traditional explanations been inadequate?

2. Discuss the patriarchal, class, and racial contexts of female delinquency.

3. According to the author, there is more childhood sexual and physical abuse among females. Why is this the case? How does this impact adolescent female delinquency?

APPLICATIONS

1. Is American society dominated by a patriarchal system? Cite examples from your own experience to support your response.

2. Stereotyping is a significant part of "genderizing" beliefs, attitudes, and behaviors about females and males. Construct a list of common stereotypes regarding females. Construct a similar list for males. Compare your lists to another class member's lists (preferably someone gender different than yourself). Discuss the similarities and differences. Do you foresee any of the stereotypes you have listed changing in the near future? Why?

KEY TERMS

androcentric dominated by or emphasizing a masculine interest or point of view.

egalitarian one who asserts or advocates the removal of inequalities among people.

patriarchal a characteristic of a social organization where men disproportionately control a large share of power; may refer to the head of a household or to beliefs and values that control institutions of government, industry, religion, and education.

status offense refers to an offense committed by a youth that if committed as an adult would not be illegal; illegal because of the status of being young.

stereotype a mental picture or attitude held by an individual or group, typically about another individual or group, which is an oversimplified opinion, a prejudiced appraisal, or a critical judgment.

symbiotic relationship a cooperative interaction between two individuals or groups.

venerate to honor or regard with reverence and/or acts of devotion.

13

Foundation for a General Strain Theory of Crime and Delinquency

Robert Agnew
Emory University

This paper presents a general strain theory of crime and delinquency that is capable of overcoming the criticisms of previous strain theories. In the first section, strain theory is distinguished from social control and differential association/social learning theory. In the second section, the three major types of strain are described: (1) strain as the actual or anticipated failure to achieve positively valued goals, (2) strain as the actual or anticipated removal of positively valued stimuli, and (3) strain as the actual or anticipated presentation of negatively valued stimuli. In the third section, guidelines for the measurement of strain are presented. And in the fourth section, the major adaptations to strain are described, and those factors influencing the choice of delinquent versus nondelinquent adaptations are discussed.

After dominating deviance research in the 1960s, strain theory came under heavy attack in the 1970s (Bernard, 1984; Cole, 1975), with several prominent researchers suggesting that the theory be abandoned (Hirschi, 1969; Kornhauser, 1978). Strain theory has survived those attacks, but its influence is much diminished (see Agnew, 1985a; Bernard, 1984; Farnworth and Leiber, 1989). In particular, variables derived from strain theory now play a very limited role in explanations of crime/delinquency.

"Foundation for a General Theory of Crime and Delinquency," *Criminology*, 30:1 (1992), pp. 47–87. Reprinted with permission of The American Society of Criminology.

Several recent causal models of delinquency, in fact, either entirely exclude strain variables or assign them a small role (e.g., Elliott et al., 1985; Johnson, 1979; Massey and Krohn, 1986; Thornberry, 1987; Tonry et al., 1991). Causal models of crime/delinquency are dominated, instead, by variables derived from differential association/social learning theory and social control theory.

This paper argues that strain theory has a central role to play in explanations of crime/delinquency, but that the theory has to be substantially revised to play this role. Most empirical studies of strain theory continue to rely on the strain models developed by Merton (1938), A. Cohen (1955), and Cloward and Ohlin (1960). In recent years, however, a wealth of research in several fields has questioned certain of the assumptions underlying those theories and pointed to new directions for the development of strain theory. Most notable in this area is the research on stress in medical sociology and psychology, on equity/justice in social psychology, and on aggression in psychology—particularly recent versions of frustration-aggression and social learning theory. Also important is recent research in such areas as the legitimation of stratification, the sociology of emotions, and the urban underclass. Certain researchers have drawn on segments of the above research to suggest new directions for strain theory (Agnew, 1985a; Bernard, 1987;

Elliott et al., 1979; Greenberg, 1977), but the revisions suggested have not taken full advantage of this research and, at best, provide only incomplete models of strain and delinquency. (Note that most of the theoretical and empirical work on strain theory has focused on delinquency.) This paper draws on the above literatures, as well as the recent revisions in strain theory, to present the outlines of a general strain theory of crime/delinquency.

The theory is written at the social-psychological level: It focuses on the individual and his or her immediate social environment—although the macroimplications of the theory are explored at various points. The theory is also written with the empirical researcher in mind, and guidelines for testing the theory in adolescent populations are provided. The focus is on adolescents because most currently available data sets capable of testing the theory involve surveys of adolescents. This general theory, it will be argued, is capable of overcoming the theoretical and empirical criticisms of previous strain theories and of complementing the crime/delinquency theories that currently dominate the field.

The paper is in four sections. In the first section, there is a brief discussion of the fundamental traits that distinguish strain theory from the other two dominant theories of delinquency: social control and differential association/social learning theory (in the interest of brevity, the term *delinquency* is used rather than *crime and delinquency*). In the second section, the three major sources of strain are described. In the third section, guidelines for the measurement of strain are provided. And in the final section, the major adaptations to strain are listed and the factors influencing the choice of delinquent versus nondelinquent adaptations are discussed.

Strain Theory as Distinguished from Control and Differential Association/Social Learning Theory

Strain, social control, and differential association theory are all sociological theories: They explain delinquency in terms of the individual's social relationships. Strain theory is dis-

tinguished from social control and social learning theory in its specification of (1) the type of social relationship that leads to delinquency and (2) the motivation for delinquency. First, strain theory focuses explicitly on *negative relationships with others*: relationships in which the individual is not treated as he or she wants to be treated. Strain theory has typically focused on relationships in which others prevent the individual from achieving positively valued goals. Agnew (1985a), however, broadened the focus of strain theory to include relationships in which others present the individual with noxious or negative stimuli. Social control theory, by contrast, focuses on the *absence of significant relationships with conventional others and institutions*. In particular, delinquency is most likely when (1) the adolescent is not attached to parents, school, or other institutions; (2) parents and others fail to monitor and effectively sanction deviance; (3) the adolescent's actual or anticipated investment in conventional society is minimal; and (4) the adolescent has not internalized conventional beliefs. Social learning theory is distinguished from strain and control theory by its focus on *positive relationships with deviant others*. In particular, delinquency results from association with others who (1) differentially reinforce the adolescent's delinquency, (2) model delinquent behavior, and/or (3) transmit delinquent values.

Second, strain theory argues that adolescents are *pressured into delinquency by the negative affective states—most notably anger and related emotions—that often result from negative relationships* (see Kemper, 1978, and Morgan and Heise, 1988, for topologies of negative affective states). This negative affect creates pressure for corrective action and *may* lead adolescents to (1) make use of illegitimate channels of goal achievement, (2) attack or escape from the source of their adversity, and/or (3) manage their negative affect through the use of illicit drugs. Control theory, by contrast, denies that outside forces pressure the adolescent into delinquency. Rather, the absence of significant relationships with other individuals and groups *frees the adolescent to engage in delinquency*. The freed adolescent either drifts into delinquency or, in some versions of control theory, turns to delinquency in response to inner forces or situational inducements (see Hirschi, 1969:31–34). In differential association/social learning theory, the adolescent commits delinquent acts because group forces lead the adolescent to *view delinquency as a desirable or at least justifiable form of behavior* under certain circumstances.

Strain theory, then, is distinguished by its focus on negative relationships with others and its insistence that such relationships lead to delinquency through the negative affect—especially anger—they sometimes engender. Both dimensions are necessary to differentiate strain theory from control and differential association/social learning theory. In particular, social control and social learning theory sometimes examine negative relationships—although such relationships are not an explicit focus of these theories. Control theory, however, would argue that negative relationships lead to delinquency not because they cause negative affect, but because they lead to a reduction in social control. A control theorist, for example, would argue that physical abuse by parents leads to delinquency because it reduces attachment to parents and the effectiveness of parents as socializing agents. Likewise, differential association/social learning theorists sometimes examine negative relationships—even though theorists in this tradition emphasize that imitation, reinforcement, and the internalization of values are less likely in negative relationships. Social learning theorists, however, would argue that negative relationships—such as those involving physically abusive parents—lead to delinquency by providing models for imitation and implicitly teaching the child that violence and other forms of deviance are acceptable behavior.

Phrased in the above manner, it is easy to see that strain theory complements the other major theories of delinquency in a fundamental way. While these other theories focus on the absence of relationships or on positive relationships, strain theory is the only theory to focus explicitly on negative relationships. And while these other theories view delinquency as the result of drift or of desire, strain theory views it as the result of pressure.

The Major Types of Strain

Negative relationships with others are, quite simply, relationships in which others are not treating the individual as he or she would like to be treated. The classic strain theories of Merton (1938), A. Cohen (1955), and Cloward and Ohlin (1960) focus on only one type of negative relationship: relationships in which others prevent the individual from achieving positively valued goals. In particular, they focus on the goal blockage experienced by lower-class individuals trying to achieve monetary success or middle-class status. More recent versions of strain theory have argued that adolescents are not only concerned about the future goals of monetary success/middle-class status, but are also concerned about the achievement of more immediate goals—such as good grades, popularity with the opposite sex, and doing well in athletics (Agnew, 1984; Elliott and Voss, 1974; Elliott et al., 1985; Empey, 1982; Greenberg, 1977; Quicker, 1974). The focus, however, is still on the achievement of positively valued goals. Most recently, Agnew (1985a) has argued that strain may result not only from the failure to achieve positively valued goals, but also from the inability to escape legally from painful situations. If one draws on the above theories—as well as the stress, equity/justice, and aggression literatures—one can begin to develop a more complete classification of the types of strain.

Three major types of strain are described—each referring to a different type of negative relationship with others. Other individuals may (1) prevent one from achieving positively valued goals, (2) remove or threaten to remove positively valued stimuli that one possesses, or (3) present or threaten to present one with noxious or negatively valued stimuli. These categories of strain are presented as ideal types. There is no expectation, for example, that a factor analysis of strainful events will reproduce these categories. These categories, rather, are presented so as to ensure that the full range of strainful events are considered in empirical research.

STRAIN AS THE FAILURE TO ACHIEVE POSITIVELY VALUED GOALS

At least three types of strain fall under this category. The first type encompasses most of the major strain theories in criminology, including the classic strain theories of Merton, A. Cohen, and Cloward and Ohlin, as well as those modern strain theories focusing on the achievement of immediate goals. The other two types of strain in this category are derived from the justice/equity literature and have not been examined in criminology.

Strain as the Disjunction between Aspirations and Expectations/Actual Achievements

The classic strain theories of Merton, A. Cohen, and Cloward and Ohlin argue that the cultural system encourages everyone to pursue the ideal goals of monetary success and/or middle-class status. Lower-class individuals, however, are often prevented from achieving such goals through legitimate channels. In line with such theories, adolescent strain is typically measured in terms of the disjunction between *aspirations* (or ideal goals) and *expectations* (or expected levels of goal achievement). These theories, however, have been criticized for several reasons (see Agnew, 1986, 1991b; Clinard, 1964; Hirschi, 1969; Kornhauser, 1978; Liska, 1987; also see Bernard, 1984; Farnworth and Leiber, 1989). Among other things, it has been charged that these theories (1) are unable to explain the extensive nature of middle-class delinquency, (2) neglect goals other than monetary success/middle-class status, (3) neglect barriers to goal achievement other than social class, and (4) do not fully specify why only *some* strained individuals turn to delinquency. The most damaging criticism, however, stems from the limited empirical support provided by studies focusing on the disjunction between aspirations and expectations (see Kornhauser, 1978, as well the arguments of Bernard, 1984; Elliott et al., 1985; and Jensen, 1986).

As a consequence of these criticisms, several researchers have revised the above theories. The most popular revision argues that there is a youth subculture that emphasizes a variety of immediate goals. The achievement of these goals is further said to depend on a variety of factors besides social class: factors such as intelligence, physical attractiveness, personality, and athletic ability. As a result, many middle-class individuals find that they lack the traits or skills necessary to achieve their goals through legitimate channels. This version of strain theory, however, continues to argue that strain stems from the inability to achieve certain ideal goals emphasized by the (sub)cultural system. As a consequence, strain continues to be measured in terms of the disjunction between *aspirations* and *actual achievements* (since we are dealing with immediate rather than future goals, actual achievements rather than expected achievements may be examined).

It should be noted that empirical support for this revised version of strain theory is also weak (see Agnew, 1991b, for a summary). At a later point, several possible reasons for the weak empirical support of strain theories focusing on the disjunction between aspirations and expectations/achievements will be discussed. For now, the focus is on classifying the major types of strain.

Strain as the Disjunction between Expectations and Actual Achievements

As indicated above, strain theories in criminology focus on the inability to achieve *ideal* goals derived from the cultural system. This approach stands in contrast to certain of the research on justice in social psychology. Here the focus is on the disjunction between *expectations* and *actual achievements* (rewards), and it is commonly argued that such expectations are existentially based. In particular, it has been argued that such expectations derive from the individual's past experience and/or from comparisons with referential (or generalized) others who are similar to the individual (see Berger et al., 1972, 1983; Blau, 1964; Homans, 1961; Jasso and Rossi, 1977; Mickelson, 1990; Ross et al., 1971; Thibaut and Kelly, 1959). Much of the research in this area has focused on income expectations, although the above theories apply to expectations regarding all manner of positive stimuli. The justice literature argues that the failure to achieve such expectations may lead to such emotions as anger, resentment, rage, dissatisfaction, disappointment, and unhappiness—that is, all the emotions customarily associated with strain in criminology. Further, it is argued that individuals will be strongly motivated to reduce the gap between expectations and achievements—with deviance being commonly mentioned as one possible option. This literature has not devoted much empirical research to deviance, although limited data suggest that the expectations-achievement gap is related to anger/hostility (Ross et al, 1971).

This alternative conception of strain has been largely neglected in criminology. This is unfortunate because it has the potential to overcome certain of the problems of current strain theories. First, one would expect the disjunction between expectations and actual achievements to be more emotionally distressing than that between aspirations and achievements. Aspirations, by definition, are *ideal* goals. They have something of the utopian in them, and for that reason, the failure to achieve aspirations may not be taken seriously. The failure to achieve expected goals, however, is likely to be taken seriously since such goals are rooted in reality—the individual has previously experienced such goals or has seen similar others experience such goals. Second, this alternative conception of strain assigns a central role to the social comparison process. As A. Cohen (1965) argued in a follow-up to his strain theory, the neglect of social comparison is a major shortcoming of strain theory. The above theories describe one way in which social comparison is important: Social comparison plays a central role in the formation of individual goals (expectations in this case; also see Suls, 1977). Third, the assumption that goals are culturally based has sometimes proved problematic for strain theory (see Kornhauser, 1978). Among other things, it makes it difficult to integrate strain theory with social control and cultural deviance theory (see Hirschi, 1979). These latter theories assume that the individual is weakly tied to the cultural system or tied to alternative/oppositional subcultures. The argument that goals are existentially based, however, paves the way for integrations involving theory.[1]

Strain as the Disjunction between Just/Fair Outcomes and Actual Outcomes

The above models of strain assume that individual goals focus on the achievement of specific outcomes. Individual goals, for example, focus on the achievement of a certain amount of money or a certain grade-point average. A third conception of strain, also derived from the justice/equity literature, makes a rather different argument. It claims that individuals do not necessarily enter interactions with specific outcomes in mind. Rather, they enter interactions expecting that certain distributive justice rules will be followed, rules specifying how resources should be allocated. The rule that has received the most attention in the literature is that of equity. An equitable relationship is one in which the outcome/input ratios of the actors involved in an exchange/allocation relationship are equivalent (see Adams, 1963, 1965; Cook and Hegtvedt, 1983; Walster et al., 1978). Outcomes encompass a broad range of positive and negative consequences, while inputs encompass the individual's positive and negative contributions to the exchange. Individuals in a relationship will compare the ratio of their outcomes and inputs to the ratio(s) of specific others in the relationship. If the ratios are equal to one another, they feel that the outcomes are fair or just. This is true, according to equity theorists, even if the outcomes are low. If outcome/input ratios are not equal, actors will feel that the outcomes are unjust and they will experience distress as a result. Such distress is especially likely when individuals feel they have been underrewarded rather than overrewarded (Hegtvedt, 1990).

The equity literature has described the possible reactions to this distress, some of which involve deviance (see Adams, 1963, 1965; Austin, 1977; Walster et al., 1973, 1978; see Stephenson and White, 1968, for an attempt to recast A. Cohen's strain theory in terms of equity theory). In particular, inequity may lead to delinquency for several reasons—all having to do with the restoration of equity. Individuals in inequitable relationships may engage in delinquency in order to (1) increase their outcomes (e.g., by theft); (2) lower their inputs (e.g., truancy from school); (3) lower the outcomes of others (e.g., vandalism, theft, assault); and/or (4) increase the inputs of others (e.g., by being incorrigible or disorderly). In highly inequitable situations, individuals may leave the field (e.g., run away from home) or force others to leave the field.[2] There has not been any empirical research on the relationship between equity and delinquency, although much data suggest that inequity leads to anger and frustration. A few studies also suggest that insulting and vengeful behaviors may result from inequity (see Cook and Hegtvedt, 1991; Donnerstein and Hatfield, 1982; Hegtvedt, 1990; Mikula, 1986; Sprecher, 1986; Walster et al., 1973, 1978).

It is not difficult to measure equity. Walster et al. (1978:234–242) provide the most complete guide to measurement.[3] Sprecher (1986) illustrates how equity may be measured in social surveys; respondents are asked who contributes more to a particular relationship and/or who "gets the best deal" out of a relationship. A still simpler strategy might be to ask respondents how fair or just their interactions with others, such as parents or teachers, are. One would then predict that those involved in unfair relations will be more likely to engage in current and future delinquency.

The literature on equity builds on the strain theory literature in criminology in several ways. First, all of the strain literature assumes that individuals are pursuing some specific outcome, such as a certain amount of money or prestige. The equity literature points out that individuals do not necessarily enter into interactions with specific outcomes in mind, but rather with the expectation that a particular distributive justice rule will be followed. Their goal is that the interaction conform to the justice principle. This perspective, then, points to a new source of strain not considered in the criminology literature. Second, the strain literature in criminology focuses largely on the individual's outcomes. Individuals are assumed to be pursuing a specific goal, and strain is judged in terms of the disjunction between the goal and the actual outcome. The equity literature suggests that this may be an oversimplified conception and that the individual's *inputs* may also have to be considered. In particular,

an equity theorist would argue that inputs will condition the individual's evaluation of outcomes. That is, individuals who view their inputs as limited will be more likely to accept limited outcomes as fair. Third, the equity literature also highlights the importance of the social comparison process. In particular, the equity literature stresses that one's evaluation of outcomes is at least partly a function of the outcomes (and inputs) of those with whom one is involved in exchange/allocation relations. A given outcome, then, may be evaluated as fair or unfair depending on the outcomes (and inputs) of others in the exchange/allocation relation.

Summary: Strain as the Failure to Achieve Positively Valued Goals

Three types of strain in this category have been listed: strain as the disjunction between (1) aspirations and expectations/actual achievements, (2) expectations and actual achievements, and (3) just/fair outcomes and actual outcomes. Strain theory in criminology has focused on the first type of strain, arguing that it is most responsible for the delinquency in our society. Major research traditions in the justice/equity field, however, argue that anger and frustration derive primarily from the second two types of strain. To complicate matters further, one can list still additional types of strain in this category. Certain of the literature, for example, has talked of the disjunction between "satisfying outcomes" and reality, between "deserved" outcomes and reality, and between "tolerance levels" or minimally acceptable outcomes and reality. No study has examined all of these types of goals, but taken as a whole the data do suggest that there are often differences among aspirations (ideal outcomes), expectations (expected outcomes), "satisfying" outcomes, "deserved" outcomes, fair or just outcomes, and tolerance levels (Della Fave, 1974; Della Fave and Klobus, 1976; Martin, 1986; Martin and Murray, 1983; Messick and Sentis, 1983; Shepelak and Alwin, 1986). This paper has focused on the three types of strain listed above largely because they dominate the current literature.[4]

Given these multiple sources of strain, one

might ask which is the most relevant to the explanation of delinquency. This is a difficult question to answer given current research. The most fruitful strategy at the present time may be to assume that all of the above sources are relevant—that there are several sources of frustration. Alwin (1987), Austin (1977), Crosby and Gonzalez-Intal (1984), Hegtvedt (1991b.), Messick and Sentis (1983), and Tornblum (1977) all argue or imply that people often employ a variety of standards to evaluate their situation. Strain theorists, then, might be best advised to employ measures that tap all of the above types of strain. One might, for example, focus on a broad range of positively valued goals and, for each goal, ask adolescents whether they are achieving their ideal outcomes (aspirations), expected outcomes, and just/fair outcomes. One would expect strain to be greatest when several standards were not being met, with perhaps greatest weight being given to expectations and just/fair outcomes.[5]

STRAIN AS THE REMOVAL OF POSITIVELY VALUED STIMULI FROM THE INDIVIDUAL

The psychological literature on aggression and the stress literature suggest that strain may involve more than the pursuit of positively valued goals. Certain of the aggression literature, in fact, has come to deemphasize the pursuit of positively valued goals, pointing out that the blockage of goal-seeking behavior is a relatively weak predictor of aggression, particularly when the goal has never been experienced before (Bandura, 1973; Zillman, 1979). The stress literature has largely neglected the pursuit of positively valued goals as a source of stress. Rather, if one looks at the stressful life events examined in this literature, one finds a focus on (1) events involving the loss of positively valued stimuli and (2) events involving the presentation of noxious or negative stimuli (see Pearlin, 1983, for other topologies of stressful life events/conditions).[6] So, for example, one recent study of adolescent stress employs a life-events list that focuses on such items as the loss of a boyfriend/girlfriend, the death or serious illness of a friend, moving to a new school district, the divorce/separation of one's parents, suspension from school, and the presence of

a variety of adverse conditions at work (see Williams and Uchiyama, 1989, for an overview of life-events scales for adolescents; see Compas, 1987, and Compas and Phares, 1991, for overviews of research on adolescent stress).[7] Drawing on the stress literature, then, one may state that a second type of strain or negative relationship involves the actual or anticipated removal (loss) of positively valued stimuli from the individual. As indicated above, numerous examples of such loss can be found in the inventories of stressful life events. The actual or anticipated loss of positively valued stimuli may lead to delinquency as the individual tries to prevent the loss of the positive stimuli, retrieve the lost stimuli or obtain substitute stimuli, seek revenge against those responsible for the loss, or manage the negative affect caused by the loss by taking illicit drugs. While there are no data bearing directly on this type of strain, experimental data indicate that aggression often occurs when positive reinforcement previously administered to an individual is withheld or reduced (Bandura, 1973; Van Houten, 1983). And as discussed below, inventories of stressful life events, which include the loss of positive stimuli, are related to delinquency.

STRAIN AS THE PRESENTATION OF NEGATIVE STIMULI

The literature on stress and the recent psychological literature on aggression also focus on the actual or anticipated presentation of negative or noxious stimuli.[8] Except for the work of Agnew (1985a), however, this category of strain has been neglected in criminology. And even Agnew does not focus on the presentation of noxious stimuli per se, but on the inability of adolescents to escape legally from noxious stimuli. Much data, however, suggest that the presentation of noxious stimuli may lead to aggression and other negative outcomes in certain conditions, even when legal escape from such stimuli is possible (Bandura, 1973; Zillman, 1979). Noxious stimuli may lead to delinquency as the adolescent tries to (1) escape from or avoid the negative stimuli; (2) terminate or alleviate the negative stimuli; (3) seek revenge against the source of the negative stimuli or related targets, although the evidence on displaced aggression is somewhat mixed (see Berkowitz, 1982; Bernard, 1990; Van Houten, 1983; Zillman, 1979); and/or (4) manage the resultant negative affect by taking illicit drugs.

A wide range of noxious stimuli have been examined in the literature, and experimental, survey, and participant observation studies have linked such stimuli to both general and specific measures of delinquency—with the experimental studies focusing on aggression. Delinquency/aggression, in particular, has been linked to such noxious stimuli as child abuse and neglect (Rivera and Widom, 1990), criminal victimization (Lauritsen et al., 1991), physical punishment (Straus, 1991), negative relations with parents (Healy and Bonner, 1969), negative relations with peers (Short and Strodtbeck, 1965), adverse or negative school experiences (Hawkins and Lishner, 1987), a wide range of stressful life events (Gersten et al., 1974; Kaplan et al., 1983; Linsky and Straus, 1986; Mawson, 1987; Novy and Donohue, 1985; Vaux and Ruggiero, 1983), verbal threats and insults, physical pain, unpleasant odors, disgusting scenes, noise, heat, air pollution, personal space violations, and high density (see Anderson and Anderson, 1984; Bandura, 1973, 1983; Berkowitz, 1982, 1986; Mueller, 1983). In one of the few studies in criminology to focus specifically on the presentation of negative stimuli, Agnew (1985a) found that delinquency was related to three scales measuring negative relations at home and school. The effect of the scales on delinquency was partially mediated through a measure of anger, and the effect held when measures of social control and deviant beliefs were controlled. And in a recent study employing longitudinal data, Agnew (1989) found evidence suggesting that the relationship between negative stimuli and delinquency was due to the *causal* effect of the negative stimuli on delinquency (rather than the effect of delinquency on the negative stimuli). Much evidence, then, suggests that the presentation of negative or noxious stimuli constitutes a third major source of strain.

Certain of the negative stimuli listed above, such as physical pain, heat, noise, and pollution, may be experienced as noxious largely for biological reasons (i.e., they may be unconditioned negative stimuli). Others may be conditioned negative stimuli, experienced as noxious largely because of their association with unconditioned negative stimuli (see Berkowitz, 1982). Whatever the case, it is assumed that such stimuli are experienced as noxious regardless of the goals that the individual is pursuing.

THE LINKS BETWEEN STRAIN AND DELINQUENCY

Three sources of strain have been presented: strain as the actual or anticipated failure to achieve positively valued goals, strain as the actual or anticipated removal of positively valued stimuli, and strain as the actual or anticipated presentation of negative stimuli. While these types are theoretically distinct from one another, they may sometimes overlap in practice. So, for example, the insults of a teacher may be experienced as adverse because they (1) interfere with the adolescent's aspirations for academic success, (2) result in the violation of a distributive justice rule such as equity, and (3) are conditioned negative stimuli and so are experienced as noxious in and of themselves. Other examples of overlap can be given, and it may sometimes be difficult to disentangle the different types of strain in practice. Once again, however, these categories are ideal types and are presented only to ensure that all events with the potential for creating strain are considered in empirical research.

Each type of strain increases the likelihood that individuals will experience one or more of a range of negative emotions. Those emotions include disappointment, depression, and fear. Anger, however, is the most critical emotional reaction for the purposes of the general strain theory. Anger results when individuals blame their adversity on others, and anger is a key emotion because it increases the individual's level of felt injury, creates a desire for retaliation/revenge, energizes the individual for action, and lowers inhibitions, in part because individuals believe that others will feel their aggression is justified (see Averill, 1982; Berkowitz, 1982; Kemper, 1978; Kluegel and Smith, 1986: Ch. 10; Zillman, 1979). Anger, then, affects the individual in several ways that are conducive to delinquency. Anger is distinct from many of the types of negative affect in this respect, and this is the reason that anger occupies a special place in the general strain theory.[9] It is important to note, however, that delinquency may still occur in response to other types of negative affect—such as despair, although delinquency is less likely in such cases.[10] The experience of negative affect, especially anger, typically creates a desire to take corrective steps, with delinquency being one possible response. Delinquency may be a method for alleviating strain, that is, for achieving positively valued goals, for protecting or retrieving positive stimuli, or for terminating or escaping from negative stimuli. Delinquency may be used to seek revenge; data suggest that vengeful behavior often occurs even when there is no possibility of eliminating the adversity that stimulated it (Berkowitz, 1982). And delinquency may occur as adolescents try to manage their negative affect through illicit drug use (see Newcomb and Harlow, 1986). The general strain theory, then, has the potential to explain a broad range of delinquency, including theft, aggression, and drug use.

Each type of strain may create a *predisposition* for delinquency or function as a *situational event* that instigates a particular delinquent act. In the words of Hirschi and Gottredson (1986), then, the strain theory presented in this paper is a theory of both "criminality" and "crime" (or to use the words of Clarke and Cornish [1985], it is a theory of both "criminal involvement" and "criminal events"). Strain creates a predisposition for delinquency in those cases in which it is chronic or repetitive. Examples include a continuing gap between expectations and achievements and a continuing pattern of ridicule and insults from teachers. Adolescents subject to such strain are predisposed to delinquency because (1) nondelinquent strategies for coping with strain are likely to be taxed; (2) the threshold for adversity may be lowered by chronic strains (see Averill, 1982:289); (3) repeated or chronic strain may lead to a hostile attitude—a general dislike and suspicion of others and an associated tendency to respond in an aggressive manner (see Edmunds and Kendrick, 1980:21); and (4) chronic strains increase the likelihood that individuals will be high in negative affect/arousal at any given time (see Bandura, 1983; Bernard, 1990). A particular instance of strain may also function as the situational event that ignites a delinquent act, especially among adolescents predisposed to delinquency. Qualitative and survey data, in particular, suggest that particular instances of delinquency are often instigated by one of the three types of strain listed above (see Agnew, 1990; also see Averill, 1982, for data on the instigations to anger).

Measuring Strain

As indicated above, strain theory in criminology is dominated by a focus on strain as goal blockage. Further, only one type of goal blockage is typically examined in the literature—the failure to achieve *aspirations*, especially aspirations for monetary success or middle-class status. The general strain theory is much broader than current strain theories, and measuring strain under this theory would require at least three sets of measures: those focusing on the failure to achieve positively valued goals, those focusing on the loss of positive stimuli, and those focusing on the presentation of negative stimuli. It is not possible to list the precise measures that should be employed in these areas, although the citations above contain many examples of the types of measures that might be used. Further, certain general guidelines for the measurement of strain can be offered. The guidelines below will also highlight the limitations of current strain measures and shed further light on why those measures are typically unrelated to delinquency.

DEVELOPING A COMPREHENSIVE LIST OF NEGATIVE RELATIONS

Strain refers to negative or adverse relations with others. Such relations are ultimately defined from the perspective of the individual. That is, in the final analysis adverse relations are whatever individuals say they are (see Berkowitz, 1982). This does not mean, however, that one must employ an idiosyncratic definition of adverse relations—defining adverse relations anew for each person one examines. Such a strategy would create serious problems for (1) the empirical study of delinquency, (2) the prediction and control of delinquency, and (3) efforts to develop the macroimplications of the general strain theory. Rather, one can employ a strategy similar to that followed by stress researchers.

First, one can draw on theory and research to specify those objective situations that might reasonably be expected to cause adversity among adolescents. This parallels stress research, which relies on inventories of stressful life events, and several standard inventories are in wide use. The items in such inventories are based, to varying degrees, on the perceptions and judgments of researchers, on previous theory and research, and on reports from samples of respondents (see Dohrenwend, 1974). In developing inventories of strainful events, criminologists must keep in mind the fact that there may be important group differences in the types of strain or negative relations most frequently encountered. A list of negative relations developed for one group, then, may overlook certain negative relations important for another group (see Dohrenwend, 1974). It may eventually be possible, however, to develop a comprehensive list of negative relations applicable to most samples of adolescents.

Second, criminologists must recognize that individuals and groups may experience the strainful events in such inventories differently (see Thoits, 1983). Limited data from the stress literature, for example, suggest that the impact of family stressors is greatest among young adolescents, peer stressors among middle adolescents, and academic stressors among old adolescents (Compas and Phares, 1991). Stress researchers have responded to such findings not by abandoning their inventories, but by investigating those factors that determine why one group or individual will experience a given event as stressful and another will not. And researchers have identified several sets of variables that influence the perception and experience of negative events (e.g., Compas and Phares, 1991; Pearlin, 1982; Pearlin and Schooler, 1978). Many of the variables are discussed in the next section, and they represent a major set of conditioning variables that criminologists should consider when examining the impact of strainful events on delinquency.

EXAMINING THE CUMULATIVE IMPACT OF NEGATIVE RELATIONS

In most previous strain research in criminology, the impact of one type of negative relation on delinquency is examined with other negative relations ignored or held constant. So, for example, researchers will examine the impact of one type of goal blockage on delinquency, ignoring other types of goal blockage and other potential types of strain. This stands in sharp contrast to a central assumption in the stress literature, which is that stressful life events have a cumulative impact on the individual. Linsky and Straus (1986:17), for example, speak of the "accumulation theory," which asserts that "it is not so much the unique quality of any single event but the *cumulation* of several stressful events within a relatively short time span" that is consequential. As a result, it is standard practice in the stressful life-events literature to measure stress with a composite scale: a scale that typically sums the number of stressful life events experienced by the individual.

The precise nature of the cumulative effect, however, is unclear. As Thoits (1983:69) points out, stressful events may have an additive or interactive effect on outcome variables. The additive model assumes that each stressor has a fixed effect on delinquency, an effect independent of the level of the other stressors. Somewhat more plausible, perhaps, is the interactive model, which assumes that "a person who has experienced one event may react with even more distress to a second that follows soon after the first . . . two or more events . . . results in more distress than would be expected from the simple sum of their singular effects."

Whether the effect is additive or interactive, there is limited support for the idea that the level of stress/strain must pass a certain threshold before negative outcomes result (Linsky and Straus, 1986; Thoits, 1983). Below that level, stress/strain is unrelated to negative outcomes. Above that level, stress/strain has a positive effect on negative outcomes, perhaps an additive effect or perhaps an interactive effect.

Given these arguments, one should employ a composite index of strain in all analyses or examine the interactions between strain variables. Examining interactions can become very complex if there are more than a few indicators of strain, although it does allow one to examine the differential importance of various types of strain. If stressors have an interactive effect on delinquency, the interaction terms should be significant or the composite index should have a nonlinear effect on delinquency (see the discussion of interactions and nonlinear effects in Aiken and West, 1991). If the effect is additive, the interaction terms should be insignificant or the composite index should have a linear effect on delinquency (after the threshold level is reached). These issues have received only limited attention in the stress literature (see the review by Thoits, 1983), and they should certainly be explored when constructing measures of strain for the purpose of explaining delinquency. At a minimum, however, as comprehensive a list of negative events/conditions as possible should be examined.

There is also the issue of whether positive events/experiences should be examined. If prior stressors can aggravate the negative effect of subsequent stressors, perhaps positive events can mitigate the impact of stressors. Limited evidence from the stress literature suggests that lists of negative events predict better than lists examining the balance of negative and positive events (usually negative events minus positive events) (see Thoits, 1983:58–59; Williams and Uchiyama, 1989:101; see Gersten et al., 1974, for a possible exception). This topic, however, is certainly in need of more research. In addition to looking at the *difference* between desirable and undesirable events, researchers may also want to look at the *ratio* of undesirable to desirable events.

It should be noted that tests of strain theory in criminology typically examine the disjunction between aspirations and expectations for one or two goals and ignore all of the many other types of strain. The tests also typically assume that strain has a linear effect on delinquency, and they never examine positive as well as negative events. These facts may constitute additional reasons for the weak empirical support given to strain theory in criminology.

EXAMINING THE MAGNITUDE, RECENCY, DURATION, AND CLUSTERING OF ADVERSE EVENTS

Limited research from the stress and equity literatures suggest that adverse events are more influential to the extent that they are (1) greater in magnitude or size, (2) recent, (3) of long duration, and (4) clustered in time.

Magnitude

The magnitude of an event has different meanings depending on the type of strain being examined. With respect to goal blockage, magnitude refers to the size of the gap between one's goals and reality. With respect to the loss of positive stimuli, magnitude refers to the amount that was lost. And with respect to the presentation of noxious stimuli, magnitude refers to the amount of pain or discomfort *inflicted*.[11] In certain cases, magnitude may be measured in terms of a standard metric, such as dollars or volts delivered. In most cases, however, there is no standard metric available for measuring magnitude and one must rely on the perceptions of individuals (see Jasso, 1980, on quality versus quantity goods). To illustrate, researchers in the stress literature have asked judges to rate events according to the amount of readjustment they require or the threat they pose to the individual (see Thoits, 1983, for other weighting schemes). Such judgments are then averaged to form a magnitude score for each event. There is evidence, however, of subgroup differences in weights assigned (Thoits, 1983:53–55).

Magnitude ratings are then sometimes used to weight the events in composite scales. A common finding, however, is that lists of life events weighted by magnitude do *not* predict any better than unweighed lists (e.g., Gersten et al., 1974). This is due to the fact that the correlation between lists of weighted and unweighted events is typically so high (above .90) that the lists can be considered virtually identical (Thoits, 1983). Williams and Uchiyama (1989:99–100) explain this high correlation by arguing that severe life events, which are heavily weighted, have a low base rate in the population and so do not have a significant impact on scale scores. Studies that consider major and minor events separately tend to find that major events are in fact more consequential than minor events (Thoits, 1983:66).

It should be noted that the previous research on strain theory has paid only limited attention to the dimension of magnitude, even in those cases in which standard metrics for measuring magnitude were available. Samples, in fact, are often simply divided into strained and nonstrained groups, with little consideration of variations in the magnitude of strain.

Recency

Certain data suggest that recent events are more consequential than older events and that events older than three months have little effect (Avison and Turner, 1988). Those data focus on the impact of stress on depression, and so are not necessarily generalizable to the strain-delinquency relationship. Nevertheless, the data suggest that the recency of strain may be an important dimension to consider, and findings in this area might be of special use in designing longitudinal studies, in which the issue of the appropriate lag between cause and effect is central (although the subject of little research and theory).

Duration

Much theory and data from the equity and stress literatures suggest that events of long duration (chronic stressors) have a greater impact on a variety of negative psychological outcomes (Folger, 1986; Mark and Folger, 1984; Pearlin, 1982; Pearlin and Lieberman, 1979; Utne and Kidd, 1980). Some evidence, in fact, suggests that discrete events may be unimportant except to the extent that they affect chronic events (Cummings and El-Sheikh, 1991; Gersten et al., 1977; Pearlin, 1983). Certain researchers in the equity/justice literature have suggested that the expected duration of the event into the future should also be considered (Folger, 1986; Mark and Folger, 1984; Utne and Kidd, 1980; see especially the "likelihood of amelioration" concept).

Clustering

Data from the stress literature also suggest that events closely clustered in time have a greater effect on negative outcomes (Thoits, 1983). Such events, according to Thoits (1983), are more likely to overwhelm coping resources than events spread more evenly over time. Certain data, in particular, trace negative outcomes such as suicide and depression to a series of negative events clustered in the previous few weeks (Thoits, 1983).

Adaptations to (Coping Strategies for) Strain

The discussion thus far has focused on the types of strain that might promote delinquency. Virtually all strain theories, however, acknowledge that only *some* strained individuals turn to delinquency. Some effort has been made to identify those factors that determine whether one adapts to strain through delinquency. The most attention has been focused on the adolescent's commitment to legitimate means and association with other strained/delinquent individuals (see Agnew, 1991b).

The following discussion builds on this effort and is in two parts. First, the major adaptations to strain are described. This discussion points to a number of cognitive, emotional, and behavioral coping strategies that have not been considered in the criminology literature. Second, those factors that influence whether one adapts to strain using delinquent or nondelinquent means are described. This discussion also expands on the criminology literature to include several additional factors that affect the choice of adaptation.

ADAPTATIONS TO STRAIN

What follows is a typology of the major cognitive, emotional, and behavioral adaptations to strain, including delinquency.

Cognitive Coping Strategies

Several literatures suggest that individuals sometimes cognitively reinterpret objective stressors in ways that minimize their subjective adversity. Three general strategies of cognitive coping are described below; each strategy has several forms. These strategies for coping with adversity may be summarized in the following phrases: "It's not important," "It's not that bad," and "I deserve it." This typology represents a synthesis of the coping strategies described in the stress, equity, stratification, and victimization literatures (Adams, 1963, 1965; Agnew, 1985b; Agnew and Jones, 1988; Averill, 1982; Della Fave, 1980; Donnerstein and Hatfield, 1982; Pearlin and Schooler, 1978; Walster et al., 1973, 1978). The stress literature, in particular, was especially useful. Stress has been found to have a consistent, although weak- to-moderate, main effect on outcome variables. Researchers have tried to explain this weak-to-moderate effect by arguing that the impact of stressors is conditioned by a number of variables, and much of the attention has been focused on coping strategies (see Compas and Phares, 1991; Thoits, 1984).

Ignore/Minimize the Importance of Adversity. The subjective impact of objective strain depends on the extent to which the strain is related to the central goals, values, and/or identities of the individual. As Pearlin and Schooler (1978:7) state, individuals may avoid subjective strain "to the extent that they are able to keep the most strainful experiences within the least valued areas of their life." Individuals, therefore, may minimize the strain they experience by reducing the absolute and/or relative importance assigned to goals/values and identities (see Agnew, 1983; Thoits, 1991a).

In particular, individuals may claim that a particular goal/value or identity is unimportant in an absolute sense. They may, for example, state that money or work is unimportant to them. This strategy is similar to Merton's adaptations of ritualism and retreatism, and it was emphasized by Hyman (1953). Individuals may also claim that a particular goal/value or identity is unimportant in a relative sense—relative to other goals/values or identities. They may, for example, state that money is less important than status or that work is less important than family and leisure activities.

The strategy of minimizing strain by reduc-

ing the absolute and/or relative emphasis placed on goals/values and identities has not been extensively examined in the strain literature. Certain evidence, however, suggests that it is commonly employed and may play a central role in accounting for the limited empirical support for strain theory. In particular, research on goals suggests that people pursue a wide variety of different goals and that they tend to place the greatest absolute and relative emphasis on those goals they are best able to achieve (Agnew, 1983; McClelland, 1990; Rosenberg, 1979:265–269; Wylie, 1979).

Maximize Positive Outcomes/Minimize Negative Outcomes. In the above adaptation, individuals acknowledge the existence of adversity but relegate such adversity to an unimportant area of their life. In a second adaptation, individuals attempt to deny the existence of adversity by maximizing their positive outcomes and/or minimizing their negative outcomes. This may be done in two ways: lowering the standards used to evaluate outcomes or distorting one's estimate of current and/or expected outcomes.

Lowering one's standards basically involves lowering one's goals or raising one's threshold for negative stimuli (see Suls, 1977). Such action, of course, makes one's current situation seem less adverse than it otherwise would be. Individuals may, for example, lower the amount of money they desire (which is distinct from lowering the importance attached to money). This strategy is also related to Merton's adaptations of ritualism and retreatism, and many of the critics of strain theory in criminology have focused on it. Hyman (1953) and others have argued that poor individuals in the United States are not strained because they have lowered their success goals—bringing their aspirations in line with reality. The data in this area are complex, but they suggest that this adaptation is employed by some—but not all—lower-class individuals (see Agnew, 1983, 1986; Agnew and Jones, 1988; see Cloward and Ohlin, 1960, and Empey, for data on "relative" aspirations).

In addition to lowering their standards, individuals may also cognitively distort their estimate of outcomes. As Agnew and Jones (1988) demonstrate, many individuals exaggerate their actual and expected levels of goal achievement. Individuals with poor grades, for example, often report that they are doing well in school. And individuals with little objective chance of attending college often report that they *expect* to attend college. (See Wylie, 1979, for additional data in this area.) In addition to exaggerating positive outcomes, individuals may also minimize negative outcomes—claiming that their losses are small and their noxious experiences are mild.

The self-concept literature discusses the many strategies individuals employ to accomplish such distortions (see Agnew and Jones, 1988; Rosenberg, 1979). Two common strategies, identified across several literatures, are worth noting. In "downward comparisons," individuals claim that their situation is less worse or at least no worse than that of similar others (e.g., Brickman and Bulman, 1977; Gruder, 1977; Pearlin and Schooler, 1978; Suls, 1977). This strategy is compatible with the equity literature, which suggests that one's evaluation of outcomes is conditioned by the outcomes of comparison others. Temporal comparisons may also be made, with individuals claiming that their situation is an improvement over the past. Recent research on the social comparison process suggests that individuals often deliberately make downward comparisons, especially when self-esteem is threatened (Gruder, 1977; Hegtvedt, 1991b; Suls, 1977). In a second strategy, "compensatory benefits," individuals cast "about for some positive attribute or circumstance within a troublesome situation . . . the person is aided in ignoring that which is noxious by anchoring his attention to what he considers the more worthwhile and rewarding aspects of experience" (Perlin and Schooler, 1978:6–7). Crime victims, for example, often argue that their victimization benefited them in certain ways, such as causing them to grow as a person (Agnew, 1985b).

Accept Responsibility for Adversity.

Third, individuals may *minimize* the subjective adversity of objective strain by convincing themselves that they *deserve* the adversity they have experienced. There are several possible reasons why *deserved* strain is less adverse than undeserved strain.

Undeserved strain may violate the equity principle, challenge one's "belief in a just world" (see Lerner, 1977), and—if attributed to the malicious behavior of another—lead one to fear that it will be repeated in the future. Such reasons may help explain why individuals who make internal attributions for adversity are less distressed than others (Kluegel and Smith, 1986; Mirowsky and Ross, 1990).

Drawing on equity theory, one may argue that there are two basic strategies for convincing oneself that strain is deserved. First, individuals may cognitively minimize their positive inputs or maximize their negative inputs to a relationship. Inputs are conceived as contributions to the relationship and/or status characteristics believed to be relevant to the relationship (see Cook and Yamagishi, 1983). Second, individuals may maximize the positive inputs or minimize the negative inputs of others. Della Fave (1980) uses both of these strategies to explain the legitimation of inequality in the United States. Those at the bottom of the stratification system are said to minimize their own traits and exaggerate the positive traits and contributions of those above them. They therefore come to accept their limited outcomes as just (also see Kluegel and Smith, 1986; Shepelak, 1987).

Behavioral Coping Strategies

There are two major types of behavioral coping: those that seek to minimize or eliminate the source of strain and those that seek to satisfy the need for revenge.

Maximizing Positive Outcomes/Minimizing Negative Outcomes.

Behavioral coping may assume several forms, paralleling each of the major types of strain. Individuals, then, may seek to achieve positively valued goals, protect or retrieve positively valued stimuli, or terminate or escape from negative stimuli. Their actions in these areas may involve conventional or delinquent behavior. Individuals seeking to escape from an adverse school environment, for example, may try to transfer to another school or they may illegally skip school. This rather broad adaptation encompasses Merton's adaptations of innovation and rebellion, as well as those coping strategies described in the equity literature as "maximizing one's outcomes," "minimizing one's inputs," and "maximizing the other's inputs."

Vengeful Behavior. Data indicate that when adversity is blamed on others it creates a desire for revenge that is distinct from the desire to end the adversity. A second method of behavioral coping, then, involves the taking of revenge. Vengeful behavior may also assume conventional or delinquent forms, although the potential for delinquency is obviously high. Such behavior may involve efforts to minimize the positive outcomes, increase the negative outcomes, and/or increase the inputs of others (as when adolescents cause teachers and parents to work harder through their incorrigible behavior).

Emotional Coping Strategies

Finally, individuals may cope by acting directly on the negative emotions that result from adversity. Rosenberg (1990), Thoits (1984, 1989, 1990, 1991b), and others list several strategies of emotional coping. They include the use of drugs such as stimulants and depressants, physical exercise and deep-breathing techniques, meditation, biofeedback and progressive relaxation, and the behavioral manipulation of expressive gestures through play-acting or "expression work." In all of these examples, the focus is on alleviating negative emotions rather than cognitively reinterpreting or behaviorally altering the situation that produced those emotions. Many of the strategies are beyond the reach of most adolescents (Compas et al., 1988), and data indicate that adolescents often employ illicit drugs to cope with life's strains (Labouvie, 1986a, 1986b; Newcomb and Harlow, 1986). Emotional coping is especially likely when behavioral and cognitive coping are unavailable or unsuccessful.

It should be noted that individuals may employ more than one of the above coping strategies (see Folkman, 1991). Also, still other coping strategies, such as distraction, could have been listed. It is assumed, however, that the above strategies constitute the primary responses to strain.

PREDICTING THE USE OF DELINQUENT VERSUS NONDELINQUENT ADAPTATIONS

The above typology suggests that there are many ways to cope with strain—only some of which involve delinquency. And data from the stress literature suggest that individuals vary in the extent to which they use the different strategies (Compas et al., 1988; Menaghan, 1983; Pearlin and Schooler, 1978). These facts go a long way toward explaining the weak support for strain theory. With certain limited exceptions, the strategies are not taken into account in tests of strain theory.

The existence of the above coping strategies poses a serious problem for strain theory. If strain theory is to have any value, it must be able to explain the selection of delinquent versus nondelinquent adaptations. This issue has, of course, been raised before. Critics contend that Merton and other strain theorists fail to explain adequately why only *some* strained individuals turn to delinquency. This issue, however, is all the more pressing when one considers the full range of nondelinquent adaptations to strain listed above. It is therefore important to specify those factors that influence the choice of delinquent versus nondelinquent coping strategies.

The following discussion of influencing factors draws on the aggression, equity, and stress literatures (see especially Adams, 1965; Menaghan, 1982; Pearlin and Schooler, 1978; Walster et al., 1978). The aggression literature in psychology is especially useful. Adversity is said to produce a general state of arousal, which can facilitate a variety of behaviors. Whether this arousal results in aggression is said to be determined by a number of factors, many of which are noted below (see Bandura, 1973, 1983; Berkowitz, 1978, 1982). Those factors affect the choice of coping strategies by affecting (1) the constraints to nondelinquent and delinquent coping and (2) the disposition to engage in nondelinquent versus delinquent coping.

Constraints to Nondelinquent and Delinquent Coping

While there are many adaptations to objective strain, those adaptations are not equally available to everyone. Individuals are constrained in their choice of adaptations(s) by a variety of internal and external factors. The following is a partial list of such factors.

Initial Goals/Values/Identities of the Individual. If the objective strain affects goals/values/identities that are high in absolute and relative importance, and if the individual has few alternative goals/values/identities in which to seek refuge, it will be more difficult to relegate strain to an unimportant area of one's life (see Agnew, 1986; Thoits, 1991a). This is especially the case if the goals/values/identities receive strong social and cultural support (see below). As a result, strain will be more likely to lead to delinquency in such cases.

Individual Coping Resources. A wide range of traits can be listed in this area, including temperament, intelligence, creativity, problem-solving skills, interpersonal skills, self-efficacy, and self-esteem. These traits affect the selection of coping strategies by influencing the individual's sensitivity to objective strains and ability to engage in cognitive, emotional, and behavioral coping (Agnew, 1991a; Averill, 1982; Bernard, 1990; Compas, 1987; Edmunds and Kendrick, 1980; Slaby and Guerra, 1988; Tavris, 1984). Data, for example, suggest that individuals with high self-esteem are more resistant to stress (Averill, 1982; Compas, 1987; Kaplan, 1980; Pearlin and Schooler, 1978; Rosenberg, 1990; Thoits, 1983). Such individuals, therefore, should be less likely to respond to a given objective strain with delinquency. Individuals high in self-efficacy are more likely to feel that their strain can be alleviated by behavioral coping of a nondelinquent nature, and so they too should be less likely to respond to strain with delinquency (see Bandura, 1989, and Wang and Richarde, 1988, on self-efficacy; see Thoits, 1991b, on perceived control).

Conventional Social Support. Vaux (1988) provides an extended discussion of the different types of social support, their measurement, and their effect on outcome variables. Thoits (1984) argues that social support is important because it facilitates the major types of coping. The major types of social support, in fact, correspond to the major types of coping listed above.

Thus, there is informational support, instrumental support, and emotional support (House, 1981). Adolescents with conventional social supports, then, should be better able to respond to objective strains in a nondelinquent manner.

Constraints to Delinquent Coping. The crime/delinquency literature has focused on certain variables that constrain delinquent coping. They include (1) the costs and benefits of engaging in delinquency in a particular situation (Clarke and Cornish, 1985), (2) the individual's level of social control (see Hirschi, 1969), and (3) the possession of those "illegitimate means" necessary for many delinquent acts (see Agnew, 1991a, for a full discussion).

Macro-Level Variables. The larger social environment may affect the probability of delinquent versus nondelinquent coping by affecting all the above factors. First, the social environment may affect coping by influencing the importance attached to selected goals/values/identities. For example, certain ethnographic accounts suggest that there is a strong social and cultural emphasis on the goals of money/status among certain segments of the urban poor. Many poor individuals, in particular, are in a situation in which (1) they face strong economic/status demands, (2) people around them stress the importance of money/status on a regular basis, and (3) few alternative goals are given cultural support (Anderson, 1978; MacLeod, 1987; Sullivan, 1989). As such, these individuals should face more difficulty in cognitively minimizing the importance of money and status.

Second, the larger social environment may affect the individual's sensitivity to particular strains by influencing the individual's beliefs regarding what is and is not adverse. The subculture of violence thesis, for example, is predicated on the assumption that young black males in urban slums are taught that a wide range of provocations and insults are highly adverse. Third, the social environment may influence the individual's ability to minimize cognitively the severity of objective strain. Individuals in some environments are regularly provided with external information about their accomplishments and failings (see Faunce, 1989), and their attempts at cognitively distorting such information are quickly challenged. Such a situation may exist among many adolescents and among those who inhabit the "street-corner world" of the urban poor. Adolescents and those on the street corner live in a very "public world"; one's accomplishments and failings typically occur before a large audience or they quickly become known to such an audience. Further, accounts suggest that this audience regularly reminds individuals of their accomplishments and failings and challenges attempts at cognitive distortion.

Fourth, certain social environments may make it difficult to engage in behavioral coping of a nondelinquent nature. Agnew (1985a) has argued that adolescents often find it difficult to escape legally from negative stimuli, especially negative stimuli encountered in the school, family, and neighborhood. Also, adolescents often lack the resources to negotiate successfully with adults, such as parents and teachers (although see Agnew, 1991a). Similar arguments might be made for the urban underclass. They often lack the resources to negotiate successfully with many others, and they often find it difficult to escape legally from adverse environments—by, for example, quitting their job (if they have a job) or moving to another neighborhood.

The larger social environment, then, may affect individual coping in a variety of ways. And certain groups, such as adolescents and the urban under-class, may face special constraints that make nondelinquent coping more difficult. This may explain the higher rate of deviance among these groups.

Factors Affecting the Disposition to Delinquency

The selection of delinquent versus nondelinquent coping strategies is not only dependent on the constraints to coping, but also on the adolescent's disposition to engage in delinquent versus nondelinquent coping. This disposition is a function of (1) certain temperamental variables (see Tonry et al., 1991), (2) the prior learning history of the adolescent, particularly the extent to which delinquency

was reinforced in the past (Bandura, 1973; Berkowitz, 1982), (3) the adolescent's beliefs, particularly the rules defining the appropriate response to provocations (Bernard's, 1990, "regulative rules"), and (4) the adolescent's attributions regarding the causes of his or her adversity. Adolescents who attribute their adversity to others are much more likely to become angry, and as argued earlier, that anger creates a strong predisposition to delinquency. Data and theory from several areas, in fact, suggest that the experience of adversity is most likely to result in deviance when the adversity is blamed on another.[12] The attributions one makes are influenced by a variety of factors, as discussed in recent reviews by Averill (1982), Berwin (1988), R. Cohen (1982), Crittenden (1983, 1989), Kluegel and Smith (1986), and Utne and Kidd (1980). The possibility that there may be demographic and subgroup differences in the rules for assigning blame is of special interest (see Bernard, 1990; Crittenden, 1983, 1989).

A key variable affecting several of the above factors is association with delinquent peers. It has been argued that adolescents who associate with delinquent peers are more likely to be exposed to delinquent models and beliefs and to receive reinforcement for delinquency (see especially, Akers, 1985). It may also be the case that delinquent peers increase the likelihood that adolescents will attribute their adversity to others.

The individual's disposition to delinquency, then, may condition the impact of adversity on delinquency. At the same time, it is important to note that continued experience with adversity may create a disposition for delinquency. This argument has been made by Bernard (1990), Cloward and Ohlin (1960), A. Cohen (1955), Elliott et al. (1979), and others. In particular, it has been argued that under certain conditions the experience of adversity may lead to beliefs favorable to delinquency, lead adolescents to join or form delinquent peer groups, and lead adolescents to blame others for their misfortune.

Virtually all empirical research on strain theory in criminology has neglected the constraints to coping and the adolescent's disposition to delinquency. Researchers, in particular, have failed to examine whether the effect of adversity on delinquency is conditioned by factors such as self-efficacy and association with delinquent peers. This is likely a major reason for the weak empirical support for strain theory.

Conclusion

Much of the recent theoretical work in criminology has focused on the integration of different delinquency theories. This paper has taken an alternative track and, following Hirschi's (1979) advice, has focused on the refinement of a single theory. The general strain theory builds upon traditional strain theory in criminology in several ways. First, the general strain theory points to several new sources of strain. In particular, it focuses on three categories of strain or negative relationships with others: (1) the actual or anticipated failure to achieve positively valued goals, (2) the actual or anticipated removal of positively valued stimuli, and (3) the actual or anticipated presentation of negative stimuli. Most current strain theories in criminology only focus on strain as the failure to achieve positively valued goals, and even then the focus is only on the disjunction between aspirations and expectations/actual achievements. The disjunctions between expectations and achievements and just/fair outcomes and achievements are ignored. The general strain theory, then, significantly expands the focus of strain theory to include all types of negative relations between the individual and others.

Second, the general strain theory more precisely specifies the relationship between strain and delinquency, pointing out that strain is likely to have a cumulative effect on delinquency after a certain threshold level is reached. The theory also points to certain relevant dimensions of strain that should be considered in empirical research, including the magnitude, recently, duration, and clustering of strainful events.

Third, the general strain theory provides a more comprehensive account of the cognitive, behavioral, and emotional adaptations to strain. This account sheds additional light on the reasons why many strained individuals do *not* turn to delinquency, and it may prove useful in devis-

ing strategies to prevent and control delinquency. Individuals, in particular, may be taught those nondelinquent coping strategies found to be most effective in preventing delinquency.

Fourth, the general strain theory more fully describes those factors affecting the choice of delinquent versus nondelinquent adaptations. The failure to consider such factors is a fundamental reason for the weak empirical support for strain theory.

Most of the above modifications in strain theory were suggested by research in several areas outside of traditional criminology, most notably the stress research in medical sociology and psychology, the equity/justice research in social psychology, and the aggression research in psychology. With certain exceptions, researchers in criminology have tended to cling to the early strain models of Merton (1938), A. Cohen (1955), and Cloward and Ohlin (1960) and to ignore the developments in related fields. And while these early strain models contain much of value and have had a major influence on the general strain theory in this paper, they do not fully exploit the potential of strain theory.

At the same time, it is important to note that the general strain theory is not presented here as a fully developed alternative to earlier theories. First, the macroimplications of the theory were only briefly discussed. It would not be difficult to extend the general strain theory to the macro level, however; researchers could focus on (1) the social determinants of adversity (for an example, see Bernard, 1990, on the urban underclass) and (2) the social determinants of those factors that condition the effect of adversity on delinquency. Second, the theory did not concern itself with the nonsocial determinants of strain, such as illness. It seems doubtful that adversity caused by nonsocial sources is a major source of delinquency because, among other things, it is unlikely to generate anger (see Averill, 1982). Nevertheless, nonsocial sources of adversity should be investigated. Third, the relationship between the general strain theory and other major theories of delinquency must be more fully explored. As hinted earlier, the relationship is rather complex. While the general strain theory is clearly distinct from control and differential

association theory, strain may lead to low social control and association with delinquent others. Further, variables from the three theories may interact with one another in producing delinquency. Individuals with delinquent friends, for example, should be more likely to respond to strain with delinquency. The general strain theory then, is presented as a foundation on which to build.

It is not possible to test the general strain theory fully with currently available data sets, but it is possible to test core sections of the theory. Most data sets dealing with delinquency contain at least some measures of adversity and at least some measures of those factors said to condition the effect of adversity on delinquency. Given this fact, researchers could focus on the following core hypotheses derived from the theory:

First, adverse relations with others will have a positive effect on both general and specific measures of delinquency, with measures of social control and differential association held constant. This is especially true of adverse relations that are severe and that provide limited opportunities for nondelinquent coping. Prime examples, as discussed earlier, are adverse relations involving family, school, and neighborhood. It is hoped research will point to several measures of strain that are especially relevant to delinquency. Such measures can then be made a routine part of delinquency research, just as the elements of the social bond and measures of differential association are now routinely included in empirical studies.

Second, adverse relations will have a cumulative impact on delinquency after a certain threshold level is reached. Further, this cumulative impact will likely be interactive in nature; each additional increment in strain will have a greater impact than the one before.

Third, the impact of strain or adverse relations on delinquency will be conditioned by several variables, as listed above.

Strain theory is the only major theory to focus explicitly on negative relations with others and to argue that delinquency results from the negative affect caused by such relations. As such, it complements social control and differential association/social learning theory in a fundamental way. It is hoped that the general strain theory will revive interest in negative relations and cause criminologists to "bring the bad back in."

NOTES

1. One need not assume that expectations are existentially based; they may derive from the cultural system as well. Likewise, one need not assume that aspirations derive from the cultural system. The focus in this paper is on *types* of strain rather than *sources* of strain, although a consideration of sources is crucial when the macroimplications of the theory are developed. Additional information on the sources of positively valued goals—including aspirations and expectations—can be found in Alves and Rossi, 1978; Cook and Messick, 1983; Hochschild, 1981; Jasso and Rossi, 1977; Martin and Murray, 1983; Messick and Sentis, 1983; Mickelson, 1990; and Shepelak and Alwin, 1986.

2. Theorists have recently argued that efforts to restore equity need not involve the specific others in the inequitable relationship. If one cannot restore equity with such specific others, there may be an effort to restore "equity with the world" (Austin, 1977; Stephenson and White, 1968; Walster et al., 1978.) That is, individuals who feel they have been inequitably treated may try to restore equity in the context of a totally different relationship. The adolescent who is inequitably treated by parents, for example, may respond by inequitably treating peers. The concept of "equity with the world" has not been the subject of much empirical research, but it is intriguing because it provides a novel explanation for displayed aggression. It has also been argued that individuals may be distressed not only by their own inequitable treatment, but also by the inequitable treatment of others (see Crosby and Gonzalez-Intal, 1984; Walster et al., 1978). We may have, then, a sort of vicarious strain, a type little investigated in the literature.

3. The equity literature has been criticized on a number of points, the most prominent being that there are a variety of distribution rules besides equity—such as equality and need (Deutsch, 1975; Folger, 1984; Mikula, 1980; Schwinger, 1980; Utne and Kidd, 1980). Much recent research has focused on the factors that determine the preference for one rule over another (Alves and Rossi, 1978; Cook and Hegtvedt, 1983; Deutsch, 1975; Hegtvedt, 1987, 1991a; Hochschild, 1981; Lerner, 1977; Leventhal, 1976; Leventhal et al., 1980; Schwinger, 1980; Walster et al., 1978). Also, the equity literature argues that individuals compare themselves with similar others with whom they are involved in exchange/allocation relations. However, it has been argued that individuals sometimes compare themselves with dissimilar others, make referential (generalized) rather than local (specific) comparisons, make internal rather than external comparisons, make group-to-group comparisons, or avoid social comparison altogether (see Berger et al.,

1972; Hegtvedt, 1991b; Martin and Murray, 1983; see Hegtvedt, 1991b, and Suls and Wills, 1991, for a discussion of the factors affecting the choice of comparison objects). Finally, even if one knows what distribution rule individuals prefer and the types of social comparisons they make, it is still difficult to predict whether they will evaluate their interactions as equitable. Except in unambiguous situations of the type created in experiments, it is hard to predict what inputs and outcomes individuals will define as relevant, how they will weight those inputs and outcomes, and how they will evaluate themselves and others on those inputs and outcomes (Austin, 1977; Hegtvedt, 1991a; Messick and Sentis, 1979, 1983; Walster et al., 1973, 1978). Fortunately, however, the above three problems do not prohibit strain theory from taking advantage of certain of the insights from equity theory. While it is difficult to predict whether individuals will define their relationships as equitable, it is relatively easy to measure equity after the fact.

4. To add a still further complication, it has been suggested that anger may result from the violation of *procedural* as well as distributive justice rules (Folger, 1984, 1986; Lind and Tyler, 1988). Procedural justice does not focus on the fairness of outcomes, but rather on the fairness of the procedures by which individuals decide how to distribute resources. A central issue in procedural justice is whether all individuals have a "voice" in deciding how resources will be distributed. One might, then, ask adolescents about the fairness of the procedures used by parents, teachers, and others to make rules.

5. This strategy assumes that all standards are relevant in a given situation, which may not always be the case. In certain situations, for example, one may make local comparisons but not referential comparisons (see Brickman and Bulman, 1977; Crosby and Gonzales-Intal, 1984). In other situations, social comparison processes may not come into play at all; outcomes may be evaluated in terms of culturally derived standards (see Folger, 1986).

6. The stress literature has also focused on positive events, based on the assumption that such events might lead to stress by overloading the individual. Accumulating evidence, however, suggests that it is only undesirable events that lead to negative outcomes such as depression (e.g., Gersten et al., 1974; Kaplan et al., 1983; Pearlin et al., 1981; Thoits, 1983).

7. Certain individuals have criticized the stress literature for neglecting the failure of individuals to achieve positively valued goals. In particular, it has been charged that the stress literature has neglected "nonevents," or events that are desired or anticipated but do not occur (Dohrenwend and Dohrenwend, 1974; Thoits, 1983). One major distinction between the strain literature in criminology and the stress literature in medical sociology, in fact, is that the former has focused on "nonevents" while the latter has focused on "events."

8. Some researchers have argued that it is often diffi-

cult to distinguish the presentation of negative stimuli from the removal of positive stimuli (Michael, 1973; Van Houten, 1983; Zillman, 1979). Suppose, for example, that an adolescent argues with parents. Does this represent the presentation of negative stimuli, (the arguing) or the removal of positive stimuli (harmonious relations with one's parents)? The point is a valid one, yet the distinction between the two types of strain still seems useful since it helps ensure that all major types of strain are considered by researchers.

9. The focus on blame/anger represents a major distinction between the general strain theory and the stress literature. The stress literature simply focuses on adversity, regardless of whether it is blamed on another. This is perhaps appropriate because the major outcome variables of the stress literature are inner-directed states, like depression and poor health. When the focus shifts to outer-directed behavior, like much delinquency, a concern with blame/anger becomes important.

10. Delinquency may still occur in the absence of blame and anger (see Berkowitz, 1986; Zillman, 1979). Individuals who accept responsibility for their adversity are still subject to negative affect, such as depression, despair, and disappointment (see Kemper, 1978; Kluegel and Smith, 1986). As a result, such individuals will still feel pressure to take corrective action, although the absence of anger places them under less pressure and makes vengeful behavior much less likely. Such individuals, however, may engage in inner-directed delinquency, such as drug use, and if suitably disposed, they may turn to other forms of delinquency as well. Since these individuals lack the strong motivation for revenge and the lowered inhibitions that anger provides, it is assumed that they must have some minimal disposition for deviance before they respond to their adversity with outer-directed delinquency (see the discussion of the disposition to delinquency).

11. As Empey (1956) and others have pointed out, magnitude may also be measured in *relative* terms. For example, suppose an individual earning $10,000 a year and an individual earning $100,000 both lose $100 in a burglary. In absolute terms, the magnitude of their loss is the same. Relative to their current income, however, the magnitude of their loss is quite different. In most cases, it would be difficult to develop precise measures of relative magnitude. Nevertheless, researchers should at the very least be sensitive to this issue when analyzing and interpreting data.

12. This is a major theme in the psychological research on aggression, in much of the recent research on equity, and in the emotions literature, and it is a central theme in Cloward and Ohlin's (1960) strain theory (e.g., Averill, 1982; Berkowitz, 1982; R. Cohen, 1982; Crosby and Gonzalez-Intal, 1984; Garrett and Libby, 1973; Kemper, 1978; Leventhal, 1976; Mark and Folger, 1984; Martin and Murray, 1984; Weiner, 1982; Zillman, 1979).

REFERENCES

ADAMS, J. STACY
1963   Toward an understanding of inequity. Journal of Abnormal and Social Psychology 67:422–436.
1965   Inequity in social exchange. In Leonard Berkowitz (ed.), Advances in Experimental Social Psychology. New York: Academic Press.

AGNEW, ROBERT
1983   Social class and success goals: An examination of relative and absolute aspirations. Sociological Quarterly 24:435–452.
1984   Goal achievement and delinquency. Sociology and Social Research 68:435–451.
1985a   A revised strain theory of delinquency. Social Forces 64:151–167.
1985b   Neutralizing the impact of crime. Criminal Justice and Behavior 12:221–239.
1986   Challenging strain theory: An examination of goals and goal-blockage. Paper presented at the annual meeting of the American Society of Criminology, Atlanta.
1989   A longitudinal test of the revised strain theory. Journal of Quantitative Criminology 5:373–387.
1990   The origins of delinquent events: An examination of offender accounts. Journal of Research in Crime and Delinquency 27:267–294.
1991a   Adolescent resources and delinquency. Criminology 28:535–566.
1991b   Strain and subcultural crime theory. In Joseph Sheley (ed.), Criminology: A Contemporary Handbook. Belmont, Calif.: Wadsworth.

AGNEW, ROBERT AND DIANE JONES
1988   Adapting to deprivation: An examination of inflated educational expectations. Sociological Quarterly 29:315–337.

AIKEN, LEONA S. AND STEPHEN G. WEST
1991   Multiple Regression: Testing and Interpreting Interactions. Newbury Park, Calif.: Sage.

AKERS, RONALD L.
1985   Deviant Behavior: A Social Learning Approach. Belmont, Calif.: Wadsworth.

ALVES, WAYNE M. AND PETER H. ROSSI
1978   Who should get what? Fairness judgments of the distribution of earnings. American Journal of Sociology 84:541–564.

ALWIN, DUANE F.
1987   Distributive justice and satisfaction with material well-being. American Sociological Review 52:83–95.

ANDERSON, CRAIG A. AND DONA C. ANDERSON
1984   Ambient temperature and violent crime: Tests of the linear and curvilinear hypotheses. Journal of Personality and Social Psychology 46:91–97.

ANDERSON, ELIJAH
1978   A Place on the Corner. Chicago: University of Chicago Press.

AUSTIN, WILLIAM
1977   Equity theory and social comparison processes. In Jerry M. Suls and Richard L. Miller (eds.), Social Comparison Processes. New York: Hemisphere.

AVERILL, JAMES R.
1982   Anger and Aggression. New York: Springer-Verlag.

AVISON, WILLIAM R. AND R. JAY TURNER
1988   Stressful life events and depressive symptoms: Disaggregating the effects of acute stressors and chronic strains. Journal of Health and Social Behavior 29:253–264.

BANDURA, ALBERT
1973   Aggression: A Social Learning Analysis. Englewood Cliffs, N.J.: Prentice-Hall.
1983   Psychological mechanisms of aggression. In Russell G. Geen and Edward Donnerstein (eds.), Aggression: Theoretical and Empirical Reviews. New York: Academic Press.
1989   Human agency and social cognitive theory. American Psychologist 44:1175–1184.

BERGER, JOSEPH, MORRIS ZELDITCH, JR., BO ANDERSON, AND BERNARD COHEN
1972   Structural aspects of distributive justice: A status-value formulation. In Joseph Berger, Morris Zelditch, Jr., and Bo Anderson (eds.), Sociological Theories in Progress. New York: Houghton Mifflin.

BERGER, JOSEPH, M. HAMIT FISCK, ROBERT Z. NORMAN, AND DAVID G. WAGNER
1983   The formation of reward expectations in status situations. In David M. Messick and Karen S. Cook (eds.), Equity Theory: Psychological and Sociological Perspectives. New York: Praeger.

BERKOWITZ, LEONARD
1978   Whatever happened to the frustration-aggression hypothesis? American Behavioral Scientist 21:691–708.
1982   Aversive conditions as stimuli to aggression. In Leonard Berkowitz (ed.), Advances in Experimental Social Psychology. Vol. 15. New York: Academic Press.
1986   A Survey of Social Psychology. New York: Holt, Rinehart & Winston.

BERNARD, THOMAS J.
1984   Control criticisms of strain theories: An assessment of theoretical and empirical adequacy. Journal of Research in Crime and Delinquency 21:353–372.
1987   Testing structural strain theories. Journal of Research in Crime and Delinquency 24:262–280.
1990   Angry aggression among the "truly disadvantaged." Criminology 28:73–96.

BLAU, PETER
1964   Exchange and Power in Social Life. New York: John Wiley & Sons.

BREWIN, CHRIS R.
1988   Explanation and adaptation in adversity. In Shirley Fisher and James Reason (eds.), Handbook of Life Stress, Cognition and Health. Chichester, England: John Wiley & Sons.

BRICKMAN, PHILIP AND RONNIE JANOFF BULMAN
1977   Pleasure and pain in social comparison. In Jerry
        M. Suls and Richard L. Miller (eds.), Social Com-
        parison Processes. New York: Hemishpere.

CLARKE, RONALD V., AND DEREK B. CORNISH
1985   Modeling offenders' decisions: A framework for
        research and policy. In Michael Tonry and Nor-
        val Morris (eds.), Crime and Justice: An Annual
        Review of Research. Vol. 6. Chicago: University of
        Chicago Press.

CLINARD, MARSHALL B.
1964   Anomie and Deviant Behavior. New York: Free
        Press.

CLOWARD, RICHARD A. AND LLOYD E. OHLIN
1960   Delinquency and Opportunity. New York: Free
        Press.

COHEN, ALBERT K.
1955   Delinquent Boys. New York: Free Press.
1965   The sociology of the deviant act: Anomie theory
        and beyond. American Sociological Review
        30:5–14.

COHEN, RONALD L.
1982   Perceiving justice: An attributional perspective.
        In Jerald Greenberg and Ronald L. Cohen (eds.),
        Equity and Justice in Social Behavior. New York:
        Academic Press.

COLE, STEPHEN
1975   The growth of scientific knowledge: Theories of
        deviance as a case study. In Lewis A. Coser (ed.),
        The Idea of Social Structure: Papers in Honor of
        Robert K. Merton. New York: Harcourt Brace
        Jovanovich.

COMPAS, BRUCE E.
1987   Coping with stress during childhood and adoles-
        cence. Psychological Bulletin 101:393–403.

COMPAS, BRUCE E., VANESSA L. MALCARNE, AND KAREN M.
        FONDACARO
1988   Coping with stressful events in older children and
        young adolescents. Journal of Consulting and Clin-
        ical Psychology 56:405–411.

COMPAS, BRUCE E. AND VICKY PHARES
1991   Stress during childhood and adolescence: Sources
        of risk and vulnerability. In E. Mark Cummings,
        Anita L. Greene, and Katherine H. Karraker
        (eds.), Life-Span Developmental Psychology: Per-
        spectives on Stress and Coping. Hillsdale, N.J.:
        Lawrence Erlbaum.

COOK, KAREN S., AND KAREN A. HEGTVEDT
1983   Distributive justice, equity, and equality. Annual
        Review of Sociology 9:217–241.
1991   Empirical evidence of the sense of justice. In Mar-
        garet Gruter, Roger D. Masters, Michael T.
        McGuire (eds.), The Sense of Justice: An Inquiry
        into the Biological Foundations of Law. New York:
        Greenwood Press.

COOK, KAREN S. AND DAVID MESSICK
1983   Psychological and sociological perspectives on dis-
        tributive justice: Convergent, divergent, and par-
        allel lines. In David M. Messick and Karen S. Cook

(eds.), Equity Theory: Psychological and Sociological Perspectives. New York: Praeger.

COOK, KAREN S. AND TOSHIO YAMAGISHI
1983   Social determinants of equity judgments: The
        problem of multidimensional input. In David M.
        Messick and Karen S. Cook (eds.), Equity Theory:
        Psychological and Sociological Perspectives. New
        York: Praeger.

CRITTENDEN, KATHLEEN S.
1983   Sociological aspects of attribution. Annual Review
        of Sociology 9:425–446.
1989   Causal attribution in sociocultural context: Toward
        a self-presentational theory of attribution
        processes. Sociological Quarterly 30:1–14.

CROSBY, FAYE AND A. MIREN GONZALEZ-INTAL
1984   Relative deprivation and equity theories: Felt in-
        justice and the undeserved benefits of others. In
        Robert Folger (ed.), The Sense on Injustice: Social
        Psychological Perspectives. New York: Plenum.

CUMMINGS, E. MARK AND MONA EL-SHEIKH
1991   Children's coping with angry environments: A
        process-oriented approach. In E. Mark Cummings,
        Anita L. Greene, and Katherine H. Karraker
        (eds.), Life-Span Developmental Psychology: Per-
        spectives on Stress and Coping. Hillsdale, N.J.:
        Lawrence Erlbaum.

DELLA FAVE, L. RICHARD
1974   Success values: Are they universal or class-differ-
        entiated? American Journal of Sociology
        80:153–169.
1980   The meek shall not inherit the earth: Self-evalua-
        tions and the legitimacy of stratification. Ameri-
        can Sociological Review 45:955–971.

DELLA FAVE, L. RICHARD AND PATRICIA KLOBUS
1976   Success values and the value stretch: A biracial
        comparison. Sociological Quarterly 17:491–502.

DEUTSCH, MORTON
1975   Equity, equality, and need: What determines which
        value will be used as the basis of distributive justice.
        Journal of Social Issues 31:137–149.

DOHRENWEND, BARBARA SNELL AND BRUCE P. DOHRENWEND
1974   Overview and prospects for research on stressful
        life events. In Barbara Snell Dohrenwend and
        Bruce P. Dohrenwend (eds.), Stressful Life Events:
        Their Nature and Effects. New York: John Wiley
        & Sons.

DOHRENWEND, BRUCE P.
1974   Problems in defining and sampling the relevant
        population of stressful life events. In Barbara Snell
        Dohrenwend and Bruce P. Dohrenwend (eds.),
        Stressful Life Events: Their Nature and Effects.
        New York: John Wiley & Sons.

DONNERSTEIN, EDWARD AND ELAINE HATFIELD
1982   Aggression and equity. In Jerald Greenberg and
        Ronald L. Cohen (eds.), Equity and Justice in
        Social Behavior. New York: Academic Press.

EDMUNDS, G. AND D.C. KENDRICK
1980   The Measurement of Human Aggressiveness. New
        York: John Wiley & Sons.

ELLIOTT, DELBERT AND HARWIN VOSS
1974   Delinquency and Dropout. Lexington, Mass.: Lexington Books.

ELLIOTT, DELBERT, SUZANNE AGETON, AND RACHEL CANTER
1979   An integrated theoretical perspective on delinquent behavior. Journal of Research in Crime and Delinquency 16:3–27.

ELLIOTT, DELBERT, DAVID HUIZINGA, AND SUZANNE AGETON
1985   Explaining Delinquency and Drug Use. Beverly Hills, Calif.: Sage.

EMPEY, LAMAR
1956   Social class and occupational aspiration: A comparison of absolute and relative measurement. American Sociological Review 21:703–709.

1982   American Delinquency: Its Meaning and Construction. Homewood, Ill.: Dorsey.

FARNWORTH, MARGARET AND MICHAEL J. LEIBER
1989   Strain theory revisited: Economic goals, educational means, and delinquency. American Sociological Review 54:263–274.

FAUNCE, WILLIAM A.
1989   Occupational status-assignment systems: The effect of status on self-esteem. American Journal of Sociology 95:378–400.

FOLGER, ROBERT
1984   Emerging issues in the social psychology of justice. In Robert Folger (ed.), The Sense of Injustice: Social Psychological Perspectives. New York: Plenum.

1986   Rethinking equity theory: A referent cognitions model. In Hans Werner Bierhoff, Ronald L. Cohen, and Jerald Greenberg (eds.), Justice in Social Relations. New York: Plenum.

FOLKMAN, SUSAN
1991   Coping across the life-span: Theoretical issues. In E. Mark Cummings, Anita L. Greene, and Katherine H. Karraker (eds.), Life-Span Developmental Psychology: Perspectives on Stress and Coping. Hillsdale, N.J.: Lawrence Erlbaum.

GARRETT, JAMES AND WILLIAM L. LIBBY, JR.
1973   Role of intentionality in mediating responses to inequity in the dyad. Journal of Personality and Social Psychology 28:21–27.

GERSTEN, JOANNE C., THOMAS S. LANGER, JEANNE G. EISENBERG, AND LIDA OZEK
1974   Child behavior and life events: Undesirable change or change per se. In Barbara Snell Dohrenwend and Bruce P. Dohrenwend (eds.), Stressful Life Events: Their Nature and Effects. New York: John Wiley & Sons.

GERSTEN, JOANNE C., THOMAS S. LANGER, JEANNE G. EISENBERG, AND ORA SMITH-FAGON
1977   An evaluation of the etiological role of stressful life-change events in psychological disorders. Journal of Health and Social Behavior 18:228–244.

GREENBERG, DAVID F.
1977   Delinquency and the age structure of society. Contemporary Crises 1:189–223.

GRUDER, CHARLES L.
1977   Choice of comparison persons in evaluating oneself. In Jerry M. Suls and Richard L. Miller (eds.), Social Comparison Processes. New York: Hemisphere.

HAWKINS, J. DAVID AND DENISE M. LISHNER
1987   Schooling and delinquency. In Elmer H. Johnson (ed.), Handbook on Crime and Delinquency Prevention. New York: Greenwood.

HEALY, WILLIAM AND AUGUSTA F. BONNER
1969   New Light on Delinquency and Its Treatment. New Haven, Conn.: Yale University Press.

HEGTVEDT, KAREN A.
1987   When rewards are scarce: Equal or equitable distributions. Social Forces 66:183–207.

1990   The effect of relationship structure on emotional responses to inequity. Social Psychology Quarterly 53:214–228.

1991a   Justice processes. In Martha Foschi and Edward J. Lawler (eds.), Group Processes: Sociological Analyses. Chicago: Nelson-Hall.

1991b   Social comparison processes. In Edgar F. Borgotta and Marie E. Borgotta (eds.), Encyclopedia of Sociology. New York: Macmillan.

HIRSCHI, TRAVIS
1969   Causes of Delinquency. Berkeley: University of California Press.

1979   Separate and unequal is better. Journal of Research in Crime and Delinquency 16:34–38.

HIRSCHI, TRAVIS AND MICHAEL GOTTFREDSON
1986   The distinction between crime and criminality. In Timothy F. Hartnagel and Robert A. Silverman (eds.), Critique and Explanation. New Brunswick, N.J.: Transaction Books.

HOCHSCHILD, JENNIFER L.
1981   What's Fair: American Beliefs about Distributive Justice. Cambridge, Mass,: Harvard University Press.

HOMANS, GEORGE C.
1961   Social Behavior: Its Elementary Forms. New York: Harcourt, Brace and World.

HOUSE, JAMES S.
1981   Work Stress and Social Support. Reading, Mass.: Addison-Wesley.

HYMAN, HERBERT
1953   The value systems of the different classes: A social-psychological contribution to the analysis of stratification. In Reinhard Bendix and Seymour Martin Lipset (eds.), Class, Status, and Power. New York: Free Press.

JASSO, GUILLERMINA
1980   A new theory of distributive justice. American Sociological Review 45:3–32.

JASSO, GUILLERMINA AND PETER H. ROSSI
1977   Distributive justice and earned income. American Sociological Review 42:639–651.

JENSEN, GARY
1986   Dis-integrating integrated theory: A critical analy-

sis of attempts to save strain theory. Paper presented at the annual meeting of the American Society of Criminology, Atlanta.

JOHNSON, RICHARD E.
1979   Juvenile Delinquency and Its Origins. London: Cambridge University Press.

KAPLAN, HOWARD B.
1980   Deviant Behavior in Defense of Self. New York: Academic Press.

KAPLAN, HOWARD B., CYNTHIA ROBBINS, AND STEVEN S. MARTIN
1983   Toward the testing of a general theory of deviant behavior in longitudinal perspective: Patterns of psychopathology. In James R. Greenley and Robert G. Simmons (eds.), Research in Community and Mental Health. Greenwich, Conn.: Jai Press.

KEMPER, THEODORE D.
1978   A Social Interactional Theory of Emotions. New York: John Wiley & Sons.

KLUEGEL, JAMES R. AND ELIOT R. SMITH
1986   Beliefs about Inequality. New York: Aldine De Gruyter.

KORNHAUSER, RUTH ROSNER
1978   Social Sources of Delinquency. Chicago: University of Chicago Press.

LABOUVIE, ERICH W.
1986a   Alcohol and marijuana use in relation to adolescent stress. International Journal of the Addictions 21:333–345.

1986b   The coping function of adolescent alcohol and drug use. In Rainer K. Sibereisen, Klaus Eyfeth and George Rudinger (eds.), Development as Action in Context. New York: Springer.

LAURITSEN, JANET L., ROBERT J. SAMPSON, AND JOHN LAUB
1991   The link between offending and victimization among adolescents. Criminology 29:265–292.

LERNER, MELVIN J.
1977   The justice motive: Some hypotheses as to its origins and forms. Journal of Personality 45:1–52.

LEVENTHAL, GERALD S.
1976   The distribution of rewards and resources in groups and organizations. In Leonard Berkowitz and Elaine Walster (eds.), Advances in Experimental Social Psychology: Equity Theory: Toward a General Theory of Social Interaction. New York: Academic Press.

LEVENTHAL, GERALD S., JURGIS KARUZAJR, AND WILLIAM RICK FRY
1980   Beyond fairness: A theory of allocation preferences. In Gerald Mikula (ed.), Justice and Social Interaction. New York: Springer-Verlag.

LIND, E. ALLAN AND TOM R. TYLER
1988   The Social Psychology of Procedural Justice. New York: Plenum.

LINSKY, ARNOLD S. AND MURRAY A. STRAUS
1986   Social Stress in the United States. Dover, Mass.: Auburn House.

LISKA, ALLEN E.
1987   Perspectives on Deviance. Englewood Cliffs, N.J.: Prentice-Hall.

MCCLELLAND, KATHERINE
1990   The social management of ambition. Sociological Quarterly 31:225–251.

MACLEOD, JAY
1987   Ain't No Makin' It. Boulder, Colo.: Westview Press.

MARK, MELVIN M. AND ROBERT FOLGER
1984   Responses to relative deprivation: A conceptual framework. In Philip Shaver (ed.), Review of Personality and Social Psychology. Vol. 5. Beverly Hills, Calif.: Sage.

MARTIN, JOANNE
1986   When expectations and justice do not coincide: Blue collar visions of a just world. In Hans Weiner Bierhoff, Ronald L. Cohen, and Jerald Greenberg (eds.), Justice in Social Relations. New York: Plenum.

MARTIN, JOANNE AND ALAN MURRAY
1983   Distributive injustice and unfair exchange. In David M. Messick and Karen S. Cook (eds.), Equity Theory: Psychological and Social Perspectives. New York: Praeger.

1984   Catalysts for collective violence: The importance of a psychological approach. In Robert Folger (ed.), The Sense of Injustice: Social Psychological Perspectives. New York: Plenum.

MASSEY, JAMES L. AND MARVIN KROHN
1986   A longitudinal examination of an integrated social process model of deviant behavior. Social Forces 65:106–134.

MAWSON, ANTHONY R.
1987   Criminality: A Model of Stress-Induced Crime. New York: Praeger.

MENAGHAN, ELIZABETH
1982   Measuring coping effectiveness: A panel analysis of marital problems and coping efforts. Journal of Health and Social Behavior 23:220–234.

1983   Individual coping efforts: Moderators of the relationship between life stress and mental health outcomes. In Howard B. Kaplan (ed.), Psychosocial Stress: Trends in Theory and Research. New York: Academic Press.

MERTON, ROBERT
1938   Social structure and anomie. American Sociological Review 3:672–682.

MESSICK, DAVID M. AND KEITH SENTIS
1979   Fairness and preference. Journal of Experimental Social Psychology 15:418–434.

1983   Fairness, preference, and fairness biases. In David M. Messick and Karen S. Cook (eds.), Equity Theory: Psychological and Sociological Perspectives. New York: Praeger.

MICHAEL, JACK
1973   Positive and negative reinforcement, a distinction that is no longer necessary; or a better way to talk about bad things. In Eugene Ramp and George Semb (eds.), Behavior Analysis: Areas of Research and Application. Englewood Cliffs, N.J.: Prentice-Hall.

MICKELSON, ROSLYN ARLIN
1990   The attitude-achievement paradox among black adolescents. Sociology of Education 63:44–61.

MIKULA, GEROLD
1980   Justice and Social Interaction. New York: Springer-Verlag.
1986   The experience of injustice: Toward a better understanding of its phenomenology. In Hans Werner Bierhoff, Ronald L. Cohen, and Jerald Greenberg (eds.), Justice in Social Relations. New York: Plenum.

MIROWSKY, JOHN AND CATHERINE E. ROSS
1990   The consolation-prize theory of alienation. American Journal of Sociology 95:1505–1535.

MORGAN, RICK L. AND DAVID HEISE
1988   Structure of emotions. Social Psychology Quarterly 51:19–31.

MUELLER, CHARLES W.
1983   Environmental stressors and aggressive behavior. In Russell G. Geen and Edward I. Donnerstein (eds.), Aggression: Theoretical and Empirical Reviews. Vol. 2. New York: Academic Press.

NEWCOMB, MICHAEL D. AND L.L. HARLOW
1986   Life events and substance use among adolescents: Mediating effects of perceived loss of control and meaninglessness in life. Journal of Personality and Social Psychology 51:564–577.

NOVY, DIANE M. AND STEPHEN DONOHUE
1985   The relationship between adolescent life stress events and delinquent conduct including conduct indicating a need for supervision. Adolescence 78:313–321.

PEARLIN, LEONARD I.
1982   The social contexts of stress. In Leo Goldberger and Shlomo Berznitz (eds.), Handbook of Stress. New York: Free Press.
1983   Role strains and personal stress. In Howard Kaplan (ed.), Psychosocial Stress: Trends in Theory and Research. New York: Academic Press.

PEARLIN, LEONARD I. AND CARMI SCHOOLER
1978   The structure of coping. Journal of Health and Social Behavior 19:2–21.

PEARLIN, LEONARD I. AND MORTON A. LIEBERMAN
1979   Social sources of emotional distress. In Robert G. Simmons (ed.), Research in Community and Mental Health. Vol. I. Greenwich, Conn.: Jai Press.

PEARLIN, LEONARD I., ELIZABETH G. MENAGHAN, MORTON A. LIEBERMAN, AND JOSEPH T. MULLAN
1981   The stress process. Journal of Health and Social Behavior 22:337–356.

QUICKER, JOHN
1974   The effect of goal discrepancy on delinquency. Social Problems 22:76–86.

RIVERA, BEVERLY AND CATHY SPATZ WIDOM
1990   Childhood victimization and violent offending. Violence and Victims 5:19–35.

ROSENBERG, MORRIS
1979   Conceiving the Self. New York: Basic.

1990   Reflexivity and emotions. Social Psychology Quarterly 53:3–12.

ROSS, MICHAEL, JOHN THIBAUT, AND SCOTT EVENBACK
1971   Some determinants of the intensity of social protest. Journal of Experimental Social Psychology 7:401–418.

SCHWINGER, THOMAS
1980   Just allocations of goods: Decisions among three principles. In Gerald Mikula (ed.), Justice and Social Interaction. New York: Springer-Verlag.

SHEPELAK, NORMA J.
1987   The role of self-explanations and self-evaluations in legitimating inequality. American Sociological Review 52:495–503.

SHEPELAK, NORMA J. AND DUANE ALWIN
1986   Beliefs about inequality and perceptions of distributive justice. American Sociological Review 51:30–46.

SHORT, JAMES F. AND FRED L. STRODTBECK
1965   Group Process and Gang Delinquency. Chicago: University of Chicago Press.

SLABY, RONALD G. AND NANCY G. GUERRA
1988   Cognitive mediators of aggression in adolescent offenders: 1. Developmental Psychology 24:580–588.

SPRECHER, SUSAN
1986   The relationship between inequity and emotions in close relationships. Social Psychology Quarterly 49:309–321.

STEPHENSON, G.M. AND J.H. WHITE
1968   An experimental study of some effects of injustice on children's moral behavior. Journal of Experimental Social Psychology 4:460–469.

STRAUS, MURRAY
1991   Discipline and deviance: Physical punishment of children and violence and other crimes in adulthood. Social Problems 38:133–154.

SULLIVAN, MERCER L.
1989   Getting Paid. Ithaca, N.Y.: Cornell University Press.

SULS, JERRY M.
1977   Social comparison theory and research. An overview from 1954. In Jerry M. Suls and Richard L. Miller (eds.), Social Comparison Processes. New York: Hemisphere.

SULS, JERRY M. AND THOMAS ASHBY WILLS
1991   Social Comparison: Contemporary Theory and Research. Hillsdale, N.J.: Lawrence Erlbaum.

TAVRIS, CAROL
1984   On the wisdom of counting to ten. In Philip Shaver (ed.), Review of Personality and Social Psychology: 5. Beverly Hills, Calif.: Sage.

THIBAUT, JOHN W. AND HAROLD H. KELLEY
1959   The Social Psychology of Groups. New York: John Wiley & Sons.

THOITS, PEGGY
1983   Dimensions of life events that influence psychological distress: An evaluation and synthesis of the literature. In Howard B. Kaplan (ed.), Psychosocial

Stress: Trends in Theory and Research. New York: Academic Press.

1984   Coping, social support, and psychological outcomes: The central role of emotion. In Philip Shaver (ed.), Review of Personality and Social Psychology: 5. Beverly Hills, Calif.: Sage.

1989   The sociology of emotions. In W. Richard Scott and Judith Blake (eds.), Annual Review of Sociology. Vol. 15. Palo Alto, Calif.: Annual Reviews.

1990   Emotional deviance research. In Theodore D. Kemper (ed.), Research Agendas in the Sociology of Emotions. Albany: State University of New York Press.

1991a   On merging identity theory and stress research. Social Psychology Quarterly 54:101–112.

1991b   Patterns of coping with controllable and uncontrollable events. In E. Mark Cummings, Anita L. Greene, and Katherine H. Karraker (eds.), Life-Span Developmental Psychology: Perspectives on Stress and Coping. Hillsdale, N.J.: Lawrence Erlbaum.

THORNBERRY, TERENCE P.
1987   Toward an Interactional Theory of Delinquency. Criminology 25:863–891.

TONRY, MICHAEL, LLOYD E. OHLIN, AND DAVID P. FARRINGTON
1991   Human Development and Criminal Behavior. New York: Springer-Verlag.

TORNBLUM, KJELL Y.
1977   Distributive justice: Typology and propositions. Human Relations 30:1–24.

UTNE, MARY KRISTINE AND ROBERT KIDD
1980   Equity and attribution. In Gerald Mikula (ed.), Justice and Social Interaction. New York: Springer-Verlag.

VAN HOUTEN, RON
1983   Punishment: From the animal laboratory to the applied setting. In Saul Axelrod and Jack Apsche (eds.), The Effects of Punishment on Human Behavior. New York: Academic Press.

VAUX, ALAN
1988   Social support: Theory, Research, and Intervention. New York: Praeger.

VAUX, ALAN AND MARY RUGGIERO
1983   Stressful life change and delinquent behavior. American Journal of Community Psychology 11:169–183.

WALSTER, ELAINE, ELLEN BERSCHEID, AND G. WILLIAM WALSTER
1973   New directions in equity research. Journal of Personality and Social Psychology 25:151–176.

WALSTER, ELAINE, G. WILLIAM WALSTER, AND ELLEN BERSCHEID
1978   Equity: Theory and Research. Boston: Allyn & Bacon.

WANG, ALVIN Y. AND R. STEPHEN RICHARDE
1988   Global versus task-specific measures of self-efficacy. Psychological Record 38:533–541.

WEINER, BERNARD
1982   The emotional consequences of causal attributions. In Margaret S. Clark and Susan T. Fiske (eds.), Affect and Cognition: The Seventeenth Annual Carnegie Symposium on Cognition. Hillsdale, N.J.: Lawrence Erlbaum.

WILLIAMS, CAROLYN L. AND CRAIGE UCHIYAMA
1989   Assessment of life events during adolescence: The use of self-report inventories. Adolescence 24:95–118.

WYLIE, RUTH
1979   The Self-Concept. Vol. 2. Lincoln: University of Nebraska Press.

ZILLMAN, DOLF
1979   Hostility and Aggression. Hillsdale, N.J.: Lawrence Erlbaum.

QUESTIONS FOR DISCUSSION

1. Give a general explanation of strain theory. In what ways does strain theory differ from the following?
   a. control theory
   b. differential association

2. Discuss the three major types of strain.

3. How does the concept of equity effect the disjunction between just/fair outcomes and actual outcomes?

4. Discuss the following temporal components of stress and equity:
   a. magnitude
   b. recency
   c. duration
   d. clustering

5. Discuss three coping mechanisms that help a person adapt to stress/strain. How might we predict delinquent and non-delinquent outcomes?

APPLICATIONS

1. List ten situations or events that cause you stress or strain. Then, describe how you managed or attempted to lessen the stress for each of the ten items you have listed. Finally, explain how strain theory explains the adaptation or mechanism you used to reduce stress.

2. Using the list and explanations from the previous application, compare your adaptations to another class member's list. Do your adaptations and mechanisms match? How have you and the other class member used strain theory differently to explain stress reduction?

KEY TERMS

amelioration refers to making something better or more tolerable.

equity theory asserts that individuals engage in an interaction not with specific goals or outcomes in mind, but rather with an expectation of equality in what they give to and take from the relationship. An equitable relationship is one in which the outcome/input ratios of the actors involved in an exchange/allocation relationship are equivalent.

ethnographic refers to systematic research about culture.

idiosyncratic refers to a particularly peculiar characteristic of a human; an eccentricity or unusual temperament.

legitimation refers to giving something a legal status or authorization; showing or affirming that something is justified.

mediation intervening between conflicting individuals or groups to promote a settlement or compromise.

mitigate causing something to become less severe or harsh; relieving or alleviating by intervention.

predisposition having a preconceived suceptibility to an idea, an attitude, or a behavior.

self-efficacy refers to an individual's ability or power to produce a desired effect; one's ability to control outcomes.

typology an analysis or classification based on types or categories.

III

THE SOCIAL CONTEXT
OF JUVENILE DELINQUENCY

Perhaps one of the greatest needs of every human being is to be accepted by other human beings. The desire for acceptance shapes our personalities and influences the choices we make concerning the people with whom we associate. The social context of human behavior is of great importance to understanding ourselves and subsequently delinquency or any behaviors considered wrong by other groups or our own group members. In our lifetimes we belong to literally hundreds of groups and throughout our lives we are continually influenced by others. Some of the most influential groups are those small, intimate groups such as families or peers. The influence of the family on the young child's life and personality is so significant that there is virtually nothing that has a more lasting impact. The peer group and the need to be accepted by others are keys to understanding delinquency and youth culture. The articles in this section deal with the complicated social contexts in which delinquency is produced, experienced, and controlled.

Part III begins with "At the Roots of Violence: The Progressive Decline and Dissolution of the Family" by George B. Palermo and Douglas Simpson. The family has been a dynamic force in virtually every society and the tremendous changes in the American family are at the roots of much of the violence in our social landscape. The decline of the family in America often translates into problems of transferring primary social values such as honesty and responsibility to new members. It is this major breakdown in primary group socialization that has contributed significantly to the larger nexus of violence in the streets of America. The addition of easily available guns and drugs in the streets creates an increasingly violent social world in which citizenship is denuded and violence only increases. This article is extremely important for students to absorb as they examine the complex nature of delinquency, and especially, violence among youth.

David F. Greenburg, in "Delinquency and the Age Structure of Society," offers not only an analysis of age and delinquency but discusses the crucial issue of adolescents being excluded from the world of adult work. Greenburg integrates several elements of the structural theories into his discussions providing some very lucid insights.

School failure could be the most important predictor of delinquency and continues to be of serious concern to researchers. Stephen A. Cernovich and Peggy C. Giordano present some very interesting data in "School Bonding, Race, and Delinquency." Focusing on black youth, the authors examine social bonding and the school in relation to delinquency. Of particular interest here are the reasons why this has not been examined as well as it should be in delinquency theory or research. Generalizations about black youth are difficult to make based on research conducted on whites. The related foci on family and peers is especially important for students of delinquency.

Research targeting female delinquency is relatively new. Just a few decades ago females were all but ignored in delinquency research and theory. Today, however, females are increasingly becoming the focus of many new researchers in the field. Females have become involved in traditional delinquency as well as strictly female misbehavior. George Calhoun, Janelle Jurgens, and Fengling Chen present some very fresh and new ideas concerning females in "The Neophyte Female Delinquent: A Review of the Literature." These authors focus especially on the definitions, etiology, and treatment regarding female delinquency. With female delinquency reaching epic proportions, the areas of research that need to be addressed are monumental.

Gangs: Just the mention of the word brings many images to mind; often images of the most disturbing aspects of the American culture. Yet, gangs are perhaps some of the most misunderstood entities in the research regarding delinquency. The influence of peers on delinquency has been established over the years, but the stereotype of gangs has clouded the reality of the phenomenon and the related influence on delinquency. James C. Howell, in "Recent Gang Research: Program and Policy Implications," points out the limited nature of our knowledge and sheds light on the implications of a clearer understanding of gangs in relation to policy and program development. A major priority, Howell suggests, is to distinguish between true gangs and other collective youth groups. In addition, the author suggests that ethnographic studies will be required to answer the many complicated questions regarding gangs.

In many ways, the groups to which we belong in our lives are not family groups in a technical biological or adopted sense, but they often appear as pseudo-families. Our friendship groups serve as some of the most influential and important social factors in our lives. Many adolescents serve as the semi-adult role models to children who are only a few years younger. For many of these children, a delinquent role model serves as their mentor as they enter the adult world. The urban gang has become almost synonymous with violence, greed, and to many, family. This is not to suggest that all groupings of adolescents are hell-bent on societal or self-destruction, but rather to point out the complex nature and structure of youth misbehavior in relation to the larger societal evolution. As a whole, American society has so dramatically changed over the last century that no social institution, from family to government, even remotely resembles the rather simple structures of a hundred years ago.

The subcultural world of teenage prostitution is examined by Terry Williams and William Kornblum in "Players and Ho's." The backgrounds, attitudes, and prospects for the future of both the pimps and prostitutes make this a lively but complicated piece of research. An entirely different, confusing and frightening subculture unfolds to expose the wasted human potential that is often the by-product of the larger social context.

Our final selection, "The Saints and the Roughnecks" by William J. Chambliss, has become a classic in delinquency research. Pointing out that much of delinquency is a result of ascription rather than behavior is the real power of this fine article. The societal reaction theory, or labeling perspective, became popular during the 1960s and Chambliss offers great insight into the application of this perspective.

14

At the Roots of Violence: The Progressive Decline and Dissolution of the Family

George B. Palermo

Douglas Simpson

Abstract: *The authors reflect on the origin of the family and its traditional dynamic force in the social and moral education, and in the affective support and protection of its members. They expound on their thesis that since the institution of the family is progressively crumbling under the pressures of ever changing socioeconomic events, people feel more insecure and frustrated. It is their belief that the present day family often does not pass on to its members those traditional high moral values of honesty and responsibility so important for good citizenship and self-esteem, and that the above, compounded by unemployment and the widespread presence of psychoactive drugs in our streets, may be a basic factor in the upsurge of violence and criminal behavior in our homes and our cities. Sociological and psychological thoughts are offered in support of their theories on the importance of the family as a germ-cell of society. Even though violence in the streets is multifactorial and the too easy availability of guns and the drug culture are certainly important factors, the authors believe that the family and its value deficit are basic to the problem of disruptive violence in our streets. They envision a modern functional family whose members uphold personal responsibility together with cultural, religious, and moral values. They believe that their adherence to the above values would enable them to be better motivated and disciplined for good citizenship. Crime would then be fought at its roots.*

HISTORICAL NOTES

Existentialism proposes as the basis of human life a dynamic adaptational psychobiological force, and changing cultural and social patterns, and continuous scientific discoveries are its obvious expressions (Lavine, 1984). Humans and the human family have been, and are, subject to this dynamic force. The original functions of the human family as a group that pre-existed the *civitas* were to maintain order and readiness for defense, and to carry out, even though in a microstructure, the essential functions of the later State. Studies of Babylonian, Assyrian, Egyptian, Islamic, Indian, Greek, and Roman early civilizations strongly support this assertion. The early Roman family was patriarchal and authoritarian and, as in the primordial family, the father had the power of life and death over family members to such an unconscionable degree that unwanted children were exposed in public or abandoned, and family name and industriousness were more important than blood. We are told that strict rules

International Journal of Offender Therapy and Comparative Criminology 38 (2):105–116, 1994. Reprinted by Permission of Sage Publications, Inc.

were to be observed by the family members who gave up a certain amount of freedom for a portion of security. It was only during the middle and late Medieval era when the church championed the nuclear family that 'family' began to denote "a complex ramified community whose essential function was one of protection" (Rouche, 1987, p. 404) and its fabric allowed "large numbers of children . . . [to have] frequent contact with the elderly whose words were heeded by the young" (Duby, Barthelemy & LaRoncière, 1987, p. 169). Throughout history, the structure of the family was so strongly rooted and so well accepted that not even the social upheaval of the French revolution was able to destabilize it. It was a natural institution. "The newest political idea of the day was probably that the family is the basic cell of society. Domesticity had a fundamental regulatory function; it played the role of the hidden god" (Perrot & Martin-Fugieri, 1987, p. 100).

In more recent times, however, families—and in this case we take into consideration those in the western hemisphere—stable and united for many years, fully supporting of and supported by the Judeo-Christian tradition, have been shaken at their roots by a multitude of socioeconomic factors, radical social changes and rejection of previous religious conformism. The concept of the family as a psychobiological group, matriarchal or patriarchal in type, basic component of society, has tended to crumble and at times has reached dissolution. Fortunately, the process is not widespread and the majority of families are still united.

Originally, the family provided for the needs of its members, and also offered certain protective boundaries. Eventually, it was recognized that the structure of the family should not be a fixed and static one, but that "[It] can and must vary widely to fit into, and assure the continuity of, the very divergent societies of which it is a subsystem" (Lidz, 1963, p. 3). Its functions are basic and vital for society. It helps its members to internalize institutions and teaches them *social and moral values* and responsible roles. It passes on to them basic adaptive techniques proper to their culture, as well as the *sense of social responsibility* so important for

proper human development and humane, civic interaction. Also, as a basic component of society, the family is bound to play a role in the dissolution of cultures when it no longer carries out its basic functions.

SOCIOLOGICAL REFLECTIONS

A family is as healthy as its members, and factors leading to a healthy family and its maintenance are numerous. Scott and Scott (1983) state that while trust, affection, autonomy, and initiative are basic psychological components for the formation of a lasting group, the presence of a good genetic and psychogenetic pool, of a private and a mutual territory for the spouses, and the existence of a family myth that provides symbolism, values, and structure seem to be essential to it. It is evident that, "A family without values is a non-directed, goal changing, grasping small group" (Scott & Scott, 1983, p. 73).

Today, social violence is soaring. Its presence is multifactorial. It occurs both in communities and within the single family. There, within the home, the clash between spouses or live-in members often proves to be highly disruptive to physical and emotional well-being. Many members of society, both young and old, show the negative consequences of family violence and of its effect on the family group. They show difficulty in adaptation, communication, and in establishing relationships, and children may not be helped to develop their inborn capacities. "Many of our insecurities in living and the instabilities of individuals surely arise from the contemporary family's difficulties in finding a secure structure and satisfactory ways of raising children" (Lidz, 1963, p. 28).

The ever increasing succession of new expedients to the problem of living, the secularization of religion, the industrial, and postindustrial revolutions with their migration of workers—blue and white collar alike, the fear of losing a job or the anxiety of not finding one, and an overstressed personal autonomy and hedonistic goals contribute to social confusion and irresponsible living. Many people, possibly overwhelmed by sociocultural changes and devoting their energy to personal needs and desires, distance themselves from one another, and this lack of communication at times leads to a different family structure, a new family structure or no family at all. The one-parent family has appeared on the social scene and is steadily growing in number. Statistics speak clearly about the decline of the institution of the traditional family. "According to the Census Bureau half of all marriages end in divorce. Births to single mothers now make up one-quarter of total births. One in four Americans over age 18 have never married" ("Married with Children," 1992). Married couples with children under age 18 make up 25.9% of American households; married couples without children, 29.4%; people living alone, 25.05%; unrelated people living together, 4.7%; other families without children, 6.5%; other families with children, 8.5%. It is a statistical fact that married couples with a child under age 18 have become a shrinking minority. In 1970 married couples with a child under 18 constituted 40.3% of all American households; that became 30.9% in 1980 and a mere 25.9% in 1991. Concentrations of families made up of a married couple with children are "primarily in areas with large numbers of Hispanic, Indian, or Mormon families, in parts of Appalachia and in some suburbs" ("Married with Children," 1992).

A closer look at today's family shows that the paternal figure has often been deprived of authority as in a society of bees, and perhaps as a consequence of the misinterpretation of some of Freud's psychological theories.

One can portray many present-day families, even those nuclei still apparently intact, regardless of race, age group, or socioeconomic status, as groups of separate, individual members within a hypothetical circle. Each of the family members looks toward a different horizon— almost staring into infinity. That infinity often equates to emptiness, solitude, and frustration, and frustrated emotional needs are often at the basis of aggressive behavior.

As stated by Parsons, "Society is a system of inter-related parts" (Collins & Makowsky, 1980, pp. 205–206), and the idea that at the basis of society there should be a functional interdependence of its parts seems quite logical and acceptable. However, during the past 50 years drastic and rapid economic and value changes have taken place, contributing to a lack of stability of family structure and emotional ties. Reproduction, biological maintenance, socialization, social control, status placement and emotional maintenance are no longer the prerogative of a family nucleus (Goode, 1960). "The three pillars of *gemeinschaft*—blood, place (land), and mind, or kinship, neighborhood, and friendship . . . all encompassed in the family . . . united in spite of all separating factors" (Nisbet, 1966, p. 75) seem to have lost their importance, and communities have been supplanted by what sociologists call *gesellschaft*— a society, held together by codified laws and certificated advisors—from financial counselors to mental therapists.

Not only have people and their families changed, but so have the architectural design of modern cities and towns. The public square, seat of people's encounters and ever ongoing democratic conversation (Hill et al., 1990), is no longer present. Parks are often unusable because of the fear of human violence, and cold, consumer-oriented malls, expressions of an object-oriented, robotized society, have poorly replaced them. Neatly packaged and promoted consumerism has facilitated the progressive alienation of people from one another and a void is felt in this still orderly and extremely envied American way of living. The decline of human values and wholesome relationships leads to a rush to own material objects that will fill the days and hopefully will lend meaning to existence. In many families both parents must work just in order to maintain a marginal family menage. In other families, however, both spouses work in order to possess more things.

Even forms of communication have changed. They have evolved from the direct personal contact of meetings, discussions, and letters to the remote, electronic means of the telephone, answering machine, and FAX. To the extent that people are still drawn to common areas (e.g., to shop) there is little chance that actual contact/communication will occur, and the contact that occurs will be with mirror-image individuals. People experience a sense of loss and an increasing inability to relate to one another. Human isolation is ubiquitous.

In a frenetic tempo of life the child, at times still an infant, is often placed in a preschool kindergarten, and there, like a partially abandoned being, attempts to socialize with other similarly frustrated children, all of them frustrated in their most important affective needs. An increasing number of children are being born into homes where no family, in the traditional sense of the word, has been established, or into homes where the family, because of divorce or separation, dissolves soon after birth. Because children learn parenting and other skills by observation/experience, we have a generation of children being raised without adequate role models. This is a particular problem for black children. Male black children, especially, often have to make the transition from boyhood to manhood under the guidance of a woman/mother. In his book *The Truly Disadvantaged*, black sociologist Wilson shows that in 1940, toward the end of the Great Depression, only 17.19% of black American families were headed by women, and, in those that were, the reason was usually that the husbands were dead. By 1988, the percentage was more than 50 and rising, but widowhood was no longer the cause (Hamill, 1988).

Not only may children suffer because of the loss of parents to the needs of two-income families, but an erosion of grandparent-grandchild relationships has also become common. The elderly, simply by their presence in the family, have always taught the young about suffering and humanness. They taught about death and the meaning of our existence. Once a powerful source of values and meaning, the elderly are now often shoved to one side in order that other family members can seek out the "good life," and they are unable to pass on to the younger generation the experiences of their lives. The affective alienation of the young and the old has been beautifully rendered in the poem "The Little Boy and the Old Man" (Silverstein, 1983), in which each describes his respective, and similar, loneliness.

Lidz's (1963, p. 37) statement of 30 years ago, "A larger proportion of the population is married than ever before," contrasts with the above-mentioned common occurrence in today's society—the one-parent family. The one-parent family, however, still holding good socio-moral values, should not be regarded in a negative way, even though "It becomes increasingly evident scientifically, as it has been through common sense, that children require two parents with whom they interact and who optimally are of opposite sexes in temperament and outlook, but who together form a parental coalition complementing and completing one another" (Lidz, 1963, p. 34).

One could certainly wonder whether emancipation and individualism have contributed to excessive egocentrism and to a gradual dissolution of the nuclear family. That the world changes because people change is normal. It is the acceptable consequence of people's becoming more aware of themselves, their environment, their position in life. They become better educated, more constructive, more interested in creating a better world to live in for both themselves and for their children. But too drastic and sudden a social change such as society has experienced during the past few decades has created chaos, insecurity, and directionless activity for many. A supervening discomfort and anxiety became fertile ground for drugs, and crime followed, unconscionable, and motiveless.

AT THE BASIS OF SOCIAL VIOLENCE

Violence is often the expression of frustration and hostility, at times generated by a profound dissatisfaction with the business of life. Unchecked by moral values, it may erupt and become highly destructive. Those basic moral values which serve to direct one's personal or group libidinal energy constructively are usually learned in the family that upholds them, and their importance is reinforced by civic laws. The functions of the family should lie primarily in offering to its members the affective, social, and educational arena that promote the personal and social growth and emotional stability of is members. As the nonfunctioning or noncoordination of the various organ systems creates sickness in the human body, so the disruption of the family is producing a nonfunctioning society. To this effect, Zimmerman's various parallels on the relation between family and society through the centuries, and his ideas of a possible connection between the decline of the modern family and the general breakdown of society is quite appealing (Goode, 1960).

People may be manipulated by social systems. Today, a good percentage of them seem to direct themselves, inappropriately and unsuccessfully, towards those ever-changing goals that culture and society incessantly manufacture for them. Bureaucracy, extreme rationalism, and utilitarianism have reduced "man to a pure subject, an organism with behaviors that can be predicted, manipulated, and controlled" (Kendall, 1990). Frustrated individuals and a similarly frustrated society alternate in a fruitless search for an existential answer. *Social frustration creates insecurity, hostility and confusion, and all too often hostility and violence find their outlet in the family itself.* Within the home, people are victimized by their own family members. "[T]he one place on earth where they should feel safe and secure has become a place of danger" (Herrington, 1984, p. iv). More unconscionable violence floods our streets.

Families should be the result of togetherness, sharing, love, work, lack of selfishness, and awareness of the physical, emotional, and spiritual needs of their members and of others. Healthy families help to form healthy communities. The family may find it difficult to keep itself healthy when the woman/mother has been drawn into the large cauldron of competitive work outside the home and the man/father must often procure a second job. That does not mean, however, that it is not possible. It only means that the family may be under more stress. Achieving better material goods is part of the American heritage. "The achievement society cannot love a man or a woman who is without zeal" (Watson, 1991, p. 113). Fear of failure and abhorrence of idleness and boredom have contributed to the development of a society of workaholics and worried overachievers. They are the frustrated possessors of fleeting "goods." They seem to "look both upward and downward, applauding

and reproaching themselves daily and hourly for their success in having climbed so far, their failure in not having climbed further" (Watson, 1991, p. 116). De Tocqueville already noticed that Americans had "a cloud habitually upon their brow . . . forever brooding over advantages they do not possess" (Watson, 1991, p. 114). The above can still be observed a century and a half later.

Today, almost half of the working class is composed of women, some by choice, considering it, correctly, their right to pursue their chosen career, and some by necessity. Many of these women are mothers. That is in tune with present sociocultural mores. One should be aware of the impact that this present-day social reality will have on the structure, functioning, and nurturing of the family and the development of resentment, frustration, and a hostility in many people. The child may feel deprived of parental affection and possibly that he/she is a secondary consideration to his/her parents' position in society. The child's formative years, often controlled by a series of commercial arrangements, leave the strong impression that there are no relationships in society other than those that are contracted. The parents themselves also become prey to guilt feelings and restlessness. The child may grow up with no concept of warm, human, spontaneous relationship, and, in some instances, a lack of parental presence may throw them into unhealthy streets where crime is high.

Basic cultural patterns are usually maintained through the family, its socialization and its moral education. Respect and duties towards self and others should be taught in the family and not by superficial conditioning of laws and policing. Families often seem to lack the emotional cohesiveness necessary for good personal and social growth and are no longer that "zone of immunity to which we may fall back or retreat, a place where we may set aside arms and armor needed in the public place, relax, take our ease, and lie about unshielded by the ostentatious carapace worn for protection in the outside world. This is the place where the family thrives, the realm of domesticity" (Duby, 1987, p. viii). In this atmosphere of increasing alienation many people, full of conscious and subconscious frustration, move around and about like automatons. They are under pressure—inner and outer, and run through the days, the months, and the years like goal-directed projectiles, going through life almost unaware of the world of affective interaction. Frequently, solitude makes them prey to inner anxiety and agitation and *frustrated rebelliousness.*

Is this the consequence of our technological discoveries? If that is the case, then one should realize that either technology is not good for society or that society is not making good use of technology. A technological society may tend to create a mechanical type of cooperation among its robotized members. Life becomes more organized but also more monotonously Orwellian. Monotony may also breed the upsurge of disruptive interests. Present-day social engineering and an ultrarational approach to life have created the image of a "[t]runcated . . . man, a less than fully human" (Kendall, 1990, p. 105) who, by logical consequence, will dehumanize anyone who comes in contact with him. It is a fact that present-day messy urban realities are a source of deep dissatisfaction and frustration for the majority of people. Daily, people must contend with the aggressive tempo of urban life—its traffic, its lack of jobs, its costly housing, increasing prostitution, use of drugs or sudden, uncalled-for, violent behavior. Does this social panorama breed frustration, rebellion, and violence in the family and society? Probably so. Does it justify violence in our society? Certainly not.

SUGGESTIONS AND CONCLUSIONS

Laws are in a continuous flux in an attempt to rectify the personal and social confusion that often breeds crime and violence, forgetting that "Legislation cannot save society. Legislation cannot rectify society. . . . [T]he law that would work . . . is the successful embodiment of unselfish citizenship" (Wilson, 1915). If our assumption is correct, that the dissolution of the family is one of the major factors at the roots of violence in our homes and neighborhoods, the reintegration of the family in a modern and functional structure, upholding high

moral values, is central to the stabilization of present-day society. We believe that responsibility and civic duties are as important as personal or group rights but that, more basically, human beings should become more humane in their dealings with one another. Indeed, "the duties of a person towards others are the same as his duties towards himself. . . . Natural obligation is absolutely unchangeable" (Wolff, 1955, pp. 1234–1235). If the family group will emphasize the values of honesty, respect, love, and responsibility for others, criminality and violence in our homes and chaotic streets may be lessened. As a consequence of that, the number of prisoners in our jails, many of them young people—social offenders and victims themselves of early emotional and affective deprivation will diminish. "[T]runcated beings . . . inevitably end up being mired in social disorder, because their souls are disordered and spiritual disorder leads, in the end, to social disorder" (Kendall, 1990, p. 106). As roots are essential for the growth of good, healthy trees so "[f]amilies stand at the center of society . . . [and] building our future must begin by preserving family values" (Reagan, 1984, p. 11). In the midst of present-day social confusion it is of comfort to know that the majority of American families are still united, loving, and responsible. These families silently and stoically oppose their disintegration because they believe in those traditional values passed on to them by previous generations. Myriad low-income families are successfully protecting their members from the ravages of drugs, alcohol, and violence because they are honest, civil, and moral. It is the lack of values in a rapidly changing society that creates the propensity to crime in an individual, not poverty, and the family is an essential supporting structure for both the young an the old. Ackermann clearly pointed this out: "The essence of life is change, growth, learning, adaptation to new conditions, and creative evolution of new levels of interchange between persons and environment. . . . The matrix of human relationship, whether healthy or sick, is the family . . . [and] intrapsychic equilibrium cannot be divorced from interpersonal equilibrium" (Ackerman, 1966, p. 203). The family is a natural social group, preexisting any state organization, with a proper set of internal rules, rights, and duties, destined to carry out a function that goes beyond personal interests to favor the interests of the group. We believe that a new, modern, well-integrated, wholesome loving family, enriched by the knowledge and experience acquired in the recent past, may be the agency capable of eliminating, at its roots, that sense of despair and confusion that leads to the violence that often seems to be dominant in our streets and in many homes. Even though its structure may, at times, be different from the traditional mold, the family will benefit from retaining traditional values. We certainly wish to take issue with the statement that "contrary to popular opinion, there is no scientific evidence for the application of our Euro-American concepts of family, house, home or household to the entire known spectrum of human domestic arrangements" (Harris, 1971, p. 266). We believe, indeed, that in confronting the problems facing today's families, it would be wise to take popular opinion into consideration, as well as clinical experience, statistical and scientific evidence (especially when it has to do with things of the heart), deep feelings, and values. We like to look at people not just as cold data. The majority of people are sensitive, and, sensibly, they know how much they suffer, how alienated they feel, how frightened they are, how capable or incapable they are to change axioms that serve to manipulate their actions and reactions. People know what they want and the average American citizen does not deny the natural importance of the family and its value system in our society.

Recently, the political scene has raised the issue of family values, and the press and public opinion have dealt with it extensively. However, it seems to us that a great deal of confusion exists concerning the meaning of the term. We believe that a family unit is primarily an entity that holds people from a similar biological background together, generally residing under the same roof until the children reach late adolescence. It developed naturally for protective and nurturing reasons and has been found to be essential for a smoother running of communities and states. However, when we talk about family values we mean a family, regardless of its structure and membership, holding within itself the values of love, respect, and responsibility for self and others, a part of those larger values that have come to be known as human rights and duties. These values are handed down from generation to generation and are exemplified in the sacred books of the world's religions. We, as a society formed by family groups, have made those values an integral part of our *modus vivendi* to the point that a family, in its purest sense, is not a family unless those values are an integral part of it. Without them, it is just an aggregation of people, held together by biological, nurturing, and defensive factors. The present-day upsurge of violent crimes perpetrated by adolescents whose age ranges from 14 to 17 may be an example of the partial failure of the family to pass on to its children good values to live by, or of the family giving them mixed value messages.

Freud understood that people in general have a certain "inclination to aggression" (Freud, 1950, p. 114) and he thought of the family as the "germ-cell of civilization" (Freud, 1950, p. 116) essential to counteract man's aggressive instinct. In *Civilization and Its Discontents,* he beautifully expressed that the human aggressive instinct, which we consider to be at the basis of family and societal violence, opposes the course of civilization: "[C]ivilization is a process in the service of Eros whose purpose is to combine single human individuals, and after that families, then races, peoples and nations, into one great unity, the unity of mankind . . . [but] man's natural aggressive instinct, the hostility of each against all and of all against each, opposes this programme of civilization (Freud, 1950, p. 122). Sixty years later a pastoral voice reaffirmed the importance of the family in facing the present violent destructive trend: "It is necessary to go back to seeing the family as the sanctuary of life. The family is indeed sacred: it is the place in which life, the gift of God, can be properly welcomed and protected against the many attacks to which it is exposed, and can develop in accordance with what constitutes authentic human growth. In the face of the so-called culture of death, the family is the heart of the culture of life" (John Paul II, 1991, p. 76). That should be true for a two-parent family, the single-parent family, and for any group that considers itself a family.

Halting the progression of the dissolution of the family should be a concerted effort involving sociologists, educational and religious leaders, politicians, and parents. The reintegration of the family unit in some areas may be helped by the presence of the "man of the house" thus far kept away by certain regulations of welfare legislation. Fathers should not be forced out of the home as an eligibility requirement; we should not encourage additional births by benefit structures that reward subsequent pregnancies; we must stop contributing to the abandonment of all hope for employment and self-sufficiency. The combination of these systemic defects is a moral tragedy, and a lack of parental guidance and moral support contributes to indolence, crime, and violence. Organized religion should also become more involved and accept leadership in this crusade while, at the same time, a "'social-environmental" . . . 'human-ecological' . . . strategy which includes interventions on the level of individuals and families 'at risk' [should be implemented] . . . to exert social control over those larger forces which now are increasingly undermining communities" (Currie, 1989). We believe it possible that by tackling these many factors, society will be able to effectively diminish the wave of violence in the country and people will have directed their energies constructively and purposefully and their social conscience will be at ease. Imbert stated that "In the long term, the solution [to social violence] will almost certainly lie in a greater sense of social responsibility, instilled through family, school, church, and all those other institutions which share the burden of the moral development of society" (Imbert, 1990, p. 425).

REFERENCES

ACKERMAN, N. W. (1966). Family therapy. In S. Arieti (Ed.), *American handbook of psychiatry* (Vol. 3, pp. 201–212). New York: Basic Books.

COLLINS, R., & MAKOWSKY, M. (1989). *The discovery of society.* New York: Random House.

CURRIE, E. (1989). Confronting crime: Looking toward the twenty-first century. *Justice Quarterly, 6,* 5–25.

DUBY, G. (1987). Foreword. In P. Aries & G. Duby (Gen. Eds.), P. Veyne (Ed.), *A history of private life* (Vol. 1, p. viii). Cambridge, MA: Belknap Press of Harvard University Press.

DUBY, G., BARTHÉLEMY, D., & LA RONCIÈRE (1987). Portraits. In P. Aries & G. Duby (Gen. Eds.), P. Veyne (Ed.), *A history of private life* (Vol. 2, p. 169). Cambridge, MA: Belknap Press of Harvard University Press.

FREUD, S. (1950). *The standard edition of the complete psychological works of Sigmund Freud* (Vol. 11, J. Strachey, Trans.). London: Hogarth Press.

GOODE, W. (1960). The sociology of the family. In R. Merton, L. Broom, & L. Cottrell, Jr. (Eds.), *Sociology today. Problems and prospects* (pp. 188–190). New York: Basic Books.

HAMILL, P. (1988, March). America's black underclass: Can it be saved? *Esquire.*

HARRIS, M. (1971). *Culture, man and nature.* New York: Crowell.

HERRINGTON, H. (1984, September). In *Attorney general's task force on family violence. Final report* (p. iv). Washington, DC: U. S. Government Printing Office.

HILL, J., FLEMING, R., PLATER, E., ZYBERK, R., WINES, J., & ZIMMERMAN, E. (1990, July). Whatever became of the public square? *Harper's Magazine,* pp. 49–60.

IMBERT, P. (1990). Policing a violent society. *Journal of the Royal Society of Medicine, 83,* 425–426.

JOHN PAUL II (1991, May 1). *On the hundredth anniversary of rerum novarum—centesimus annus.* Encyclical Letter, Publication No. 436-8. Washington, DC: United States Catholic Conference.

KENDALL, G. (1990). Bureaucracy and welfare: The enslavement of the spirit. *Social Justice Review,* May/June, 104–107.

LAVINE, T. (1984). *From Socrates to Sartre—The philosophical quest.* New York: Bantam Books.

LIDZ, T. (1963). *The family and human adaptation.* New York: International University Press. Married with children: The waning icon. (1992, August 23). *The New York Times,* Section 4, p. 2.

NISBET, R. (1966). *The sociological traditions.* New York: Basic Books.

PERROT, M., & FUGIER-MARTIN, A. (1987). The actors. In P. Aries & G. Duby (Gen. Eds.), P. Veyne (Ed.), *A history of private life* (Vol. 4, p. 100). Cambridge, MA: Belknap Press of Harvard University Press.

REAGAN, R. (1984, September). In *Attorney general's task force on family violence. Final report* (p. 11). Washington, DC: U.S. Government Printing Office.

ROUCHE, M. (1987). The early middle ages in the West. In P. Aries & G. Duby (Gen. Eds.), P. Veyne (Ed.), *A his-*

tory of private life (Vol. 1, pp. 464–465). Cambridge, MA: Belknap Press of Harvard University Press.

SCOTT, E., & SCOTT, K. (1983). Healthy families. *International Journal of Offender Therapy and Comparative Criminology, 27,* 71–78.

SILVERSTEIN, S. (1983). The littleboy and the old man. In *Poetry for children.* New York: Random House.

WATSON, G. (1991). The decay of idleness. *The Wilson quarterly,* Spring, 110–116.

WILSON, W. (1915, May 31). Memorial Day address. *The Wilson quarterly,* Spring, 110–116.

WOLFF, C. (1955). Duties toward others. In D. Runes (Ed.), *Treasury of philosophy* (pp. 1234–1236). New York: Philosophical Library.

QUESTIONS FOR DISCUSSION

1. What has been the historical function of the family? What modern-day factors have presented families with a significant increase in stress?

2. How is the progressive disintegration of the family and the increase in violence related? Cite examples to support your response.

3. When identifying the genesis of violence in our society, much of the focus has been on discouraging violence with tougher laws and more severe punishment. Will this approach work? Cite examples to support your response.

4. If Palermo and Simpson are correct, implementing changes in social policy that strengthen families should have an immediate and long-term effect in reducing violence. Do you agree or disagree? Why?

5. Other than the family unit, are there any other social institutions that may be able to fight the rising tide of violence in society? If so, in what ways?

APPLICATIONS

1. Consider your own family. What kinds of changes might you propose to bring your family members closer together into a stronger social bond? Is there any proposal you might make for all families?

2. What are several ways that families in your neighborhood might develop a greater sense of community? Discuss these with members of your class.

KEY TERMS

carapace a shield or cover.

gemeinschaft a social relationship that is spontaneous and characterized by strong reciprocal bonds on kinship and sentiment within a common tradition.

modus vivendi a feasible arrangement or practical compromise.

stoically refers to someone who can bear hardship and adversity with fortitude.

ubiquitous present everywhere at the same time.

15

Delinquency and the Age Structure of Society

David F. Greenberg

An extraordinary amount of crime in America is the accomplishment of young people, . . . [although] delinquents commonly abandon crime in late adolescence, . . . [and] arrest rates for vandalism and [nonviolent] property crimes . . . decline with age . . . [more] rapidly . . . than . . . arrest rates for narcotics violations and [violent] offenses. . . .[1] This pattern is a fairly recent development. The peak ages for involvement in crime seem to have been higher in nineteenth-century America than they are today. Other industrialized capitalist nations, such as England, seem to have undergone a similar shift in the age distribution of involvement in crime. By contrast, comparatively few crimes are committed by young people in the less industrialized nations of the modern world.[2]

The increasingly disproportionate involvement of juveniles in major crime categories is not readily explained by current sociological theories of delinquency, but it can be readily understood as a consequence of the historically changing position of juveniles in industrial societies. This changing position has its

"Delinquency and the Age Structure of Society," *Contemporary Crises: Crime, Law, and Social Policy*, 1 (1977), pp. 189–223. Reprinted by permission of Kluwer Academic Publishing Group.

origin, at least in Europe and the United States, in the long-term tendencies of a capitalist economic system.

DELINQUENCY THEORY AND THE AGE DISTRIBUTION OF CRIME

Since neither the very young nor the very old have the prowess and agility required for some types of crime, we might expect crime rates to rise and then fall with age. But the sharp decline in involvement in late adolescence cannot be explained in these terms alone. If age is relevant to criminality, the link should lie primarily in its social significance. Yet contemporary sociological theories of delinquency shed little light on the relationship between crime and age. If, for example, lower class male gang delinquency is simply a manifestation of a lower class subculture, as Miller (1958) has maintained, it would be mysterious why 21-year-olds act in conformity with the norms of their subculture so much *less* often than their siblings just a few years younger—unless the norms themselves were age-specific. While age-specific expectations may contribute to desistance from some forms of delinquent play, such as vandalism and throwing snowballs at cars, as Clark and Haurek (1966) suggest, there is no social class in which felony theft and violence receive general *approval* for persons of any age. Moreover, adult residents of high crime areas often live in fear of being attacked by teenagers, suggesting that if delinquency is subcultural, community does not form the basis of the subculture.

The difficulty of accounting for "maturational reform" within the framework of the motivational theories of Cloward and Ohlin (1960) and Cohen (1955) has already been noted by Matza (1964:24–27). In both theories, male delinquents cope with the problems arising from lower class status by entering into and internalizing the norms of a subculture which repudiates conventional rules of conduct and *requires* participation in crime. As with other subcultural theories, it is not at all clear why most subculture carriers abandon activities that are so highly prized within the subculture with such haste.

This desistance is especially perplexing in anomie or opportunity theories (Merton, 1957; Cloward and Ohlin, 1960) because the problem assumed to cause delinquency, namely the anticipation of failure in achieving socially inculcated success goals through legitimate means, does not disappear at the end of adolescence. At the onset of adulthood, few lower and working class youths are close to conventionally defined "success," and their realization that opportunities for upward mobility are drastically limited can only be more acute. Students can perhaps entertain fantasies about their future prospects, but graduates or dropouts must come to terms with their chances.

Cloward and Ohlin do note that many delinquents desist, but explain this in ad hoc terms unrelated to the main body of their theory. Writing of neighborhoods where violence is common, they assert:

> As adolescents near adulthood, excellence in the manipulation of violence no longer brings status. Quite the contrary, it generally evokes extremely negative sanctions. What was defined as permissible or tolerable behavior during adolescence tends to be sharply proscribed in adulthood. New expectations are imposed, expectations of "growing up," of taking on adult responsibilities in the economic, familial, and community spheres. The effectiveness with which these definitions are imposed is attested by the

tendency among fighting gangs to decide that conflict is, in the final analysis, simply "kid stuff.". . . In other words, powerful community expectations emerge which have the consequence of closing off access to previously useful means of overcoming status deprivation (Cloward and Ohlin, 1960:185).

In view of Cloward and Ohlin's characterization of neighborhoods where gang violence is prevalent as so disorganized that no informal social controls limiting violence can be exercised (1960:174–75), one can only wonder whose age-specific expectations are being described. Cloward and Ohlin do not say. This explanation, for which Cloward and Ohlin produce no supporting evidence, is inconsistent with their own larger theory of delinquent subcultures. In addition, it seems inconsistent with the *slowness* of the decline in the violence offense categories.

In a departure from the emphasis placed on social class membership in most motivational theories of delinquency, Bloch and Niederhoffer (1958) interpret such forms of delinquency as adolescent drinking, sexual experimentation, and "wild automobile rides" as responses to the age status problems of adolescence. Denied the prerogatives of adulthood, but encouraged to aspire to adulthood and told to "act like adults," teenagers find in these activities a symbolic substitute which presumably is abandoned as soon as the genuine article is available. As an explanation for joy-riding and some status offenses, this explanation has manifest plausibility. For other categories it is more problematic, since it assumes that delinquents interpret activities engaged in largely by adolescents as evidence of adult stature. When Bloch and Niederhoffer turn to more serious teenage crime, their explanations are vague and difficult to interpret, but in any event seem to depend less on the structural position of the juvenile.

In *Delinquency and Drift*, Matza (1964) provides an alternative approach to the explanation of desistance. His assumption that many delinquents fully embrace neither delinquent nor conventional norms and values, but instead allow themselves to be easily influenced without deep commitment, makes desistance possible when the delinquent discovers that his companions are no more committed to delinquency than he is. This discovery is facilitated by a reduction in masculinity anxiety that accompanies the attainment of adulthood. There are valuable insights in this account, but unresolved questions as well. Insofar as the discovery of a shared misunderstanding depends on chance events, as Matza suggests (1964:54–58), *systematic* differences in desistance remain unexplained. Why does desistance from violence offenses occur later and more slowly than for theft offenses? Why are some juveniles so much more extensively involved in delinquency than others? Matza's remarkable presentation of the subjective elements in delinquency must be supplemented by an analysis of the objective, structural elements in causation, if such questions are to be answered.

That is the approach I will take. I will present an analysis of the position of juveniles in American society and elaborate the implications of that position for juvenile involvement in crime. The explanation of high levels of juvenile involvement in crime will have two major components. The first, a theory of motivation, locates sources of motivation toward criminal involvement in the structural position of juveniles in American society. The second, derived from control theory, suggests that the willingness to act on the basis of criminal motivation is distributed unequally among age groups because the cost of being apprehended are different for persons of different ages. Although some of the theoretical ideas (e.g., control theory) on which I will be drawing have already appeared in the delinquency literature, each by itself is inadequate as a full theory of delinquency. When put together with some new ideas, however, a very plausible account of age and other systematic sources of variation in delinquent involvement emerges.

ANOMIE AND THE JUVENILE LABOR MARKET

Robert Merton's discussion of anomie has provided a framework for a large volume of research on the etiology of crime. Although Merton observed that a disjunction between socially inculcated goals and legitimate means for attaining them would produce a strain toward deviance, *whatever the goal* (Merton, 1957:166), specific application of the perspective to delinquency has been restricted to an assessment of the contribution to delinquency causation of the one cultural goal Merton considered in depth, namely occupational success. Cloward and Ohlin for example, attribute lower class male delinquency to the anticipation of failure in achieving occupational goals as adults. These youths' involvement in theft is interpreted as a strategy for gaining admission to professional theft and organized crime circles, that is, a way of obtaining the tutelage and organizational affiliations necessary for the successful pursuit of *career* crime, rather than for immediate financial return. Crime is thus seen as a means toward the attainment of *future* goals rather than *present* goals.

The assumption that delinquency is instrumentally related to the attainment of adult goals is plausible only for limited categories of delinquency, however; e.g., students who cheat on exams in the face of keen competition for admission to college or graduate school, and youths who save what they earn as pimps or drug merchants to capitalize investment in conventional business enterprises. For other forms of delinquency this assumption is less tenable. Delinquents would have to be stupid indeed to suppose that shoplifting, joy-riding, burglary, robbery or drug use could bring the prestige or pecuniary rewards associated with high status lawful occupation. Nor is there evidence that most delinquents seek careers in professional theft or organized crime. In the face of Cohen's characterization of delinquents as short-run hedonists (1955:25), and the difficulty parents and teachers encounter in attempting to engage delinquent youths in activities which could improve chances of occupational success (like school homework), the future orientation assumed in opportunity theory is especially farfetched.

The potential explanatory power of anomie theory, is, however, not exhausted by Cloward and Ohlin's formulation, because delinquency can be a response to a discrepancy between aspirations and expectations for the attainment of goals other than occupational ones. Most people have a multiplicity of goals, and only some of them are occupational. As the salience of different life goals can vary with stages of the life cycle, our understanding of delinquency may be advanced more by examining those goals given a high priority by adolescents than by considering the importance attached to different goals in American culture generally.

The transition from childhood to adolescence is marked by a heightened sensitivity to the expectations of peers and a reduced concern with fulfilling parental expectations (Blos, 1941; Bowerman and Kinch, 1959; Tuma and Livson, 1960; Conger, 1973:282–92). Popularity with peers becomes highly valued, and exclusion from the most popular cliques leads to acute psychological distress.

Adolescent peer groups and orientation to the expectations of peers are found in many societies (Eisenstadt, 1956; Bloch and Neiderhoffer, 1958); but the natural tendency of those who share common experiences and problems to prefer one another's company is accentuated in American society by the importance that parents and school attach to popularity and to developing social skills assumed to be necessary for later occupational success (Mussen et al., 1969). In addition, the exclusion of young people from adult work and leisure activity forces adolescents into virtually exclusive association with one another, cutting them off from alternative sources of validation for the self (as well as reducing the degree of adult supervision). A long-run trend toward increased age segregation created by changing patterns of work and education has increased the vulnerability of teenagers to the expectations and evaluations of their peers (Panel on Youth, 1974).

This dependence on peers for approval is not itself criminogenic. In many tribal societies, age-homogeneous bands of youths are functionally integrated into the economic and social life of the tribe and are not considered deviant (Mead, 1939; Eisenstadt, 1956:56–92). In America, too, many teenage clubs and cliques are not delinquent. Participation in teenage social

life, however, requires resources. In addition to personal assets and skills (having an attractive appearance and "good personality," being a skilled conversationalist, being able to memorize song lyrics and learn dance steps, and in some circles, being able to fight), money is needed for buying clothes, cosmetics, cigarettes, alcoholic beverages, narcotics, phonograph records, transistor radios, gasoline for cars and motorcycles, tickets to films and concerts, meals in restaurants, and for gambling. The progressive detachment of teenage social life from that of the family and the emergence of advertising directed toward a teenage market (this being a creation of post-war affluence and the "baby boom") have increased the importance of these goods to teenagers and hence have inflated the costs of their social activities.

When parents are unable or unwilling to subsidize their children's social life at the level required by local convention, when children want to prevent their parents from learning of their expenditures, or when they are reluctant to incur the obligations created by taking money from their parents, alternative sources of funds must be sought. Full or part-time employment once constituted such an alternative, but the long-run, persistent decline in teenage employment and labor force participation has progressively eliminated this alternative. During the period from 1870 to 1920, many states passed laws restricting child labor and establishing compulsory education. Therefore, despite a quadrupling of the "gainfully employed" population from 1870 to 1930, the number of gainfully employed workers in the 10- to 15- year-old age bracket *declined*. The Great Depression resulted in a further contraction of the teenage labor force and increased the school-leaving age (Panel on Youth, 1974:36–38). In 1940 the U.S. government finally stopped counting all persons over the age of 10 as part of the labor force (Tomson and Fiedler, 1975)!

In recent years, teenage labor market deterioration has been experienced mainly by black teenagers. From 1950 to 1973, black teenage labor force participation declined from 67.8% to 34.7%, while white teenage labor force participation remained stable at about 63%. The current recession has increased teenage unemployment in the 16- to 19-year-old age bracket to about 20%, with the rate for black teenagers being twice as high.

This process has left teenagers less and less capable of financing an increasingly costly social life whose importance is enhanced as the age segregation of society grows. Adolescent theft then occurs as a response to the disjunction between the desire to participate in social activities with peers and the absence of legitimate sources of funds needed to finance this participation.

Qualitative evidence supporting this explanation of adolescent theft is found in those delinquency studies that describe the social life of delinquent groups. Sherif and Sherif noted in their study of adolescent groups that theft was often instrumentally related to the group's leisure-time social activities:

> In several groups . . . stealing was not the incidental activity that it was in others. It was regarded as an acceptable and necessary means of getting needed possessions, or, more usually, cash. Members of the aforementioned groups frequently engaged in theft when they were broke, usually selling articles other than clothing, and *often using the money for group entertainment and treats* (1964:174).

Similarly, Werthman (1967) reports that among San Francisco delinquents,

> shoplifting . . . was viewed as a more instrumental activity, as was the practice of stealing coin changers from temporarily evacuated buses parked in a nearby public depot. In the case of shoplifting, most of the boys wanted and wore the various items of clothing they stole; and when buses were robbed, either the money was divided among the boys, or it was used to buy supplies for a party being given by the club.

Studies of urban delinquent gangs or individuals in England (Fyvel, 1962; Parker, 1974), Israel and Sweden (Toby, 1967), Taiwan (Lin, 1959), Holland (Bauer, 1964), and Argentina (DeFleur, 1970) present the same uniform picture: unemployed or employed-but-poorly-paid male youths steal to support their leisure-time, group-centered social activities. Only to a very limited extent are the proceeds of theft used for biological survival (e.g., food).

Where parents subsidize their children adequately, the incentive to steal is obviously reduced. Because the cost of social life can increase with class position, a strong correlation between social class membership and involvement in theft is not necessarily predicted. Insofar as self-reporting studies suggest that the correlation between participation in nonviolent forms of property acquisition and parental socioeconomic status is not very high, this may be a strong point for my theory. By contrast, the theories of Cohen, Miller, and Cloward and Ohlin all clash with the self-reporting studies.

In view of recent suggestions that increases in female crime and delinquency are linked with changing gender roles (of which the women's liberation movement is taken either as a cause or a manifestation), it is of interest to note that the explanation of adolescent theft presented here is applicable to boys and girls, and in particular, allows for female delinquency in support of *traditional* gender roles related to peer involvement in crime. The recent increases in female crime have occurred largely in those forms of theft where female involvement has traditionally been high, such as larceny (Simon, 1975), and are thus more plausibly attributed to the same deteriorating economic position that males confront than to changes in gender role.

As teenagers get older, their vulnerability to the expectations of peers is reduced by institutional involvements that provide alternative sources of self-esteem; moreover, opportunities for acquiring money legitimately expand. Both processes reduce the motivation to engage in acquisitive forms of delinquent behavior. Consequently, involvement in theft should fall off rapidly with age, and it does.

DELINQUENCY AND THE SCHOOL

To explain juvenile theft in terms of structural obstacles to legitimate sources of money at a time when peer-oriented leisure activities require it is implicitly to assume that money and goods are stolen because they are useful. Acts of vandalism, thefts in which stolen objects are abandoned or destroyed, and interpersonal violence not necessary to accomplish a theft cannot be explained in this way. These are the activities that led Albert Cohen to maintain that much delinquency is "malicious" and "non-utilitarian" (1955:25) and to argue that the content of the delinquent subculture arose in the lower class male's reaction to failure in schools run according to middle class standards.

Although Cohen can be criticized for not indicating the criteria used for assessing rationality—indeed, for failure to find out from delinquents themselves what they perceived the goals of their destructive acts to be—and though details of Cohen's theory (to be noted below) appear to be inaccurate, his observation that delinquency may be a response to school problems need not be abandoned. Indeed, the literature proposing a connection between one or another aspect of school and delinquency is voluminous (see for example, Polk and Schafer, 1972). I believe that two features of the school experience, its denial of student autonomy, and its subjection of some students to the embarrassment of public degradation, are especially important in causing "non-utilitarian" delinquency.

In all spheres of life outside the school, and particularly within the family, children more or less steadily acquire larger measures of personal autonomy as they mature. Over time, the "democratization" of the family has reduced the age at which given levels of autonomy are acquired. The gradual extension of freedom that normally takes place in the family (not without struggle!) is not accompanied by parallel deregulation at school. Authoritarian styles of teaching, and rules concerning such matters as smoking, hair styles, manner of dress, going to the bathroom, and attendance, come into conflict with expectations students derive from the relaxation of controls in the family.[3] The delegitimation of hierarchical authority structures brought about by the radical movements of the 1960s has sharpened student awareness of this contradiction.

The symbolic significance attached to autonomy exacerbates the inherently onerous burden of school restrictions. Parents and other adults invest age-specific rights and expectations with moral significance by disapproving "childish" behavior and by using privileges to reward behavior they label "mature." Because of this association, the deprivation of autonomy is experienced as "being treated like a baby," that is, as a member of a disvalued age-status.

All students are exposed to these restrictions, and to some degree, all probably resent them. For students who are at least moderately successful at their schoolwork, who excel at sports, participate in extracurricular school activities, or are members of popular cliques, this resentment is likely to be more than compensated for by rewards associated with school attendance. These students tend to conform to school regulations most of the time, rarely collide with school officials, and are unlikely to feel overtly hostile to school or teachers. Students who are unpopular, and whose academic record, whether from inability or disinterest, is poor, receive no comparable compensation. For them, school can only be a frustrating experience: it brings no current gratification and no promise of future payoff. Why then should they put up with these restrictions? These students often get into trouble, and feel intense hostility to the school.

Social class differences must of course be taken into account. Preadolescent and early adolescent middle and upper class children are supervised more closely than their working class counterparts, and thus come to expect and accept adult authority, while working class youths, who enter an unsupervised street life among peers at an early age, have more autonomy to protect, and guard their prerogatives jealously (Psathas, 1957; Kobrin, 1962; Werthman, 1967; Rainwater, 1970:211–34; Ladner, 1971:61–63). To the extent that they see in the school's denial of their autonomy, preparation for a future in occupations that also deny autonomy, and see in their parents' lives the psychic costs of that denial, they may be more prone to rebel than middle class students, who can generally anticipate entering jobs that allow more discretion and autonomy.

Middle class youths also have more to gain

by accepting adult authority than their working class counterparts. Comparatively affluent parents can control their children better because they have more resources they can withhold and are in a better position to secure advantages for their children. Children who believe that their future chances depend on school success are likely to conform even if they resent the school's attempt to regulate their lives. On the other hand, where returns on school success are reduced by class or racial discrimination (or the belief that these will be obstacles, even if the belief is counter to fact), the school loses this source of social control. For similar reasons, it loses control over upper class children, since their inherited class position frees them from the necessity of doing well in school to guarantee their future economic status.

Only a few decades ago, few working class youths—or school failures with middle class family backgrounds—would have been exposed to a contradiction between their expectations of autonomy and the school's attempts to control them, because a high proportion of students, especially working class students, left school at an early age. However, compulsory school attendance, low wages and high unemployment rates for teenagers, along with increased educational requirements for entry-level jobs, have greatly reduced dropout rates. Thus in 1920, 16.8% of the 17-year-old population were high school graduates; and in 1956, 62.3% (Toby, 1967). In consequence, a greater proportion of students, especially those who benefit least from school, is exposed to this contradiction.[4]

Common psychological responses to the irritation of the school's denial of autonomy range from affective disengagement ("tuning out" the teacher) to smoldering resentment, and at the behavioral level responses range from truancy to self-assertion through the flouting of rules. Such activities as getting drunk, using drugs, joy riding, truanting, and adopting eccentric styles of dress, apart from any intrinsic gratification these activities may provide, can be seen as forms of what Gouldner has called "conflictual validation of the self" (1970:221–22). By helping students establish

independence from authority (school, parents, etc.), these activities contribute to self-regard. Their attraction lies in their being forbidden.

As a status system, the school makes further contributions to the causation of delinquency. Almost by definition, status systems embody invidious distinctions. Where standards of evaluation are shared, and position is believed to reflect personal merit, occupants of lower statuses are likely to suffer blows to their self-esteem (Cohen, 1955:112–13; Sennett and Cobb, 1972). The problem is somewhat alleviated by a strong tendency to restrict intimate association to persons of similar status. If one's associates are at roughly the same level as oneself, they provide the standards for self-evaluation (Hyman, 1968). In addition, "democratic" norms of modesty discourage the flaunting of success and boasting of personal merit, thereby insulating the less successful from an implied attribution of their failures to their own deficiencies.

These niceties are not, however, universal in applicability. In our society, certification as a full-fledged social member is provided those whose commitment to the value of work and family is documented by spouse, home, car and job (for women, children have traditionally substituted for job). Institutional affiliations are thus taken as a mark of virtue, or positive stigma. Those who meet these social criteria are accorded standards of respect in face-to-face interaction not similarly accorded members of unworthy or suspect categories (e.g., prison and psychiatric hospital inmates, skid row bums, the mentally retarded). In particular, these full-fledged members of society are permitted to sustain self-presentations as dignified, worthy persons, regardless of what may be thought or said of them in private.

Students, especially failing students, and those with lower class or minority origins, are accorded no comparable degree of respect. As they lack the appropriate institutional affiliations, their moral commitment to the dominant institutions of society is suspect. In this sense, they are social strangers; we don't quite know what we can expect from them. They are, moreover, relatively powerless. In consequence, they are exposed to evaluations from which adults are ordinarily shielded. School personnel continuously communicate their evaluations of students through grades, honor rolls, track positions, privileges, and praise for academic achievement and proper deportment. On occasion, the negative evaluation of students conveyed by the school's ranking systems is supplemented by explicit criticism and denunciation on the part of teachers who act as if the academic performance of failing students could be elevated by telling them they are stupid, or lazy, or both. Only the most extreme failures in the adult world are subjected to degradation ceremonies of this kind.

Cohen (1955) has argued that working class youths faced with this situation protect their self-esteem by rejecting conventional norms and values. Seeking out one another for mutual support, they create a delinquent subculture of opposition to middle class norms in which they can achieve status. This subculture is seen as supporting the non-utilitarian acts of destructiveness that alleviate frustration. There is little difficulty in finding evidence of adolescent destructiveness, but the choice of target may be more rational (or less non-utilitarian) than Cohen allows. If the school is a major source of the juvenile's frustration, then the large and growing volume of school vandalism and assaults on teachers may, in the perpetrator's own frame of reference, not be irrational at all, even though it may be targeted on those who themselves are not necessarily to blame for what the school does. Other targets may be chosen because of their symbolic value, such as members of a despised racial group or class stratum, or adults, who represent repressive authority. Even random violence, though comparatively rare, can be a way of experiencing the potency and autonomy that institutions—the school among them—fail to provide (Silberman, 1978).

Self-reporting studies of delinquency indicate the association between class and most forms of delinquency to be weaker than Cohen supposed. School failure, though class-linked, is not the monopoly of any class, and the self-esteem problems of middle class youths who fail are not necessarily any less than those of working class schoolmates; indeed since parental expectation for academic achievement may be higher in middle class families, and since school failure may augur downward mobility, their problems could conceivably be worse. If delinquency restores self-esteem lost through school failure, it may serve this function for students of all class backgrounds.

The impact of school degradation ceremonies is not limited to their effect on student's self-esteem. When a student is humiliated by a teacher the student's attempt to present a favorable self to schoolmates is undercut. Even students whose prior psychological disengagement from the value system of the school leaves their self-esteem untouched by a teacher's disparagement may react with anger at being embarrassed before peers. It is the situation of being in the company of others whose approval is needed for self-esteem that makes it difficult for teenagers to ignore humiliation that older individuals, with alternative sources of self-esteem, could readily ignore.

Visible displays of independence from, or rejections of, authority can be understood as attempts to reestablish moral character in the face of affronts. This can be accomplished by direct attacks on teachers or school, or through daring illegal performances elsewhere. These responses may or may not reflect anger at treatment perceived to be unjust, may or may not defend the student against threats to self-esteem, may or may not reflect a repudiation of conventional conduct norms. What is crucial is that these activities *demonstrate* retaliation for injury and the rejection of official values to an audience of peers whose own resentment of constituted authority causes it to be appreciative of rebels whom it would not necessarily dare to imitate. Secret delinquency and acts that entailed no risk would not serve this function.

Field research on the interaction between teachers and delinquent students (Werthman, 1967), and the responses of delinquent youths to challenges to their honor (Short and Strodtbeck, 1965; Horowitz and Schwartz, 1974), support this dramaturgical interpretation of delinquency. Most gang violence seems not to erupt spontaneously out of anger, but is chosen and manipulated for its ability to impress others.

Non-utilitarian forms of theft, property destruction and violence may well be understood as quite utilitarian if their purpose is the establishment or preservation of the claim to be a certain sort of person, rather than the acquisition of property.

Goffman (1974) has called attention to the common features of other, mainly non-criminal activities in which participants establish moral character through risk-taking. Such activities as dueling, bull fighting, sky diving, mountain climbing, big game hunting, and gambling for high stakes are undertaken for the opportunity they provide to carve out a valued social identity by exhibiting courage, daring, pluck and composure.

These qualities are those the industrial system (factory and school) tend to disvalue or ignore: the concept of seeking out risks and "showing off" is antithetical to the traditional ethos of capitalism, where the emphasis has been placed on minimizing risk, using time productively, and suppressing the self to demonstrate moral character. Consequently, those who seek prestige through risk-taking traditionally come from classes not subject to the discipline and self-denial of industrial production, e.g., the European nobility, bohemian populations, and the unemployed poor.

More recently, as production has come to require less sacrifice and self-denial from large sectors of the work force, and to require the steady expansion of stimulated consumption for its growth, the more affluent sectors of the labor force are increasingly encouraged to seek an escape from the routine of daily life through mild forms of risk-taking (e.g., gambling and skiing) as well as through the leisure use of drugs and sex.

The similarity between the subculture of delinquency and that of the leisurely affluent, noted by Matza and Sykes (1961), makes sense in view of the position of the delinquent vis à vis the school. Like the factory, the school frequently requires monotonous and meaningless work. Regimentation is the rule. Expressions of originality and spontaneity are not only discouraged, but may be punished. Sociability among students is prohibited by the discipline of the classroom. Students who reap no pre-sent rewards from their schoolwork or who anticipate only the most limited occupational returns as a compensation for their adherence to the onerousness of school discipline are free to cultivate the self-expressive traits which the school fails to reward, because they will lose nothing that is important to them by doing so. As Downes (1966) points out, they may come to regard adults who work as defeated and lifeless because of their subordination to a routine that necessitates self-suppression, and hence try to avoid work because of the cost in self-alienation.

Traditionally this has been especially true of students with lower class backgrounds; however, when the political and economic institutions of sectors of society lose their legitimacy, students of other classes may find the prospect of entering conventional careers in those sectors so repugnant that they lose the motivation to achieve in school, and also cultivate lifestyles based on self-expression or politically motivated risk-taking. The bright hippies and radicals from white middle class backgrounds in the late 1960s are a case in point.

The similarity between delinquent and non-criminal recreational risk-taking warns us that the pursuit of status through risk-taking does not *necessarily* arise from problems in self-esteem. Once a status system rewarding delinquent activity exists, students may act with reference to it in order to *increase* prestige in the group, not only to prevent prestige from falling. Thus teachers may be provoked (Werthman, 1967), gang rivals taunted, and daring thefts and assaults perpetrated, even in the absence of humiliation.

When students drop out or graduate from high school, they enter a world that, while sometimes inhospitable, does not restrict their autonomy and assault their dignity in the same way the school does. The need to engage in crime to establish a sense of an autonomous self and to preserve moral character through risk-taking is thus reduced. In addition, the sympathetic audience of other students of the same age is taken away. Thus school-leaving eliminates major sources of motivation toward delinquency. Indeed, American studies indicate that the self-esteem of dropouts rises after they leave school (Bachman et al., 1972) and that dropping out produces an immediate decline in delinquency involvement (Mukherjee, 1971; Elliot and Voss, 1974). In England, when the school-leaving age was raised by one year, the peak age for delinquency rose simultaneously by one year (McClean and Wood, 1969). These findings are especially ironic, in thatnineteenth-century reformers touted the extension of public schooling as a way of reducing delinquency; and present-day delinquency prevention programs have involved campaigns to keep delinquents in school.[5]

MASCULINE STATUS ANXIETY AND DELINQUENCY

Many observers have remarked on the disproportionate involvement of males in delinquency, and the exaggerated masculine posturing that characterizes their involvement, particularly where violence offenses are concerned. This behavior pattern has been explained as a "masculine protest" against maternal domination and identification, especially in the female-based households of the lower class (Parsons, 1947; Cohen, 1955: 162–69; Miller, 1958). In such households, the argument goes, boys will tend to identify with the mother, and hence will experience uncertainty and anxiety in later years in connection with their identification as a male. To allay this anxiety, they reject the "good" values of the mother and engage in "masculine" forms of delinquency.

Application of the theory to delinquency in the United States has not been entirely successful. Male delinquency does appear to be associated with what has been interpreted as anxiety over masculinity, but it is independent of whether the household in which the child is raised lacks an adult male (Monahan, 1957; Tennyson, 1967; Rosen, 1969). This finding points to the need for a revision in the argument.

Hannerz (1969) has pointed out that children raised in homes without fathers may still have alternative male role models. Indeed, children raised in a community where adult male

unemployment rates are high may spend more of their time in the company of adult males who could serve as role models than their middle class peers. Males who are not in doubt about their identity as males may nevertheless feel anxiety in connection with anticipated or actual inability to fulfill traditional sex role expectations concerning work and support of family. This masculine *status* anxiety can be generated by a father who is present but ineffectual, and by living in a neighborhood where, for social-structural reasons, many men are unemployed—regardless of whether one's own father is present in the household.

Men who experience such anxiety because they are prevented from fulfilling conventional male role expectations may attempt to alleviate their anxiety by exaggerating those traditionally male traits that *can* be expressed. Attempts to dominate women (including rape) and patterns of interpersonal violence can be seen in these terms. In other words, crime can be a response to masculine status anxiety no less than to anxiety over male identity; it can provide a sense of potency that is expected and desired but not achieved in other spheres of life.

In this interpretation, a compulsive concern with toughness and masculinity arises not from a hermetically sealed lower-class subculture "with an integrity of its own" nor from the psychodynamics of a female-headed household (Miller, 1958), but as a response to a contradiction between structural economic-political constraints on male status attainment and the cultural expectations for men that permeate American society. The role of the subculture Miller describes is to make available the behavioral adaptations that previous generations have developed in response to this contradiction.

If I am correct in assuming that delinquents in the last years of elementary school and early years of high school are not excessively preoccupied with their occupational prospects, but become more concerned with their futures toward the end of high school, then masculine anxiety during these early years must stem from other sources. One plausible source lies in the contradiction between the school's expectations of docility and submission to authority, and more widely communicated social expectations of masculinity. While the school represses both boys and girls, the message that girls get is consistent with society's message; the message boys receive is contradictory. This difference would help to explain sex differences in delinquency in early adolescence. Most of the male behavior that can be explained plausibly in this way—smoking, sexual conquest, joy-riding, vandalism, fighting—is fairly trivial, and either becomes legal in mid to late adolescence or abates rapidly. Anxiety over inability to fulfill traditional male occupational roles would be expected to show up late in adolescence.

One would expect masculine status anxiety to appear with greatest intensity and to decline most slowly in those segments of the population in which adult male unemployment is exceptionally high. This conforms to the general pattern of arrests for violent offenses such as homicide, forcible rape and assaults—offenses often unconnected with the pursuit of material gain, and hence most plausibly interpreted as a response to masculine status anxiety. Rates of arrest for these offenses peak in the immediate post–high school age brackets (several years later than for the property offenses) and the decline is slower than for property offenses. Moreover, blacks are overrepresented in violence offense arrests to a much greater degree than in arrests for property offenses.

COST OF DELINQUENCY

So far, some possible sources of age-linked variation in motivation to participate in criminal activity have been identified, but this is only half the story, for one may wish to engage in some form of behavior but nevertheless decide not to do so because its potential costs are deemed unacceptably high. Costs can be a consequence of delinquency, and must be taken into account. Control theorists have begun to do so (Briar and Piliavin, 1965; Hirschi, 1969; Piliavin et al. 1969).

In early adolescence the potential costs of all but the most serious forms of delinquency are relatively slight. Parents and teachers are generally willing to write off a certain amount of misbehavior as "childish mischief," while enormous caseloads have forced juvenile courts in large cities to adopt a policy that comes very close to what Schur (1973) has called "radical nonintervention." Given the slight risk of apprehension for any single delinquent act, the prevalence of motivations to violate the law, and the low cost of lesser violations, we should expect minor infractions to be common among juveniles, and the self-reporting studies generally suggest that they are. As teenagers get older, the potential costs of apprehension increase: victims may be more prone to file a complaint, and police to make an arrest. Juvenile court judges are more likely to take a serious view of an older offender, especially one with a prior record. Older offenders risk prosecution in criminal court, where penalties tend to be harsher, and where an official record will have more serious consequences for later job opportunities.

Delinquents are acutely sensitive to these considerations. According to several youthful offenders testifying before the New York State Select Committee at a hearing on assault and robbery against the elderly, "If you're 15 and under you won't go to jail. . . . That's why when we do a 'Rush and Crib'—which means you rush the victim and push him or her into their apartment, you let the youngest member do any beatings. See, we know if they arrest him, he'll be back on the street in no time" (Williams, 1976). Thus the leniency of the juvenile court contributes to high levels of juvenile crime.

Just as the costs of crime are escalating, new opportunities in the form of jobs, marriage, or enlistment in the armed forces create stakes in conformity and, as Matza points out (1964:55), may also relieve problems of masculine status anxiety. Toward the end of high school, when student concern about the future increases, the anticipation of new opportunities is manifested in desistance from delinquency and avoidance of those who do not similarly desist. Consistent with this interpretation is the fact that in both England and the United States, the peak year for delinquent involvement is the year *before* school-leaving.

Those whose opportunities for lucrative employment are limited by obstacles associated with racial and/or class membership, however, will have far less reason to desist from illegal activity than those whose careers are not similarly blocked. The jobs available to young members of the lower strata of the working class tend to be limited, tedious, and low paying. Marriage may appear less appealing to young men whose limited prospects promise inability to fulfill traditional male expectations as breadwinner. Even an army career may be precluded by an arrest record, low intelligence test scores, physical disability, or illiteracy. Thus the legitimate opportunity structure, even if relatively useless for understanding entrance into delinquency, may still be helpful in understanding patterns of desistance.

The same may be said of the illegal opportunity structure. Those few delinquents who are recruited into organized crime or professional theft face larger rewards and less risk of serious penalty than those not so recruited, and their personal relationships with partners may be more satisfying. They should be less likely to desist from crime, but their offense patterns can be expected to change.

This reasoning suggests that the association between criminal involvement on the one hand and race and class on the other should be stronger for adults than for juveniles. If this is so, arrest rates in a given offense category should decline more rapidly for whites and youths with middle class backgrounds than for blacks and youths with working class and lower class backgrounds, and they do (Wolfgang et al., 1972).

DELINQUENCY AND THE SOCIAL CONSTRUCTION OF THE JUVENILE

Among the structural sources of adolescent crime identified here, the exclusion of juveniles from the world of adult work plays a crucial role. It is this exclusion that simultaneously exaggerates teenagers' dependence on peers for approval and eliminates the possibility of their obtaining funds to support their intensive, leisure-time social activities. The disrespectful treatment students receive in school depends on their low social status, which in turn reflects their lack of employment and income. In late adolescence and early adulthood, their fear that this lack of employment will persist into adulthood evokes anxiety over achievement of traditional male gender role expectations, especially among males in the lower levels of the working class, thus contributing to a high level of violence.

Institutionalized leniency to juvenile offenders, which reduces the potential costs of delinquency, stems from the belief that teenagers are not as responsible for their actions as adults. The conception of juveniles as impulsive and irresponsible gained currency around the turn of the century, when organized labor and Progressive reformers campaigned for child labor laws to save jobs for adults, a goal given high priority after the Depression of 1893. This conception was, in a sense, self-fulfilling. Freed from ties to conventional institutions, teenagers *have* become more impulsive and irresponsible.

The exclusion of teenagers from serious work is not characteristic of all societies. Peasant and tribal societies could not afford to keep their young idle as long as we do. In such societies, juvenile crime rates were low. Under feudalism, too, children participated in farming and handicraft production as part of the family unit beginning at a very early age.

In depriving masses of serfs and tenant farmers of access to the means of production (land), European capitalism in its early stages of development generated a great deal of crime, but in a manner that cut across age boundaries. Little of the literature on crime in Elizabethan and Tudor England singles out juveniles as a special category.

The industrial revolution in the first half of the nineteenth century similarly brought with it a great deal of misery, but its effect on crime was not restricted to juveniles. Children of the working class in that period held jobs at an early age and in some sectors of the economy were given preference. Only middle and upper class children were exempt from the need to work, and they were supervised much more closely than they are nowadays. As far as can be judged, juvenile crime in that period was a much smaller fraction of the total than at present, and was more confined to the lower classes than it is now.

In modern capitalist societies, children of all classes share, for a limited period, a common relationship to the means of production (namely exclusion) which is distinct from that of most adults, and they respond to their common structural position in fairly similar ways. Although there are class differences in the extent and nature of delinquency, especially violent delinquency, they are less pronounced than for adults, for whom occupational differentiation is much sharper.

The deteriorating position of juveniles in the labor market in recent years has been ascribed to a variety of causes, among them the inclusion of juveniles under minimum wage laws; changes in the structure of the economy (less farm employment); teenage preference for part-time work (to permit longer periods of education), which makes teenage labor less attractive to employers; and the explosion in the teenage labor supply, created by the baby boom, at a time when women were entering the labor market in substantial numbers (Kalacheck, 1973). Whatever contribution these circumstances may have made to shifting teenage employment patterns in the short run, the exclusion of juveniles from the labor market has been going on for more than a century, and may more plausibly be explained in terms of the failure of the oligopoly-capitalist economy to generate sufficient demand for labor than to these recent developments (Carson, 1972; Bowers, 1975).[6]

In both the United States and England, the prolongation of education has historically been associated with the contraction of the labor market, casting doubt on the view that more education is something that the general population has wanted for its own sake. Had this been true, the school-leaving age would have jumped upward in periods of prosperity, when a larger proportion of the population could afford more education, not during depressions. Moreover, the functionalist argument that increased education is necessary as technology becomes more complex would apply at best to a small minority of students, and rests on the dubious assumption that full-time schooling is pedagogically superior to alternative modes of organizing the education of adolescents.

The present social organization of education, which I have argued contributes to delinquency, has also been plausibly attributed to the functional requirement of a capitalist economy for a docile, disciplined and stratified labor force, as well as to the need to keep juveniles out of the labor market. Thus the high and increasing level of juvenile crime we are seeing in present-day United States and in other Western countries originates in the structural position of juveniles in an advanced capitalist economy.

Delinquency is not, however, a problem of capitalism alone. Although there are many differences between crime patterns in the United States and the Soviet Union, the limited information available indicates that delinquency in the Soviet Union is often associated with leisure-time consumption activities on the part of youths who are academic failures, and who either are not working or studying, or are working at or preparing for unrewarding jobs (Connor, 1970; Polk, 1972, This suggests that some of the processes described here may be at work in the Soviet Union. Since Soviet society is based on hierarchical domination and requires a docile, disciplined and stratified labor force, this parallel is not surprising. Yet it must not be forgotten that the parallel is only partial. The Soviet economy, for example, does not generate unemployment the way the capitalist economies of the West do. Insofar as can be learned from Soviet sources, juvenile delinquency has declined in recent decades, whereas it has increased rapidly in most of the capitalist nations.

DISCUSSION

For decades, criminologists have proposed such reforms as eliminating poverty and racial discrimination to solve the crime problem (see Silberman, 1978, for the latest of this genre). None of them seriously addresses how the serious obstacles to achieving this task are to be overcome within the framework of a capitalist society. To suppose that the writing of an article or a book calling for an end to poverty and racism will actually contribute to ending poverty and racism is to betray a whimsical bit of utopianism. Marxist theorists tend to see these problems as largely produced by a class society, and insoluble within it. Efforts to tackle these problems may certainly be worthwhile, but not because they can be expected to achieve full success.

My analysis of delinquency suggests that most proposed "solutions" to the delinquency problem would have limited impact. Thoroughly integrating teenagers into the labor force, on at least a part-time basis, would go far toward reducing delinquency. But the jobs for adolescents are not there; and the drastic restructuring of education that would be required is hardly to be expected in the forseeable future.

If young people had a good understanding of the structural sources of their frustration and oppression, their response might well be different. Instead of individualistic and predatory adaptations, we might see collective, politicized, and non-predatory challenges to their exclusion. It seems unlikely that such a radical transformation in consciousness would develop spontaneously, but in the context of a mass socialist movement, it could well occur.

NOTES

1. Arrest rates broken down by age can be found in any recent edition of the FBI's *Uniform Crime Reports.*
2. See, for example, Christiansen (1960), Toby (1967), DeFleur (1970), and Christie (1978).
3. These expectations are derived from young peoples' knowledge of family arrangements in our society generally, not from their own family circumstances alone. When controls in their own family are not relaxed, this can provide an additional source of conflict.
4. The emphasis given to school problems as a cause of delinquency in the criminological literature of the 1950s and 1960s was probably due at least in part to there being more delinquents *in* school then than in earlier decades.
5. Although this evidence confirms that the school does contribute to delinquency, it is hardly necessary. In Argentina, patterns of delinquency are fairly similar to those in the U.S., even though the school-leaving age for working class children is 10, and delinquents report favorable attitudes toward school (DeFleur, 1970). In the United States, unsatisfactory school

experiences simply add to the economic motivations created by the exclusion of juveniles from the labor market.

6. The theory of supply and demand in economics demonstrates that with a given demand for a product, profits will be maximized at a lower level of production if the producing firm is a monopoly than if it is faced with competition.

Thus the demand for labor has declined relative to the volume of production as American business has become more concentrated in a small number of giant corporations. The replacement of workers by machinery further reduces employment. Monopolization speeds up this process because large firms can more easily afford large investments in machinery. Large corporations can also relocate in other parts of the country or overseas to reduce costs of production, generating unemployment where disinvestment occurs. Since the labor market is not fully competitive, wages do not fall to a level that would permit full employment; such factors as minimum wage laws, labor unions, welfare for the unemployed, and illegal income all help to maintain wages above the competitive level.

REFERENCES

BACHMAN, J.G., S. GREEN AND I. WIRTANEN
1972   *Dropping Out: Problem or Symptom.* Ann Arbor: Institute for Social Research.

BAUER, E.J.
1964   "The Trend of Juvenile Offenses in the Netherlands and the United States." *Journal of Criminal Law, Criminology and Police Science* 55:359–69.

BLOCH, H.A., AND A. NIEDERHOFFER
1958   *The Gang.* New York: Philosophical Society.

BLOS, P.
1941   *The Adolescent Personality: A Study of Individual Behavior.* New York: Appleton.

BOWERMAN, C.E., AND J.W. KINCH
1959   "Changes in Family and Peer Orientation of Children between the Fourth and Tenth Grades." *Social Forces* 37:206.

BOWERS, N.
1975   "Youth and the Crisis of Monopoly Capitalism." In *Radical Perspectives on the Economic Crisis in Monopoly Capitalism.* New York: Union of Radical Political Economics.

BRIAR, S., AND I. PILIAVIN
1965   "Delinquency, Situational Inducements, and Commitment to Conformity." *Social Problems* 13:35–45.

CARSON, R.B.
1972   "Youthful Labor Surplus in Disaccumulationist Capitalism." *Socialist Revolution* 9:15 – 44.

CHRISTIANSEN, K.
1960   "Industrialization and Urbanization in Relation

to Crime and Juvenile Delinquency." *International Review of Criminal Policy* 16:3.

CHRISTIE, N.
1978   "Youth as a Crime-Generating Phenomenon." In Barry Krisberg and James Austin (eds.), *The Children of Ishmael.* Palo Alto, Calif.: Mayfield.

CLARK, J.P., AND E.W. HAUREK
1966   "Age and Sex Roles of Adolescents and Their Involvement in Misconduct: A Reappraisal." *Sociology and Social Research* 50:495–503.

CLOWARD, R., AND L. OHLIN
1960   *Delinquency and Opportunity.* New York: Free Press.

COHEN, A.
1955   *Delinquent Boys.* New York: Free Press.

CONGER, J.J.
1973   "A World They Never Knew: The Family and Social Change." *Daedalus* 100:1105–38.

CONNOR, W.
1970   *Deviance in Soviet Society.* New York: Columbia University Press.

DEFLEUR, L.
1970   *Delinquency in Argentina.* Pullman: Washington State University Press.

DOWNES, D.M.
1966   *The Delinquent Solution: A Study in Subcultural Theory.* New York: Free Press.

EISENSTADT, S.N.
1956   *From Generation to Generation: Age Groups and Social Structures.* New York: Free Press.

ELLIOTT, D.S., AND H.L. VOSS
1974   *Delinquency and Dropout.* Lexington: D.C. Health.

FYVEL, T.R.
1962   *Troublemakers.* New York: Schocken Books.

GOFFMAN, E.
1974   "Where the Action Is." In *Interaction Ritual.* Garden City: Anchor Books.

GOULDNER, A.
1970   *The Coming Crisis in Western Sociology.* New York: Basic Books.

HANNERZ, U.
1969   *Soulside: Inquiries into Ghetto Culture.* New York: Columbia University Press.

HIRSCHI, T.
1969   *The Causes of Delinquency.* Berkeley: University of California Press.

HOROWITZ, R., AND G. SCHWARTZ
1974   "Honor, Normative Ambiguity and Gang Violence." *American Sociological Review* 39:238–51.

HYMAN, H.H.
1968   "The Psychology of Status." In H.H. Hyman and E. Singer (eds.). *Readings in Reference Group Theory and Research.* New York: Free Press.

KALACHECK, E.
1973   "The Changing Economic Status of the Young." *Journal of Youth and Adolescence* 2:125–32.

KOBRIN, S.
1962   "The Impact of Cultural Factors in Selected Prob-

lems of Adolescent Development in the Middle and Lower Class." *American Journal of Orthopsychiatry* 33:387–90.

LADNER, J.
1971   *Tomorrow's Tomorrow: The Black Woman.* Garden City: Doubleday.

LIN, T.
1959   "Two Types of Delinquent Youth in Chinese Society." In Martin K. Opler (ed.), *Culture and Mental Health.* New York: Macmillan.

MCCLEAN, J.D., AND J.C. WOOD
1969   *Criminal Justice and Treatment of Offenders.* London: Sweet and Maxwell.

MATZA, D.
1964   *Delinquency and Drift.* New York: Wiley.
———   and G. Sykes 1961 "Juvenile Delinquency and Subterranean Values." *American Sociological Review* 26:712–19.

MEAD, M.
1939   *From the South Seas: Part III. Sex and Temperament in Three Primitive Societies.* New York: Morrow.

MERTON, R.K.
1957   *Social Theory and Social Structure*, rev. ed. New York: Free Press.

MILLER, W.B.
1958   "Lower Class Subculture as a Generating Milieu of Gang Delinquency." *Journal of Social Issues* 14:5–19.

MONAHAN, T.P.
1957   "Family Status and the Delinquent: A Reappraisal and Some New Findings." *Social Forces* 35:251–58.

MUKHERJEE, S.K.
1971   *A Typological Study of School Status and Delinquency.* Ann Arbor, Mich.: University Microfilms.

MUSSEN, P.H., J.J. CONGER AND J. KAGAN
1969   *Child Development and Personality.* New York: Harper and Row.

PANEL ON YOUTH OF THE PRESIDENT'S SCIENCE ADVISORY COMMITTEE
1974   *Youth: Transition to Adulthood.* Chicago: University of Chicago Press.

PARKER, H.H.
1974   *View from the Boys.* North Pomfret, Vt.: David and Charles.

PARSONS, T.
1947   "Certain Primary Sources and Patterns of Aggression in the Social Structure of the Western World." *Psychiatry* 10:167– 81.

PILIAVIN, I.M., A.C. VADUM AND J.A. HARDYCK
1969   "Delinquency, Personal Costs and Parental Treatment: A Test of a Reward-Cost Model of Juvenile Criminality." *Journal of Criminal Law, Criminology and Police Science* 60:165–72.

POLK, K.
1972   "Social Class and the Bureaucratic Response to Youthful Deviance." Paper presented to the American Sociological Association.

POLK, K., AND W.E. SCHAFER
1972   *Schools and Delinquency.* Englewood Cliffs, N.J.: Prentice-Hall.

PSATHAS, G.
1957   "Ethnicity, Social Class, and Adolescent Independence from Parental Control." *American Sociological Review* 22:415–23.

RAINWATER, L.
1970 *Behind Ghetto Walls.* Chicago: Aldine.

ROSEN, L.
1969 "Matriarch and Lower Class Negro Male Delinquency." *Social Problems* 17:175–89.

SCHUR, E.M.
1973   *Radical Non-Intervention: Rethinking the Delinquency Problem.* Englewood Cliffs, N.J.: Prentice-Hall.

SENNETT, R., AND J. COBB
1972   *The Hidden Injuries of Class.* New York: A. Knopf.

SHERIF, M., AND C.W. SHERIF
1964   *Reference Groups: Exploration into Conformity and Deviation of Adolescents.* New York: Harper and Row.

SHORT, J.F., AND F.L. STRODTBECK
1965   *Group Process and Gang Delinquency.* Chicago: University of Chicago Press.

SILBERMAN, C.
1978   *Criminal Violence, Criminal Justice.* New York: Random House.

SIMON, R.J.
1975   *Women and Crime.* Lexington, Mass.: Lexington Books.

TENNYSON, R.A.
1967   "Family Structure and Delinquent Behavior." In M.W. Klein (ed.), *Juvenile Gangs in Context.* Englewood Cliffs, N.J.: Prentice-Hall.

TOBY, J.
1967   "Affluence and Adolescent Crime." In *Task Force Report: Juvenile Delinquency and Youth Crime*, pp. 132–44. Washington, D.C.: Government Printing Office.

TOMSON, B., AND E.R. FIEDLER
1975   "Gangs: A Response to the Urban World," Part II. In D.S. Cartwright, Barbara Tomson, and Hershey Schwartz (eds.), *Gang Delinquency.* Monterey, Calif.: Brooks/Cole.

TUMA, E., AND N. LIVSON
1960   "Family Socioeconomic Status and Attitudes toward Authority." *Child Development* 31.

WERTHMAN, C.
1967   "The Function of Social Definitions in the Development of Delinquent Careers," pp. 155–70. In *Task Force Report: Juvenile Delinquency.* Washington, D.C.: Government Printing Office.

WILLIAMS, L.
1976   "Three Youths Call Mugging the Elderly Profitable and Safe." *New York Times*, December 8, p. B2.

WOLFGANG, M.E., R.M. FIGLIO AND T. SELLIN
1972   *Delinquency in a Birth Cohort.* Chicago: University of Chicago Press.

QUESTIONS FOR DISCUSSION

1. Discuss how juveniles are affected by the financial costs of their social lives and the labor market.

2. How do typical schooling practices actually contribute to delinquency?

3. What is meant by "masculine status anxiety"?

4. In what ways do the status of age and a capitalist economy contribute to delinquency?

APPLICATIONS

1. Were you employed during your years in high school?
   a. If "yes," why did you work? Were you able to engage in other activities as a result of working? Do you think working kept you out of "trouble"?
   b. If "no," why didn't you work? Do you think that as a result of not working you got into more "trouble" than someone who worked? Explain.

2. Based on your experience, through twelve years of public school, do you think that the way in which schools are conducted contributes to delinquency? Why? How would you change the school system in your community?

KEY TERMS

dramaturgical refers to an individual presenting him or herself to others in a manner analogous to a stage actor's presentation to an audience. This social "presentation of self" may be authentic or unauthentic depending on such things as the audience, the role expectation, or how the actor chooses to manipulate other social actors.

ethos of capitalism the guiding beliefs or principles of an economy based on the accumulation of capital and profit.

genre a category of something that is characterized by a particular style, form, or content.

pecuniary rewards rewards that consist of payment with money.

pedagogical relating to or befitting education or teaching; refers to how and in what order educational materials are disseminated by an instructor.

plausibility when something appears worthy of belief or an assertion that is logically constructed.

prerogative an exclusive right, privilege, or power.

repugnant when something is distasteful or adverse; inconsistent or incompatible.

16

School Bonding, Race, and Delinquency

Stephen A. Cernkovich
Peggy Giordano

School and school-related variables assume prominent roles in most major theories of delinquency: disorganized schools (cultural deviance theory), school environments that frustrate students' goals and aspirations (strain theory), a lack of attachment and commitment to the school (control theory), an educational system that provides an inferior education to poor and minority children (conflict theory), and the negative labeling of school failures and "troublemakers" (societal reaction theory)— all increase the likelihood of delinquency (Empey 1982:289; Siegel and Senna 1988:300) and/or school dropout (see Bachman and O'Malley 1978; Elliott 1966; Elliott and Voss 1974; Hathaway et al. 1969; Polk et al. 1981; Thornberry et al. 1985). Siegel and Senna (1988:302) note the considerable research showing school failure to be a stronger predictor of delinquency than socioeconomic status (also see Kelly and Balch 1971), race or ethnic background, and peer relations. Further, school failure is predictive of delinquency for middle and upper status youngsters as well as

for lower status ones (Braithwaite 1981; Siegel and Senna 1988:305), and it is especially common among chronic offenders (see Shannon 1982; West and Farrington 1977; Wilson and Hernstein 1985; Wolfgang et al. 1972). Liska and Reed (1985:548) note that "delinquent youth are less likely to complete assigned work at home or in school, to get good grades, to enjoy school, to aspire to higher education, to get along with their teachers, and even to be in school than are more conventional youth." In his popular textbook, Empey (1982) suggests that difficulties in school may be the single best predictor of delinquent behavior in American society today, although there is some debate as to whether school problems are a cause or an effect of involvement in delinquency (see Elliott 1966; Hargreaves 1967; Hirschi 1969; Kelly 1971, 1874; Kelly and Balch 1971; Liska and Reed 1985; Phillips and Kelly 1979; Polk et al. 1974; Polk and Halferty 1966; Polk and Schafer 1972; Rhodes and Reiss 1969; Schafer and Polk 1967; Stinchcombe 1964; Toby 1957).

The purpose of this research is to describe the manner in which school bonding affects delinquent conduct, focusing in particular on the role of the school in the delinquent involvement of black youths. Paralleling the "gender gap" that characterizes the school-delinquency

Stephen A. Cernkovich and Peggy C. Giordano, "School Bonding, Race, and Delinquency," *Criminology* 30(2) (1992):261–90. Reprinted with permission of the American Society of Criminology.

literature (Rosenbaum and Lasley 1990:493) is a "racial gap"—a failure to examine racial variation in the impact of school factors on juvenile misconduct. In fact, the research literature is surprisingly silent in general on the issue of racial differences in delinquency. Matsueda and Heimer (187:826) suggest that three factors are primarily responsible for this lack of attention: the politically sensitive nature of examining racial differences in crime and delinquency; the belief that racial differences in official measures of crime and delinquency do not reflect real differences, but rather are the result of criminal justice system bias; and the difficulty of measuring delinquency and its correlates reliably because of racial differences in the validity of self-report data.

Regardless of the reasons underlying it, this neglect of blacks in delinquency research is challenged both by the more general literature on black adolescence and by a number of empirical realities that suggest that there are important racial differences in schooling—differences that may, in turn, result in differential levels of delinquency involvement: the higher drop-out rate of black compared with white adolescents[1]; charges of racially biased testing, classification, and tracking; negative teacher attitudes toward black students and lower teacher expectations for black than for white students (Ogbu 1988:177); and the pejorative label of "acting white" by peers of those blacks who are successful in school (Fordham and Ogbu 1986). Further, research has indicated that race/ethnicity may be an important factor affecting the balancing act between deviant and conventional behavior that is so common during adolescence. Jessor (1982) contends that early involvement in deviant activities may block future participation in educational and occupational pursuits. Clayton and Voss (1981:164) suggest that whites may be better able than blacks to flirt with deviant behavior in adolescence without suffering long-term deleterious effects. There also is evidence from the status-attainment literature that some of the strongest predictors of achievement among whites, such as family status and parental encouragement and influence, are not as powerful in predicting the status attain-

ment of blacks (Burke and Hoelter 1988; Clark 1983; Kerckhoff and Campbell 1977; Porter 1974; Prom-Jackson et al. 1987).

The considerable ambivalence among blacks regarding the role of education in their lives similarly belies the neglect of race in the school-delinquency equation. While many blacks view the American educational system as the embodiment of the culture's false promise of equality and therefore withhold any serious commitment, there are significant numbers who see it as a means to greater opportunity and an improved social and economic future—as the only means by which they can acquire the skills necessary to compete with whites (see Liska and Reed, 1985:557–558). Ogbu (1988:170–81) has noted that while education is valued among blacks, several realities mitigate against their commitment to educational achievement: a "job ceiling" that restricts the employment of blacks, regardless of their level of education; socialization and life experiences that reinforce the reality of this job ceiling and create considerable disillusionment about the merit of expending effort on academic pursuits; and an objectively inferior education which prohibits blacks from competing for more desirable jobs and blocks significant social mobility. Ironically, the response of many blacks to these realities may further increase the likelihood of school failure: disillusionment and alienation; withdrawal of commitment to educational activities that are perceived as having no payoff; the use of "survival strategies" (e.g., nonconventional economic activities) that are incompatible with middle-class classroom behavior; and a general attitude of suspicion, distrust, and hostility toward the school system. To the extent that black youths adopt such a frame of reference early in their lives, they enter school with certain predispositions that inhibit commitment to school and that result in a greater probability of experiencing school difficulties.

Thus, there is considerable evidence suggesting that blacks experience school in a qualitatively different way than whites (also see McAdoo 1988a, 1988b; McAdoo and McAdoo 1985). To the extent that school factors are predictive of delinquency involvement—and previous research has shown that they are, at least for white males—such racial variation in school experiences may well be reflected in differential delinquent outcomes. Whether this is the case empirically, however, is largely unknown because of the failure of prior research to examine the role of race in the school-delinquency equation.[2] While quite a bit is known about the role school plays in the lives of white adolescents, very little is known about its role among blacks, unless one is willing to assume that the effects are relatively constant across racial boundaries. As we have noted above, there are several good reasons for guarding against accepting such a characterization in the absence of more direct empirical evidence.

THEORETICAL ORIENTATION

To a greater degree than the other major delinquency theories, strain and control models see school problems as critical correlates of delinquent involvement. Strain theory (Cloward and Ohlin 1960; Cohen 1955; Merton 1938) suggests that unpleasant school experiences and school failure, especially among lower class and, by implication, minority youths are important precursors of delinquency involvement. Further, the insensitivity of the educational system to the needs of underprivileged youths is seen as exacerbating the problems they have in adapting to the school environment (Bartol and Bartol 1989:245–246). Among low-status youths, school is perceived as unrelated to future success; as a result, they see little reason to conform to the demands of the school environment. In this model, school failure leads to the frustration of long-range ambitions, which in turn reduces the students' commitment to conformity, thus increasing the probability of delinquency (Cohen 1955; Empey 1982: 271–272; Seigel and Senna 1988:308–309; Stinchcombe 1964).

Control theory (Hirschi 1969) also conceptualizes the delinquent as someone who experiences school failure, but it suggests an alternative time ordering of the variables. Lack of attachment to parents and teachers and a weak commitment to educational and occupational goals are prior causally to both school failure

and involvement in delinquency (Empey 1982:272–272; Hirschi 1969). Adolescents who do not care what their teachers think of them, who do not care about getting good grades, who do not spend much time on homework, who do not have high aspirations for the future, and who generally do not want to be in school—these are the youths who are the most likely candidates for delinquency. From a control theory perspective, lack of school bonding is a critical link in the causal chain leading to delinquency involvement, and this relationship is held to be invariant across class, race, and gender boundaries (Rosenbaum and Lasley 1990:497).

While control theory arguably has become the dominant perspective for examining the school-delinquency relationship in recent years (Rosenbaum and Lasley 1990:496), the legacy of strain theory (with its emphasis on the structural sources of crime and delinquency) provides an important framework for any research on blacks. Although not addressed directly by strain theorists, the social context within which schooling takes place is a critical component of the American educational system. Years of attempts to achieve school integration notwithstanding, the American school system continues to be made up of an amalgam of various racial environments along a continuum from complete segregation to complete integration, with considerable variation in school culture, quality, funding, and teacher expertise across types. We believe it is important to understand the effects these different racial environments may have on the behavior and attitudes of the students attending them, particularly black students. Insofar as schools of varying racial composition subject those attending them to differential experiences and cultures, and to strains, frustrations, and failures that vary in both type and magnitude, it is reasonable to believe that individual levels of school bonding will be correspondingly conditioned.

While racial composition of the school setting most probably affects all students to some degree, it may be particularly important for blacks because of the distinct educational experiences they have had in this country and the consequent meaning of education in the black culture. Fordham and Ogbu (1986:177, 181–182) suggest that school achievement historically has been viewed by both blacks and whites as an arena in which only whites can succeed, in which minorities have rarely been given the opportunity to achieve, and in which few minorities were rewarded if they did succeed. That is, many blacks define certain activities and behaviors, among them academic striving and success, as the domain of white Americans. Among the behaviors identified as "acting white" by the students in Fordham and Ogbu's study were "spending a lot of time in the library studying," "working hard to get good grades," and actually "getting good grades." Blacks who engage in such behaviors are labeled by their peers as "acting white" and are negatively sanctioned.

Further, commitment to education is a *subtractive process:* The black student who succeeds in school not only is "acting white" but also is doing so at the cost of "acting black." Academic success places a particularly onerous stigma on the black male: His manhood is questioned by the suspicion that he may be gay. Because it threatens the minority identity on both a cultural and an individual level, academic achievement is opposed socially by the peer group and psychologically by the individual. On a social level the peer group discourages educational striving by negative labeling, exclusion, or even physical assault. On a personal level, individuals resist educational striving out of fear of such responses and to avoid psychological dissonance (Fordham and Ogbu 1986:182–183, 186, 194).

Given this cultural definition of education, many blacks face a serious dilemma: On the one hand, education clearly is viewed by many as their best avenue to success; on the other hand, success in the school context often is devalued by the peer group. Considerable ambivalence about expending effort and succeeding in school is the result. How do youths finding themselves in this predicament adapt? The best evidence suggests that black students use a variety of strategies to cope with the ambivalence associated with their desire to perform well in school, on the one hand, and the demands of the peer group that they conform in attitude and behavior to the black cultural frame of reference, on the other. Underachievers avoid conflict altogether by limiting academic effort; high achievers minimize negative labeling via such mechanisms as pretending to be someone who does not expend much effort to earn good grades, choosing bullies as friends/protectors in exchange for help with schoolwork, and maintaining a low profile by not joining academic clubs or by cutting classes (Fordham 1988:60–61; Fordham and Ogbu 1986:187–187, 184–197). These and other mechanisms allow black students to succeed in school without incurring the wrath of their peers.

School context (i.e., racial composition of the school) is related to this cultural definition of education in that varying racial environments are likely to exert differential pressures on black students toward or away from school commitment and achievement. For example, if Fordham and Ogbu are correct, one would expect blacks attending predominantly black schools to face overwhelming pressure against school success. Highly committed or high-achieving students in this kind of environment would have to possess strong coping mechanisms indeed. On the other hand, black students attending predominantly white schools presumably would find greater levels of support for educational commitment and achievement (or at least lower levels of negative sanctioning from their black peers in the school environment; still, they may be negatively sanctioned for their school success by black peers in other contexts). Those attending racially mixed schools might by the most conflicted of all—receiving mixed messages from their white and black peers. The interaction dynamics on these varying racial contexts are sufficiently complex, however, to make prediction of the pressures, conflicts, and resulting effects on behavior difficult. Nonetheless, there is good reason to believe that school context has something other than a neutral effect on bonding, and as such, it represents an important variable to include in any analysis of school bonding, race, and delinquency.[3]

On the basis of this background, the purpose of this research is to examine the impact of school bonding on the delinquent behavior of black and white youths. Specifically, we are concerned with the relationship between two separate dimensions of school bonding—the *level* of school bonding among black and white youths and the *effect* of school bonding on delinquent conduct. Although there need by no necessary relationship between the level of bonding and the effect of bonding (i.e., differential levels of school bonding do not necessarily result in differential levels of delinquency involvement), there certainly is sufficient theoretical justification for expecting such an association. That is, control theory suggests that the greater the level of school bonding—as evidenced by high degrees of attachment to the school and to teachers, high grades, high aspirations and a commitment to the future, and involvement in such school and school-related activities as homework, athletic teams, school clubs, and school-sponsored events—the lesser the likelihood of involvement in delinquent activities (Hirschi 1969:16–34, 110–134, 170–182, 191–192). In addition, insofar as school bonding varies by race and according to the racial composition of the school environment, we hypothesize that the school bonding-delinquency relationship will be correspondingly conditioned.

RESEARCH DESIGN

Sample

Johnson (1979:73) has noted that studies of the relationship between school bonding and delinquent behavior often are based on school samples—samples that are inherently biased. Adolescents who attend school are more likely to have higher levels of school bonding than those who do not attend regularly, who have dropped out, or who are institutionalized. However, since our sample is neighborhood-based it is not limited by the school-based bias articulated by Johnson. In order to obtain a cross-section of youths between twelve and nineteen years of age and geographically dispersed throughout the Toledo, Ohio, metropolitan area, we used a multistage, modified probability sample design in which geographically defined area segments were selected with known probability. We stratified the segments using the most up-to-date census data available (1980), on the basis of racial composition and average housing value. Within the segments, we selected households and eligible respondents for interview to fill specified sex and race quotas; no specific age quotas were allocated, although the ages of respondents were tracked as the interviews were conducted to ensure adequate representation of teens of all ages. A total of 942 face-to-face interviews were successfully completed. Of those, 51 percent were with adolescent females, 45 percent of the respondents were white, the remaining non-whites being predominantly black (50 percent of the neighborhood sample). The respondents ranged in age from twelve through nineteen: 21 percent were either twelve or thirteen; 32 percent, fourteen or fifteen; 32 percent, sixteen or seventeen; and 15 percent, eighteen or nineteen years of age.[4]

Dependent Variable

Delinquency involvement was measured by a modified version of Elliott and Ageton's (1980) self-report delinquency scale. Twenty-seven individual delinquent behaviors were represented in the scale. Subjects indicated how many times during the previous year they had committed each act: never (coded as 0), once or twice a year (1), once every two to three months (2), once a month (3), once every two to three weeks (4), once a week (5), and two to three times a week, once a day, or more than once a day (all coded 6). Each offense item also was assigned a ratio-score seriousness weight derived from the National Survey of Crime Severity (Wolfgang et al. 1985:46–50), ranging from 0.25 for such status offenses as truancy and cheating on tests to 25.85 for rape.[5] The total delinquency score for a respondent is the mean of the sum of the products of each item's frequency and its seriousness weight. Scale scores range from 0 to 13.72, with a mean of 1.16. The alpha reliability coefficient for the scale is 0.875.

School-Bonding Scales

While school bonding typically is viewed as something other than a unidimensional phenomenon (see, for example, Agnew 1985; LaGrange and White 1985; Polk and Halferty 1966), prior attempts at conceptualization and measurement have fallen short of reflecting the true complexity of the construct. Much of the previous research on the school and delinquency has operationalized school bonding as a combination of attachment, involvement, performance, and commitment, and has indexed such bonding by one or two variables representing this amalgamation. In contrast, our operationalization of school bonding is much more multidimensional in nature.[6]

We initially identified several school-bonding dimensions by means of an orthogonal (Varimax) factor analytic solution of thirty-three school-related items included in our interview schedule. Using this mathematical solution as a starting point, we then modified the scales in an effort to derive a set of substantively meaningful, theoretically justifiable, and empirically reliable scales. That is, once the scales were defined mathematically by the factor analysis, we performed a series of reliability analyses and examined each item and scale for its face and construct validity. Items that detracted from the internal consistency of the scale in question, and/or those that were not theoretically consistent with the other items composing the scale were eliminated. Similarly, items were added to a scale if it made empirical or theoretical sense to do so. For example, although "Getting good grades is not important to me at all" and "Homework is a waste of time" did not "load" at a mathematically acceptable level on the school-commitment dimension in the factor analysis, these items certainly seemed to be consistent with the theoretical meaning of the control theory concept of commitment. In addition, including them in the commitment scale increased the alpha reliability coefficient from .721 to .749. Thus, although we generally maintained the dimensional structure of school bonding identified in the factor analysis, we modified this structure when it was empirically and/or conceptually appropriate to do so. This process resulted in the following seven school-bonding scales, all ranging in value from 1 to 5, and all constructed as the arithmetic mean of the items composing them.

School attachment refers to the degree to which students care about school and have positive feelings for it. This is the most general of all the factors, and it is composed of the following two items, both taken from Minor (n.d.): "I feel as if I really don't belong at school" and "I wish I could drop out of school." Both of these negatively worded items are reverse scored so that high scale scores reflect high levels of school attachment. The alpha reliability coefficient for the scale is 0.744.[7]

Attachment to teachers (alpha = 0.702) is a two-item scale—"Most of my teachers treat me fairly" (Elliott and Voss 1974) and "I like my teachers" (Minor, n.d.)—reflecting feelings of admiration and respect for one's teachers. High scale scores are indicative of high levels of attachment to teachers.

School commitment (alpha = 0.749) refers to the degree to which the student has a "stake in conformity" that insulates him or her from involvement in delinquency. This is reflected by such matters as the extent to which he or she invests time and effort in academic activities, gets good grades, shows concern for future achievement, and has high aspirations for the future. This scale is composed of the following items: "How many hours a week to you usually spend doing homework?" "What grades to you usually get in school?" (Hirschi 1969). "How far would you *like* to go in school?" "How far do you think you *will* go in school?" (Elliott and Voss 1974). "Getting good grades is not important to me at all" (reverse scored). "I try hard in school" (Minor, n.d.). "School work is very important" (Minor, n.d.). "Homework is a waste of time" (reverse scored). The composition of this scale is generally consistent with Krohn and Massey's (1980:530–533) argument that such variables as grades and amount of time spent doing homework should be conceptualized as part of the commitment variable rather than as aspects of attachment or involvement. High scale scores indicate high levels of educational commitment.

Perceived risk of arrest (alpha = 0.672) is a two-item scale—"If you were arrested for something, how likely would it be to hurt your chances of going as far as you would like in school?" and "If you were arrested for something, how likely would it be to hurt your chances of getting the kind of job you want?"—indexing the effect the respondent believes formal arrest would have on educational and occupational opportunities. Both items are taken from Minor (n.d.). While these items clearly are related to the control theory concept of commitment, they performed better (as indexed by their alpha reliabilities) as a separate dimension than as part of the commitment scale. High scale scores indicated a high level of perceived risk.

School involvement (alpha = 0.548) refers to the amount of behavioral participation in various school activities. As the temporal dimension of attachment, involvement in an activity or set of activities suggests commitment to that activity (Krohn and Massey 1980). As Hirschi (1969:191) has noted, however, it is important to know what *kind* of activity the youth is involved in; most conventional activities are neutral—they neither inhibit nor produce delinquency. As a consequence, rather than ask youths whether they are involved in school activities in general, we gauge involvement in several different kinds of school activities, all based on earlier research by Minor (n.d.): "How many days a week (outside of class time) do you spend time on athletic teams?" "Attending athletic events, plays, or school dances" "On honor society activities?" "On newspaper/yearbook activities?" "On music/band activities?" "On student government?" High scale scores represent high levels of involvement in school activities.

Parental communication (alpha = 0.622) is a measure of the level of parental interest in and support for school-related activities. The theoretical logic of this variable rests on the assumption that the degree of communication between an adolescent and his or her parent(s) regarding school activities both reflects and reinforces the student's bonding to the school. The scale is made up of four items: "How often do you talk with your parents about problems you have at school?"; "How often do you talk with your parents about how well you get along with your teachers?", "How often do you talk with your parents about your job plans for the future?" (all from West and Zingle 1969), and "My parents often ask about what I am doing in school." High levels of parental interest and communication are indicated by high scale scores.

Perceived opportunity (alpha = 0.672) refers to the respondent's perception of opportunities for future success. The two items composing this scale (both reverse scored)—"I'll never have as much opportunity to succeed as kids from other neighborhoods" (Landis et at. 1963) and "My chances of getting ahead and being successful are not very good"—make no direct reference to school, but our assumption is that perception of future opportunities is very much conditioned by one's attachment and commitment to school. While such items traditionally have been used to index strain theory, we believe that they are consistent with control theory as well, especially the concept of commitment. High scale scores are indicative of a positive perception of future opportunities.

Control Variables

Because our review of the literature suggests that the racial environment of the school is an important consideration for understanding school bonding, we created a *school-context* variable. We classified the schools attended by the youths in our sample as one of three types: predominantly white (defined as at least 80 percent white), predominantly black (at least 80 percent black), and racially mixed (20 to 79 percent white). Cross-classifying respondents' race with the racial composition of the school they attended resulted in six school-context categories: blacks attending predominantly white schools (*n* = 76), blacks in mixed-race schools (*n* = 260), blacks in predominantly black schools (*n* = 78), whites attending predominantly white schools (*n* = 126), whites in racially mixed schools (*n* = 156), and whites in predominantly black schools (*n* = 3).[8] The school-context variable permits us to determine whether the strength of the school-bonding dimensions varies for blacks in predominantly white schools as opposed to those attending predominantly black or racially mixed schools. We are ultimately interested, of course, in whether any such differential bonding across school contexts is associated with differential levels of delinquency involvement.

Other control variables include *age, sex, race, and socioeconomic status* (SES). With the exception of socioeconomic status, all are self-explanatory. Because lower class children are overrepresented among both school failures and those involved in serious and repetitive delinquent conduct, and because race is strongly associated with social status, it is essential that SES be included in this analysis. Our measure of social status is based on the Hollingshead and Redlich (1958) Two-Factor Index of Social Position, which considers both occupation and education in the computation of a single SES score.[9]

Before proceeding to the data analysis, the possibility of differential measurement error by race must be addressed. Hindelang et al. (1981) have presented evidence that black males' self-reports of their delinquency involvement are less valid than the reports of other groups. Specifically, they found that black males underreport involvement at every level of delinquency, but especially at the high end of the continuum. They also found that self-reported grades are least valid among black males. This obviously has serious implications for our analysis. It would be a mistake, however, to conclude that such measurement error invalidates the data provided by the black males in our sample. There are several good reasons to believe that it does not.

First, Hindelang and his colleagues conclude that while differential validity by race means that self-reports are poor *social indicators* of the absolute extent of delinquency among black males, such data can still be quite useful in *etiological research*. That is, etiological research is less interested in the absolute frequency of delinquency than with how individual or group rankings on delinquency are associated with individual or group rankings on various independent variables of interest (1981:215–16). The latter is clearly the focus of our research. Second, if black males do indeed

underreport their delinquency involvement, then our measure of their misbehavior is a conservative one. This implies that some of the relationships we report would be even stronger if blacks reported a truer and therefore greater level of involvement. Third, Hindelang and colleagues note that while the differential-validity problem makes comparison *across groups* potentially misleading, analysis *within groups* is not compromised. This means that we can have confidence in the relative explanatory power of our independent variables within race and race-sex subgroups. A fourth mitigating factor is our reliance on face-to-face interviews in the collection of these data—the method Hindeland and colleagues found to produce the least biased self-reports among black males (1981:178). finally, our research incorporates the most basic implications of the Hindelang et al. findings (1981:214)—the necessity of stratifying by race in both sampling and data analysis.

In general, we believe we have done virtually everything possible to minimize the bias of differential self-reporting by race. While we have no illusions that we have eliminated the problem entirely, we believe it preferable to proceed with research on black adolescents with our eyes open to such problems than to take the more radical approach to throwing the data out because the respondents may be less than completely candid. Although the differential-validity issue means that comparisons across racial groups must be made with caution, we can have considerable confidence in our within-group analyses. Confidence in these data also is bolstered by our previous research on the relationship between delinquency and family and peer relations (Cernkovich and Giordano 1987; Giordano et al. 1986), which suggests that if black males are misreporting, they certainly are not doing so in consistent and predictable directions. That is, the several family, peer school, and delinquency scales we have created evoke among black males (as among the other subjects in our sample) the full range of responses, in both positive and negative directions, and in ways that do not suggest social-desirability or response-set biases.

ANALYSIS AND FINDINGS

Table 1 is derived from a one-way analysis of variance and presents mean levels of delinquency involvement and school bondings by race-sex subgroups.[10] There are significant differences across the four groups in delinquency involvement and for four of the seven school-bonding scales.[11] Both black and white males report significantly more delinquency than do black and white females; there is no significant difference, however, in the delinquent involvement of black and white males. Black females report significantly higher levels of school attachment, commitment, and perceived risk of arrest than do other groups. In addition, while black females report significantly higher levels of school involvement than do white females, it is black males who report the highest levels of involvement. Importantly, for none of the school-bonding variables do whites, male or female, report significantly higher scores than blacks. This challenges the common presumption that blacks are not bonded to the school to the same degree as whites. The data in Table 1 leave unanswered, however, the question of whether school bonding varies according to the racial composition of the school attended by these youths.

Table 2 presents the results of a one-way analysis of variance for delinquency and the seven school-bonding dimensions of school context. While there is variation in levels of delinquency involvement across the five school-context categories, none of the differences is statistically significant. However, blacks in mixed-race school environments do report significantly higher levels of school commitment than do whites in racially mixed schools. Similarly, blacks in racially mixed schools report greater school involvement than whites in mixed schools and whites in predominantly white schools; blacks attending predominantly white schools also report significantly higher levels of involvement than do whites in mixed-race environments. Finally, blacks attending predominantly white schools are more likely than blacks attending mostly black schools to believe that arrest will negatively affect their future educational and occupational opportunities. As was true of the previous data presented by race-sex subgroups, these data do not reveal a single instance of greater school bonding among whites than blacks across the five school contexts. The data in Table 2 suggest that blacks are at least as strongly bonded to the educational system as are whites, and in some cases are more strongly bonded than are whites. This is true regardless of the racial composition of the school, although the bonding scores of blacks tend to be higher in mixed-race or predominantly white school environments than in predominantly black schools.

Table 3 presents the results of the regression of delinquency on the seven school-bonding factors, SES, age, and school context for each of the four race-sex subgroups.[12] Overall, the model explains from 16.2 percent (for

TABLE 1   Mean Delinquency and School-Bonding Scores, by Race-Sex Subgroups

	Black males (n = 233)	White Males (n = 196)	Black Females (n = 238)	White Females (n = 217)	F-Value
Delinquency	1.39	1.60	0.86	0.84	11.33**
School attachment	4.16	4.11	4.35	4.25	3.50*
Attachment to teachers	3.63	3.62	3.70	3.77	1.59
School commitment	3.57	3.48	3.80	3.62	12.05**
Risk of arrest	3.65	3.47	3.76	3.53	3.01*
School involvement	1.89	1.71	1.79	1.56	9.98**
Parental communication	3.73	3.63	3.81	3.67	2.42
Perceived opportunity	3.79	3.81	3.97	3.82	2.09

*$p<.05$
**$p<.001$

TABLE 2   Mean Delinquency and School-Bonding Scores, by School Context

	Black/White (n = 76)	Black/Mixed (n = 260)	Black/Black (n = 78)	White/White (n = 126)	White/Mixed (n = 156)	F-Value
Delinquency	1.31	1.06	1.13	1.12	1.32	0.72
School attachment	4.25	4.28	4.10	4.15	4.16	1.10
Attachment to teachers	3.60	3.68	3.65	3.68	3.67	0.15
School commitment	3.69	3.65	3.63	3.48	3.49	3.45*
Risk of arrest	3.84	3.71	3.36	3.44	3.61	3.24*
School involvement	1.81	1.85	1.74	1.60	1.55	6.44**
Parental communication	3.68	3.78	3.71	3.66	3.60	1.42
Perceived opportunity	3.84	3.90	3.67	3.70	3.75	1.83

*$p < .01$
**$p < .001$

white females) to 11.9 percent (for black females) of the variance in delinquency involvement. For white males, only school commitment (beta = -.213) is a statistically significant predictor of delinquency, and attending a predominantly black school (beta = -.233) is the only noteworthy correlate among black females. Perceived risk of arrest (beta = -.239) and age (beta = .162) are significant predictors among white females. Among black males, school commitment (beta = -.211) and school attachment (beta = -.196) are significant predictors of delinquency in the expected direction: The higher the degree of commitment and attachment, the lower the level of delinquency involvement. School involvement is also a significant correlate among black males (beta = .151), but in a direction contrary to expectations: Greater levels of involvement in sports and other school-related activities are associated with greater levels of delinquency involvement. Our initial explanation of this was based on the supposition that involvement in extracurricular activities might detract from the more academic dimensions of school bonding, which in turn, are more important inhibitors of delinquent involvement. An analysis of the zero-order correlations among the independent variables (not shown) does not bear this out, however: Involvement is associated to approximately the same degree with the other school-bonding measures across all four race-sex subgroups. This analysis did show, however, that the association of school involve-

ment with delinquency is lowest for the two black subgroups, particularly black males; -.180 for white males, -.155 for white females, -.016 for black females, and -.001 for black males. Unfortunately, our data do not allow us to determine the precise mechanism by which involvement is differentially related to the delinquency of blacks and whites.

In many respects, the data in Table 3 are more important for what they fail to demonstrate than for that they reveal. First, while the school-bonding model explains a reasonable amount in variance in delinquency involvement, it is not a powerful predictor. Nonetheless, school factors appear to be as important as peer and family factors in explaining delinquent involvement (see for comparison, Cernkovich and Giordano 1987; Giordano et al. 1986), and we believe it would be a mistake to neglect the role of the school in both producing and inhibiting delinquent behavior. Second, and more important, there is no significant variation across race-sex groups in the general explanatory power of the model.[13] While the relative importance of the individual dimensions of school bonding varies across the four subgroups, as indicated by the magnitudes of the respective unstandardized coefficients, none of these differences is statistically significant.[14] Thus, the most general conclusion from these data is that school bonding plays substantially the same role in the delinquency involvement of blacks and whites. This is not all what our review of the literature and

TABLE 3 Delinquency Regressed on School-Bonding Scales, SES, Age, and School Context, by Race-Sex Subgroups

	Black Males		White Males		Black Females		White Females	
	b	Beta	b	Beta	b	Beta	b	Beta
School attachment	-.509	-.196*	-.198	-.089	-.118	-.068	-.091	-.066
Attachment to teachers	-.045	-.017	-.139	-.054	-.036	-.023	.107	.064
School commitment	-.769	-.211*	-.621	-.213*	-.493	-.180	-.273	-.146
Risk of arrest	-.015	-.008	.012	.006	.013	.010	-.284	-.239***
School involvement	.459	.152*	-.236	-.079	.076	.036	-.142	-.064
Parental communication	.137	.048	-.066	-.025	-.220	-.117	-.071	-.043
Perceived opportunity	-.372	-.144	.291	.132	-.040	-.025	.161	.121
Socioeconomic status	-.013	-.099	-.015	-.118	-.002	-.022	.006	.078
Age	-.025	-.023	.105	.103	.023	.029	.101	.162*
Black/black context	-.440	-.075	—	—	-1.050	-.233**	—	—
Black/mixed context	-.384	-.091	—	—	-.407	-.137	—	—
Black/white context	.090	.016	—	—	.634	-.166	—	—
White/white context	—	—	.272	.066	—	—	-.141	-.054
White/mixed context	—	—	.452	.116	—	—	.051	.021
R²		.154		.133		.119		.162

*p<.05
**p<.01
***p<.001

theoretical orientation led us to hypothesize. Rather, we expected to find lower *levels* of school bonding among blacks compared with whites, and consequent differential *effects* by race of school bonding on delinquent behavior. This clearly is not the case. Rather, it is more accurate to conclude that whites are not more strongly bonded to the school than blacks, and that race does not condition the relationship between school bonding and delinquency.

Further, while the levels of several school-bonding dimensions vary according to the racial composition of the school (Table 2), the finding (Table 3) that school context is generally unimportant in predicting delinquency (with the exception of black females attending predominantly black schools) also was surprising. Because of this, we computed separate regression equations for the five school contexts to determine whether different variables or different patterns of variables are more important in one context than in another.

The analyses reported in Table 4 reveal that the model explains considerably more of the variance in the delinquency of blacks attending predominantly black (34.4 percent) and predominantly white schools (17.5 percent) than of those attending racially mixed schools (9.4 percent). In addition, the explanatory power of the model is somewhat greater for whites attending predominantly white school (19.6 percent) than for those at racially mixed schools (15.6 percent). An examination of the standardized coefficients within the school-context categories shows that attachment to teachers, perceived opportunity, sex, and commitment are the strongest correlates of delinquency in the black/white context. Among blacks attending racially mixed schools, commitment and school attachment are the best predictors. For blacks in predominantly black schools, however, several variables produce sizable coefficients: school attachment, perceived risk of arrest, commitment, sex, SES, and attachment to teachers. Among whites, sex and school commitment are important correlates in the predominantly white context, and sex and school attachment are the best predictors in the racially mixed context. With only

a few exceptions, however, most of these coefficients are not significantly associated with delinquency. Despite this absence of statistical significance, these data do suggest that the influence of the school-building variables is not constant across school contexts.

In fact, a comparison of the unstandardized coefficients across school-context categories reveals considerable variability in the influence of most of the school-bonding variables. For example, school attachment ($b = -.707$) appears to be much more important in the black/black context than in any of the other school environment. Similarly, attachment to teachers ($b = -.578$) and perceived opportunity ($b = -.574$) are much better predictors in the black/white context than in the other four. Perceived risk of arrest ($b = -.335$) and school involvement ($b = .340$) have their strongest influence in the black/black environment. On the other hand, commitment appears to be a strong predictor across all contexts[15] (although its impact is somewhat weaker for the two white groups), and sex is strongly related to delinquency in all contexts except the black/mixed. None of these differences in the relative magnitude of the unstandardized coefficients across school contexts is statistically significant, however, and the reader should exercise caution in making such comparisons.

In addition, because of the relatively small sample sizes for two of the school-context categories (i.e., seventy-six blacks attending predominantly white schools, seventy-eight blacks in predominantly black schools), because school context is most certainly confounded with variables we have not been able to control in our analysis (e.g., neighborhood crime, school size, neighborhood SES), and because the number of schools in three of the five contexts is relatively small (i.e., 81 percent of the students in the two predominantly white contexts came from only four schools, and 60 percent of those in the predominantly black context attended just two different schools), these findings regarding the influence of school context should be viewed as exploratory in nature. Still, our data do suggest that the racial composition of the school may indeed have some impact on the role school bonding plays in

TABLE 4 Delinquency Regressed on School-Bonding Scales, SES, Age, and Sex, by School Context

	Black/White		Black/Mixed		Black/Black		White/White		White/Mixed	
	b	Beta	b	Beta	b	Beta	b	Beta	b	Beta
School attachment	-.132	-.053	-.258	-.131	-.707	-.301	.195	.091	-.296	-.165
Attachment to teachers	-.578	-.270	-.029	-.016	.398	.184	.012	.005	.014	.006
School commitment	.673	.182	-.602	-.196*	-.727	-.238	-.440	-.178	-.233	-.092
Risk of arrest	.057	.030	.056	.037	-.335	-.251	-.183	-.124	-.074	-.039
School involvement	.117	.041	.149	.060	.340	.162	-.313	-.117	-.288	-.101
Parental communication	-.102	-.041	.001	.001	-.127	-.056	-.235	-.096	.005	.003
Perceived opportunity	-.574	-.254	-.115	-.059	-.157	-.083	-.262	.146	.118	.061
Socioeconomic status	-.012	-.073	-.006	-.050	-.025	-.200	-.016	-.121	-.002	-.013
Age	.014	.012	-.025	-.025	.014	.019	.108	.125	.122	.124
Sex	.909	.221	.082	.024	.732	.232	.845	.253*	.883	.262**
R²	.175		.094		.344		.196		.156	

*p<.05
**p<.01

252

delinquency involvement, particularly for black adolescents. At the very least, school context is a potentially important variable that should be included in future research efforts.

SUMMARY AND DISCUSSION

Blacks are surprisingly underrepresented in research on the school and delinquency. This is due in part to the politically sensitive nature of the race issue in American society, to the belief by some researchers that while race is related to official processing it is not an important correlate of self-reported delinquency, and to validity problems associated with the self-reports of blacks (Matsueda and Heimer 1987:826). The neglect of blacks is due also to the role of race in major delinquency theories. Although control and strain theory have been the dominant theoretical models informing empirical analyses of the school-delinquency relationship historically, neither has spawned a systematic study of the role of race in the casual equation. This is because neither model directly addresses the role of race theoretically: control theory because its key predictors are held to be invariant across racial boundaries, and strain theory because it is a class-based model that deals with race only by implication.[16]

This research introduced race as a key variable in the school bonding-delinquency equation. For some, our findings of no significant differences in the effect of school bonding on delinquency across race-sex subgroups and school racial environments will be interpreted as support for the continued neglect of blacks. That is, our findings appear to vindicate control theory, a model that purports to be constant across racial, sex, and socioeconomic boundaries. We believe such a conclusion would be both premature and mistaken. This is because our research has left unanswered some important questions and has raised additional ones that must be addressed before we can say with any degree of certainty that there are or are not race-specific differentials in the relationship between school bonding and delinquency.

For example, while our final regression analyses suggested that racial context may indeed have an impact on school bonding and delinquency after all, subsample size issues and the potential confounding of school context with several unmeasured variables prohibited asserting this with a great deal of confidence. Similarly, we were unable in this research to examine directly whether our subjects perceived a "job ceiling" regarding their future employability, and whether such a perception conditioned their bonding to the school, or their behavior independent of such bonding. Nor did we investigate whether blacks, especially males, felt pressured by their peers to temper their school achievement out of fear of being labeled as "acting white," and whether this was in any way related to delinquency.

While our earlier research revealed that several dimensions of family and peer relations were differentially related to delinquency involvement among blacks and whites, the most general conclusion from the present data is that there are no important racial differences in the impact of school bonding on delinquency. We believe it is important to understand why this is the case. Perhaps it is because school bonding is qualitatively distinct from family and peer bonding. While family and peer relationships are by definition affective, immediate, and interpersonal, school relationships are more impersonal, future-oriented, and competitive. The school is the major arena for adolescent status competition in American society, an arena where universalistic rules apply, and many blacks, especially those from lower status backgrounds, enter at a competitive disadvantage. As a result, they face a unique set of problems and frustrations (Cohen 1955). While we have not in this research investigated what it is that minority youths bring to the school that results in their experiencing school in ways that are qualitatively different from white experiences, it is clear that future research needs to examine how cultural and interpersonal relations in the family and among peers influence school bonding and, in turn, delinquency.

An excellent model for the sort of research that is needed is MacLeod's (1987) ethnographic study of lower class teenagers. In marked contrast to the white youths he studied, MacLeod's black respondents believed strongly in the worth and value of education. They viewed the school as a level playing field, an environment in which hard work would pay off to remedy the problems created by racial inequality. Black parents encouraged high aspirations among their children, and the peer group was clearly achievement oriented, valued school success, encouraged high aspirations, and rewarded behavior consistent with these values and goals.[17] Even though the parents of these youths had failed in their quests to succeed, all had renewed hope for the young—an abiding belief that the racial environment had changed substantially to provide more equality of opportunity. The school, in turn, was viewed as the primary mechanism for "making it." Even though they were only moderately successful in school, these black youths did not blame the school or its discriminatory tracking system, its partiality toward higher status youths, or the self-fulfilling consequences of low teacher expectations for minority youths. Rather, they tended to blame themselves for not working hard enough or being smart enough. And despite the objective lack of economic opportunities for those adults around them, these students maintained their commitment to education; for many their aspirations were tempered only after they had finished high school and confronted the harsh realities of the job market (MacLeod 1987:97–101, 110, 126–30).

Even if we accept this characterization of a strong belief among many blacks in the value and practicality of education (an assumption confirmed by recent empirical studies showing blacks to have higher aspirations than whites from the same socioeconomic background—a reversal of the pattern prevailing in the 1960s and early 1970s [MacLeod 1987:129–30]), our research has highlighted some troubling questions: If blacks are at least as strongly bonded to the school as whites, why does the black dropout rate continue to outstrip the white rate by a wide margin? Why do blacks continue to be disciplined, suspended, and expelled in greater numbers than whites? Why isn't school bonding more effective in moderating delinquency involvement among blacks? Why is school involvement positively related to delinquency among black males, an association opposite to that found among the other race-sex subgroups?

In framing responses to such questions, we believe our findings on school bonding should be juxtaposed against our earlier research regarding family and peer relationships (Cernkovich and Giordano 1987; Giordano et al. 1986). Although much research historically has emphasized the dysfunctional features of the black family, our findings point to areas of greater intimacy between black adolescents and their families, in contrast to the lower levels of intimacy and higher levels of conflict we found to characterize white adolescents and their families. Similarly, while their peer relations were quite similar to those of whites in many respects, blacks scored significantly lower on our friendship scale measuring "basic caring and trust," they were less likely to feel pressured by peers into behaving in ways contrary to their wishes, and they were less likely to lie in order to protect their friends. This appears to be due, in part at least, to a somewhat more intimate family base, which results in black adolescents being less likely to seek out peer support or to experience peer pressure with the same degree of intensity as their white counterparts. Such findings clearly challenge the traditional model of black family and peer relationships. We believe our school findings likewise question the accuracy of the dysfunctional model. The black youths in our sample are not isolated and alienated from school; rather they are just as committed and attached as whites, if not more so.

None of these findings means, of course, that black adolescents do not experience peer pressures, are not intimate with their peers, do not have family conflicts, or do not have difficulties in school. But these clearly are matters of degree, and our research suggests that while black adolescent social relations—in the family, with peers, and in school—are quite similar to those of whites in several respects, they also are in many important ways qualitatively different. Such findings reveal the hazards of making generalizations about blacks on the basis of research conducted on whites, and they underscore the necessity for more research directly examining the role of race in the complex processes leading to delinquency involvement.

NOTES

1. Contrary to the common belief that the black dropout problem is enormous and worsening yearly, however, is a recent study reporting that the high school graduation rate of blacks has improved much faster than that of whites and Hispanics over the past two decades. Thus, the critical question may not be why so many black youths drop out of school, but rather, given all the problems of crime, poverty, discrimination, drugs, and pregnancy, why so many stay in school and graduate (DeParle 1991:1, 14).

2. While Hirschi (1969:120), for example, does examine racial differences in the impact of some school factors on delinquency, such analyses are used to illustrate a point other than the importance of race in his model. He makes it clear that his model applies across racial, gender, and class boundaries.

3. The evidence regarding the influence of the school's racial environment on black children is equivocal, and two conflicting hypotheses have emerged. We note these not with the intention of evaluating their relative efficacy, but because they underscore the importance of the school's racial context. The "contact hypothesis" asserts that school segregation is harmful to the development and self-esteem of black youths. Contact with whites through school integration is seen as bolstering black self-esteem and increasing levels of school achievement. The "insulation hypotheses," however, holds that contact with whites may in fact lower levels of black self-esteem and achievement: Blacks in an integrated school setting may internalize whites' negative image of blacks (Krause 1985:257–258). Citing Rosenberg (1977), Krause discusses three mechanisms by which this occurs: (1) minority youths in majority group settings are more likely to be exposed to negative communication about themselves or about their group (i.e., racial teasing or putdowns); (2) minority youths in integrated settings come to realize that their norms and values are different from those of the majority group and are considered inferior by the dominant group; (3) minority youths in integrated environments also suffer because of the reference group against which they compare themselves regarding academic performance. Insofar as the academic performance of blacks is below that of whites, blacks in white-dominated schools are comparing themselves to the higher achieving whites, with a consequent lowering of self-esteem when they find their achievement levels lagging. Because the homogeneous environment reduces the magnitude of such discrepancies in academic performance in segregated schools, students making such comparisons do not perceive the

lag observed in integrated schools—the reference group is different (Krause 1985:258–259).

4. The neighborhood survey was managed by National Analysts, Inc. Interviews were conducted from late April through late June of 1982. Informed consent and written permission were obtained from each respondent and parent/guardian prior to the interview. The National Analysis staff validated 54% of the interviews to ensure that proper protocol was followed.

5. The twenty-seven items and their seriousness weights are as follows: vandalism (2.88), motor vehicle theft (8.05), theft more than $50 (3.59), buying/selling/possessing stolen goods (5.00), throwing objects at cars or people (1.14), running away (0.85), lying about age (0.25), carrying hidden weapon (4.64), theft less than $5 (1.78), aggravated assault (6.17), prostitution (2.07), sexual intercourse (1.60), gang fighting (11.74), selling marijuana (8.53), cheating on tests (0.25), simple assault (1.47), disturbing the peace (1.14), selling hard drugs (20.65), joyriding (4.45), rape (25.85), unarmed robbery (5.12), public drunkenness (1.75), theft $5–$50 (2.88), breaking and entering (3.22), truancy (0.25), drug use (1.42), and alcohol use (1.06).

6. While we have used several different theoretical models (i.e., social control, strain, social learning, deterrence, and subcultural theory), to identify a number of school-bonding variables, this work is not an attempt at theoretical integration. Rather, we have sought to operationalize school bonding as thoroughly as possible, and in doing so have refused to be limited to a single theoretical orientation. While our conceptualization is most compatible with social control theory, the reader should recognize that it contains elements of these other models as well.

7. Since we will be making comparisons across race and sex groups in our analysis, it is important to know if our scales are differentially reliable across subgroups. The alpha reliability coefficients for delinquency involvement and the seven school-bonding scales are as follows for the total sample, whites, blacks, males, and females, respectively: Delinquency involvement: .875, .883, .836, .850, .811; school attachment: .774, .737, .740, .732, .742; attachment to teachers: .702, .692, .711, .599, .795; school commitment: .749, .789, .713, .716, .685; perceived risk of arrest: .672, .640, .683, .652, .712; school involvement: .548, .532, .549, .556, .570; parental communication: .622, .622, .615, .543, .673; perceived opportunity: .672, .694, .676, .615, .723. While the coefficients vary somewhat, none of the group alphas is so low as to create problems of reliability in the data. The reader should be aware, however, of evidence indicating that self-reports of delinquency and school performance may be differentially *valid* across demographic subgroups (Hindelang et al. 1981).

8. Nonwhites other than blacks were excluded in the construction of the school-context variable. The predominantly white school context consists of students

who attended eighteen different schools; however, 81% of the respondents came from only four of the eighteen schools. The racially mixed context is represented by twenty-two schools, with 92% of the respondents coming from ten of them. Finally, eleven schools make up the predominantly black context, with 60% of the respondents attending two of the eleven. One hundred ninety-nine of our respondents attended private schools, for which we were not able to obtain data on racial composition. As a result, these cases are counted as missing data in the school-context portion of the analysis.

9.   Parental occupations as reported by the respondents were coded according to the Census Bureau's Index of Industries and Occupations (Bureau of the Census 1980). Parental education level also was based on subject response. For each respondent, education was weighted by a factor of 4, occupation by a factor of 7; the two scores were then summed to form a single SES score. Father's education and occupation were used to compute SES scores except in cases where data were not available for the father; in these cases, mother's education and occupation were used in the computation. For the purpose of describing the socioeconomic characteristics of the sample, we collapsed individual scores into four categories: I = 11–31, II = 32–47, III = 48–63, and IV = 64–77 (Bonjean et al. 1967:381–385). Class I represents the highest SES category, class IV the lowest. The sample distribution across the four SES categories is as follows: I (upper) = 13%, II (middle) = 13%, III (working) = 41%, and IV (lower) = 33%. In the regression analyses to follow, the social-status variable assumes its noncollapsed distribution.

Johnson (1979:56–57) has noted several ways in which social class affects school success. Two are of special interest here: (1) middle-class teachers expect little achievement from lower status youngsters, and through a self-fulfilling prophecy, find little; (2) lower status parents place less emphasis on school success, a lack of emphasis that translates into lack of commitment and achievement on the part of the youths. If this is true it would mean, for instance, that lower status youths spend less time talking to their parents about school-related problems, and that their parents do not inquire very often about how they are doing in school. On the other hand, it may be that school difficulties and failure among middle-status adolescents is more strongly associated with delinquency than among lower status youths. Middle-status youths may have higher aspirations than lower status youngsters, so that school failure among the former may reflect a greater discrepancy between future aspirations and current indications of success (Braithwaite 1981). Whatever the direction and magnitude of the effect of SES, it is essential that it be controlled in our analyses.

10.   Because almost all previous research has shown sex to be a strong correlate of delinquency, our data are presented by race-sex subgroups. Although there is no reason to suspect differential validity of self-reports by gender, the reader should be cautious in interpreting comparisons across groups because of the possibility of underreporting of delinquency by black males. We believe our methodology has minimized the magnitude of this problem, however, and there is no evidence of a differential reporting problem for the school-bonding items.

11.   Based on the TukeyB statistic, which permits multiple comparisons between means for polychotomous variables.

12.   A correlation matrix (not shown) of delinquency involvement, age, sex, race, SES, and the school-bonding measures indicates that while many of the independent variables are significantly associated with one another, none of the coefficients is of sufficient magnitude to create problems of multicollinearity in the regression analyses. In addition, a collinearity analysis produced no variance inflation factor greater than 3.4. Using the rule of thumb that a variance inflation factor of 10 or more is indicative of multicollinearity problems, we conclude that the level of association among our independent variables is not sufficient to produce unstable or uninterpretable regression coefficients or to present other problems of interpretation.

13.   The R^2 statistic is partly a function of the subgroup's variance. As a result, the reader is reminded that comparisons across groups should be made with caution.

14.   In order to test whether there are statistically significant differences in the relative magnitude of the unstandardized coefficients across the race-sex subgroups, we computed a series of regression equation for the full and restricted models: The full models included interaction terms for race and sex with the remaining independent variables, while the restricted models included all variables except the interaction terms (Jaccard et al. 1990:47). All possible subgroup comparisons were made. None of the equations containing the interaction terms resulted in statistically significant increments in the explained variance over the models without the interaction terms. However, the equations comparing black and white males came very close to reaching statistical significance at the .05 level, as did the equations comparing black and white females. For readers who wish to pursue these differences, we note that the individual *t*-tests showed the impact of the school involvement variable to be significantly different for black males ($b = .459$) compared with white males ($b = .236$); the same was true for the opportunity variable ($b = -.372$) for black males and .291 for white males). Among the females, the individual *t*-tests revealed significant differences for involvement ($b = .076$ for black females and .291 for white males). Among the females, the individual *t*-tests revealed significant differences for involvement ($b = .076$ for black females, $-.142$ for white females) and perceived risk of arrest ($b = .013$ for black females, $-.284$ for white females). The reader should be cautious in making such comparisons, however. Because

the equations with and without the interaction terms are not significantly different from one another suing the global incremental R^2 test, comparing individual t-test differences is technically inappropriate. They are reported here for heuristic purposes only.

15. In addition, school commitment is positively associated with delinquency in the black/white context, but negatively correlated (as expected) in all the other contexts (as it was for the four race-sex groups in table 10.3). Since it is out of line with the direction of all of the other relationships, we suspect that this positive association is an anomalous function of the relatively small sample size ($n = 76$) for the black/white context and the resulting large standard error for the commitment variable (.649).

16. To the extent that class differences overlap with and/or are accepted (rightly or wrongly) as proxy measures of race, however, strain theory is less guilty than the control model of failing to incorporate race. Still, race does not assume a prominent role in strain theory.

17. Clearly, not all black youths fit the mold of those studied by MacLeod; he recognizes that many others are pessimistic about their futures and are quite cynical about the equality-of-opportunity ideology symbolized by the educational system (1987:132). Still, the sharp contrast between the positive image of school commitment and achievement within the black peer group portrayed by MacLeod and the negative "acting white" image portrayed by Fordham and Ogbu (1986) further underscores the need for more basic research on black adolescents.

REFERENCES

AGNEW, ROBERT. 1985. Social control theory and delinquency: A longitudinal test. *Criminology* 23:47–61.

BACHMAN, JERALD G. AND PATRICK M. O'MALLEY. 1978. *Youth in Transition.* Vol. VI: *Adolescence to Adulthood: Change and Stability in the Lives of Young Men.* Ann Arbor: University of Michigan Press.

BARTOL, CURT R. AND ANNE M. BARTOL. 1989. *Juvenile Delinquency: A Systems Approach.* Englewood Cliffs, NJ: Prentice-Hall.

BONJEAN, CHARLES M., RICHARD J. HILL, AND S. DALE MCLEMORE. 1967. *Sociological Measurement: An Inventory of Scales and Indices.* San Francisco, CA: Chandler Publishing.

BRAITHWAITE, JOHN. 1981. The myth of social class and criminality reconsidered. *American Sociological Review* 46:36–57.

BUREAU OF THE CENSUS. 1980. *Alphabetical Index of Industries and Occupations.* 1st ed. 1980 Census of Population. U.S. Department of Commerce. Washington, DC: U.S. Government Printing Office.

BURKE, PETER J. AND JON W. HOELTER. 1988. Identity and sex-race differences in educational and occupational aspirations formation. *Social Science Research* 17:29–47.

CERNKOVICH, STEPHEN A. AND PEGGY C. GIORDANO. 1987. Family relationships and delinquency. *Criminology* 25:401–427.

CERNKOVICH, STEPHEN A., PEGGY C. GIORDANO, AND M.D. PUGH. 1985. Chronic offenders: The missing cases in self-report delinquency research. *Journal of Criminal Law and Criminology* 76:705–732.

CLARK, REGINALD. 1983. *Family Life and School Achievement.* Chicago: University of Chicago Press.

CLAYTON, RICHARD R. AND HARWIN L. VOSS. 1981. *Young Men and Drugs in Manhattan: A Causal Analysis.* NIDA Research Monography No. 39. Washington, DC: U.S. Government Printing Office.

CLOWARD, RICHARD AND LLOYD OHLIN. 1960. *Delinquency and Opportunity.* New York: Free Press.

COHEN, ALBERT K. 1955. *Delinquent Boys.* New York: Free Press.

DEPARLE, JASON. 1991. Without fanfare, blacks march to greater high school success. *New York Times,* June 9, 1991, pp. 1, 14.

ELLIOTT, DELBERT S. 1966. Delinquency, school attendance and dropout. *Social Problems* 13:307–1–314.

ELLIOTT, DELBERT AND SUZANNE AGETON. 1980. Reconciling race and class differences in self-reported and official estimates of delinquency. *American Sociological Review* 45:95–110.

ELLIOTT, DELBERT AND HARWIN VOSS. 1974. *Delinquency and Dropout.* Lexington, MA: Heath.

EMPEY, LAMAR T. 1982. *American Delinquency: Its Meaning and Construction.* Rev. ed. Homewood, IL: Dorsey.

FORDHAM, SIGNITHIA. 1988. Racelessness as a factor in black students' school success: Pragmatic strategy or pyrrhis victory? *Harvard Educational Review* 58:54–84.

FORDHAM, SIGNITHIA AND JOHN U. OGBU. 1986. Black students' school success: Coping with the "burden of acting white." *Urban Review* 18:176–206.

GIORDANO, PEGGY C., STEPHEN A. CERNKOVICH, AND M.D. PUGH. 1986. Friendships and delinquency. *American Journal of Sociology* 91:1170–1202.

HARGREAVES, DAVID H. 1967. *Social Relations in a Secondary School.* London: Routledge and Kegan Paul.

HATHAWAY, STARKE R., PHILLIS C. REYNOLDS, AND ELIO D. MONACHESI. 1969. Follow-up of later careers and lives of 1,000 boys who dropped out of high school. *Journal of Consulting and Clinical Psychology* 33:370–380.

HINDELANG, MICHAEL J., TRAVIS HIRSCHI, AND JOSEPH G. WEISS. 1981. *Measuring Delinquency.* Beverly Hills, CA: Sage.

HIRSCHI, TRAVIS. 1969. *Causes of Delinquency.* Berkeley: University of California Press.

HOLLINGSHEAD, AUGUST B. AND FREDERICK C. REDLICH. 1958. *Social Class and Mental Illness: A Community Study.* New York: Wiley.

JACCARD, JAMES, ROBERT TURRISI, AND CHOI K. WAN. 1990. *Interaction Effects in Multiple Regression.* Berkeley, CA: Sage.

JESSOR, RICHARD. 1982. Problem behavior and developmental transition in adolescence. *Journal of School health*, May, pp. 295–300.

JOHNSON, RICHARD E. 1979. *Juvenile Delinquency and Its Origins*. New York: Cambridge University Press.

KELLY, DELOS H. 1971. School failure, academic self-evaluation and school avoidance and deviant behavior. *Youth and Society* 2:489–503.

———. 1974. Track position and delinquent involvement: A preliminary analysis. *Sociology and Social Research* 58:380–386.

KELLY, DELOS H. AND R.W. BALCH. 1971. Social origins and school failure: A reexamination of Cohen's theory of working-class delinquency. *Pacific Sociological Review* 14:413–430.

KERCKHOFF, ALAN C. AND RICHARD T. CAMPBELL. 1977. Black-white differences in the educational attainment process. *Sociology of Education* 1:15–27.

KRAUSE, NEAL. 1985. Interracial contact in schools and black children's self-esteem. In *Black Children: Social, Educational, and Parental Environments*. Newbury Parek, CA: Sage.

KROHN, MARVIN AND JAMES MASSEY. 1980. Social control and delinquent behavior. An examination of the elements of the social bond. *Sociological Quarterly* 21:529–543.

LAGRANGE, RANDY AND HELENE RASKIN WHITE. 1985. Age differences in delinquency: A test of theory. *Criminology* 23:19–45.

LANDIS, JUDSON, SIMON DINITZ, AND WALTER C. RECKLESS. 1963. Implementing two theories of delinquency: Value orientation and awareness of limited opportunity. *Sociology and Social Research* 47:408–416.

LISKA, ALLEN E. AND MARK D. REED. 1985. Ties to conventional institutions and delinquency: Estimating reciprocal effects. *American Sociological Review* 50:547–560.

MACLEOD, JAY. 1987. *Ain't No Makin' It*. Boulder, CO: Westview Press.

MCADOO, HARRIETTE PIPES (ED). 1988a. *Black Families*, 2d ed. Newbury Park, CA: Sage.

———. 1988b. Transgenerational patterns of upward mobility in African-American families. In Harriette Pipes McAdoo (ed.), *Black Families*. 2d ed. Newbury Park, CA: Sage.

MCADOO, HARIETTE PIPES AND JOHN L. MCADOO (EDS.). 1985. *Black Children: Social, Educational, and Parental Environments*. Newbury Park, CA: Sage.

MATSUEDA, ROSS L. AND KAREN HEIMER. 1987. Race, family structure, and delinquency: A test of differential association and social control theories. *American Sociological Review* 52:826–840.

MERTON, ROBERT K. 1938. Social structure and anomie. *American Sociological Review* 52:826–840.

MINOR, WILLIAM. n.d. Maryland Youth Survey. Institute of Criminal Justice and Criminology. College Park: University of Maryland.

OGBU, JOHN U. 1988. Black education: A cultural-ecological perspective. In Hariette Pipes McAdoo (ed.), *Black Families*. 2d ed. Newbury Park, CA: Sage.

PHILLIPS, JOHN C. AND DELOS H. KELLY. 1979. School failure and delinquency: Which causes which? *Criminology* 17:194–207.

POLK, KENNETH AND DAVID HALFERTY. 1966. School cultures, adolescent commitments, and delinquency. *Journal of Research in Crime and Delinquency*. Englewood Cliffs, NJ: Prentice-Hall.

POLK, KENNETH, DEAN FREASE, AND F. LYNN RICHMOND. 1974. Social class, school experience, and delinquency. *Criminology* 12:84–96.

POLK, KENNETH, CHRISTINE ADLER, GORDON BAZEMORE, GERALD BLAKE, SHEILA CORDRAY, GARRY COVENTRY, JAMES GALVIN, AND MARK TEMPLE. 1981. Becoming Adult: An Analysis of Maturational Development from Age 16 to 30 of a Cohort of Young Men. Final Report of the Marion County Youth Study. Eugene: University of Oregon.

PORTER, JAMES N. 1974. Race, socialization and mobility in educational and early occupational attainment. *American Sociological Review* 39:303–316.

PROM-JACKSON, SYLVIA, T. JOHNSON, AND MICHAEL B. WALLACE. 1987. Home environment, talented minority youth, and school achievement. *Journal of Negro Education* 56:111–121.

RHODES, ALBERT L. AND ALBERT J. REISS, JR. 1969. Apathy, truancy and delinquency as an adaptation to school failure. *Social Forces* 48:12–22.

ROSENBAUM, JILL LESLIE AND JAMES R. LASLEY. 1990. School, community context, and delinquency: Rethinking the gender gap. *Justice Quarterly* 7:493–513.

ROSENBERG, MORRIS. 1977. Contextual dissonant effects: nature and causes. *Psychiatry* 40:205–217.

SCHAFER, WALTER E. AND KENNETH POLK. 1967. Delinquency and the schools. Appendix M to Task Force Report: Juvenile Delinquency and Youth Crime. President's Commission on Law Enforcement and Administration of Justice. Washington, DC: U.S. Government Printing Office.

SHANNON, LYLE. 1982. *Assessing the Relationship of Adult Criminal Careers to Juvenile Careers: A Summary*. Washington, DC: U.S. Government Printing Office.

SIEGEL, LARRY J. AND JOSEPH J. SENNA. 1988. *Juvenile Delinquency: Theory, Practice, and Law*. 3d ed. St. Paul, MN: West.

STINCHCOMBE, ARTHUR L. 1964. *Rebellion in a High School*. Chicago: Quadrangle Books.

THORNBERRY, TERENCE, MELANIE MOORE, AND R.L. CHRISTENSON. 1985. The effect of dropping out of high school on subsequent criminal behavior. *Criminology* 23:3–18.

TOBY, JACKSON. 1957. Social disorganization and stake in conformity. *Journal of Criminal Law, Criminology and Police Science* 48:12–17.

WEST, DAVID J. AND DAVID P. FARRINGTON. 1977. *The Delinquent Way of Life*. London: Heineman.

WEST, LLOYD AND HARVEY W. ZINGLE. 1969. A self-disclosure inventory for adolescents. *Psychological Reports* 23:439–445.

WILSON, JAMES Q. AND RICHARD J. HERNSTEIN. 1985. *Crime and Human Nature.* New York: Simon and Schuster.

WOLFGANG, MARVIN E., AND ROBERT M. FIGLIO, AND THORSTEN SELLIN. 1972. *Delinquency in a Birth Cohort.* Chicago: University of Chicago Press.

WOLFGANG, MARVIN E., ROBERT M. FIGLIO, PAUL E. TRACY, AND SIMON L. SINGER. 1985. *The National Survey of Crime Severity.* U.S. Dept. of Justice. Washington, DC: Bureau of Justice Statistics.

QUESTIONS FOR DISCUSSION

1. Discuss how school bonding affects the likelihood of involvement in delinquent activity. Provide examples to support your response.

2. In what ways may black and white youth view the role of education in their lives differently? Provide examples.

3. Summarize the findings of the research presented in this article. What suggestions are given by the authors for future research?

APPLICATIONS

1. Construct a list of five to ten reasons explaining why you are in school. Compare your list with other members of your class. Are there any differences? Are all of the lists generally in agreement?

2. During our years in high school most of us notice those peers who were "good" or "bad" students. What were the major differences between these two groups of students? Do you think these differences impacted the amount of these students' delinquent involvement?

KEY TERMS

amalgamation   refers to a joining together; to unite.

ethnographic   related to the description of the races of mankind.

etiological   related to the cause of something.

exacerbating   making something more serious.

juxtaposed   when things or facts are placed side by side.

pejorative   making worse; disparaging.

vindicate   to prove something to be true or valid after it has been questioned or denied.

17

The Neophyte Female Delinquent: A Review of the Literature

George Calhoun

Janelle Jurgens

Fengling Chen

ABSTRACT

During the 1950s, most of the attention on juvenile delinquency concentrated on males. Recently, however, the incidence of female delinquency has escalated. Female delinquency that did exist a generation ago centered primarily on sexual misconduct; today much greater numbers of females are involved in armed robbery, gang activity, drug trafficking, burglary, weapons possession, aggravated assault, and prostitution. Research on the etiology of this behavior is inconclusive, with some of the theories centering around dysfunctional families, victimization, aggression, neglect, rejection, physical and sexual abuse, self-perception, gender role, and intellectual ability. This paper attempts to ascertain the status of female delinquency, with special focus on definition, etiology, and treatment.

INTRODUCTION

For nearly a century, researchers have been concerned about juvenile delinquency. Initially, much of the research centered around ado-

Adolescence, Vol. 28 No. 110, Summer 1993. Libra Publishers, Inc., 3089C Clairemont Dr., Suite 383, San Diego, CA 92117. Reprinted by permission of the publisher.

lescent males from lower socioeconomic backgrounds living in metropolitan areas (Cohen, 1955; Glueck & Glueck, 1950). However, during the past generation, youth from all socioeconomic backgrounds have been involved in antisocial activities, with the norm being behavior disorders ranging from truancy to shoplifting. Those acts were classified merely as status offenses; however, a new type of antisocial behavior has arisen. Today's youth are involved in sophisticated gang activity centered around lucrative drug trafficking, armed robbery, drive-by shooting, and murder. These newly adopted felonies are classified as delinquent offenses.

During the 1950s, most attention directed toward juvenile delinquency focused on males. Female delinquency was much less common during this era, and primarily involved sexual misconduct. This is no longer the case. Balthazar and Cook (1984) state:

> The formerly held belief that delinquency among girls is predominantly sex-related no longer squares with official statistics. It is noted that less than 1% of the total arrests of females under 18 were for specifically sex-related offenses such as prostitution, commercialized vice, or sex offenses....In contrast, 33% of these arrests were for violent crime or property crime. (pp. 105–106)

Although large numbers of females are still identified as delinquent due to sexual misconduct, according to annual reports from some of the larger U.S. police departments (Chicago, Detroit, Los Angeles, San Francisco, Houston, and Washington, D.C.), a greater proportion of females are now involved in armed robbery, gang activity, and drug trafficking.

Female delinquency is escalating, and many of these girls tend to be the products of dysfunctional families (Bowker & Klein, 1983; Henggeler et al., 1987). According to Henggeler et al. (1987):

> Although the family relations of female delinquents have not been studied extensively, some investigators have supported the view that families of female delinquents are more dysfunctional than those of male delinquents. Roff and Wirt (1984) found that teachers' reports of disturbed family relationships strongly predicted future delinquent activity among girls. (p. 200)

There has been considerable flux in female deviance as it relates to antisocial behavior, and changes in attitudes, mores, and gender role acceptance have brought about an emergence of a new female juvenile delinquent. This paper attempts to ascertain the status of female juvenile delinquency. A review of the literature focusing on definition, etiology, and treatment is presented.

DEFINITION

"Juvenile delinquency" is a term that was once predominantly applied by the courts to adolescent male offenders. Recently, female delinquency has experienced an upsurge. Within the past five years, female convictions related to gang activity, sexual misconduct, and drug offenses have quadrupled. Denmark and Rutschmann-Jaffe (1979) pointed out that, while women represent less than 5% of the prison population in the United States, "in all categories women's crime is rising between three and five times as rapidly as males'" (p. 51). Campbell (1984) revealed that, between 1970 and 1974, crimes committed by females

were up drastically; aggravated assault was up 75% and weapons possession was up 107%.

However, there appears to be a disparity in the degree and types of felonies for which male and female offenders tend to be arraigned (Schwartz et al., 1990; Figueira-McDonough, 1985). Females are more likely to be incarcerated for sexual misdemeanors, such as promiscuity and prostitution, even though a large percentage have reported being victims of sexual abuse themselves. Since there is a differentiation in the types of acts which result in the identification of males and females as juvenile delinquents, considerable attention should be directed to the definition of the term.

According to the 1987 Juvenile Detention and Correction Facility Census (JDCFC), "delinquent offenses" are acts which would be considered crimes if committed by adults, whereas "status offenses" are delinquent acts which would not be considered crimes if committed by adults. The JDCFC classified the various offenses and placed them in the following categories by degree of severity: Part-I Violent, Part-I Property, and Part-II Status Offenses. Crimes listed under Part-I Violent include murder, nonnegligent manslaughter, aggravated assault, robbery, and forcible rape. Felonies listed under Part-I Property include burglary, arson, larceny-theft, and motor-vehicle theft. In contrast, misdemeanors associated with Part-II Status Offenses include truancy, running away, breaking curfew, vandalism, and sexual misconduct such as promiscuity.

The classification of felonies by severity as practiced by the JDCFC is analogous to that described by Calhoun et al. (1984). While the JDCFC employs the term "juvenile offenses" for serious crimes, Calhoun et al. identify these behaviors as "hard-core." Minor offenses are depicted as "status offenses" by the JDCFC and "soft-core" by Calhoun et al.

Calhoun et al. (1984) found that young offenders committed crimes which were related to their immediate needs. Thus, adolescents of middle and upper socioeconomic status (SES) were more likely to engage in acts classified as status offenses, or soft-core. These misdemeanors are generally committed to get parental attention or to relieve boredom by following the lead of the peer group. In contrast, lower SES youths tended to become involved in serious delinquent offenses, or hard-core crimes. Their crimes are committed primarily for economic reasons and include armed robbery, burglary, or drug-related murder. Because ethnic minorities are overrepresented in the lower SES, a proportionately larger number of these adolescents appear to be convicted for more serious offenses than are their counterparts from middle and higher SES.

According to Calhoun et al. (1984):

> When defining juvenile delinquency, special consideration should be given to the age of the offender and the nature of the crime. Extreme scrutiny should be exercised when labeling acts committed by children as crimes; thus, problems related to "disobedience," "loitering," "running away," and "breaking curfew" should be recognized as simple misdemeanors. Actually, "juvenile delinquency" is a legal term that identifies youths as juvenile criminals. Therefore, a juvenile delinquent is a youth between the ages of 10 and 16 who was apprehended by law officials for committing a crime, arraigned in court, adjudicated, and incarcerated. (p. 323)

Offenders whose crimes do not match the criteria established for identification, and are not arraigned in court, adjudicated, and incarcerated, officially are not juvenile delinquents. Thus, these individuals have only engaged in delinquent behavior, which is thirty times more prevalent than juvenile delinquency. Delinquent behavior involves crimes committed which were not recorded by the courts, and there are thousands of antisocial acts committed by youth regularly which are not brought to the attention of law enforcement officials. While these acts should warrant attention by the courts, many tend to go undetected; therefore, these offenders cannot legally be labeled as juvenile delinquents.

Tidwell (1981) identified serious problems with the definition and types of acts committed by delinquents. Tidwell suggested that these issues should be reviewed: "Not only is there diversity in the language employed to describe those who manifest inappropriate behaviors,

but the behaviors themselves are highly diversified—ranging from innocuous acts, such as truancy, to major felonies, such as grand theft" (p. 335).

ETIOLOGY

The etiology of delinquency has been associated with many psychological and sociocultural factors. Some of the popular theoretical causes involve gender role, dysfunctional families, intellectual ability, self-perception, and parental neglect. While these are believed to be associated with delinquency, there are many other related variables. In addition, these variables may be interrelated. For example, within the framework of dysfunctional families, sexual and physical abuse, running away, parental neglect, and abandonment may be involved.

Gender Role

Researchers are beginning to investigate the relationship between female delinquency and recent changes in gender role. Female delinquents have become more daring in their efforts to enter territory once considered the domain of "bad boys." However, research on gender role is both sparse and contradictory.

Hansen (1975) suggested that female delinquents have very little in common with the new liberated woman because of their poor self-perception. Rather, they tend to become involved in deviant behavior as a result of their subservient relationship with men. He believed that poor economic conditions and the proliferation of drugs are partly responsible for the escalation of crimes committed by females.

Balthazar and Cook (1984) indicated that female delinquency has increased because (1) a greater percentage of girls have become more masculine, (2) some are caught between the stereotypical traditional female role and the newer, more active role, and (3) some are unable to live up to their role expectations at home, school, or among peers. Chesney-Lind (1989) disagreed, and pointed out that the ways in which agencies and courts deal with female delinquency should be examined. Berger (1989) indicated that male family members usually have more freedom, while females are more often protected by the family, thus keeping their behavior in check. He further stated:

> Traditional family arrangements have kept females, in comparison to males, dependent and cloistered, and females have been expected to provide support and nurturance to others....As a result, girls have been more closely supervised by their parents than boys and have had less opportunity to commit delinquent acts. (p. 377)

Self-Perception

Some theorists have indicated that female delinquents tend to exhibit poor self-perception as compared to their nondelinquent cohorts (Bour, Young, & Henningsen, 1984; Power & Beveridge, 1990; James & Meyerding, 1977). However, many variables can influence self-perception, including sexual victimization and parental abuse or neglect. However, of the factors which could be linked to poor self-perception, few have the impact of sexual victimization on adolescent females. James and Meyerding (1977) discovered that early sexual abuse tended to have a profound impact on the development of self-identity. It may lead to sexual or even occupational deviance, including prostitution in later adulthood. Researchers who have indicated that sexual abuse might be the most significant cause of delinquency in girls include Bour, Young, and Henningsen (1984), MacVicar and Dillion (1980), James and Meyerding (1977), and Bracey (1983).

Intellectual Ability

Some social theorists argue that female delinquents may be suffering from limited intellectual functioning. White, Moffitt, and Silva (1989) found that both male and female delinquents had significantly lower IQ scores than did their nondelinquent counterparts. Haynes and Bensch (1983) found that both male and female delinquents had higher performance (P) than verbal (V) scores on the Wechsler Intelligence Scale for Children (WISC). They stated: "It may be that the salience of academic

difficulties is greater for females than for males and contribute to low female verbal IQ" (p.143).

Dysfunctional Family

With respect to delinquency, the dysfunctional family often involves a single-parent household or "broken home." However, most researchers agree that any home situation where children are not valued, protected, and loved could be considered dysfunctional. Research has consistently shown a positive correlation between female juvenile delinquency and the dysfunctional family. Relevant variables include physical and/or sexual abuse, incest involving the father or other close relative, and parental neglect or abandonment. Morris (1964) found that significantly more female delinquents were reared in single-parent households than either male delinquents or male and female nondelinquents. Hardy and Cull (1975) suggested that inadequate family structure could exacerbate the child's problems and even affect school performance. Kroupa (1988) shared that contention, stating that delinquent girls "scored lower on mental age, came from families of lower SES, scored lower on the social desirability scale, and came from broken homes more often than did the nondelinquent girls" (p. 177). It was also revealed that female delinquents tended to perceive their parents more negatively than did their nondelinquent counterparts. Rosenbaum (1989) noted that many of the girls suffered from broken marriages, multiple relationships, alcoholism, and mental illness: "It appears that not only were these women victims, they were double victims: victims of their families and victims of the criminal justice system as well. Most of these girls were sentenced to the CYA for status offenses (mostly running away)" (p.40). Toby (1957) pointed out that the relationship between delinquency and broken homes was greater for females than males. Henggeler, Edwards and Borduin (1987) studied the effect of family relations on female delinquency:

> It was observed that mother-adolescent dyads and parents in families of female delinquents had

higher rates of conflict than their counterparts in families of male delinquents. In addition, the fathers of female delinquents were more neurotic than the fathers of male delinquents. These findings provide some support for the view that the families of female delinquents are especially dysfunctional. (p. 199)

However, Bowker and Klein (1983) provided contradictory results, suggesting that delinquent females were not any more apt than nondelinquents to come from broken homes or from homes where parents had low-income jobs. Chesney-Lind (1989) also held an interesting and contrary perspective of female-headed households:

There is no evidence to suggest that as women's labor force participation has increased, girls' delinquency has increased. Indeed, during the last decade when both women's labor force participation accelerated and the number of female-headed households soared, aggregate female delinquency measured by self-report and official statistics either declined or remained stable (Ageton, 1983; Chilton & Datesman, 1987; Federal Bureau of Investigation, 1987). (p. 20)

Berger (1989) indicated that several factors have resulted in the proliferation of felonies committed by females. First, there is a greater percentage of female delinquents from broken homes. In the vast majority of cases, the father is usually the absent parent. In addition, more mothers are either working or involved with their own personal problems (i.e., drugs). Second, the young males remaining in the home are not as protective of their sisters today as they were a generation ago. Many homes are plagued with so many problems that everyone is forced to "look out for himself." Therefore, "the man of the house" (usually a young adolescent male) is not likely to accept the role of protector of his vulnerable sister.

Running Away

As mentioned previously, a large percentage of female delinquents have been found to be "victims of circumstances" and share the common characteristic of sexual abuse (Chesney-

Lind, 1989; Bracey, 1983; Figueira-McDonough, 1985). Research consistently shows that over 75 percent of all girls identified as juvenile delinquent by the courts have been sexually abused at an early age and forced to endure the traumatic experience until they were old enough to run away.

Ironically, however, running away is recognized by the courts as delinquent behavior even though the girls may be trying to escape from abuse. Once they turn to the streets, there is a greater chance that they will become involved in deviant behaviors, such as prostitution. MacVicar and Dillion (1980) found that at least three out of ten prostitutes in their investigation revealed that they were sexually abused as children. Once girls are abused in this fashion, they eventually lose what limited self-respect they held for themselves and begin to commit more serious crimes. A large number of these girls are exploited by pimps who force them to become drug addicts. Once they are dependent on narcotics, they must continue a life of prostitution to support their drug habit.

TREATMENT

Prisoner-Run Delinquency Prevention Programs

The rehabilitation of juvenile delinquents has had only limited success. While working as a recreational supervisor at a boy's training school in Michigan, it became evident to the first author that incarceration was not an effective deterrent. There he observed innocent and hostile young men gentle adolescents being transformed into hardened, aggressive, and hostile young men by the end of their short sentences. From being victims of sexual abuse by older and physically stronger delinquents, they eventually became victimizers of the new arrivals. As depicted in the motion pictures *Lock Up* and *An Innocent Man*, sexual abuse is a way of life in prison, and this behavior is practiced by both male and female delinquents in detention centers.

Prompted by the trauma associated with prison life, a group of inmates from Rahway State Prison in New Jersey assisted in the making of the educational, correctional film *Scared*

Straight. The program was called the "Lifers' Juvenile Awareness Project." The award-winning film was made in an attempt to deter adolescents from becoming juvenile delinquents. Buckner and Chesney-Lind (1983) pointed out that the Rahway plan was effective because of the format employed to depict the realities of prison life:

> The Rahway program utilized a confrontational style, with tough prisoners subjecting the youths to sordid stories of prison life, including the loss of privacy and individualism and the constant threat of physical and/or sexual assault. The project's appeal was based in large part on the assumption that the harsh style of the prison life would challenge naive expectations of "doing easy time." (p. 228)

The effectiveness of this project can be appreciated only by acknowledging the success rate of the program. According to researchers who studied the Rahway plan, the program was approximately 90% successful (Buckner & Chesney-Lind, 1983). As a result, a replication of the Scared Straight Program has been adopted by Hawaii's Oahu Correctional Center. According to Buckner and Chesney-Lind (1983), Hawaii's Stay Straight/Youth Awareness Program avoided the confrontational style of the Scared Straight model, and allowed the prisoners to describe some of the events in their lives and the crimes they committed as youths which ultimately resulted in their arrest and incarceration. After investigating the Stay Straight Program, Buckner and Chesney-Lind concluded that "a program aimed at reducing delinquency through persuasion, even if it does involve prisoners speaking in a prison setting, is not going to have a substantial impact on previously arrested youths—those who are probably most in need of help" (p. 245).

Juvenile Group Home

Because incarceration has limited effectiveness in preventing further delinquency, the group home concept was adopted and is in use throughout the state of California. Here, families open up their homes to adolescents who have been identified and institutionalized as

being delinquent. Such group homes must be licensed by the state and also conform to other local and county ordinances. The average group home generally provides services for six delinquents. The caretaker is funded by the state, but homes with nonprofit status can also receive some federal funding.

The group home concept provides juvenile delinquents with a family atmosphere which cannot be replicated in a training school or correctional facility. While assigned to a group home, delinquents are expected to attend school, counseling, or any other service provided by the group home. In addition, they must adhere to the regulations established by the parole office of the correctional facility to which they are assigned.

Delinquents guilty of crimes or group home violations may be returned to the correctional institution (either a minimum or maximum security detention facility) to complete their sentence. As a result, youngsters who got to a group home are likely to make the best of the opportunity. Juveniles who fail in a group home setting usually have more emotional and psychological problems and therefore will fair poorly in most types of incarceration. In light of the limited success of other treatment plans employed to deter delinquency, the group home setting appears to deserve wider application.

CONCLUSION

As the literature substantiates, female delinquency has reached epic proportions. In addition, the degree and types of acts committed by this new generation have become more serious, resembling those of males. There is a need for more research on female delinquency. There should also be greater efforts at developing programs and services to assist these youngsters to cope with personal, educational, and employment concerns.

REFERENCES

BALTHAZAR, M. L., & COOK, R. J. (1984). An analysis of the factors related to the rate of violent crimes committed by incarcerated female delinquents. In *Gender issues, sex offenses, and criminal justice* (pp. 103–118). Binghamton, NY: The Haworth Press.

BERGER, R. J. (1989). Female delinquency in the emancipation era: A review of the literature. *Sex Roles, 21,* 375–399.

BERZONSKY, M. D. (1978). Ausubel's satellization theory: Application to some research on adolescents. *Adolescence, 13,* 167–186.

BOUR, D. S., YOUNG, J. P., & HENNINGSEN, R. (1984). A comparison of delinquent prostitutes and delinquent non-prostitutes on self-concept. In *Gender issues, sex offenses, and criminal justice* (pp. 89–101). Binghamton, NY: The Haworth Press.

BOWKER, L. H., & KLEIN, M. W. (1983). The etiology of female juvenile delinquency and gang membership: A test of psychological and social structural explanations. *Adolescence, 18,* 739–751.

BRACEY, D. H. (1983). The juvenile prostitute: Victim and offender. *Victimology, 8,* 151–160.

BUCKNER, J. C., & CHESNEY-LIND, M. (1983) Dramatic cures for juvenile crime: An evaluation of a prisoner-run delinquency prevention program. *Criminal Justice and Behavior, 10,* 227–247.

CALHOUN, G., CONLEY, S., & BOLTON, J. A. (1984). Comparison of delinquents and non-delinquents in ethnicity, ordinal position, and self-perception. *Journal of Clinical Psychology, 40,* 323–328.

CAMPBELL, A. (1984). Girls' talk: The social representation of aggression by female gang members. *Criminal Justice and Behavior, 11,* 139–156.

CHESNEY-LIND, M. (1989). Girls' crime and woman's place: Toward a feminist model of female delinquency. *Crime & Delinquency, 35,* 5–29.

COHEN, A. K. (1955). *Delinquent boys: The culture of the gang.* Glencoe, IL: Free Press.

DENMARK, F. L., & RUTSCHMANN-JAFFE, R. (1979). The emerging female criminal. *International Journal of Group Tensions, 1–4,* 50–58.

FIGUEIRA-MCDONOUGH, J (1985). Are girls different? Gender discrepancies between delinquent behavior and control. *Child Welfare, 64,* 273–288

GLUECK, S., & GLUECK, E. (1050). *Unraveling juvenile delinquency.* Cambridge, MA: Harvard University Press.

HANSEN, J. (1975, March 17). Woman's rights and wrongs. *The New York Times,* p. 29.

HARDY, R. E., & CULL, J. G. (1975). *Fundamentals of juvenile criminal behavior and drug abuse: The female delinquent and her behavior.* Springfield, IL: Charles C. Thomas, Publisher.

HAYNES, J. P., & BENSCH, M. (1983). Female delinquent recidivism and the PV sign on the WISC-R. *Journal of Clinical Psychology, 39,* 141–144.

HENGGELER, S. W., EDWARDS, J., & BORDUIN, C. M. (1987). The family relations of female juvenile delinquents. *Journal of Abnormal Child Psychology, 15,* 199–209.

JAMES, J., & MEYERDING, J. (1977). Early sexual experience and prostitution. *American Journal of Psychiatry, 134,* 1381–1385.

KROUPA, S. E. (1988). Perceived parental acceptance and female juvenile delinquency. *Adolescence, 23,* 171–185.

MACVICAR, K., & DILLION, M. (1980). Childhood and adolescent development of ten prostitutes. *Journal of the American Academy of Child Psychiatry, 19,* 14–59.

MORRIS, R. R. (1964). Female delinquency and relational problems. *Social Forces, 43,* 82–89.

POWER, K. G., & BEVERIDGE, L. (1990). The effects of custody in a Scottish detention centre on inmates' self-esteem. *International Journal of Offender Therapy and Comparative Criminology, 34,* 177–186.

ROSENBAUM, J. L. (1989). Family dysfunction and female delinquency. *Crime & Delinquency, 35,* 31–44,

SCHWARTZ, I. M., STEKETEE, M, W., & SCHNEIDER, V. W. (1990). Federal juvenile justice policy and the incarceration of girls. *Crime & Delinquency, 36,* 503–520.

TIDWELL, R. (1981). Schooling of youthful offenders: Theory and practice. *Urban Education, 16,* 333–347.

TOBY, J. (1957). The differential impact of family disorganization. *American Sociological Review, 22,* 505–512.

WHITE, J. L., MOFFITT, T. E., & SILVA, P. A. (1989). A prospective replication of the protective effects of IQ in subjects at high risk for juvenile delinquency. *Journal of Consulting and Clinical Psychology, 57,* 719–724.

QUESTIONS FOR DISCUSSION

1. Discuss how each of the following are related to delinquency:
   —Gender roles
   —Dysfunctional families
   —Self-perception
   —Intellectual ability
   —Running away

2. According to the authors, rehabilitation programs for juveniles have limited success. Why?

3. Why is a "group home" possibly the best environment to treat juvenile delinquents?

APPLICATIONS

1. Traditionally, males have accounted for much of the serious delinquency. Recently, females are engaging in more serious delinquency. What changes in our society have effected this change?

2. Recall your years in high school. Can you think of any females in your school that were delinquent? What indication did you have that they were delinquent? Write a description of these delinquent females and share your description with the class.

KEY TERMS

arraigned   being called to court to answer an indictment; to be formally charged.

cloistered   being isolated or confined.

dysfunctional   when something cannot operate or exist as intended or expected.

flux   constantly changing.

salience   the quality of being the most important or prominent.

stereotypical   a characteristic or attribute considered to be common or endemic among a particular group.

18

Recent Gang Research: Program and Policy Implications

James C. Howell

Current knowledge of street gangs and related crime is limited. Media reports would have us believe that they account for the recent increase in juvenile violence; that they are spreading, mostly through establishment of satellite operations in other cities; that they have become extensively involved in drug trafficking; and that they are actively expanding these operations to other cities. This article reviews recent gang studies that shed light on the above assertions and increase our knowledge of gangs. Program and research implications for federal, state, and local entities along with recommended next Steps are offered.

Public officials and criminologists have been struggling to explain the recent increase in youth violence in the United States. Aside from widely recognized factors, which may also be the result of youth violence, including family deterioration, school failure, poverty, drugs, availability of firearms, and disorganized communities, a popular answer is gangs. This article reviews available empirical evidence concerning several popular notions about street gangs.

Crime and Delinquency, Vol. 40 No. 4, October 1994 495–515
© 1994 Sage Publications, Inc.

First, gangs are viewed as accounting for much of the increase in violence, especially among juveniles, by virtue of sheer numbers, as they have presumably grown. Is the gang problem indeed growing? Or, is the increase in youth violence accounted for by other law-violating youth?

Second, gangs are believed to have spread eastward from the West Coast, from larger cities to smaller ones, and from central cities to suburban areas. Law enforcement officials believe that much of this presumed gang migration is for the purpose of expanding drug trafficking operations. Do we have evidence of gang migration and for drug trafficking purposes?

Third, gangs are thought to have become more active in violent crime because they have presumably become more involved in the distribution of drugs. Much inner-city street violence, especially homicides, is believed to be associated with disputes over drug distribution territory. Is there evidence to support the interconnection of gangs, drugs, and violence?

The purpose of this article is to review recent gang research in an effort to shed light on the above issues. More generally, we are interested in policy, program, and research implications of recent gang study results.

MILLER'S NATIONAL SURVEYS

We begin with Miller's study (1982) because it provides the original national baseline. His research was conducted against a backdrop of very limited knowledge of gangs in the United States. Only two previous efforts had been made to assess the gang problem across the country. Bernstein (1964) surveyed gang problems in nine major cities in 1962, although not for the purpose of assessing gang characteristics. Klein (1969) reviewed all available literature on gangs in conjunction with the report of the National Commission on the Causes and Prevention of Violence. Needle and Stapleton (1983) surveyed 60 police departments in 1980 primarily for the purpose of assessing methods they were using to control gangs.

At the time of Miller's study, gang knowledge was based largely on a New York-centered picture of gang evolution: growth in the 1950s, demise in the 1960s, revival in the early 1970s, and dormancy in the later 1970s. The popular perception was that the New York sequence of events applied to other cities. Miller's pilot study (1975) found this assumption to be radically wrong. He found high levels of gang violence in 6 of the 12 largest cities. The results led the Office of Juvenile Justice and Delinquency Prevention (OJJDP) to support Miller's national gang survey (1982).

Limitations of space preclude a comprehensive summary of Miller's landmark report (1982) that resulted from his 26-city study. Rather, we shall focus on the most significant features and results that provide guidance to future gang research and program development. The reader is referred to his report for the richness of its details and references to numerous other products. Miller initially set out to address only the first of three research questions he posed: What is the nature of the violent gang phenomenon? How can it be explained? and What can be done about it? However, he addressed the other two questions as well.

Early in his study, Miller realized that the gang problem could not be accurately assessed without taking a broader approach. He titled his research "A National Survey of Collective Youth Crime." His study was unique in scope in that it was the first detailed assessment of *collective youth crime* as a national phenomenon. For decades, criminologists and sociologists have known that, unlike adult crime, most juvenile crime is committed in groups (Zimring 1981). Therefore, Miller felt it necessary to distinguish gang behavior, as one form of group delinquency, from other varieties. Having made this decision, he was able to make an enormous contribution to identifying and understanding youth gangs and other law-violating youth groups.

Miller used the law-violating youth group, rather than *gang* as his major unit of analysis. He defined a law-violating youth group as "an association of three or more youths whose members engage recurrently in illegal activities with the cooperation and/or moral support of their companions." He identified 12 types of law-violating youth groups, of which three are types of gangs: *turf gangs, gain-oriented gangs*, and *fighting gangs*.

Miller (1982) concluded that, to some extent, gang problems ebbed and flowed during the 1970s. Mysteriously, gang violence in New York and Philadelphia decreased substantially during the decade. He observed that "Nationwide, the prevalence of gangs at any given time more closely resembles that of, say, influenza rather than blindness" (Miller 1982, p. 51).

Selected findings from Miller's study (1982) presented below are particularly relevant to future research and programming regarding gangs. Two caveats are necessary before proceeding. First, the reader should be aware that Miller focused on *problems with*, rather than the *presence of*, gangs. Second, beginning with the 26 largest cities, he expanded the scope of the study to 36 metropolitan areas. Some of the findings pertain to the largest cities, or a subset of them; others, to the large metropolitan areas.

Prevalence and Location. All of the 26 cities studied were site visited. Problems with youth gangs were reported by all or almost all respondents in nine cities, by a majority in eight cities, and by a minority in five. Gang problems were reported for 18 of the 36 metropolitan areas. For large cities, prevalence rates were 52%; for metropolitan areas, 62%; and for California metropolitan areas, 80%. The proliferation of gangs in smaller California cities was especially pronounced, along with their spread to other smaller cities across the country.

Collective Youth Crime Problems. In all of the 26 surveyed localities, virtually all respondents reported problems with groups other than gangs. Except in a few cities experiencing the most severe gang problems, problems with nongang youth groups were generally considered to be more serious than were gang problems.

Law-Violating Youth Groups and Group Members. Systematic collection of information on groups other than gangs by law enforcement and other officials has been practically nonexistent. Usable information was obtained for 13 of the 26 cities. Membership in *disruptive youth groups* consisted of about 17% of all youth aged 10-19 in those cities, and percentages ranged from about 3% for Denver to about 40% for Miami and Boston. The average size of groups was about 11. Miller estimated that in the 1970s there were about 120,000 law-violating youth groups, with a membership of about 1.5 million, in the 2,100 American cities and towns of 10,000 and over. About 7 1/2 times as many communities had problems with disruptive youth groups, but not with gangs, as had problems with gangs alone. There were seven times as many disruptive youth groups as gangs in the typical locality.

Gangs. During the late 1970s, there were about 2,300 gangs with 98,000 members located in approximately 300 U.S. cities and towns. The average gang had about 57 members. The number of gang members averaged about 5% of all males aged 10–19 in the 10 large cities. Gangs made up about 2% of the total number of law-violating youth groups, and gang members about 7% of all group members. Gangs

were disproportionately concentrated in the largest cities. The 10 largest gang-problem cities—New York, Chicago, Los Angeles, Philadelphia, Detroit, San Diego, San Antonio, Phoenix, San Francisco, and Boston—contained about one half of the nation's gangs and two thirds of its gang members. However, about one half of all gangs and one third of all gang members were found in cities with populations of one-half million or less, indicating an increasing probability of finding gangs in smaller cities toward the end of the decade.

Social Characteristics of Youth Gang Members. Gang members ranged from 10 to 21 years of age. The peak age for gang membership was about 17. About 19% of arrested gang members in the four largest cities were aged 14 or 15; nearly 38% were 16 or 17; 25% were 18 or 19; and 9% were 20–21. Few autonomous female gangs existed, and those that did posed far less of a threat than did male gangs.

The ethnic composition of gangs had changed considerably from previous decades. In the past, the majority of gangs were White, composed of various European backgrounds. By the 1970s, about four fifths of all gang members were Black or Hispanic. The increase in Hispanic gangs and the emergence of Asian gangs represented new developments. However, the ethnic composition (recently migrated) and social class position (lower levels) of gang populations remained constant.

Criminal Activity. Gang members, whose numbers equaled about 6% of males age 10 to 19 in the three largest cities, accounted for about 11% of all arrests of male youth and 42% of arrests for serious and violent crimes. On the other hand, nongang members accounted for 89% of all arrests and 58% of all arrests for serious and violent offenses. About 6% of gang member arrests were for drug offenses. Gang members were much less likely to be arrested for drug offenses than were nongang youth. However, there was evidence of increasing involvement of gang members in the drug trade.

An estimated 71% of all serious crimes committed by juveniles were attributed to law-violating youth groups. These groups were particularly active in such offenses as larceny, burglary, robbery, drug and alcohol violations, assault, disruption, disorderly conduct, vandalism, and arson. However, gang members were arrested in significantly higher proportions for more violent crimes, including robbery, rape, assault, and weapons violations. Victims of gang violence in the 1970s were gang members in about 60% of the cases.

Between 1975 and 1979, the number of known gang homicides made up about 23% of all juvenile homicide arrests. During the 1970s, homicide arrests of juveniles increased by 40%, whereas gang killings increased by over 200%. A significant finding from Miller's trend analysis was that peak years for gang killings in various cities were spread evenly over the decade, rather than clustering or consistently increasing. He noted that "this makes it very difficult to explain trends in gang violence on the basis of any set of nationwide developments such as changing economic conditions, unemployment rates, or patterns of drug use" (Miller 1982, p. 102).

Weaponry. Guns were more readily available, more prevalent, and far more widely used toward the end of the 1970s than earlier in the decade. In addition, gangs were beginning to use automobiles in their assaultive attacks. Miller (1982) concluded that "the prevalence, use, quality, and sophistication of weaponry in the gangs of the 1970s far surpassed anything known in the past, and is probably the single most significant characteristic distinguishing the gangs of the 1970s from their predecessors" (p. 115).

Policy, Research, and Program Implications. According to Miller (1982), the finding that problems with nongang youth groups were generally considered to be more serious than gang problems, except in the worst gang problem cities, "suggests that much greater attention be devoted to this type of crime problem and that substantially increased resources be allocated both to information gathering and program

development with respect to crime by youth groups other than gangs" (p. 48). To address these and other gang issues, Miller (1976, 1990) recommended a new federal initiative.

SPERGEL'S NATIONAL SURVEY OF RESPONSES TO GANGS

Irving Spergel and his colleagues, David Curry and Ronald Chance, conducted the first comprehensive national survey of organized agency and community group *responses* to gang problems in the United States (Spergel 1990, 1991; Spergel et al. 1991; Spergel and Curry 1993). It is the only national assessment of efforts to combat gangs.

The National Youth Gang Survey began with a universe of 101 cities in which the presence of gangs was suspected. Contacts with police regarding the presence of gangs and the existence of an organized agency or community response reduced the number to 74 cities. Among these, 39% had no organized gang program or strategy in response. The gang responses of the remaining 45 cities, of which 21 were classified as chronic and 24 as emerging gang cities, were studied in detail in 1987.

A total of 254 respondents were surveyed in the 45 cities, involving three main categories: law enforcement, school officials, and community service agencies. Respondents were asked to identify the best ways employed by their organizations to deal with gang problems. These responses were classified into five main strategies: (a) community organization or community mobilization, (b) social intervention, (c) opportunities provision, (d) suppression, and (e) organizational change and development.

Chronic gang problem cities relied mainly on community organization and suppression strategies, whereas emerging gang problem cities used primarily suppression strategies. Also, Spergel (1992) has noted a shift in preferred strategies over the past 40 years from social intervention strategies in the 1950s and 1960s to suppression strategies in the 1970s and 1980s of a high-risk group of urban youths. Thornberry et al. (1993) did not report the percentage of gang members in the Rochester Youth Development Study.

Illegal Gang Activities.   Esbensen and Huizinga (1993) found that male gang members were considerably more involved in all types of delinquent activity than were their nongang male counterparts. Male gang members reported levels of delinquent activity two to three times greater than those of nongang males, except for drug sales. Male gang members accounted for only 33% of street offenders in the last year of the study, yet they reported committing 57% of the street offenses reported by the entire sample. Peripheral members reported the same level of delinquent activity as did core members. Although female gang members were more likely than female nongang members to be involved in delinquency, their level of delinquent activity was similar to nongang females.

Gang members were asked in the Denver study about the kinds of activities in which the gang was involved. Although fights with other gangs was the most frequently mentioned form of illegal activity, about three fourths of the gang members reported that their gang was involved in the following offenses: robberies. assaults, theft, and drug sales.

Dynamics of Gang Membership.   Esbensen and Huizinga (1993) found a lack of stability in gang membership. Very few youths reported being a gang member for more than a year: 67% were members for only 1 year, 24% belonged for 2 years, 6% belonged for 3 years, and only 3% belonged for all 4 years. By contrast, Thornberry et al. (1993) found that 55% of the gang members in Rochester were members for only 1 year; but 21 % were members in all 3 years. Many of the active Denver gang members indicated that they would prefer *not* to be a gang member and anticipated leaving the gang in the near future. Thus the majority of gang members were found to be peripheral or transitory members who drift in and out of the gang.

In both cities, gang members were much more likely to be involved in street offenses during the period in which they were gang members, with lower levels of involvement both before and after their time in the gang. Esbensen and Huizinga (1993, p. 583) noted that the trend toward increasing delinquency was prevalent at least 2 years before youths joined a gang. They speculated that gang membership may be a more formalized form of co-offending initiated within a delinquent peer group.

Thornberry and his colleagues (1993) were particularly interested in *why* gang members are more likely to have higher rates of serious and violent crime than do nongang members. They examined three explanatory hypotheses: (a) a selection or *kind of person* model, (b) a social facilitation or *kind of group* model, and (c) an enhancement model that combined aspects of the selection and social facilitation models. The kind of person model posits that gangs recruit adolescents who are already delinquent, whereas the kind of group model holds that the group processes and normative structure of gangs bring about high rates of delinquency among initially nondelinquent youths who join.

Thornberry et al. (1993) found the social facilitation or kind of group model to receive the strongest support. This was especially true for transient gang members whose membership lasted 1 year or less. Among stable gang members who remained in the gang for at least 2 years, the social facilitation model and, to a lesser extent, the enhancement model appeared to be operating. The social facilitation model also was supported in their examination of offense-type categories. Among gang members with high rates of violent crimes and involvement in drug sales, both transient and stable gang members showed higher rates only when they were active gang members. This was not the case for property crimes. This pattern was particularly pronounced for violent offenders but not for property offenders. Violent offenders' rates were at least twice as high while they were gang members than before and after gang participation. Although Thornberry and his colleagues found offense patterns in Rochester before and after gang membership to be similar to those Esbensen and Huizinga

(1993) found in Denver, the before and during membership differences they observed were not as great as among Denver youths.

Thornberry and his colleagues (1993) argued that the normative structure and dynamics of the gang must be the central focus of attempts to explain why gang members have higher rates of delinquency than do nongang members. They contend that efforts should be made to identify factors that separate the more transient from the more permanent gang members because participation in the gang appears to be a more important process than recruitment of particular types of persons. They rightly suggested that the implications for prevention and intervention efforts are important.

These Denver and Rochester investigations should give us pause. First, these are the largest representative samples of gang members interviewed in recent studies. Second, the longitudinal designs permitted examination of transitions both in and out of gangs. Third, the examination of temporal relationships of gang membership and delinquency involvement is unique in gang research. One must wonder, however, whether Denver and Rochester gangs differ from those in more established gang cities.

CURRY'S LAW ENFORCEMENT SURVEY

Curry, Fox, Ball, and Stone(1993) conducted a 1992 National Assessment Survey of law enforcement agencies. Their findings are presented below with comparisons they made to other studies.

Presence of Gangs in Cities. Officials in 91% of the 79 largest U.S. cities reported the presence of gang problems, 5% (4) reported no problem, and nearly 4% (3) reported a gang-like problem only. Curry et al. (1993) conservatively estimated that during 1991 there were 4,881 gangs with 249,324 gang members. However, only an estimated 46,359 criminal gang incidents were reported to police.

By comparison, Miller's 1975 survey of the 12 largest cities found one half to be gang problem cities. Curry et al.'s (1993) study found 10

of the 12 to have gang problems in 1992—an increase of 33%. Compared to Miller's 1982 survey of 26 cities (in the largest Standard Metropolitan Statistical Areas), Curry et al.'s study found increases in gang problems in cities of all sizes: Cities over one million population had an increase of 17%, cities from 500,000 to one million had an increase of 40%, and cities from 200,000 to 500,000 had an increase of 63%. Needle and Stapleton's 1983 law enforcement survey found 27 of 60 cities included in the study to be gang problem cities. Curry et al.'s study of 44 cities included in both surveys found 91% to be gang problem cities—an increase of 41% over the 50% among these 44 cities that Needle and Stapleton found to be gang problem cities. Spergel and Curry's 1988 survey found 73% of 85 U.S. cities to have a gang problem. Curry et al. (1993) found nearly 91% of these cities to be gang problem cities in 1992. For the 50 largest cities included in both surveys, the change was from 74% to 92% reporting gang problems; and for the 35 smaller cities, the change was from over 71% to nearly 89%.

Gang Member Characteristics. Only 8 of the 72 large city police departments reporting gang problems could provide statistics on the number of gang incidents, broken down by juveniles and adults, within their jurisdictions. Sixteen others were willing to provide estimates. In general, cities with relatively recent gang problems reported much higher proportions (up to 90%) of juvenile membership, whereas more established gang cities, such as Chicago, reported much higher proportions (74%) of adult members.

Twenty-seven cities reported the presence of female gangs. Forty large police departments reported a total of 7,205 female gang members. The number of male gang members in these 40 jurisdictions was not reported.

Among 26 large city police jurisdictions, the ethnicity of gang members was estimated to be 4% for Whites, 47% for Blacks, 43% for Hispanics, and 6% for Asians. White gang members showed the largest proportional growth from 1990 to 1991: a 62% increase. A number of jurisdictions reported emerging gang problems attributable to newly arrived immigrant groups such as refugees from Southeast Asia and Central America.

Law Enforcement Responses. The 65 reporting police departments were as likely to use suppression as they were to use community organization liaison activities. Suppression strategies perceived to be the most effective by the departments were identifying gang members (64%), case management of gang member files (63%), increased enforcement against gang members (60%), and increased law enforcement liaison (55%).

Recommendations. Curry et al. (1993) made two major recommendations, based on their survey. First, they recommended that technical assistance be provided to law enforcement agencies to transform their databases into management information systems. Such technical assistance should reflect (a) an awareness of the need for a focus on accurate and routine reporting as well as recording gang-related information, (b) a greater emphasis on the importance of gang-related incident data, and (c) the need to address local information requirements.

Second, Curry et al. (1993) recommended regular federal assessment of gang problems. They suggested that this assessment focus on gang incidents, not the number of gangs, because gang violence is of the most concern. They note that surveys since Miller's baseline study have been sporadic and conducted for different purposes. Regular comprehensive assessments were urged to provide the knowledge base for prevention and intervention efforts, including targeted technical assistance.

BLOCK AND BLOCK'S CHICAGO HOMICIDE STUDY

A unique Chicago homicide study conducted by Block and Block (1993) made use of detailed Chicago Police Department data files to geographically locate police-recorded offenses and to determine not only the street gang affiliation of the offender and victim but

also whether or not homicides were gang motivated. They were able to spatially locate offenses within the boundaries of gang turfs based on maps drawn by street gang officers in Chicago's 26 districts. Gang-related neighborhoods were classified into three types: turf hot spots, drug hot spots, or turf and drug hot spots. The study focused on Chicago's four largest and most criminally active street gangs during 1987-1990.

Block and Block (1993) found that gang involvement in violence and homicide was more often turf-related than drug-related. Only 8 of 288 gang-motivated homicides between 1987 and 1990 were related to drugs. The larger gangs were extensively engaged in acts of instrumental violence (such as theft, burglary, or possession or sale of drugs), whereas most of the criminal activity in smaller street gangs centered on turf defense. The most lethal gang-related crimes were along disputed boundaries between small street gangs. They also found that the predominant type of street gang activity in neighborhoods often changed from year to year, or even month to month, and tended to occur in spurts.

Block and Block (1993, p. 9) concluded that street gang membership and violence patterns could be explained by such social conditions as racial and class discrimination and adjustment of immigrants, and also by such community and contextual factors as weapon availability, drug markets, and the spatial arrangement of street gang territories across a city.

OTHER RECENT STUDIES

Gang Migration. Several field studies in the 1980s sought evidence of gang migration (Hagedorn 1988; Huff 1989; Rosenbaum and Grant 1983), yet none has documented the establishment of satellite gangs in distant locations. These studies invalidated migration rumors, finding instead that local gangs consisted of local youths in Midwestern cities.

Maxson and Klein (1993) are currently conducting a nationwide gang migration study, which involves a survey of law enforcement agencies in over 1,100 U.S. cities. Among these, 713 reported some gang migration. Preliminary analyses indicate that the movement of gang units to other cities is a much less frequent phenomenon than is relocation of gang members with their families. In 39% of the cases, gang members moved because of family relocation; whereas, in 20% of the cases, expansion of drug markets was cited as the main reason for migration.

Female Participation.   Several recent studies have documented the increasing number of females in gangs and exclusive female gangs (Harris 1988; Fagan 1990; Campbell 1984, 1990, 1991). The Denver study (Esbensen and Huizinga 1993) produced a surprising finding on this issue. During the 4-year study period, from 20% to 46% of gang members were females. None of the other studies found levels even near this high. In Curry et al.'s (1993) survey, 27 cities reported the presence of female gangs and 40 large police departments reported a total of 7,205 female gang members.

Gangs and Crime.   Beginning with the earliest gang studies, gang members have been shown to have higher crime rates than nongang members. Other recent studies, beyond the Denver and Rochester research, include Block (1985); Fagan (1989); Hagedorn (1988); Maxson and Klein (1990); Maxson, Klein, and Gordon (1985); Quicker (1981); Rand (1987); Spergel (1983, 1991); Taylor (1990); Vigil (1988).

Gangs, Drugs, and Crime.   A United States Congress study (General Accounting Office 1989) concluded that during the latter part of the 1980s the Crips and Bloods gained control of 30% of the crack cocaine market in the United States. Another federal agency, the Drug Enforcement Administration (1988) has claimed that Los Angeles streetgangs have been identified with drug sales in 46 states.

Over the last decade, little empirical research has documented organizational operation of drug trafficking networks by true youth gangs. Police and FBI officials have reported that the Los Angeles Bloods and Crips have migrated to 45 other cities and set up crack operations (Skolnick 1989). This prompted the *New York Times* to announce that drug gangs

had spread to rural areas (Johnson 1989). According to Skolnick (1989), most of the drug trafficking in the two cities most often said to be gang migration cities, Kansas City and Seattle, attributed to Crips and Bloods has been carried out by older, former members of these gangs and by "wannabees," although they may be supplied by the Los Angeles gangs.

The Klein, Maxson, and Cunningham (1991) Los Angeles study specifically examined crack dealing in a city where gangs had been widely reputed to be involved. This study, conducted in 1985, found that drug trafficking was not a primary gang activity, although many of the gang members were involved in crack distribution (in about 25% of the instances). Klein and his colleagues also concluded that the connection between street gangs, drugs, and homicide was weak and could not account for the recent increase in Los Angeles homicides.

Because gang involvement in drug trafficking was said by the police, the media, and other sources to have increased, become more violent, and spread to smaller cities, Klein and his colleagues (Maxson, Klein, and Cunningham 1993) conducted a similar study in Pasadena and Pomona, California. Data comparing arrest records and the cities' police files of gang membership were gathered between 1989 and 1991. Among cocaine sales incidents, gang members were involved in about 27% of arrests. Comparison of gang and nongang drug sales arrests revealed similar characteristics: Relatively small amounts of cocaine were involved, sales occurred on the street or in open settings, and firearms were rarely involved. Gang members were less frequently involved in noncocaine drug sales (about 12% of arrests). The mean age of gang cocaine arrestees was 22. Violence was present in only 5% of the incidents. Firearms were involved in only 10% of the sale incidents. Klein and his colleagues characterized gang involvement in drug distribution in these two smaller cities as "substantial, but not overwhelming." Regarding police implications, they (Maxson, Klein, and Cunningham 1993) concluded that "the clearest policy implication . . . is a recommendation to move away from gang specialization in narcotics enforcement" (p. 27).

Miller's (1994) assessment of gangs and drugs in Boston showed that only about 10% of violent crimes including homicides involving gangs in the Boston area between 1984 and 1994 involved drug dealing or drug use. During this period, 9% of 75 reported homicides, which were categorized as definitely gang related, involved drug use or dealing. Of another 138 reported homicides categorized as probably or definitely gang related, 10% involved drug use or dealing. Of 545 violent incidents involving gangs, drug use or dealing were involved in nearly 9%.

Other studies have found very high levels of drug use, along with some evidence of drug dealing, among gang members. Fagan (1989) interviewed 151 gang members from Chicago, Los Angeles, and San Diego to learn about their involvement in drug dealing and whether or not violence was associated with drug sales. Although gang members reported extensive involvement in drug trafficking, little association with violence was evident. Fagan also found a small group of gangs that were extensively involved in both drug use and trafficking but avoided collective violence altogether.

Dolan and Finney (1984), Vigil (1988), and Skolnick (1989) have also conducted studies showing gang involvement in drug dealing. Certain investigators have found gang specialization in drug trafficking. Skolnick (1988) has reported involvement of Chicano gangs in the crack cocaine trade in Chicago. Philibosian (1989) has documented involvement of White motorcycle gangs in methamphetamine trafficking and Hispanic gang use and sales of PCP and marijuana. Chin (1989) has reported active involvement of Chinese gang leaders in the New York City heroin trade.

Despite these reports of gang involvement in drug trafficking, Huff (Goldstein and Huff 1993) recently concluded that "the most common scenario appears to involve *individual* gang members in drug distribution networks that are neither gang controlled nor organized gang activities" (P. 10).

Johnson, Williams, Dei, and Sanabria's (1988) analysis of New York City drug trafficking suggested that entrepreneurs often recruit persons with violence histories who then may recruit groups such as gangs into the enterprise. Gang members possess unique qualifications because of their sense of group identification and solidarity. Hagedorn (1991) found that, among the 37 original members of the three African American gangs in Milwaukee, 59% graduated, over a 5-year period, from the gang into drug posses or small drug trafficking enterprises.

Klein (forthcoming) has argued that typical street gang structures do not organizationally support drug distribution but that drug-selling cliques may operate within gangs. Spergel (1991) has drawn the same conclusion and has contended that "traditional turf-related gang violence and gang crisis inspired cohesion are not directly functional to drug use, selling, and associated criminal enterprise, which requires more rational kinds of organization, communication and distribution" (Sec. II, p. 29).

CONCLUSION

What do the reviewed studies suggest regarding the three popular assumptions about gangs in the United States that we noted at the outset?

Is the violent youth gang problem growing? Yes. Surveys conducted over the past decade (primarily of law enforcement agencies) have found gangs in more and more cities. The gang problem is also increasing from the standpoint of more violent offenses being committed by gang members, more serious injuries, and more lethal weapons employed. However, it is unclear whether the growth in urban violence should be attributed largely to gangs, law-violating youth groups, or nongang youths. Although several studies have documented higher levels of violence among gang members compared to nongang youths, the research necessary to clarify this issue has not been conducted since Miller's study in the 1970s. To untangle this situation, more definitive data must be collected, delineating truly violent gangs from other types of co-offending youth groups.

Are gangs spreading eastward from the West Coast and to smaller cities? Local police and the FBI have reported the migration of Los Angeles Crips and Bloods to as many as 45 western and midwestern cities. The migration of gangs is being studied by Maxson and Klein (1993). Preliminary results of their survey indicated considerable emergence of gangs in smaller cities. However, family migration, not gang unit relocation, and local genesis appear to be the main explanatory factors.

Are gangs increasingly involved in drug trafficking and increased violence as a result? Empirical research has not documented extensive involvement of gangs in drug trafficking as an organizational activity of gangs. Gang members are extensively involved in drug trafficking just as are nongang youths who are serious and violent juvenile offenders using drugs extensively. Studies have not documented a significant amount of violence associated with gang members' drug trafficking. Most gang violence appears to be related to turf disputes. Some episodes of gang violence related to turf wars may be mistaken for drug wars. A few drug trafficking gangs and cliques within gangs established for drug distribution purposes have been identified.

This review suggests that an overlooked question should be given equal priority. Raised most recently by Curry et al. (1993), it is: Are youth gang incidents increasing? The answer is unclear. Curiously, the law enforcement agencies Curry et al. (1993) surveyed reported over five times as many gang members as gang incidents. However, the excess of members over incidents may be partially explained by the fact that gang rosters maintained by police departments are cumulative, whereas the reported incidents were not.

Data necessary to answer these general questions are woefully lacking. Much more definitive data collection and research must be carried out to document national trends and provide a basis for sound program and police decisions in dealing with violent gangs.

WHERE DO WE START?

The following are recommendations for federal action, based on this review of recent research.

Information Gathering and Dissemination. A gang assessment and research center should be established to perform two primary functions: (a) collection, assessment, and synthesis of information on gangs; and (b) dissemination of information that would support federal, state, and local planning and program development. In lieu of periodic surveys, the center would track gangs and gang-related serious and violent crime incidents nationwide. A replication of Miller's 1982 study would provide the necessary information base to establish the center's data collection function. Such a broad survey is necessary to identify true gangs, distinguishing them from other forms of collective youth crime. These survey results would also provide the necessary information to target intervention efforts in emerging and chronic gang cities.

Gang center staff would work directly with police, other juvenile justice system officials, and youth serving agencies, regularly updating information on the emergence, growth, and demise of gangs. At the same time, the center would provide information to such organizations and agencies that would profile gangs and connecting agencies to training, technical assistance, and other federal, state, and local program development and implementation resources.

As an integral part of the gang center's activities, compatible definitions must be developed and promulgated across the country. Data collection procedures and information systems should be developed at the state and local levels to provide gang tracking data. These must be coordinated with juvenile justice system data collection efforts. Technical assistance would be coordinated by the center.

The center's youth gang tracking activities must be coordinated with those of other federal agencies that perform tracking operations, including the Federal Bureau of Investigation; the Drug Enforcement Administration; the Bureau of Alcohol, Tobacco and Firearms; and the Bureau of Justice Assistance's Regional Information Sharing System.

Federal Coordination. Better coordination among federal agencies is urgently needed, especially among the main sources of funding for gang programs and research—the Bureau of Justice Assistance; the U.S. Department of Health and Human Services' Administration for Children, Youth and Families; the National Institute of Justice; and OJJDP. Gang intervention efforts must also be coordinated with the Department of Housing and Urban Development, the Labor Department, the Department of Education, and the Office for Substance Abuse Prevention.

Program Tests and Demonstrations. Field tests and demonstrations of the effectiveness of gang prevention and intervention models should be expanded. Top priority should be given to evaluating existing models rather than developing new ones. Communitywide interventions should include a focus on gang prevention and intervention (Wilson and Howell 1993).

State- and city-level program planning and interagency coordination should be supported with state and local resources. State-level responsibility for youth gang coordination should be designated by the governor of each state. These offices would conduct their activities in liaison with the gang center. Local coordinators would report to the state offices. At the local level, community planning and implementation would be the responsibility of neighborhood planning teams.

Training and Technical Assistance. Training and technical assistance for police and other local community agencies should be expanded, primarily through the addition of technical training teams, which would provide a broader range of gang diagnosis and program development expertise. These teams would assist communities in which emerging, and particularly chronic, youth gang problems have been documented through the gang center's database.

Research. Federally sponsored research will be required to answer a plethora of questions regarding gangs.

Distinguishing true gangs from other collective youth groups is a research priority. Much group delinquency appears to be erroneously labeled as violent gang delinquency. Are nonviolent gangs identifiable? How are they char-

acterized? Do youths graduate from group delinquency to gang membership? Do small groups or cliques often join gangs?

How are different types of gangs distinguished? How do they vary by geographical location? What proportion of members are juveniles or adults in different gang types? What distinguishes juvenile from young adult gangs? How does gang formation relate to community characteristics?

The dynamics of gang membership have not been systematically examined. Why do youths join gangs? Have the reasons changed over the decades? What factors distinguish transitory from stable members? Why do youths leave gangs after memberships as brief as 1 year? Is the recruitment stage the most propitious intervention point?

What proportion of violent youth crimes is accounted for by gangs? What proportion of juvenile homicides are gang related? By law-violating youth groups?

What are the major motives for gang crimes? Honor? Turf defense? Drug turfs? Control? Economic gain? How are violence motives related to neighborhood characteristics, including population composition?

Why are gang problems increasing, generally? Why are we seeing increasing problems in some large cities but not in others? What factors are related to the ebb and flow of gangs? To the formation of gangs in new communities? Ethnographic studies will be required to answer these questions.

REFERENCES

BERNSTEIN, SAUL. 1964. *Youth on the Streets: Work with Alienated Youth Groups.* New York: Association Press.

BLOCK, CAROLYN R. 1985. "Lethal Violence in Chicago Over Seventeen Years: Homicides Known to the Police, 1965–1981." Report to the Illinois Criminal Justice Information Authority.

BLOCK, RICHARD AND CAROLYN R. BLOCK. 1993. *Street Gang Crime in Chicago.* Research in Brief. Washington, DC: U.S. Department of Justice, National Institute of Justice.

CAMPBELL, ANNE. 1984. *The Girls in the Gang: A Report from New York City.* Oxford: Blackwell.

———.1990. "Female Participation in Gangs." Pp. 163–82 in *Gangs in America,* edited by C. R. Huff. Newbury Park, CA: Sage.

———.1991. *The Girls in the Gang,* 2nd ed. Cambridge, MA: Blackwell.

CHIN, KO-LIN. 1989. "Triad Subculture and Criminality: A Study of Triads, Tongs, and Chinese Gangs." Report to the New York City Criminal Justice Department.

CURRY, G. DAVID, ROBERT J. FOX, RICHARD A. BALL, AND DARRYL STONE. 1993. "National Assessment of Law Enforcement Anti-Gang Information Resources." Report to the U.S. Department of Justice, National Institute of Justice.

DOLAN, EDWARD R. AND SHAN FINNEY. 1984. *Youth Gangs.* New York: Simon & Schuster.

DRUG ENFORCEMENT ADMINISTRATION. 1988. "Crack Cocaine Availability and Trafficking in the United States." Washington, DC: U.S. Department of Justice, Drug Enforcement Administration.

ESBENSEN, FINN-AAGE AND DAVID HUIZINGA. 1993. "Gangs, Drugs, and Delinquency in a Survey of Urban Youth." *Criminology* 31:565–89.

FAGAN, JEFFERY. 1989. "The Social Organization of Drug Use and Drug Dealing Among Urban Gangs." *Criminology* 27:633–69.

———. 1990. "Social Process of Delinquency and Drug Use Among Urban Gangs." Pp. 183–219 in *Gangs in America,* edited by C. R. Huff. Newbury Park, CA: Sage.

GENERAL ACCOUNTING OFFICE. 1989. *Nontraditional Organized Crime.* Washington, DC: U.S. Government Printing Office.

GOLDSTEIN, ARNOLD AND C. RONALD HUFF. 1993. *The Gang Intervention Handbook.* Champaign, IL: Research Press.

HAGEDORN, JOHN M. 1988. *People and Folks: Gangs, Crime and the Underclass in a Rustbelt City.* Chicago: Lakeview.

———. 1991. "Gangs, Neighborhood, and Public Policy." Unpublished manuscript, University of Wisconsin-Milwaukee.

HARRIS, MARY G. 1988. *Cholas: Latino Girls and Gangs.* New York: AMS.

HUFF, RONALD C. 1989. "Youth Gangs and Public Policy." *Crime & Delinquency* 35:524–37.

JOHNSON, BRUCE D., TERRY WILLIAMS, KOJO DEI, AND HARRY SANABRIA. 1988. "Drug Abuse and the Inner City: Impact of Hard Drug Use and Sales on Low Income Communities." New York State Division of Substance Abuse Research.

JOHNSON, JULIE. 1989. "Drug Gangs Are Now Operating in Rural States, Justice Dept. Says." *New York Times,* August 4, p. A1.

KLEIN, MALCOLM W. 1969. "Violence in American Juvenile Gangs." Pp. 1427-60 in *Crimes of Violence,* vol. 13, edited by D. J. Mulvihill and M. M. Tumin. Washington, DC: National Commission on the Causes and Prevention of Violence.

———. Forthcoming. *The American Street Gang.* New York: Lexington Free Press.

KLEIN, MALCOLM W., CHERYL L. MAXSON, AND LEA C. CUNNINGHAM. 1991. "Crack, Street Gangs, and Violence." *Criminology* 29:623–50.

MAXSON, CHERYL L. AND MALCOLM W. KLEIN. 1990. "Street Gang Violence: Twice as Great, or Half as Great?" Pp. 71–100 in *Gangs in America,* edited by C. R. Huff. Newbury Park, CA: Sage.

———. 1993. "The Scope of Street Gang Migration in the U.S.: An Interim Report to Survey Participants." Los Angeles: University of Southern California.

MAXSON, CHERYL L., MALCOLM W. KLEIN, AND LEA C. CUNNINGHAM. 1993. "Street Gangs and Drug Sales." Report to the National Institute of Justice.

MAXSON, CHERYL L., MALCOLM W. KLEIN, AND M. A. GORDON. 1985. "Differences Between Gang and Nongang Homicides." *Criminology* 23:209–22.

MILLER, WALTER B. 1975. "Violence by Youth Gangs and Youth Groups as a Crime Problem in Major American Cities." Washington, DC: U.S. Department of Justice, Office of Juvenile Justice and Delinquency Prevention.

———. 1976. "New Federal Initiatives Re: Serious Collective Youth Crime." Pp. 262–66 in *Hearings before the Subcommittee to Investigate Juvenile Delinquency of the Committee on the Judiciary,* United States Senate, 95th Cong. 2nd Sess., April 10 and 12.

———. 1982. *Crime by Youth Gangs and Groups in the United States.* Washington, DC: U.S. Department of Justice, Office of Juvenile Justice and Delinquency Prevention. Rev. 1992.

———. 1990. "Why the United States has Failed to Solve its Youth Gang Problem." Pp. 263–87 in *Gangs in America,* edited by C. R. Huff. Newbury Park, CA: Sage.

———. 1994. "Boston Assaultive Crime." Memorandum: Author.

NEEDLE, JEROME AND W. VAUGHAN STAPLETON. 1983. *Police Handling of Youth Gangs.* Washington, DC: U.S. Department of Justice, Office of Juvenile Justice and Delinquency Prevention.

PHILIBOSIAN, ROBERT H. 1989. "Report of the State Task Force on Gangs and Drugs." Report to the California Department of Justice.

QUICKER, JOHN C. 1981. "Seven Decades of Gangs." Report to the California Commission on Crime Control and Violence Prevention.

RAND, ALICE. 1987. "Transitional Life Events and Desistence From Delinquency and Crime." Pp. 134–62 in *From Boy to Man, From Delinquency to Crime,* edited by M. E. Wolfgang, T. Thornberry, and R. M. Figlio. Chicago: University of Chicago Press.

ROSENBAUM, DENNIS P. AND LANE A. GRANT. 1983. "Gangs and Youth Problems in Evanston." Center for Urban Affairs, Northwestern University.

SKOLNICK, JEROME H. 1988. "The Social Structure of Street Drug Dealing." Unpublished manuscript, University of California, Berkeley.

———. 1989. "Gang Organization and Migration—Drugs, Gangs, and Law Enforcement." Unpublished manuscript, University of California, Berkeley.

SPERGEL, IRVING A. 1983. "Violent Gangs in Chicago: Segmentation and Integration." Unpublished manuscript, University of Chicago.

————. 1990. "Youth Gangs: Continuity and Change." Pp. 171–275 in *Crime and Justice: A Review of Research*, vol. 12, edited by M. Tonry and N. Morris. Chicago: University of Chicago Press.

————. 1991. "Youth Gangs: Problem and Response." Report to the U.S. Department of Justice, Office of Juvenile Justice and Delinquency Prevention.

————. 1992. "Youth Gangs: An Essay Review." *Social Service Review* 66:121–40.

SPERGEL, IRVING A., RONALD CHANCE, KENNETH EHRENSAFT, THOMAS REGULUS, CANDICE KANE, ROBERT LASETER, ALBA ALEXANDER, AND SANDRA OH. 1991. "Executive Summary: Models." Report to the U.S. Department of Justice, Office of Juvenile Justice and Delinquency Prevention.

SPERGEL, IRVING A. AND G. DAVID CURRY. 1993. "The National Youth Gang Survey: A Research and Development Process." Pp. 359–400 in *The Gang Intervention Handbook*, edited by A. Goldstein and C. R. Huff. Champaign, IL: Research Press.

TAYLOR, CARL S. 1990. "Gang Imperialism." Pp. 103–15 in *Gangs in America*, edited by C. R. Huff. Newbury Park: Sage.

THORNBERRY, TERENCE P., MARVIN D. KROHN, ALAN J. LIZOTTE, AND DEBORAH CHARD-WIERSCHEM. 1993. "The Role of Juvenile Gangs in Facilitating Delinquent Behavior." *Journal of Research in Crime and Delinquency* 30:55–87.

VIGIL, JAMES D. 1988. *Barrio Gangs*. Austin: University of Texas Press.

WILSON, JOHN J. AND JAMES C. HOWELL. 1993. *A Comprehensive Strategy for Serious, Violent and Chronic Juvenile Offenders*. Washington, DC: U.S. Department of Justice, Office of Juvenile Justice and Delinquency Prevention.

ZIMRING, FRANKLIN. 1981. "Kids, Groups and Crime: Some Implications of a Well-Known Secret." *Journal of Criminal Law and Criminology* 72:867–85.

NOTES

JAMES C. HOWELL: Director of Research and Program Development, Office of Juvenile Justice and Delinquency Prevention (OJJDP), in the U.S. Department of Justice. He has recently headed OJJDP's Gangs Task Force, charged with responsibility for developing a comprehensive youth gang program for the office. His current interests extend more broadly to encompass other forms of serious, violent, and chronic juvenile crime. He recently authored, with John J. Wilson, *A Comprehensive Strategy for Serious, Violent, and Chronic Juvenile Offenders*, published by the U.S. Department of Justice. This publication is available free of charge from the Juvenile Justice Clearinghouse (800-638-8736).

The author is indebted to Don Gibbons for his extremely detailed editorial review and substantive contributions. Other reviewers who were very helpful include Barry Krisberg, Rolf Loeber, Walter Miller, Joan McCord, Malcolm Klein, Cheryl Maxson, and Irving Spergel. The views expressed in this article are those of the author and do not necessarily represent the official policies or positions of the U.S. Department of Justice.

QUESTIONS FOR DISCUSSION

1. What were the major findings of Miller's national survey with respect to:
   —the social characteristics of gang members
   —criminal activity
   —weaponry

2. Discuss the major findings of Spergel's survey on "responses to gangs."

3. A major concern in our society is the migration of gangs to new communities where there has been no previous gang activity. What accounts for this migration?

4. List and discuss Howell's recommendations for effectively curtailing gang activity.

APPLICATIONS

1. Visit your local police department and ask about the prevalence of gang activity in your community. What reasons do law enforcement personnel give for the absence or presence of gang activity? Do they believe gang activity migrated to the community? If so, how?

2. Given your knowledge and/or experience of gangs, what recommendation would you make to reduce gang activity?

KEY TERMS

autonomous self-governing or directed.

contextual refers to a condition or circumstance that affects some occurrence or condition.

genesis origin or where something was created.

plethora a great quantity or variety.

posits to set into context or assume.

promulgated made publicly known; proclaimed.

19
Players and Ho's

Terry Williams

William Kornblum

I don't exactly fill out a W2 form after I turn a trick.—*Margo Sharp*

Cooksey's, D's Inferno, Club 437, McDonald's, and the mall are familiar hangouts for teenagers in Louisville. The mall is located in downtown Louisville; although it is integrated, it is a meeting place for black youth from all over the city. Many of the teenagers hustle in the pool rooms and discos, peddling marijuana and sex.

For the young women, hustling is synonymous with prostitution. Indeed, in all the cities we studied, prostitution is the main occupation for girls in the underground economy—girls like Donna White, who hustles in Louisville's mall area.

I am 19 years old. About two years ago my parents moved to a little town called Madisonville, Kentucky. I hated that place. But I stayed long enough to finish school at Norman Hopkins [High School]. I wanted to go places and see different things and not stay in that damn place. I wanted to make something out of myself so I left

"Players and Ho's," *Growing Up Poor* (New York: Lexington Books, 1985), pp. 61–72. Reprinted by permission of Lexington Books, an imprint of Macmillan Publishing Company. Copyright © 1985 by Lexington Books.

and came here to Louisville. I couldn't find no job for nine months here so I met up with some friends who told me I could hustle and make some money. They said they would show me how. All I had to do was learn.

So I first started hustling in the pool rooms and pushing a few petty drugs. My boyfriend and/or his friend would stand in the pool room or out in the hall and wait till they saw some men, soldiers, businessmen, or whatever, and ask them if they wanted to have some sex. If they said yes, he would steer them over to the pool room and then tell me where to go meet them.

In the Hough district of Cleveland, dilapidated, burned-out structures from the 1960s riots are still visible. The housing consists mainly of single-family units. It is odd to see so many old houses, many in the grand style, decaying, unpainted, and broken. Hough is the ghetto of Cleveland. Its citizens, black and white alike, seem helpless to change it. The community is bankrupt economically, politically, and socially. Many feel that Hough is being punished for the "sins" it committed in the 1960s.

Pearl Varnedoe has worked as a prostitute in the Hough area and downtown near the University of Cleveland since she was fourteen. Pearl left home in order to "make money and live free." She says hustling came easily to her because "my parents had a club that always had pimps, whores, and gamblers in it."

> My mother was always beating me. My father tried to make her stop but he couldn't. My mother was always drunk and she couldn't stop that either. My father ran this after-hours club and when I left home I met up with some of them from his joint and they turned me out [set me up as a prostitute]. I always had real big titties and a nice body. As a matter of fact, the vice squad know me on sight and arrest me sometimes just to have something to do. I've been arrested about 21 times. They never knew I was a minor during all the time I spent there. When I went home to check on my father, I found out my mother had been beating my brothers and sisters too. Our neighbor had called in a child-abuse worker to talk to her, she told me she knew about my being on the street and filed a delinquency report with the juvenile authorities.

In Meridian, Mississippi, a large naval base on the outskirts of town has created a thriving market for drugs and sex. Thus the young people in Meridian perceive numerous opportunities in the illegal economy. The young men between the ages of 16 and 20 are the players or pimps, and the young women between the ages of 13 and 20 are the prostitutes—making prostitution the main source of illegal income for youths. Teenagers like Curly and his girls make up the "supply side" of prostitution in Meridian.

Curly is eighteen years old. His hustle is young women. He's a "player" and they are "ho's" or "tricks." (In Meridian "trick" refers to the prostitute or seller of sex; in New York the converse is true—"trick" refers to the buyer of sex.)

> I have one or two girls on the street. I still got a couple of them doing things for me. You know I gotta have that paper [money]. The only rule I have is that my main lady don't go out there. The others I have them boosting, tricking, whatever, as long as they keep giving up the money. See, baby, you do what you have to do to survive in this world now. The more money they have, the more I have. They do what they want to to get it. And when I ask them for it, I get it. Sometimes I'll help out if I get hip to someone who wants

to make a buy. I'll let them know. But it depends on how much they get and how much I need. But I don't take all of their money. I usually leave them a little. And I don't feel I'm responsible for putting no ho on the street. Look, they are out there trying to be grown. They put themselves out there. If I didn't take their money, they would give it to someone else. Them tricks ain't gonna be nothing but whores. All I did was fuck them a couple of times and they started giving me money. See, a woman doesn't have to sell her body for a man to pimp her. There are plenty of women that are smart and pretty with good jobs and taking care of men. That's pimping.

Among Curly's "tricks" are Maylee Jones, Clara Thompson, and Dorothea Caddy, aged sixteen, sixteen, and seventeen, respectively. Here's what they have to say about "the life":

> *Maylee*: There ain't no jobs around here. Besides I can make more money doing this. Sometimes I make one hundred or two, sometimes more, sometimes less. If I had a job, I wouldn't make that much. If I could make as much money in a job as I do hustling, I would work. The Navy boys they spend a lot of money. All these old white men do too. Anyway around here they give all the good jobs to the white people.
> The most important thing in my life right now is surviving. That's all I believe in. Well, I believe in God but not preachers 'cause all the preachers do is ride around in Cadillacs and wear silk suits.
> *Clara*: I have four boyfriends who give me $15 a week to go to bed with them. I only go out with one of them. The money I get I just spend it on clothes and stuff to get high with. I don't like to do it too much. I think it might do something to me. All the men are young, in their 20s. I give them a bit here and there but they give me the money on time. I like to show my legs and breast. It fascinates me to watch men cream.
> *Dorothea*: I started tricking because I didn't know what time it was. I was at a friend's house getting high and they said, hey, you want to turn a trick for someone? And I said, it depends on the cash, what time, and who. At that time, I needed the money, you know. My boyfriend was there and I didn't know he was no pimp. But he kept encouraging me to do it. Anyway, after that I set my own thing up with one of my girlfriends. I have them [johns] call her. I used to have them call my pimp till I got rid of him. He got mad, but he knew I could fight him if he tried some

shit like hitting on me. I didn't need him any-more, you know. I only had him for protection and the first time I went to jail for fighting, the man was out of town. I would make $150 or so and put $75 back and show him the rest, and he would give me $25 of that plus what I had, you know. He didn't know what time it was.

Dorothea dropped out of school in the ninth grade. At seventeen she organized a group of teenage prostitutes and set up a brothel in a fashionable black section of town.

Young women in each of these cities—and in New York as well—are shocked and depressed by the bleakness of their situation. Many do not believe they have a choice between getting a job and hustling. Hustling—meaning prosti-tution—is the only choice. (Theft and prosti-tution are often combined, but prostitution is by far the easiest, most convenient, and most profitable form of illegal activity for these teenagers.)

Most girls are recruited into prostitution, but some are tricked, coerced, or charmed into the life. The latter are talked into believing that it is an exciting life complete with fine cars and endless amounts of money. There is a note of self-delusion in some of their comments, like "A lot of the men are lonely and I feel I can help them" or "Most of the time the tricks don't know what time it is, so you can get their money."

While there are adult role models and com-munity institutions that try to steer teenagers away from the life, many find the incentives too strong. Margo Sharp's life as a prostitute in Harlem illustrates the careers young women pursue in the underground economy.

Margo's parents separated when she was four years old. Her mother remarried, and dur-ing the ensuing years her father made sporadic appearances. When Margo was twelve or thir-teen her mother became embroiled in domes-tic problems with her stepfather. Arguments and fights were common. Margo's mother began to have relationships with other men, including some of her husband's friends. One of those men had a traumatic impact on Margo.

My mother had an affair with this man who was later to become my stepfather. Well, he had this friend, best friend no less, who was this little horny Dominican motherfucker. I was 12 years old then and I knew about sex and all of that, although I had never had sex. He would come around the house all the time and even though my mother was seeing my stepfather, this guy would come over some-times and they would laugh and drink and my stepfather would leave them alone sometimes because he trusted his friend so much. Well, my mother and this little Dominican started to have a thing behind my stepfather's back. And this little motherfucker was so horny, he wound up fucking my mother's best friend too.

Anyhow, one day I was upstairs doing my homework and he comes into my room and tells me he wants to talk to me. I don't remember if anybody was home or not that day, but I assumed he was gonna talk about my mother and their lit-tle thing, you know. So he told me to sit on the bed next to him. And I did. Still not thinking any-thing about it. Well the next thing I know he's taking my blouse off. And all the time he's ask-ing me if I feel anything. Well I don't know why I didn't scream or anything but I just sat there. After he had taken off my panties, the only thought I had in my mind was not to panic. Not to scream because I had read all about how men had killed women and kids molesting them or something, and I wasn't about to say a thing. So he took off my panties and the only thing that stood out in my mind was how big he was. It seemed like he was as big as a tree trunk, I swear to God, I was hurting so bad, I was so sore. I felt, my God, what did he do to me? Well, when it was over, he helped me put back on my clothes and I sat on the bed for a long time just thinking.

I never told my mother anything for two years. And when I did her reaction was typical of women in love. She slapped me. She thought I was lying for years after I told her this. She didn't believe nothing I told her. One day two years later this little bastard drove up to my house to see my mother. Well my mother told me to come out and say hello to him. But I was not too excited about seeing the little fucker ever again. So I refused. But she insisted so I went out to say hello. But when I saw his face I just got angry. The win-dow of the car door was down. And he reached his face out to kiss me and I spat in it. My mother jerked me away and slapped me. But I grabbed her arm and told her I was no kid any more. I was 14 years old and that she had no reason to protect a man who had not only cheated on her by fucking her friend but had cheated on her by fucking her daughter. She didn't believe me. Like I said, she thought I was lying. She was so in love with this faggot that she didn't believe her own daughter. I hated him for that more than his act against me because it made my relationship with my mother a stormy one for years to come.

Margo was fourteen then. Her mother was unwilling to assume responsibility for her wayward daughter, so she sent Margo to a social worker at the Children's Aid Society. After a series of bad experiences in a variety of schools, Margo finally dropped out. Considered gifted by her teachers, she could not make herself sit still long enough to complete her studies. Instead, she was habitually absent. Her lateness and absenteeism eventually resulted in expulsion.

Margo's attitudes about men were formed early. She was more game than most men could handle. Standing tall and shapely with big eyes and a warm, inquisitive intelligence, she was no child and knew it. After leaving school, she refused to work but always seemed to have money. Her mother occasionally asked her how she was able to get along without working, but Margo always had an explanation.

> I would have $200, $300, $400 and my mother knew nothing about it. I wouldn't tell her where I had been. So half the time she didn't know. I didn't buy a lot of stuff or give her money because I was afraid she would ask me where I got it from. I tried to explain it to her one day. I told her a friend of hers, Mr. George, who was about 50 years old had hinted he wanted to have sex with me. So I jokingly told my mom that if he wanted it, it would cost him a hundred bucks. Well, she laughed and said, "Yeah, that's better than giving it to him for free." So in a way, I guess, she didn't really object to what I was doing.

By the time Margo was fifteen she was involved in casual prostitution, averaging two hundred dollars per customer. She was in the life as an "outlaw," that is, without benefit of a pimp. Her method was bit unorthodox. When a man approached her, she would take the money from the transaction and give it to one of her male friends.

Sometimes my friend would look at me funny when I told him to hold the cash. It would be a few hundred dollars. And that I would be back later. I would go to a hotel and after it was over I'd go back to pick up my money. If a guy approached me and said I was beautiful and asked how much would it cost him to have me, I would tell him whatever came to my mind. If he looked well dressed and clean I would say $200, $300, $400. It depended on my mood. If I was real horny, I would react quicker but that didn't mean the price went down. I would just choose someone who I thought was good looking. Someone who I thought would be pleasant to fuck. Sometimes I would get off with these guys but most of the time I would pretend.

At least some liked it enough to pay high prices for it. It started out with offers of $100 or more for an hour or two. When they first started asking me I would decline, and then decided to stop being such a fool. I started accepting, not only money, but gifts, trips, etc. It was sort of like getting your cake and eating it too. I was not only compensated for time, but I was spent time with as well. The sexual acts were sexual acts. But if they brought on a smile, a kiss or hug the morning after, it was worthwhile. I felt not only wanted but needed. At the same time, a lot of lonely hearts were warmed. Call it what you will, I see my actions in a benevolent light. I enjoyed the money, spending highly, indulging in things I wouldn't normally have. The gifts were sweet. They showed a touch more of consideration. The men were usually much older than myself. I, in some cases, portrayed a prized china doll that they flaunted.

Yes, I did get tired of the life at times, but it was an experience, and I learned a lot. I met some very interesting people. I always tried to establish a good rapport with my friends. One never knows who one may need some day. But only as friends. My intimate relationships were always kept separate and never came about from a trick night. It was difficult at times having both a main man and my pastime, but I managed. In some cases, where I felt the person I was dealing with was due more respect, I would cool off my friendly encounters and devote myself to that one person.

For young women like Margo, prostitution becomes a distinctive lifestyle, known as "the life." But for the pimps or players, hustling sex isn't very different from any other kind of hustle. The young man usually has tried a variety of ways of earning money, finally settling on pimping as involving the least effort for the greatest reward. Ray-Ray Southern is typical.

I came to Meridian when I was 11 years old. I went to Oakland Heights Elementary School in the fifth grade. I got along very well with the teachers. We caught the city bus every day to school. I got out of school one day by playing sick and stole a bicycle. I had to go by the babysitter's house to pick up my little sister and brother. They were very happy to see me. My momma came home by the babysitter's house and found out about the bicycle. She asked me where it was and I told her somewhere else, but I didn't know where. Momma took me home and whipped me. The police came and talked to me and we got over that.

About three weeks later our house caught on fire. My sister was smoking a cigarette and threw the butt on the floor. After the fire, we changed schools and I met the wrong type of friends. I had a fight the first day of school. Later on, I stole another bicycle and I didn't get caught. I began to turn out with this girl I was running with. We would do things like stealing, smoking, drinking, and breaking out people's windows.

Everything was happening to me then. My girlfriend and I got caught in the act of love making. My mother was very upset. She wanted to whip me but my dad talked her out of it. She was upset because she didn't know I knew too much about sex. My mother talked to us about it but I wasn't listening. I liked what I was doing. After a few more incidents, we broke up because of her mother. So I met another girl. I was going over there every day. I was going to school but I would play hooky with her. We didn't stay together because all she wanted was sex. The first day of the next term I was kissing this girl and they said I had to go. This happened too many times. So I left because there was too many rules anyhow. You couldn't hold hands, you couldn't talk to white girls, etc.

I got into trouble again and this time they sent me to Columbia Training School. I was there for four months and two weeks. Three months later I was in more trouble—breaking and entering. I got some items out and sold them to the wrong person. I had to go back to the juvenile center. I was out one day and the next one I was in.

I got a job when I got out working at Morrison's [Restaurant] as a cook. But at $1.95 an hour,

that's bullshit. At Morrison's they thought they had a real nigger working 'cause I really tried to keep that job. But that damn man [boss] was crazy. He started bitching with me. Now he knows a cook don't wash no damn dishes. I wouldn't do that shuffling routine, so I quit. I started stealing hams and making some money. I would take my girlfriend with me to the supermarket and I'd have a box underneath the cart. We'd walk around filling the box with steaks, pork chops, hams, chickens, all kinds of shit. I'd have tape in my pocket and some stamps with rope. This is so it would look like a package. That don't never fail to work. I'd steal about $1,500 worth of meat and sell it for $800. Sometimes I buy a little weed to sell. I pay $45 for an ounce or $150 for a pound and make more than $300 every three or four days. All I want is a Cadillac, two tons of weed, five pounds of crystal T, a nice house, and be financially well off. I would much rather work than hustle because working is steady. When you work you know where the money is coming from.

We did not find any consistent pattern in the backgrounds of young men who become pimps. Husbands, boyfriends, and transient players all play the role. Young boys sometimes identify with the player image—New York players set standards of dress and lifestyle that are widely imitated—but in most cases the motivation is economic necessity. Frances H., a close observer of the street scene in Meridian, described the situation of teenage pimps in this southern town as follows:

It's not that all these kids want to be players or hustlers. The first thing you think is they don't want to work. That's misleading. Most of them, and I mean the major portion of them, have tried at one time or another to get a job. They have beat down the doors of the unemployment offices. They have been in these stores, dealing with all these crackers who constantly make wisecracks and comments about how dumb they are and stuff like that. And they, rightly so, get tired of it. Then they come back out here on the street and say, "Fuck it. I'll make it any way I can. I'll be a player. I'll be a hustler. I'll be cool. I'll be clean." They want to have that paper. Just like everybody else does. You can't tell 'em they don't know what time it is because they think they do. So it ain't like they ain't tried. It's just that they got tired of all the bullshit. A lot of what this is about is discrimination. It's prejudice against these kids. Them young white boys can go to daddy and say, "I need a job" or "I need money" and get it. But these black kids have to kiss ass and then be told, "Ain't no jobs for you, nigger boy." So you know it ain't about not wanting to work.

The experiences of young people in other regions of the country reveal few differences in lifestyle and some basic similarities in values and outlook toward their immediate future. Most teenagers in the underground economy, regardless of region, maintain the traditional values of work, money, and success. Although these are limited commodities, the youths are as desperate in their search as anyone else.

One thing is clear—teenagers like Ray-Ray will more often than not find illegal opportunities more attractive than legal ones. Those who have had negative experiences in the work place, no matter how brief, will move on to the underground economy and try to forge an identity there. Ray-Ray, however, is the first to admit that he is not going to get rich stealing meat, selling marijuana, or even pimping.

Some teenage hustlers do manage to find jobs. But often they leave within a few months because the demands of the job appear to be too great, especially when hustling seems to offer an easier life. Here's what Margo has to say about her brief career in the nine-to-five world:

> If you're the type that can never be without a job, not having one may cause a problem. I'm not that type. I can live with or without one. I've never been one to worry about work. Occasionally I might find myself in a jam, but I believe things work themselves out and they usually do. Not working doesn't bother me so much as having to do that regular nine to five. I hate straight hours, time clocks and suspicious bosses. I enjoy not having to deal with the same environment and people within that structure on a daily basis. That type of contact, being constant, tires me. I love to free-lance. I enjoy change in work situations. I'm trying other ways to make money, not necessarily legal ways, and I'm open to ideas.
>
> Not working steadily, I will admit, causes problems for me. Because the cash flow isn't there all the time. Naturally I will find other ways to make up for this lack of money, but the market isn't

> always open to me. When I say this, I'm speaking of the people I may be with at that particular time in my life, or my access to the street. Making illegal money is a whole different scene. It's part of what I categorized before as free-lancing. Some examples of free-lancing would be anything from hocking your personal property or someone else's, to dealing drugs or selling yourself, borrowing, mediating, touting, you know. If you can do any of these and hold down a tax-paying job, you're alright. But if you can keep this life up and survive from it alone, you're doing better.
>
> One thing about prostitution, it's a tax-free job. The risk is the thrill. I feel one has to be adventurous, daring, and mischievous to a point. The first thing one has to keep in mind is that you're going to get caught. Not by the authorities, no! That's the last thing in my mind. When I say get caught, I mean by the street. If you're dealing in anything against the law, you always have heavy competition. If your game is good, people want to tear it down. It's a constant battle in the streets for survival. There is a lot of planning, scheming, lying, cheating, and a little bit of fear out there. The fear has to be natural or you're doomed. You have to love danger.
>
> I hate what society considers normal. So I find other ways of living within this world, without letting it bother me. If it bothers others, that's their problem. Every man for himself. When it comes to money you will find very few are going to help you make it. And if you're the type that helps others, you'll find yourself taken for a sucker. So you resign to helping yourself. The advantages of this street business, hustling, it's on you. You wake up, eat, sleep, you don't punch no clocks, you don't conform to no rules and regulations or courtesy to co-workers, customers, bosses, clients, patients, staff, etc. Best of all, you don't pay taxes either.

Margo's work history includes both legitimate and illegitimate roles. Although she possesses the skills to work in a mainstream occupation, she has not developed the discipline to remain in a job very long. This is partly a result of immaturity. However, it is a well-known fact that few teenagers maintain jobs for more than a few months at a time. It is Margo's street and family values that have kept her at odds with the straight world. Her forays into the regular workaday routine are always of short duration because there is more money to be made on the streets. There is always an available market of older men who will buy her services, yet she sees the weakness of her own game. She knows that a prostitute's life—even a high-class call girl's life—is a short one. She knows she won't always have a youthful face and body. And when things get tough—for instance, after a brutal trick—she looks for work in a regular job. Margo sees no discernible difference between her straightout prostitution and what other women do as secretaries or as wives at home.

Margo's views are not shared by the parents and friends of most of the teenage prostitutes we met. There appears to be a double standard operating in this area: the pimps/players are seen as smooth, slick, and smart, the girls as stupid and dirty. Feelings of revulsion and pity were expressed by some of the parents, while others did not seem to know or care what their children were doing. Many of the girls turned to prostitution after becoming pregnant and being rejected by their boyfriends and parents.

Once a girl enters the life, ties with family and friends are usually broken. It is common practice for a pimp to insist that his girls sever all such relationships. Independent prostitutes like Margo may maintain contact with their friends but tend not to explain to them what they do for a living.

In addition to the availability of prostitution as an option and the perceived disadvantages of straight jobs, certain experiences during childhood and adolescence can lead to a career in prostitution. Rose M. of Hough is a case in point.

> Things were okay at home until I turned 13. I moved out when I turned 13 and quit school. My stepfather and I couldn't get along any more. I kept moving in and out until I was 15. My mother didn't mind because I always let her know where I was and went by to see her when my stepfather was at work. I didn't have to worry about supporting myself then. When I was 14 I got put on probation for not going to school. At 15, when my mother died, my stepfather sent my sister and myself down south to stay with our real father. I didn't like my father so I came back to Cleveland to stay with a friend. I was getting a social security check from my father so I had money.
> The girl I was staying with worked the streets.

> She was only 16. I didn't have to but I started working with her. It was scary but it was a living. I grew up very fast in the streets. I shot dope but I never got hooked. At 16 I got pregnant and left my man. I went to the Safe Space Station, a runaway shelter. The people were really nice. They tried to help, but I was used to being on my own. So I went back to my man and worked until I was seven months. I also shot dope while I was pregnant. The dope only made my baby small.
> We moved from place to place after that. Then my stepfather had me put in D.H. and tried to take my baby. I stayed there for ten days, then went to a child-care center for three weeks. I turned 17 in there. The court placed me in the custody of the county. My social worker took me down and got me on welfare. Before that I was still turning tricks. I still worked some even though I was on welfare and got social security because I wasn't used to getting money once a month. I still moved from place to place. My son has never had a stable home until now, and he'll be two next month.
> Now I'm 18 and I'm three months pregnant. One thing I promised myself, with this baby I'm not going to go through the things I went through with the first. I feel I have an advantage over most people my age and older because I know and have experienced things they'll never know. The only disadvantage is I don't have as much interest in men like I had. My pimp beat me up and tried to make me have an abortion. But I ran away from him because I was tired of the streets and let myself get pregnant on purpose. I know I wasn't forced to get into the life. Because I used to do it a lot with my girlfriends after school to get money to buy extra clothes. When my mother would ask me where I got the clothes from I would tell her I exchanged them with friends. After my mom died and I wasn't going to my stepfather's anymore, I lived with the rest of the girls at my pimp's stable.

For some teenage girls, incestuous relationships with their fathers and encounters with pimps at school may have started them on the road to prostitution. Kate Strolls is a seventeen-year-old dropout who moved away from home after a series of incidents with her father.

> I dropped out of school in the ninth grade. At this point I have no interest in going back. I used to live in the Woodland Projects apartments. It was ugly as hell. It had all these empty houses,

old buildings, and winos everywhere. I first hooked up with this pimp at school. I started turning tricks in the afternoon and bringing some of the money home to my mother. She took the money and never asked me where I got it from. She just told me not to get myself killed.

My father moved away after we, my sister and me, got together and told my mother that he had been having sex with both of us and then threatening to kill us if we told anybody. I feel okay about the whole thing but my sister turned real mean and won't talk to nobody. She has no friends and stays at home with my brother even though she is old enough to be on her own. I don't feel that way about men. I just don't develop feelings for them when I'm working. And I prefer to be with women anyhow.

I had this woman stop me one night down on Prospect and give me $100 to go with her. I was scared but, shit, I figured I could outfight the broad if it got too crazy. She had this nice place to stay and all this nice furniture and a man. She turned me out that night.

For many young women, a crucial factor is the lifestyles of the adult women who are closest to them. This was the case for Margo. Her adult role models were her mother, her aunt, and a very close friend of her mother who was active in civil rights, all of whom were rebels and fought private battles at home or public battles against society. Unlike many of the other girls in our study, Margo had a relatively stable home and social environment. She had opportunities to travel, to attend school and do well. But the examples set by her family, her early experiences, and the complexities of her own personality led her to choose the fast life. There is no doubt that young women like Margo could lead successful lives in a professional career were it not for one or two incidents that shaped their life patterns. As she herself explains:

As a baby, not from what I recall, but only hearsay, I was alert, smart, too fast for my britches, and loved to party and drink. One might say that I haven't changed a bit. I was walking at the age of six months, but didn't let go of my bottle till around four years. I was a year old and one still couldn't tell whether I was a girl or a boy, since I still had not grown hair. There was no way to add

ribbons, bows or clips to my scalp. So I spent my first year as a child with an undefined sexuality. At eight months my mom was fed up with me, so I say. She claims that it was in my best interest for her to have sent me to my grandparents in South America. This was for a period of three years. I've been told that as a toddler, I spoke too much, knew too much, ate too much, and never liked going to bed on time. I was spoiled, having been the first granddaughter, and yet was very charming and lovable.

At 3 ½, I was sent back home to my mother, who by this time I'd forgotten. This, of course, was after having traveled throughout South America and the Virgin Islands. I wish they would have saved those trips now. I arrived at Kennedy International Airport via Avianca Airlines, escorted by my aunt, and was received by everyone from a to z that was a member of my family or knew someone in it.

My room was filled with an accumulation of toys over the past three years. Most of them I still have. One that I loved in particular was a teddy bear named Moy-Moy. He used to be white and fluffy, nowadays he is skinned of all his hair, dyed and ripped. One of the dolls I used to have was four feet tall. Now I was a tiny 3 ½-year-old, so you can imagine in comparison to me this thing was a giant. Sometimes I honestly feel that parents are not practical. An example is that by the time I was five, my father, whom I rarely saw, had given me a collection of dolls from all different nations. By the time I was seven, the collection was destroyed. To this day, my mother still curses me out over it and calls me irresponsible.

I may sound ungrateful, but I'm really not. I really can't complain about my childhood. It's my teen years that I hated the most. I knew my real father as the man who came to give me money, or to take me shopping to buy things. He was very well off and he proved it to me. But I didn't want his fucking money. He deprived me of his presence. He deprived me of his love. What is money to try and replace that? I'll tell ya, it ain't shit. So I threw all of that in his face. I guess that's why he's been so reluctant to contact me now. He knows I hate what he did. All my life I've had negative feelings about my father due to the fact that in my eyes his time was too precious to spend with me. All these years I've denied ever having needed him, loved him, missed him, or wanting him. Now I wonder. I remember when I was real small. He would come in, pick me up, and put me on his shoulders. You see, my father was real tall and skinny and when he would lift me up, it seemed like—oh God—it was to the ceiling. It seemed so high to me. But I would hold my breath and close my eyes and in a few seconds I was on top of the world.

Teenage prostitutes, and the men who exploit them, have developed a negative self-image and considerable hostility toward members of the opposite sex. They are at risk of remaining in the criminal subculture as adults, and if they do not find better role models and opportunities that is the most likely prognosis. But these teenagers, street wise and cynical as they are, are not "lost" or "fallen," even though they may think of themselves in such terms. Timely intervention by caring adults could counteract the experiences that led them into prostitution and could guide them onto more constructive paths to maturity.

QUESTIONS FOR DISCUSSION

1. What motivated these young people to engage in prostitution and/or pimping? Were the motivations the same for the women as for men? If yes, in what ways?

2. Margo saw no difference between prostitution and what other women do as secretaries or wives. Why?

3. The authors suggest that teenage prostitutes and the men who exploit them have a negative self-image and hostility toward members of the opposite sex. Do you agree? Why? Cite examples from this article to support your response.

APPLICATIONS

1. Based on what you have read, what kinds of changes in the social environment might we make to curtail teenage prostitution?

2. If you had an opportunity to talk with Margo about her "life style," what would you tell her to encourage her to make positive changes away from prostitution? (Remember that you and she are more than likely from very different social settings and experiences.)

KEY TERMS

benevolent marked by good will or disposed to doing good for others.

commodity an economic good or product.

foray to make a raid or an invasion for the purpose of obtaining spoils or others' possessions.

revulsion a sense of utter distaste or repugnance.

self-delusion a persistent false belief regarding oneself; often results in a bizarre or distorted perception of reality.

underground economy an unofficial, unsanctioned, or illegal system of exchanging goods and services.

20

The Saints
and the Roughnecks

William J. Chambliss

Eight promising young men—children of good, stable, white upper-middle-class families, active in school affairs, good pre-college students—were some of the most delinquent boys at Hanibal High School. While community residents and parents knew that these boys occasionally sowed a few wild oats, they were totally unaware that sowing wild oats completely occupied the daily routine of these young men. The Saints were constantly occupied with truancy, drinking, wild driving, petty theft and vandalism. Yet not one was officially arrested for any misdeed during the two years I observed them.

This record was particularly surprising in light of my observations during the same two years of another gang of Hanibal High School students, six lower-class white boys known as the Roughnecks. The Roughnecks were constantly in trouble with police and community even though their rate of delinquency was about equal with that of the Saints. What was the cause of this disparity? The result? The following consideration of the activities, social class and community perceptions of both gangs may provide some answers.

"The Saints and the Roughnecks," *Society*, 11:11 (November–December 1973), pp. 24–31. Reprinted by permission of the author and publisher. Copyright © 1973 by Transaction Publishing.

THE SAINTS FROM MONDAY TO FRIDAY

The Saints' principal daily concern was with getting out of school as early as possible. The boys managed to get out of school with minimum danger that they would be accused of playing hooky through an elaborate procedure for obtaining "legitimate" release from class. The most common procedure was for one boy to obtain the release of another by fabricating a meeting of some committee, program or recognized club. Charles might raise his hand in his 9:00 chemistry class and ask to be excused— a euphemism for going to the bathroom. Charles would go to Ed's math class and inform the teacher that Ed was needed for a 9:30 rehearsal of the drama club play. The math teacher would recognize Ed and Charles as "good students" involved in numerous school activities and would permit Ed to leave at 9:30. Charles would return to his class, and Ed would go to Tom's English class to obtain his release. Tom would engineer Charles' escape. The strategy would continue until as many of the Saints as possible were freed. After a stealthy trip to the car (which had been parked in a strategic spot), the boys were off for a day of fun.

Over the two years I observed the Saints, this pattern was repeated nearly every day. There were variations on the theme, but in one form

291

or another, the boys used this procedure for getting out of class and then off the school grounds. Rarely did all eight of the Saints manage to leave school at the same time. The average number avoiding school on the days I observed them was five.

Having escaped from the concrete corridors the boys usually went either to a pool hall on the other (lower-class) side of town or to a cafe in the suburbs. Both places were out of the way of people the boys were likely to know (family or school officials), and both provided a source of entertainment. The pool hall entertainment was the generally rough atmosphere, the occasional hustler, the sometimes drunk proprietor and, of course, the game of pool. The cafe's entertainment was provided by the owner. The boys would "accidentally" knock a glass on the floor or spill cola on the counter—not all the time, but enough to be sporting. They would also bend spoons, put salt in sugar bowls and generally tease whoever was working in the cafe. The owner had opened the cafe recently and was dependent on the boys' business which was, in fact, substantial since between the horsing around and the teasing they bought food and drinks.

THE SAINTS ON WEEKENDS

On weekends the automobile was even more critical than during the week, for on weekends the Saints went to Big Town—a large city with a population of over a million 25 miles from Hanibal. Every Friday and Saturday night most of the Saints would meet between 8:00 and 8:30 and would go into Big Town. Big Town activities included drinking heavily in taverns or nightclubs, driving drunkenly through the streets, and committing acts of vandalism and playing pranks.

By midnight on Fridays and Saturdays the Saints were usually thoroughly high, and one or two of them were often so drunk they had to be carried to the cars. Then the boys drove around town, calling obscenities to women and girls; occasionally trying (unsuccessfully so far as I could tell) to pick girls up; and driving recklessly through red lights and at high speeds with their lights out. Occasionally they played

"chicken." One boy would climb out the back window of the car and across the roof to the driver's side of the car while the car was moving at high speed (between 40 and 50 miles an hour); then the driver would move over and the boy who had just crawled across the car roof would take the driver's seat.

Searching for "fair game" for a prank was the boys' principal activity after they left the tavern. The boys would drive alongside a foot patrolman and ask directions to some street. If the policeman leaned on the car in the course of answering the question, the driver would speed away, causing him to lose his balance. The Saints were careful to play this prank only in an area where they were not going to spend much time and where they could quickly disappear around a corner to avoid having their license plate number taken.

Construction sites and road repair areas were the special province of the Saints' mischief. A soon-to-be repaired hole in the road inevitably invited the Saints to remove lanterns and wooden barricades and put them in the car, leaving the hole unprotected. The boys would find a safe vantage point and wait for an unsuspecting motorist to drive into the hole. Often, though not always, the boys would go up to the motorist and commiserate with him about the dreadful way the city protected its citizenry.

Leaving the scene of the open hole and the motorist, the boys would then go searching for an appropriate place to erect the stolen barricade. An "appropriate place" was often a spot on the highway near a curve in the road where the barricade would not be seen by an oncoming motorist. The boys would wait to watch an unsuspecting motorist attempt to stop and (usually) crash into the wooden barricade. With saintly bearing the boys might offer help and understanding.

A stolen lantern might well find its way onto the back of a police car or hang from a street lamp. Once a lantern served as a prop for a reenactment of the "midnight ride of Paul Revere" until the "play," which was taking place at 2:00 AM in the center of a main street of Big Town, was interrupted by a police car several blocks away. The boys ran, leaving the lanterns on the street, and managed to avoid being apprehended.

Abandoned houses, especially if they were located in out-of-the-way places, were fair game for destruction and spontaneous vandalism. The boys would break windows, remove furniture to the yard and tear it apart, urinate on the walls and scrawl obscenities inside.

Through all the pranks, drinking and reckless driving the boys managed miraculously to avoid being stopped by police. Only twice in two years was I aware that they had been stopped by a Big City policeman. Once was for speeding (which they did every time they drove whether they were drunk or sober), and the driver managed to convince the policeman that it was simply an error. The second time they were stopped they had just left a nightclub and were walking through an alley. Aaron stopped to urinate and the boys began making obscene remarks. A foot patrolman came into the alley, lectured the boys and sent them home. Before the boys got to the car one began talking in a loud voice again. The policeman, who had followed them down the alley, arrested this boy for disturbing the peace and took him to the police station where the other Saints gathered. After paying a $5.00 fine, and with the assurance that there would be no permanent record of the arrest, the boy was released.

The boys had a spirit of frivolity and fun about their escapades. They did not view what they were engaged in as "delinquency," though it surely was by any reasonable definition of that word. They simply viewed themselves as having a little fun and who, they would ask, was really hurt by it? The answer had to be no one, although this fact remains one of the most difficult things to explain about the gang's behavior. Unlikely though it seems, in two years of drinking, driving, carousing and vandalism no one was seriously injured as a result of the Saints' activities.

THE SAINTS IN SCHOOL

The Saints were highly successful in school. The average grade for the group was "B," with two of the boys having close to a straight "A" average. Almost all of the boys were popular

and many of them held offices in the school. One of the boys was vice-president of the student body one year. Six of the boys played on athletic teams.

At the end of their senior year, the student body selected ten seniors for special recognition as the "school wheels"; four of the ten were Saints. Teachers and school officials saw no problem with any of these boys and anticipated that they would all "make something of themselves."

How the boys managed to maintain this impression is surprising in view of their actual behavior while in school. Their technique for covering truancy was so successful that teachers did not even realize that the boys were absent from school much of the time. Occasionally, of course, the system would backfire and then the boy was on his own. A boy who was caught would be most contrite, would plead guilty and ask for mercy. He inevitably got the mercy he sought.

Cheating on examinations was rampant, even to the point of orally communicating answers to exams as well as looking at one another's papers. Since none of the group studied, and since they were primarily dependent on one another for help, it is surprising that grades were so high. Teachers contributed to the deception in their admitted inclination to give these boys (and presumably others like them) the benefit of the doubt. When asked how the boys did in school, and when pressed on specific examinations, teachers might admit that they were disappointed in John's performance, but would quickly add that they "knew that he was capable of doing better," so John was given a higher grade than he had actually earned. How often this happened is impossible to know. During the time that I observed the group, I never saw any of the boys take homework home. Teachers may have been "understanding" very regularly.

One exception to the gang's generally good performance was Jerry, who had a "C" average in his junior year, experienced disaster the next year and failed to graduate. Jerry had always been a little more nonchalant than the others about the liberties he took in school. Rather than wait for someone to come get him from class, he would offer his own excuse and leave. Although he probably did not miss any more classes than most of the others in the group, he did not take the requisite pains to cover his absences. Jerry was the only Saint whom I ever heard talk back to a teacher. Although teachers often called him a "cut up" or a "smart kid," they never referred to him as a troublemaker or as a kid headed for trouble. It seems likely, then, that Jerry's failure his senior year and his mediocre performance his junior year were consequences of his not playing the game the proper way (possibly because he was disturbed by his parents' divorce). His teachers regarded him as "immature" and not quite ready to get out of high school.

THE POLICE AND THE SAINTS

The local police saw the Saints as good boys who were among the leaders of the youth in the community. Rarely, the boys might be stopped in town for speeding or for running a stop sign. When this happened the boys were always polite, contrite and pled for mercy. As in school, they received the mercy they asked for. None ever received a ticket or was taken into the precinct by the local police.

The situation in Big City, where the boys engaged in most of their delinquency, was only slightly different. The police there did not know the boys at all, although occasionally the boys were stopped by a patrolman. Once they were caught taking a lantern from a construction site. Another time they were stopped for running a stop sign, and on several occasions they were stopped for speeding. Their behavior was as before: contrite, polite and penitent. The urban police, like the local police, accepted their demeanor as sincere. More important, the urban police were convinced that these were good boys just out for a lark.

THE ROUGHNECKS

Hanibal townspeople never perceived the Saints' high level of delinquency. The Saints were good boys who just went in for an occasional prank. After all, they were well dressed, well mannered and had nice cars. The Rough-necks were a different story. Although the two gangs of boys were the same age, and both groups engaged in an equal amount of wild-oat sowing, everyone agreed that the not-so-well-dressed, not-so-well-mannered, not-so-rich boys were heading for trouble. Townspeople would say, "You can see the gang members at the drugstore, night after night, leaning against the store-front (sometimes drunk) or slouching around inside buying cokes, reading magazines, and probably stealing old Mr. Wall blind. When they are outside and girls walk by, even respectable girls, these boys make suggestive remarks. Sometimes their remarks are downright lewd."

From the community's viewpoint, the real indication that these kids were in for trouble was that they were constantly involved with the police. Some of them had been picked up for stealing, mostly small stuff, of course, "but still it's stealing small stuff that leads to big time crimes." "Too bad," people said. "Too bad that these boys couldn't behave like the other kids in town; stay out of trouble, be polite to adults, and look to their future."

The community's impression of the degree to which this group of six boys (ranging in age from 16 to 19) engaged in delinquency was somewhat distorted. In some ways the gang was more delinquent than the community thought; in other ways they were less.

The fighting activities of the group were fairly readily and accurately perceived by almost everyone. At least once a month, the boys would get into some sort of fight, although most fights were scraps between members of the group or involved only one member of the group and some peripheral hanger-on. Only three times in the period of observation did the group fight together: once against a gang from across town, once against two blacks and once against a group of boys from another school. For the first two fights the group went out "looking for trouble"—and they found it both times. The third fight followed a football game and began spontaneously with an argument on the football field between one of the Roughnecks and a member of the opposition's football team.

Jack had a particular propensity for fighting

and was involved in most of the brawls. He was a prime mover of the escalation of arguments into fights.

More serious than fighting, had the community been aware of it, was theft. Although almost everyone was aware that the boys occasionally stole things, they did not realize the extent of the activity. Petty stealing was a frequent event for the Roughnecks. Sometimes they stole as a group and coordinated their efforts; other times they stole in pairs. Rarely did they steal alone.

The thefts ranged from very small things like paperback books, comics and ballpoint pens to expensive items like watches. The nature of the thefts varied from time to time. The gang would go through a period of systematically shoplifting items from automobiles or school lockers. Types of thievery varied with the whim of the gang. Some forms of thievery were more profitable than others, but all thefts were for profit, not just thrills.

Roughnecks siphoned gasoline from cars as often as they had access to an automobile, which was not very often. Unlike the Saints, who owned their own cars, the Roughnecks would have to borrow their parents' cars, an event which occurred only eight or nine times a year. The boys claimed to have stolen cars for joy rides from time to time.

Ron committed the most serious of the group's offenses. With an unidentified associate the boy attempted to burglarize a gasoline station. Although this station had been robbed twice previously in the same month, Ron denied any involvement in either of the other thefts. When Ron and his accomplice approached the station, the owner was hiding in the bushes beside the station. He fired both barrels of a double-barreled shotgun at the boys. Ron was severely injured; the other boy ran away and was never caught. Though he remained in critical condition for several months, Ron finally recovered and served six months of the following year in reform school. Upon release from reform school, Ron was put back a grade in school, and began running around with a different gang of boys. The Roughnecks considered the new gang less delinquent than themselves, and during the

following year Ron had no more trouble with the police.

The Roughnecks, then, engaged mainly in three types of delinquency: theft, drinking and fighting. Although community members perceived that this gang of kids was delinquent, they mistakenly believed that their illegal activities were primarily drinking, fighting and being a nuisance to passersby. Drinking was limited among the gang members, although it did occur, and theft was much more prevalent than anyone realized.

Drinking would doubtless have been more prevalent had the boys had ready access to liquor. Since they rarely had automobiles at their disposal, they could not travel very far, and the bars in town would not serve them. Most of the boys had little money, and this, too, inhibited their purchase of alcohol. Their major source of liquor was a local drunk who would buy them a fifth if they would give him enough extra to buy himself a pint of whiskey or a bottle of wine.

The community's perception of drinking as prevalent stemmed from the fact that it was the most obvious delinquency the boys engaged in. When one of the boys had been drinking, even a casual observer seeing him on the corner would suspect that he was high.

There was a high level of mutual distrust and dislike between the Roughnecks and the police. The boys felt very strongly that the police were unfair and corrupt. Some evidence existed that the boys were correct in their perception.

The main source of the boys' dislike for the police undoubtedly stemmed from the fact that the police would sporadically harass the group. From the standpoint of the boys, these acts of occasional enforcement of the law were whimsical and uncalled for. It made no sense to them, for example, that the police would come to the corner occasionally and threaten them with arrest for loitering when the night before the boys had been out siphoning gasoline from cars and the police had been nowhere in sight. To the boys, the police were stupid on the one hand, for not being where they should have been and catching the boys in a serious offense, and unfair on the other hand, for trumping up "loitering" charges against them.

From the viewpoint of the police, the situation was quite different. They knew, with all the confidence necessary to be a policeman, that these boys were engaged in criminal activities. They knew this partly from occasionally catching them, mostly from circumstantial evidence ("the boys were around when those tires were slashed"), and partly because the police shared the view of the community in general that this was a bad bunch of boys. The best the police could hope to do was to be sensitive to the fact that these boys were engaged in illegal acts and arrest them whenever there was some evidence that they had been involved. Whether or not the boys had in fact committed a particular act in a particular way was not especially important. The police had a broader view: their job was to stamp out these kids' crimes; the tactics were not as important as the end result.

Over the period that the group was under observation, each member was arrested at least once. Several of the boys were arrested a number of times and spent at least one night in jail. While most were never taken to court, two of the boys were sentenced to six months' incarceration in boys' schools.

THE ROUGHNECKS IN SCHOOL

The Roughnecks' behavior in school was not particularly disruptive. During school hours they did not all hang around together, but tended instead to spend most of their time with one or two other members of the gang who were their special buddies. Although every member of the gang attempted to avoid school as much as possible, they were not particularly successful and most of them attended school with surprising regularity. They considered school a burden—something to be gotten through with a minimum of conflict. If they were "bugged" by a particular teacher, it could lead to trouble. One of the boys, Al, once threatened to beat up a teacher and, according to the other boys, the teacher hid under a desk to escape him.

Teachers saw the boys the way the general community did, as heading for trouble, as being uninterested in making something of themselves. Some were also seen as being incapable of meeting the academic standards of the school. Most of the teachers expressed concern for this group of boys and were willing to pass them despite poor performance, in the belief that failing them would only aggravate the problem.

The group of boys had a grade point average just slightly above "C." No one in the group failed either grade, and no one had better than a "C" average. They were very consistent in their achievement or, at least, the teachers were consistent in their perception of the boys' achievement.

Two of the boys were good football players. Herb was acknowledged to be the best player in the school and Jack was almost as good. Both boys were criticized for their failure to abide by training rules, for refusing to come to practice as often as they should, and for not playing their best during practice. What they lacked in sportsmanship they made up for in skill, apparently, and played every game no matter how poorly they had performed in practice or how many practice sessions they had missed.

TWO QUESTIONS

Why did the community, the school and the police react to the Saints as though they were good, upstanding, nondelinquent youths with bright futures but to the Roughnecks as though they were tough, young criminals who were headed for trouble? Why did the Roughnecks and the Saints in fact have quite different careers after high school—careers which, by and large, lived up to the expectations of the community?

The most obvious explanation for the differences in the community's and law enforcement agencies' reactions to the two gangs is that one group of boys was "more delinquent" than the other. Which group *was* more delinquent? The answer to this question will determine in part how we explain the differential responses to these groups by the members of the community and, particularly, by law enforcement and school officials.

In sheer number of illegal acts, the Saints were the more delinquent. They were truant from school for at least part of the day almost every day of the week. In addition, their drinking and vandalism occurred with surprising regularity. The Roughnecks, in contrast, engaged sporadically in delinquent episodes. While these episodes were frequent, they certainly did not occur on a daily or even a weekly basis.

The difference in frequency of offenses was probably caused by the Roughnecks' inability to obtain liquor and to manipulate legitimate excuses from school. Since the Roughnecks had less money than the Saints, and teachers carefully supervised their school activities, the Roughnecks' hearts may have been as black as the Saints', but their misdeeds were not nearly as frequent.

There are really no clear-cut criteria by which to measure qualitative differences in antisocial behavior. The most important dimension of the difference is generally referred to as the "seriousness" of the offenses.

If seriousness encompasses the relative economic costs of delinquent acts, then some assessment can be made. The Roughnecks probably stole an average of about $5.00 worth of goods a week. Some weeks the figure was considerably higher, but these times must be balanced against long periods when almost nothing was stolen.

The Saints were more continuously engaged in delinquency but their acts were not for the most part costly to property. Only their vandalism and occasional theft of gasoline would so qualify. Perhaps once or twice a month they would siphon a tankful of gas. The other costly items were street signs, construction lanterns and the like. All of these acts combined probably did not quite average $5.00 a week, partly because much of the stolen equipment was abandoned and presumably could be recovered. The difference in cost of stolen property between the two groups was trivial, but the Roughnecks probably had a slightly more expensive set of activities than did the Saints.

Another meaning of seriousness is the potential threat of physical harm to members of the community and to the boys themselves. The Roughnecks were more prone to physical violence; they not only welcomed an opportunity to fight; they went seeking it. In addition, they

fought among themselves frequently. Although the fighting never included deadly weapons, it was still a menace, however minor, to the physical safety of those involved.

The Saints never fought. They avoided physical conflict both inside and outside the group. At the same time, though, the Saints frequently endangered their own and other people's lives. They did so almost every time they drove a car, especially if they had been drinking. Sober, their driving was risky; under the influence of alcohol it was horrendous. In addition, the Saints endangered the lives of others with their pranks. Street excavations left unmarked were a very serious hazard.

Evaluating the relative seriousness of the two gangs' activities is difficult. The community reacted as though the behavior of the Roughnecks was a problem, and they reacted as though the behavior of the Saints was not. But the members of the community were ignorant of the array of delinquent acts that characterized the Saints' behavior. Although concerned citizens were unaware of much of the Roughnecks' behavior as well, they were much better informed about the Roughnecks' involvement in delinquency than they were about the Saints'.

VISIBILITY

Differential treatment of the two gangs resulted in part because one gang was infinitely more visible than the other. This differential visibility was a direct function of the economic standing of the families. The Saints had access to automobiles and were able to remove themselves from the sight of the community. In as routine a decision as to where to go to have a milkshake after school, the Saints stayed away from the mainstream of community life. Lacking transportation, the Roughnecks could not make it to the edge of town. The center of town was the only practical place for them to meet since their homes were scattered throughout the town and any noncentral meeting place put an undue hardship on some members. Through necessity the Roughnecks congregated in a crowded area where everyone in the community passed frequently, including teachers and law enforcement officers. They could easily see the Roughnecks hanging around the drugstore.

The Roughnecks, of course, made themselves even more visible by making remarks to passersby and by occasionally getting into fights on the corner. Meanwhile, just as regularly, the Saints were either at the cafe on one edge of town or in the pool hall at the other edge of town. Without any particular realization that they were making themselves inconspicuous, the Saints were able to hide their time-wasting. Not only were they removed from the mainstream of traffic, but they were almost always inside a building.

On their escapades the Saints were also relatively invisible, since they left Hanibal and travelled to Big City. Here, too, they were mobile, roaming the city, rarely going to the same area twice.

DEMEANOR

To the notion of visibility must be added the difference in the responses of group members to outside intervention with their activities. If one of the Saints was confronted with an accusing policeman, even if he felt he was truly innocent of a wrongdoing, his demeanor was apologetic and penitent. A Roughneck's attitude was almost the polar opposite. When confronted with a threatening adult authority, even one who tried to be pleasant, the Roughneck's hostility and disdain were clearly observable. Sometimes he might attempt to put up a veneer of respect, but it was thin and was not accepted as sincere by the authority.

School was no different from the community at large. The Saints could manipulate the system by feigning compliance with the school norms. The availability of cars at school meant that once free from the immediate sight of the teacher, the boys could disappear rapidly. And this escape was well enough planned that no administrator or teacher was nearby when the boys left. A Roughneck who wished to escape for a few hours was in a bind. If it were possible to get free from class, downtown was still a mile away, and even if he arrived there, he was still very visible. Truancy for the Roughnecks meant almost

certain detection, while the Saints enjoyed almost complete immunity from sanctions.

BIAS

Community members were not aware of the transgressions of the Saints. Even if the Saints had been less discreet, their favorite delinquencies would have been perceived as less serious than those of the Roughnecks.

In the eyes of the police and school officials, a boy who drinks in an alley and stands intoxicated on the street corner is committing a more serious offense than is a boy who drinks to inebriation in a nightclub or a tavern and drives around afterwards in a car. Similarly, a boy who steals a wallet from a store will be viewed as having committed a more serious offense than a boy who steals a lantern from a construction site.

Perceptual bias also operates with respect to the demeanor of the boys in the two groups when they are confronted by adults. It is not simply that adults dislike the posture affected by boys of the Roughneck ilk; more important is the conviction that the posture adopted by the Roughnecks is an indication of their devotion and commitment to deviance as a way of life. The posture becomes a cue, just as the type of the offense is a cue, to the degree to which the known transgressions are indicators of the youths' potential for other problems.

Visibility, demeanor and bias are surface variables which explain the day-to-day operations of the police. Why do these surface variables operate as they do? Why did the police choose to disregard the Saints' delinquencies while breathing down the backs of the Roughnecks?

The answer lies in the class structure of American society and the control of legal institutions by those at the top of the class structure. Obviously, no representative of the upper class drew up the operational chart for the police which led them to look in the ghettoes and on streetcorners—which led them to see the demeanor of lower-class youth as troublesome and that of upper-middle-class youth as tolerable. Rather, the procedures simply developed from experience—experience with irate and influential upper-middle-class parents insisting that their son's vandalism was simply a prank and his drunkenness only a momentary "sowing of wild oats"—experience with cooperative or indifferent, powerless, lower-class parents who acquiesced to the laws' definition of their son's behavior.

ADULT CAREERS OF THE SAINTS AND THE ROUGHNECKS

The community's confidence in the potential of the Saints and the Roughnecks apparently was justified. If anything, the community members underestimated the degree to which these youngsters would turn out "good" or "bad."

Seven of the eight members of the Saints went on to college immediately after high school. Five of the boys graduated from college in four years. The sixth one finished college after two years in the army, and the seventh spent four years in the air force before returning to college and receiving a B.A. degree. Of these seven college graduates, three went on for advanced degrees. One finished law school and is now active in state politics, one finished medical school and is practicing near Hanibal, and one boy is now working for a Ph.D. The other four college graduates entered submanagerial, managerial or executive training positions with larger firms.

The only Saint who did not complete college was Jerry. Jerry had failed to graduate from high school with the other Saints. During his second senior year, after the other Saints had gone on to college, Jerry began to hang around with what several teachers described as a "rough crowd"—the gang that was heir apparent to the Roughnecks. At the end of his second senior year, when he did graduate from high school, Jerry took a job as a used-car salesman, got married and quickly had a child. Although he made several abortive attempts to go to college by attending night school, when I last saw him (ten years after high school) Jerry was unemployed and had been living on unemployment for almost a year. His wife worked as a waitress.

Some of the Roughnecks have lived up to community expectations. A number of them were headed for trouble. A few were not.

Jack and Herb were the athletes among the Roughnecks and their athletic prowess paid off handsomely. Both boys received unsolicited athletic scholarships to college. After Herb received his scholarship (near the end of his senior year), he apparently did an about-face. His demeanor became very similar to that of the Saints. Although he remained a member in good standing of the Roughnecks, he stopped participating in most activities and did not hang around the corner as often.

Jack did not change. If anything, he became more prone to fighting. He even made excuses for accepting the scholarship. He told the other gang members that the school had guaranteed him a "C" average if he would come to play football—an idea that seems far-fetched, even in this day of highly competitive recruiting.

During the summer after graduation from high school, Jack attempted suicide by jumping from a tall building. The jump would certainly have killed most people trying it, but Jack survived. He entered college in the fall and played four years of football. He and Herb graduated in four years, and both are teaching and coaching in high schools. They are married and have stable families. If anything, Jack appears to have a more prestigious position in the community than does Herb, though both are well respected and secure in their positions.

Two of the boys never finished high school. Tommy left at the end of his junior year and went to another state. That summer he was arrested and placed on probation on a manslaughter charge. Three years later he was arrested for murder; he pleaded guilty to second degree murder and is serving a 30-year sentence in the state penitentiary.

Al, the other boy who did not finish high school, also left the state in his senior year. He is serving a life sentence in a state penitentiary for first degree murder.

Wes is a small-time gambler. He finished high school and "bummed around." After several years he made contact with a bookmaker who employed him as a runner. Later he acquired his own area and has been working it ever since. His position among the bookmakers is almost identical to the position he had in the gang; he is always around but no one is really aware of him. He makes no trouble and he does not get into any. Steady, reliable, capable of keeping his mouth closed, he plays the game by the rules, even though the game is an illegal one.

That leaves only Ron. Some of his former friends reported that they had heard he was "driving a truck up north," but no one could provide any concrete information.

REINFORCEMENT

The community responded to the Roughnecks as boys in trouble, and the boys agreed with that perception. Their pattern of deviancy was reinforced, and breaking away from it became increasingly unlikely. Once the boys acquired an image of themselves as deviants, they selected new friends who affirmed that self-image. As that self-conception became more firmly entrenched, they also became willing to try new and more extreme deviances. With their growing alienation came freer expression of disrespect and hostility for representatives of the legitimate society. This disrespect increased the community's negativism, perpetuating the entire process of commitment to deviance. Lack of a commitment to deviance works the same way. In either case, the process will perpetuate itself unless some event (like a scholarship to college or a sudden failure) external to the established relationship intervenes. For two of the Roughnecks (Herb and Jack), receiving college athletic scholarships created new relations and culminated in a break with the established pattern of deviance. In the case of one of the Saints (Jerry), his parents' divorce and his fail-

ing to graduate from high school changed some of his other relations. Being held back in school for a year and losing his place among the Saints had sufficient impact on Jerry to alter his self-image and virtually to assure that he would not go on to college as his peers did. Although the experiments of life can rarely be reversed, it seems likely in view of the behavior of the other boys who did not enjoy this special treatment by the school that Jerry, too, would have "become something" had he graduated as anticipated. For Herb and Jack outside intervention worked to their advantage; for Jerry it was his undoing.

Selective perception and labelling—finding, processing and punishing some kinds of criminality and not others—means that visible, poor, nonmobile, outspoken, undiplomatic "tough" kids will be noticed, whether their actions are seriously delinquent or not. Other kids, who have established a reputation for being bright (even though underachieving), disciplined and involved in respectable activities, who are mobile and monied, will be invisible when they deviate from sanctioned activities. They'll sow their wild oats—perhaps even wider and thicker than their lower-class cohorts—but they won't be noticed. When it's time to leave adolescence most will follow the expected path, settling into the ways of the middle class, remembering fondly the delinquent but unnoticed fling of their youth. The Roughnecks and others like them may turn around, too. It is more likely that their noticeable deviance will have been so reinforced by police and community that their lives will be effectively channeled into careers consistent with their adolescent background.

QUESTIONS FOR DISCUSSION

1. In what ways are the Saints and the Roughnecks similar? How are they dissimilar?

2. How does "visibility" affect the delinquent definitions that are applied to the two groups of adolescents?

3. Discuss how money, success in school, and demeanor can influence and insulate being labeled "delinquent" by the community and the police.

APPLICATIONS

1. Draw upon your own experience, and try to recall a positive or negative label that was applied to you.
   a. Who assigned the label to you (friends, parents, a teacher, the police)?
   b. Did the label affect the way you felt about yourself?
   c. Was the label, good or bad, reinforced by others around you?
   d. Do you feel today that your life is a product of the labels that were applied to you and repeatedly reinforced?

2. Try to remember the different groups of student in your high school. Can you think of any groups that were considered to be "saints" or "roughnecks"? Write a short summary about your school describing the characteristics of a saint group and a roughneck group.

KEY TERMS

accomplice someone who aids or abets another person in committing a criminal act.

bias a preconceived or prejudiced belief.

cognitive dissonance a theory that states that individuals strive to maintain internal consistency so that values, beliefs, and opinions maintain consonance. Dissonance occurs when new information does not coincide with an existing perception of the world. To reduce the associated stress caused by this conflict, the individual often redefines or rationalizes the new information to fit existing beliefs.

escapade a breaking loose from restraints; flight from confining rules.

labeling theory a theory that holds that deviant behavior is not a quality of the act a person commits, but rather a consequence of the applications, by others, of rules and sanctions on the offender. Nothing is inherently deviant but only becomes deviant when others apply a deviant label.

reinforcement an event or some reward whose occurrence increases the likelihood that certain behaviors will continue.

social class a category of people who have been grouped together based on one or more common characteristics. A class is a stratum in a societal hierarchy. Classes may be determined by wealth, power, or prestige and other socioeconomic indicators such as income, occupation, and educational attainment.

vagrancy the state of a person who wanders from place to place without a fixed home or livelihood. Usually considered to be a public nuisance. Vagrants often engage in begging, stealing, and even prostitution to obtain income.

IV

INSTITUTIONAL RESPONSES TO JUVENILE DELINQUENCY

The reactions to youth and youth behavior have created a multitude of ideas and programs intended to change either the individual, social institutions, or the societal reactions toward many youth. Some, such as the creation of public schools, were good ideas and have led to some of the greatest successes in history. Although not a panacea for all social problems, youth involvement in education continues to be a positive foundational aspect of our society. Other ideas and programs are just as meritorious and yet the societal consensus as to how the society should respond to youth and especially youth deviance remains elusive, complex, and frustrating.

Part IV includes six articles which cover some of the most important institutional responses to youth behavior and all tend to deal with the issue of status to one degree or another. Should juveniles be treated as adults by the police, courts, or correctional systems? Should our reactions to youths be more tolerant than our reactions to adults? Are race, gender, or socioeconomic status more important in determining societal reactions than behavior? These questions and issues have not only shaped the present juvenile justice system but continue to be some of the most pertinent.

Alan Neigher describes one of the most important legal cases in the history of juvenile justice with his article "The Gault Decision: Due Process and the Juvenile Courts." Neigher examines the case, decision, and the impact of affording juveniles protections once reserved for "adults only." The impact of the *Gault* decision is still being felt and the due process issue brought forth as a result of the decision grows ever more complicated.

The legal responses often are the most formal and least effective in solving human problems. An interesting example of how the formal or manifest functions of an institution for juveniles is subverted by the informal organizations of both inmates and staff is provided by Barry C. Feld in "A Comparative Analysis of Organizational Structure and Inmate Subcultures in Institutions for Juvenile Offenders."

Kenneth Polk, rather than focusing on juvenile institutions, turns his attention to diverting juveniles away from the formal system in "Juvenile Diversion: A Look at the Record." The issues brought up by Polk include recidivism, sexism, and the power of these diversionary programs. Diversion away from the formal adult criminal justice system, in many ways, created the juvenile justice system and helps to maintain the working assumptions that juveniles are less responsible, culpable, and indeed, salvageable.

"Juvenile Parole Policy in the United States: Determinate Versus Indeterminate Models," by Ashford and LeCroy points out that ideational shifts within the juvenile system since the 1960s have still not led to the resolution of the aftercare issues. The move towards determinacy has not affected aftercare as much as it has affected the formalization process in juvenile justice.

The unequal treatment of juveniles based on sex is addressed by Gail Armstrong in "Females Under the Law—Protected but Unequal." She claims that a "double standard of morality" exists wherein females experience differential sentencing results and in fact are not equal under the law. The way in which justice is applies cannot be discriminatory or justice will not exist.

Our last article focuses on the recidivism issue in relation to custody type and indirectly examines the deeper issue of correctional outcome. Anne L. Schneider, in "Restitution and Recidivism Rates of Juvenile Offenders: Results from Four Experimental Studies," examines the effects of restitution on recidivism. Her results were encouraging and she suggests that future research needs to focus on attitudes and future behaviors. Accepting total responsibility for one's behavior and attitudes underlies much of the success of the juveniles in these experiments.

21

The Gault Decision: Due Process and the Juvenile Courts

Alan Neigher

On May 15, 1967, the Supreme Court of the United States ruled that juvenile courts must grant to children many of the procedural protections required in adult criminal trials by the Bill of Rights. In this, the *Gault*[1] decision, the Supreme Court for the first time considered the constitutional rights of children in juvenile courts.

It is not questioned that *Gault* will have a major impact on the future of juvenile courts in this country, many of which having for years operated under a philosophy that made ordinary procedural safeguards seem evil. It is submitted, however, that the *Gault* decision is neither a panacea for children in trouble nor an onerous burden for juvenile law enforcement officers. The decision will hopefully protect young people from being given indeterminate "correctional" sentences for making allegedly obscene phone calls that no one thinks necessary to verify. The decision may make life a bit more difficult for judges and probation officers. It is clear that at the very least, *Gault* will

grant some semblance of consistent legal protection to the child.

But there are some popular misconceptions concerning the scope of *Gault*. As an example, the front page of the May 16, 1967, *New York Times* headlined an otherwise excellent summary of the decision as follows: "High Court Rules Adult Code Holds in Juvenile Trials . . . Finds Children Are Entitled to the Basic Protections Given in Bill of Rights."[2] But the decision does not accord to juveniles all of the protections of the Bill of Rights. All juvenile courts—with the exception of the District of Columbia—are, in fact, state courts. The Bill of Rights has not yet been made applicable in its entirety to state criminal proceedings. Further, the *Gault* decision was limited to but a few Bill of Rights issues. This must be kept in mind, although, as will be later noted, the decision was as significant for what it *suggested* as it was for what it actually held as binding legal precedent.

Thus, before the decision may be discussed in terms of its implications for the juvenile courts, a brief examination is in order as to what the "basic protections" of the Bill of Rights are, and whether these protections have been extended to state (and thereby juvenile) proceedings.

"The Gault Decision: Due Process and the Juvenile Courts," *Federal Probation*, 31 (December 1967) pp. 8–18. Reprinted by permission of Federal Probation.

BILL OF RIGHTS AND THE FOURTEENTH AMENDMENT

The Bill of Rights[3] means the first Ten Amendments to the newly written Federal Constitution, proposed to the state legislatures by the First Congress in 1789. The Bill of Rights was intended to be a series of limitations on the three *federal* branches: the Congress, the Executive, and the Judiciary. These proposed limitations were a practical political necessity, to mollify local concern over the sanctity of state autonomy in many areas of the law, and thereby speed ratification by the necessary nine state legislatures.

Of these Ten Amendments, six are not directly related to the criminal process. These are the First, Second, Third, Seventh, Ninth, and Tenth. Left for consideration, therefore, are the Fourth, Fifth, Sixth, and Eighth Amendments. And of these four, the Fourth and Eighth were not at issue in *Gault* and will be treated briefly.

Before these Amendments are discussed, the Fourteenth Amendment must be considered because it is closely related to the concept of federalism and because it affects not only those Amendments related to the criminal process, but also the entire Ten Amendments and their applicability to the states.

The Bill of Rights was expressly intended to be a check on federal power. There was nothing in the original Constitution to prevent the states from formulating their own systems of criminal administration, and indeed, the Tenth Amendment provides that "The powers not delegated to the United States by the Constitution; nor prohibited by it to the States, are reserved to the States respectively, or to the people."

After the Civil War, almost a century after the ratification of the Constitution (which included the Bill of Rights), Amendments Thirteen, Fourteen, and Fifteen were enacted, largely for the benefit of the newly emancipated slaves. Amendment Thirteen abolished slavery; Amendment Fifteen provided that race, color, or previous condition of servitude shall not be a disability for voting.

Amendment Fourteen was written partly to assure fair and equitable treatment on the part of state authorities to the newly emancipated. For our purposes, its most pertinent part is Section 1, which provides: ". . . No State shall make or enforce any law which shall abridge the privileges or immunities of citizens of the United States; nor shall any State deprive any person of life, liberty, or property, *without due process of law,* nor deny to any person within its jurisdiction the equal protection of the laws."

Thus, the "due process" clause of the Fifth Amendment was made applicable to the states. However, the vague and sweeping concept of due process was slow in making its impact felt on the states which had been left virtually autonomous in formulating criminal procedures. But in recent years, on a case-by-case basis, the Supreme Court has made *some* of the Bill of Rights protection binding on the states through the due process clause of the Fourteenth Amendment. Of those protections now applicable to the states included are several under those Amendments not relevant to the criminal process (especially freedom of speech under the First Amendment), and these need not be considered here.

The Fourth Amendment was largely a reaction to the Writs of Assistance issued in the colonies prior to the Revolution, which gave British revenue officers nearly unlimited authority to search private dwellings and to seize goods. Consequently, the Fourth Amendment reflects the Founders' jealous regard of the right to privacy—to be secure against unreasonable invasion of one's person, property, and home. The Fourth Amendment now applies in full to both federal and state authorities.

The Fourth Amendment provides for the security of people "in their persons, houses, papers, and effects against unreasonable searches and seizures." The laws pertaining to warrants—for both search and arrest—are too technical to be set out here. Suffice it to say that, as to searches and seizures of property, unless there is consent, individuals and their possessions or dwellings cannot be searched or seized without a warrant, except when this is justified by the surrounding circumstances and is done in a reasonable manner.

The Fourth Amendment prohibits unwarranted and unreasonable arrests, but it does not require that the police obtain a warrant for every arrest. The police may arrest without a warrant where the arresting officer actually sees the commission of a misdemeanor or a felony; also, the arresting officer may arrest without a warrant when he has "probable cause" to believe a felony has been committed. Probable cause is difficult to define precisely, but it may generally be stated that it is the existence of such facts and circumstances as would lead a reasonable person to believe that the suspect to be arrested is guilty of the offense.

Where a warrant must be obtained, it must specifically describe the person to be arrested. A general warrant—one that is to be filled in at the arresting officer's convenience—is not valid. An arrest made pursuant to an invalid warrant is unlawful. A warrant for either arrest or search and seizure may be issued only by a magistrate or judge; police officers have no authority to issue warrants.

THE FIFTH AMENDMENT

The First Congress included a specific provision regarding grand jury indictments as the first clause of the Fifth Amendment. The purpose of the provision is to insure that persons will not be brought to trial arbitrarily when there is no reasonable basis for believing they are guilty of a crime, and that those who are brought to trial will be adequately informed of the charges against them. The Supreme Court has held that the due process clause of the Fourteenth Amendment does not require a state to provide grand jury indictment, so long as the state provides other means of insuring justice to the accused.

The next clause provides that no person "shall . . . be subject for the same offense to be twice put in jeopardy of life or limb." The Founders' sense of fair play led them to include in the Fifth Amendment the concept that the Government should not be able to harass and persecute a man by trying him repeatedly for the same offense. The double jeopardy prohibition has not yet been binding on the states. However, the states are bound by the due process clause of the Fourteenth Amendment; thus, successive trials which flaunt the principles of justice and fair play are not permitted.

The Fifth Amendment next provides that no person "shall be compelled in any criminal case to be a witness against himself. . . ." The history of inquisition and torture in the Old World gave the Founders ample reason to provide against the idea that a man should be forced to incriminate himself by his own words. The privilege has two aspects: (1) the right to be free from coercion designed to extract a confession; and (2) the right to remain silent without having an inference of guilt drawn from that silence.

Freedom from coerced confessions has long been recognized as basic to due process and neither federal nor state governments may extract a confession by force. Force need not be physical; mental coercion such as threats or interrogation to the point of exhaustion would make a confession coerced, and thereby invalid.

The second aspect of the privilege against self-incrimination is the right to remain silent. This is the right invoked by those who "take the Fifth." This right, too, has recently been extended to apply to the states under the Fourteenth Amendment. A criminal defendant has the right to refuse to testify entirely; his failure to take the stand may not even be commented upon by the prosecution in either the federal or state courts. A witness, on the other hand, must take the stand if called, and must claim the privilege one question at a time. The privilege applies not only to criminal trials, but extends also to those before congressional committees, grand juries, and administrative agencies.[4]

The privilege against self-incrimination was highly relevant to the *Gault* decision.

Following the self-incrimination provision appears the most sweeping concept of American jurisprudence: that no person shall "be deprived of life, liberty or property without due process of law." We have seen that the "due process" concept was later duplicated in the Fourteenth Amendment.

If there exists a legal concept not susceptible of precise definition it is due process. It means justice; it means judicial fair play. It is perhaps the very essence of our constitutional tradition. It is both "substantive" and "procedural"—it prohibits the making of laws that are unfair in themselves, and it prohibits unfair application of the law.

Due process applies to Congress in its law-making authority, and forbids laws that are arbitrary or unreasonable. And when the Executive Branch exercises a law-making or rule-making function, it, too, must exercise substantive due process.

Procedural due process requires that the laws, once made, be applied fairly. It means that an individual has the right to be fairly heard before he stands to lose life, liberty, or property. It requires a fair trial in a criminal case and a hearing by an impartial tribunal in a property case.

Procedural due process considerations were at the heart of the *Gault* decision.

THE SIXTH AMENDMENT

The Sixth Amendment is of particular importance to the *Gault* decision. Of the entire Bill of Rights, it is the one most particularly concerned with the rights of an accused in a Federal criminal trial. The text of the Sixth Amendment follows:

> In all criminal prosecutions, the accused shall enjoy the right to a speedy and public trial, by an impartial jury of the State and District wherein the crime shall have been committed, which District shall have been previously ascertained by law, *and to be informed of the nature and cause of the accusation; to be confronted with the witnesses against him;* to have compulsory process for obtaining witnesses in his favor, *and to have the assistance of Counsel for his defense.* [Emphasis added.]

The right to a jury trial in criminal prosecutions was considered so important to the Founders that they included the right in the main body of the Constitution as well as in the Bill of Rights: Article III, Section 2, commands that the "Trials of all Crimes, except in Cases of Impeachment, shall be by Jury. . . ."

The Sixth Amendment establishes the basic requirement that the accused be tried by the traditional jury of 12. On the other hand, the states are *not* required to provide trial by jury, although many do by virtue of their own constitutions. Some states provide for juries of 8 or 10, rather than 12. However, the Fourteenth Amendment mandate that the states provide due process requires that whatever form of trial the states do provide must be fair.

Not "all criminal prosecutions" by the Federal Government require jury trials. Military trials, criminal contempt proceedings, or petty offenses punishable by small fines or short periods of imprisonment may be conducted without juries. When the right to jury trial applies, this right may be waived, and the defendant may be tried by a judge alone, where both the defendant and the Government so agree, with the consent of the trial judge.

The Sixth Amendment further provides that "the accused enjoy . . . a speedy and public trial." The history of the Inquisition and the Court of the Star Chamber was not lost on the Founding Fathers. These Courts were notorious for their practices of detaining accused persons for long periods, and interrogating witnesses in secret. The Sixth Amendment provided against these abuses by insuring that the accused has the right to defend himself while witnesses and evidence are still available. The wisdom of this protection is readily apparent if one considers the anxiety involved in a prolonged criminal prosecution. Thus, if an accused is not afforded a speedy trial, he may not be tried at all. As to what constitutes a "speedy trial" suffice it to say that standards of reasonableness must govern. The right to a speedy trial has not yet been held binding upon the states under the Fourteenth Amendment, although an obvious prolongment would probably violate due process.

The right to a *public* trial is a basic right under due process, and this right does extend to defendants in trials conducted by the states. The presence of the public and representatives of the press acts as a guarantee that the court will proceed appropriately. The Supreme Court has not yet determined whether all trials must be freely open to the public or whether circumstances will permit a limitation on the type of spectators allowed.

The next protection afforded under the

Sixth Amendment is the right to an impartial jury. The definition of "impartial" as used here has two aspects. First, there must be an opportunity for a cross section of the community to serve as jurors. Exclusion because of race, religion, national origin, or economic status violates the defendant's Sixth Amendment rights, whether the trial be federal or state. The cross-section concept does *not* require that every jury be composed of all the various racial, religious, ethnic, or economic groups of the community. It does prohibit court officials from *systematically* excluding any of these groups.

Second, the right to an impartial jury also involves the problem of publicity surrounding the trial. The First Amendment guarantees of free speech and freedom of the press must be balanced against the accused's right to be accorded a jury that will consider his case with an open mind. Modern communications techniques have added great complexity to this problem. The Supreme Court held in the case of Dr. Sam Sheppard that due process is violated where widespread newspaper publicity saturates the community so as to make it virtually impossible to find a panel of impartial jurors.

The Sixth Amendment next requires that a person be tried by "an impartial jury of the State and District wherein the crime shall have been committed, which District shall have been previously ascertained by law." This provision insures that a person will be tried only in that area where the crime was committed—where evidence and witnesses should be readily available, unless circumstances dictate that an impartial trial can only be had elsewhere. It is also required that Congress define in advance the boundaries of the Districts in which crimes shall be tried. The Supreme Court has not yet dealt with the issue of whether the due process clause of the Fourteenth Amendment limits the states in determining where trials for state offenses may be held.

Of great relevance to the *Gault* decision is the next phrase of the Sixth Amendment, which provides that the accused shall enjoy the right "to be informed of the nature and cause of the accusation." Thus, the accused must be informed of the charges against him sufficiently in advance of the court proceedings to allow him a reasonable opportunity to prepare a defense. Also, such notice must specify the alleged misconduct with reasonable particularity. Again this guarantee obtains, whether the trial be federal or state.

The second clause of the Sixth Amendment also was critical to the *Gault* decision. It provides that the accused shall enjoy the right "to be confronted with the witnesses against him." The philosophy underlying this clause is that the accused should be met by his accusers face-to-face, and be able to subject the testimony of the witnesses against him to cross-examination. The right to confrontation is a basic due process protection and applies to state, as well as to federal courts.

The Sixth Amendment next provides that an accused be entitled to have the court compel witnesses to appear and testify if they are unwilling to come voluntarily. A refusal to so compel witnesses to testify on behalf of the accused violates the right to a fair trial, and consequently offends the due process clause. Although the Supreme Court has not dealt directly with the issue, it does not seem likely that such a basic fair trial protection would bail to be held binding on the states under the Fourteenth Amendment.

Finally, the Sixth Amendment provides that the accused shall "have the assistance of counsel for his defense." There was no right to counsel prior to the enactment of the Bill of Rights, and the accused had to rely on the graces of the trial judge to act as his counsel. The inclusion of this right in the Sixth Amendment reflected the belief of the Founders that most defendants are vastly unprepared to protect themselves against the resources of the state's prosecution machinery. The accused today in both federal and state proceedings has the right to counsel in felony cases, and in misdemeanor cases where the accused is in jeopardy of incarceration. In such cases, the recent *Escobedo* and *Miranda* decisions have extended the right to counsel beyond the trial state; the accused is now entitled to counsel when the investigation focuses upon him so as to attempt to elicit incriminating statements. The reader should note that it is at this point, also, that the Fifth Amendment's privilege against self-incrimination attaches.

THE EIGHTH AMENDMENT

Statutes prohibiting excessive bail and cruel and unusual punishment had been enacted in precolonial England and in the constitutions of a number of colonies. These prohibitions were reflected in the Eighth Amendment which reads: "Excessive bail shall not be required, nor excessive fines imposed, nor cruel and unusual punishment inflicted."

It has not been definitely settled whether the provisions of the Eighth Amendment are applicable to the states under the Fourteenth Amendment.

Bail is a mechanism designed to insure the appearance of a defendant in court; by posting bail, the defendant undertakes to guarantee his appearance in court or else forfeit a sum of money. The amount of bail required is generally set by the magistrate who commits an arrested person to custody. Not every accused person is entitled to bail—military personnel and those accused of capital crimes are generally denied such release. But where the accused is entitled to bail, the Eighth Amendment requires that it not be "excessive." Such factors as the defendant's criminal history, the seriousness of the crime and ability to pay are relevant to the issue of excessiveness. There is generally no right to bail after conviction pending appeal; requests for such bail are left largely to the discretion of the trial judge.

As to the excessive fine provision, it is generally left to Congress to prescribe the limits of fines and to the trial courts to decide what fine should be imposed in a particular case. The Supreme Court has refused to review fines levied by the lower federal courts.

There are no precise standards as to what constitutes cruel and unusual punishment. The death penalty is not of itself cruel and unusual; what is forbidden by very early tradition of Anglo-American law is the infliction of unnecessary pain in the execution of the death sentence.

It is apparent that the Eighth Amendment, like its companions, leaves many problems unanswered, especially because the Eighth Amendment's prohibitions are not yet binding on the states. The law of bail—especially as it applies to the indigent accused—is in a state of re-evaluation. There are those who have argued, in the wake of the Chessman case, that long delay in execution is cruel and unusual punishment; indeed, there are many who argue that by modern standards, the death penalty is itself cruel and unusual punishment.

It is not pretended that the above summary of certain of the Bill of Rights criminal protections is an authoritative treatise. Indeed, entire volumes have been written on some individual Amendments. It is only hoped that the reader be informed of these protections so that the *Gault* decision might be placed in its proper constitutional perspective.

THE CASE OF THE "LEWD AND INDECENT" PHONE CALL

Gerald and another boy were taken into custody in the morning of June 8, 1964, by the Sheriff of Gila County, Arizona. The police were acting upon a verbal complaint from a Mrs. Cook, a neighbor of the boys, that she received a lewd and indecent phone call. Both of Gerald's parents were at work that morning and no notice of the police action was left at their home. Gerald's mother learned of his being taken to the Children's Detention House only after Gerald's older brother went to look for him at the home of the other boy. At the Detention Home, the mother and brother were told "why Jerry was there" and that a hearing would be held the next day at 3 o'clock.

A petition praying for a hearing was filed on June 9 by an Officer Flagg which recited that "said minor is under the age of 18 years and in need of protection of this Honorable Court [and that] said minor is a delinquent minor." The petition was not served on the Gaults and they first saw it 2 months later.

On June 9, a hearing was held in the chambers of Juvenile Judge McGhee with Gerald, his mother, his brother and the probation officers being present. No formal or informal record of this hearing was made. Judge McGhee questioned Gerald about the telephone calls without advising him of a right to counsel or a privilege against self-incrimination. There is conflicting testimony as to Gerald's answers. Both Officer Flagg and Judge McGhee stated that Gerald admitted making at least one of the indecent remarks while Mrs. Gault recalled that her son only admitted dialing Mrs. Cook's number.

Gerald was released from the detention home without explanation on either the 11th or the 12th (again the memories of Mrs. Gault and Officer Flagg conflict) pending further hearings; a hearing was held before Judge McGhee on June 15th. Mrs. Gault asked that Mrs. Cook be present but was told by the Judge that "she didn't have to be present." Neither the Gaults nor Officer Flagg remembered any admission by Gerald at this proceeding of making the indecent remarks, though the judge did remember Gerald's admitting some of the less serious statements. At the conclusion of the hearing, Gerald was committed as a juvenile delinquent to the State Industrial School "for the period of his minority [6 years] unless sooner discharged by due process of law."

No appeal is permitted under Arizona law in juvenile cases. Gerald filed a writ of habeas corpus with the Supreme Court of Arizona which was referred to the Superior Court for hearing. Among other matters, Judge McGhee testified that he acted under a section of the Arizona Code which defines a "delinquent child" as one who (in the judge's words) is "habitually involved in immoral matters." The basis for the judge's conclusion seemed to be a referral made 2 years earlier concerning Gerald when the boy allegedly had "stolen" a baseball glove "and lied to the Police Department about it." No petition or hearing apparently resulted from this "referral." The judge testified that Gerald had violated the section of the Arizona Criminal Code which provides that a person who "in the presence of or hearing of any woman or child . . . uses vulgar, abusive or obscene language, is guilty of a misdemeanor. . . ." The penalty for an adult convicted under this section is a fine of $5 to $50, or imprisonment for not more than 2 months.

The Superior Court dismissed the habeas corpus petition, and Gerald sought review in the Arizona Supreme Court on many due process grounds. The Arizona Supreme Court affirmed the dismissal of the petition.

The appellants, in their appeal to the United States Supreme Court, did not raise all of the issues brought before the Supreme Court of Arizona. The appeal was based on the argument that the Juvenile Code of Arizona is invalid because, contrary to the due process clause of the Fourteenth Amendment, the juvenile is taken from the custody of his parents and committed to a state institution pursuant to proceedings where the Juvenile Court has virtually unlimited discretion, and in which the following basic rights are denied: Notice of the charges; right to counsel; right to confrontation and cross-examination; privilege against self-incrimination; right to a transcript of the proceedings; and right to appellate review.

These were the questions before the Supreme Court in the *Gault* decision. The Court explicitly noted that other issues passed upon by the Supreme Court of Arizona, but not presented by the appellants to the Supreme Court of the United States, would not be considered. This is consistent with the Court's strict practice of reviewing—if it chooses to review at all—only those issues actually presented to it.

THE DECISION

The *Gault* decision was handed down May 15, 1967, a little over 5 months after its oral argument was heard by the Supreme Court. Mr. Justice Fortas wrote the opinion for the majority which was, in effect, 8 to 1. Justice Fortas was joined by Chief Justice Warren and Justices Brennan, Clark, and Douglas. Mr. Justice Black concurred with the result but argued that juveniles in jeopardy of confinement be tried in accordance with all of the Bill of Rights protections made applicable to the states by the Fourteenth Amendment.[5] Mr. Justice White concurred with the majority except for Part V concerning self-incrimination, confrontation, and cross-examination which he felt need not be reached, since the decision would be reversed on other grounds.[6] Mr. Justice Harlan concurred in part and dissented in part: he concurred with the majority insofar as it held that Gerald was deprived of due process of law by being denied adequate notice, record of the proceedings, and right to counsel; he dissented on the grounds that the other procedural safeguards imposed by the Court might discourage "efforts to find more satisfactory solutions for the problems of juvenile crime, and may thus now hamper enlightened development of juvenile courts."[7]

Only Mr. Justice Stewart dissented in full. Although acknowledging the shortcomings of many of the juvenile and family courts, he maintained that the procedural safeguards imposed by the decision would abolish the flexibility and informality of juvenile courts and would cause children again to be treated as adults.[8]

In summary form, the decision held as follows:

Notice of Charges.[9]—A petition alleging in general terms that the child is "neglected, dependent or delinquent" is sufficient notice under Arizona law.[10] It is not required that the petition be served upon the parents. No facts need be alleged in the initial petition; the Arizona Supreme Court held that such facts need not be alleged until the close of the initial hearing. No petition at all was served upon Gerald or his parents prior to the initial hearing.

The Arizona Supreme Court rejected Gerald's claim that due process had been denied because of failure to provide adequate notice on the following grounds: that "Mrs. Gault knew the exact nature of the charge against Gerald from the day he was taken to the detention home"; that the Gaults had appeared at the two hearings "without objection"; that advance notice of the specific charges or basis for taking the juvenile into custody and for the hearing is not necessary because "the policy of the juvenile law is to hide youthful errors from the full gaze of the public and bury them in the graveyard of the forgotten past."

The Supreme Court rejected these arguments, noting that the "initial hearing" in this case was in fact a hearing on the merits of the case. The Court stated that even if there was validity to the practice of deferring specific notice on the grounds of protecting the child from the public eye, it must yield to the due process requirement of adequate notice. Therefore, a hearing where a youth's freedom and the parent's right to custody are in jeopardy may not be held unless the child and his parents or guardian be first notified in writing of the specific issues that must be met at that hearing. Such notice must be given at the earliest practicable time and sufficiently in advance of the hearing to permit preparation. Mere "knowledge" of the kind Mrs. Gault allegedly had of the charges against Gerald does not constitute a waiver of the right to adequate notice because of its lack of particularity.

Right to Counsel.[11]—The Arizona Supreme Court had held that representation of counsel for a minor is discretionary with the trial judge. The Supreme Court disagreed, noting that neither probation officer nor judge can adequately represent the child. Since a proceeding where a child stands to be found "delinquent" and subject to loss of liberty is comparable in gravity to an adult felony prosecution, the juvenile needs the assistance of counsel for the same reasons underlying the inclusion of the right in the Sixth Amendment: The juvenile—even less than the average adult criminal defendant—is not prepared to cope with the complexities of the law or of building an adequate defense. Thus, the due process clause of the Fourteenth Amendment requires that in state proceedings which may result in commitment the child and his parent must be notified of the child's right to be represented by counsel. If they are unable to afford a lawyer, one must be appointed for them.[12]

The Court discounted the holding of the Arizona Supreme Court that since Mrs. Gault knew that she could have appeared with counsel, her failure to do so was a waiver of the right. Notification of the right to counsel plus "specific consideration" of whether to waive the right must precede a valid waiver. Without being expressly advised of the right (and Mrs.

Gault was not so advised) there can be no "specific consideration" and thus, no waiver.

Self-Incrimination, Confrontation, and Cross-Examination.[13]—It will be recalled that at the June 9 hearing, Judge McGhee questioned Gerald about the telephone calls without advising him of his right to counsel or his right to remain silent. The judge and Officer Flagg stated that Gerald admitted making at least one of the indecent remarks; Mrs. Gault recalled only that her son admitted dialing Mrs. Cook's number. The Arizona Supreme Court rejected Gerald's contention that he had a right to be advised that he need not incriminate himself, saying that the "necessary flexibility for individualized treatment will be enhanced by a rule which does not require the judge to advise the infant of a privilege against self-incrimination."

The Supreme Court rejected this view and held that any admissions that Gerald allegedly made were improperly obtained in violation of the Fifth Amendment's privilege against self-incrimination. The Court traced the history underlying the privilege, and observed: "one of its purposes is to prevent the State, whether by force or by psychological domination, from overcoming the mind and will of the person under investigation and depriving him of the freedom to decide whether to assist the State in securing his conviction." The Court implied that no less than the freedom from coerced confessions is the importance of the reliability, especially as to alleged admissions or confessions from those of Gerald's age, must undergo careful scrutiny for in the Court's words: "It would indeed be surprising if the privilege against self-incrimination were available to hardened criminals but not to children. The language of the Fifth Amendment, applicable to the States by peration of the Fourteenth Amendment, is unequivocal and without exception. And the scope of the privilege is comprehensive."[14]

The State of Arizona argued that the Fifth Amendment provides only that no person "shall be compelled in any *criminal case* to be a witness against himself" and should therefore not apply through the Fourteenth Amendment to state juvenile proceedings. The Supreme Court held that the privilege is not based upon the *type* of proceeding in which it is involved, "but upon the nature of the statement or admission made, the exposure which it invites." Since the privilege may be invoked in a civil or administrative proceeding, the court noted that it would make no difference whether juvenile proceedings are deemed "civil" or "criminal." The Court took the opportunity to express its disapproval with these labels, and noted that in over half of the states juveniles may be placed in adult penal institutions after findings of delinquency.[15] The Court stated: "For this purpose, at least, commitment is a deprivation of liberty. It is incarceration against one's will, whether it is called 'criminal' or 'civil.' And our Constitution guarantees that no person shall be 'compelled' to be a witness against himself when he is threatened with deprivation of his liberty. . . ."

The Court noted that "special problems may arise with respect to waiver of the privilege by or on behalf of children, and that there may well be some differences in technique—but not in principle—depending upon the age of the child and the presence and competence of parents." And as special care must be taken before the privilege is validly waived, so also must admissions obtained without the presence of counsel be subject to the greatest scrutiny. Here we see the Fifth Amendment's self-incrimination provision to be vitally interwoven with the Sixth Amendment's right to counsel.

The "confession" of Gerald, made without counsel, outside of the presence of his parents, and without advising him of his right to remain silent served as a basis for Judge McGhee's finding of delinquency. Since this "admission" or "confession" was obtained in violation of those rights noted above, the Supreme Court searched for another basis on which the judgment might rest. There was none to be found. There was no sworn testimony. The complainant, Mrs. Cook, did not appear. The Arizona Supreme Court held that "sworn testimony must be required of all witnesses" including those related to the juvenile court system. The Supreme Court held that this is not sufficient: In the absence of a valid confession adequate to support the determination of the Court, confrontation and sworn testimony by witnesses available for cross-examination were essential for a finding of "delinquency" and a subsequent order depriving Gerald of his liberty.[16] The court made it clear, therefore, that an adjudication of "delinquency" or a commitment to an institution is invalid unless the juvenile is afforded the same protections respecting sworn testimony that an adult would receive in a criminal trial.

Appellate Review and Transcript of Proceedings.[17]—The Supreme Court did not specifically decide whether there is a right to appellate review in a juvenile case[18] or whether juvenile courts are required to provide a transcript of the hearings for review, because the decision of the Arizona Supreme Court could be reversed on other grounds. Notwithstanding its failure to rule directly on this issue, the Court pointed out the undesirable consequences of the present case, where: no record of the proceedings was kept; no findings or grounds for basing the juvenile court's conclusions were stated; and the reviewing courts were forced to reconstruct a record while Judge McGhee had the "unseemly duty of testifying under cross-examination as to the events that transpired in the hearings before him."[19]

EPILOGUE

It should be evident to the reader that the legal precedents handed down by the *Gault* decision are neither numerous nor complex. At any proceeding where a child may be committed to a state institution, that child and his parent or guardian must be given notice in writing of the specific charges against the child sufficiently in advance of the proceedings to permit adequate preparation. The child and his parent must be notified of the child's right to be represented by counsel, and if financial considerations so require, counsel must be appointed for them. The child and his parents or guardian must be advised of the child's right to remain silent. Admission or confessions obtained from the child without the presence of counsel must undergo the greatest scrutiny in order to insure reliability. In the absence of a valid confession, no finding of "delinquency" and no order of commitment of the child for any length of time may be upheld unless such finding is supported by confrontation and

sworn testimony of witnesses available for cross-examination.

If indeed the *Gault* decision were significant only for the black-letter law, summarized above, the demands made upon our juvenile judges and probation officers would be rather easy to comply with. The few mandates of *Gault* would eventually become implemented (with, of course, varying degrees of enthusiasm). However, the decision cannot be read solely in the light of its few binding precedents.

Some may recall that it was the same Justice Fortas who wrote for the majority in the *Kent*[20] decision, which a year prior to *Gault* considered the requirement for a valid waiver of "exclusive" jurisdiction of the juvenile court of the District of Columbia so that a youth could be tried in the District's adult criminal court. The essence of *Kent* was that the basic requirements of due process and fairness be met in such a proceeding. But although confined to the narrow issue of waiver proceedings, *Kent* was a prologue to *Gault* insofar as it expressed disenchantment with the course of juvenile justice in this country, which was expressed in an often-quoted sentence: "There is evidence . . . that there may be grounds for concern that the child receives the worst of both worlds: that he gets neither the protections accorded to adults nor the solicitous care and regenerative treatment postulated for children."[21]

With this warning, an alert was sounded in *Kent* for what would become in *Gault* an indictment of the juvenile courts. Despite the limitation of issues actually adjudicated in the decision, *Gault*, taken as a whole, is a comprehensive note of concern over the administration of juvenile justice in this country. Part II of the decision[22] dealing largely with background and history contains 41 footnotes citing materials covering the entire ambit of juvenile justice, from custody to treatment, from probation to psychiatric care, and including numerous books, studies, and articles critical of virtually every aspect of the juvenile process. In Part II the *parens patriae* doctrine—the concept of the state assuming the role of substitute parent—was challenged on both historical grounds ("its meaning is murky and its historic credentials are of dubious relevance") and on legal grounds

("[T]he constitutional and theoretical basis for this peculiar system is—to say the least—debatable"). The nomenclature attached to "receiving homes" or "industrial schools" did not, in the Court's view, alter the practical reality that these are institutions of confinement where juveniles may for years be deprived of their liberty. The Court was careful to note that the "substitute parents" of the early reformers' ideology have, in fact, become guards, state employees, and fellow juveniles incarcerated for offenses ranging in scope from "waywardness" to rape and murder.

It is therefore apparent to the reader of Part II of the *Gault* decision that the case was not, as the narrow scope of its holding might wrongly suggest, decided in the abstract. Part II was a harsh and critical prelude to the decision. It was tempered with concern for a system of justice that the Court suggests has fallen short of its early hopes and aspirations, and it was laced with documentation of these failings. It is submitted that the marked distaste for the course of juvenile justice in this country, which permeated the decision, was of itself a prologue (as *Kent* was for *Gault*) for further decisions by the Supreme Court extending the due process clause into other aspects of juvenile proceedings. To speculate on the direction of such hypothetical extensions would be indeed foolish. As noted earlier, the Supreme Court selects only a small fraction of those cases submitted to it for review, and of these, only those issues necessary to dispose of a case are actually adjudicated (the appellate review and transcript issue in *Gault* is an example).

For those who are understandably concerned with the present, the *Gault* decision leaves many questions unanswered. Mr. Justice Fortas wrote in *Gault* that "neither the Fourteenth Amendment nor the Bill of Rights is for adults alone." But if indeed they are not for adults only, the Fourteenth Amendment and the Bill of Rights are not yet for children completely. The *Gault* decision did not cover the procedures or constitutional rights applicable to the pre-judicial or post-adjudicative stages of the juvenile process.[23] Thus, the body of law now pertaining to the rights of the adult criminal suspect when he is first brought into custody does not yet apply to the juvenile suspect. It is yet to be decided whether the Fourth Amendment's prohibitions against unreasonable searches and seizures, protections made fully binding upon the states, will affect the kind of evidentiary matter admissible against the child in an adjudicatory proceeding. The Fifth Amendment's right to a grand jury indictment and the double jeopardy prohibition have not yet been made fully binding upon the states by the Supreme Court, and their relevance to juvenile proceedings are uncertain.

One may ponder whether prolonged confinement in a "receiving home" pending a hearing on the merits would violate the Sixth Amendment's guarantee of a *speedy* trial, if this right is held to be firmly binding upon the states. The Sixth Amendment's guarantee to a *public* trial, which is binding upon the states, may have significant implications for juvenile hearings, which have by statute in a large proportion of the states been closed to the public. The Sixth Amendment's guarantee that the accused be entitled to have the court compel witnesses to appear and testify, a right closely related to the right of confrontation, has potential relevance to juvenile hearings, and cannot be ignored (although this right is not yet firmly binding upon the states under the Fourteenth Amendment).

One might further consider the Eighth Amendment and its prohibitions against cruel and unusual punishment, excessive fines, and excessive bail. If any or all of the Eighth Amendment is eventually made binding upon the states, how will the course of juvenile justice be affected? Is it cruel and unusual punishment to deny to a child those safeguards not considered by *Gault* and then subject that child to confinement in an institution of limited treatment facilities? Does unconditional relegation to a "receiving home" pending a hearing infringe on the prohibition against excessive bail?

That these issues may legitimately be framed, in the light of the Supreme Court's refusal in *Gault* to accept the traditional noncriminal label attached to juvenile proceedings is, in the writer's opinion, the greatest significance of the decision. It is not possible to even speculate as to the extent to which the Supreme Court is prepared to go in according to juveniles the procedural safeguards available to adults in criminal proceedings. All that is clear is that the sweeping, intangible concept of due process has at last been officially introduced to our juvenile courts.

NOTES

1. *In Re Gault*, 387 U.S. 1 (1967).

2. *New York Times*, May 16, 1967, p. 1, col. 1 (city ed.).

3. For excellent summaries of the entire Constitution from which much of the following material on the Bill of Rights is drawn, see Antieau, *Commentaries on the Constitution of the United States* (1960), and The Younger Lawyers Committee of the Federal Bar Association, *These Unalienable Rights* (1965).

4. The privilege has one notable exception: A person has no right to remain silent if a statute (federal or state) gives him immunity from prosecution—that is, if the government is prevented from prosecuting him on the basis of his testimony.

5. *In Re Gault*, supra note 1, at 59–64.

6. *Id.* at 64–65.

7. *Id.* at 77.

8. *Id.* at 78–81.

9. *Id.* at 31–34.

10. Ariz. Rev. Stat. ANN. tit. 8, 222 (1955).

11. *In Re Gault*, supra note 1, at 34–42.

12. The Court emphasized as "forceful" the Report of the President's Commission on Law Enforcement and Administration of Justice, *The Challenge of Crime in a Free Society*, pp. 86–7 (hereinafter cited as NAT'L CRIMECOMM'N REPORT) (1967), which recommended: "Counsel should be appointed as a matter of course wherever coercive action is a possibility without requiring any affirmative choice by child or parent." In *Re Gault*, supra note 1, at 38–40 n. 65. Also cited was HEW, *Standards for Juvenile and Family Courts*, Children's Bureau Pub. No. 437–1966, p. 57 (1966) (hereinafter cited as *Standards*) which states: "As a component part of a fair hearing required by due process guaranteed under the 14th Amendment, notice of the right to counsel should be required at all hearings and counsel provided upon request when the family is financially unable to employ counsel." In *Re Gault*, supra note 1, at 39.

13. *Id.* at 42–57.

14. The Court cited to this point *Standards, supra* note 12, at 49, for authority that prior to a police interview, the child and his parents should be informed of his right to have legal counsel present and to refuse to answer questions. This provision of the *Standards* also suggests that the parents and child be informed of their right to refuse to be fingerprinted, but the Court refused to express any opinion as to fingerprinting as this issue was not before the Court. In *Re Gault, supra* note 1, at 49.

15. HEW, *Delinquent Children in Penal Institutions*, Children's Bureau Pub. No. 415–1964, p. 1 (1964).

16. For this point, the Court again cited *Standards, supra* note 12, at 72–73, which states that all testimony should be under oath and that only competent material and relevant evidence under rules applicable to civil cases should be admitted into evidence. Also cited was, *e.g.*, Note, "Rights and Rehabilitation in Juvenile Courts," 67 Colum. L. Rev. 281, 336 (1967): "Particularly in delinquency cases, where the issue of fact is the commission of a crime, the introduction of hearsay—such as the report of a policeman who did not witness the events—contravenes the purpose underlying the Sixth Amendment right of confrontation." (Footnote omitted.) in *Re Gault, supra* note 1, at 56–57 n. 98.

17. *Id.* at 57–59.

18. The Supreme Court has yet to hold that a state is required to provide any right to appellate review, *Griffin v. Illinois*, 351 U.S. 12, 18 (1956).

19. The Court cited, *e.g.*, *Standards*, supra note 12, at 8, which recommends "written findings of fact, some form or record of the hearing" "and the right to appeal." It recommends verbatim recording of the hearing by stereotypist or mechanical recording. *Id* at 76. Finally, it urges that the judge make clear to the child and family their right to appeal. *Id.* at 78. Also cited was, *e.g.*, NAT'L CRIME COMM'N REPORT, supra note 12, at 86, which states that "records make possible appeals which, even if they do not occur, import by their possibility a healthy atmosphere of accountability." In *Re Gault, supra* note 1, at 58–69, n. 102.

20. *Kent v. United States*, 383 U.S. 541 (1966).

21. *Id.* at 556, citing Handler. "The Juvenile Courts and the Adversary Systems: Problems of Function and Form," 1965 WIS. L. REV. 7 (other citations omitted).

22. *In Re Gault, supra* note 1, at 12–31.

23. *Id.* at 13.

QUESTIONS FOR DISCUSSION

1. The *Gault* Decision afforded juveniles specific protections of the Bill of Rights. What were those protections?

2. What "protections" were adults afforded by the Bill of Rights that juveniles did not receive?

3. Explain what is meant by an "impartial jury."

APPLICATIONS

1. The *Gault* decision, handed down in 1967, was the first time in American history that the Supreme Court granted procedural protections to juveniles under the Bill of Rights. In your opinion, why did the extension of these rights to juveniles take so long?

2. Since 1967, have any other constitutional rights been extended to or broadened by the Supreme Court? Explain.

KEY TERMS

ambit refers to a sphere of action or influence; the scope of one's control.

mandate a directive or requirement.

mollify to soothe in temper or disposition; to soften or pacify.

nomenclature designation or description with a particular and agreed-upon set of terms.

onerous characterizes something that is troublesome or that causes a burden.

panacea a cure-all; a remedy for all ills or problems.

permeate to diffuse through or to penetrate.

postulate to assume or claim to be true, existent, or necessary.

pursuant to in conformity with or according to a pre-existing condition.

22

A Comparative Analysis of Organizational Structure and Inmate Subcultures in Institutions for Juvenile Offenders

Barry C. Feld

The penological debate over the origins, processes, and characteristics of inmate subcultures in correctional facilities has attributed the qualities of subcultures either to features of the formal organization or to preimprisonment characteristics of the incarcerated offenders.[1] Observers of adult and juvenile correctional facilities confirm the emergence of inmate subcultures within institutions, and most studies of prison cultures document their oppositional qualities, with the hostility and antagonism between inmates and staff subsumed in an "inmate code."[2]

The two competing explanations of the inmate social system are commonly referred to as the "indigenous origins" model and the "direct importation" model.[3] The former provides a functionalist explanation that relates the values and roles of the subculture to the inmates' responses to problems of adjustment posed by institutional deprivations and conditions of confinement.[4] Accordingly, the formal organization of the prison shapes the informal inmate social system. While earlier studies of

adult maximum-security prisons described a monolithic inmate culture of collective opposition to staff values and goals,[5] more recent studies suggest that a modification of organizational structure in pursuit of treatment goals results in considerably greater variability in the inmate social system and the processes of prisonization.[6]

An alternative interpretation attributes the normative order of adult prisons to the identities, roles, and values held by the inmates before incarceration.[7] Accordingly, inmates' personal characteristics shape the subculture, and in a population of incarcerated offenders an oppositional, criminal value system predominates. Differences in social characteristics such as sex, race, or criminal involvement before incarceration influence both the subculture's qualities and any individual inmate's adaptations to it.[8]

INMATE VIOLENCE IN INSTITUTIONS

The prevalence of inmate violence and its significance for stratification, role differentiation, and subcultural processes represent a recurring theme.[9] However, the relationships between organizational variables, inmate violence, and other characteristics of the subculture have not been adequately explored.

"A Comparative Analysis of Organizational Structure and Inmate Subcultures in Institutions for Juvenile Offenders," *Crime and Delinquency*, 27:3 (1981), pp. 336–363. Reprinted by permission of the publisher, Sage Publications, Inc.

Physical aggression, verbal abuse, or psychological intimidation can be used to create or reestablish relationships of domination and submission within the subculture.[10] Many maxims of the inmate code are attempts to regulate violence and exploitation among inmates, and many of the "argot" roles differentiate inmates on the basis of their use of or response to aggression.[11] For individual inmates, many of the "pains of imprisonment"—material deprivations, sexual isolation, and threats to status, self-esteem, and personal security—cited in functionalist explanations of subcultures can be alleviated by the use of violence. While imprisonment imposes deprivations, violence and exploitation provide at least some inmates with a potential solution, albeit at the expense of other inmates.[12]

The prevalence of inmate violence also reflects characteristics of the incarcerated. Many adult and juvenile inmates are drawn from social backgrounds or cultures that emphasize toughness, manliness, and the protection of one's own physical integrity.[13] Preincarceration experiences equip in different ways inmates from diverse social, economic, criminal, racial, or sexual backgrounds to participate in the violent subcultures within some institutions.[14] Thus, a predisposition to violence among the inmate subculture also reflects influences of cultural importation which organizational features may aggravate or mitigate.

Neither functionalist nor importation explanations alone adequately explain the characteristics of the inmate subculture or an inmate's adaptations to it. The functionalist model does not account for the influence of pre- and postimprisonment variables on inmates' adaptations, while the importation model does not fully explicate the connections between preprison characteristics and the subcultures that arise within institutions that are not custodial or punitive. Although some recent research attempts to integrate the two perspectives by identifying the ways in which preprison characteristics influence inmates' adaptations to adjustment problems created by the organization,[15] most subculture studies suffer from the common shortcoming of focusing on prisonization within only a single insti-

tution. In contrast, a comparison of organizations would permit a fuller exploration of the relationships between formal organizational structure and the ensuing inmate culture, as well as of the influence of preprison characteristics on the adaptations of inmates in diverse settings.[16] Controlling for the effects of preincarceration characteristics on inmates' perceptions and adaptations, this study presents a comparative analysis of the ways in which variations in organizational goals and intervention strategies in institutions for juvenile offenders produce differences in the informal inmate social system.

Organizational features affect the inmate subculture and the prevalence of inmate violence both by creating incentives for inmates to resort to violence and by providing inmates with opportunities to use violence. Organizational variations in the nature and extent of deprivations may motivate inmates in different ways to exploit others. Various organizational control strategies differ in the degree to which they provide an environment conducive to the use of violence to relieve these deprivations. The deprivations and control strategies also influence many other aspects of the subculture. This comparative analysis examines the variations in organizational goals, staff intervention strategies, and social control practices that influence the levels of violence and the structure of the inmate social system.

CORRECTIONAL TYPOLOGY

There are several descriptions of the organizational variations in juvenile and adult correctional facilities that can be used as tools to classify systematically and compare the relationships between organizational structure and inmate subculture.[17] A common classification distinguishes juvenile correctional organizations on the basis of their custody or treatment goals,[18] distinguishing differences in goals on the basis of the relative emphases staff place on custody and containment, and on vocational and academic education versus clinical or group treatment.[19] The intervention strategies used to achieve either custodial or therapeutic goals range from group-oriented practices to those more attuned to individuals' character-istics.[20] Group-oriented strategies reflect efforts to change or control an inmate through the group of which he is a member, while individ-ualized methods of intervention focus more directly on the person, without comparable manipulation of the social environment.

Organizational goals—custody or treat-ment—and strategies of change—group or individual—may vary independently; thus, four different types of correctional organizations may be distinguished on the basis of both their correctional goals and the means used to attain those goals (see Figure 1).

Every juvenile correctional institution con-fronts the same necessity to explain both what its clients' problems are and how the clients should be rehabilitated.[21] The answers to the questions of cause and cure in turn determine the organizational goals and the intervention strategies and social control practices required to achieve them. The typology in Figure 1 illus-trates four different kinds of correctional solu-tions to the problems of juvenile offenders. It also suggests several interrelated organizational variables: a staff ideology defining inmates and their needs, organizational goals serving those needs, intervention strategies implemented through programs and social control practices, and the structure of relationships between inmates and staff.

A degree of internal consistency among these organizational variables is necessary. Methods of intervention and social control practices must be complementary, since efforts to ensure compliance that alienate the inmate are incompatible with change strategies requir-ing commitment on the part of that inmate.[22] Compliance strategies and programs will vary with the correctional goals and inmate changes sought and determine the kinds of relation-ships staff develop with inmates. Amitai Etzioni's compliance framework provides a basis for a comparative organizational analysis of staff control strategies and inmates' responses in coercive and normative-coercive settings.[23] The primary correctional social con-trol strategies are (1) the threat or use of phys-ical coercion, (2) the threat or use of transfer to less desirable units or isolation cells, (3) the use of a privilege system,[24] and (4) collabora-tion between inmates and staff, which may be either informal[25] or formal.[26]

METHODS

The data for this study were collected in ten cottage units located in four juvenile institu-tions administered by the Massachusetts Depart-ment of Youth Services before the closing of the training schools.[27] A process of institutional decentralization initiated to transform the var-ious cottage settings into small, therapeutic communities[28] provided considerable auton-

FIGURE 1 Correctional Typology

Organizational Means	Organizational Goals	
	Custody	Treatment
Group-Oriented Intervention Strategy	Group Custody Custodial[a] Obedience/Conformity[b] Protective custody[c]	Group Treatment Group treatment[a] Treatment[b] Therapeutic community[c]
Individual-Oriented Intervention Strategy	Individual Custody Educational[a] Reeducation/Development[b] Protective custody[c]	Individual Treatment Psychotherapeutic[a] Treatment[b,c]

a. Organization corresponding to typology in Studt, Messinger, and Wilson, *C-Unit*, p. 12.
b. Organization corresponding to typology in Street, Vinter, and Perrow, *Organization for Treatment*, p. 12.
c. Organization corresponding to typology in Ohlin, "Organizational Reform in Correctional Agencies," p. 1000.

omy and independence for each individual unit. Clinical, vocational, academic, and cottage personnel either formed staff teams or were assigned to cottages to develop coordinated treatment programs. Decentralization resulted in a number of diverse "mini-institutions" in which staff pursued a variety of goals using different intervention strategies.

Since inmate assignments to the various cottages were not randomized, the ten cottages studied were selected to maximize the comparability of inmate populations and the variety of treatment strategies used. The ten cottages studied included seven units for males, two for females,[29] and one coeducational facility, located in four different state institutions. Cottage populations were matched on the basis of age, race, past criminal histories (both official and self-reported), present commitment offense, age at initial contact and number of prior juvenile court appearances, and prior commitments to institutions. The inmate characteristics in the various cottages are summarized in Table 1. The cottages sampled produced comparable inmate groups. Although cottage assignments were not randomized, there was no systematic effort by administrators to match inmate "needs" with particular treatment programs, and the primary determinants were the availability of bed space and the need to maintain a population balance among the various cottages.

In addition to the matching of populations, statistical controls for the effects of background characteristics within each cottage were used to establish cottage comparability. Controls for each background variable were used to determine whether a particular characteristic was systematically associated with differences within each cottage population and whether the differences among cottages were a product of these population differences. In addition to tests for relationships between background variables and attitudes, sign tests were used to allow for interaction effects between inmates' characteristics and cottage treatment strategies. Despite some variations in the respective cottage populations, these techniques support the conclusion that the substantial differences between cottages were not a function of varia-

TABLE 1   Inmate Background Characteristics

| | Custody-Oriented Cottages | | | | | Treatment-Oriented Cottages | | | |
| | Group | Individual | | | | Individual | Group | | |
	Cottage 9 (n = 27)	Cottage 8 (n = 15)	Elms (n = 40)	Westview (n = 29)	Lancaster (F) (n = 28+22)[a]	Topsfield (coed) (n = 15)	Sunset (n = 15)	Shirley (n = 16)	"I Belong" (n = 8)
Mean age	15.7	16.3	15.6	15.6	14.9	16.2	15.5	16.3	14.2
Percentage black inmates	19%	27%	35%	21%	11%	32%	25%	19%	25%
Mean age at first juvenile court appearance	12.6	13.2	12.7	13.1	13.1	14.1	12.5	13.8	12.4
Seriousness of present offense (percentage of residents)									
High [b]	24%	36%	35%	27%	9%	0%	23%	21%	29%
Moderate [c]	68	43	60	54	34	60	77	57	43
Low [d]	8	21	5	19	57	40	0	21	28
Prior institutional experience (percentage of residents)	92%	82%	90%	62%	60%	87%	73%	67%	50%

a.   Institutional decentralization and the development of cottage-based programs occurred later and, when this study was conducted, were less complete at the Industrial School for Girls, Lancaster, than at the corresponding male institutions. The school still functioned as a traditional training school without any significant program differentiation by cottage. Separate analysis of inmate and staff data in the two cottages sampled (n = 28 + 22) revealed virtually no differences. Consequently, the Lancaster questionnaire data are presented in the aggregate.

b.   Offenses against the person—murder, manslaughter, rape, assaults, robbery, and the like.

c.   Property offenses—burglary, theft, forgery, unauthorized use of a motor vehicle, and drug offenses.

d.   Misdemeanor-level public misbehavior, such as disorderly conduct, as well as juvenile status offenses.

tions in the inmate populations and are properly attributed to the cottages' social structures.[30] In institutions with young populations (averaging approximately sixteen years of age), who are presumably less committed to criminal careers than are imprisoned adults and who are incarcerated for an average of four months, it is not surprising that background characteristics or preimprisonment experiences are subordinate to the more immediate, organizational imperatives. (Because the sample is not random, no tests of significance are reported.)

Data were collected in each of the ten cottages by a team of five trained researchers who spend about six weeks in each unit administering questionnaires and interview schedules to both staff members and residents. Between 90 and 100 percent of the staff and residents in each cottage completed hour-long closed-ended questionnaires and equally extensive open-ended structural interviews. Most of the researchers' time was spent in participant observation and unstructured interviews, with field notes transcribed onto standardized forms to simplify analysis, coding, and comparison of observations from different settings.

FINDINGS

Organizational Structure

Although the administrators of the Massachusetts Department of Youth Services told the institutional staff to "do good things for kids," they did not specify what the staff members should do or how they should do it. The process of institutional decentralization allowed staff to pursue a variety of goals using diverse treatment strategies within the autonomous cottages. In structuring programs for how their clients should be handled and changed, staff were guided by their own assumptions about the causes of and cures for delinquent behavior. Although there was some diversity among staff within the respective cottages, recruitment, self-selection, and cottage assignments resulted in relatively homogeneous correctional ideologies among cottage personnel; the focus of this study is on the substantial differences among the various units in programs and goals that

emerged and the effects of these differences on the respective inmate cultures.

Cottage Programs and Social Control Strategies

Maximum Security (Group Custody) Cottage Nine was a unit used for juveniles who had run away from the institution and for youths who had committed other disciplinary infractions. About half of all residents escaped from the institution at some time during their stay; there were no significant differences between those who absconded and those who did not. There was no vocational training, academic education, or clinical program in the maximum-security setting. Intervention consisted of punishment and deprivation, with periods of enforced idleness interrupted only for meals, routine clean-up and cottage maintenance. All the cottage activities took place in a highly controlled, structured environment, and virtually all activities occurred in a group setting. Staff attempted to coerce inmate conformity and obedience, and punished recalcitrance or resistance. At a result, a typical three- to four-week stay in Cottage Nine before return to an open cottage was an unpleasant experience which residents had little choice but to endure.

Staff used physical coercion and isolation cells—"the Tombs"—to enforce obedience, conformity, and respect. These techniques were feasible since there was no program in which staff needed to obtain active inmate participation, and the staff's physical domination made coercion practicable. Staff members used their limited repertoire of controls to counter major forms of deviance such as riots and fights, as well as inmate provocation, disrespect, or recalcitrance. They also used mass lockups and other forms of group punishment.

Other control techniques were virtually absent, since there were no amenities or privileges that might be lost, and strategies designed to ensure group control precluded the development of individualized relationships necessary for collaborative controls. The use of coercive tactics alienated inmates, who minimized contacts with staff. Personnel ignored considerable inmate misbehavior that did not challenge their authority, and did not encourage inmates to report deviance that occurred outside the presence of staff members.

Industrial Training School (Individual Custody)

Despite considerable program diversity, each of the individual custody settings—Cottage 8, Elms, Westview, and the Lancaster Industrial School for Girls—used vocational training as the primary strategy of change. Most of the trades programs consisted of either institutional maintenance or services for residents—a cafeteria program, laundry program, institutional upkeep, painting, landscaping and groundskeeping, and the like. There were limited academic and clinical programs in some of the cottages. However, individual counseling sessions were not scheduled regularly, and inmates initiated contact with clinical staff primarily to secure a weekend furlough or early parole.

Compared with those in the maximum-security unit, residents of the training school cottages enjoyed greater physical freedom within the institution, which rendered staff control more difficult. Inmate cooperation in the work programs was also problematic. Staff used a privilege system to induce conformity, coupling this with the threat of transfer to more punitive, maximum-security settings. The privilege system was a security-graded progression, with inmates at different levels accorded different privileges or governed by different restrictions. Passage from one level to another reflected the amount of time served and an inmate's general behavior and conformity. Because of the relatively limited privileges available, staff members exercised considerable discretion in the rules they enforced, against whom, and under what circumstances. The staff also collaborated informally with inmate leaders to maintain order, manipulating the privilege system to confer additional status and rewards on the elite. Informal collaboration between staff members and the inmate elite is a common training school control strategy because of the availability of privileges, the discretionary bases upon which rewards are manipulated, and the problems of maintaining order posed by program individualization, the need to secure cooperation, and increased inmate freedom.[31]

Individual Treatment

The individual treatment program used all types of clinical treatment, including both individual counselling and individual therapy in a group setting. The cottage program was free and open with few restrictions. Staff minimized deprivations and maximized amenities to encourage inmate commitment and involvement in the clinical process. Staff eschewed universal rules, responding to each inmate or the basis of individualized therapeutic considerations.

Staff relied almost exclusively on a rich privilege system to secure the cooperation and participation of inmates. Although the threat of transfer to a less desirable setting was a possibility, the penalty was never invoked. There was virtually no physical coercion or informal collaboration used to obtain conformity or obedience. In response to inmate deviance, additional clinical sessions were prescribed to reinforce the privilege system—not as sanctions, but to provide additional supports for the recalcitrant resident.

Group Treatment

All of the group treatment cottages used a therapeutic community treatment model,[32] which was supplemented with either vocational or academic educational programs. The therapeutic community treatment model used both daily staff-inmate community meetings and group therapy sessions. A daily log provided the agenda for cottage community discussions, with staff and residents encouraged to record incidents that required the community's attention. At these meetings, staff integrated observations of residents on work, school, or cottage living. They then divided the cottage populations into smaller treatment groups and used a type of guided group interaction to deal with interpersonal problems or to resolve issues raised during the community meetings.

Formal collaborations between staff and inmates was the primary means of social control. Staff used the group problem-solving process to define and enforce cottage norms and to mobilize group pressures to deal with specific instances of deviance. Rules and consequences were elaborated in a privilege system that was jointly enforced; each inmate's privileges and freedoms were more dependent upon performance and participation and were less a function of the length of time served than was the case in the more custodial settings. The gradations of privileges and freedom and the responsibilities associated with each level were consistently and energetically enforced.

The strength of the formal collaboration process was the pressure staff placed upon residents to motivate other inmates to change. The concept of "responsibility" was crucial, and residents were responsible both for their own progress and behavior and for that of others. This principle of third-party responsibility provided a therapeutic rationale that significantly transformed subcultural norms governing informing and greatly increased the amount of information received by staff about the inmate group.

The Relationship between Staff Correctional Ideology and Cottage Program Characteristics
The differences in correctional programs and control strategies stemmed from various assumptions staff made about appropriate ways to treat inmates. Since staff members were allowed to form their own cottage teams, there was substantial interpersonal and ideological compatibility within units. For purposes of explaining

the diversity in the cottage programs and subcultures, the more important differences were among the different units. (See Table 2 for a presentation of some of the dimensions on which they differed.)

One component of a correctional ideology is the emphasis placed by staff on inmates' obedience, respect for authority, and submission to external controls. Custodial staff were much more concerned with obedience and respect than were treatment personnel, and subscribed more extensively to the use of external controls to achieve inmate conformity.

Cottage staff members also differed in their views of deviance. Personnel in the treatment-oriented cottages attributed delinquency to emotional or psychological problems, while custody staff rejected psychopathology or emotional dysfunction, emphasizing as a cause of delinquency such factors as a youth's exercise of free will, which could be deterred by punishment. Because the custody staff rejected psychological interpretations, they found delinquent or bizarre inmate behavior considerably more difficult to understand than did treatment staff. Staff members also disagreed over whether delinquents were capable of establishing "normal" relationships, with those emphasizing custody far more likely than treat-

TABLE 2   Selected Indicators of Staff Ideology and Goals (as a percentage of total staff in setting)

Scale	Custody-Oriented Cottages					Treatment-Oriented Cottages			
	Group	Individual				Individual	Group		
	Cottage 9 (n = 9)	Cottage 8 (n = 16)	Elms (n = 15)	Westview (n = 10)	Lancaster (F) (n = 14)	Topsfield (coed) (n = 9)	Sunset (n = 5)	Shirley (n = 16)	"I Belong" (n = 8)
Respect for authority	89%	88%	73%	67%	54%	11%	0%	25%	25%
Free will and deterrence	79	81	60	78	50	0	40	38	13
Delinquents cannot be understood	67	75	67	67	43	0	0	19	13
Inmates are dangerous	67	63	47	56	43	0	20	38	13
Conformity to staff orders	56	69	71	63	50	0	20	6	13
Custody-oriented goals	37	34	32	37	38	15	13	21	10
Personnel acting in clinical capacity	0	18	7	10	21	56	20	44	50

NOTE: Each scale contains three or more items, with an interitem correlation greater than .5 and significant at the .001 significance level.

ment personnel to regard the inmates in their cottages as "hard-core delinquents" who were dangerous and untrustworthy.

A correctional ideology both rationalizes deviance and its control and describes the end result sought—the "changed" inmate. Institutional behavior provides the staff with an indicator of an inmate's "rehabilitation" and readiness to return to the community. Custody staff strongly preferred inmates who followed orders, kept to themselves, and stayed out of trouble, which reflected their greater emphasis on external conformity rather than internalized controls. Their more negative perceptions of inmates and apprehension about collusion also led the custody staff members to disrupt informal inmate associations and encourage self-isolation, while treatment personnel encouraged inmate involvement with other inmates.

These alternative analyses of delinquency led staffs to pursue different correctional goals. When personnel were asked to choose among various correctional goals for incarcerated delinquents, significantly more of the custody-oriented staff members subscribed to custodial institutional objectives—isolation, respect and discipline, and training and educating—than did treatment personnel. Allocation of institutional resources provides another indicator of organizational goals; in juvenile institutions, personnel are the primary resource. Organizations pursuing custodial goals assign personnel to control and containment, or vocational and educational functions; treatment-oriented organizations, in contrast, assign more staff members to clinical and treatment functions. The greatest proportion of personnel in the custodial cottages served as guards, work supervisors, and academic instructors, while the treatment-oriented cottages assigned a larger percentage of the staff to treatment roles, with a corresponding reduction in purely supervisory personnel.

The Inmate Subcultures

An inmate subculture develops within the confines of a correctional institution, and its norms and values reflect the focal concerns of insti-

tutional life and the inmate population. Inmate roles and subculture stratification reflect conformity to or deviation from these norms, and newly entering inmates are socialized into this system and adapt to the expectations of their fellow inmates. The informal social system often mediates the effectiveness of the formal organization, aiding or thwarting staff members in the pursuit of their goals.[33]

A feature of correctional organization that influences the character of the inmate social systems is the extent to which staff members successfully control inmate violence and exploitation. Institutional characteristics influence the prevalence of inmate aggression by varying the levels of deprivation, a condition that gives some inmates an incentive to direct predatory behavior at others, and by providing the opportunities under which such exploitation may be carried out successfully. Inmate violence is directly related to the quality of relations between inmates and staff and to the information available to personnel about the workings of the subculture. Thus, controlling violence is a sine qua non of effective correctional programming and administration.

There was a clear relationship between the type of formal organization and the informal inmate culture. In the punitive, group custody setting, inmates experienced the greatest deprivation and were the most alienated from other inmates and staff members. Inmate alienation prevented the development of effective staff controls and allowed aggressive inmates to exploit their fellows through diverse forms of violent behavior. In the training school settings, the staff members used a privilege system coupled with informal cooperation of the inmate elite to bring potentially aggressive inmates under some degree of control. This reduced the effectiveness of inmate violence and exploitation, although aggression remained the dominant mode of interaction within the subculture. In the treatment-oriented cottages, especially in the group treatment programs, formal collaboration between inmates and staff members reduced the level of inmate violence and provided a therapeutic rationale for informing that made the workings of the subculture more visible to staff. The greater visibility, combined with significantly reduced deprivation, lowered the necessity for and effectiveness of inmate aggression and exploitation and allowed for the emergence of a more positive inmate culture.

Inmate Perceptions of Staff and Inmates Problems of institutional living influence inmates' motives for interaction and the types of solutions they can develop. Just as correctional personnel structure their relationships with inmates, residents attempt to structure and control their relationships with staff and other inmates to resolve the problems of the informal organization. The types of relationships and collective solutions available depend upon the inmates' perceptions of the program, staff, and other inmates. Inmate cooperation with staff augers for a more open, visible, and manageable social system. If staff cannot obtain inmate cooperation through either formal or informal collaboration, then a more closed, subterranean, and violent social system emerges.

Cottage Purposes The cottage goals and programs define the organizational context to which inmates must adapt. Table 3 provides a breakdown of inmates' perceptions of the goals, staff, and other aspects of life in the different cottages. When asked about cottage purposes and staff expectations, residents of the custody-oriented cottages described the cottages as places for punishment, while inmates in the treatment-oriented settings regarded the cottages as places for rehabilitation and for gaining self-awareness. As a further indicator of organizational purposes and adaptive constraints, inmates were asked whether staff encouraged them to conform or to gain insight into their own motivation and behavior. Responding to staff expectations (see Table 2), inmates in the custody-oriented settings were more than twice as likely to view the staff as demanding obedience and conformity as were those in the treatment cottages, while the latter were almost three times as likely as the residents of custody-oriented settings to describe staff expectations in terms of treatment and self-understanding.

A corollary of the differences in custodianship and punitiveness was the "pain of imprisonment" that inmates described. While some of the problems inmates confront are inherent in incarceration—loss of liberty, separation from family and friends, increased dependency and submission to authority, and the like—other pains of confinement, such as material deprivations, are attributable to characteristics of a particular setting. By virtually every measure, the inmates in the custody-oriented cottages reported far more extensive and severe problems associated with their confinement—boredom, living with other residents, and material deprivations—than did the inmates in the treatment cottages. These reported differences in institutional amenities resulted from staff actions, since treatment personnel tried to minimize the unpleasant, alienating aspects of incarceration to a greater extent than did custody-oriented staff.

Inmate Perceptions of Staff Inmates' views of staff paralleled staff members' perceptions of inmates. In those settings where staff had negative views of inmates, describing them as dangerous, unreliable, abnormal, or incorrigible, the inmates held correspondingly negative views of staff, regarding them as untrustworthy, unhelpful or indifferent. In those settings where the staff expressed more favorable views of inmates, residents shared more positive views of the staff. Virtually every inmate in the maximum-security setting and over half the inmates in the individual custody settings, as contrasted with only about one-fifth of those in the treatment settings, regarded staff as neither concerned nor helpful. Inmates readily equated punitive programs with unconcerned staff and therapeutic programs with committed staff. Likewise, residents of the custody-oriented cottages initiated fewer contacts with personnel and talked with them less about personal problems than did those in the treatment settings.

Inmate Perceptions of Other Inmates Characteristics of the inmate social system also reflect the extent to which inmates can cooperate with one another to ease the hardship of adjusting to the institution. The residents of the custody-

TABLE 3 Selected Indicators of Inmate Attitudes (as a percentage of total residents)

| | Custody-Oriented Cottages | | | | | Treatment-Oriented Cottages | | | |
| | Group | Individual | | | | Individual | Group | | |
	Cottage 9 (n = 27)	Cottage 8 (n = 15)	Elms (n = 40)	Westview (n = 29)	Lancaster (F) (n = 28 + 22)	Topsfield (coed) (n = 15)	Sunset (n = 15)	Shirley (n = 16)	"I Belong" (n = 8)
Inmate perceptions of cottage goals: What is this place trying to do for you?									
Gain understanding	11%	20%	23 (23)[a]	24%	28%	73%	53%	63 (64)	86%
Train and educate	11	7	0 (1)	0	0	13	7	13 (8)	0
Respect for authority	0	13	13 (15)	21	13	13	13	13 (13)	14
Punish for the wrong things they did	78	60	64 (61)	55	60	0	27	13 (15)	0
Staff emphasis									
Obey the rules and don't get into any trouble	63	86	74 (78)	79	73	7	46	43 (37)	0
Understand your personal problems	37	14	26	21	27	93	54	57	100
Staff do not help or care about inmates	96	87	46 (58)	59	51	13	20	25 (18)	0
Positive perception of staff	0	0	39 (30)	35	40	80	73	63 (74)	100
Negative perception of other inmates	70	47	41 (41)	38	51	7	27	25 (21)	0
Regardless of what the adults say, the best way to get along here is—									
Stay out of the way of the adults, but get away with what you can	37	7	23 (18)	17	20	0	13	6 (8)	0
Don't break any rules and keep out of trouble	26	53	54 (54)	55	33	33	27	44 (38)	50
Show that you are really sorry for what you did	0	7	7	10	11	13	13	6	13
Try to get an understanding of yourself	37	33	13 (22)	28	37	53	47	44 (44)	37
Prisonized adoption	59	60	56 (51)	38	53	7	40	13 (21)	0
Approval of informing	7	20	21 (18)	14	36	80	33	50 (51)	88
Positive inmate role	33	33	48 (45)	48	47	64	60	56 (66)	100
Inmate leaders negative	52	73	48 (49)	38	48	13	33	31 (26)	0

a. The numbers in parentheses denote the average percentage of residents in each type of cottage responding as shown to the attitudinal indicator. The responses are mutually exclusive; thus the totals will be 100 percent (with slight variation because of rounding).

oriented cottages reported substantially lower levels of trust and concern on the part of other inmates than did those in the treatment-oriented settings. Residents of the treatment cottages also reported greater inmate solidarity than did their custody cottage counterparts. Since predatory behavior and subcultural violence were more prevalent in the custody-oriented settings, the differences in inmate perceptions also reflect the extent to which inmates were exploited and victimized by others.

Inmate Adaptations Differences among the programs in staff expectations constitute an additional organizational constraint on inmates' adaptations. Custodial staff emphasized inmate conformity and obedience, whereas treatment staff emphasized gaining insight and solving personal problems (see Table 2). In response, inmates in the custody-oriented settings chose either overt conformity and covert deviance or obedience and conformity as adaptive strategies, while those in the treatment-oriented settings chose self-understanding. Similarly, adaptations reflecting elements of prisonization—prompt obedience, conformity, and self-isolation—were chosen by twice as many residents of custody-oriented settings as those in treatment programs, closely paralleling the staff expectations.

Social Structure of the Inmate Subculture Inmates interact more frequently and intensely with residents of their own cottage than they do with those in other settings, and a set of norms and roles based upon those norms govern their interactions with other inmates and staff. Differences in staff intervention practices are strongly related to variations in inmates' perceptions of other inmates, staff, and institutional adaptation, and to corresponding differences in inmate norms, subculture roles, and interaction patterns.

The inmates' and staff's responses to violence and aggression are among the most important determinants of subculture processes. In the absence of effective controls, violence and aggression underlie most interactions within the inmate subculture.[34] Direct action, toughness, and defense of personal integrity are focal concerns of many delinquent inmates,[35] and even a few aggressive inmates can immediately make the control of violence a major concern within the institution. Moreover, the prevalence of violence is closely related to other subcultural norms, particularly those related to informing.

Inmate norms governing interactions with staff and the acceptability of informing personnel of other inmates' activities have been frequently described.[36] Informing and subcultural violence are closely linked, since uncontrolled violence can deter informing, while informing, if properly encouraged by staff, can reduce it. The regulation of the flow of information between inmates and staff thus emerges as a critical determinant of inmate roles and subculture structure.

Inmates' views of staff and inmates and their adaptations to the institution influence the amount of information staff members receive about the inmate social system, which in turn conditions the staff members' ability to control the subcultural violence. Residents of the treatment cottages held relatively favorable views of other inmates and staff. Because of the greater availability of privileges and amenities, they had less incentive to engage in covert deviance to relieve deprivations and thus had less to hide. Almost three times as many inmates in the treatment settings as in the custody-oriented settings approved of informing. In fact, a virtual majority of residents of the former approved of informing.

As indicated previously, the treatment inmates' support for informing stemmed, in part, from the staff members' redefinition of informing as "helping" or "being responsible for others" as part of the treatment program. Formal collaboration reinforced the therapeutic rationale for informing and gave inmates greater protection from intimidation by increasing the visibility of informal pressures by other inmates. By legitimating and fostering informing, staff members received an enormous amount of information about the hidden processes of the subculture, which better enabled them to control inmate violence.

Participant observation and structured interviews provided an insight into "strong-arming" and "bogarting"—the subterranean violence among residents. "You have to fight" was a norm in the custody-oriented cottages, and the levels of verbal abuse and physical violence were considerably higher there than in the treatment-oriented settings. Inmates emphasized toughness, resisting exploitation or provocation, and maintaining one's position in the subculture through physical means. Physical and verbal testing and scuffles were daily occurrences, although actual fights were less frequent. The inmate did not have to be a successful fighter, but a willingness to fight to protect himself, his position, and his property was essential. Fighting and defending against exploitation were as important for female inmates as for males in comparable custodial cottages.

An inmate's readiness and ability to defend personal integrity and property were tested very early during confinement as new residents were subtly or overtly challenged for whatever material goods they possessed. As mentioned above, the greater deprivation in the custody-oriented settings made exploitation a profitable strategy for the more aggressive inmates. Residents who fought back could insulate themselves from chronic exploitation, while failure to do so left them and their possessions vulnerable.

There was significantly less exploitation in the treatment-oriented cottages than in the custody-oriented cottages. The field observers recorded fewer incidents of fights, physical confrontations, or expropriation of property. All the observers commented on the virtual absence here of "ranking"—verbal abuse—as compared with the custody cottages. There was less normative support for fighting, and when it did occur most of the inmates condemned it in the community meetings.

The differences in subcultural violence resulted from the steps staff took to control it. In the custody cottages, inmates retaliated with violence to punish those who informed to staff and to discourage other inmates from doing so. Given their limited social control repertoire, custody staff did not encourage inmates to inform, since it only forced them to confront violent inmates directly. When staff members

learned of inmate violence or victimization, they seldom took steps to prevent its recurrence. More frequently, they reinforced the values of the violent subculture by encouraging the resident to fight back and defend himself. In view of the unsympathetic and unsupportive staff response to complaints and the retaliatory inmate violence that followed, inmates had little incentive to cooperate with staff. Custody staff were isolated from the workings of the subculture, and unable to combat the violence that stifled the flow of information. In the treatment-oriented cottages, formal collaboration and inmate support for informing provided channels of communication and a mechanism for coping with incidents of violence.

While inmate approval of informing afforded greater control over inmate violence, there were differences in other subcultural norms as well. Responses to a series of hypothetical stories concerning common incidents in correctional institutions demonstrated a further contrast in the norms that prevailed in the various cottages. About two-thirds of the inmates in the treatment-oriented settings, as compared with less than half of those in the custody-oriented settings, supported "positive" inmate behavior—cooperation with staff, refusal to aid escapes, and the like.

Different inmate roles and subcultural stratification accompanied the differences in cottage norms. In the more violent custodial cottages, the roles of superior and inferior were allocated on the basis of an inmate's ability to "out-fight, outthink, or out-talk" fellow inmates. Since most inmates were neither complete successes nor complete failures in out-fighting, out-thinking, or out-talking their peers, the distribution of roles resulted in a stratification system with a few aggressive leaders at the top, a few "punks"—chronic victims—at the bottom, and most of the inmates occupying a more intermediate status, neither "one-up" nor "one-down." In the treatment-oriented settings, inmate roles and stratification were not as tied to physical or verbal prowess.

The differences in cottage norms and inmate relations were reflected in the characteristics of the inmate leadership as well. A majority of inmates in the custody-oriented cottages, as contrasted with about one-quarter of the residents of the treatment cottages, described the leaders as filling a negative and violent role in cottage life. Both observations and interviews revealed that leaders were those inmates who "strong-armed" and exploited lower-status inmates. There was greater normative support for negative inmate behavior in these cottages, and the leaders reflected and perpetuated the dominate values of the subculture.

Norms governing violence and informing constrained inmate leaders in the treatment-oriented cottages. Formal collaboration between inmates and staff reduced the leaders' ability to maintain covert physical control over the inmate group, and they played a more positive and supportive role in the institution. Formal collaboration increased their visibility and required that they at least appear to adopt a cooperative attitude in their relations with staff, which enabled other inmates to establish more positive relationships with inmates and staff.

At the bottom of the custody cottages' social structure were the "punks," inmates who were bullied and exploited and who acquiesced in the role of victim. Since the first rule of survival in the violent subculture was to defend oneself, inmates who were unable or unwilling to fight were at the mercy of those who would do so. Punks were chronically victimized, both psychologically and physically, and were the victims of merciless taunting and pummeling. In the custodial settings, the strong norm against informing prevented either the victims or other inmates from revealing what occurred. The inability of staff to control the violence prevented inmates from revealing their victimization and left them at the mercy of their exploiters.

Homosexual rape was the ultimate act of physical aggression by tough cottage leaders against punks. More than exploitative sexual satisfaction, rape entailed conquest and domination of the victim by the aggressor.[37] Every incident of homosexual assault discovered during this study could be analyzed in terms of leader-punk role relationships; such assaults occurred only in the violent custody-oriented cottages.

In the treatment-oriented settings, punks did not suffer as much physical or verbal abuse. Although other inmates regarded them as weak, immature, and lacking self-respect, formal collaboration provided a substantial check on the extent of their victimization. At least by contrast with those custody-oriented settings, low-status inmates in the treatment cottages enjoyed a comparatively benign incarceration experience.

DISCUSSION AND CONCLUSIONS

Organizational structure has a major effect on the informal inmate social system. The cottage programs varied in both the levels of deprivation and the effectiveness of staff controls and confronted the inmates with markedly different organizations to which to adapt. The respective cottage cultures reflected these differences in inmates' perceptions of cottage purposes and goals, in their adaptations to the institution, in their views of staff and other inmates, and in their norms, values, and interaction patterns.

Punishment and isolation were the reasons given by the inmates in maximum security for their incarceration. They suffered the greatest deprivation within the institution, which gave them the greatest incentive to improve their circumstances through violent exploitation and covert deviance. Staff sought inmate obedience and conformity and used physical control to obtain compliance and suppress challenges to their authority. Inmates were alienated by the staff's repressive controls, and the absence of programs prevented the development of individualized relationships, perpetuating the negative stereotypes of one another held by inmates and staff. Motivated by their poor opinion of inmates, staff attempted to disrupt informal groups. The inmates' isolation hindered them from cooperating with one another in the institutional adjustment or in resisting exploitation, while predatory violence reinforced inmates' negative views of one another. Inmates adapted by isolating themselves, avoiding other inmates and appearing to obey staff.

In developing covert deviant solutions to relieve their material deprivation, particularly in exploiting weaker inmates for their possessions, tough inmates reinforced their own dominant status and provided themselves with a measure of safety and security. They discouraged inmate contact that would reveal their own deviant and violent behavior and physically punished inmates who informed to discourage the communication of information that would improve staff control. And the dominance of aggressive inmates reinforced staff efforts to isolate inmates within the culture by making inmates distrustful and fearful of one another. The inmates' ability to use violence determined their various roles within the group, and prevented them from engaging in positive forms of social behavior. The failure of staff to support informing or to control violence forced the inmates to seek accommodation with the primary source of power, the aggressive inmate leaders. This, in turn, reinforced their alienation from one another, precluded collective resistance to aggression, and left each individual inmate at the mercy of those who were more aggressive.

Subculture characteristics in the training school cottages were similar to those in maximum security, although organizational differences reduced the extremes of staff-inmate alienation and antagonism. Program individualization engendered more contacts between staff and inmates that tempered somewhat their negative perceptions of one another. The use of vocational programs required staff to obtain the active cooperation of inmates in productive work. Staff induced at least minimal cooperation and participation in work programs through privileges and rewards that reduced the levels of institutional deprivation. The necessity to obtain voluntary compliance limited the utility of punitive forms of social control, and a privilege system provided staff with a more flexible means of responding to inmates than did the use of force and isolation cells. The forms of adaptation among inmates reflected staff members' primary emphasis on obedience and conformity. Staff informally collaborated with and coopted the potentially violent inmate elite, and thus obtained some con-

trol over aggression within the subculture. By coopting the inmate leaders through informal collaboration, staff enlisted their aid in maintaining order within the subculture. In the course of protecting their privileged status, the leaders informally maintained control for staff, suppressed some forms of anti-institutional activities, and reduced the levels of violence within the inmate group. The privileges available reduced the levels of deprivation, and covert inmate deviance declined accordingly. With less to hide, there was less need among the inmates to restrict contact with staff. Although inmates disapproved of informing, this was not as ruthlessly suppressed as was the case in maximum security. The lesser degree of deprivation and violent exploitation reduced the inmates' isolation and alienation from one another.

The differences in organizational goals and intervention strategies in the treatment-oriented cottages had a significant effect on the inmates' incarceration experience. Staff both elevated treatment expectations over custodial considerations and successfully communicated their expectations to inmates. Rehabilitation, gaining insight, and solving personal problems were seen as the purposes of incarceration, and these goals required change rather than simply conformity. Staff emphasized more rewarding experiences and privileges, and residents of the treatment setting suffered less punishment, deprivation, or alienation than did their custody cottage counterparts. The reduced material deprivation also lowered inmates' incentive to engage in deviant activities within the institution.

In both the individual and group treatment settings, positive contact between staff and inmates was considerable, occurring in individual counseling and through formal collaboration, resulting in markedly more favorable inmate perceptions of staff than in other settings. Formal collaboration allowed inmates and staff to make decisions collectively about cottage life and provided them with a common context in which to meet. Formal collaboration fostered greater equality among staff members, between staff and inmates, and among inmates, and reduced inmates' alienation from staff and encouraged more favorable views of fellow inmates.

Formal collaboration coupled with individual and group treatment increased the visibility of the inmate subculture and provided staff and inmates with a mechanism for controlling inmate violence. Staff provided a rehabilitation-based rationale for informing, enabling the norm governing this behavior to become more positive than was the case in the custody cottages. Equally important, staff members defined the program itself in such a way as to convince the inmates that personnel were committed to treatment rather than punishment.

The increased communication of information enabled staff to control inmate violence, which reinforced this communication. The reduced deprivation, increased freedom, and support provided by formal collaboration for controlling inmate violence combined to foster more positive, less exploitative inmate relationships.

NOTES

1. See Hugh Cline, "The Determinants of Normative Patterns in Correctional Institutions," in *Scandinavian Studies in Criminology*, vol. 2, Nils Christie, ed. (Oslo, Norway: Oslo University Press, 1968), pp. 173–84; Barry Schwartz, "Pre-institutional vs. Situational Influence in a Correctional Community," *Journal of Criminal Law, Criminology and Police Science*, December 1971, pp. 532–42; Charles W. Thomas and Samuel C. Foster, "The Importation Model Perspective on Inmate Social Roles," *Sociological Quarterly*, Spring 1973, pp. 226–34; Charles W. Thomas, "Theoretical Perspectives on Alienation in the Inmate Society," *Pacific Sociological Review*, vol. 18 (1975), pp. 483–99; Charles W. Thomas and Matthew Zingraff, "Organizational Structure as a Determinant of Prisonization," *Pacific Sociological Review*, January 1976, p. 98.

2. Donald Clemmer, *The Prison Community* (Boston: Christopher, 1940); Norman S. Hayner and Ellis Ash, "The Prison as a Community," *American Sociological Review*, vol. 4 (1940), pp. 577–83; Howard Polsky, *Cottage 6* (New York: Russell Sage, 1962); David A. Ward and Gene Kassebaum, *Women's Prison: Sex and Social Structure* (Chicago: Aldine, 1965); Clemens Bartollas, Stuart J. Miller, Simon Dinitz, *Juvenile Victimization: The Institutional Paradox* (Beverly Hills, Sage: 1976).

3. Thomas, "Theoretical Perspectives on Alienation in the Inmate Society"; Charles W. Thomas, "Theoretical Perspectives on Prisonization: A Comparison of the Importation and Deprivation Models," *Journal of Criminal Law and Criminology*, March 1977, pp. 135–45.

4. Lloyd W. McCorkle and Richard Korn, "Resocialization with Walls," *Annals of the American Academy of Political and Social Science*, May 1954, pp. 88–98; Gresham Sykes, *Society of Captives* (Princeton, N.J.: Princeton University Press, 1958); Gresham Sykes and Sheldon Messinger, "The Inmate Social System," in *Theoretical Studies in Social Organization of the Prison*, Richard Cloward et al., eds. (New York: Social Science Research Council, 1960), pp. 5–19; Irving Goffman, *Asylums* (Garden City, N.Y.: Anchor, 1961).

5. Haner and Ash, "Prison as a Community"; Clarence Schrag, "Leadership among Prison Inmates," *American Sociological Review*, vol. 19 (1954), pp. 37–42; Clarence Schrag, "Some Foundations for a Theory of Corrections," in *The Prison: Studies in Institutional Organization and Change*, Donald Cressey, ed. (New York: Holt, Rinehart and Winston, 1961), pp. 309–58; Gresham Sykes, "The Corruption of Authority and Rehabilitation," *Social Forces*, vol. 34 (1956), pp. 257–62.

6. Oscar Grusky, "Organizational Goals and the Behavior of Informal Leaders," *American Journal of Sociology*, vol. 65 (1959), pp. 59–67; Oscar Grusky, "Role Conflict in Organizations: A Study of Prison Camp Officials," *Administration Science Quarterly*, March 1959, pp. 452–72; Stanton Wheeler, "Socialization in Correctional Communities," *American Sociological Review*, October 1961, pp. 707–11; Mayer N. Zald, "Organizational Control Structures in Five Correctional Institutions," *American Journal of Sociology*, November 1962, pp. 335–45; Mayer N. Zald, "Comparative Analysis and Measurement of Organizational Goals: The Case of Correctional Institutions of Juveniles, *Sociological Quarterly*, Summer 1963, pp. 206–30; Peter G. Garabedian, "Social Roles and Processes of Socialization in the Prison Community," *Social Problems*, Fall 1963, pp. 139–52; Peter G. Garabedian, "Social Roles in a Correctional Community," *Journal of Criminal Law, Criminology and Police Science*, September 1964, pp. 338–47; Daniel Glaser, *The Effectiveness of a Prison and Parole System* (Indianapolis, Ind.: Bobbs-Merrill, 1964); Mayer N. Zald and David A. Street, "Custody and Treatment in Juvenile Institutions," *Crime and Delinquency*, July 1964, pp. 249–56; Bernard Berk, Organizational Goals and Inmate Organization," *American Journal of Sociology*, March 1966, pp. 522–34; David A. Street, Robert D. Vinter, and Charles Perrow, *Organization for Treatment* (New York: Free Press, 1966); Ronald L. Akers, Norman S. Hayner, and Werner Gruniger, "Homosexual and Drug Behavior in Prison," *Social Problems*, vol. 21 (1974), pp. 410–22; Ronald L. Akers, Norman S. Hayner, and Werner Gruniger, "Prisonization in Five Countries," *Criminology*, February 1977, pp. 527–54; Barry C. Feld, *Neutralizing Inmate Violence: Juvenile Offenders in Institutions* (Cambridge, Mass.: Ballinger, 1977).

7. John Irwin and Donald Cressey, "Thieves, Convicts, and the Inmate Culture," *Social Problems*, Fall 1962, p. 142; Ward and Kassebaum, *Women's Prison*.

8. Ward and Kassebaum, *Women's Prison*; James Jacobs, "Stratification and Conflict among Prison Inmates," *Journal of Law & Criminology*, vol. 66 (1976), p. 476; Leo Carroll, *Hacks, Blacks, and Cons* (Lexington, Mass.: Lexington Books, 1974); Thomas and Foster, "Importation Model Perspective on Inmate Social Roles"; Thomas, "Theoretical Perspectives on Prisonization."

9. Polsky, *Cottage 6*; Bartollas, Miller, and Dinitz, *Juvenile Victimization*; Jacobs "Stratification and Conflict among Prison Inmates."

10. Social control by inmates within the subculture may be maintained by verbal as well as physical manipulation. Verbal assaults—"ranking"—provide a mechanism by which relative status is fixed by verbal rather than physical aggression. Howard Polsky described rankings as "verbal, invidious distinctions based on values important to the group. . . . Ranking fixes antagonistic positions among three or more persons by placing one member in a target position" (Polsky, *Cottage 6*, p. 62). David Matza describes the same process as "sounding," which entails an "imputation of negative characteristics. . . wherein the recipient concurs with the perpetrator in the negative evaluation of the substance of the remark." (David Matza, *Delinquency and Drift* [New York: John Wiley, 1964], p. 43.) This process of verbal denigration is prevalent in female inmate interactions as well (Rose Giallombardo, *Society of Women* [New York: John Wiley, 1966]; Rose Giallombardo, *Social World of Imprisoned Girls* [New York: John Wiley, 1974]). The target of scornful, mocking, or negative statements made in the presence of a social audience can either concur in the negative imputations, establishing subordination, or resist the characterization. Acquiescence or resistance defines relative social status.

11. Sykes, *Society of Captives*; Sykes and Messinger, "Inmate Social System."

12. Polsky, *Cottage 6*; Bartollas, Miller, and Dinitz, *Juvenile Victimization*; Feld, *Neutralizing Inmate Violence*.

13. Walter Miller, "Lower Class Culture as a Generating Milieu of Gang Delinquency," *Journal of Social Issues*, vol. 14, no. 3 (1958), pp. 5–19; Marvin Wolfgang and Franco Ferracuti, *The Subculture of Violence* (London, England: Tavistock, 1967).

14. Jacobs, "Stratification and Conflict among Prison Inmates"; Giallombardo, *Social World of Imprisoned Girls*; Feld, *Neutralizing Inmate Violence*.

15. Charles W. Thomas and Samuel C. Foster, "Prisonization in the Inmate Contraculture," *Social Problems*, Fall 1972, pp. 229–39; Thomas and Foster, "Importation Model Perspective on Inmate Social Roles"; Akers, Hayner, and Gruniger, "Homosexual and Drug Behavior in Prison"; Feld, *Inmate Violence*.

16. Street, Vinter, and Perrow, *Organization for Treatment*; Akers, Hayner, and Gruniger, "Homosexual and Drug Behavior in Prison"; Feld, Neutralizing *Inmate Violence*.

17. Donald R. Cressey, "Prison Organization," in *Handbook of Organizations*, J. March, ed. (Chicago: Rand McNally), pp. 1023–70; Street, Vinter, and Perrow, *Organization for Treatment*; Elliot StudT, Sheldon Messinger, and Thomas Wilson, *C-Unit: Search for Community in Prison* (New York: Russell Sage, 1968).

18. Street, Vinter, and Perrow, *Organization for Treatment*; Lloyd Ohlin, "Organizational Reform in Correctional Agencies," in *Handbook of Criminology*, Daniel Glaser, ed. (Chicago: Rand McNally, 1974), pp. 995–1020; Feld, *Neutralizing Inmate Violence*.

19. Zald, "Organizational Control Structures in Five Correctional Institutions"; Zald, "Comparative Analysis and Measurement of Organizational Goals"; Zald and Street, "Custody and Treatment in Juvenile Institutions."

20. Corresponding to distinctions between custody and treatment, there is also a tension in the organization between tendencies toward bureaucratization and tendencies toward individualization. The pressures of bureaucratization lead personnel to deal with inmates according to gross characteristics. The pull toward individualization leads to nonroutinized treatment with potentially disruptive consequences for the organization. The nonuniform nature of individual behavior results either in individualized, nonroutinized staff responses *or* in an effort to increase predictability through regimentation. While bureaucratization increases regimentation and clearly defined expectations for inmate behavior, individualization requires either specifying norms for every eventuality or delegating discretion and authority to low-level staff to enable them to deal with unpredictable situations and individual variations. The resolution of these countervailing pressures constitutes a primary source of variation in organizations. See Goffman, *Asylums*; Cressey, "Prison Organization."

21. Street, Vinter, and Perrow, *Organization for Treatment*.

22. Amitai Etzioni, *A Comparative Analysis of Complex Organizations* (New York: Free Press, 1961); Amitai Etzioni, *A Comparative Analysis of Complex Organizations* (New York: Free Press, 1975).

23. Ibid.

24. Goffman, *Asylums*.

25. Lacking complete physical domination of inmates, staff members rely upon the inmate elite to maintain social order, in return for which the staff allow the elite certain privileges and immunities. Richard Cloward describes one way in which this process occurs. He notes that the two primary groups in the prison—custodians and inmates—seek, respectively, social order and escape from deprivation. The custodian employs a coercion and inducement, force and incentive to secure order from the inmates, but "in the absence of absolute force, the prisoner must be led to share in the process of social control." Disruptive behavior is avoided by guards who provide access to illegitimate means whereby the prisoners can reduce the deprivation. "The official system accommodates to the inmate system in ways that have the consequence of creating illegitimate opportunity

structures." To some extent the guards can determine which prisoners will have access to these opportunities, and in turn these prisoners maintain order for the guards as a means of protecting their own privileged positions. This occurs because "certain prisoners, as they become upwardly mobile in these structures, tend to become progressively conservative. . . . Seeking to entrench their relative advantage over other inmates, they are anxious to suppress any behavior that might disturb the present arrangements." Richard Cloward, "Social Control in Prison," in *Theoretical Studies in Social Organization of the Prison* (New York: Social Science Research Council, 1960), pp. 20–48.

This process is also described by Richard McCleary, "Communication Patterns as Bases of Systems of Authority and Power," in *Theoretical Studies in Social Organization of the Prison* (New York: Social Science Research Council, 1960), pp. 49–77; Richard McCleary, "The Governmental Process and Informal Social Control," in *The Prison*, Donald Cressey, ed. (New York: Holt, Rinehart and Winston, 1961), pp. 149–88; and Sykes, *Society of Captives*. According to Sykes ("Corruption of Authority and Rehabilitation"), the guards must rely on the inmates to maintain order because of the "lack of a sense of duty among those who are held captive, the obvious fallacies of coercion, the pathetic collection of rewards and punishments to induce compliance, the strong pressures toward the corruption of the guard in the form of friendship, reciprocity, and the transfer of duties into the hands of trusted inmates—all are structural defects in the prison's system of power rather than individual inadequacies." The same processes operate in institutions for juvenile offenders. See Polsky, *Cottage 6*; Feld, *Neutralizing Inmate Violence*; Bartollas, Miller, and Dititz, *Juvenile Victimization*.

26. Formal collaboration between staff and inmates as a means of social control occurs when a social structure allows both to participate, at least to some degree, as members of a common group in defining deviance, determining the appropriate sanctions, or both. Formal collaboration differs from informal collaboration in a number of critical respects. It is explicit and overt, with parties visibly engaged in the process. Since the process is formalized and given organizational sanction, it is legitimate and consistent with the declared principles of the organization, rather than covert, *sub rosa*, and basically subversive of the formal organization. Formal collaboration is universalistic and democratic, with all members of both groups potentially involved, rather than elitist and particularistic, confined only to the inmate leadership.

27. Feld, *Neutralizing Inmate Violence*; Robert Coates, Alden Miller, and Lloyd Ohlin, *Diversity in a Youth Correctional System* (Cambridge, Mass.: Ballinger, 1978); Craig McEwen, Designing Correctional Organizations for Youth (Cambridge, Mass.: Ballinger, 1978).

28. Maxwell Jones, *Beyond the Therapeutic Community* (New Haven, Conn.: Yale University Press, 1968); Maxwell Jones, *Social Psychiatry in Practice* (Baltimore, Md.: Penguin Books, 1968).

29. The Lancaster Industrial Schools for Girls was not converted to a decentralized, cottage-based institution to nearly the same degree as were the Shirley Industrial School and the Lyman Schools. It still operated as a traditional training school and there were virtually no differences in the social structure of the individual cottages. Accordingly, questionnaire data from Lancaster are aggregated for tabular presentation.

30. Feld, *Neutralizing Inmate Violence*, pp. 207–11.

31. Polsky, *Cottage 6*; Bartollas, Miller, and Dinitz, *Juvenile Victimization*; Feld, *Neutralizing Inmate Violence*.

32. Jones, *Beyond the Therapeutic Community*; Jones, *Social Psychiatry in Practice*.

33. Sykes and Messinger, "The Inmate Social System"; Sheldon Messinger, "Issues in the Study of the Social System of Prison Inmates," *Issues in Criminology*, vol. 4 (1970), pp. 133–44; Street, Vinter and Perrow, *Organization for Treatment*.

34. Polsky, *Cottage 6*; Bartollas, Miller, and Dinitz, *Juvenile Victimization*; Feld, *Neutralizing Inmate Violence*.

35. Miller, "Lower Class Culture as a Generating Milieu of Gang Delinquency"; Wolfgang and Ferracuti, *Subculture of Violence*.

36. Sykes, *Society of Captives*; McCleary, "Communication Patterns as Bases of Systems of Authority and Power"; McCleary, "Governmental Process and Informal Social Control"; Sykes and Messinger, "Inmate Social System."

37. Susan Brownmiller, *Against Our Will: Men, Women and Rape* (New York: Simon & Schuster, 1975).

QUESTIONS FOR DISCUSSION

1. Discuss the two major competing explanations of the inmate social system.

2. Discuss the characteristics of inmate violence in institutions. Specifically consider the organizational structure and how this affects the social interactions of inmates.

3. Discuss the specific findings of Feld's research pertaining to cottage programs and social control strategies.

APPLICATIONS

1. Assuming that the majority of incarcerated offenders will be returning to society, which type of treatment strategy or institutional setting, in your opinion, would be the most effective in producing law-abiding and socially responsible individuals. Why?

2. If you were in a position to make decisions about which types of institutional settings to place inmates in, what kinds of settings would you choose? What criteria would you use to decide whether an inmate needed a custody-oriented facility or a treatment-oriented facility?

KEY TERMS

albeit   conceding the fact that; even though.

eschewed   when something is avoided, particularly on moral or practical grounds.

explicate   to give a detailed explanation.

pummel   to physically pound or beat.

recalcitrance   stubborn or obstinate defiance, particularly to authority.

subterranean   existing or working in secret; hidden.

23

Juvenile Diversion: A Look at the Record

Kenneth Polk

What are the accomplishments of juvenile diversion? In their recent review, Binder and Geis (1984) provide a spirited and proactive defense of diversion, noting that many of those finding fault with the concept base their observations on "polemical and ideological conclusions lacking a firm anchorage in fact" (p. 326). In their attempt to "rehabilitate the record of diversion," Binder and Geis (p. 326) express dismay at the fact that the response to diversion seems to be "inconsistent with the actual record." Their conclusion is that the criticisms of diversion originate in the personal motivations of sociologists and are the result of disciplinary narrowness, distrust of the police, and overidentification with the underdog.

That there have been questions raised about the success of diversion, and that the strongest of these seem to come from sociologists, cannot be disputed. Is it possible, however, that the source of these questions resides not so much in the motivations of sociologists, but in the record of diversion itself? A brief review of some of the empirical work on diversion may help

to clarify and give shape to the features of the debate opened up by Binder and Geis.

DIVERSION AND SUBSEQUENT DELINQUENCY

A starting point for many analyses of diversion consists of assessing the outcomes of diversion in terms of its impact on subsequent delinquency. What is that record? It is clearly mixed. There are many studies which show that diversion is successful in reducing subsequent deviance (e.g., Duxbury, 1973; Thornton et al., 1972; Forward et al., 1975; Quay and Love, 1977; Palmer et al., 1978; Palmer and Lewis, 1980). These results are at least equally balanced, however, by findings of no impact. One of the most methodologically rigorous evaluations of diversion concluded that: "The hypothesis that diversion leads to lower rates of subsequent delinquent behavior than traditional processing was not supported" (Elliott et al., 1978: 10). In their review of several California diversion programs, Haapanen and Rudisill report that the programs

were found to have no measurable effect on the self-report delinquency, the attitudes, the family relations, or the minor misbehavior of their clients. Nor did they have a measurable effect

"Juvenile Diversion: A Look at the Record," *Crime and Delinquency*, 30:4 (1989), pp. 648–859. Reprinted by permission of the publisher, Sage Publications, Inc.

on the official delinquency of their clients over a six-month or twelve-month follow-up period [1980:139].

In their evaluation of several programs in Wisconsin, after making comparisons of records of subsequent delinquency between diversion and control clients, it was concluded by Venezia and Anthony (1978:121) that "none of the comparisons resulted in a significant difference being demonstrated." Similarly, in a review of the outcomes of one diversion program it was concluded that "no strong inference can be made" . . . that diversion "had a significant impact on youths' subsequent delinquent behavior" (Quincy, 1981:127; although it should be noted that this investigation did find consistent positive results on self-report measures of delinquency).

Even more important for the present argument, however, are indications of diversion as having harmful effects. In one analysis of a police diversion program, it was concluded that diversion served to aggravate rather than to deter recidivism (Lincoln, 1976). Elliott and colleagues (1978) report that receiving service, regardless of whether the intervention was in a traditional justice setting or in the diversion agency, resulted in higher levels of perceived labeling and self-report delinquency. Similarly, Lincoln (1977) found that although persons who were diverted had lower rates of recidivism than was true for persons who received a court petition, their rates were also higher than those released outright without any form of service. It further should be noted that these studies suggesting harmful effects of diversion are among the most methodologically rigorous in the diversion literature.

After analyzing this mixed pattern of research, and reviews of evaluations, Alder and Polk (1982:105) suggested that studies showing positive effects "have not stood up under careful scrutiny of their methodology." Binder and Geis profess that it "is inconceivable to us how one can so cavalierly dismiss" the works which show positive results, because this array of research "is no poorer in overall methodology than the array that has produced the negative results upon which the antidiversionists

focus their attention" (Binder and Geis, 1984:324–325).

There are three curious features of this response. One, Binder and Geis scrupulously avoid mention of the major empirical investigations which show either negative or harmful effects of diversion. Although they assert that one set of studies is "no poorer," they provide no literature, data, or rationale in support of that assertion. Second, Binder and Geis fail to inform the reader that at least Alder and Polk cite a basis for their conclusion; namely methodological reviews of diversion research (Alder and Polk, 1982: 105). One of these reviews, after examining a study cited by Binder and Geis as an illustration of the positive effects of diversion, comments:

The Quay and Love (1977) report presented information on group characteristics, including the mean number of prior arrests for each group within fairly specific categories of offense. Within these narrow categories, the two groups did not differ significantly from one another, and the authors concluded that the two groups were equivalent. However, when the submeans were added together to produce a mean for the total number of priors in each group, the control group mean was 34% higher than that of clients. Given the importance of prior offenses as a predictor of subsequent offenses, this suggests that the groups cannot be compared without taking this difference into account. There were other problems with this study, the most glaring being the different follow-up periods of clients and controls; the control group had a longer period in which to get arrested. If (a) the proportion of youths arrested in each group and (b) the mean number of arrests per individual are standardized with respect to exposure time, the differences between the groups disappear. Given the fact that clients had fewer prior arrests (were better "risks"), this lack of actual difference calls into question the positive treatment effects that were claimed by the authors (Haapanen and Rudisill, 1980:8).

Similarly, Gibbons and Blake (another source cited by Alder and Polk) carry out an analysis of several evaluations of diversion programs, finding such problems in one typical study as too short a time period for impact assessment, the failure to describe the handling of control cases, and an absence of a range of impact data (Gibbons and Blake, 1976:415). This review concludes:

> Clearly, there is insufficient evidence in the nine studies examined here for one to have much confidence in diversion arguments and contentions (Gibbons and Blake, 1976:420).

Third, is not the posture assumed by Binder and Geis at variance with what is generally accepted within the research community? Assume for a moment that the intervention being proposed were some form of medical treatment. What would the response of the scientific community be if there was evidence that suggests that the form of treatment may be either: (1) beneficial, (2) of no benefit, or (3) potentially harmful? How compelling would the argument appear, advanced by an obvious advocate of the treatment, that the research showing positive results is "no poorer in overall methodology" than research showing negative or harmful effects? Would not the rules of evidence which apply in such cases place a particular burden of proof on those who advocate the treatment? Is not some caution to be urged, especially when harm has been found in experimentation? How telling is an attack which makes no reference whatsoever to the data and evidence showing negative or harmful results, and instead leaps immediately to challenging the motives of the researchers?

DIVERSION AND NET-WIDENING

A major feature of the defense of diversion provided by Binder and Geis is their rejection of the concern that diversion may result in a widening of the net of juvenile justice. Their position seems based in the following propositions:

1. Diversion is beneficial in the sense that many or most clients are helped through the services provided by diversion programs.

2. Because diversion is helpful, then the proposition that doing nothing, rather than doing something, is unacceptable. Being precise, Binder and Geis find the argument that it is more desirable to ignore deviant behavior than to seek remedial help in diversion "a dubious proposition at best and a downright harmful one at worst" (Binder and Geis, 1984:316).

3. Diversion programs in most cases are voluntary because "offenders and their families may refuse services without consequences" (Binder and Geis, 1984:313).

4. When coercion is present, we are reminded that coercion has essentially been invited by the offender's choice of behavior. "If he or she wished to retain maximum freedom of choice, it would have been prudent either to have abstained from the earlier behavior or not to have gotten caught at it" (Binder and Geis, 1984:313).

5. Because there is actual offense behavior at issue, then some form of social control is desirable and probably inevitable. There is nothing pernicious about social control in the view of Binder and Geis because it consists not simply of law, but of etiquette, norms, regulations, customs and ethics, and takes place in the home, street, school, or family. Not only is social control broadly conceived, but so is the notion of an agent of social control, which consists of the following:

> Any person who attempts to influence behavior that is considered unacceptable in a normative sense. This may be a mother, a minister, a friend, indeed anyone with physical or psychological authority, or presumably anyone who interacts with another person, since it is a given of human intercourse that each of us in our actions attempts to influence another to behave in a particular way or to desist from behaving in a certain manner. (Binder and Geis, 1984:316).

For Binder and Geis, given these premises, diversion becomes a reasonable and responsible form of expanding the devices of social control available to a community for coping with adolescent offense behavior and is worthy of an energetic defense. Because diversion is an effective, voluntary, and appropriate response to delinquent behavior, they find no merit in the concern that net-widening may result from diversion, observing instead:

> The phrase "widening the net" is, of course, employed pejoratively, with the intent to evoke an emotional response. It conjures up visions of a mesh net that is thrown over thrashing victims, incapacitating them as they flail about, desperately seeking to avoid captivity. The net is maneuvered by "agents of social control," another image provoking term, this one carrying a Nazi-like connotation. Both terms are employed for purposes of propaganda rather than to enlighten (Binder and Geis, 1984:315).

Unfortunately, however vivid the imagery, a case rejecting the net-widening argument is built by Binder and Geis which avoids reference to the empirical record. The first two premises are challenged by the evidence of the impact of diversion on subsequent behavior as cited above. If further research confirms either that diversion has no impact or that it is harmful, then the assumption that it is better to do something (in the form of diversion) than to do nothing becomes unsupportable.

Evidence exists which also raises questions about the voluntary nature of diversion services. Early in the development of diversion, Klapmuts (1972) cautioned that if being referred to the diversion program was backed by a threat of referral to court, then the allegedly nonpunitive agency in reality becomes an extension of the justice system and the diversion is a legal fiction. After reviewing the practices of a few diversion programs, Nejelski (1976:410) warned that: "there is a danger that diversion will become a means of expanding coercive intervention in the lives of children and families without proper concern for their rights." A national survey of over 300 youth service bureaus (YSBs), which included more intensive site analyses and interviews with 27 of the diversion agencies, provides some empirical support for such concerns (Polk and Schuchter, 1975:92):

> Data from our field visits suggest that diver-

sionary referrals from court intake and courts to YSBs essentially facilitate deferred prosecution; generally are contingent upon admission of guilt without the advice of counsel; that "voluntary agreements" or consent decrees are obtained under coercive circumstances which vitiate the meaning of voluntariness; that throughout the diversionary and referral process the youth inhabits a legal limbo which increases his vulnerability to subsequent punishment for offenses previously committed, and which is a much more subtle and pernicious problem than double jeopardy.

A further problem in the viewpoint of Binder and Geis is their undifferentiated view of the sources of social control. In its original intent, as should be clear from the term "diversion," there was a recognition that control within the juvenile justice system should be sharply differentiated from other forms of social control. The basic assumed thrust of diversion would be to shift responsibility and intervention for some individuals who had entered juvenile justice processing outside of that system into some form of nonjustice, community alternative.

A major concern of many of the researchers who write about net-widening is the question of whether this is, in fact, what diversion programs accomplish. Is diversion serving as a process for moving young persons who have "penetrated" the justice network outward and away from that system, or has it become a device for incorporating a whole new class of clients inside an expanding justice system? Some have questioned whether it is offense behavior at all that brings clients to diversion agencies, pointing out that the attributes of diversion referrals (age, sex, reason for referral) suggest that a population quite different from delinquent offenders is being tapped by diversion programs. From his analysis of evaluations and descriptions of over 50 diversion programs, Klein (1979:165) was able to comment that:

> The conclusion seems unavoidable: among projects reporting on the characteristics of diversion clients, no reasonable case can be made that these projects are carrying out diversion as its

rationale suggested they should. The bulk of "diversion cases" are young people who are normally counseled and released by the police, if indeed they have any dealings with the police. With clients like these, we cannot truly be testing the efficacy of diversion.

Further, Empey (1982) argues that because a majority of diversion projects have actually been connected with, or even operated by, traditional justice agencies, one of the major functional goals of diversion has been subverted:

> Diversion was supposed to turn the flow of juveniles away from the juvenile justice system and back toward the community. But rather than doing that, several studies reveal that as many as half of all referrals have come, not from police and intake officers, but from schools, welfare agencies, and parents—the very people and institutions that were supposed to be mobilized to serve youth in lieu of legal processing (p. 482).

One of the persons most closely identified with the origins of the concept of diversion has been concerned enough about the control of the diversion process by the justice system to comment that:

> The cooptation of the diversion movement by law enforcement leaves the rather sour conclusion that not only have the purposes of diversion been perverted but, moreover, police power has been extended over youths and types of behavior not previously subjected to control (Lemert, 1981:43).

Perhaps because the discipline makes them more sensitive to the organizational level of analysis, sociologists then become concerned with two issues. One, does the record of diversion show that responsibility for handling of cases is being shifted away from the justice system? When the data indicate that the programs are controlled by justice agencies, that referrals are coming from rather than to schools, families, and other community resources, and that the cases are those that would not under ordinary circumstances come to the attention of justice authorities, then diversion may be

functioning in quite a different way than its originators intended and the term would imply.

Second, if clients come to diversion agencies for help with personal and social problems far removed from offense behavior, and if the diversion agency is part of the justice system, then, whatever the motivation, young persons are coming under the control of the justice system for behavior that, prior to the introduction of diversion, would not have led to such control.

The concern for net-widening is, in short, a concern about whether diversion is meeting its original goal of deflecting cases away from juvenile justice processing. A solid, data-grounded argument can be made which suggests that this goal is not being met, and that instead the juvenile justice system, under the banner of diversion, is taking on both more cases and expanded functions (for a recent review, see Blomberg, 1983). It is not a question of whether services should be available for young persons, but one of where those services should be located. The underlying theory of diversion is that both the individuals served and the community itself would be better off if more of the responsibility for youth behavior were shifted to the community and away from juvenile justice. Is it really inappropriate to discuss an apparent inconsistency between what was planned and what resulted when the inconsistency is revealed by data and evidence?

DIVERSION AND HIDDEN SEXISM

The comments of Binder and Geis regarding the suggestion of Alder and Polk (1982; see also Alder, forthcoming) [to] examine such propositions . . . provide a further illustration of their apparent unwillingness to confront the empirical record of diversion. In their statement, Alder and Polk . . . examine such propositions as: diversion clients are more likely to be female than are clients at other points of formal justice processing; the female clients are being referred to diversion programs disproportionately for the same kinds of behaviors (status offenses) that have provoked concern for sexism within the juvenile justice system; diversion programs may be expanding their network of social control; and finally, diversion may increase the probability of further deviance (and, thus, subsequent formal contact with the juvenile justice system). Literature and extensive data are presented to substantiate these points. Alder and Polk warn, however, that the data are not completely consistent with each point of their argument. They are forced to rely on secondary analysis, and data on some key points of a more complete argument chain are not available. Accordingly, they alert the reader to the conjectural nature of the argument. They then observe that if the above observations are accurate (and at least some data are available to support each point), then a reasonable derivative conclusion is that diversion may represent a form of hidden sexism which results in an increase in the number of girls who ultimately come under the control of juvenile justice agencies.

Binder and Geis profess astonishment at this conclusion, and observe that "in truth, virtually the entire argument is conjectural and rhetorical" (1984:324). In what sense is this the case? Do not Alder and Polk present evidence at each point of their argument? Is not the conclusion logically consistent with the premises established? This is not to say that Alder and Polk are correct. Binder and Geis may have discussed how the data cited by Alder and Polk are in error or where in the chain of argumentation leading to the conclusion an important flaw or inconsistency exist. This they did not do. Instead, they observe the following:

> What diversion does, according to Alder and Polk, when it is successful in resolving the family, personal, or school problems of females is to contribute to "sex-role maintenance." When it fails to provide help, then, of course, the intervention may be regarded as unsuccessful, and evidence of inflicted labeling harm (p. 324).

Alder and Polk make no such claims. The reader will look in vain for any reference whatsoever in their work to conditions either where diversion is "successful in resolving . . . problems" or where "it fails to provide help." It is difficult to see how this disturbing misrepresentation of the work of others, or a dismissal of several pages of empirical data as "rhetoric" either meets minimal standards of scholarly fairness or serves to clarify the record of diversion.

CONCLUSION

The contradictory record of juvenile diversion is not easy to read or interpret. Because individuals will approach the evidence from different experiential bases and differential disciplinary paradigms, some disagreements are probably unavoidable. Consider, for example, the following description of diversion (which can be presumed to come from experience) as seen by Binder and Geis (1984:325):

> Some . . . troubling youngsters will be arrested, some will be referred to probation and the courts. Among the group simply arrested and among those referred upward in the justice system, many will be released or redirected to the community. Among those redirected, at least some would benefit from such services as employment counseling, family counseling, a requirement of restitution, a relationship with a Big Brother or Big Sister, substance abuse education, or even psychotherapy. And that is diversion.

This is, of course, precisely the sense of diversion as it was originally intended (i.e., a process which results in removal of individuals from justice system processing, with supportive community experiences substituted). Because Binder and Geis also see the alternative services as both beneficial and voluntary, the vigor with which they defend diversion becomes more explainable.

Unfortunately, the empirical record suggests that this is not diversion in general practice. Study after study suggests that the programs are often run by, or closely connected to, the justice system, and that most of the clients are not offenders being referred outward, but are youngsters with a variety of personal problems far removed from offense behavior who are being referred into this system. The evidence suggests that a large proportion of the programs may be coercive rather than voluntary. The data on impact do not permit us at this time to reject the hypothesis that the services may be either of no benefit or even harmful to the clients experiencing the diversion program. Several bits of evidence can be woven together to suggest that unanticipated consequences of diversion may be occurring in terms of hidden sexist processes.

Despite their professed desire to explain why the response to diversion is "so inconsistent with the actual record," Binder and Geis themselves choose to ignore that record. Crucial evidence contrary to their position receives no mention. Arguments firmly anchored in fact and data are dismissed as "rhetorical," without presentation of alternative evidence. The concerns about diversion are seen as originating not from the research findings, but from the petty motivations of antidiversionist sociologists. There is an alternative view. Many sociologists, despite what Binder and Geis allege, are firmly committed to the goals of diversion as defined in its original conception. These investigators read the patterns of the empirical record, however, and are dismayed by the drift of diversion from its intended course. They document that drift with data. If Binder and Geis have alternative evidence, they could provide a valuable service by presenting it.

REFERENCES

ALDER, C.
"Gender bias in juvenile justice." Crime and Delinquency 30 (forthcoming).

ALDER, C. AND K. POLK
"Diversion and hidden sexism." Australian and New Zealand J. of Criminology 15: 100–108 (1982).

BINDER, A. AND G. GEIS
"*Ad Populum* argumentation in criminology: juvenile diversion as rhetoric." Crime and Delinquency, 30:309–333 (1984).

BLOMBERG, T. G.
"Diversions, disparate results, and unresolved questions: an integrative evaluation perspective." J. of Research in Crime and Delinquency 20:24–38 (1983).

DUXBURY, E.
Evaluation of Youth Service Bureaus. Sacramento: California Youth Authority, 1973.

ELLIOTT, D. S., F. W. DUNFORD, AND B. KNOWLES
Diversion: A Study of Alternative Processing Prac-

tices. Boulder, CO: Behavioral Research Institute, 1978.

EMPEY, L. T.
American Delinquency: Its Meaning and Construction. Homewood, IL: Dorsey, 1982.

FORWARD, J. R., M. KIRBY, AND K. WILSON
Volunteer Intervention with Court-Diverted Juveniles. Denver: Partners' Court Diversion Program, 1975.

GIBBONS, D. AND G. BLAKE
"Evaluating the impact of juvenile diversion programs." Crime and Delinquency 22:411–420 (1976).

HAAPANEN, R. AND D. RUDISILL
The Evaluation of Youth Service Bureaus: Final Report, Sacramento: California Youth Authority, 1980.

KLAPMUTS, N.
"Children's rights: the legal rights of minors in conflict with law of social custom." Crime and Delinquency Literature (September, 1972).

KLEIN, M. W.
"Deinstitutionalization and diversion of juvenile offenders: a litany of impediments," pp. 145–201 in N. Morris and M. Tonry (eds.), Crime and Justice. Chicago: Univ. of Chicago Press, 1979.

LEMERT, E. M.
"Diversion in juvenile justice: what hath been wrought?" J. of Research in Crime and Delinquency 18:34–46 (1981).

LINCOLN, S. B.
"Juvenile referral and recidivism," in R. M. Carter and M. W. Klein (eds.), Back on the Street: Diversion of Juvenile Offenders. Englewood Cliffs, NJ: Prentice-Hall, 1976.

——— "Recidivism rates of diverted juvenile offenders." Paper presented at the National Conference on Criminal Justice Evaluation, Washington, DC, 1977.

NEJELSKI, P.
"Diversion: the promise and danger." Crime and Delinquency 22: 393–410 (1976).

PALMER, T., M. BOHNSTEDT, AND R. LEWIS
The Evaluation of Juvenile Diversion: Final Report. Sacramento: California Youth Authority, 1978.

PALMER, T. AND R. LEWIS
"A differentiated approach to juvenile diversion." J. of Research in Crime and Delinquency 17:209–277 (1980).

POLK, K. AND A. SCHUCTER
Report: Phase I Assessment of Youth Service Bureaus. A report prepared for the National Institute of Law Enforcement and Criminal Justice, Washington, DC, 1975.

QUAY, H. C. AND C. T. LOVE
"The effect of a juvenile diversion program on rearrests." Criminal Justice and Behavior 4: 377–396 (1977).

QUINCY, R. L.
An Evaluation of the Effectiveness of the Youth Service Bureau Diversion Concept. Unpublished Ph.D. dissertation, Michigan State University at East Lansing, 1981.

THORNTON, W., E. BARRETT, AND L. MUSOLF
The Sacramento County Probation Department 601 Diversion Project. Sacramento: Sacramento County Probation Department, 1972.

VENEZIA, P. AND D. ANTHONY
A Program Level Evaluation of Wisconsin's Youth Service Bureaus. Tuscon, AZ: Associates for Youth Development, 1978.

QUESTIONS FOR DISCUSSION

1. Explain how diversion should ideally be implemented and how, according to this article, it actually is implemented.

2. Explain "net-widening." What are several criticisms of net-widening?

3. Alder and Polk suggest that the practice of diversion for juveniles contains hidden sexism. Why?

APPLICATIONS

1. In your opinion, is diversion an effective mechanism for ensuring that juveniles do not become "hardened" by institutionalization? Why?

2. For what types of juvenile delinquency might we effectively use diversion? Explain.

KEY TERMS

conjectural involving or based on a conclusion deduced or surmised by guesswork.

derivative something made up of or formulated by varying elements.

perjorative something that tends to belittle or disparage.

pernicious highly injurious or destructive.

polemical characterizes something controversial, opposite, or disputed.

24

Juvenile Parole Policy in the United States: Determinate Versus Indeterminate Models

Jose B. Ashford
Craig Winston LeCroy

This paper presents an overview of eight approaches in juvenile parole policy for terminating, extending, and discharging youths from juvenile parole or after-care. These types were derived from the results of a national survey of juvenile parole policy in the United States. This survey was sent to the departments of correction, youth service bureaus, and legislative service agencies for the 50 states. The survey sought comparative data on trends in substantive and procedural approaches for handling parole duration and discharge issues for juvenile offenders. These trends are evaluated in relation to movements toward formalism in corrections, recent reforms in juvenile sentencing, standards promulgated by various standard-setting groups, and recent shifts in juvenile justice philosophy in the United States.

Since the cases of *Kent v. United States* (1966) and *Gault* (1967), juvenile justice philosophy gradually has shifted toward a fairness or a justice paradigm (Aultman and Wright 1982). This paradigm stresses the fundamental images of "just deserts," equality in sentencing, and crime control. It has ushered in many reforms in sentencing and in release policy (Forst, Fisher and

"Juvenile Parole Policy in the United States: Determinate versus Indeterminate Models," *Justice Quarterly*, 10:2 (June 1993), pp. 179–195. Reprinted by Permission of the Publisher and the Authors.

Coates 1985) designed to improve the exercise of judicial and correctional discretion. Most of these reforms advocate using some form of determinate sentencing, presumptive sentencing, or administrative guidelines.

Determinate sentencing refers to any sentencing or disposition system in which the length of a commitment is determined when the initial disposition is imposed (Tonry 1987). Presumptive sentencing, on the other hand, is any scheme entailing a presumed range of dispositions or sentences that are deemed proportionate to the seriousness of the defendant's offense (Singer 1978; Tonry 1987). Administrative guidelines refer to any approaches in sentencing in which agencies establish guidelines or standards that determine a person's length of confinement in a correctional facility.

The specification of the length of a confinement in a determinate sentence does not necessarily mean that the offender will serve the specified duration of the sentence (Singer 1978). In some determinate sentencing systems, offenders still may be released on parole or may receive reductions in the duration of their sentence for good time. In other systems, provisions for supervised release have been abolished or reduced significantly. The function and the role of parole are unclear in this determinate sentencing movement primarily

343

because of the "variety" of determinate sentencing schemes (Singer 1978; von Hirsh and Hanrahan 1981). In particular, considerable confusion surrounds the purpose of the community supervision component of juvenile and adult parole (Clear 1979; von Hirsh and Hanrahan 1984; Wheeler 1978). Does the option of a desert model or of a philosophy of determinate or presumptive sentences necessarily rule out parole supervision (von Hirsch and Hanrahan 1984)? How have the determinacy and accountability movements in sentencing for juveniles affected the minimizing of disparities in duration on parole or aftercare?

Between 1979 and 1980, Forst, Fisher, and Coates (1985) conducted a national survey on juvenile determinate and indeterminate commitment and release practices in the United States. This survey provided invaluable insights into the types of approaches used in juvenile sentencing since the demise of the rehabilitative ideal. Since Forst and his colleagues published the results of their survey, many states have continued to reform their juvenile codes.

> Reformed codes usually include one or more of the following provisions: provisions which broaden the offense age requirements in waiver, allowing a greater number of youth to the criminal court; lowered ages of jurisdiction, which allow the criminal court to routinely handle younger offenders without the need for certification; serious delinquent statutes, which ensure the prolonged incarceration of repeat offenders and sentencing guidelines or administrative guidelines governing institutional exit (Harris and Graff 1988: 66).

Still, it is unclear how parole duration issues are being handled in the reformed and the nonreformed states.

The primary aim of this paper is to examine current trends in juvenile parole policy in view of the inchoate shifts in juvenile sentencing philosophy. In this examination we focus on identifying present variations in determinate and indeterminate approaches to terminating, extending, and discharging youths from parole. We also examine the sources and the patterns of authority involved in the setting of parole standards. This analysis is based on an examination of data from a national survey of youth service bureaus, departments of youth corrections, and legislative service agencies for the 50 states.

HISTORICAL PERSPECTIVE ON JUVENILE AFTERCARE OR PAROLE

"Aftercare in the juvenile justice system is the equivalent of parole in the adult criminal justice system" (Siegel and Senna 1985: 512). Traditionally, juvenile aftercare placed greater emphasis on achieving rehabilitative and treatment ends than was necessarily true of adult parole. To some extent, this difference was due to basic jurisprudential differences between the adult and the juvenile justice systems. In the juvenile justice system, authority for parole services is derived primarily from the *parens patriae* powers of the state and from its attendant to social welfare orientation. In contrast, authority for adult parole is derived primarily from the police powers of the state and from its attendant orientation to crime control. Nonetheless, the rationales used to differentiate between these two systems of justice are less sharp today than immediately after the inception of the juvenile court movement.

Some policy makers assume that it is not legitimate to consider all juveniles as victims of social conditions and as needing the protection and care of the state. This viewpoint was emphasized recently in the Model Juvenile Code of the American Legislative Exchange Council (1987). This group advocated holding juveniles responsible for their actions because they are represented dispportionately in current statistics for serious crime. Similarly, Siegel and Senna (1985:viii) pointed out that "those with a law enforcement orientation suggest that efforts to treat children under the concept of parens patriae have neglected the victims of delinquency, and that serious offenders need to be punished rather than rehabilitated." These viewpoints obviously conflict with the original intent of the founders of the juvenile justice system: "Although there is dispute about the motives of the founders—whether they set out to engage in child-saving or in a less benevolent pursuit based on economic and religious beliefs—it is agreed that the movement's basic philosophy was to exempt the young offender from criminal punishment" (Kittrie & Zenoff 1981:308).

Krisberg et al. (1986:26) argue that the current trend in juvenile justice reform reveals "a system growing more formal, restrictive and punitive." It is unclear, however, how these trends are affecting the provision of aftercare services. If rehabilitative ends are being supplanted by punitive objectives, we should expect substantial increases in the formalization of aftercare decisionmaking processes. These increases are expected primarily because approaches to justice which emphasize principles of punishment generally assume that the ends of justice are served best if decisions are limited by formal criteria. (Daivs 1979; Rothman 1983). Still, it is not clear to what extent punishment has replaced rehabilitation as the raison d'etre in aftercare decision-making processes. Probation and parole officials still justify many of their broad discretionary powers by appealing to rehabilitation (Porter 1980).

"In most states, aftercare is the least developed aspect of correction; in the opinion of many observers, it is less adequate than its counterpart, adult parole" (Presi-dent's Commission on Law Enforcement and the Administration of Justice 1967:149). This view of juvenile aftercare, presented by the President's Commission on Law Enforcement and the Administration of Justice, was based in part on evidence gathered in a survey of aftercare services in the United States. The findings in this survey showed wide variation in the structure and the program content of juvenile aftercare. It was argued in the Commission's report that their survey revealed "the harsh realities of the nation's failure to come to grips with the juvenile aftercare problem" (Newman 1968:201).

As in the 1960s, the problem with juvenile aftercare in the early 1980s was one of gross neglect (Daum 1981; Simonsen and Gordon 1982). In most jurisdictions, aftercare remained the phase of the correctional process that escaped extensive formalization by correctional authorities (Baird 1981) and intervention by the courts (Bailey and Rothblatt 1982). In fact, aftercare workers in many jurisdictions still had unfettered discretion in making decisions

restricting the liberty and the life chances of youths released from correctional institutions. For instance, decisions involving the placement of youths in residential treatment or substitute care were not guided by explicit criteria. Similarly, reclassification or even initial classification decisions were not restricted sufficiently by explicit standards (Baird 1981). Aftercare workers had the power to employ whatever criteria they deemed appropriate in distributing burdens and benefits (Ashford and LeCroy 1988).

Coffey (1973) observed as early as 1957 that authorities were troubled by the lack of national standards for juvenile parole. Under indeterminate sentencing principles and the rehabilitative ideal, parole agencies and agents were granted broad discretion in making decisions about aftercare supervision, termination, and discharge. These decisions generally were justified by individualized treatment or predictive considerations. Experts in these matters were presumed to be better equipped than either judges or legislators to decide when to terminate parole. It was also assumed that these experts could predict the likelihood of a youth's recidivating while on parole or could determine whether the youth needed further treatment. This confidence of early exponents of parole in professional judgment is illustrated in the following quotation from a historical source in the field:

> As to the length of this trial visit and time when the former offender shall be formally discharged from the custody of the institution, it seems that on account of the greater variety of character disorder with which the reformatory has to deal, and with the great dependence upon the manner in which the former offender conducts himself during the parole, that the time of termination of the parole should rest with this board of experts. It should be for them to determine when the paroled delinquents ought to be returned to the reformatory and when the conduct of any paroled offender was such as to warrant final discharge (Haines 1920: 165–66).

This broad discretion granted to juvenile authorities was not subjected to close scrutiny until the late 1970s. At that time, individuals in academic and policy circles began to examine the aftercare problem. Romig (1978) reviewed eight studies that assessed the effectiveness of juvenile parole. In his review of the literature he found that "in not one of the studies were the results overwhelmingly favorable" (Romig 1978:190). Hudson's (1973) study, which was included in Romig's review, explicitly questioned the effectiveness of traditional parole programming. Hudson reached this position after discovering that low-risk youths released without parole supervision fared as well as youths released with supervision on parole.

Hudson's indictment of the effectiveness of parole supervision was shared by Wheeler (1978). In a study of parole in a midwestern state, Wheeler uncovered several key disparities in the ability of parole to achieve its stated mission. He stated:

> Of the three assumptions of parole, the nature of supervision in the community most dramatically illustrates the negative consequences of the indeterminate parole. Regardless of offense, blacks generally received the longer parole than whites. The same trend of longer parole was observed for younger offenders and females. Also, youth with the least serious offense at commitment were subject to equal or longer supervision in the community than index offenders. . . . These research findings present a strong case against continuing the indeterminate sentence. While many lawyers and criminologists agree with this conclusion, correctional practitioners appear highly skeptical of adopting a "fixed" sentence for juveniles (Wheeler 1978:80–82).

On the basis of these findings, Wheeler concluded that indeterminate sentences and juvenile aftercare should be abolished. His recommendations, however, included the suggestion that "authorities may consider making parole services optional" (1978:132).

Wheeler's (1978) recommendation for a just deserts model in sentencing juveniles also was made by the Joint Commission on Juvenile Justice Standards, appointed in 1979 by the Institute of Judicial Administration and the American Bar Association (IJA-ABA). This prestigious group developed a set of juvenile standards for

corrections administration that stressed determinate sentences. Melton et al. observed that the IJA/ABA standards were important primarily because they served as a significant "model for the new post-Gault juvenile court" (1987:294).

For its policy on dispositions, this standard-setting group recommended that states classify offense types and limit dispositions for each class of offense. The IJA/ABA's Standard 2.1 states that "in choosing among statutory permissible disposition, the court should employ the least restrictive category and duration of disposition that is appropriate to the seriousness of the offense . . ." (1980:34). This group was less specific, however, about limits on parole duration because it intended to replace offender-based dispositions with dispositions based on principles of just deserts. As of 1987, no state had adopted the entire code recommended by the IJA/ABA. "Offender-based dispositions are still the rule, except for the most serious offense by the oldest juveniles" (Melton et al. 1987:295–96).

The subject of parole discharge or termination decisions in juvenile justice has received minimal scrutiny. Several standard-setting groups beside the IJA/ABA, however, have developed broad goals and standards to direct policy-making behavior in these areas. The Commission on Accreditation for Corrections of The American Correctional Association (ACA) recommended in Standard 7173 that it is essential for correctional authorities to develop written policy and procedure regarding recommendations for early termination of aftercare.

> The agency should develop . . . criteria for early termination of probation/aftercare. These may include demonstrated successful adjustment in terms of nonarrest and demonstrate stability in terms of home adjustment, school attendance, employment, social relationships, etc. Procedure should include specific time frames and careful case reviews. . . . Supervision should be terminated when it is clear that delivery of services to the youth is no longer required to protect the community or to enhance the youth's overall performance (ACA 1978:34).

In addition, the U.S. government established parole policy guidelines that were designed to "promote a more consistent exercise of discretion and enable fairer and more equitable decision making without removing individual case considerations" (28 C.F.R., Part II, 1990: 96). This national parole policy established early termination guidelines from parole supervision for juvenile delinquents and youthful offenders. These guidelines specify that "absent case specific factors to the contrary, termination of supervision shall be considered indicated when:

(i) A parolee originally classified in the very good risk category (pursuant to @ 2.20) has completed two continuous years of supervision free from any indication of new criminal behavior or serious parole violation; and

(ii) A parolee originally classified in other than the very good risk category (pursuant to @ 2.20) has completed three continuous years of supervision free from any indications of new criminal behavior or serious parole violation" (28 C.F.R. Part II, 1990:122–23).

These policy guidelines limit the decision-making processes by asserting the principle of a presumed termination of parole. That is, the parolee should be terminated presumptively after serving the minimum period of parole in the absence of specific factors to the contrary. The policy was asserted initially in the Model Penal Code (1968) developed for adult offenders (Morris 1988; Tonry 1988).

The Model Juvenile Justice Court Act (1968) did not subscribe to this principle of a presumed termination of parole at the end of a specified period. It limited commitment dispositions by recommending that commitments should "continue in force for 2 years or until the child is sooner discharged" (36(b)). Unlike the Model Penal Code, the Model Juvenile Justice Court Act advocates a discretionary minimum with a fixed maximum period of supervision. In addition, it includes special standards that allow for the extension of supervision up to a two-year maximum. In 1985 this act officially

was renamed the Uniform Law Commissioners' Model Act. The 1987 table for adopting jurisdictions for the Model Act showed that it had not been adopted completely by any of the states.

This review of the literature suggests that since the Model Juvenile Justice Court Act (1968), several standard-setting groups have emphasized the need to limit the duration of sentences for juvenile offenders. Most of these groups have advocated making decision criteria explicit and for setting limits on duration of parole. We do not know, however, how much variation exists among the states in their policy approaches to parole duration. Furthermore, we do not know to what extent states have chosen to adopt the recommendations of the various national standard-setting groups.

PROCEDURE

Between November 1987 and November 1988 we conducted a national survey to understand the current trends and patterns in juvenile parole/aftercare policy in the United States. This survey consisted of a questionnaire and a request for supporting documentation from the departments of correction, the youth service bureaus, and the legislative service agencies for the 50 states. It requested comparative information on the standards and criteria used to structure the discretion of aftercare decision makers and asked whether these criteria could be found in legislation, administrative rules, or formal agency or departmental procedures. We asked the authorities to respond to six questions. The following question was relevant to this paper:

> Does your state have formal policies and procedures governing the discharge/termination of youth from parole or aftercare services?

If the respondents replied "yes" to this question, they were requested to check boxes indicating where these policies were located. We also asked them to cite appropriate legislation and to enclose relevant statutes or guidelines when appropriate. Finally, we asked the respondents to indicate whether their state had any pending policy or legislation that would address these concerns. Of the 50 states surveyed, we received adequate information from 47, a 94 percent response rate.

We analyzed each of these questionnaires and all supporting documentation. In addition, in spring 1991 we reexamined selected state statutes identified in the survey. We also analyzed secondary sources such as law review articles.

The results of this study cannot be considered an up-to-date account of existing policy because agencies and states are constantly modifying their policy practices. Even so, they represent the best available information since the survey performed by Forst and his colleagues in 1979 and 1980. In fact, this is the first analysis of many of these issues since standards were recommended by several national standard-setting groups in the late 1970s. The findings should benefit policy analysts interested in evaluating the range and variety of approaches to terminating, extending, and discharging youths from supervised release to the community. They present a view of policy practices a decade after significant policy recommendations by juvenile justice authorities.

FINDINGS

We examined all of the materials from the survey to classify state policies affecting the duration of a youth's period on supervised release or aftercare. We used the following variables to classify types of parole; these were derived from the literature on juvenile aftercare and on adult and juvenile sentencing: 1) the amount of discretion allowed to youth service or aftercare workers in making termination and discharge decisions; 2) whether the parole period was determinate or indeterminate; and 3) who set the standards and criteria limiting parole termination or discharge decisions (Forst et al. 1985; Singer 1978; von Hirsch and Hanrahan 1981; Wheeler 1978). Given these variables, we identified eight types of parole supervision:

Type 1 is a determinate parole. In this system, length of parole is related to the period of commitment specified by the committing court. The court commits a youth for a specified period of time and the juvenile may serve a specified portion of this commitment on supervised release in the community. The range of time allowed for supervised release is specified in the initial judicial commitment and is proportionate to the youth's offense. If the youth engages in identified infractions while in the institution, he or she may lose the benefit of supervised release. In these circumstances, the youth will serve in the institution the specified length of time prescribed in the initial judicial commitment.

Juvenile parole authorities have no discretion to extend the period of supervision beyond the period prescribed in the judicial commitment. As a result, the decision to discharge a youth involves a straightforward computation of time since the beginning of the youth's commitment. This period is commensurate with the offender's offense, prior criminal history, and other factors considered significant by the legislature or sentencing commission. Furthermore, the legislature is the authority that generally sets the standards governing the range of parole duration deemed commensurate with established classes of offenses. Washington was the only state that fit this type of parole. Washington also was one of the few states that had special provisions allowing for voluntary supervision following the expiration of the youth's commitment. This voluntary supervision could last up to six months.

Type 2 is a determinate parole set by administrative agency. In this approach, the parole release date is set immediately after the youth arrives at the institution. This date includes a parole of fixed length that is considered proportionate to the youth's offense classification. This type of approach has much in common with Type 1; parole length in both types is commensurate with the seriousness of the youth's commitment offense and with his or her criminal history. The authority that sets the standards for length of confinement, release dates, and ranges of parole duration is the key distinguishing factor between Type 1 and Type 2. In Type 2, the standards governing the decision to terminate supervision rest with the parole or aftercare agency. Georgia and New

Jersey were the only states that belonged to this type. At the time of the survey, Maryland was developing a classification system that prescribed parole lengths proportionate to the youth's classification.

Utah has developed administrative guidelines, but supervision under these guidelines is not determinate. Youths may be kept under supervision because of adjustment difficulties. Nevada also employs a variant of parole duration and supervision that presented some coding difficulties. The statutory language suggests that length of parole is indeterminate. Agency policy developed to implement the statutory language, however, prescribes fixed lengths of supervision and defines three types of discharge that are based on behavioral performance: positive termination, general termination, and negative termination. In Nevada, six months of supervision are prescribed for youths over 18, and nine months under 18. Although these paroles are of fixed lengths, the coders did not believe that Nevada should be coded as a state with determinate parole because the court maintained the discretion to continue youths on parole supervision. Therefore we categorized the fixed period as a presumptive minimum rather than as fixed length.

Type 3 is a presumptive minimum with limits on the extension of the supervision period for a fixed or a determinate length of time. This approach involves the presumption that parole should terminate after the youth completes a minimum period of supervised release. For example, the youth should be terminated presumptively from parole after completing at least six months on supervised release unless established factors or standards indicate otherwise. In effect, the agent or worker cannot depart from the prescribed six-month parole without evidence of behavior that fits standards governing the extension of parole. These specified factors, which limit agents' and workers' authority to extend the period of parole supervision, generally are found in statutes or in agency policies. If the aftercare worker presents evidence of factors indicating a need to extend the parole, this extension is limited to a fixed or determinate period such as six months. For example, supervised release terminates pre-

sumptively in Arkansas after six months of supervision, but can be extended only for a maximum of six months.

For the purposes of this study, we considered Type 3 a determinate approach to parole duration. Three states fit the definition for this classification: Arkansas, Kansas, and Mississippi. Presumptive durations in Kansas differed somewhat from those in the other two states. The standard term in Kansas is a presumptive six-month minimum and a maximum of 12 months. Superintendents or directors, however, may set different minimum and maximum lengths of time at the point of release. Another interesting variation in policy was found in Florida, which has a special sentencing provision for youths adjudicated delinquent for first-degree misdemeanurs. For these youths, supervision should terminate presumptively after six months of supervision, but it can be extended for not longer than six additional months.

Type 4 is a presumptive minimum with limits on the extension of supervision for an indeterminate period. This approach also presumes that parole should terminate after a minimum period, absent factors indicating otherwise. In this approach, the discretion to extend parole is limited by explicit standards, but the period of extension is indeterminate. The aftercare worker has the discretion to extend parole supervision for an unspecified length of time until the maximum age for automatic termination of the juvenile court's jurisdiction. Because the presumptive length of parole involves explicit standards governing extensions, we considered this type determinate even though it becomes indeterminate after a finding of poor adjustment on parole. Four state fit the criteria for this classification: Massachusetts, Michigan, Montana, and Nevada.

In Texas the policies include an approach for conventional delinquency commitments that caused some classification difficulties. A youth is committed indeterminately to the Texas Youth Commission until age 18 for conventional acts of delinquency. The institution, however, can release a youth at any time and can place him or her on parole. These youths on parole may be removed from active supervision after they have successfully completed

180 days at the lowest level of supervision. This presumptive discharge occurs after the youth meets the presumptive 180 days free of difficulties at Level 3 supervision. The presumptive discharge is indeterminate, however, because it is contingent on the youth's performance at each level of supervision. Performance difficulties translate into additional time at a given level. As a result, Texas aftercare for conventional commitments was not classified as determinate parole. A similar presumptive element is present in New Mexico; we also coded it under an indeterminate classification, however, because of its discretionary minimum.

Type 5 is a presumptive minimum with discretionary extension of supervision for an indeterminate period. This approach includes the assumption that parole should terminate after a minimum period, but can be extended at the discretion of the supervising authority. No limits are placed on the discretion of aftercare workers to extend the parole. Although the minimum length is specified, the factors allowing for indeterminate extension of supervision up to the maximum period of the commitment or the maximum age for termination are not specified. Because this approach lacks explicit standards limiting the extension of parole, we consider it indeterminate for the purposes of this paper. Five states fit the criteria for this type of parole: Arizona, Florida, New Hampshire, New York, and Pennsylvania. Although New York sets presumptive minimums with discretionary extension of supervision, it also has special determinate sentencing provisions for serious offense categories.

Type 6 is an indeterminate parole with a specified maximum and a discretionary minimum length of supervision. This approach is consistent with the approach advocated by the Model Juvenile Court Act of 1968. It limits the maximum level of commitment, but leaves the length of confinement and the period of supervised release to the discretion of parole authorities. Eleven states fit the criteria emphasizing a specified maximum and a discretionary minimum: Alabama, Colorado, Connecticut, Delaware, Louisiana, New Mexico, North Carolina, North Dakota, Tennessee, Vermont, and Wisconsin. This category encompasses a broad range of philosophies and approaches to determining a youth's readiness for discharge. Some states in this category have not formalized the early release decisions. States such as Wisconsin and Vermont, however, have introduced highly formalized agency policies that structure these decision-making processes.

Type 7 is an indeterminate parole with legal minimum and maximum periods of supervision. In this approach, the parole authority is granted the discretion to discharge the youth from parole within a broad range of time. That is, the range between the minimum and the maximum term of commitment is much larger than in either Type 1 or Type 2. This approach was dominant in adult sentencing before the determinacy movement in sentencing in the mid-1970s. Seven states fit this classification: Alaska, California, Kentucky, Maine, Ohio, Texas, and Utah. We classified Utah under this option because minimum and maximum ranges in their administrative guidelines are not determinate. That is, their procedures grant authorities the discretion not to release any youth whose behavior does not merit release. In Utah's system, youths are reviewed every three months; the findings of these reviews can affect discharge from parole.

Type 8 is indeterminate or purely discretionary. In this approach, the length of parole is unspecified and there is no legal minimum to limit decisions about discharging a youth from parole. In states in this category, expiration of commitment at the age of majority is the only specified limit. Discharge decisions are based on the discretion of the aftercare staff, who possess the authority to assess the youth's readiness for discharge from parole supervision. Fourteen states fit this classification: Hawaii, Idaho, Illinois, Maryland, Missouri, Nebraska, Oklahoma, Oregon, Rhode Island, South Carolina, South Dakota, Virginia, West Virginia, and Wyoming.

Figure 1 displays the percentages of the distributions of these types of parole across the United States. These results do not include information about special sentencing provisions for serious or nonserious youth offend-

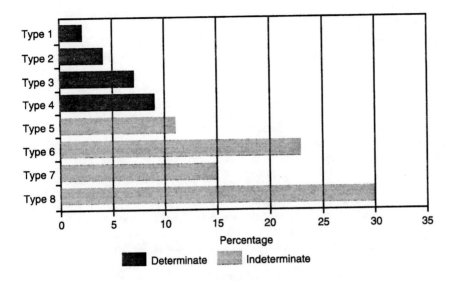

FIGURE 1 **Percentages of Parole Types across the United States**

ers. They show that indeterminate approaches to duration of parole supervision remain the dominant type in juvenile aftercare.

Although a number of states have instituted determinate sentencing provisions for serious juvenile offenders, the parole periods under many of these statutes also are subject to substantial discretion and indeterminacy. Of the 47 states surveyed here, 66 percent had standards for discharge from parole in their statutes, 28 percent in administrative rules, and 76 percent in agency policies. Finally, in 19 percent of the states, standards for aftercare policy were located in statutes and in administrative rules.

DISCUSSION

When Washington State enacted its Juvenile Justice Act in 1978, authorities responsible for parole services acknowledged that parole lacked a clear direction in a justice framework. Nonetheless, they took positive steps to avoid the arbitrary termination of aftercare services when commitment orders expired. That is, they confronted the possibility that equal parole lengths for offenses in the same classification "might be detrimental to the rehabilitation of certain youth" (Division of Juvenile Rehabilitation 1987:7). They recommended that youths be entitled to request continued services after completing a length of supervision deemed commensurate with their criminal history, age, and committing offense. Although commensurate approaches to parole length based on principles of desert were advocated by reformers (Wheeler 1978) in the late 1970s and were implemented in Washington State, few states have adopted these recommendations for a desert approach to supervised release. Most states maintain indeterminate approaches to parole supervision.

In addition, few states have adopted fixed or presumptive approaches to parole length. Policy governing length of supervision has been influenced more by principles of crime control and accountability than by principles of consistency or equality in lengths of parole. For example, many states have introduced determinate sentencing provisions that subject youths to extended surveillance and supervision in the community. Thus lengths of parole have not diminished as a result of the determinacy movement. Youths with determinate sentences can be placed on extensive periods of parole supervision. This finding was unexpected primarily because justice models initially were rationalized on the grounds that they would eliminate the unnecessary expansion of the therapeutic state and its disparities in duration (Wheeler 1978). Thus goals of incapacitation and punishment appear to be playing a more important role in policy reforms involving length of parole than are principles of equality or justice.

Similarly, few states have adopted graduated release practices that allow for individualized assessments of a youth's reintegration into the community and readiness for termination from supervision. The states that include systems of levels of parole (Illinois, New Mexico, Texas, Utah) subscribe to various justifying aims ranging from rehabilitative punishment to individualized treatment and rehabilitation. We expected that differential levels of supervision and formalized procedures for assessing readiness for discharge would play an increased role in discharge decisions, in view of the concerns about discretionary abuses voiced by reformers in the late 1970s. Yet the results of the survey revealed that only a few indeterminate states (e.g., Wisconsin and Vermont) give substantial attention to the results of formal risk, needs, and reassessment instruments. In fact, Vermont is the only state that bases termination decisions strictly on evidence of sufficient rehabilitation as indicated by "a reduction in risk factors and treatment needs." The lack of systems of levels also was unexpected because the National Council of Juvenile and Family Court Judges (1984) recommended the adoption of phased reentry into the community for serious offenders.

Our findings from the survey show that the terms of postrelease supervision in the United States still are justified on multiple grounds. Lengths of supervision vary from jurisdiction to jurisdiction; no clear standard of time presently exists for achieving aftercare objectives. States specify from six months to two years as a minimum period for achieving release objectives. Our results also show that the recommendations of standard-setting groups have not been adopted widely by juvenile justice authorities. In fact, the modal type of parole

in the United States remains highly indeterminate and discretionary. In addition, few innovations from the formalization movements in classification and in correctional rule making are influencing state discharge policies. In particular, no state classified under Type 8 has introduced rule-making practices to formalize the decision-making processes involved in their discharge decisions.

Our analysis of state parole policies identifies eight types of approaches to terminating, extending, and discharging youths from supervised release. Although our categorization of some states may be questioned on substantive grounds, our findings are significant primarily in that they illustrate the diversity of parole policies in the United States. This diversity presented obvious coding difficulties. It is reasonable to conclude, however, that the states have no standard approach to reducing disparities in lengths of parole. Furthermore, we find no evidence of a clear trend toward a desert approach to terminating youths from parole supervision.

In sum, postrelease supervision has not been abolished in the juvenile justice system since the onset of the determinacy and the accountability movements. Most states retain some form of supervised release regardless of their philosophy of sentencing. Texas and New York, for example, have passed determinate sentencing provisions, but youths committed under these provisions still may be released on conditional supervision. Although supervised released has been maintained even in determinate-parole jurisdictions such as Washington State, the underlying justification remains unspecified. Few states have articulated a coherent policy that includes the aftercare or parole aspect of the correctional process. As in the late 1960s, aftercare remains the least developed area of the juvenile justice process.

REFERENCES

AMERICAN CORRECTIONAL ASSOCIATION
1978   *Manual of Standards for Juvenile Probation and Aftercare Services*. Rockville, MD: Commission on Accreditation for Corrections.

AMERICAN LEGISLATIVE EXCHANGE COUNCIL
1987   "Model Juvenile Justice Code" (draft). Claremont, CA: Rose Institute of Justice.

ASHFORD, J.B., AND C.W. LECROY
1988   "Decision-Making for Juvenile Offenders in Aftercare." *Juvenile and Family Court Journal* 39:47–53.

AULTMAN, M.G. AND K.N. WRIGHT
1985   "The Fairness Paradigm: An Evaluation of Change in Juvenile Justice." *Canadian Journal of Criminology* 24:13–24.

BAILEY, F.L. AND H.B. ROTHBLATT
1982   *Handling Juvenile Delinquency Cases.* Rochester, NY: Lawyers Co-operative Publishing Co.

BAIRD, C.S.
1981   "Classifying Juveniles: Making the Most of an Important Management Tool." *Corrections Today* 43:36–41.

CLEAR, T.R.
1979   "Three Dilemmas in Community Supervision." *Prison Journal* 59:2–16.

28 C.F.R., PART II
1987   pp. 91–118.

COFFEY, A.R.
1975   *Juvenile Corrections: Treatment and Rehabilitation.* Englewood Cliffs, NJ: Prentice-Hall.

DAUM, J.M.
1981   "Aftercare: the Neglected Phase of Adolescent Treatment." *Juvenile and Family Court Journal* 32:43–48.

DAVIS, K.C.
1971   *Discretionary Justice: A Preliminary Inquiry,* Urbana: University of Illinois Press.

DIVISION OF JUVENILE REHABILITATION
1987   Juvenile Parole Program Standards. Olympia: Department of Social and Health Services.

FORST, M.L., B.A. FISHER, AND R.B. COATES
1985   "Indeterminate and Determinate Sentencing of Juvenile Delinquents: A National Survey of Approaches to Commitment and Release Decision Making." *Juvenile and Family Court Journal* 36:1–11.

HAINES, T.H.
1920   "Lessons from the Principles Governing the Parole Procedure in Hospitals for the Insane." In *Conference on Social Work,* pp. 159–66. Chicago: University of Chicago Press.

HARRIS, P.M. AND GRAFF L.G.
1988   "A Critique of Juvenile Sentences Reform." *Federal Probation* 52:66–71.

HUDSON, C.H
1973   Summary Report: An Experimental Study of the Different Effects of Parole Supervision for A Group of Adolescent Boys and Girls. Minneapolis: Minnesota Dept. of Corrections.

INSTITUTE OF JUDICIAL ADMINISTRATION/AMERICAN BAR ASSOCIATION
1980   *Dispositions.* Cambridge, MA: Ballinger.

KITTIRE, N.N. AND E.H. ZENOFF
1981   *Sanctions, Sentencing and Corrections: Law, Policy, and Practice.* Mineola, NY: Foundation Press.

KRISBERG, B., I.M. SCHWARTZ, P. LITSKY, AND J. AUSTIN
1986   "The Watershed of Juvenile Justice Reform." *Crime and Delinquency* 32:5–38.

MELTON, G.B., J. PETRILA, N.G. POYTHRESS, AND C. SLOBOGIN
1987   *Psychological Evaluations for the Courts.* New York: Guilford Press.

MODEL JUVENILE JUSTICE COURT ACT
1968   (36).

MODEL PENAL CODE AND COMMENTARIES, PART I
1962

MORRIS, N.
1988   "Sentencing under the Model Penal Code: Balancing the Concerns." *Rutgers Law Journal* 19:811–21.

NATIONAL COUNCIL OF JUVENILE AND FAMILY COURT JUDGES
1984   "The Juvenile Court and Serious Offenders." *Juvenile and Family Court Journal* 35:1–22.

NEWMAN, C.L.
1968   *Sourcebook on Probation, Parole and Pardons.* Springfield, IL: Thomas.

PORTER, J.B.
1983   "Grievance Mechanisms in Community Based Corrections." *Journal of Probation and Parole* 12:29–42.

PRESIDENT'S COMMISSION ON LAW ENFORCEMENT AND THE ADMINISTRATION OF JUSTICE
1967   *Task Force Report: Corrections.* Washington, DC: U.S. Government Printing Office.

ROMIG, D.A.
1978   *Justice for Children.* Lexington, MA: Heath.

ROTHMAN, D.
1986   "Sentencing Reform in Historical Perspective." *Crime and Delinquency* 29:631–51.

SIEGEL, L.J. AND J.J. SENNA
1985   *Juvenile Delinquency: Theory Practice, and Law.* St. Paul: West.

SIMONSEN, C.E. AND M.S. GORDON III
1982   *Juvenile Justice in America.* New York: Macmillan.

SINGER, R.
1978   "In Favor of 'Presumptive Sentences' Set by a Sentencing Commission." *Crime and Delinquency* 24:401–27.

TONRY, M.H.
1987   *Sentencing Reform Impacts.* Washington, DC.: National Institute of Justice.
1988   "Sentencing Guidelines and The Model Penal Code." *Rutgers Law Journal* 19:823–47.

VON HIRSH, A. AND K. HANRAHAN
1981   "Determinate Penalty Systems in America: An Overview." *Crime and Delinquency* 27:289–316.
1984   "Abolish Parole." In. R.M. Carter, D. Glaser, and

L.T. Wilkins (eds.), *Probation, Parole, and Community Corrections*, pp. 184–94. New York: Wiley.

WHEELER, G.R.
1978   *Counter-Deterrence.* Chicago: Nelson Hall.

CASES CITED

Gault, 387 U.S. 1 at 7 (1967).
Kent v. United States, 383, U.S. 541, 86 S. Ct. 1045, 16 L. Ed. 2d 84 (1966).

QUESTIONS FOR DISCUSSION

1. What are the differences between determinate and indeterminate sentencing? Provide examples of each.

2. What is presumptive sentencing? Give an example of this type of sentencing.

3. Discuss the most common type of juvenile parole in the United States.

APPLICATIONS

1. Aftercare for juveniles is the least developed area of the juvenile justice process. Based on your opinion and what you have read, why is this the case?

2. What kinds of programs and/or activities would you recommend for juveniles during aftercare that would improve their chances of successful reintegration into the community?

KEY TERMS

discretionary when something is left to individual choice or judgment.

explicit expressed without vagueness or ambiguity; leaving nothing questionable or unclear.

implicit not specifically revealed or expressed, but understood in context with something else.

inchoate imperfectly formed or formulated; hazy or unclear.

raison d'etre reason or justification for existence.

recidivism a return or relapse to prison by virtue of the commission of more criminal acts.

supplanted when something is removed and substituted or superceded with something else.

unfettered unrestrained; free.

25

Females under the Law— "Protected" but Unequal

Gail Armstrong

Graduate Student, Department of Forensic Studies, Indiana University

The sex of the offender is a significant determinant of the length and type of the sentence imposed. Many sentencing statutes and judges make sex distinctions that are transmitted into different sentences for male and female offenders found guilty of the same offense. Sometimes this discrimination on the basis of sex works in favor of females before the law; most of the time it works against them; all of the time, whether the sentence is more lenient or more severe than the one imposed on a male, the misbegotten motive is chivalry or special protectiveness. Our statutes and sentencing practices incorporate a double standard of morality. Males and females are not equal under the law.

Sentencing is a crucial step in the processing of an offender through the criminal justice system. In some cases the sentencing judge may use discretion and choose from several modes of punishment. In other cases this discretionary power is pre-empted by the dictates of the state legislature. Both instances bear evidence of discrimination on the basis of the offender's sex. Women are sentenced both more severely and less severely than men are for the same offenses.

"Females under the Law—'Protected' but Unequal," *Crime and Delinquency*, 23:2 (1977), pp. 109–120. Reprinted by permission of the publisher, Sage Publications, Inc.

Some states have special sentencing provisions, enacted at the turn of the century to "protect" females, under which the length of a woman's sentence is determined not by the judge but by correctional authorities within the limits set by statute.[1] The result is denial of equal protection for women: under these statutes, female offenders often serve longer sentences than male offenders convicted of the same criminal conduct.[2]

Discrimination in favor of female offenders often occurs when judges have discretionary power. Many judges believe, erroneously, that women are better able than men to reform themselves[3] and that, though given to crimes of passion, they seldom possess the pervasive criminal tendencies that characterize male criminals.[4]

SENTENCING ADULT FEMALES

The Chivalry Factor

Our society is thought to have an especially protective attitude toward women,[5] and it is a widely held belief that women fare much better than men when the trial court has discretion. This selective application of the law is attributed to the "chivalry factor." Pollak states that traditional chivalry in the courtroom has led to acquittals that did not accord with the evidence but rather reflected our cultural attitudes toward women.[6] Compared with men, women are considered to be less liable to be detected, arrested, convicted, and committed, and those who are processed all the way through the criminal justice system are regarded as extraordinarily distasteful or dangerous: "Those who are ultimately sent to prison are the very worst of the total crop."[7]

"Protective" Statutes

In effect today are statutes which reflect the belief that something in the very nature of being a woman justifies her being incarcerated for a longer period than a man would be for the same offense.[8] Between 1869 and 1915, ten states (Indiana, Iowa, Maine, Massachusetts, Minnesota, New Jersey, New York, Ohio, Pennsylvania, and Wisconsin) enacted legislation that created separate facilities for convicted women and established the use of the indeterminate sentence for them, a logical consequence of the legislators' belief that women have psychological characteristics which make longer periods of incarceration necessary.[9] After 1915 three other states (Alabama, Arkansas, and California) enacted sentencing statutes applicable only to women and requiring indeterminate sentences. These statutes usually result in sentences more severe for women than for men guilty of the same offense. Thus there is an interim period during which the male defendant is either under consideration for parole or out on parole, whereas the female defendant remains "protected" in prison, where she is denied a great many fundamental rights.[10]

For example, Iowa law allows women to be confined up to five years for a misdemeanor but, unless an exception is made in the statute defining the particular offense, limits the imprisonment of male misdemeanants to one year.[11] In Maine, women between the ages of seventeen and forty can be sentenced to reformatories for up to three years even if the statutory maximum for the offense is less.[12]

Muncy Act

In Pennsylvania the Muncy Act (1913) required that all women over the age of sixteen who had been convicted of an offense punishable by more than one year in prison must be given a general sentence to the Muncy State Industrial Home for Women. The Muncy Act did not permit the trial judge to use discretion to impose a shorter maximum sentence than the maximum punishment prescribed by law for the offense or to fix a minimum sentence at the expiration of which the female prisoner would be eligible for parole. But he had discretionary power to make these decisions in the case of a male.[13]

Specifically, the Muncy Act discriminated against women in the following ways:

1. A woman could be sentenced to a term of three years even if the maximum was less; a man could not be sentenced over the maximum prescribed by law.
2. A woman was sentenced to the maximum legal penalty if convicted of a crime punishable by more than three years; a man could be sentenced to less than the maximum prescribed by law.
3. A woman could not receive a minimum sentence; not only could a man receive a minimum term but that term could not be more than half the maximum.
4. Under Pennsylvania law, the authority to grant parole lies with the sentencing judge when the sentence is less than two years; it lies with the parole board when the sentence is two years or more. Since all sentences to Muncy were for at least three years, women imprisoned there came under the jurisdiction of the parole board, which does not permit representation by counsel at its hearings.
5. Only if her offense was punishable by a sentence of one year or less could a woman serve the term in a county jail, but she was sent to Muncy, separated from relatives and friends, for the same kind of offense that would have sent a man to the county jail.[14] "Women sentenced under

the Act actually spend more than 50 per cent longer in jail than do men sentenced for like offenses. . . ."[15]

The philosophy upon which the Muncy Act was originally founded has been expressed as follows:

All delinquent women are sexually immoral and breed feeble-minded bastards; prolonged confinement deters delinquency and impedes sexual immorality; the conclusion drawn from this reasoning is that women should be given indefinite sentences.[16]

Many equal-protection challenges to special sentencing statutes for women have failed because the courts concluded that, since women have a rehabilitative capacity different from men's, they *can* reasonably be sentenced differently. No case in court has ever *shown* that women take longer to be rehabilitated than men do.[17]

Daniels.—On May 3, 1966, Jane Daniels was convicted of robbery in Pennsylvania. The trial court sentenced her to one-to-four years in the Philadelphia County Prison. Thirty-one days later, the judge realized that the Muncy Act deprived him of the power to fix Daniels' term at less than the statutory maximum. He then sent her to the State Industrial Home for Women without fixing a minimum or maximum period of imprisonment. This allowed for the possibility that Daniels would serve ten years (the maximum for robbery) instead of her original maximum of four years.[18]

Theoretically, under the Muncy Act women received discriminatorily favorable treatment with regard to parole. Men were required to sere their minimum sentences before becoming eligible for parole, but women, because their sentences were indeterminate, were eligible for immediate parole. Under her original sentence, Daniels could have been paroled in one year, like a male sentenced to one-to-four years for the same offense.[19] However, under the parole policy of Muncy officials, she would not be paroled for at least three years.

Jane Daniels appealed.[20] The issue presented was the constitutionality of the Muncy Act—specifically, the differences of punishment imposed on male and female offenders convicted of the same offense. Unequal treatment, the United States Supreme Court has said, is permissible only when it is reasonable in the light of its purpose.[21]

Daniels was the first attack ever launched against the Muncy Act. All earlier attacks on similar statutes had failed.[22] Pre-*Daniels* opinions upheld sentencing schemes identical to the Muncy Act and indicated that the indeterminate sentence for female offenders was considered essential to a purpose of reform associated with treatment rather than punishment.[23] In 1946 the Maine Supreme Court, citing a legislative need to experiment with prison reform, upheld an unequal sentencing statute, which provided that women be incarcerated for potentially longer terms than men for identical offenses.[24]

The Pennsylvania Superior Court majority opinion ruled that there was a "rational basis" for the unequal treatment of women committed to Muncy—"i.e., a reasonable connection between the classification by sex and the purpose of the legislation":

The broad purpose of the legislation was to provide for the punishment and rehabilitation of prisoners. Different types of incarceration for the same crimes are regularly imposed both for classes of individuals (e.g., juveniles, sex offenders, recidivists, criminally insane), as well as among separate individuals where judicial discretion in imposing sentence may be allowed by the legislature. The only requirement for different classes of persons is that the class exhibits characteristics that justify the different treatment. . . . This court is of the opinion that the legislature reasonably could have concluded that indeterminate sentences should be imposed on women as a class, allowing the time of incarceration to be matched to the necessary treatment in order to provide more effective rehabilitation. Such a conclusion could be based on the physiological and psychological makeup of women, the type of crime committed by women, their relation to the criminal world, their roles in society, their unique vocational skills and pursuits, and their reaction as a class to imprisonment as well as the number and type of women who are sentenced to imprisonment rather than given suspended sentences. Such facts could have led the legislature to conclude that a different manner of punishment and rehabilitation was necessary for women sentenced to confinement. . . .[25]

The majority opinion justified discrimination on the basis of sex, not on the presumption that the Muncy facility provided effective treatment rather than punishment.

The Supreme Court of Pennsylvania unanimously reversed the Superior Court decision on July 1, 1968, saying that there is no difference between the sexes that justifies a shorter maximum sentence for men committing the same offenses as women. It did *not* altogether reject classification by sex.[26]

The inability of the women's reformatory system to offer its inmates a rehabilitative and curative experience—its failure to achieve the penological purposes that might have justified a special sentencing structure—may have been at the bottom of the state Supreme Court's willingness to strike down the sentencing provisions of the Muncy Act as violative of equal protection.[27]

Two weeks after the Pennsylvania Supreme Court handed down this decision, the legislature passed a revision of the Muncy Act. According to the new version, women would not necessarily receive longer maximum sentences than men but were still denied the right to have a minimum sentence set by the judge; consequently, they would remain in prison awaiting parole while men with fixed minimum sentences became eligible for parole.[28] Challenges to the 1968 amendment to the Muncy Act have been unsuccessful.[29]

Douglas.—The *Douglas* case helped persuade the Supreme Court of Pennsylvania to permit an appeal from the superior court decision on *Daniels.* Daisy Douglas and Richard Johnson were convicted of aggravated robbery. Under the Muncy Act, Douglas was sentenced to Muncy for twenty years—the maximum legal penalty; Johnson was sentenced to three-to-ten years in the men's penitentiary. Statistics kept by the Pennsylvania Board of Probation and Parole showed that male parolees convicted of a second equally serious offense were rarely sentenced to the maximum. Douglas filed a petition under Pennsylvania's Post-Conviction Hearing Act, maintaining that her sentence was a denial of her Fourteenth Amendment rights. Her petition was dismissed but her case was consolidated with *Daniels* and was accepted for argument before the Supreme Court of Pennsylvania.[30]

Douglas provided convincing evidence of the discriminatory effect of the Muncy Act. Douglas and Johnson were co-defendants, jointly tried and convicted of the same offense. Johnson, unlike Douglas, had a serious criminal record. Johnson was eligible for parole after three years; under her indeterminate sentence Douglas was technically eligible for parole at any time but in practice would not be eligible for 3 ½ years. The consolidated appeals of *Douglas* and *Daniels* were successfully argued. Both cases were remanded for resentencing.

Robinson.—In Connecticut, 38-year-old Carrie Robinson pleaded guilty to breach of the peace and resisting arrest. Ordinarily these are misdemeanors carrying maximum terms of one year and six months, respectively.[31] However, under a Connecticut statute,[32] women over sixteen who commit such misdemeanors were to be sentenced to an indefinite term not to exceed three years or to the offense maximum, if longer; the statute allowed women to be sentenced for longer terms than men for identical offenses. Robinson claimed that sentencing only women, not men, to indefinite sentences deprived them of equal protection.

The federal district court decision in *Robinson*[33] struck down the statute, finding it a violation of the equal protection clause of the Fourteenth Amendment. The state argued that the longer terms for women involved treatment and rehabilitation, not punishment; but the court followed the U.S. Supreme Court decision in *In re Gault,*[34] which stated that confinement by any other name is still confinement.

Like *Daniels*, *Robinson* did not reject all sex-based classifications. Some sex-based classifications, it said, are reasonable—e.g., limiting women's working hours. *Robinson* and *Daniels* emphasize that unequal deprivation of a *basic* civil right must be sustained by a valid justification.[35]

Costello **and** ***Chambers*.**—In New Jersey, males convicted on gambling charges get minimum-maximum terms in the state prison, and the judge can set the maximum; for identical offenses, females were sentenced (until 1973) to an indeterminate term of up to five years in the Correctional Institution for Women, and the judge had no discretion to lower the maximum.[36] The actual term served by the female offender was determined entirely by the institution's board of managers, while males earned earlier release through "good time" provisions or application to the state parole board.[37]

Mary Costello pleaded guilty in Camden County Court to gambling offenses. She was sentenced to an indeterminate term not to exceed five years at the New Jersey Correctional Institution for Women. For the same offense, a male would probably be sentenced to one-to-two years. Costello appealed, contending that her constitutional rights to equal protection under the law had been violated.[38]

Though New Jersey's sentencing scheme for women was similar to Pennsylvania's and Connecticut's (which had already been held unconstitutional[39]), it was deemed by the court in *Costello* not violative of the equal protection clause of the Fourteenth Amendment. The court cited cases in which sex-based discrimination in sentencing had been found constitutional, even though most of the statutes vindicated in those cases were no longer on the books.

In *State v. Chambers*,[40] a composite of six cases (including *Costello*), each involving females who had been convicted of gambling offenses and had been given indeterminate sentences, the New Jersey Supreme Court held that disparate sentencing based on sex-based classifications violates the equal protection clause of the Fourteenth Amendment. Where a fundamental right of liberty is restrained in conjunction with a classification system based on sex, a state statute is unconstitutional unless a compelling state interest exists. The state's claim that females were better subjects for rehabilitation was insufficient to justify the infringement upon liberty.

COMMITTING JUVENILE FEMALES

The Chivalry Factor

Many believe that female delinquents are not likely to be treated harshly when they come before the courts. Like their adult counterparts, female delinquents are considered to be the beneficiaries of chivalrous treatment. "Our police are inclined to treat unofficially all minor offenses of young girls in order to save them from the social stigma which follows an appearance in court."[41]

Enforcing the Double Standard

Most juvenile courts have broad discretionary powers vested in them by statutes that give them jurisdiction over a wide variety of juvenile activity. Theoretically these statutes apply equally to males and females; actually they are allied in accordance with our double standard of juvenile morality and lend themselves to discriminatory enforcement against females.[42]

Many of the young women who come into contract with the adjudicatory process are "turned in" by their parents or relatives rather than "arrested" by law enforcement officials. The juvenile court is very much concerned with obedience to familial demands. Because of the vastly different parental expectations regarding appropriate behavior for male and female children, there is a corresponding differential response from the juvenile court toward male and female children. Females have a much narrower range of acceptable behavior.[43] For example, in the tradition that a woman's place is in the home, judges often decide that it is delinquent for a young woman, but not a young man, to return home at an "unreasonable" hour.[44]

Most male delinquency consists of statute violation. Most female delinquency involves violation of sex-role expectations *and* is more severely punished than male delinquency. There are basically five offenses that lead to commitment for the juvenile female: (1) running away, (2) incorrigibility, (3) sexual offenses, (4) probation violation, and (5) truancy. Although the official record may read differently, sexual misconduct usually underlies all of these female offenses.[45] A study of 252 young women committed to a correctional school for girls in Wisconsin during the early thirties said that "75.4 percent had records of sex irregularity. Over 40 percent of the total number had been promiscuous, and approximately 40 per cent had a history of venereal disease. Sex delinquency was the most frequent offense."[46]

A few years ago in Connecticut a sixteen-year-old girl was sent to the State Farm for Women because her parents and the court agreed that she was "in danger of falling into habits of vice." The law under which she was committed was upheld on the grounds that her commitment was not punishment but a "protective safeguard."[47]

All girls brought into Family Court in New York, including those brought before the court for nonsexual offenses, are given vaginal Wasserman smears to test for venereal disease. This procedure is terrifying for many young girls who have not engaged in sexual activity.[48]

Statistics

More than 50 percent of the girls—in contrast, only 20 percent of the boys—are institutionalized for "noncriminal" offenses. Because the offenses committed by girls are not very serious (over one-half are noncriminal) one would expect their dispositions to be shorter than those generally given to boys for criminal offenses. Actually, girls usually get longer dispositions than boys.[49] A 1958 study of 162 training schools throughout the United States showed that the average time served by a juvenile delinquent was 9.7 months. Separating the sexes, the study showed that the average for

female delinquents was 12 months; for male delinquents, 9.3 months. In 1962 the overall average for both sexes was 9.5 months (10.8 months for females; 9.2 months for males). In 1964 the overall average declined to 9.3 months. Females averaged 10.7 months; males, 8.2 months.[50]

In 1964, nation-wide statistics put the male-female ratio in juvenile institutions at 3 to 1. The male-female ratio for all juvenile offenses was 4 to 1; for major criminal offenses, 15.3 to 1. There were more juvenile females in institutions than the number of their offenses warranted. "The 'saving' or 'helping' of a girl often justifies more radical and severe 'treatment' than does the punishment of a male law violator."[51]

Statistics published by the Children's Bureau indicate that training schools serving only non-white children or only females keep a child for a longer period of time.[52]

Morals Statutes

Juvenile morals statutes are (1) unconstitutionally vague, (2) impermissibly overbroad because they inhibit constitutionally protected behavior, (3) unconstitutionally overbroad because they encourage selective enforcement against female juveniles according to a double standard of sexual morality, and (4) impermissible in that they punish a status.[53]

Most jurisdictions in the United States have statutes that allow a finding of juvenile delinquency when it is established that the defendant engaged in immoral conduct. Few distinctions are made between juveniles according to the grade of offense seriousness. Most jurisdictions lump them all together—all juveniles who break the law are delinquents. Kansas and Illinois are the only states that do not send runaways to state reform schools.[54]

Morality statutes enable the states to place any juvenile under custody for almost any act for a period ranging from six months to eleven years. Vague delinquency provisions based on subjective determinations of "immorality" and unsupported predictions of future criminal conduct have no legal or practical justification.

The due process clause of the Fourteenth Amendment requires that statutes provide fair warning. Delinquency statutes should be more precisely defined.[55]

Sex-Neutral Statutes

Courts have been reluctant to rule that juvenile morals statutes are unconstitutionally vague. According to the Texas juvenile morals statute, any child who "habitually so comports himself as to injure or endanger the morals of himself or others" can be adjudged a juvenile delinquent. Because our society believes that *female* sexual morals should be more restricted, such vague statutes will tend to enforce the double standard of morality. Sexual delinquency is the most common offense of female juveniles. Male juveniles are usually not adjudicated for such behavior and to this extent the vague language incorporated within sex-neutral juvenile morals statutes permits discriminatory enforcement of different sexual standards for males and females.[56]

Sexually Discriminatory Statutes

Juvenile court statutes that differentiate on their face between male and female juveniles fall into three categories:

1. Some juvenile statutes assume that females need more supervision than males and therefore establish higher jurisdictional age limits for females. At the same time, recognizing the earlier emotional maturity of females, many states with such statutes permit females to marry two or three years earlier than males. Jurisdictional statutes providing for higher age limits for females reflect the attitude that young men should be independent and that young women should graduate from parental supervision directly to marriage. These statutes enforce the double standard of morality.[57] Society is obsessed with the notion of protecting unmarried females from themselves.

   Most states are moving toward a common jurisdictional age for both male and female juveniles.[58]

2. The juvenile court system is civil and its purported goal is rehabilitation. Delinquents within the custody of the court may be "treated" by any of several means defined in the disposition and confinement statutes of the state juvenile court act. The integrity of the juvenile court judge determines whether these statutes are applied equally to males and females.[59]

   Several states allow for discrepancies between the permissible length of confinement for female and male juveniles. In New York a female adjudged a "person in need of supervision" may be committed to the state training school to remain until age twenty. A male must be released by age eighteen.[60]

3. A few state legislatures have provided for special treatment of juvenile females. Until recently, Connecticut and Tennessee had provisions in their juvenile codes permitting institutional commitment of any female between certain ages who is leading a "vicious" or "criminal" life.[61] Now, only Tennessee allows juvenile courts to take custody of girls where they may not take charge of boys.[62]

PINS in New York State

The New York State Family Court Act provides:

Persons in need of supervision means a male less than sixteen years of age and a female less than eighteen years of age who does not attend school in accordance with the provisions of part one of article sixty-five of the education law or who is incorrigible, ungovernable or habitually disobedient and beyond the lawful control of parent or other lawful authority.[63]

Successive extensions [of the original placement] may be granted, but no placement may be made or continued under this section beyond the child's eighteenth birthday, if male, or twentieth birthday, if female.[64]

Under these provisions females are liable for two extra years of original liability and two extra years of placement. It is clear that these provisions deprive females of fundamental rights and liberties.

Court Tests

Courts have applied the equal protection clause to juveniles to invalidate sexually discriminatory juvenile statutes.[65] A statute that distinguishes between two or more classes of people is not always in violation of the equal protection clause of the Fourteenth Amendment. The state must establish that it has a compelling state interest which justifies the law and that the distinctions made by the law are necessary to further its purpose.[66]

The constitutional right to liberty is the major concern in cases challenging sexually discriminatory juvenile statutes. Juvenile laws that discriminate on the basis of sex do affect the liberty of juveniles. The imposition of longer confinement on one sex than on the other is no more permissible with juveniles than it is with adults.[67]

Sex-based discrimination, like racial discrimination, tends to create and perpetuate inferior status and second-class citizenship.[68] In 1972, the United States Supreme Court declared discrimination on the basis of sex to be a "suspect classification."[69]

SENTENCING PROVISIONS THAT DISCRIMINATE AGAINST MALES

Dr. John MacDonald tells the following "apocryphal" story to illustrate "society's divergent attitudes toward the same behavior in males and females":

> If a man walking past an apartment stops to watch a woman undressing before the window, the man is arrested as a peeper. If a woman walking past an apartment stops to watch a man undressing before a window, the man is arrested as an exhibitionist.[70]

It would be a misrepresentation not to mention a few of the rare sentencing provisions that discriminate against males.

1. *Wark.*—A male escapee from the Maine State Prison Farm received a longer sentence for his escape than a woman would have. He asserted that his Fourteenth Amendment rights had thus been violated. Denying his appeal in *Wark v. State,*[71] the court said:

> Viewing statutory provisions for punishment as in part a deterrent to criminal conduct, the legislature could logically and reasonably conclude that a more severe penalty should be imposed upon a male prisoner escaping from the State Prison than upon a woman confined at the "Reformatory" while serving a State Prison sentence who escapes from that institution. We conclude that a classification based on sex under these circumstances is neither arbitrary nor unreasonable but is a proper exercise of legislative discretion which in no way violates the constitutional right to equal protection of the law.[72]

2. *Assault under Arizona Law.*—Under an Arizona law, men are sentenced more severely than women when the victim of the crime is a woman. Arizona defines aggravated assault as an assault made by a male upon a female *or* by a person over age eighteen on a child under fifteen.[73] Under this law, if an adult female spits in the face of another adult female, she will probably be charged with simple assault and pay a $300 fine or serve up to three months. A male who commits the same offense can be charged with aggravated assault and be punished by imprisonment of one to five years and a fine of $100 to $200. North Carolina and Texas have similar assault statutes.[74]

3. *Oklahoma Juvenile Law.*—Under Oklahoma juvenile court law, females who have been adjudged delinquent and have been institutionalized are discharged at age eighteen; males adjudged delinquent and institutionalized are discharged at age twenty-one.[75]

THE EQUAL RIGHTS AMENDMENT

In Oklahoma male delinquents can be confined for a longer period than female delinquents; the reverse is true in New York State.

How can the discrepancy between Oklahoma and New York juvenile court laws be rationally justified? Is there some factual difference between males in Oklahoma and males in New York? Or between males and females anywhere that justifies punishment more or less severe for one sex than for the other? Such inconsistencies in our laws demonstrate the need for the proposed Twenty-Seventh Amendment to the U.S. Constitution—the Equal Rights Amendment.

Sexually discriminatory laws and the unequal application of many sex-neutral statutes coerce females to conform to society's conception of the female sex role. It does not make sense, however, to design training programs in domestication for women who have, by breaking the law, shown their reluctance to adjust to an inferior sex role. Yet, institutions for women and girls offer no programs that teach independent trades. Confined females are trained as housekeepers, seamstresses, and waitresses.

Passage of the Equal Rights Amendment would render *any* discrimination on the basis of sex a "suspect classification." this would hold for juveniles as well as adults, for males as well as females. More comprehensive than an extension of the equal protection clause of the Fourteenth Amendment, the Equal Rights Amendment would be a mandate by the American people. But until that amendment is passed and goes into effect (two years after ratification) the equal protection approach should be rigorously pursued to challenge sexually discriminatory statutes.

CONCLUSION

Special sentencing statutes, sentencing judges, and society's conception of the female sex role are all responsible for the unjust sentencing of females. The disparate sentences received by males and females found guilty of the same offenses provide the most blatant evidence of this unequal treatment. Special sentencing statutes enacted at the turn of the century to "protect" women deny them their fundamental rights. The juvenile justice system enforces society's double standard of morality and severely sanctions only females for "sexual misconduct."

These inconsistencies in the application of our laws and in our system of justice can be swiftly diminished and rendered unconstitutional with the passage of the proposed Twenty-Seventh Amendment to the U.S. Constitution. The Equal Rights Amendment can bring us all a *long* way.

NOTES

1. Brown, Emerson, Falk, & Freedman, *The Equal Rights Amendment: A Constitutional Basis for Equal Rights for Women*, 80 YALE, L.J. 871, 965 (1971).
2. Clements, *Sex and Sentencing*, 26 Sw. L.J. 890 (1972).
3. *Ibid.*
4. Baab & Furgeson, *Texas Sentencing Practices: A Statistical Study*, 45 TEXAS L. REV. 471, 496–97 (1967).
5. W. Reckless, THE CRIME PROBLEM 99 (4th ed. 1967).
6. O. Pollak, THE CRIMINALITY OF WOMEN 4 (1950).
7. Kay & Schultz, *Divergence of Attitudes toward Constituted Authorities between Male and Female Felony Inmates*, in INTERDISCIPLINARY PROBLEMS IN CRIMINOLOGY 209–16 (W. Reckless & C. Newman eds. 1967).
8. Temin, *Discriminatory Sentencing of Women Offenders: The Argument for the ERA in a Nutshell*, 11 AM. CRIM. L. REV. 355 (1973).
9. Clements, *supra* note 2, at 891.
10. Clements, *supra* note 2, at 901.
11. Iowa Code Ann. § 245.7 (1969).
12. Me. Rev. Stat. Ann. tit. 34, § 853–54 (Supp. 1972).
13. Pa. Stat. Ann. tit. 61, ch. 7 (1964).
14. Temin, *supra* note 8.
15. Brief for Appellee at 20–22, Commonwealth v. Daniels, 210 Pa. Super. 156, 232 A.2d 247 (1967).
16. *Id.* at 19.
17. Clements, *supra* note 2.
18. L. Kanowitz, WOMEN AND THE LAW: THE UNFINISHED REVOLUTION 167 (1969).
19. Gold, *Equal Protection for Juvenile Girls in Need of Supervision in New York State*, 17 N.Y.L.F. 570 (1971).
20. Commonwealth v. Daniels, 210 Pa. Super. 156, 232 A.2d 247 (1967).
21. Calloway, *Constitutional Law—Indeterminate Sentences for Women*, 22 ARK. L. REV. 524 (1968).
22. State v. Heitman, 105 Kan. 136, 181 P. 630 (1919); *Ex parte* Dunkerton, 104 Kan. 481, 179 P. 347 (1919); Platt v. Commonwealth, 256 Mass. 539, 152 N.E. 914 (1926); *Ex parte* Brady, 116 Ohio St. 512, 157 N.E. 69 (1927); *Ex parte* Gosselin, 141 Me. 412, 44 A.2d 882 (1945), *cert. denied sub. nom.* Gosselin v. Kelley, 328 U.S. 817 (1946).
23. Note, *Equal Protection—Longer Sentences for Women than for Males Convicted of the Same Offenses Denies Equal Protection*, 82 HARV. L. REV. 921 (1969).

24. Gosselin v. Kelley, *supra* note 22.
25. Commonwealth v. Daniels, *supra* note 20, 232 A.2d at 247, 251–52.
26. Commonwealth v. Daniels, 243 A.2d 400 (1968).
27. *Supra* note 23.
28. Temin, *supra* note 8.
29. Commonwealth v. Blum, 220 Pa. Super. 703, —— A.2d —— (1972); Commonwealth v. Piper, 221 Pa. Super. 187, 289 A.2d 193 (1972).
30. Commonwealth v. Daniels (II), 430 Pa. 642, 243 A.2d 400 (1968).
31. Gold, *supra* note 19.
32. Conn. Gen. Stat. Ann. ch. 309, § 17-360 (1960), as transferred, ch. 323, § 18–65 (Supp. 1972).
33. United States *ex rel.* Robinson v. York, 281 F. Supp. 8 (D. Conn. 1968).
34. 387 U.S. 1 (1967).
35. Kanowitz, *op cit. supra* note 18.
36. N.J. Stat. Ann. § 2A: 164-17 (1971); N.J. Stat. Ann. § 30: 4-155 (Supp. 1973).
37. Lillehaug, *Constitutional Law—Equal Protection–Sex Discrimination in Sentencing Criminal Offenders Is Unconstitutional,* 50 N. Dak L. Rev.. 359 (1974).
38. State v. Costello, 59 N.J. 334, 282 A.2d 748 (1971).
39. *See* notes 26 and 33 *supra* and accompanying text.
40. 63 N.J. 287, 307 A.2d 78 (1973).
41. Pollack, *op. cit. supra* note 6.
42. Comment, *Juvenile Delinquency Laws: Juvenile Women and the Double Standard of Morality,* 19 U.C.L.A.L. Rev. 313 (1971).
43. Chesney-Lind, *Judicial Enforcement of the Female Sex Role: The Family Court and the Female Delinquent,* 8 Issues in Criminology 51 (1973).
44. *Supra* note 42.
45. C. Vedder & D. Somerville, The Delinquent Girl 147 (1970).
46. Lumpkin, *Factors in the Commitment of Correctional School Girls in Wisconsin,* 37 Am. J. Sociology 222 (1931–32).
47. *To Be Minor and Female,* Ms., August 1972, at 74.
48. *Ibid.*
49. Gold, *supra* note 19.
50. W. Lunden, Statistics On Delinquents And Delinquency 258–59 (1964).
51. Chesney-Lind, *supra* note 43, at 57.
52. Children's Bureau, U.S. Dept. of Health,Education and Welfare, Statistical Series No. 81, Statistics on Public Institutions for Delinquent Children—1964, at 7 (1965).
53. *Supra* note 42.
54. Note, *An Aspect of the Texas Juvenile Delinquency Law—"Morals,"* 24 Sw. S.J. 698 (1970).
55. Note, *Statutory Vagueness in Juvenile Law: The Supreme Court and Mattiello v. Connecticut.* 118 U. Pa. L. Rev. 152 (1969).
56. *Supra* note 42.
57. Davis & Chaires, *Equal Protection for Juveniles: The Present Status of Sex-based Discrimination in Juvenile Court Laws,* 7 Ga. L. Rev. 494 (1973).
58. New York's Family Court Act is an exception; it has two provisions which subject females to the authority of the court for a longer period than males. *See* notes 63 and 64 *infra* and accompanying text.
59. Davis & Chaires, *supra* note 57.
60. See notes 63 and 64 *infra* and accompanying text.
61. Conn. Rev. Stat. § 2761 (1949); Tenn. Code Ann. § 37-440 (1955).
62. Davis & Chaires, supra note 57.
63. N.Y. *Judiciary-Family Court Act* § 712(b) (McKinney Supp. 1971).
64. N.Y. *Judiciary-Family Court Act* § 756(c) (McKinney Supp. 1963).
65. *E.g.,* Long v. Robinson, 316 F. Supp. 22 (D. Md. 1970): Lamb v. Brown, 456 F.2d 18 (10th Cir. 1972).
66. Davis & Chaires, *supra* note 57.
67. *Ibid.*
68. *Ibid.*
69. Frontiero v. Richardson, 41 U.S.L.W. 4609, 4613-14 (U.S. May 14, 1972).
70. J. MacDonald, Psychiatry and the Criminal 353 (3rd ed. 1976).
71. 266 A.2d 62 (Me. 1970).
72. *Id.* at 65.
73. Ariz. Rev. Stat. Ann. § 3-245 (1972).
74. Note, *Sex Discrimination in the Criminal Law: The Effect of the ERA,* 11 Am. Crim. L. Rev. 469, 503 (1973).
75. *Okla. Stat. Ann. tit. 10, § 1139(b) (Supp. 1973).*

QUESTIONS FOR DISCUSSION

1. Discuss the "chivalry factor" and its impact on the juvenile justice system.
2. What are the five offenses that lead to commitment for the juvenile female? What do these offenses have in common?
3. Cite examples of enforcement and sentencing disparity for both females and males presented in this article.

APPLICATIONS

1. The author contends that the passage of the Equal Rights Amendment would result in significant changes in the way juvenile females are "protected under the law." Do you agree or disagree with this notion? Why?

2. In your opinion, will America always have a "chivalry factor"? Why?

KEY TERMS

apocryphal when something is spurious or of doubtful authenticity.

chivalry the system, spirit, or customs of a knight or king; in this case, chivalry refers to a male-dominated justice system and society.

conjunction the act or instance that two or more elements are combined.

erroneous refers to anything that has been found to have errors in substance or logic.

impede to interfere with or to slow the progress of something.

penitentiary a term applied to early American prisons whose founders were from religious sects. The penitentiary was thought to be a place where offenders could reflect upon their transgressions and repent of their sins.

preempted replaced with something considered to be of greater value or priority.

vindicate to free from allegation or blame by providing a justification or defense.

26

Restitution and Recidivism Rates of Juvenile Offenders: Results from Four Experimental Studies

Anne L. Schneider

Oklahoma State University

One of the major changes in juvenile justice during the past decade has been the increased reliance on restitution as a sanction for juvenile offenders. Although a great deal has been learned during the past 10 years about the operation of restitution programs, much remains unknown regarding its impact on recidivism rates. This report contains the results from four random-assignment experiments conducted simultaneously in four communities: Boise, Idaho, Washington, D.C., Clayton County, Georgia, and Oklahoma County, Oklahoma.

In all four studies, youths were randomly assigned into restitution and into traditional dispositions. On the whole, the results show that restitution may have a small but important effect on recidivism. However, not all programs will be able to achieve this effect, either because of program management and strategy, community circumstances, or other factors.

Youths in the restitution groups never had higher recidivism rates than those in probation or detention conditions. In two of the four studies, the juveniles in restitution clearly had fewer subsequent recontacts with the court during the two-to-three-year follow-up.

"Restitution and Recidivism Rates of Juvenile Offenders: Results from Four Experimental Studies," *Criminology*, 24:3 (1986), pp. 533–552. Reprinted by permission of The American Society of Criminology.

The use of restitution as a sanction for juvenile delinquents is one of the most marked changes in juvenile justice during the past decade. In 1977, a survey of juvenile courts identified fewer than 15 formal restitution programs (Schneider and Schneider, 1977). By 1985, formal programs are known to exist in more than 400 jurisdictions, and more than 35 states now have explicit statutory authority to order restitution—either monetary or community service or both (Schneider, 1985).

The emergence of restitution as a distinct dispositional alternative can be attributed to several factors. For one, restitution is attractive to the proponents of more servere sanctions for juvenile offenders as well as to those who believe that increasingly heavy-handed intervention only exacerbates the delinquency problem (Armstrong, 1980). The former group views restitution as a more servere response than probation, whereas the latter views it as more appropriate than incarceration. The specificity of restitution as well as its emphasis on accountability also have contributed to its popularity among judges and juvenile justice professionals (Beck-Zierdt, 1980; Cannon and Stanford, 1981; Klein and Kramer, 1980).

The second factor contributing to the rapid spread of restitution has been massive federal efforts to improve and expand the use of this disposition. These efforts began during the Carter administration by the Office of Juvenile Justice and Delinquency Prevention and have continued—albeit at a reduced level—during the Reagan administration.[1]

ISSUES IN THE USE OF RESTITUTION

Restitution has not been without its critics, however. Concerns about restitution have focused on its philosophy, the practical difficulties in implementing restitution programs, and its effectiveness.

From a philosophical perspective, there were initial concerns that restitution would be interpreted as punishment and, even though that interpretation might increase its popularity with the private sector, it could reduce its acceptability with juvenile justice professionals. Treatment-oriented juvenile justice professionals, for example, could thwart the rehabilitative potential of restitution by failing to implement the restitution requirements. It was not at all clear during the early development of programs whether restitution would become a part of the "treatment" perspective or of the "punishment" perspective. Complicating the situation even further was the fact that restitution could be justified from a nonutilitarian perspective grounded in the principles of "justice" and victims rights, thereby avoiding both the "treatment" and "punishment" labels.

What has emerged over the past five years is a growing consensus among juvenile justice professionals that the underlying rationale of restitution is to hold juveniles accountable (to the victims) for the crimes they have committed. This perspective seems to have arisen from the basic logic and practice of restitution throughout the country as literally dozens of programs began focusing on the concepts of accountability and responsibility rather than debating whether restitution is "punishment" or "treatment."

A 1985 survey of restitution programs showed that accountability was by far the most important goal of restitution programs as it was rated 9.7 on a 10-point scale (Schneider, 1985).

Treatment of juveniles was rated 7.9 on the same scale; services to victims was rated 7.6, and punishment averaged a 3.3 rating.

From a practical point of view, one of the most pressing issues was how local jurisdictions would finance the development of formal restitution programs once the federal program funds were exhausted. This problem is far from being solved, but the lack of funds to implement new programs almost certainly has contributed to the fact that in many jurisdictions, implementing and monitoring restitution orders has become the primary responsibility of probation officers, replacing their more traditional tasks of counseling and monitoring curfew, school work, and the like.

Another set of practical concerns revolved around whether judges would be willing to order restitution and whether juveniles would be able to pay. This type of issue has become far less prominent over the years as the results from evaluations of the federal programs indicated high completion rates (85%) and overwhelming support from the judiciary. The average order, in most jurisdictions, was slightly over $200 (Schneider, Schneider, Griffith, and Wilson, 1982).

The issue of racial and social class bias was confronted directly by some programs as they sought to obtain subsidies that would insure that no youth was denied the opportunity for restitution (rather than a more severe sanction) solely on the grounds of inability to pay. This practice has continued even beyond the federal funding with programs establishing subsidy funds through private donations, restitution "fines," and state-wide appropriations.

The third issue involves not only whether restitution is effective, but also the criteria against which it should be judged. Proponents of restitution tend to use a justice-based argument: the primary goal of restitution is to hold juveniles accountable for their acts and to return full or partial payment to victims of crimes. When there is no specific victim or no outstanding loss, the goal is to hold the youth accountable through symbolic restitution (community service work).

A strict adherence to justice-based principles would relieve restitution of any responsibility vis-à-vis longer-term effects on the youths. From this perspective, restitution is ordered because it is "right" and "fair" and constitutes a fundamental principle of justice. Most observers of juvenile justice, however, recognize the inherent weaknesses of justifying a dispositional alternative solely on justice-based principles. Any intervention which must rely solely on fairness or justice-based arguments rather than its therapeutic, rehabilitative, or deterrence value, will soon be replaced by a different intervention which promises to reduce the incidence of juvenile crime. Hence, the effect of restitution on recidivism of juvenile offenders will strongly influence the ultimate fate of this alternative.

RESTITUTION AND RECIDIVISM

Empirical studies of restitution have been reported only since the late 1970s, and most of these defined the effectiveness of restitution in terms of its impact on victims (Galaway and Hudson, 1978; Hudson and Galaway, 1977). The amount of loss returned, the number of proportion of victims provided with restitution, victim satisfaction with the outcome of the case, and victim perceptions of the fairness or "justice" of the sentence were the common performance indicators included in the early empirical studies.

The first two studies which sought to link restitution with reduced recidivism were both conducted with adult parolees after their release from prison. Heinz, Galaway, and Hudson in 1976 reported that the restitution group had fewer convictions after release than a matched group of incarcerated offenders. Similar results were found by Hudson and Chesney (1978) in their two-year follow-up of adult offenders released from the Minnesota Restitution Center.

In a study conducted by Bonta, Boyle, Motiuk, and Sonnichsen (1983), adult offenders in a restitution program had higher recidivism rates that those in a control group, although the differences were not statistically significant. Both groups were housed in a community resource center, and most persons in

both groups were employed. The control program permitted offenders to maintain employment by serving their sentences in the community resource center. The authors point out that the restitution group was a higher-risk group than the others prior to the intervention and that this could have diminished the true impact of the program.

The first two tests of restitution's effect on recidivism of juvenile offenders were undertaken by doctoral candidates. In one of these, conducted by Wax at Washington State, juveniles were randomly assigned into one of three groups: monetary restitution (with the victim present at sentencing), community service restitution, and a control group which had no contact with victims and paid no restitution. No differences in recidivism rates were found to be statistically significant, although restitution was observed to have positive effects on some of the psychological tests (Wax, 1977). The size of the sample in this study, however, was so small (36 total) that the possibility of finding an impact, even if one existed, was exceptionally low.

The second doctoral study examined recidivism rates of approximately 250 offenders in the Tulsa County juvenile restitution program (Guedalia, 1979). Variables found to be significantly related to reduced recidivism were victim contact and restitution orders of less than $100. The latter, of course, could simply be a reflection of a less serious immediate offense (hence the lower amount of the restitution order).

Two recent studies of recidivism rates among juvenile delinquents sentenced to restitution reported positive effects. Cannon and Stanford (1981) found a 19% rearrest rate among restitution cases over a six-month time period compared with a 24% rates for the nonrestitution groups. Hofford (1981) reported an 18% recidivism rate for youths in the juvenile restitution program compared with a 30% rate for those on regular probation.

The results from these studies are instructive, although they are far from being definitive. As is the case with virtually all field research, serious methodological problems confound most of the studies, making it necessary to rely more heavily on replication of findings than on any single study. With the exception of Wax's study and the adult study by Heinz et al. (1976), none achieved a satisfactory degree of equivalence between the comparison group and the recidivism group. In the juvenile studies, little information was provided on whether the groups were equivalent, and multivariate analysis was not conducted in an attempt to hold constant other differences between the groups that could have produced different recidivism rates.

THE EXPERIMENTS

The research reported in this paper is based on experimental studies undertaken simultaneously in four different juvenile court jurisdictions.[2]

Although there were numerous problems involved in establishing the random assignment procedure and insuring the integrity of the data, tests eventually were developed which permitted direct comparisons of restitution against traditional dispositions in Boise, Idaho, Washington, D.C., Clayton County, Georgia, and Oklahoma City, Oklahoma.

Boise, Idaho

The experiment in Boise was structured to provide a comparison of restitution against short-term detention. Youths randomly selected for the treatment group were required to pay monetary restitution to the victims of their crimes or, if there was no outstanding monetary loss, they were required to complete a specified number of community service hours. Juveniles assigned to the control group were sentenced to several successive weekends of detention in a local detention facility. All juveniles were on probation (in addition to their requirements regarding restitution or weekend detention).

The eligible group included all youths referred to court for adjudication on a delinquent offense, except those who were held in detention during their pretrial period. These cases were excluded from eligibility because the youths had already experienced incarceration, and thus would not represent a proper

test of the restitution condition if they later were randomly assigned to it.

After the fact-finding hearing, all youths for whom the charges were substantiated were then randomly assigned either to the restitution or the detention group. At the disposition hearing, the probation officer presented the results of the random selection. The judge was able to either follow the recommendation or give a different disposition. In Boise, the assignment was followed for 89% of those recommended for restitution and for 97% of the detention recommendations.

Case management in Boise was handled by restitution counselors. The average length of time in the restitution program was two months, and the average length of time under court jurisdiction was nine months. Although these youths were technically on probation, there was little if any active supervision by probation officers.

The control group youths were incarcerated for an average of eight days. The incarcerations took place in a local detention facility and usually involved being locked up for several successive weekends. After release from the local facility, the youths were on probation for an average of nine months.

Washington, D.C.

The Washington, D.C., design provided a comparison of victim-offender mediation restitution against probation for a group of serious offenders. One of the eligibility criteria in this study was that the youths have at least one felony conviction.

After the presentence investigation had been completed, the probation officers recommended the youths either for incarceration or for probation. Those recommended for probation were then randomly assigned either into probation or into victim-offender mediation and the restitution program.

The D.C. program rested on the premise that restitution would be effective only if juveniles accepted responsibility for their offenses and were committed to the principal of making amends to the victim. If a youth did not feel responsible for his or her behavior, then restitution was not expected to be effective. Furthermore, serious complications were expected in the mediation sessions if youths were required to participate in this part of the program. Thus, the program wished to permit the youths who had been randomly selected for victim-offender mediation to voluntarily reject their assignment in favor of probation only.

Although this aspect of the program design clearly would create serious problems with the evaluation, it was accepted since it was an integral and "natural" part of their program. A design which did not permit juveniles to choose or reject restitution would not be generalizable after the experiment was over because the program would not continue to operate with youths who had been "coerced" into the mediation process. Furthermore, it is difficult to envision any victim-offender mediation program anywhere in the United States that would require youths or victims to participate. Thus, voluntary participation was essential to the program and to the generalizablity of the research results.

Although various inducements were attempted throughout the program period to encourage juveniles selected for restitution to actually participate in it, there were many refusals—approximately 40%. An analysis of the reasons for the refusals indicated that defense lawyers were an important source of information for the youths and that they were the ones usually suggesting that the youths eschew the restitution/mediation program.

As in the other sites which have "crossovers" or other kinds of violations in the random assignment, the analysis was greatly complicated by these deviations.

Clayton County

The restitution experiment in Clayton County was designed to compare four distinct treatment strategies: restitution, counseling, restitution and counseling combined, and a control condition which consisted of the normal disposition which could be either probation or incarceration. All youths in the first three groups were on probation. Thus, the actual test was the marginal impact of restitution. An additional feature of this design was the ability to test the marginal impact of counseling.

Cases were randomly assigned into the four conditions after the adjudication hearing. As with the other experiments, the actual placement of the youths into the groups was done by the judge at disposition. The judge could overrule the random assignment, but this was seldom done. Of the cases that were included in the study, 7% received an actual sentence that differed from the randomly assigned one.

The treatments associated with the four groups can be summarized as follows:

Restitution. Youths in this group were ordered at disposition to pay monetary restitution and/or to do community service restitution. Service restitution was more common, involving 60% of the youths. Of the 40% who paid monetary restitutions, slightly more than half found their own jobs and the rest obtained employment through the efforts of the restitution program.

The youths kept some of their earnings— on the average, about 40%. There were no program subsidies in Clayton County, and youths generally were not permitted to pay the restitution from their savings or to have family members assist in the payment. Restitution cases were monitored by restitution case workers who also were responsible for insuring their compliance with normal probation requirements. The average period of supervision was 3.5 months.

Counseling. Juveniles with a counseling disposition were assigned to a mental health therapist on the county social service staff. The counseling consisted of a diagnostic session followed by assignment to one of several special kinds of therapy: recreational, family, and so forth. The average supervision period was 5.6 months.

Restitution and Counseling. For this group, both restitution and mental health therapy were ordered at disposition. The restitution requirements were quite similar to those for the restitution-only group: 63% were ordered to do community service and 44% had monetary restitution requirements. Families were not permitted to pay and most of the youths found employment in private or public sector jobs. These youths were under supervision for an average of 5.8 months.

Control. Any court-approved disposition was considered appropriate for this group, and most were placed on probation (78%). Only 5% were incarcerated, and the remainder either received some other disposition or were dismissed with no sanction.

Oklahoma County

Eligible cases in Oklahoma County included all adjudicated delinquents except those convicted of murder and rape for whom a monetary value could be placed on victim losses. Following the fact-finding hearing, these youths were randomly assigned into one of three groups: the restitution only group; restitution and probation; and a control group which would receive whatever sanction the judge deemed appropriate, so long as it did not include restitution. For those who were to be in either of the restitution groups, program staff developed restitution recommendations which were presented to the judge along with other presentencing information.

One important compromise reached in the negotiation about random assignment was that the judge would be able to sentence youths in any one of the three groups to an incarceration sanction if this was deemed necessary. Although this had an adverse impact on the power of the design (when the youths were left in their assigned groups for the analysis), it does not appear that the effect would be harmful enough to abandon the experiment. Since the youths were randomly assigned into the three groups, each group would contain youths of approximately equal seriousness and would have an approximately equal proportion of their more serious offenders removed for incarceration. This type of "crossover" does not introduce bias into the final groups if the youths are left in their assigned treatment for analysis, but it does reduce the power of the design. Decisions to incarcerate were about equally likely in all three groups: 9% for the

restitution-only group were committed to the state for incarceration; 10% of the restitution-plus probation group were given this disposition, and 11% of the control group were committed to the state.

Approximately half of the youths were ordered to pay monetary restitution and the others did community work service.

Randomization

The randomization procedure varied from one program to another, although in each site the procedure guaranteed that any deviations would be immediately obvious. The formulas were all based on some combination of day-of-birth, a random number starter, and a final assignment which allocated cases into groups in accordance with predetermined proportions.

The list of numbers and their assignment was kept by the researchers rather than program staff to insure that persons responsible for identifying the eligible pool would not have prior knowledge of the group to which the youth would be assigned if he or she were determined to be eligible.

The random assignment formulas were not necessarily set to achieve equal number of cases in the treatment and control conditions. Instead, the proportions were established so that the program could take a sufficient number of cases to fulfill its grant obligations and to achieve as nearly an equal distribution of cases as feasible under the circumstances.

METHODOLOGY

Measuring Recidivism

Recidivism was defined as crimes committed after entry into the treatment or control conditions which resulted in contact with the county juvenile or adult court, except incidents which were dismissed due to a lack of evidence or those for which the youth was found not guilty. Crimes that were committed after the immediate offense but before entry into the program were counted as "concurrent" incidents and were not included in the analysis.

A complete search of all juvenile and adult

court records was undertaken by a team of trained individuals from the national evaluation group. The follow-up period varied from 22 to 36 months, depending on when the youths entered the program and when the final official records check was conducted.

Multiple measures of recidivism were used to incorporate both the seriousness and frequency of reoffending as well as to minimize possible misinterpretations based on single-indicator analysis. The measures used were:

Prevalence. Prevalence refers to the percentage of juveniles in each group who committed a subsequent offense which resulted in a referral to adult or juvenile court during the follow-up period. Excluded from this figure were any recontacts for which the records definitely established that the case was dismissed for lack of evidence or the youth was found not guilty.

Annual Offense Rate. The annual offense (contact) rate was calculated by summing all of the recontacts for the group, dividing by the time at risk (in days), and then correcting to an average annual rate per 100 youths. Both the pre- and postoffense rates were calculated.

Recontact Frequency. Recontact frequency was used as an individual-level measure of overall recidivism in the regression analyses. Recontact frequency refers to the total number of recontacts for each youth. This is a badly skewed variable, and several transformations were tested in the multiple regression analysis. Although very few differences were noted in the results, the most stable measure was a natural log transformation, and this was employed in the analysis reported here.

Recontact Rate. This is also an individual-level measure used in the multiple regression analysis. It was calculated by dividing the total number of offenses for each youth by the total time at risk, thereby creating an individual-level "rate" of recontact. Juveniles with no reoffenses had differing follow-up periods, however, because they entered the programs at different points in time. A simple rate involves dividing zero reoffenses by the risk time which, of course, produces a score of zero regardless of whether the youth had six months of time at risk or four years. To distinguish among the nonrecidivists so that those with longer periods of time at risk have lower scores, a small constant (.01) was added to the numerator of this measure.

Seriousness Indices. Three variables representing seriousness were used in the initial data analysis. One of these was an ordinally coded variable representing the most serious offense committed by the juvenile. Violent personal offenses were coded "6," followed by serious property offenses "5," other felony property offenses "4," minor personal offenses "3," minor property offenses "2," and trivial offenses, "1."

The second variable representing seriousness was created by scoring each reoffense in terms of its seriousness and then summing these to obtain an overall measure of frequency and seriousness of reoffense. The final variable was a seriousness rate in which the overall score for each youth was divided by the amount of time at risk, thereby taking into account that youths with longer follow-up periods would be expected to have more reoffenses.

Because these three measures yielded almost identical results and because these results were similar to those produced by the frequency variables, only the last seriousness measure is included in this paper.

In all instances, the rate of reoffending (frequency divided by time at risk) was actually an adjusted rate in which a small constant (.01) was added to the numerator so that the scores of persons who had no recidivist offenses would be scaled in terms of their time at risk.

Establishing Causality

Juveniles were randomly assigned into the program and control conditions in all four sites. In an ideal experiment, the random assignment alone would be sufficient to insure that the statistical measure of program impact was not confounded with other variable. Field experiments, however, seldom meet the rigid requirements of experimental conditions, and the ones in this evaluation were no exception.

The major problem was with cross overs—cases which were assigned to one condition but which ended up in the other. In most of the sites, these cross overs constituted fewer than 5% of the total, but in Washington, D.C., approximately half of the youths randomly selected for the victim offend mediation–restitution program voluntarily decided not to participate and to accept traditional probation instead.

It is always difficult to know what to do with crossover cases, but the analysis here follows the common recommendation, which is to consider a case in the group to which it was assigned, even if the actual treatment was something different. This is generally viewed as a conservative approach due to the expectation that those who violate the random assignment do so to protect the program by "creaming." Hence, the more difficult cases are directed away from the program, leaving only the easier ones. To include all cases, as originally assigned, protects against "creaming."

In the analysis reported below, however, the precaution was also taken of testing all the regression models with the cases in the actual, rather than assigned, groups. The results of these analyses in sites with small numbers of crossovers were no different from the results when the cases were kept in their original groups, and are not reported. However, in Washington, D.C., the crossover group (juveniles who voluntarily selected probation rather thatn restitution) was so sizable that the entire analysis is reported.

For the analysis, bivariate regressions were conducted and, to insure that potentially confounding effects did not interfere with the interpretation, multiple regression analysis also was undertaken in which priors, age, race, school status, and sex were controlled. In all of the regression tests, the independent variable is the treatment/control condition with restitution being scored "zero" and control scored "one."

FINDINGS

Table 1 contains descriptive data for juveniles in the restitution and the control group in all

TABLE 1 Background Characteristics, Prevalence Rates, and Incident Rates [a]

Site	No. Cases	Full-Time Student %	Ethnic Minority %	Gender (Male) %	Repeat Offender %	Age %	Referral Offense Felony %	Months of Followup	Prevalence %	Annual Incident Rate Per 100 Youths Pre	Post
Boise											
Restitution	86	81	5	86	66	15.0	41	22	53	103	86
Detention	95	85	1	84	80	15.3	32	22	59	137	100
Washington, D.C.											
Restitution	143	75	99	97	63	15.4	65	32	53	61	54
Restn. Refused	131	72	98	87	65	15.5	57	31	55	62	52
Probation	137	72	99	91	61	15.5	59	31	63	61	65
Clayton County											
Restitution	73	76	6	86	60	15.1	24	35	49	101	74
Restn. + Counseling	74	82	4	80	43	15.2	40	35	46	55	47
Prob. + Counseling	55	75	4	78	56	15.1	49	36	60	64	84
Probation	55	86	0	80	54	15.2	30	37	52	75	75
Oklahoma County											
Sole Sanction Restn.	104	65	34	91	59	15.2	50	23	49	66	72
Restn. + Prob.	116	69	46	87	59	15.4	48	24	50	56	64
Probation	78	72	32	85	68	15.5	40	24	52	75	74

[a] In all sites, the information on prior and subsequent offenses was based on an official records search of juvenile and adult court records.

four sites. Table 2 has the results of the multivariate analyses.

Boise

There were no statistically significant differences in the background characteristics of youths in the two groups. Most were full-time students (81% and 85%, respectively); the average age was just over 15 years, and more than 80% were males.

The population from which the random assignment was made included primarily serious offenders. In the restitution group, 66% were repeat offenders and 80% were repeaters in the detention group. This difference, which appears to indicate that the detention group contained somewhat more serious offenders than the restitution group, is offset by the fact that 41% of the restitution youths entered the

program as a result of a felony conviction compared with 32% of the incarceration group.

The recidivism analysis suggests that the restitution group did somewhat better (that is, had fewer reoffenses), but the differences are not very large and they may have been produced by chance. The observed significance levels in most of the analyses, although favoring the restitution group, were between .25 and .30.

Specifically, in the 22 months of follow-up, 53% of the restitution group had one or more subsequent contacts with the court compared with 59% of the incarceration group. The post-program annual rate of subsequent contacts per 100 youths was 86 for the restitution group compared with 100 for the incarceration group. Differences of this magnitude would be expected, by chance alone, approximately one fourth to one third of the time.

TABLE 2   Multiple Regression Analysis of Restitution and Recidivism

Site	Prevalence			Incidence			Seriousness		
	r [a]	bwt [b]	osl [c]	r	bwt	osl	r	bwt	osl
Boise									
(a) Restitution vs. Detention	.05	.44	.27	.02	.02	.33	.04	.04	.29*
Washington, D.C.									
(a) Restitution and Restitution Refused vs. Probation	.08	.10	.04	.07	.10	.05	.02	.05	.25
(b) Restitution vs. Probation	.09	.11	.03	.08	.11	.04	.03	.04	.20
Clayton County									
(a) Restitution vs. Probation	.11	.11	.07	.11	.13	.04	.08	.09	.16
(c) Restitution vs. (Restitution + Counseling)	−.10	−.07	.38	−.09	−.05	.60	.01	.07	.42
(d) Without Counseling vs. With Counseling	.03	−.02	.77	.02	−.03	.69	−.09	−.12	.06
Oklahoma Co.									
(a) Sole-Sanction Restitution vs. (Restitution + Probation)	−.08	.02	.77	−.03	.14	.84	.00	.00	.99
(b) Restitution vs. Probation	.00	.00	.97	.00	.00	.99	.07	.00	.87

[a] The zero-order correlation coefficient.
[b] The standardized regression coefficient (beta weight) with priors, age, race, sex, and school status controlled. Time at risk also was controlled in the equations utilizing prevalence.
[c] The observed significance level (for the restitution variable in the multivariate equation, two-tailed test).
* Positive scores indicate the restitution group did better (that is, had lower recidivism rates). Positive scores in other comparisons indicate the group named first did better.

The multiple regression analysis (see Table 2) indicated a difference of about the same magnitude, but it too would occur by chance about 25% to 30% of the time.

The pre/post comparison shows that the intervention may have slowed the annual offense rate for both groups. The average number of offenses committed, per 100 youths per year, dropped from 103 for the restitution group to 86. For the incarceration group, the annual preprogram rate dropped from 137 to 100. Although maturation of the youths obviously could influence the pre/post change in annual rates, the groups were randomly selected and were about the same age. Hence, the maturation effects should be about the same for both groups and the cross-comparison of pre/post rates yields interesting information. It also should be recalled that the data collected included tracking into adult courts. Thus, there is no cutoff of subsequent incidents as the youths reach 18 years of age.

On balance, the Boise experiment indicates the restitution youths did just as well as those who were in detention and that there was a relatively good probability (about two out of three) that the participation in the restitution program actually yielded a slightly lower recidivism rate. This conclusion, however, must be balanced against the fact that the control group had a higher level of priors before the intervention (but slightly less serious immediate offenses), and the reduction in incidence was actually somewhat higher for the control group.

Washington, D.C.

Referrals to the Washington, D.C., program were serious offenders. More than 60% were repeat offenders, and for approximately 60%, the immediate incident which resulted in their referral was a felony (see Table 1). These youths were predominately black (99%) and male (95%).

There were no statistically significant differences between the restitution and control groups in terms of background characteristics. This held true when the crossovers were grouped with the restitution youths and when they were kept separate. It should be noted,

however, that the crossovers contained substantially more females (13%) than either of the other two groups.

The results of the recidivism analysis are interesting, but perplexing. The restitution group (all those randomly assigned restitution, including the "crossovers") had reoffense prevalence rates considerably below the probation group—53% to 63%, a statistically significant difference—and annual reoffense rates similarly lower than the control group (54 to 65). The multiple regression analysis also shows that the youths assigned to restitution had lower overall contact (both frequency and rates) after controlling for the number of priors, age, race, school status, and sex.

As mentioned previously, substantial treatment contamination occurred in the randomization, with about half of the randomly assigned restitution youths receiving probation instead of restitution. With this issue in mind, three additional sets of multiple regression analyses were conducted. In each instance, different evaluation groups were included or excluded, creating different treatment and comparison groups. In each case, the independent (treatment) variable was dichotomous (scored as zero for the control condition and one for the treatment). These results show the following:

Restitution versus Restitution Refused (Crossovers). This comparison indicates that the restitution group had slightly fewer recidivist offenses, but the differences were not significant.

Restitution versus Probation. In this analysis, the crossovers were omitted entirely and the restitution youths had significantly lower recidivism rates on almost all measures.

Restitution versus Restitution Refused (Plus Probation). The crossovers actually received probation and in these analyses were grouped with the probation youths who were randomly assigned. The restitution group had somewhat better scores on most of the indicators, but the differences were only marginally significant (for example, in the .15 to .25 range).

Three major findings stand out. First, youths

who were randomly assigned into restitution—whether they actually participated in it or not—had lower recidivism rates than youths randomly assigned probation. Second, those who actually participated in restitution generally had lower recidivism levels than those in probation. And, third, those who had participated in restitution never had higher rates than those who participated in probation.

Why then did youths who were randomly selected for restitution but refused (the crossovers) have lower recidivism rates that those on probation? Both actually participated in probation. Differences in the background characteristics do not appear to account for these differences.

Perhaps the reason for the differences is that youths selected for restitution were given realistic choices and involvement in the determination of their disposition which the probation youth did not have. All juveniles selected for restitution were presented with two choices of roughly equivalent severity (probation or restitution) and they were allowed some involvement in the process of determining their disposition. It is possible that this choice component allowed them to select a treatment somewhat better suited to their individual interests and motivations and thus one which was more efficacious in impacting their future behaviors.

Clayton County

Clayton County youths were overwhelmingly white (as is the population in that suburban area near Atlanta), approximately 15 years of age, and predominately male (see Table 1). Between one fourth and one half of the youths were referred for felony offenses and most of the others had been involved in misdemeanor property crimes.

The restitution-only group was compared with the restitution-counseling group to determine whether the latter produced any improvement in the successful completion rates. As shown in Table 1, the completion rates were very high for both groups and the small difference observed (86% for-restitution-only ver-

sus 82% for restitution-counseling) was not statistically significant.

Both restitution groups were somewhat less likely to commit subsequent offenses resulting in court contacts during the three-year follow-up period as 49% of the restitution-only group and 46% of the restitution-counseling group were again referred to court. These figures compare with a 60% and 52% recidivism rates for the two probation groups.

The postprogram offense rates also show similar differences with the restitution groups having lower annual offense rates.

The multiple regression analyses, controlling for number of priors, age, school statues, race, and sex indicate an effect with a high likelihood of being produced by the program (significance levels of .07, .04, and .16 on a two-tailed test). In these tests, the two restitution groups were combined and compared with the two probation groups.

The group reoffense rates before and after the intervention indicate some interesting differences. For the restitution-only group, the preprogram rate was 101 offenses. After the intervention, this dropped to 74. Drops in the postintervention rates of similar magnitudes were not observed for any of the other groups. The restitution and counseling group had a preprogram rate of 55, which dropped only to 47 afterward. The probation and counseling group actually showed an increase from 64 to 84, and the probation only group showed no change (75 to 75).

A second multiple regression analysis was undertaken to determine whether counseling had an impact on recidivism when contrasted with the noncounseling dispositions. For this analysis, both counseling groups were compared with the noncounseling alternatives and no significant differences were found. A final comparison was between the restitution-only condition and restitution-counseling. Again, no significant differences were found.

The results from Clayton County show that youths required to make restitution to their victims either through community service or monetary payments had lower recidivism rates than those given the more traditional juvenile court disposition. These results show that restitution works quite well on its own and that it does not need to be combined with mental health counseling.

Oklahoma County

Most of the juveniles in Oklahoma County were relatively serious offenders: 59% of the restitution youths had one or more priors and 68% of the control youths had a prior record of court contact. Many of the youths entered the experiment as a result of felony convictions: 50% of the sole-sanction group, 48% of the restitution and probation group, and 40% of the probation-only controls.

The groups did not differ on recontact with the court, regardless of the method of measuring recidivism or the type of analysis undertaken. On the average, juveniles in the sole-sanction group committed 140 offenses per 100 youths per year compared with 133 for the restitution and probation group and 150 for the controls. These differences were not great enough to be statistically significant—they were not even close, in fact.

Comparison of the pre- and postrates show that none of the interventions reduced the overall offense rates. In fact, the youths in both restitution groups tended to reoffend slightly more afterward than before whereas the control group continued at the same rate.

The multiple regression analysis effectively removed even the slight differences observed between the groups as the unstandardized regression coefficient with the other variables controlled was .00 in two of the tests and less than .02 in the other.

The findings from this experiment indicate that youths who were given restitution as a sanction, without benefit of probation requirements or probation supervision, were generally as successful as those who received probation along with restitution. Furthermore, the results indicate that youths who received restitution sanctions did no better and no worse than the control group of probation youths in terms of recidivism.

CONCLUSIONS

The results from the experiments regarding the effect of restitution on recidivism should be viewed as quite encouraging. In two of the four direct comparisons, approximately 10% fewer of the restitution group were recontacted during the follow-up. An annualized measure of recontact indicated that the restitution program cases produced almost 10 fewer crimes per 100 youth per year than the controls in these two programs (Washington, D.C., and Clayton County, Georgia). The differences in these two sites were great enough to rule out chance variation as a likely cause of the apparent program effect.

In one other jurisdiction—Boise, Idaho—the program youths did better on both measures of recidivism by six percentage points and an annual rate differential of 14 incidents per 100 youths per year. The smaller sample size, however, prevented these differences from achieving statistical significance at the .05 level. The study in Oklahoma County revealed among the three groups no differences of sufficient size to merit policy consideration. These results should not be viewed as inconclusive or as contradictory. Rather, the lesson here is that restitution can have a positive effect on recidivism, but it does not necessarily have this impact under all circumstances.

The reasons for the success of restitution in reducing recidivism—in those instances when it was successful—remain a matter of speculation and theory. As with any effective intervention, it is reasonable to assume that the intervention must have an impact on one or more variables which influence delinquency. And, since the restitution intervention was directed primarily at the juvenile (rather than his or her parents, friends, or neighborhood), it is reasonable to believe that the effect is transmitted through changes in the juvenile's perceptions or attitudes which in turn, alter behavior.

Many possible variables might be cited:

1. Youths who participate in restitution have positive experiences in "real job" situations

which not only may provide a positive adult role model, but which also may instill a sense of confidence that the youth can be successful in nondelinquent situations.

2. Restitution may have a less stigmatizing effect on the youth since it offers the juvenile the potential for "paying the debt" and for being "redeemed" for the offense.

3. The youth may have a more realistic understanding of the actual consequences of crime for victims and for the community as a result of being "held accountable" for delinquent acts.

4. Restitution is believed by many program managers to break down the postoffense rationalization (for example, the victim deserved it) and force the offender to confront the true consequences of the crime.

5. It is possible that restitution has a deterrent effect (in the sense of increasing the perception that crimes have consequences which result in costs to the offender).

6. Restitution usually involves a relatively intensive supervision since most of the youths are spending a substantial portion of their free time at work. This may break down the relationship between the youths and other delinquent peers during the supervisory period and perhaps beyond.

Future research needs to focus on the linkages between restitution, attitudes, and subsequent behavior in order to identify how restitution operates to reduce delinquency when, in fact, it has this effect.

NOTES

1. The original federal program was intended to involve six or eight juvenile courts and was viewed as a research and development program. When Ira Schwartz became administrator of the Office of Juvenile Justice and Delinquency Prevention, however, the priority given to restitution increased enormously and the program expanded to a 20 million dollar effort eventually involving 85 juvenile courts. A national evaluation was separately funded by the National Institute for Juvenile Justice and Delinquency Prevention. Under the Reagan administration, the emphasis on restitution was temporarily suspended, but was resumed by Alfred Regnery as a major training and technical assistance program (RESTTA, Resti-

tution Education, Specialized Training, and Technical Assistance).

2. The evaluation was conducted at the Institute of Policy Analysis, Eugene, Oregon. The author of this paper was one of the principal investigators of the study, along with Peter R. Schneider. William Griffith, Mike Wilson, and Gordon Bazemore also contributed enormously to the data collection and analysis upon which this paper is based.

REFERENCES

ARMSTRONG, TROY
1980   Restitution: A sanction for all seasons. Presented at the Fourth Symposium on Restitution and Community Services Sentencing.

BECK-ZIERDT, NATHANIEL
1980   Tri-county juvenile restitution program. Unpublished. St. Paul, MN: Minnesota Crime Control Planning Board Research and Evaluation Unit.

BONTA, JAMES L., JANE BOYLE, LAURENCE L. MOTIUK, AND PAUL SONNICHSEN
1983   Restitution in correctional half-way houses: Victims satisfaction, attitudes and recidivism. Canadian Journal of Correction 20: 140–152.

CANNON, A. AND R.M. STANFORD
1981   Evaluation of the juvenile alternative services project. Unpublished. Florida Department of Health and Rehabilitative Services.

GALAWAY, BURT AND JOE HUDSON (EDS.)
1978   Offender Restitution in Theory and Action. Lexington, MA: Health.

GUEDALIA, LESLIE J.
1979   Predicting recidivism of juvenile delinquents on restitutionary probation from selected background, subject, and program variables. Unpublished doctoral dissertation. Washington, D.C.: American University.

HATFIELD, ELAINE AND MARY K. UTNE
1978   Equity Theory and Restitution Programming. In Burt Galaway and Joe Hudson (eds.), Offender Restitution in Theory and Action. Lexington, MA: Heath.

HEINZ, J., BURT GALAWAY, AND JOE HUDSON
1976   Restitution or parole: A follow-up study of adult offenders. Social Service Review 50: 148–156.

HOFFORD, MERRY
1981   Juvenile restitution program. Unpublished final report. Trident. Charleston, SC: United Way.

HUDSON, JOE AND BURT GALAWAY
1977   A review of the restitution and community-service sanctioning research. In Joe Hudson and Burt

Galaways (eds.), Victims, Offenders, and Alternative Sanctions. Lexington, MA: Heath

HUDSON, JOE AND STEVE CHESNEY
1978   Research on restitution: A review and assessment. In Burt Galaway and Joe Hudson (eds.), Offender Restitution in Theory and Action. Toronto: Lexington.

KLEIN, ANDREW R. AND ALBERT L. KRAMER
1980   Earn-It: The Story So Far. Quincy, MA: Earn-It.

SCHNEIDER, ANNE L. (ED.)
1985   Guide to Juvenile Restitution Programs. Washington, D.C.: National Criminal Justice Reference Service and GPO.

SCHNEIDER, ANNE L. AND PETER R. SCHNEIDER
1977   Restitution requirements for juvenile offenders. A survey of practices in American juvenile courts. Juvenile Justice Journal 18: 43–56.

SCHNEIDER, PETER R., ANNE L. SCHNEIDER, WILLIAM GRIFFITH, AND MICHAEL WILSON
1982   Two-Year Report on the National Evaulation of the Juvenile Restitution Initiative: An Overview of Program Performance. Unpublished. Eugene, OR: Institute of Policy Analysis.

WAX, MAX L.
1977   Effects of symbolic restitution and presence of victim on delinquent shoplifter. Unpublished doctoral dissertation. Pullman, WA: Washington State University.

WILSON, MICHAEL J.
1983   The juvenile offender instruments: Administration and a description of findings. Unpublished. Eugene, OR: Institute of Policy Analysis.

QUESTIONS FOR DISCUSSION

1. Why has restitution become more popular as a sentencing alternative?

2. According to this article, how does restitution affect the recidivism rate of the juvenile offenders who were studied?

3. What criteria does the researcher use to measure recidivism?

APPLICATIONS

1. Contact a local juvenile court judge or juvenile probation officer. Find out how often restitution is used as a sentencing option or a condition of probation for the juvenile offenders in your community. What types of restitution are typically utilized?

2. Do you think restitution is an appropriate alternative to other more institutionalized forms of adjudicative action? Why?

KEY TERMS

concurrent operating or existing at the same time.

efficacious having the power to produce a desired effect.

exacerbate to make more bitter, severe, or undesirable.

non-utilitarian refers to something that is not considered to be useful or good based or its consequences.

substantiate to establish by proof or competent evidence; to verify.

V

JUVENILE DELINQUENCY AND PUBLIC POLICY

As you have seen thus far, the system of juvenile justice that has emerged over the last 150 years is an enigma. Issues such as the age of culpability, the philosophy underlying a separate juvenile justice system, and the relative importance of status offenses have shaped it. Perhaps more important than the behavior of youths over this historical period are the changing societal reactions to youths and youth culture. Many of these reactions have shaped the juvenile justice system by offering solutions directed at treating symptoms rather than causes. Most agree that the most serious forms of delinquency are perpetuated by particular social environments and influences. Solutions must aim at processes that produce greater individual responsibility, not just greater individual freedoms.

Keep in mind that the majority of the most serious career criminals in our maximum security prisons come from environments of violence, neglect, and abuse. After only a few short years of abuse and/or neglect, the individual, due to a poor self-concept, may never accept total responsibility for his or her actions and may spend a lifetime blaming others for failure. Without efforts and resources directed at making the very early years of a child's life the most positive and loving, we will only continue to react to the worst, rather than creating the best, in our nation's youths.

The expectations of reform and a reduction in delinquency are extremely high, yet the resources remain low. Perhaps the most enigmatic feature of the system is the lack of a clearly defined set of goals; a congruent set of expectations in terms of outcomes resulting from policy or program implementations. The complexity of conceptualizing outcomes has been exacerbated by rising violence among juveniles, increased public fear of juvenile crime, and a multitude of political interests. What once was a small system seeking to improve the social ills of neglected, abused, and delinquent youth has become an institution whose mission often vacillates from one extreme to another.

The enigmatic nature of the system should not, however, blind one to the successes of many programs and people who struggle daily with issues as real as life and death. The most overlooked feature in the research area, and to a lesser degree in the public perception, is that many young lives are changed in positive ways and that these youths go on to good futures. The real issues in this section on policy encompass much more than the juvenile justice system. This last section presents four articles that focus on the system, youth culture, social change, and significant ideas on how to solve the many problems that contribute to and are caused by juvenile delinquency.

"Rethinking the Juvenile Justice System," by Travis Hirschi and Michael R. Gottfredson, presents some poignant arguments regarding an issue of critical importance to students of delinquency: Responsibility for one's actions and the long-term consequences of those actions. Hirschi and Gottfredson point out the many contradictions of a separate system of justice for juveniles and suggest that it is unjustified. Especially important to their arguments is the traditional rationale utilized to create this separate system of juvenile justice. Eliminating separate systems would have extensive consequences and would have the effect of pulling the criminal justice system in the direction of the juvenile system or could, perhaps, create a crisis for prison systems across the nation.

Hunter and McHardy, in "Juvenile Justice and the Blind Lady," claim that we are setting the stage for another "quick fix" in the juvenile justice system. Change in the system is inevitable but there are no easy paths to follow. The complex nature of the issues are such that no panaceas exist. Certainly, deinstitutionalizing status offenders was a step in the right direction. The structures of juvenile justice administration and delivery remain troublesome even for the most ardent supporters of the status quo.

Many Americans know that families are really the keys to solving social problems such as delinquency and youth violence. The early years are important in shaping the life course of any one individual. The increasing illegitimacy rate, the increased number of children below the poverty line, and the growing numbers of dysfunctional families combine to negatively affect our nation. This primary institution has and will continue to change as we enter the new century. Karen E. Wright and Kevin N. Wright, in "A Policy Maker's Guide to Controlling Delinquency and Crime through Family Interventions," make several recommendations for change in this important institution. The strategies posted by the authors include parent training, family treatment of troubled youths, and a variety of proactive approaches that serve as positive and forward-thinking intervention policy considerations.

John J. Wilson and James C. Howell present 'Serious and Violent Juvenile Crime: A Comprehensive Strategy" to point out the alarming rate at which juvenile crime is affecting the criminal justice system. Juvenile crime, especially serious and violent juvenile crime, has increased sharply since 1985 and evidence increasingly suggests that a small percentage of youths are responsible for almost 75 percent of these types of crimes. Strategies must include targeting certain youths through both prevention and societal responses to youth crime.

We conclude the anthology with Michael F. Aloisi's article "Emerging Trends and Issues in Juvenile Justice." As we've seen in other readings and evidence, a major trend has been to get tough on juvenile offenders. The most important issues revolve around which juvenile offenders will be treated with greater harshness and which will be treated as youth in need of help from the formal system. Clearly, a small number of offenders create the greatest concern for the public, whereas most of them need only minimum intervention.

27

Rethinking the Juvenile Justice System

Travis Hirschi
Michael R. Gottfredson

Ten or so years ago we became concerned about the connection between juvenile delinquency and adult crime. At that time, it was widely believed that most "delinquents" stopped offending as adults and became "nondelinquents." The existence of large numbers of adult offenders thus required an explanation distinct from the explanation of juvenile delinquency. Or, at least, theories were required to account in some complex way for the delinquents who did and those who did not become adult criminals. However handled, the usual stance was that the connection between delinquency and crime was complex, and contingent on the effectiveness of the juvenile justice system.

All this was of course consistent with the assumptions of the juvenile justice system: This system from the beginning has assumed differences in the causes of crime associated with stages of development over the life course, that, as one moves from childhood, to adolescence, to adulthood, the meaning of offenses differs such that they reflect different causes and

From *Crime and Delinquency*, Volume 39, Number 2 (April 1993), pp. 262–271. Copyright © 1993 by Sage Publications, Inc. Reprinted by permission.

require different modes of "treatment" by the state.

Many of the questions now facing the justice system may be traced to the assumption of developmental stages: Should we consider the juvenile records of adult offenders; what are the proper conditions for waiver to adult court; what is the appropriate age of automatic adult jurisdiction; how should we deal with status offenses; what are the benefits of diversion from the juvenile justice system; and what should we do with juveniles who commit very serious offenses? All of these questions reflect the influence of the idea that the meaning of acts is contingent on identifiable stages of the life course. In this article, we try to approach such questions from a different point of view—from the point of view of a theory that sees the causes of all crimes as identical, whatever the age of the offender. This view is based in part on the well-established connection between age and crime, in which crime is found to follow a predictable path over the life course, reaching its high point in the late teen years. By the way, our perspective is also influenced by research showing that the general public does not see differences in the seriousness of crimes based on the age of the offender (Sellin and Wolfgang 1964).

THE THEORY

Our theory (Gottfredson and Hirschi 1990) asserts that following childhood the population can be meaningfully ranked in terms of self-control, the tendency to consider or ignore the long-term consequences of one's acts. Acts that have long-term negative consequences for the actor are more frequently engaged in by those low on self-control. Such acts include crime, delinquency, recklessness, school misconduct, and drug use. The theory posits that the continuum of self-control is created by early childhood socialization practices. Once created, self-control is a stable individual difference responsible for considerable continuity in the tendency to deviant behavior over the life course, a tendency that manifests itself in a wide variety of misconduct.

Because criminal and deviant acts satisfy ordinary motives and desires, and are defined by lack of concern for long-term consequences, it follows that they are available to everyone throughout life. They require little cognitive complexity, little learning, planning, or skill. They are available to everyone not constrained by fear of the long term. Opportunities for such

acts of course vary by age: School truancy is available to children, but auto theft is not available until adolescence, and embezzlement is usually available only to adults. Guardianship also varies by age. Given that only minimal intervention is required to deter most crime, the presence of an adult is usually sufficient to prevent crime among children. In fact, at some ages, the commission of criminal acts is prima facie evidence that adult supervision is inadequate.

What does the theory say about the issues that have traditionally plagued the juvenile justice system? Let us begin with the basic question, the age that properly marks the boundary between juveniles and adults for purposes of penal treatment.

AGE, CRIME, AND COURT JURISDICTION

Figure 1 depicts the distribution of robbery in the United States by age. Robbery is an important, serious crime. It is the offense of record for one fourth of adults in prison and about one eighth of juveniles in penal institutions. As is obvious from the figure, robbery peaks at about age 17, and declines sharply thereafter.

FIGURE 1 **Robbery Rates by Age**

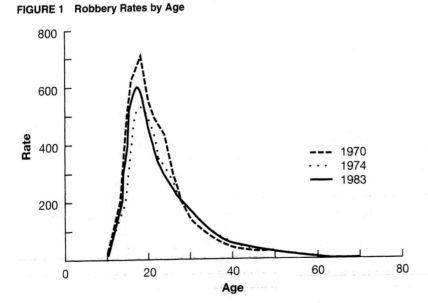

As is also obvious, the rate of decline between 29 and 34 is about as steep as the rate of decline between 19 and 24. Put another way, there is no apparent impact of justice system sanctioning (or of life course events) on the distribution of robbery. The rate would decline from its peak without intervention. Changing from juvenile to adult sanctions has no apparent impact on the rate (which begins to decline before juveniles legally become adults). As we and others have shown, we could substitute virtually any offense for robbery and achieve the same result. The decline in crime with age is continuous or monotonic throughout life, for all groups, whether or not they possess a distinct juvenile justice system. The age distribution was the same before the invention of the juvenile court. It would presumably be the same were the juvenile court abolished. (The current age distribution in the United States is for all intents and purposes identical to the distributions in England and Wales for 1842-44 and 1908—see Hirschi and Gottfredson 1983).

These distributions apply regardless of the activity level of offenders. The distinction between prevalence and incidence is not helpful in accounting for the distribution. Credible evidence disputes the belief that the crime rate declines with age because some offenders drop out, while others remain active at a high rate. In fact, crime declines with age whatever the intervention by the state and whatever the prior activity level of the offender (see, e.g., Haapanen 1990).

JUSTIFICATIONS FOR SEPARATE SYSTEMS

So how do we justify treating children differently from adults? Let us examine some possibilities. One is that the criminal behavior of children is less *serious*. One way to think about seriousness is in terms of harm or damage; another is to think about the implications of the act for the future behavior of the offender. It is common to think of adult crimes as more serious than juvenile delinquencies on both counts. However, the evidence says otherwise. Seriousness does not vary by age—offenders

do not escalate their offenses as they get older (see, e.g., Wolfgang, Figlio, and Sellin 1972). Another justification for treating offenders differentially by age is that adults but not young people are *responsible* for their acts. This is another way of saying that young people do not or cannot anticipate the consequences of their acts, particularly their effects on other people. This is what we refer to as low self-control, and we have no quarrel with the idea that it is central to an understanding of criminal behavior. But if people can be excused from the penalties of the law because they have low self-control, and if self-control is a stable individual trait, we would be forced by the same logic to excuse adult offenders as well. Daniel Glaser (1972) has indeed advanced the idea that some adult offenders are simply people who have not grown up, referring to them as "adolescent recapitulators."

Still a third reason for differential response by the justice system is the idea that young people are more malleable then adults, more receptive to treatment, and more capable of being rehabilitated. Actually, the evidence suggests that individual differences are established before the age of intervention by the juvenile court (apparently by ages 8–10, see Glueck and Glueck 1950; West and Farrington 1973), and that these differences remain remarkably stable over long periods of time. No one appears to have shown that age is a predictor of treatment success, a finding that would seem to be required by the juvenile court hypothesis. A definite theoretical advantage to early treatment is that its benefits would be enjoyed for a longer period of time. If we accept this argument, however, it seems to us that treatment would take place very early, so early that it could in no manner be sponsored by the justice system, or justified by the behavior of the child.

A fourth reason for separate treatment of juveniles is the existence of a distinct class of behaviors that are rightly considered deviant for children but which cannot reasonably be considered deviant for adults—these are of course the so-called *status offenses.*

But there are conceptual and empirical problems with the distinction between delinquent acts and status offenses. It is easily shown that behaviors analogous to status offenses among adults are also punished by the justice system or have negative consequences for those involved in them. In fact, in the United States, offenses involving alcohol and drugs are the most frequent cause of arrest *among adults*. A serious and not that uncommon offense in the United States is resisting arrest, the adult equivalent of incorrigibility. Among adults, truancy and tardiness for work can have as serious long-term consequences as the equivalent behaviors among children with respect to school. On the empirical level, it turns out that status offenses predict delinquent acts as well as delinquent acts predict delinquent acts. Put another way, juvenile offenses do not form delinquent or status clusters, but are generally highly intercorrelated. Delinquents do not specialize in one type of offense any more than adults.

The lack of clustering among offenses suggests another point too often misrepresented in the literature. Consistent with the idea of self-control, the data do not reveal specialization in particular acts or sequences of acts from one class to another. Offenders do not progress from status offenses to serious or violent acts, just as they do not progress from thievery to murder. All that we can say is that the person committing one act is more likely to commit all other acts; we cannot specify the nature or type of subsequent acts the offender is likely to commit.

Within the general theory of crime, all acts are in one sense similar (as indicators of the underlying state of the individual), and in consequence do not provide justification for differential treatment. If the number of deviant acts in a limited period of time is relevant to system response, this suggests focusing greater attention on children and adolescents and less on adults, and once again takes us outside the justice system.

Still another justification for a separate juvenile justice system is that it allows for the treatment of problem behavior without jeopardizing the life chances of the child. Currently in the United States, this question is surrounded in controversy. Some argue that juvenile

records should be made available to adult courts. Others argue for the traditional sanctity of the juvenile record. On a practical level, separate record systems compound the problem of developing, an accurate account of the offenders history (something a researcher would worry about!). But the real issue is the value of the record for criminal justice decision making vis-à-vis its negative impact on the individual's chances of success in life.

It is difficult to establish the prejudicial effect of a juvenile court record over and above the persistent effect on behavior of low self-control. This effect works in two ways to reduce the significance of information on the prior record of the offender. For one thing, it reduces the likelihood that the offender will rise to a position that would be jeopardized by information about his or her prior criminal conduct. For another, it increases the likelihood of conduct that would make knowledge of prior conduct redundant. If the offender avoids further contact with the system over a reasonable period of time, there should be no point in maintaining a file on him or her. But this is true regardless of age.

Another possible justification for a dividing line is the *dependency* of youth, that there is a point before which people require the care and attention of responsible adults and after which they should be free to take care of themselves. The juvenile court thus intervenes to insure the health and safety of pins, jins, chins, or mins, or simply dependent and neglected or abused children. We would not deny that the state has a responsibility to care for people who cannot care adequately for themselves. However, this welfare rationale differs so radically from the criminal rationale for intervention that it need not be discussed further here. Incidentally, the welfare justification does not really justify an adult/juvenile distinction, because many people in need of state assistance are not juveniles.

A historic justification for the distinction is that it provides separate facilities, where children can be isolated from the *corrupting influence* of hardened offenders. This rationale stems from the belief embodied in the saying that prisons are schools for crime. The failure to find differences in recidivism among offenders based on the amount of time served, or, for that matter, between probation and prison, casts doubt on this theory (Empey and Erickson 1972; Murray and Cox 1979) as, of course, does the age distribution of crime, which shows younger offenders being *more* criminal than adult offenders.

Perhaps the most popular justification for the distinction between juvenile delinquency and adult crime is that it provides justification for "treating" juveniles rather than punishing them, as an excuse for *leniency* toward children. This justification draws support from the recurrent tendency to demand that adult sanctions be applied to adolescents guilty of heinous acts—i.e., from the assumption that if the distinction were abandoned, the full force of the criminal law would come down on the heads of children, that the adult system would be applied to juveniles, rather than vice versa.

WHICH SYSTEM SHOULD PREVAIL?

There is good historical reason to believe that fears of excessive punitiveness toward children are unjustified. But to the extent we have a choice in these matters it seems to us that the evidence suggests that the drift of public policy should be in the other direction—i.e., that we should as far as possible attempt to replace the current system with a system modeled more on the juvenile than on the criminal justice system. Evidence in favor of this direction of change is amply provided by experience in the United States.

Statistics from the United States show that as of 1987 there were on any given day something like 41,000 juveniles detained for serious crimes; the same count for adults in the same year shows something like 600,000 incarcerated in state and federal prisons. This in spite of the fact that in any given year juveniles (those 18 or younger) account for about a third of arrests for serious crimes.

If we were applying the system to adults we now apply to children, there would be a crisis in prison construction in the United States of

unheard of proportions—but the problem would not be *insufficient* cell space. Looked at from the other direction, if we applied the adult incarceration rate to the juvenile arrest rate, we would experience a seven-fold increase in the number of juveniles behind bars.

No one would support the latter proposal. Yet the fact of the matter is—as we have shown—incarceration of juveniles should have greater impact on the crime rate than incarceration of adults. If our societies can survive a situation in which relatively high rate offenders are left on the streets, they could surely survive a situation in which relatively low rate offenders are released.

But of course the juvenile system is not fully described by the fact that it makes relatively little use of incarceration. It is also described by greater emphasis on treatment, by less procedural formality, and by less concern for the nature of specific offenses (i.e., the state of being delinquent or in need of supervision is more important than precise legal definitions of the offender's acts—e.g., second-degree burglary). All of these features of the juvenile justice system are of course now under attack. In the eyes of some, they make it inferior to the adult system, with its emphasis on deterrence and incapacitation, its insistence on legal formality, and its attendant concern for the nature of the specific offense rather than the character of the offender.

Given the current popularity of the due process-adult model, on what grounds can one argue for extension of the traditional delinquency model to adult offenders? Recall the various justifications for the current separation of the two systems discussed above. On inspection, it seems to us, all seem to point to change in the direction suggested:

1. The crimes of adults are *not* more serious than those of juveniles.
2. Adult offenders are not different from juvenile offenders in terms of self-control—i.e., neither appears to consider the long-term consequences of their acts. However, if there is a difference in likelihood of subsequent offending, it would appear to favor

adults, whose overall rate of offending is declining.

3. The idea that young people are more malleable than adults with respect to criminality has not been shown, and, again, evidence suggests that adults have a declining crime rate regardless of treatment.

4. There is no class of acts that can reasonably be considered deviant for children but not for adults. Indicators of criminality among children are also indicators of criminality among adults. Therefore, for purely crime control purposes, there is no reason to treat acts differentially according to age.

5. If benefits accrue to children from limiting the stigma attached to criminal justice proceedings (through expunging of records and the like), it is hard to see why a similar rationale would not apply to adults.

6. The welfare interest of the juvenile court would not be affected by its extension to adults who for whatever reason (i.e., mental incapacitation, temporary homelessness, spousal abuse) are unable to care for themselves.

7. As mentioned above, the corruption argument for separate facilities for juveniles and adults can be turned on its head, because there are reasons to think that juvenile offenders are as corrupt as adults. The "physical danger" argument is also usually misguided, because classification by security (or assault) risk is already widely practiced.

So, if there are no obvious costs, what would be the benefits of such a system?

One, already mentioned, would be marked reduction in the number of persons incarcerated, without corresponding increases in the crime rate. Given the extremely high costs of incarceration, the savings to taxpayers could be substantial.

Deemphasis on deterrence and incapacitation would undermine the criminal justice system more generally, leading to reduction in demand for law enforcement and court personnel, and perhaps directing attention toward prevention of criminal acts and the development of self-control.

Consolidation of the two systems would eliminate the possibility of differential treatment due to minuscule differences in age, as when a 217-month-old youth is treated as an adult while a 215-month-old youth, guilty of the same crime, is treated as a juvenile. It would eliminate the tendency of officials in the juvenile justice system to incarcerate or otherwise deal harshly with juveniles in the last year of their eligibility in order to "teach them a lesson" before they are lost forever to the adult system. It would remove the impossible task of deciding when it is appropriate to begin to treat sexually active or drug-using youngsters as adults responsible for their own behavior. All of this suggests that advantage naturally accrues to being defined as a juvenile. In fact, that is not always the case. In New York City it is said that youths overstate their age in anticipation of more lenient treatment in the adult system, and sporadic research indicates that youth waived to the adult system in anticipation of more punitive dispositions actually serve less time than their counterparts in the juvenile justice system.

Elimination of separate systems would eliminate the duplication in research, personnel, records, and facilities required by current arrangements.

Yes, but what are the costs of abolishing the distinction between adult and juvenile systems? Let us attack this question by focusing on cases that more or less define the extremes of the two systems as they now operate. For the adult system, the extreme case is the serial killer with a lengthy prior record who expresses no remorse for his or her violent acts against helpless strangers. We see no reason for complicating the issue with such cases. They should be handled with dispatch by a system of retributive justice *that makes no pretense about crime control or rehabilitation.*

At the other extreme is the 10-year-old child whose only "crime" is that she has been neglected by her family. Here too we see no reason for complicating the issue with such cases. Absent a crime control purpose, this case too can be handled easily by a system set up solely with the welfare of the client in mind—with no false pretense to a crime-prevention function.

For the run-of-the-mill case, involving theft or alcohol, effort should be devoted as now to restitution and whatever restriction or punishment the offense suggests. The assumption throughout should be that the function of the criminal justice system is to manage offenders, not to build a case against them that can be used only after they have passed beyond the age of maximal criminality.

Although our theory suggests to many that we have a profoundly pessimistic view of human nature and a profoundly cynical view of the ability of the state to change the behavior of its citizens for the better, the fact is that we see no evidence of darkly sinister motives operating behind most criminal acts, and we are actually impressed by the relatively fleeting nature of the years of high criminal activity. Given that the cause of crime is low self-control, all that is required to reduce the crime problem to manageable proportions is to teach people early in life that they will be better off in the long run if they pay attention to the eventual consequences of their current behavior.

REFERENCES

EMPEY, LAMAR AND MAYNARD ERICKSON. 1972. *The Provo Experiment.* Lexington, MA: D.C. Heath.

GASER, DANIEL. 1972. *Adult Crime and Social Policy.* Englewood Cliffs, NJ: Prentice-Hall.

GLUECK, SHELDON AND ELEANOR GLUECK. 1950. *Unraveling Juvenile Delinquency.* Cambridge MA: Harvard University Press.

GOTTFREDSON, MICHAEL AND TRAVIS HIRSCHI. 1990. *A General Theory of Crime.* Stanford, CA: Stanford University Press.

HAAPANEN, RUDY. 1990. *Selective Incapacitation and the Serious Offender.* New York: Springer Verlag.

HIRSCHI, TRAVIS AND MICHAEL GOTTFREDSON. 1983. "Age and the Explanation of Crime." *American Journal of Sociology* 89:552–84.

MURRAY, CHARLES AND LOUIS COX. 1979. *Beyond Probation.* Beverly Hills, CA: Sage.

SELLIN, THORSTEN AND MARVIN WOLFGANG. 1964. *Measurement of Delinquency.* New York: Wiley.

WEST, DONALD AND DAVID FARRINGTON. 1973. *Who Becomes Delinquent?* London: Heinemann.

WOLFGANG, MARVIN, ROBERT FIGLIO, AND THORSTEN SELLIN. 1972. *Delinquency in a Birth Cohort.* Chicago: University of Chicago Press.

QUESTIONS FOR DISCUSSION

1. Hirschi and Gottfredson assert that following childhood people can be ranked in terms of their relative degree of self-control. Explain.

2. What is the relationship of age to the frequency of criminal activity?

3. Although the juvenile justice system is becoming more like the adult system of justice, some might argue that the two systems should be different. Why? In what ways should juvenile and adult justice systems be different?

APPLICATIONS

1. Visit a local juvenile court judge. Ask how the juvenile system of justice is different than the adult system. Ask the judge what he or she sees as the future in juvenile justice.

2. If the trend in juvenile justice is toward more punition, what may be the long-term positive and/or negative consequences?

KEY TERMS

analogous similar; corresponding in some respects.

continuum a continuous series of identical components.

heinous wicked or hateful.

malleable easily affected or formed by external influences.

monotonic the same with no variation or change.

prima facie true, valid, or sufficient upon one's first impression or on the surface.

recapitulation refers to repeating or going over something again.

28

Juvenile Justice
and the Blind Lady

Hunter Hurst
Louis W. McHardy

Roscoe Pound called it the highest form of justice. That was 1940 and Mr. Pound was referring to the individualized justice of that bold social experiment known as the juvenile court. In 1967, Justice Fortas of the U.S. Supreme Court called it the worst of both worlds. Mr. Fortas was also talking about the individualized justice of the juvenile court. In 1989, writing for the majority in *Heath A. Wilkins v. Missouri*, Justice Scalia said that the Missouri juvenile court's certification procedure ensured individualized consideration of the maturity and moral responsibility of a 16-year-old youth before he was required to stand trial as an adult. The U.S. Supreme Court's determination in this regard was pivotal in its decision to uphold the death penalty imposed on Wilkins by the State of Missouri.

One hundred and twenty years after its informal founding in Suffolk County, Massachusetts, and 92 years after its formal founding in Cook County, Illinois, the U.S. juvenile court and the juvenile justice system it anchors are alive and in many ways surprisingly robust, but the ground is rapidly undulating under its foundations. As we enter the twenty-first century, there are more than a few pressing issues to be resolved in our juvenile justice system.

MISSION

Of the 38 states that articulate a mission for the juvenile court, 37 still assert acting in the interest of the child as the state's primary means of responding to the children who come within its purview, but change is in the wind (Szymanski, 1991a). Arizona, a few years back, passed the so-called PIC Act requiring juvenile courts to impose Progressively Increasing Consequences (PIC) on repeat delinquent offenders. Conceptually, this notion of progressively increasing consequences is more akin to the juvenile court's original concept of "individualized justice" than it is to the criminal court's concept of punishment proportionate to the harm caused by the criminal act. But it does not seem to be exactly what the founders had in mind when they spoke of tailored dispositions that were in the interest of the child. Other states, such as Utah, California, and Minnesota, have departed much farther from tradition by requiring that offenders be held accountable and/or responsible for their crim-

"Juvenile Justice and the Blind Lady," *Federal Probation*, 55:2 (June 1991), pp. 63–68. Reprinted by permission of the publisher and the authors.

inal law violations, while taking care to avoid any taint of criminality. None of these statutes are very eloquent on just what courts are supposed to do to avoid the taint of criminality while holding juveniles responsible for their "criminal behavior," and as might be expected the issue has become more than a little clouded, as exemplified by the recent actions of the Texas legislature authorizing juvenile courts to impose prison sentences of up to 30 years for certain classes of offenders. Texas courts are also *presumably* supposed to impose these periods of confinement while acting in the best interest of the state's children. Of course, it is at least arguable that it may be in the best interest of the child to sentence him to 30 years in prison, but the logic begins to get brittle somewhere past the age of majority since adult/criminal offenders whom courts sentence to prison for punishment rarely serve 30 years.

If the trend continues in the direction of holding youth accountable for their criminal law violations, we will soon need to re-examine our assumptions about the "criminal responsibility" of juveniles. We cannot continue to hold persons accountable for their criminal behavior without finding them culpable and therefore criminally responsible for their actions. If indeed juveniles are to be held criminally responsible for their behavior, the preferred forum for achieving that goal appears to be the criminal court—the medium that has always been available on a case-by-case waiver or transfer basis, but one that is now increasingly being prescribed by legislatures.

The Protective Side of the Mission

Although ambivalence shrouds the court's mission for delinquents, no such uncertainty exists with regard to neglected, dependent, and abused children. The decade of the eighties has witnessed an unprecedented movement of neglected children into the courtroom. The engine for this movement has been the rapidly disintegrating American family and Public Law 96-272, which requires courts or a court-approved tribunal to periodically review children in placement and assure that reasonable

efforts are being made by protective service agents to avoid placement of children in the first instance. Of course, the primary goal of these requirements is to sustain children in their families of origin where possible, but to move with dispatch in finding a permanent home for the child—if efforts to restore the family's functioning fails.

This legislation has added approximately 400,000 cases of children in foster care to the annual dockets of juvenile and family courts in the United States. This sudden increase has not been accompanied by a commensurate increase in resources and, therefore, has strained the court's capacity to the point of breaking. Typically, juvenile and family court judges now spend at least one-half of their bench time hearing such matters, when they were spending less than 20 percent on such cases prior to the advent of Public Law 96-272.

The future portends even more court involvement in protective service matters as states become more and more intrusive into family affairs by default as the family falls apart. Family theorists now insist that there are at least 13 recognizable forms of the family, as contrasted with only three such forms when we entered the decade of the sixties (Taylor, 1985). One clear implication of this rapidly changing social situation is that courts of juvenile jurisdiction are likely to be predominantly courts for protecting children by the turn of the century. In other words, they will be right back where they began 100 years ago but, this time around, the primary basis for their jurisdiction will be neglected, abused, and dependent children rather than delinquents.

STRUCTURE FOR JUVENILE JUSTICE

Before the phenomenon of specialized juvenile courts ever become pervasive in the United States, a court reform movement had already begun that sought to stamp out specialized courts. Fired by the early efforts of the Institute for Judicial Administration, the quest for unified court systems became a passion in the 1970's with the development of the National Center for State Courts and the growth of the

Institute for Court Management. For a time in the late seventies, it appeared that specialized courts of all sorts, from water courts in the West to orphans courts in the East, were slated for extinction. But, as it turns out, appearances are often deceiving. As we enter the decade of the nineties, there are only six states that are judged by the National Center for State Courts (1988) to qualify as truly unified court systems. In fact, at the moment, the momentum is in the opposite direction.

One of the trendy movements in court reorganization these days is the discovery of comprehensive family courts. Ironically, this movement begins just as we are interring the remains of the last traditional American family, but such trivialities never seem to phase court reformers. The family court has been around for some time, with the first one established in Toledo, Ohio, in 1914, followed by such communities as Baton Rouge, Louisiana, and Biloxi, Mississippi, in the decade of the fifties. In the late fifties, the then National Council of Juvenile Court Judges, the National Council on Crime and Delinquency, and the U.S. Children's Bureau combined to idealize family courts with a Model Act called the Standard Family Court Act, but the idea never really caught on. New York established a state-wide family court but did not vest it with divorce jurisdiction. Outside of that effort, no other large state attempted to establish family courts until New Jersey in 1982. In the meantime, the District of Columbia, Delaware, Rhode Island, Hawaii, and later South Carolina, had all established their own versions of family courts; but recently the States of Nevada, Missouri, Arizona, and Utah are all considering the establishment of family courts. The State of California recently rejected such a proposal.

In contrast to the family court movement, there is only one state-wide juvenile court in the United States, that being in Utah, though several other states including the State of Louisiana are actively debating the establishment of such courts. Even so, it appears that generic, one-size-fits-all, trial courts are in for rough sledding, at least for the short term. Part of the reason for this trend appears to be the

increasing complexity of court management in large urban areas; in fact, the primary reason for the rejection of a proposed family court in the State of California was the perceived difficulty of administering comprehensive family jurisdiction within one institution. California, for some time, has been moving in the direction of even further specialization of its juvenile division of superior court in large urban areas. Los Angeles County is in the process of building 27 new court facilities to house the juvenile division's "dependency courts." Other large jurisdictions, such as Philadelphia and Detroit, are moving in a similar direction though they have yet to build separate facilities to house the courts. In the words of at least one California trial lawyer, "It is impossible for even the best trained attorney to master all facets of family practice, so it seems implausible that a single court could effectually manage the entire range of jurisdiction" (Mallory, 1991).

ADMINISTRATION OF JUVENILE SERVICES

Juvenile probation is still largely a court-administered service. In spite of—or perhaps because of—the recommendations of sundry national commissions and reform organizations, the judiciary still has either appointing or supervising authority, or both, over juvenile probation officers in 41 of the 50 states (Torbet, 1989). Juvenile probation officers currently number in excess of 20,000, and the workload numbers continue to grow at an annual rate of 400,000 cases not including intake screening, investigation, and predisposition study caseloads (Hurst, 1990a).

While the administration of juvenile probation has been a rather stable phenomenon over the past two decades, the structural reorganization of juvenile corrections, other than probation, has been a rapidly changing phenomenon. As we enter the final decade of this century, there are only 14 states that administer juvenile correctional institutions within a state department of corrections. That number is down from 20 states in 1980. The current trend is in the direction of establishing a state-level department of youth services, or children and youth services, or the equivalent. Thirteen states currently organize their juvenile corrections services in such a manner. However, most state-level juvenile corrections services (23) are administered by the state departments of social service or their equivalents.

In view of the movement to hold juveniles accountable for their "criminal behavior," a movement back toward placing such services within adult departments of correction is to be expected but is not happening yet. It is quite possible that we have begun to recognize that juveniles requiring correctional institutionalization require a substantively different course of remedial action than that required by adult criminals, but in our form of democracy that is quite unlikely. What is more likely is that the current trend toward establishing separate state agencies is the result of a chance confluence between political self-interests and the always safe political harbor of more efficiency in government.

Community-Based Services

This lofty ideal ought to be catalogued under "reforms that failed because everybody liked them but no one bothered to take any action." Community re-integration, community-based services, neighborhood-based services, and the like, caught fire during the Great Society movement of the sixties but crashed and burned along with many of the programs of that era. Community-based services continue to be a part of our rhetoric but not a part of our repertoire. The primary reason for this dilemma is that juvenile correctional services, other than probation, are state-owned and administered, and state-owned services have a way of getting located where the Speaker of the House and the Governor want them located, not where it makes sense to locate them. Those states that have had the most success with achieving community-based services, such as Pennsylvania, have done so because all services for children and families are owned and operated at the local level rather than the state level. In other words, for community-based services to become

a reality, they need to be Of the Community, By the Community, and For the Community. That means total local control. That means Home Rule, a feature of our society that has been quietly interred—along with the traditional family.

Another means by which a few states have had some success in building community-based services is through the private services lobby. States—such as Massachusetts, Michigan, and New York—that have a strong private services lobby have built a range of community-based services. Ironically, even though community-based services have never been given a fair test, the logic of the idea remains compelling and has begun to fire rhetoric that transcends community-based and talks about family-based services. So far, unless you live in Scotland, it is just so much talk.

DEINSTITUTIONALIZATION OF STATUS OFFENDERS

Even though labeling as a theory of delinquency causation had largely been discredited by the time the Juvenile Justice and Delinquency Prevention Act was passed in 1974, the logic of that so-called theory permeated the provisions and requirements of the Act (Gove, 1975). Consequently, the Act required that participating states remove status offenders (runaways, truants, ungovernable) from places of secure detention and commitment. More specifically, the Act sought to remove status offenders from all association with delinquent offenders, especially in training schools and detention homes.

Seventeen years after the passage of the Juvenile Justice and Delinquency Prevention Act, states have largely succeeded in removing status offenders from state training schools and have achieved a modicum of success in removing them from pretrial detention facilities. However, the number of status offenders in out-of-home placement has not changed. There were approximately 10,000 such offenders in placement in 1975 and the number was similar in 1987 (Thornberry et al., 1991a). The place of confinement has changed though, with group homes and small residential treatment facilities being the major recipients of status offenders diverted from training schools and detention facilities.

However, the rate of juvenile court referrals for delinquency and status offenses has continued to increase—from 45 per 1,000 eligible youth in 1975 to 57 per 1,000 youth in 1988 (Snyder et al., 1987; Snyder et al., 1990a; and Snyder, 1990b). In 1975, the rate produced 1.4 million such referrals and the same number in 1988. This anomalous appearing situation was caused by a decrease in the eligible child population that equaled the increase in rate of referral. In 1975, status offenders represented 25 percent of the total, or approximately 300,000 referrals. That proportion had decreased slightly to 21 percent by 1988 but status offenders are still very much a part of the juvenile justice system workload.

FORM VERSUS SUBSTANCE

The dynamic tension between Punishing and Acting in the Interest of Children reflected in state codes has significantly affected programs for delinquent youth in the past two decades. Most significantly, Control has been pitted against Rehabilitation, and, recently, Control has been winning.

The use of risk classification instruments has gained wide acceptance in the past 10 years within the juvenile justice system. They are currently being used to screen offenders for placement on probation or placement in the institution, just as they are in the criminal justice system where they have their origins, and they are being used in institutions to segregate security risks and determine facility placement. On the other hand, needs assessment designed to determine the focus of program intervention is beginning to look like a vanishing science.

At the community level, intensive probation is showing signs of becoming the rage of the nineties; however, in today's intensive probation, "intensive tracking" and "electronic monitoring" have replaced family-based case work, home visits, and small group intervention as

preferred mediums of dealing with juvenile offenders. Community protection and individual accountability have combined to displace rehabilitation and correction of behavior in both our vocabulary and our programs. "Boot camps," "swamp camps," "gauntlet running," and maximum security institutions are the preferred mediums of community protection. Restitution, community service, fines, and short-term incarceration in secure juvenile detention facilities are the current vogue in accountability.

Competence development, translated as skill development, is as close as we currently come to designing interventions resembling rehabilitation. Literacy training, especially computer literacy, law-related education, G.E.D. training, and skills generally classified as preparation for independent living, i.e., how to open a bank account, rent an apartment, buy groceries, etc., constitute our basic repertoire of competence development.

Character development, building self-esteem, increasing moral reasoning capacity, supporting social maturation, now seem to be notions from a bygone era.

FORCES DRIVING THE CHANGE

At the dawn of the sixties, the term *family* still meant a man and a woman living in state-sanctioned matrimony. In the United States, the term was definitive legally and socially. Today, we recognize legally and socially at least 13 new family forms, including the Same-Sex Family and the Room-Mate Family (Taylor, 1985). Galimony and Palimony are now firmly-established trends in family litigation. The rapid evolution of the family has often left today's youth without an established value referent within the family and without mature adult supervision anywhere in their life. These circumstances, combined with a trend in the direction of rapidly increasing so-called Single-Parent Families and Multiple-Career Families, has cast television as the primary baby sitter and socializer of our children.

One of the behavioral outcomes of the foregoing circumstance is the continued escalation in crimes of violence, especially homicide, forcible rape, aggravated assault, and weapons offenses. All four of these crimes by youth have continued to proliferate. For example, in 1965, youth under the age of 18 were arrested at a rate of 5 per 100,000 for the crime of forcible rape; by 1989, the arrest rate had doubled. In 1965, the arrest rate for aggravated assault was 30 per 100,000; by 1989, the rate had tripled. The homicide rate increased four-fold, and the weapons rate increased three-fold (Snyder, 1991).

In addition to rapidly-increasing violence by youth, the juvenile justice system has also faced increased challenges from new types of offenders. In Marvin Wolfgang's (1972) classic study "Delinquency in a Birth Cohort," of all of the male children in the city of Philadelphia who reached age 18 in 1963 only one drug arrest was recorded from birth to age 18. His second birth cohort, born 13 years later and coming of age in 1975, recorded 737 drug arrests (Tracy et al., 1985).

Increased drug use, however, is not the most troubling part of the drug phenomenon for the juvenile justice system today. Drug dealers are. They abound in youth populations throughout the United States. As we enter the nineties, drug dealers, who are frequently no more than 13 or 14 years of age, with almost unlimited access to cash and automatic weapons, are terrorizing neighborhoods and whole communities and do not appear to be the type of delinquent offender that the founders of the juvenile court had in mind when they designed the system to give highest priority to the best interests of the child (Moore, 1991).

Another special population of juvenile offenders currently testing the resilience of the system are gangs that derive a large part of their status from criminal activity. Gangs have long been a part of the urban culture in the United States, but gangs featuring criminal enterprise as a prominent aspect of their dynamics are new to the world of youth. Cities such as Los Angeles and Chicago have had sections of their community terrorized by youth gangs in recent years in a manner reminiscent of nothing that has ever happened in this country before. The drug trade appears to be one of the engines driving gang activity, both from the standpoint of the economic gain to be had from the trade and the social abandon that can come from a good hit.

Of all the juvenile justice system's failures at rehabilitation, none is more prominent than our inability to correct the behavior of rapists. The failure of the juvenile justice system in this regard is also mirrored by the criminal justice system. That failure, combined with the continued escalation in the prevalence of all forms of sexual assault, has placed the system in an increasingly difficult dilemma (Hurst, 1988). Some states are now faced with the need to plan one in five juvenile correctional beds for serious sexual offenders, without any real optimism about our ability to alter the behavior patterns of such offenders (Hurst, 1990b).

The arrest rate for females under the age of 18 for Crime Index offenses increased 10 times as fast in the 1970s and 1980s as did the rate for males (Hurst, 1987). The system had not anticipated this change in the offending patterns of youth and is still trying to cope with the influx by developing specialized programs and modifying staffing patterns to be more responsive to female offenders. This is a trend that does not appear to be likely to reverse itself in the near term.

However, the major force driving the juvenile justice system's response to serious offenders has been the continued emphasis on legal enfranchisement of youth. In our society, rights are—of necessity—balanced by corresponding responsibilities. Reformers' zealous pursuit of a full panoply of constitutional rights for juveniles has finally confronted criminal responsibility. It is not clear to these authors whether juveniles are now, have been, or will be able in the future to fully benefit from their new-found rights, but it is painfully apparent that we have concluded that they must be held criminally responsible, diminished capacity for crime and/or freedom notwithstanding.

CONCLUSION

As we approach the end of the 20th century, the pressure on the juvenile justice system to demonstrate the efficacy of individualized justice is greater than at any time in its short history. In state after state, legislative proposals aimed at increasing the number of youth who are subjected to criminal prosecution keep being presented to legislatures and keep passing (Szymanski, 1991b). At times in the past 5 years, our legislative proposals have caused us to appear almost desperate in our pursuit of justice system solutions to the problem of juvenile violence and criminal law violations. In our desperation, we have even begun to pass laws that would make it a crime for parents to produce a delinquent child (Hurst, 1989).

Unless our families suddenly stabilize and our massive congregate school system is broken up into manageable pieces and our neighborhoods regain their sense of community within the near future (and none of these possibilities seems very probable), the juvenile justice system in the 21st century is likely to be characterized by an absence of jurisdiction over most youth age 14 and older charged with a felony crime. This change will not come about for any positive reason but rather because we have grown afraid of our own children and don't seem to know quite what else to do—other than lock them up as criminals.

We have lost much of our optimism about the capacity of youth to change—at a time when the collective need to hurt those who take unfair advantage of their fellow man is at its zenith. Curiously, our penchant for punishing young predators coincides with another social trend that is simultaneously peaking.

Protecting abused, neglected, and otherwise vulnerable children seems morally imperative at the moment. We are also beginning to recognize the insufficiency of adversarial win-lose proceedings as a decision-making medium in such cases. As a consequence, the juvenile court is lurching toward a more fiercely protective posture toward neglected children amid renewed interest in alternative decision-making models such as mediation and collaborative consensus. In many ways, today's juvenile court procedures in abuse and neglect cases are more reminiscent of the equity courts of old (which they replaced) than they are contemporary courts of law. More than a few scholars and accomplished jurists (Moore et al., 1990; Gladstone 1990; and Springer, 1991) are urging significant reforms of the juvenile court, and much of the professional juvenile justice community is sufficiently frustrated with the present system to support reasoned change. The voting public is more than ready for a new "quick fix." Everything seems to be in order for yet another social experiment along the lines of the one launched in Cook County, Illinois, in 1989.

REFERENCES

ADOPTION ASSISTANCE AND CHILD WELFARE ACT OF 1980
Public Law 96-272.

BREMNER, R.H. (ED.)
1974   *Children and youth in America: A documentary history.* (Volume III, 1933–1973. Parts 5–7). Cambridge, MA: Harvard University Press

CONFERENCE OF STATE COURT ADMINISTRATORS AND NATIONAL CENTER FOR STATE COURTS
1988   *State court organization, 1987.* Williamsburg, VA: National Center for State Courts.

Gault
1967   *In Re,* 387 U.S. 1, 87 S. Ct. 1428.

GLADSTONE, W.E.
1990   June 3. Juvenile justice—How to make it work. *Miami Herald,* Viewpoint.

GOVE, W.R. (ED.)
1975   *The labeling of deviance: Evaluating a Perspective.* New York: Holsted.

Heath A. Wilkins v. Missouri
1989   492 U.S. 361, 109 S. Ct. 2969.

HUIZINGA, D., ESBENSEN, F., & WEIHER, A.W.
1991   Are there multiple paths to delinquency? *Journal of Criminal Law and Criminology,* 82(1).

HURST, H.
1987   Sex and crime. *Juvenile and Family Court Newsletter,* 17(4).

HURST, H.
1988   More sex. *Juvenile and Family Court Newsletter,* 19(1).

HURST, H.
1989   Parent responsibility for the crimes of their children. *Juvenile and Family Court Newsletter,* 20(1).

HURST, H.
1990a   Winter. Juvenile probation in retrospect. *Perspectives*. American Probation and Parole.

HURST, H.
1990b   *Juvenile corrections at the close of the twentieth century.* Pittsburgh, PA: National Center for Juvenile Justice.

Juvenile Justice and Delinquency Prevention Act of 1974
        42 U.S.C. 5601.

Kent v. United States
1966   383 U.S. 541, 86 S. Ct. 1045 (1966).

LOEBER, R., STOUTHAMER-LOEBER, M., VAN KAMMEN, W., & FARRINGTON, D.P.
1991   Initiation, escalation and desistance in juvenile offending and their correlates. *Journal of Criminal Law and Criminology*, 82(1).

MALLORY, B.T.
1991   February. Remarks before the Advisory Committee for the Integration of Child and Family Legal Proceedings project, Institute for Court Management/National Center for State Courts, Denver, CO.

MOORE, M., FELD, B.C., GREENWOOD, P.W., & ZIMRING, F.
        The future of the juvenile court. Presentations at the 42nd Annual Meeting of the American Society of Criminology, Baltimore, MD.

MOORE, S.
1991   March 16–20. Unpublished remarks at 17th National Conference on Juvenile Justice, Albuquerque, New Mexico.

NATIONAL COUNCIL OF JUVENILE AND FAMILY COURT JUDGES.
1987   Juvenile & Family Court Journal 50th Anniversary Issue 38(2).

NATIONAL PROBATION AND PAROLE ASSOCIATION
1959   (now the National Council on Crime and Delinquency), National Council of Juvenile Court Judges, and U.S. Children's Bureau. *Standard Family Court Act.* New York: National Probation and Parole Association (now the National Council on Crime and Delinquency) 1959.

Progressively Increasing Consequences Act
        A.R.S. 8-230.01, July 1, 1984.

SNYDER, H.N., FINNEGAN, T.A., NIMICK, E.H., SICKMUND, M.H., SULLIVAN, D.P., & TIERNEY, N.J.
1987   *Juvenile court statistics 1984.* Washington, DC: U.S. Government Printing Office.

SNYDER, H.N., FINNEGAN, T.A., NIMICK, E.H., SICKMUND, M.H., SULLIVAN, D.P., & TIERNEY, N.J.
1990   *Juvenile court statistics 1988.* Pittsburgh, PA: National Center for Juvenile Justice.

SNYDER, H.N.
1990   Special Analysis of 1988 Data in the National Juvenile Court Data Archive. National Center for Juvenile Justice.

SNYDER, H.N.
1991   *Arrests of youth 1989.* Pittsburgh, PA: National Center for Juvenile Justice.

SPRINGER, C.E.
1991   Rehabilitating the juvenile court. *Notre Dame Journal of Law, Ethics and Public Policy*, 5(2).

SZYMANSKI, L.A.
1991a   *Juvenile code purpose clauses.* Pittsburgh, PA: National Center for Juvenile Justice.

SZYMANSKI, L.A.
1991b   *1990 update and statutes analysis of juvenile court jurisdiction over children's conduct.* Pittsburgh, PA: National Center for Juvenile Justice.

TAYLOR, L.S.
1985   The family as an adaptable and enduring social unit: a case for assessing delinquent behavior from a family systems perspective. *Today's Delinquent*, 4.

THE PRESIDENT'S COMMISSION ON LAW ENFORCEMENT AND ADMINISTRATION OF JUSTICE
1967   Task Force on Juvenile Delinquency. *Task force report: Juvenile delinquency and youth crime.* Washington, DC: U.S. Government Printing Office.

THORNBERRY, T.P., TOLNAY, S.E., FLANAGAN, T.J., & GLYNN, P.
1991a   *Children in custody 1987: A comparison of public and private juvenile custody facilities.* Washington, DC: Office of Juvenile Justice and Delinquency Prevention.

THORNBERRY, T.P., LIZOTTE, A.J., KROHN, M.D., FARNWORTH, M., & JANG, S.J.
1991b   Testing interactional theory: An examination of reciprocal causal relationships among family, school, and delinquency. *Journal of Criminal Law and Criminology*, 82(1).

TORBET, P.M.
1989   *Organization and administration of juvenile services: Probation, aftercare, and state delinquent institutions.* Pittsburgh, PA: National Center for Juvenile Justice.

TRACY, P.E., WOLFGANG, M.E., & FIGLIO, R.M.
1985   *Delinquency in two birth cohorts.* Washington, DC: Office of Juvenile Justice and Delinquency Prevention.

WOLFGANG, M.E., FIGLIO, F., SELLIN, T.
1972   *Delinquency in a birth cohort.* Chicago, IL: University of Chicago Press.

QUESTIONS FOR DISCUSSION

1. Given that the structure of the family has changed dramatically over the past 30 years, is the family court a realistic and practical way to approach juvenile justice?

2. According to the author, what persistent problems are associated with the administration of the juvenile court?

3. Discuss the tension that exists between punishing a child and acting in the best interest of the child.

APPLICATIONS

1. The author states that "unless our families suddenly stabilize and our massive congregate school system is broken up into manageable pieces and our neighborhoods regain their sense of community within the near future . . ., the juvenile justice system of the 21st century is likely to be characterized by an absence of jurisdiction over most youth age 14 and older charged with a felony crime." In essence we are making the age of adult criminal culpability lower and lower. In your opinion, is this a dangerous trend? Why?

2. Should we look to the family, schools, churches, and community to find solutions to juvenile delinquency? Why?

KEY TERMS

ambivalence a continual fluctuation or contradiction in attitudes or feelings.

dispatch to send off or away with promptness or speed.

interring the process of burying or depositing in a tomb.

modicum a small portion or a limited quantity.

panoply something forming a protective cover.

penchant a strong inclination or attraction to something.

pervasive that which moves or diffuses throughout something.

portend something that foreshadows a coming event.

shroud a covering for protection or a disguise to conceal.

undulating rising and falling or fluctuating.

29

A Policy Maker's Guide to Controlling Delinquency and Crime through Family Interventions

Karen E. Wright
Kevin N. Wright

For the past two decades, the trend in juvenile justice has been toward more punitive policies and laws. Implicit in these policies is a belief that children are cognizant of and wholly responsible for their behaviors, and therefore deserve the punitive responses they receive. The actions of people and institutions who surround children, however, play vital roles in their development. Therefore families appear to be a crucial, potentially productive point of intervention at which to reduce the likelihood of delinquency. This paper explores the relationship of family life to delinquency and derives five policy strategies to reduce delinquency: (1) prenatal and early childhood health care, (2) early intervention, (3) comprehensive family policy, (4) family treatment for troubled youths, and (5) parent training.

Most activities aimed at controlling crime and delinquency in the United States focus on offenders. Arrest, conviction, and punishment are sought to deter and incapacitate. At best these efforts have proved to be only marginally effective. Despite various attempts to improve the success of the criminal justice system in detecting, apprehending, and bringing to justice adult and juvenile offenders, crime rates remain high.

On the basis of examinations of the association between family life and delinquency, it appears that strengthening families may be an effective method of controlling crime. Research demonstrates clearly that families contribute to the development of delinquent and criminal patterns of life. Studies conducted during the last two decades have found, with considerable consistency, that what occurs in families is related to family members' subsequent delinquent and criminal behavior (for reviews of this literature, Henggeler 1989; Loeber and Dishion 1983; Loeber and Stouthamer-Loeber 1986; Snyder and Patterson 1987). Thus, strengthening families appears to be a viable option for improving crime control.

Barry Krisberg (1991:141), president of the National Council on Crime and Delinquency, suggests that policy leaders have not heeded recent advances in criminological research. Instead he notes that they have opted to continue allocating resources to deter and incapacitate offenders, although addressing the origins of delinquent behavior among children and within families might produce more fruitful results with substantially lower human costs.

Justice Quarterly, Vol. 11, No. 2, June 1994. Reprinted by Permission of the Academy of Criminal Justice Sciences.

Similarly, Sampson (1987b:378), a sociologist who has spent considerable time studying the relationship of family life to crime and delinquency, suggests that a "coherent family policy" would be more likely to reduce crime than present policies that lead to an ever-increasing prison population.

In this paper we outline policy responses to reduce delinquency through family intervention. These actions are grouped into five categories: (1) prenatal and early childhood health care, (2) early intervention, (3) comprehensive family policy, (4) family treatment for troubled youths, and (5) parent training.

A CAUTIONARY NOTE

We caution readers not to look to family interventions as a panacea. The causes of crime are complex; even the role of family life in the etiology of criminal behavior has been shown to be multifaceted. Although family variables consistently are found to be related to delinquency, they explain only modest amounts of the variation in delinquent outcomes.

Furthermore, programs aimed at intervening in children's lives with the expectation of reducing the risks of future delinquency and criminality have not always produced the hoped-for results. Zigler, Taussig, and Black (1992:997) observe, "Few programs directed at reducing delinquent behavior have shown lasting effects." Similarly, programs intended to prevent delinquency have generally produced few long-term successes (also see Gottfredson 1986).

Even more disturbing, at least one study (McCord 1978) discovered harmful effects of intervention in the lives of at-risk children. The Cambridge-Somerville Youth Project was initiated in 1939 to assist delinquency-prone boys and their families. Counselors worked with the boys and their families; many of the youths received academic tutoring; a significant proportion of the boys were provided with medical and psychiatric care; and some boys, who otherwise might not have participated, were brought into community programs. Involvement in the Project lasted five years on the aver-

age. A 30-year follow-up found that men who had been in the program were more likely than a control group to have sustained criminal careers, to have mental health and alcoholism problems, to have died, to have suffered stress-related diseases, to have lower-status occupations, and to be less satisfied with their jobs.

Why, asked McCord (1978:288–89), could this well-intended program have produced such subtle and unexpected effects? One explanation is that interactions with adults who possessed a different set of values from those of their families may have produced conflicting expectations in the boys. Involvement in the program may have fostered dependency on outside assistance that persisted throughout the participants' adult lives. Furthermore, the program may have raised expectations among the boys that subsequently could not be fulfilled. Finally, participation in the program may have become a self-fulfilling prophecy: receiving help led to a self-perception of needing help.

These findings led McCord to conclude, "Intervention program risk damaging the individuals they are designed to assist" (1978:289). Even so, she did not call for the cessation of programs for at-risk youths; instead she admonished practitioners and policy makers alike to proceed cautiously, to remain aware of potential harm of programs to children, and to evaluate outcomes.

We share McCord's concern about the risks of intervention, but, like her, we maintain a commitment to exploring new and we hope more successful practices. We are encouraged by recent advances in knowledge and findings about successful programs. In the following pages we outline several strategies for working with families that have the potential to reduce the incidence of delinquency and criminality. With one exception, the interventions do not deal directly with delinquents and their families; rather, they constitute early interventions in children's lives with the potential for lifelong educational, social, and behavioral effects.

These programs incorporate an ecological view of children and family life. Families are the first and among the most important institutions affecting children's development, but the interaction between parents and children takes place in a broader social and cultural environment. Schools, workplaces, community organizations, child care facilities, and health care systems play important roles in developmental processes. Zigler et al. (1992) state that "[b]y improving parents' interactions with these systems, and by helping them to support their child's physical, cognitive, and socioemotional development" (p. 997), programs can enhance the likelihood of competence in a variety of contexts during childhood and into later life.

PRENATAL AND EARLY CHILDHOOD HEALTH CARE

One way in which public policy can begin to support children's physical, cognitive, and emotional development is by ensuring that all families have access to maternal and child health care. Researchers have found considerable stability in aggressive and antisocial behavior, particularly when that behavior is extensive and begins at an early age (Huesmann et al. 1984; Loeber 1982; Olweus 1979). This evidence has led some researchers to postulate a pre-disposition toward impulsive, aggressive, and antisocial behavior which may be attributable to both genetic (Anderson, Lytton, and Romney 1986; Lytton 1990:693; Schulsinger 1980) and biological factors (Loeber 1991; Werner 1987). Many of the biological factors can be addressed directly through adequate health care.

Growing evidence suggests that low birth weight, poor nutrition, drug and alcohol abuse during pregnancy, exposure to toxins, and various other health-related factors have profound influences on children's development. They affect intelligence, impulsiveness, and aggression, all known to be related to delinquent and criminal behavior. The National Health/Education Consortium (1991) calls for a program to provide every mother and baby with early, comprehensive, preventive health care: "Unless the commitment exists to provide adequate access to comprehensive maternity and infant care, society will be forced to contend with the care and treatment of unhealthy children who,

through no fault of their own, grow up with long-term disabilities or have difficulty becoming self-supporting adults" (p. 7). Aggressive outreach programs for pregnant women at high risk of having children with developmental problems are needed to ensure adequate prenatal education and health care. Early identification of children with such problems has been shown to improve their chances for educational and social success. Waiting until they are in school may make intervention too late; early screening, diagnosis, and treatment are essential. Making sure that all children have the preventive and primary care necessary to ensure a good beginning in their developmental processes is the first step toward controlling future delinquency and criminality.

EARLY INTERVENTION

Research consistently has shown that age at onset is the single most accurate predictor of later and continued delinquency and criminality (Bell 1977; Loeber and Dishion 1983; Lytton 1990; Osborn and West 1978; Tolan 1987; Tolan and Lorion 1988; West and Farrington 1977; Wolfgang, Figlio, and Sellin 1972). Furthermore, early antisocial behavioral problems tend to be precursors to delinquency (Barnum 1987; Hanson et al. 1984; Loeber 1982; Loeber, Stouthamer-Loeber, and Green 1987).

According to the model developed at the Oregon Social Learning Center, the developmental process leading to delinquency begins in early childhood with maladaptive parent-child interactions. The components of the reciprocal relationship are complex: "The development of the child appears to be multiply determined by what the child brings to the situation, what s/he elicits from the situation, what the environment can offer and what it does offer" (Sameroff and Seifer 1983:12). Support for this model has been generated in recent years by numerous studies (Dishion 1990; Dishion et al. 1991; Larzelere and Patterson 1990; Loeber and Dishion 1983, 1984; Patterson 1980, 1986; Patterson and Dishion 1985; Patterson, Dishion, and Bank 1984; Patterson and Stouthamer-Loeber 1984; Snyder and Patterson 1987).

Parents with a difficult child may cease functioning as parents to gain superficial peace in the home. With a particularly unruly child, the parents not only may fail to supervise but actually may come to dislike the child, adding rejection to the already problematic relationship (Loeber and Stouthamer-Loeber 1986). Among the various aspects of family life, it appears that parental rejection is the most powerful predictor of juvenile delinquency (see Loeber and Stouthamer-Loeber 1986). Children raised in supportive, affectionate, accepting environments tend to become self-aware adults who can formulate their own long-term goals and can pursue socially and economically fulfilling lives (Borduin, Pruitt, and Henggeler 1986; Campbell 1987; Cernkovich and Giordano 1987; Fox et al. 1983; Henggeler et al. 1985; Johnson 1987; McCord 1979; Rodick, Henggeler, and Hanson 1986; Smith and Walters 1978; Tolan 1987, 1988; Tolan and Lorion 1988). In contrast, children of harsh, unloving, overcritical, and authoritarian parents often become self-absorbed as adults. Their impulsiveness can lead to violence and substance abuse (Bandura and Walters 1959; Chollar 1987; Glueck and Glueck 1950; Gray-Ray and Ray 1990; Kroupa 1988; Loeber and Dishion 1984; McCord 1983; Nye 1958; Pfouts, Scholper, and Henley 1981; Simons, Robertson and Downs 1989; Stouthamer-Loeber and Loeber 1986).

As a child grows older and spends more time outside the home, negative behaviors learned at home are likely to appear in other settings. In school, the child's antisocial disposition may interfere with learning and often will cause the child to be disliked by peers. The failing, disliked, and antisocial child will gravitate toward peers and social settings that reinforce his or her behavior, which in turn may further encourage the child's antisocial actions (Patterson 1982). As the child or adolescent participates or engages in more frequent antisocial behavior while associating increasingly with antisocial peers, his or her bond to conventional society will grow weaker (Hanson et al.

1984; LaGrange and White 1985; Matsueda 1982; Matsueda and Heimer 1987; Paternoster 1988; Smith and Paternoster 1987; Steinberg and Silverberg 1986). The weakening of this bond may be an initial cause of delinquency; continued and/or increased delinquent acts may become their own indirect cause as they further weaken the youth's bonds to family, school, and conventional beliefs (Thornberry 1987:876).

Longitudinal research is beginning to show that early identification of at-risk children and intervention in this process in their lives may hold great promise in preventing future delinquent behavior and criminality (Tremblay et al. 1991; Zigler et al. 1992). Staff members at the Oregon Social Learning Center have developed a procedure called "Multiple gating" to identify potentially troublesome children. The procedure uses teachers' and parents' reports to identify children likely to have later adjustment and conduct problems. This system has identified 56 percent of later delinquents (Loeber, Dishion, and Patterson 1984).

Once at-risk children have been identified, interventions in the maladaptive parent-child interactions are needed. This step may involve parents in effective child management practices; in some cases, respite may be needed for parents of particularly unruly children. Preservation of effective parental supervision, the development of social skills, and maintenance of bonds with conventional society become the goals of intervention as the children begin school.

Zigler et al. (1992) have identified four exemplary early intervention programs: the Perry Preschool Project, the Syracuse University Family Development Research Program, the Yale Child Welfare Research Program, and the Houston Parent-Child Development Center. Each of these produced long-term reductions in antisocial and aggressive behavior and delinquency. None of these four programs was started with the stated purpose of reducing delinquency; rather, the goal was to reduce the likelihood of school failure and to improve social competence. Although the programs differed, they all offered multifaceted interventions including educational assistance, health care, parent training and support, and other specific social services. Through early intervention they alleviated some of the risks in young children's lives, which thereby decreased the likelihood of future delinquency and criminality. According to Zigler and his colleagues, "the effects of successful experiences early in childhood snowballed to generate further success in school and other social contexts; the programs enhanced physical health and aspects of personality such as motivation and sociability, helping the child to adapt better to later social expectations; and family support, education and involvement in intervention improved parents' childrearing skills and thus altered the environment where children were raised" (1992:1002).

COMPREHENSIVE FAMILY POLICY

Research consistently has found that inadequate supervision is a key variable in predicting delinquency (Cernkovich and Giordano 1987; Fischer 1984; Laub and Sampson 1988; Loeber and Stouthamer-Loeber 1986; Loeber, Weiher, and Smith 1991; McCord 1979; Snyder and Patterson 1987; Van Voorhis et al. 1988; Wilson 1987). The elements necessary for effective parental supervision include the following actions: notice what the child is doing, monitor the activities over long periods, model social skills, state house rules clearly, consistently provide punishment for transgressions, provide reinforcement for conformity, and negotiate disagreement so that conflicts and crises do not escalate (Patterson 1980:81). Monitoring children involves awareness of their companions, whereabouts, and free-time activities. It also includes appropriate communication, the child's accountability to the parents, and the amount of time spent with parents (Larzelere and Patterson 1990). Monitoring becomes increasingly important as the child progresses into adolescence, when adequate supervision allows parents to influence the child's selection of friends and activities, to express disapproval, and to sanction antisocial and delinquent behavior (Snyder and Patterson 1987:227).

Some analysts advocate enhancing social services through a coherent family policy. The basis for this suggestion is that inadequate housing, a lack of income, and an inability to obtain adequate day care create stress and make it difficult to function effectively as parents and supervise children adequately.

Single-parent families have been identified as particularly in need of a comprehensive family policy. Because most of these families, and particularly those at highest risk of producing delinquents, are headed by women, the needs of mother-only families are of special interest.

A review of 50 studies on family structure and delinquency revealed that delinquency was 10 to 15 percent more prevalent in single-parent than in two-parent families (Wells and Rankin 1991:87). Experts generally agree that nothing is inherently pathological about single parenthood, but that the situation predisposes a set of conditions that may contribute to delinquency, such as greater autonomy for the adolescent (Dornbusch et al. 1985; Steinberg and Silverberg 1986), less parental control (Matsueda 1982; Steinberg 1986; Van Voorhis et al. 1988), increased susceptibility to peer pressure (Henggeler 1989:48), and poorer economic conditions (Morash and Rucker 1989:83). Furthermore, because their economic status is often poor, mother-only families may live in higher-crime neighborhoods; these may contribute to higher rates of delinquency because of increased exposure to criminal influences (Felson 1986; Felson and Cohen 1980; Sampson 1986a, 1986b, 1987a).

The Education and Human Service Consortium, composed of representatives from organizations such as the Center for Law and Social Policy, the Children's Defense Fund, the National Alliance of Business, the National Alliance of Secondary School Principals, and the U.S. Conference of Mayors, believes that the current system of social services fails children for five reasons: (1) services are crisis oriented; (2) the system separates the problems of children and of families into categories that do not take into account the interrelated causes and solutions; (3) communication among service agencies is lacking; (4) specialized agencies cannot easily produce comprehensive solutions to complex problems; and (5) existing services are not funded adequately. The Consortium calls for comprehensive delivery of a wide variety of preventive, treatment, and support services, including techniques to ensure that children and families actually receive the services they need. The focus must be on empowering the entire family (Melaville and Blank 1991).

Research has verified the beneficial effect of increased services. The provision of a coordinated set of medical and social services, including day care, had a significant impact on women and their children 10 years later. In comparison with a control group, the mothers receiving coordinated assistance were more likely to be self-supporting, had attained more education, and had smaller families. Their children performed better academically (Seitz, Rosenbaum, and Apfel 1985). The evaluators did not compare the delinquency rates of children from supported and from unsupported families; the variables they measured, however, have been linked to delinquency prevention.

In today's economically and socially stressful world, it has become increasingly difficult for all parents, not only those who are single or poor, to supervise their children adequately, to remain active participants in their children's lives, and to be nurturing and supportive caregivers. The availability of high-quality child care—day care for preschool children and after-school care for school-age youths—is essential to assist parents in supervising their children.

FAMILY TREATMENT FOR TROUBLED YOUTHS

We have shown that when parents are harsh, unloving, overcritical, and authoritarian, healthy development is impeded, and children's risks of delinquency increase. Furthermore, inadequate supervision increases the chances of delinquent behavior.

Growing up in homes with considerable conflict, marital discord, and violence also seems to increase the risks of eventual delinquent and/or criminal behavior. Witnessing violence in the home yields a consistent but modest association with delinquency (Widom 1989:22; also see Bach-y-Rita and Veno 1974; Borduin et al. 1986; Gove and Crutchfield 1982; Hanson et al. 1984; Hartstone and Hansen 1984; Hetherington, Stouwie, and Ridberg 1971; Koski 1988; Lewis et al. 1979; Mann et al. 1990; McCord 1979, 1988b, 1990; Richards, Berk, and Forster 1979; Roff and Wirt 1985; Sendi and Blomgren 1975; Simcha-Fagan et al. 1975; Sorrells 1977; Straus, Gelles, and Steinmetz 1981; Tolan 1987; Tolan and Lorion 1988; West and Farrington 1973). Moreover, being abused as a child increases the risk of becoming an abusive parent, a delinquent, or a violent adult criminal. Not only do abused children manifest more aggressive and more problematic behavior at early ages; research also shows that these children are not likely to outgrow the aggressive patterns as they mature (Widom 1989; also see Howing et al. 1990; Koski 1988; Lane and Davis 1987).

Dysfunctional families—those experiencing high levels of disorganization, conflict, dominance, hostility, lack of warmth, and authoritarian disciplinary style—do not allow children to gain insight and understanding into how their misbehavior might hurt others. In such negative family conditions, children cannot develop conventional moral reasoning with roots in acceptance of mutual expectations, positive social intentions, belief in and maintenance of the social system, and acceptance of motives that include duties and respect. Delinquency can be anticipated when children or adolescents cannot see other people's perspective and lack empathy for other people's circumstances (Arbuthnot, Gordon, and Jurkovic 1987).

Fortunately, research has identified elements of family life which may shield children from otherwise harmful circumstances. Competent mothers—those who are self-confident, consistently nonpunitive, and affectionate, and who have leadership skills—tend to protect children from criminogenic influences (Lytton 1990; McCord 1986, 1991). Similarly, the presence of one caring parent buffers children against the effect of rejection by the other parent (Minty 1988). In homes with high marital discord, the presence of one parent who maintains a warm, positive relationship with the children buffers them from conduct disorders (Rutter 1978). Although the children of alcoholic fathers are more likely than others to become alcoholics, the chances of becoming alcoholic are diminished if their mothers did not demonstrate approval or respect for the fathers (McCord 1988a). Furthermore, having a close sibling or being involved in teen sports provides social support that buffers abused children from becoming delinquent (Kruttschmitt, Ward, and Sheble 1987).

These findings suggest that even in the face of adverse family conditions, resistance to delinquency is possible. Henggeler et al. (1986) report a successful treatment experiment that used the family-ecological approach for inner-city juvenile offenders and their families. This method addressed the multidimensional nature of behavioral problems, exploring individual deficits such as poor social and problem-solving skills, inappropriate child and family interactions, and problematic transactions with extrafamilial systems such as the peer group and the school. Therapy was individualized, and focused on the most important determinants of each child's problem behavior. Observation revealed that parent-child interactions became warmer and more affectionate with treatment. In turn, parents reported a decline in their children's conduct problems, immature behavior, and association with delinquents.

Potentially the most effective response to delinquent behavior is not to treat the individual delinquent as personally responsible for his or her action, as is currently the predominant response in juvenile justice. Rather, it may lie in a more holistic strategy aimed at both the child and the family. A wide array of treatment programs has been designed to reduce family and child disorders (Hawkins et al. 1988). Teaching parents how to manage older delinquent children is one of the most promising approaches (Bank et al. 1991; Greenwood and Zimring 1985).

TRAINING IN PARENTING

Children learn to be parents from their parents. When children grow up in families where positive parental practices are modeled, they learn how to care properly for their own children. When children are raised by harsh, rejecting, and violent parents, however, inadequate and ineffective parenting may be transmitted from one generation to the next. Even individuals who were raised in caring and supportive family situations, when confronted with an impulsive or overactive child, may find it difficult to maintain effective parenting practices, particularly when they have only limited coping resources because of their familial or economic situation and when they live in relative social isolation. For people who lack parenting skills, training is a promising method for preventing delinquency. There are two possible points of intervention: in one, parents are taught how to manage difficult children; the other consists of training young people in how to be effective parents.

Programs designed for parents try to improve family management skills by teaching parents to monitor their children's behaviors, to use moderate and consistent discipline of inappropriate behavior, and to reward desired behaviors. Most of the systematic research involves programs for parents of young children with conduct problems. Four experimental tests of such programs (Karoly and Rosenthal 1977; Martin 1977; Patterson, Chamberlain, and Reid 1982; Walters and Gilmore 1973) substantiated significant reductions in problem behaviors among preadolescent children. An experimental study of a parent training program for families of serious delinquents found that the treatment group committed fewer serious crimes than the experimental group during the treatment year and spent less time in institutions. The benefits of the program, however, reportedly were achieved at substantial emotional cost to the staff (Bank et al. 1991).

Another group that might benefit from training in parental skills consists of adolescents who may lack effective role models, such as children in institutional and foster care, youths whose families are under the supervision of a family court, pregnant teenagers who choose to keep their babies, and delinquents. Some experts advocate parent training for all high school students (Farrington and West 1981).

CONCLUSIONS

Delinquent youths do not experience a set of common events that lead to delinquency; rather, multiple pathways steer some youths to inappropriate behavior. Some adolescents run away because of a bad situation in the home; some parents push their children out; some teenagers leave for the thrill; still others escape from overprotective parents (Huizinga, Esbensen, and Weiher 1991:84–85). The same apparently is true for delinquents: no certain or direct pathway emerges for all children growing up at risk (Huizinga et al. 1991).

In the lives of the children most at risk of becoming delinquent, however, some or all of the following circumstances may be operating: (l) they receive little love, affection, or warmth, and are physically or emotionally rejected and/or abandoned by their parents; (2) they are inadequately supervised by parents who fail to teach them right and wrong, who do not monitor their whereabouts, friends, or activities, and who discipline them erratically and harshly; and (3) they grow up in homes with considerable conflict, marital discord, and perhaps even violence (Farrington 1990:94; Leitenberg 1987). Families at greatest risk of delinquency are those suffering from limited coping resources, social isolation, and (among parents) poor child-rearing skills (Loeber and Southamer-Loeber 1986:97). The presence of any one of these family circumstances increases the chances of raising a delinquent child. The presence of more than one factor increases the odds further (Farrington 1990; Farrington et al. 1988; Kruttschmitt et al. 1987; Loeber and Stouthamer-Loeber 1986; Lytton 1990; McCord 1990; Minty 1988).

In this paper we have advocated five strategies for strengthening families to reduce the factors in children's lives that place them at higher risk of delinquency and criminality: (1) prenatal and early childhood health care, (2) early intervention, (3) comprehensive family policy, (4) family treatment for troubled youths, and (5) parent training. Traditional approaches to juvenile delinquency attempt to control behavior after it has become entrenched. The five strategies offered here differ in that they attempt to prevent delinquent behavior before it begins by altering the family circumstances that lead to it. The goal of this approach is not delinquency prevention as such but the development of socially competent adults. Delinquency prevention simply becomes a by-product of that process.

We have presented these five strategies separately, but attention to all five is needed. A healthy start in life is essential for educational and social success. Parent-child relations in early childhood begin the process by which children develop healthy selfconcepts, confidence, motivation, and sociability. Children who are prepared socially and academically when they begin school will be more successful and will interact more positively with teachers and peers; this point, too, has implications for continued successful development into adolescence and adulthood. Parents who have adequate social and economic support clearly would be more able to function effectively as parents than individuals who are stressed and alienated by their social and economical disadvantages and isolation. Furthermore, child-rearing skills are not a given. Some parents had successful role models, but those raised by harsh, unloving, overcritical, and authoritarian parents never had the opportunity to acquire the skills they need for effective child rearing.

To meet these requirements demands a comprehensive rather than a narrow approach. The current fragmentation in social services impedes the provision of integrated preventive approaches. Furthermore, because child development is an ongoing process, intervention also must be ongoing. It would be naive to expect a program that briefly influences children's development to alter the course of their lives. If families in fact play significant roles in the developmental processes that lead to delinquency, isn't it time to intervene systematically and comprehensively in those processes which serve as the root causes of delinquency?

REFERENCES

ANDERSON, K.E., H. LYTTON, AND D.M. ROMNEY (1986) "MOTHERS' INTERACTIONS WITH NORMAL AND CONDUCT-DISORDERED BOYS: WHO AFFECTS WHOM?" *Developmental Psychology* 22(5):604–609.

ARBUTHNOT, J., D.A. GORDON, AND G.J. JURKOVIC (1987) "Personality." In H.C. Quay (ed.), *Handbook of Juvenile Delinquency*, pp. 139–83. New York: Wiley.

BACH-Y-RITA, G. AND A. VENO (1974) "Habitual Violence: A Profile of 62 Men." *American Journal of Psychiatry* 131:1015–17.

BANDURA, A. AND R.H. WALTERS (1959) *Adolescent Aggression.* New York: Ronald Press.

BANK, L., J.H. MARLOWE, J.B. REID, G.R. PATTERSON, AND M.R. WEINROTT (1991) "A Comparative Evaluation of Parent-Training Interventions for Families of Chronic Delinquents." *Journal of Abnormal Child Psychology* 19:15–33.

BARNUM, B. (1987) "Biomedical Problems in Juvenile Delinquency: Issues in Diagnosis and Treatment." In J.Q. Wilson and G.C. Loury (eds.), *From Children to Citizens. Vol. 3: Families, Schools and Delinquency Prevention*, pp. 51–84. New York: Springer-Verlag.

BELL, R.Q. (1977) "Socialization Findings Re-Examined." In R.Q. Bell and R.V. Harper (eds.), *Child Effects on Adults*, pp. 53–84. Hillsdale, NJ: Erlbaum.

BORDUIN, C.M., J.A. PRUITT, AND S.W. HENGGELER (1986) "Family Interactions in Black, Lower-Class Families with Delinquent and Nondelinquent Adolescent Boys." *Journal of Genetic Psychology.* 147(3):333–42.

CAMPBELL, A. (1987) "Self-Reported Delinquency and Home Life: Evidence from a Sample of British Girls." *Journal of Youth and Adolescence* 16(2):167–77.

CERNKOVICH, S.A. AND P.C. GIORDANO (1987) "Family Relationships and Delinquency." *Criminology* 25(2):295–321.

CHOLLAR, S. (1987) "We Reap What We Sow." *Psychology Today* 21:12.

DISHION, T.J. (1990) "The Family Ecology of Boys' Peer Relations in Middle Childhood." *Child Development* 61:874–92.

DISHION, T.J., G.R. PATTERSON, M. STOOLMILLER, AND M.L. SKINNER (1991) "Family, School, and Behavioral Antecedents to Early Adolescent Involvement with Antisocial Peers." *Developmental Psychology* 27(1):172–80.

DORNBUSCH, S.M., J.M. CARLSMITH, S.J. BUSHWALL, P.L. RITTER, H. LEIDERMAN, A.H. HASTORF, AND R.T. GROSS (1985) "Single Parents, Extended Households, and the Control of Adolescents." *Child Development* 56:326–41.

FARRINGTON, D.P. (1990) "Implications of Criminal Career Research for the Prevention of Offending." *Journal of Adolescence* 13;93–113.

FARRINGTON, D.P., L. MORLEY, R.J. ST. LEDGER, AND D.J. WEST (1988) "Are There Any Successful Men from Criminogenic Backgrounds?" *Psychiatry* 51 (May):116–30.

FARRINGTON, D.P. AND D.J. WEST (1981) "The Cambridge Study in Delinquent Development." In S.A. Mednick and A.E. Baert (eds.), *Prospective Longitudinal Research: An Empirical basis for Primary Prevention*, Oxford: Oxford University Press.

FELSON, M. (1986) "Linking Criminal Choices, Routine Activities, Informal Control, and Criminal Outcomes." In D.B. Cornish and R.V. Clarke (eds.), *The Reasoning Criminal: Rational Choice Perspectives on Offending*, pp. 119–28. New York: Springer-Verlag.

FELSON, M. AND L.E. COHEN (1980) "Human Ecology and Crime: A Routine Activity Approach." *Human Ecology* 8(4):389–406.

FISCHER, D.B. (1984) "Family Size and Delinquency." *Perceptual and Motor Skills* 58:527–34.

FOX, R., A. F. TOATORI, F. MACKLIN, H. GREEN, AND T. FOX (1983) "Socially Maladjusted Adolescents' Perceptions of Their Families." *Psychology Reports* 52:831–34.

GLUECK, S. AND E. GLUECK (1950) *Unraveling Juvenile Delinquency.* Cambridge, MA: Harvard University Press.

GOTTFREDSON, D.C. (1986) "An Empirical Test of School-Based Environmental and Individual Interventions to Reduce the Risk of Delinquent Behavior." *Criminology* 24:705–31.

GOVE, W.R. AND R.D. CRUTCHFIELD (1982) "The Family and Juvenile Delinquency." *Sociological Quarterly* 23 (Summer):301–19.

GRAY-RAY, P. AND M.C. RAY (1990) "Juvenile Delinquency in the Black Community." *Youth and Society* 22(1):67–84.

GREENWOOD, P.W. AND F.E. ZIMRING (1985) *One More Chance: The Pursuit of Promising Intervention Strategies for Chronic Juvenile Offenders.* Santa Monica: RAND.

HANSON, C.L., S.W. HENGGELER, W.F. HAEFELE, AND J.D. RODICK (1984) "Demographic, Individual, and Family Relationship Correlates of Serious and Repeated Crime among Adolescents and Their Siblings." *Journal of Consulting and Clinical Psychology* 52(4):528–38.

HARTSTONE, E. AND K.V. HANSEN (1984) "The Violent Juvenile Offender: An Empirical Portrait." In R. A. Mathias (ed.), *Violent Juvenile Offenders: An Anthology*, pp. 83–112. San Francisco: National Council on Crime and Delinquency.

HAWKINS, J.D., J.M. JENSON, R.F. CATALANO, AND D.M. LISHNER (1988) "Delinquency and Drug Abuse: Implications for Social Services." *Social Service Review* (June): 258–84.

HETHERINGTON, E.M., R. STOUWIE, AND E.H. RIDBERG (1971) "Patterns of Family Interaction and Child Rearing

Related to Three Dimensions of Juvenile Delinquency." *Journal of Abnormal Psychology* 77:160–76.

HENGGELER, S. W. (1989) *Delinquency in Adolescence.* Newbury Park, CA: Sage.

HENGGELER, S.W., C.L. HANSON, C. BORDUIN, S.M. WATSON, AND M.A. BRUNK (1985) "Mother-Son Relationships of Juvenile Felons." *Journal of Consulting and Clinical Psychology* 53(6):942–43.

HENGGELER, S.W., J.D. RODICK, C.M. BORDUIN, C.L. HANSON, S.M. WATSON, AND J.R, UREY (1986) "Multisystemic Treatment of Juvenile Offenders: Effects on Adolescent Behavior and Family Interaction." *Developmental Psychology* 22(1):132–41.

HOWING, P.T., J.S. WODARSKI, P.D. KURTZ, J.M. GAUDIN JR., AND E.N. HERBST (1990) "Child Abuse and Delinquency: The Empirical and Theoretical Links. " *Social Work* (May):244–49.

HUESMANN, L.R., M.M. LEFKOWITZ, L.D. ERON, AND L.O. WALDER (1984) "Stability of Aggression over Time and Generations." *Developmental Psychology* 20(6):1120–34.

HUIZINGA, D., F.A. ESBENSEN, AND A.W. WEIHER (1991) "Are There Multiple Paths to Delinquency?" *Journal of Criminal Law and Criminology* 82(1):83–118.

JOHNSON, R.E. (1987) "Mother's versus Father's Role in Causing Delinquency." *Adolescence* 22(86) (Summer):305–15.

KAROLY, P. AND M. ROSENTHAL (1977) "Training Parents in Behavior Modification: Effects on Perceptions of Family Interaction and Deviant Child Behavior." *Behavior Therapy* 8:406–10.

KOSKI, P.R. (1988) "Family Violence and Nonfamily Deviance: Taking Stock of the Literature." *Marriage and Family Review* 12(1–2):23–46.

KRISBERG, B. (1991) "Are You Now or Have You Ever Been a Sociologist?" *Journal of Criminal Law and Criminology* 82(1):141–55.

KROUPA, S.E. (1988) "Perceived Parental Acceptance and Female Juvenile Delinquency." *Adolescence* 23(89) (Spring):171–85.

KRUTTSCHMITT, C., D. WARD, AND M.A. SHEBLE (1987) "Abuse-Resistant Youth: Some Factors That May Inhibit Violent Criminal Behavior." *Social Forces* 66(2):501–19.

LAGRANGE, R.L. AND H.R. WHITE (1985) "Age Differences in Delinquency: A Test of Theory." *Criminology* 23(1):19–45.

LANE, T.W. AND G.E. DAVIS (1987) "Child Maltreatment and Juvenile Delinquency: Does a Relationship Exist?" In J.D. Burchard and S.N. Burchard (eds.) *Prevention of Delinquent Behavior,* pp. 122–38. Newbury Park, CA. Sage.

LARZELERE, R.E. AND G.R. PATTERSON (1990) "Parental Management: Mediator of the Effect of Socioeconomic Status on Early Delinquency." *Criminology* 28(2):301–23.

LAUB, J.H. AND R.J. SAMPSON (1988) "Unraveling Families and Delinquency: A Reanalysis of the Gluecks' Data." *Criminology* 26(3):365–79.

LEITENBERG, H. (1987) "Prevention of Delinquency." In J.D. Burchard and S.N. Burchard (eds.), *Prevention of Delinquent Behavior,* pp. 312–31. Newbury Park, CA.: Sage.

LEWIS, D.O., S.S. SHANOK, J.H. PINCUS. AND G.H. (1979) "Violent Juvenile Delinquents: Psychiatric, Neurological, Psychological and Abuse Factors." *Journal of the American Academy of Child Psychiatry* 18:307–19.

LOEBER, R. (1982) "The Stability of Antisocial and Delinquent Child Behavior: A Review." *Child Development* 53:1431–46.

———(1991) "Antisocial Behavior: More Enduring Than Changeable?" *Journal of the American Academy of Child and Adolescent Psychiatry* 30:393–97.

LOEBER, R. AND T.J. DISHION (1983) "Early Predictors of Male Delinquency: A Review."'*Psychological Bulletin* 94(1):68–99.

———(1984) "Boys Who Fight at Home and School: Conditions Influencing Cross-Setting Consistency."'*Journal of Consulting and Clinical Psychology* 52(5):759–68.

LOEBER, R., T.J. DISHION, AND G.R. PATTERSON (1984) "Multiple Gating: A Multistage Assessment Procedure for Identifying Youth at Risk for Delinquency." *Journal of Research in Crime and Delinquency* 21:7–32.

LOEBER, R. AND M. STOUTHAMER-LOEBER (1986) "Family Factors as Correlates and Predictors of Juvenile Conduct Problems and Delinquency." In M. Tonry and N. Morris (eds.), *Crime and Justice: An Annual Review of Research,* Vol. 7, pp. 29–149. Chicago: University of Chicago Press.

LOEBER, R., M. STOUTHAMER-LOEBER, AND S.M. GREEN (1987) "Age of Onset of Conduct Problems, Different Developmental Trajectories, and Unique Contributing Factors." Paper presented at the annual meeting of the Society for Research in Child Development, Baltimore.

LOEBER, R., A.W. WEIHER, AND C. SMITH (1991) "The Relationship Between Family Interaction and Delinquency and Substance Use." In D. Huizinga, R. Loeber, and T.P. Thornberry (eds.), *Urban Delinquency and Substance Abuse: Technical Report,* Vol. 1, Washington, DC: Office of Juvenile Justice and Delinquency Prevention.

LYTTON, H. (1990) "Child and Parent Effects in Boys' Conduct Disorder. A Reinterpretation." *Developmental Psychology* 26(5):683–97.

MANN, B.J., C.M. BORDUIN, S.W. HENGGELER, AND D.M. BLASKE (1990) "An Investigation of Systemic Conceptualizations of Parent-Child Coalitions and Symptom Change." *Journal of Consulting and Clinical Psychology* 58(3):336–44.

MARTIN, B. (1977) "Brief Family Therapy Intervention: Effectiveness and the Importance of Including the Father." *Journal of Consulting and Clinical Psychology* 45:1001–10.

MATSUEDA, R.L. (1982) "Testing Control Theory and Differential Association: A Causal Modeling Approach." *American Sociological Review* 47 (August):489–504.

MATSUEDA, R.L. AND K HEIMER (1987) "Race, Family Structure, and Delinquency: A Test of Differential Association and Social Control Theories." *American Sociological Review* 52 (December):826–40.

MCCORD, J. (1978) "A Thirty-Year Follow-Up of Treatment Effects." *American Psychologist* 33:284–89.

———(1979) "Some Child-Rearing Antecedents of Criminal Behavior in Adult Men." *Journal of Personality and Social Psychology* 37:1477–86.

———(1983) "A Forty Year Perspective on Effects of Child Abuse and Neglect." *Child Abuse and Neglect* 7:265–70.

———(1986) "Instigation and Insulation: How Families Affect Antisocial Aggression." In D. Olweus, J. Block, and M. R. Yarrow (eds.), *Development of Antisocial and Prosocial Behavior*, New York: Academic Press.

———(1988a) "Alcoholism: Toward Understanding Genetic and Social Factors." *Psychiatry* 51 (May).131–41.

———(1988b) "Parental Behavior in the Cycle of Aggression." *Psychiatry* 51 (February):14–23.

———(1990) "Crime in Moral and Social Contexts—The American Society of Criminology, 1989 Presidential Address." *Criminology* 28(1):1–26.

———(1991) "Family Relationships, Juvenile Delinquency, and Adult Criminality." *Criminology* 29(3):397–418.

MELAVILLE, A.I. AND M.J. BLANK (1991) "What It Takes: Structuring Interagency Partnerships to Connect Children and Families with Comprehensive Services." Washington, DC: Education and Human Services Consortium.

MINTY, B. (1988) "Public Care or Distorted Family Relationships: The Antecedents of Violent Crime." *Howard Journal* 27(3):172–87.

MORASH, M. AND L. RUCKER (1989) "An Exploratory Study of the Connection of Mother's Age at Childbearing to Her Children's Delinquency in Four Data Sets." *Crime and Delinquency* 35(1):45–93.

NATIONAL HEALTH/EDUCATION CONSORTIUM (1991) "Healthy Brain Development: Precursor to Learning." Washington, DC: National Commission to Prevent Infant Mortality.

NYE, F.I. (1958) *Family Relationships and Delinquent Behavior.* New York: Wiley.

OLWEUS, D. (1979) "Stability of Aggressive Reaction Patterns in Males: A Review." *Psychology Bulletin* 86(4):852–75.

OSBORN, S.G. AND D.J. WEST (1978) "The Effectiveness of Various Predictors of Criminal Careers." *Journal of Adolescence* 1:101–17.

PATERNOSTER, R. (1988) "Examining Three-Wave Deterrence Models: A Question of Temporal Order and Specification." *Journal of Criminal Law and Criminology* 79(1):135–79.

PATTERSON, G.R. (1980) "Children Who Steal." In T. Hirschi and M. Gottfredson (eds.), *Understanding Crime: Current Theory and Research*, pp. 73–90. Beverly Hills: Sage.

———(1982) *Coercive Family Process*. Eugene, OR: Castalia.

———(1986) "Performance Models for Antisocial Boys." *American Psychologist* 41(4):432–44.

PATTERSON, G.R., P. CHAMBERLAIN, AND J.B. REID (1982) "A Comparative Evaluation of a Parent Training Program." *Behavior Therapy* 13:638–50.

PATTERSON, G.R. AND T.J. DISHION (1985) "Contributions of Families and Peers to Delinquency." *Criminology* 23(1):63–79.

PATTERSON, G.R., T.J. DISHION, AND L. BANK (1984) "Family Interaction: A Process Model of Deviancy Training." *Aggressive Behavior* 10;253–67.

PATTERSON, G.R. AND M. STOUTHAMER-LOEBER (1984) "The Correlation of Family Management Practices and Delinquency." *Child Development* 55:1299–1307.

PFOUTS, J.H., J.H. SCHOLPER, AND H.C. HENLEY JR. (1981) "Deviant Behaviors of Child Victims and Bystanders in Violent Families." In R.J. Hunter and Y.E. Walker (eds.), *Exploring the Relationship between Child Abuse and Delinquency*, pp. 79–99. Montclair, NJ: Allanheld.

RICHARDS, P., R.A. BERK, AND B. FORSTER (1979) *Crime As Play: Delinquency in a Middle Class Suburb*. Cambridge, MA: Ballinger.

RODICK, J.D., S.W. HENGGELER, AND C.L. HANSON (1986) "An Evaluation of the Family Adaptability and Cohesion Evaluation Scales and the Circumplex Model." *Journal of Abnormal Child Psychology* 14(1):77–87.

ROFF, J.D. AND R.D. WIRT (1985) "The Specificity of Childhood Problem Behavior for Adolescent and Young Adult Maladjustment." *Journal of Clinical Psychology* 41(4):564–71.

———(1978) "Family, Area and School Influences in the Genesis of Conduct Disorders." In L.A. Hersov, M. Berger, and D. Shaffer (eds.), *Aggression and Antisocial Behavior in Childhood and Adolescence*, Oxford: Pergamon.

SAMEROFF, A. AND R. SEIFER (1983) "Sources of Community in Parent-Child Relations." Paper presented at the meetings of the Society for Research in Child Development, Detroit.

SAMPSON, R.J. (1986a) "Crime in Cities: The Effects of Formal and Informal Social Control." In A.J. Reiss Jr. and M. Tonry (eds.), *Crime and Justice Series, Communities and Crime*, Vol. 8, pp. 271–311. Chicago: University of Chicago Press.

———(1986b) "Neighborhood Family Structure and the Risk of Personal Victimization." In J.M. Sampson and R.J. Byrne (eds.), *The Social Ecology of Crime*, pp. 25–46. New York: Springer.

———(1987a) "Doe an Intact Family Reduce Burglary Risk for Its Neighbors?" *Social Science Review* 71(3):204–207.

———(1987b) "Urban Black Violence: The Effect of Male Joblessness and Family Disruption." *American Journal of Sociology* 93(2):348–82.

SCHULSINGER, F. (1980) "Biological Psychopathology." *Annual Review of Psychology* 31:583–606.

SEITZ, V., L.K. ROSENBAUM, AND N.H. APFEL (1985) "Effects of Family Support Intervention: A Ten-Year Follow-Up." *Child Development* 56:376–91.

SENDI, I.B. AND P.G. BLOMGREN (1975) "A Comparative Study of Predictive Criteria in the Predisposition of Homicidal Adolescents." *American Journal of Psychiatry* 132:423–27.

SIMCHA-FAGAN, O., T.S. LANGER, J.C. GERSTEN, AND J.G. EISENBERG (1975) "Violent and Antisocial Behavior: A Longitudinal Study of Urban Youth." Unpublished report, Office of Child Development, Washington, DC.

SIMONS, R.L., J.F. ROBERTSON, AND W.R. DOWNS (1989) "The Nature of the Association between Parental Rejection and Delinquent Behavior." *Journal of Youth and Adolescence* 18(3):297–310.

SMITH, D.A. AND R. PATERNOSTER (1987) *The Gender Gap in Theories of Deviance: Issues and Evidence."* Journal of Research in Crime and Delinquency 24(2):140–72.

SMITH, R.M. AND J. WALTERS (1978) "Delinquent and Non-Delinquent Males' Pereptions of Their Fathers." *Adolescence* 13 (Spring):21–28.

SNYDER, J. AND G.R. PATTERSON (1987) "Family Interaction and Delinquent Behavior," In H.C. Quay (ed.), *Handbook of Juvenile Delinquency*, pp. 216–43. New York: Wiley.

SORRELLS, J.M. (1977) "Kids Who Kill." *Crime and Delinquency* 23:312–20.

STEINBERG, L. (1986) "Latchkey Children and Susceptibility to Peer Pressure: An Ecological Analysis." *Developmental Psychology* 22(4):433–39.

STEINBERG, L. AND S.B. SILVERBERG (1986) "The Vicissitudes of Autonomy in Early Adolescence." *Child Development* 57:841–51.

STOUTHAMER-LOEBER, M. AND R. LOEBER (1986) "Boys Who Lie." *Journal of Abnormal Child Psychology* 14:551–64.

STRAUS, M.A., R.J. GELLES, AND S.K. STEINMETZ (1981). *Behind Closed Doors: Violence in the American Family.* Garden City, NY: Anchor.

THORNBERRY, T.P. (1987) "Toward an Interactional Theory of Delinquency." *Criminology* 25(4):863–91.

TOLAN, P.H. (1987) "Implications of Age of Onset for Delinquency Risk." *Journal of Abnormal Psychology* 15(1):47–65.

———(1988) "Socioeconomic, Family, and Social Stress Correlates of Adolescent Antisocial and Delinquent Behavior." *Journal of Abnormal Child Psychology* 16(3):317–31.

TOLAN, P.H. AND R.P. LORION (1988) "Multivariate Approaches to the Identification of Delinquency Proneness in Adolescent Males." *American Journal of Community Psychology* 16(4):547–61.

TREMBLAY, R.E., J. MCCORD, H. BOILEAU, P. CHARLEBOIS, C. GAGNON, M. LEBLANC, AND S. LARIVEE (1991) "Can Disruptive Boys Be Helped to Become Competent?" *Psychiatry* 54:148–61.

VAN VOORHIS, P., F.T. CULLEN, R.A. MATHERS, AND C.C. GARNER (1988) "The Impact of Family Structure and Quality on Delinquency: A Comparative Assessment of Structural and Functional Factors." *Criminology* 26(2):235–61.

WALTERS, H.I. AND S.K GILMORE (1973) "Placebo versus Social Learning Effects on Parental Training Procedures Designed to Alter the Behavior of Aggressive Boys." *Behavior Therapy* 4:311–77.

WELLS, L.E. AND J.H. RANKIN (1991) "Families and Delinquency: A Meta-Analysis of the Impact of Broken Homes." *Social Problems* 38(1):71–93.

WERNER, E.E. (1987) "Vulnerability and Resiliency in Children at Risk for Delinquency: A Longitudinal Study from Birth to Young Adulthood." In J.D. Burchard and S.N. Burchard (eds.), *Primary Prevention of Psychology, Vol. 10: Prevention of Delinquent Behavior*, pp. 16–43. Newbury Park, CA: Sage.

WEST, D.J. AND D.P. FARRINGTON (1973) *Who Becomes Delinquent?* London: Heinemann.

———(1977) *The Delinquent Way of Life: Third Report of the Cambridge Study in Delinquent Development.* New York: Crane Russak.

WIDOM, C.S. (1989) "Does Violence Beget Violence? A Critical Examination of the Literature." *Psychological Bulletin* 106(1):3–28.

WILSON, H. (1987) "Parental Supervision Re-Examined." *British Journal of Criminology* 27(3):275–301.

WOLFGANG, M.E., R.M. FIGLIO, AND T. SELLIN (1972) *Delinquency in a Birth Cohort.* Chicago: University of Chicago Press.

ZIGLER, E., C. TAUSSIG, AND K. BLACK (1992) "Early Childhood Intervention: A Promising Preventative for Juvenile Delinquency." *American Psychologist* 47:997–1006.

QUESTIONS FOR DISCUSSION

1. Discuss the circumstances that may be operating in the lives of children most at risk of becoming delinquent.

2. The authors discuss five (5) strategies for strengthening families to reduce the factors that place children at higher risk of becoming delinquent and subsequently moving into adult criminality. List and discuss these factors.

3. If the primary responsibility for preventing delinquency and producing socially competent adults

belongs to parents and families, then what do government and the criminal justice system have to do, ultimately, with the prevention and reduction of crime?

APPLICATIONS

1. Create a list of characteristics that describe a dysfunctional family. Can you identify any families from an earlier period of your life that were dysfunctional? What has happened since then to the children raised in these families? Have the children of these families become criminals or have they subsequently raised dysfunctional families? In your opinion how might we best break this cycle? Discuss with other members of your class.

2. In your opinion, how has the changing role of females and males affected the social organization of the family? How has the economy affected the family? Are these changes desirable? Discuss with other members of your class.

KEY TERMS

authoritarian   favoring the theory that respect for authority is of greater importance than individual liberty; characterized by rigid adherence to conventional values and typically preoccupied with power and control of others that do not share the same preoccupation.

panacea   a cure-all; a remedy for ills or problems.

precursor   something which precedes something else; sets a condition for other things to follow.

predisposes   inclines or makes susceptible in advance.

30
Serious and Violent Juvenile Crime: A Comprehensive Strategy

John J. Wilson
James C. Howell

INTRODUCTION

The Office of Juvenile Justice and Delinquency Prevention (OJJDP) has developed a comprehensive strategy for dealing with serious, violent, and chronic juvenile offenders.[1] This program can be implemented at the state, county, or local levels. The program background, principles, rationale and components are set forth in this article.

Unfortunately, the already stressed juvenile justice system lacks adequate fiscal and programmatic resources to either identify and intervene effectively with serious, violent, and chronic offenders or to intervene immediately and effectively when delinquent conduct first occurs. The Department of Justice and its OJJDP are calling for an unprecedented national commitment of public and private resources to reverse the trends in juvenile violence, juvenile victimization, and family disintegration in our Nation.

Juvenile and Family Court Journal, 1994:3–14. Reprinted by Permission of the Publisher.

BACKGROUND

Serious and violent juvenile crime has increased significantly over the past few years, straining America's juvenile justice system.

Juvenile arrests for violent crimes are increasing. During the period 1983 to 1992, juveniles were responsible for 28% of the increase in murder arrests, 27% of rapes, 27% of robberies, and 17% of aggravated assaults (Snyder, 1994). Most of the increase in violent juvenile crimes during the 10-year period from 1983 to 1992 occurred during the second half of that decade. From 1988 to 1992, juvenile violent crime arrests increased 45%. Increases in juvenile arrests for specific offenses were: murder (52%), rape (17%), robbery (49%), and aggravated assault (47%) (FBI, 1993).

The national scope and seriousness of the youth gang problem have increased sharply since the early 1980s. Gang violence has risen drastically in a number of large cities. Youth gangs are becoming more violent, and gangs increasingly serve as a way for members to engage in illegal money-making activity, including street-level drug trafficking (Spergel et al., 1991).

Evidence continues to mount that a small proportion of offenders commit most of the serious and violent juvenile crimes. About 15% of high risk youth commit about 75% of all violent offenses (Huizinga, Loeber and Thornberry, 1993). Juveniles with four or more court referrals make up 16% of offenders but are responsible for 51% of all juvenile court cases—61% of murder, 64% of rape, 67% of robbery, 61% of aggravated assault, and 66% of burglary cases (Snyder, 1988).

Juvenile court caseloads are increasing, largely as a result of increasing violent delinquency. From 1986 through 1990, the number of delinquency cases disposed by juvenile courts increased 10%. During the same period, juvenile courts disposed of 31% more violent cases, including 64% more homicide and 48% more aggravated assault cases (Snyder, 1993).

Admissions to juvenile detention and corrections facilities are increasing, resulting in crowded facilities with attendant problems such as institutional violence and suicidal behavior. Admissions to juvenile facilities rose after 1984, reaching an all-time high in 1990 with the largest increase in detention (Krisberg et al., 1992). Forty-seven percent of confined juveniles are in detention and correctional facilities in which the population exceeds the facility design capacity. A nationwide study of conditions of confinement in juvenile detention and correctional facilities found crowding to be associated with higher rates of institutional violence, suicidal behavior, and greater reliance on the use of short-term isolation (Parent et al., 1993).

Juvenile cases handled in criminal courts have increased, resulting in increasing numbers of juveniles placed in crowded adult prisons. The number of juvenile cases handled in criminal courts is unknown, but is estimated to be as many as 200,000 in 1990 (Wilson and Howell, 1993). Judicial waivers to criminal court increased 65% between 1986 and 1990 (Snyder, 1993). Between 1984 and 1990, the number of annual admissions of juveniles to adult prisons increased 30% (OJJDP, 1991; 1994).

GENERAL PRINCIPLES

The following general principles provide a framework to guide our efforts in the battle to prevent delinquent conduct and reduce juvenile involvement in serious, violent, and chronic delinquency:

We must strengthen the family in its primary responsibility to instill moral values and provide guidance and support to children. Where there is no functional family unit, a family surrogate should be established and assisted to guide and nurture the child.

We must support core social institutions—schools, religious institutions, and community organizations—in their roles of developing capable, mature, and responsible youth. A goal of each of these societal institutions should be to ensure that children have the opportunity and support to mature into productive law-abiding citizens. A nurturing community environment requires that core social institutions be actively involved in the lives of youth.

We must promote delinquency prevention as the most cost-effective approach to dealing with juvenile delinquency. Families, schools, religious institutions, and community organizations, including citizen volunteers and the private sector, must be enlisted in the Nation's delinquency prevention efforts. These core socializing institutions must be strengthened and assisted in their efforts to ensure that children have the opportunity to become capable and responsible citizens. Communities must take the lead in designing and building comprehensive prevention approaches that address known risk factors and target other youth at risk of delinquency.

We must intervene immediately and effectively when delinquent behavior occurs to successfully prevent delinquent offenders from becoming chronic offend-

ers or progressively committing more serious and violent crimes. Initial intervention efforts, under an umbrella of system authorities (police, intake, and probation), should be centered in the family and other core societal institutions. Juvenile justice system authorities should ensure that an appropriate response occurs and act quickly and firmly if the need for formal system adjudication and sanctions has been demonstrated.

We must identify and control the small group of serious, violent, and chronic juvenile offenders who have committed felony offenses or have failed to respond to intervention and nonsecure community-based treatment and rehabilitation services offered by the juvenile justice system. Measures to address delinquent offenders who are a threat to community safety may include placements in secure community-based facilities or, when necessary, training schools and other secure juvenile facilities.

The proposed strategy incorporates two principal components: (1) preventing youth from becoming delinquent by focusing prevention programs on at-risk youth; and (2) improving the juvenile justice system response to delinquent offenders through a system of graduated sanctions and a continuum of treatment alternatives that include immediate intervention, intermediate sanctions, incorporating restitution and community service when appropriate.

Target Populations

The initial target population for prevention programs is juveniles at risk of involvement in delinquent activity. While primary delinquency prevention programs provide services to all youth wishing to participate, maximum impact on future delinquent conduct can be achieved by seeking to identify and involve in prevention programs youth at greatest risk of involvement in delinquent activity. This includes youth who exhibit known risk factors for future delinquency; drug and alcohol abuse; and youth who have had contact with the juvenile justice

system as nonoffenders (neglected, abused, and dependent), status offenders (runaways, truants, alcohol offenders, and incorrigibles), or minor delinquent offenders.

The next target population is youth, both male and female, who have committed delinquent (criminal) acts, including juvenile offenders who evidence a high likelihood of becoming, or who already are, serious, violent, or chronic offenders.

Program Rationale

What can communities and the juvenile justice system do to prevent the development of and interrupt the progression of delinquent and criminal careers? Juvenile justice agencies and programs are one part of a larger picture that involves many other local agencies and programs that are responsible for working with at-risk youth and their families. It is important that juvenile delinquency prevention and intervention programs are integrated with local police, social service, child welfare, school, and family preservation programs and that these programs reflect local community determinations of the most pressing problems and program priorities.

Establishing community planning teams that include a broad base of participants drawn from local government and the community (e.g., community-based youth development organizations, schools, law enforcement, social service agencies, civic organizations, religious groups, parents, and teens) will help create consensus on priorities and services to be provided as well as build support for a comprehensive program approach that draws on all sectors of the community for participation. Comprehensive approaches to delinquency prevention and intervention will require collaborative efforts between the juvenile justice system and other service provision systems, including mental health, health, child welfare, and education. Developing mechanisms that effectively link these different service providers at the program level will need to be an important component of every community's comprehensive plan.

Risk-focused prevention appears to be the most effective approach to preventing delinquency. The major risk factors are found in the community, family, school, and in the individual and peer group. Prevention strategies will need to be comprehensive, addressing each of the risk factors as they relate to the chronological development of children being served.

Research and experience in intervention and treatment programming suggest that a highly structured system of graduated sanctions holds significant promise. The goal of graduated sanctions is to increase the effectiveness of the juvenile justice system in responding to juveniles who have committed criminal acts. The system's limited resources have diminished its ability to respond effectively to serious, violent, and chronic juvenile crime. This trend must be reversed by empowering the juvenile justice system to provide accountability and treatment resources to juveniles. This includes gender-specific programs for female offenders, whose rates of delinquency have generally been increasing faster than males in recent years, and who now account for 23% of juvenile arrests. It will also require programs for special needs populations such as sex offenders, mentally retarded, emotionally disturbed, and learning disabled delinquents.

The graduated sanctions approach is designed to provide immediate intervention at the first offense to ensure that the juvenile's misbehavior is addressed by the family and community or through formal adjudication and sanctions by the juvenile justice system, as appropriate. Graduated sanctions include a range of intermediate sanctions and secure corrections options to provide intensive treatment that serves the juvenile's needs, provides accountability, and protects the public. They offer an array of referral and dispositional resources for law enforcement, juvenile courts, and juvenile corrections officials. The graduated sanctions component requires that the juvenile justice system's capacity to identify,

process, evaluate, refer, and track delinquent offenders be enhanced.

The Juvenile Justice System

The juvenile justice system plays a key role in protecting and guiding juveniles, including responding to juvenile delinquency. Law enforcement plays a key role by conducting investigations, making custody and arrest determinations, or exercising discretionary release authority. Police should be trained in community-based policing techniques and provided with program resources that focus on community youth.

The traditional role of the juvenile and family court is to treat and rehabilitate the dependent or wayward minor, using an individualized approach and tailoring its response to the particular needs of the child and family, with goals of: (1) responding to the needs of troubled youth and their families; (2) providing due process while recognizing the rights of the victim; (3) rehabilitating the juvenile offender; and (4) protecting both the juvenile and the public. While juvenile and family courts have been successful in responding to the bulk of youth problems to meet these goals, new ways of organizing and focusing the resources of the juvenile justice system are required to effectively address serious, violent, and chronic juvenile crime. These methods might include the establishment of unified family courts with jurisdiction over all civil and criminal matters affecting the family.

A recent NCJFCJ statement succinctly describes the critical role of the court:

> The Courts must protect children and families when private and other public institutions are unable or fail to meet their obligations. The protection of society by correcting children who break the law, the preservation and reformation of families, and the protection of children from abuse and neglect are missions of the Court. When the family falters, when the basic needs of children go unmet, when the behavior of children is destructive and goes unchecked, juvenile and family courts must respond. The Court is

society's official means of holding itself accountable for the well-being of its children and family unit (NCJFCJ, 1993).

A decade ago NCJFCJ developed 38 recommendations regarding serious juvenile offenders and related issues facing the juvenile court system. These issues included confidentiality of the juvenile offender and his or her family, transfer of a juvenile offender to adult court, and effective treatment of the serious juvenile offender (NCJFCJ, 1984). OJJDP recently funded the Council's review of the 38 recommendations for the purpose of updating them and making other modifications that might make them more consistent with the Office's Comprehensive Strategy. However, the 38 recommendations were found to be as valid today as ten years ago and also consistent with the Comprehensive Strategy.

DELINQUENCY PREVENTION

The prevention component of OJJDP's comprehensive strategy is based on a risk-focused delinquency prevention approach (Hawkins and Catalano, 1992). This approach incorporates the public health model that has been used so effectively in combating heart disease. Its premise is that in order to prevent a problem from occurring, the factors (risks) contributing to the development of that problem must be identified and then ways must be found (protective factors) to address and ameliorate those factors.

Hawkins' and Catalano's review of over 30 years of work on risk factors from various fields has identified four major risk factors for juvenile delinquency, substance abuse, school dropout, and teen pregnancy. All these problems share the following common risk factors.

Community. The more available drugs and alcohol are in a community, the higher the risk that young people will use and abuse them. More delinquency and drug problems occur in communities or neighborhoods where people have little attachment to the community, where the rates of vandalism and crime are high and where there is low surveillance of public places. Children who live in a poor, deteriorating neighborhood where the community perceives little hope for the future are more likely to develop problems with delinquency, teen pregnancy, drop out of school.

Family. Children born or reared in a family with a history of criminal activity have a higher risk for delinquency. Poor family management practices, including a lack of clear expectations for behavior, failure to monitor their children, and excessively severe or inconsistent punishment contribute to delinquency and related problems. Child abuse and family violence also increase violent behavior among offspring.

School. Boys who are aggressive in grades K-3 are at higher risk for substance abuse and juvenile delinquency. Reading problems as early as the first grade predict subsequent delinquency. Beginning in the late elementary grades, academic failure increases the risk of both drug abuse and delinquency. A lack of commitment to school is also associated with academic failure.

Individual/Peer. Children who engage in antisocial behavior (misbehaving in school, truancy, fighting) are at increased risk for engaging in drug abuse, dropping out and early sexual activity. Youngsters who associate with peers who engage in a problem behavior are more likely to engage in the same problem behavior. The earlier young people drop out of school, begin using drugs, committing crimes and becoming sexually active, the greater the likelihood that they will have problems with these behaviors later.

To counter these causes and risk factors, protective factors must be introduced. Protective factors are qualities or conditions that moderate a juvenile's exposure to risk. Hawkins and Catalano have organized protective factors into three basic categories: (1) individual characteristics such as a resilient temperament and a positive social orientation; (2) bonding with prosocial family members, teachers, and friends; and (3) healthy beliefs and clear standards for behavior. Hawkins and Catalano have organized these elements in a theory called the "Social Development Model." The theory's main premise is that, to increase bonding, children must be provided with *opportunities* to contribute to their families, schools, peer groups, and communities; *skills* to take advantage of opportunities; and *recognition* for their efforts to contribute. Simultaneously, parents, teachers, and communities need to set clear standards that endorse prosocial behavior.

The risk-focused delinquency prevention approach calls on communities to identify and understand what risk factors their children are exposed to and to implement programs that counter these risk factors. Communities must enhance protective factors that promote positive behavior, health, well-being, and personal success. Effective delinquency prevention efforts must be comprehensive, covering the causes or risk factors described above, and correspond to the social development process.

Effective/Promising Programs

The following are program models and approaches that have been demonstrated to be effective in addressing the major risk factors for delinquency, that look promising, or appear to be theoretically consistent with the "social development model."

Neighborhood and *community* programs include: community policing, safe havens for youth, neighborhood mobilization for community safety, drug-free school zones, community organization-sponsored after-school programs in tutoring, recreation, mentoring, and cultural activities, community and business partnerships, foster grandparents, job training and apprenticeships for youth, neighborhood watch, and victim programs. Community policing can play an important role in creating a safer environment. Community police officers not only help to reduce criminal activity but also become positive role models and establish caring relationships with the youth and families in a community. On-site neighborhood resource teams, composed of community police officers, social workers, health-care workers,

housing experts, and school personnel, can ensure that a wide range of problems are responded to in a timely and coordinated manner. The private-sector business community can make a major contribution through Private Industry Councils and other partnerships by providing job training, apprenticeships, and other meaningful economic opportunities for youth.

The following programs directly address negative *family* involvement factors and how to establish protective factors: teen abstinence and pregnancy prevention, parent effectiveness and family skills training, parent support groups, home instruction programs for preschool youngsters, family crisis intervention services, Court Appointed Special Advocates, surrogate families and respite care for families in crisis, permanency planning for foster children, family life education for teens and parents, and Runaway and Homeless Youth Services.

School-based prevention programs may include: drug and alcohol prevention and education, bullying prevention, violence prevention, alternative schools, truancy reduction, school discipline and safety improvement, targeted-literacy programs in the primary grades. Law-Related Education, after-school programs for latchkey children, teen abstinence-and pregnancy prevention, values development, and vocational training. School prevention programs, including traditional delinquency prevention programs not related to the school's educational mission, can assist the family and the community by identifying at-risk youth, monitoring their progress, and intervening with effective programs at critical times during a youth's development.

Programs designed to support healthy *individual* development and positive *peer* relations include gang prevention and intervention, conflict resolution—peer mediation, peer counseling and tutoring, self-help fellowship for peer groups, individual responsibility training, community volunteer service, competitive athletic team participation, Head Start, Boys and Girls Clubs, scouting, 4-H Clubs, recreational activities, leadership and personal development, health and mental health treatment, and career youth development.

Youth Leadership and Service Programs can provide such opportunities and can reinforce and help internalize in children such positive individual traits as discipline, character, self-respect, responsibility, teamwork, healthy lifestyles, and good citizenship. They can also provide opportunities for personal growth, active involvement in education and vocational training, and life skills development. The components of a Youth Leadership and Service Program may include the following types of program activities: Youth Service Corps, adventure training (leadership, endurance, and team building), mentoring, recreational, summer camp, literacy and learning disability treatment, and Law-Related Education.

The OJJDP has provided assistance to NCJFCJ in implementing risk-focused delinquency prevention planning in conjunction with the prevention priority Council President James Farris established for his presidency. OJJDP provided an orientation in risk focused prevention and resource assessment in conjunction with NCJFCJ's 21st National Conference on Juvenile Justice. This one-day session prepared conference participants to organize delinquency prevention planning efforts for possible funding under the Fiscal Year 1994 appropriation of $13 million for OJJDP's Title V Delinquency Prevention Program.

The training session on the "Communities That Care" strategy informed participants how to take the lead in organizing their communities to compete for delinquency prevention program funds. Awards will be made to units of local government in 1994 through the state agencies administering Juvenile Justice and Delinquency Prevention Act formula grant funds. Applicants must include a three-year plan describing the extent of risk factors identified in the community and how these risk factors will be addressed through prevention programs.

Beginning in April, a series of training events for local participants in risk focused prevention will be provided around the country. The first event is an orientation for key community leaders, including judges, prosecutors, lead law enforcement officers, mayors, school superintendents, business leaders, and other civic leaders. The second event is a three-day training session on risk and resource assessment for community planning teams, to provide a foundation for development of comprehensive risk-focused delinquency prevention plans necessary to secure funding under the OJJDP Title V program. These training events will be organized by the state agencies administering the JJDP Act formula grant program, and are to be provided in up to 45 sites across the nation to 5,000 participants during the spring and summer of this year.

GRADUATED SANCTIONS

An effective juvenile justice system program model for the treatment and rehabilitation of delinquent offenders is one that combines accountability and sanctions with increasingly intensive treatment and rehabilitation services. These graduated sanctions must be wide-ranging to fit the offense and include both intervention and secure corrections components. The intervention component includes the use of immediate intervention and intermediate sanctions, and the secure corrections component includes the use of community confinement and incarceration in training schools, camps, and ranches.

Each of these graduated sanctions components should consist of sublevels, or gradations, that together with appropriate services constitute an integrated approach. The purpose of this approach is to stop the juvenile's further penetration into the system by inducing law-abiding behavior as early as possible through the combination of appropriate intervention and treatment sanctions. The juvenile justice system must work with law enforcement, courts, and corrections to develop reasonable, fair, and humane sanctions.

At each level in the continuum, the family must continue to be integrally involved in treatment and rehabilitation efforts. Aftercare must be a formal component of all residential placements, actively involving the family and the community in supporting and reintegrating the juvenile into the community.

Programs will need to use Risk and Needs Assessments to determine the appropriate placement for the offender. Risk assessments should be based on clearly defined objective criteria that focus on: (1) the seriousness of the delinquent act, (2) the potential risk for re-offending, based on the presence of risk factors; and (3) the risk to the public safety. Effective risk assessment at intake, for example, can be used to identify those juveniles who require the use of detention as well as those who can be released to parental custody or diverted to nonsecure community-based programs. Needs assessments will help ensure that: (1) different types of problems are taken into account when formulating a case plan; (2) a baseline for monitoring a juvenile's progress is established; (3) periodic reassessments of treatment effectiveness are conducted; and (4) a system-wide data base of treatment needs can be used for the planning and evaluation of programs, policies, and procedures. Together, risk and needs assessments will help to allocate scarce resources more efficiently and effectively. A system of graduated sanctions requires a broad continuum of options.

For intervention efforts to be most effective, they must be swift, certain, consistent, and incorporate increasing sanctions, including the possible loss of freedom. As the severity of sanctions increases, so must the intensity of treatment. At each level, offenders must be aware that, should they continue to violate the law, they will be subject to more severe sanctions and could ultimately be confined in a secure setting, ranging from a secure community-based juvenile facility to a training school camp, or ranch.

The juvenile court plays an important role in the provision of treatment and sanctions. Probation has traditionally been viewed as the court's main vehicle for delivery of treatment services and community supervision. However, traditional probation services and sanctions have not had the resources to effectively target delinquent offenders, particularly serious, violent, and chronic offenders.

The following graduated sanctions are proposed within the intervention component.

Immediate intervention. First-time delinquent offenders (misdemeanors and nonviolent felonies) and nonserious repeat offenders (generally misdemeanor repeat offenses) must be targeted for system intervention based on their probability of becoming more serious or chronic in their delinquent activities. Nonresidential community-based programs, including prevention programs for at-risk youth, may be appropriate for many of these offenders. Such programs are small and open, located in or near the juvenile's home, and maintain community participation in program planning, operation, and evaluation. Community police officers, working as part of Neighborhood Resource Teams, can help monitor the juvenile's progress. Other offenders may require sanctions tailored to their offense(s) and their needs to deter them from committing additional crimes.

The following programs apply to these offenders: Neighborhood Resource Teams, diversion, informal probation, school counselors serving as probation officers, home on probation, mediation (victims), community service, restitution, day-treatment programs, alcohol and drug abuse treatment (outpatient), and peer juries.

Intermediate sanctions. Offenders who are inappropriate for immediate intervention (first-time serious or violent offenders) or who fail to respond successfully to immediate intervention as evidenced by re-offending (such as repeat property offenders or drug-involved juveniles) would begin with or be subject to intermediate sanctions. These sanctions may be nonresidential or residential.

Many of the serious and violent offenders at this stage may be appropriate for placement in an intensive supervision program as an alternative to secure incarceration. OJJDP's Intensive Supervision of Probationers Program Model is a highly structured, continuously monitored individualized plan that consists of five phases with decreasing levels of restrictiveness:

(1) Short-Term Placement in Community Confinement; (2) Day Treatment; (3) Outreach and Tracking; (4) Routine Supervision; and (5) Discharge and Follow-up.

Other appropriate programs include: drug testing, weekend detention, alcohol and drug abuse treatment (inpatient), challenge outdoor, community-based residential, electronic monitoring, and boot camp facilities and programs.

Secure corrections. Large congregate-care juvenile facilities (training schools, camps, and ranches) have not proven to be particularly effective in rehabilitating juvenile offenders. Although some continued use of these types of facilities will remain a necessary alternative for those juveniles who require enhanced security to protect the public, the establishment of small community-based facilities to provide intensive services in a secure environment offers the best hope for successful treatment of those juveniles who require a structured setting. Secure sanctions are most effective in changing future conduct when they are coupled with comprehensive treatment and rehabilitation services.

Standard parole practices, particularly those that have a primary focus on social control, have not been effective in normalizing the behavior of high-risk juvenile parolees over the long-term, and consequently, growing interest has developed in intensive aftercare programs that provide high levels of social control and treatment services. OJJDP's Intensive Community-Based Aftercare for High-Risk Juvenile Parolees Program provides an effective aftercare model.

The following graduated sanctions strategies are proposed within the Secure Corrections component:

Community confinement. Offenders whose presenting offense is sufficiently serious (such as a violent felony) or who fail to respond to intermediate sanctions as evidenced by continued re-offending, may be appropriate for community confinement. Offenders at this level represent the more serious (such as repeat felony drug trafficking or property offenders) and violent offenders among the juvenile justice system correctional population.

The concept of community confinement provides secure confinement in small community-based facilities that offer intensive treatment and rehabilitation services. These services include individual and group counseling, educational programs, medical services, and intensive staff supervision. Proximity to the community enables direct and regular family involvement with the treatment process as well as a phased re-entry into the community that draws upon community resources and services.

Incarceration in training schools, camps, and ranches. Juveniles whose confinement in the community would constitute an ongoing threat to community safety or who have failed to respond to community-based corrections may require an extended correctional placement in training schools, camps, ranches, or other secure options that are not community-based. These facilities should offer comprehensive treatment programs for these youth with a focus on education, skills development, and vocational or employment training and experience. These juveniles may include those convicted in the criminal justice system prior to their reaching the age at which they are no longer subject to the original or extended jurisdiction of the juvenile justice system.

Transfer to the criminal justice system. Public safety concerns are resulting in increasing demands for transfer of the most violent juvenile offenders to the criminal justice system. These demands will grow as long as American society perceives juveniles to present a disproportionate threat to the public safety. Although state legislatures are increasingly excluding certain categories of juvenile offenders from the jurisdiction of the juvenile court, judicial waiver holds the most promise as the mechanism for determining that a particular juvenile cannot be rehabilitated in the juvenile justice system. This consideration should be paramount, consistent with the original aims of the juvenile justice system and the juvenile court.

Effective/Promising Programs

Recent reviews of all known experimental evaluations of treatment programs have identified effective program approaches (Lipsey 1992). Interventions that appear to be the most effective include highly structured programs providing intensive treatments over extended periods of time. Juvenile justice system programs that have been effective in treating and rehabilitating serious, violent, and chronic juvenile offenders include intensive supervision programs; day treatment and education programs operated by Associated Marine Institutes (AMI); the Florida Environmental Institute's (FEI) wilderness camp for juveniles who would otherwise be sent to adult prisons; and intensive family-based, multisystemic therapy (MST) programs, which have been effective with serious juvenile offenders in several localities. OJJDP's Violent Juvenile Offender Program demonstrated that most violent juvenile offenders could be successfully rehabilitated through intensive treatment in small secure facilities. OJJDP has also developed an intensive after-care model designed to successfully reintegrate high-risk juvenile parolees back into the community.

NCJFCJ has completed a nationwide assessment of promising and effective juvenile justice system programs under OJJDP's new "what works" series. Nearly 1,000 program models were identified. These have been computerized in Pittsburgh, at NCJJ. A comprehensive report is being prepared for Department of Justice distribution.

Under a competitive award, the National Council on Crime and Delinquency (NCCD) is currently reviewing program models to identify the most effective/promising ones for local jurisdictions in implementing OJJDP's Comprehensive Strategy. This review will include programs reported to be effective in the NCJJ "what works" project. The main product of the NCCD program development work: an operations manual, including a blueprint for assessing their present juvenile justice system and for planning new programs that respond to community needs; and a collection of effective promising programs, from which jurisdictions can choose, for implementation.

At the same time, new-program models are under development. For example, OJJDP has supported NCJFCJ's development of a domestic violence program model for early intervention in families troubled by domestic violence. This program model, which will complement OJJDP's Comprehensive Strategy, will incorporate policies, programs and practices that serve to coordinate the efforts of police, court, social service agencies, schools and child protective services in addressing domestic violence through early intervention. This domestic violence model will help preclude the onset of serious, violent and chronic juvenile offending.

EXPECTED BENEFITS

Jurisdictions that implement OJJDP's Comprehensive Strategy can expect the following benefits:

- **Delinquency prevention.** Effective delinquency prevention will result in fewer children entering the juvenile justice system in demonstration sites. This would, in turn, permit concentration of system resources on fewer delinquents, thereby increasing the effectiveness of the graduated sanctions component and improving the operation of the juvenile Justice system.
- **Increased juvenile justice system responsiveness.** This program will provide additional referral and dispositional resources for law enforcement, juvenile courts, and juvenile corrections. It will also require these system components to increase their ability to identify, process, evaluate, refer, and track juvenile offenders.
- **Increased juvenile accountability.** Juvenile offenders will be held accountable for their behavior, decreasing the likelihood of their development into serious, violent, or

chronic offenders and tomorrow's adult criminals. The juvenile justice system will be held accountable for controlling chronic and serious delinquency while also protecting society. Communities will be held accountable for providing community-based prevention and treatment resources for juveniles.

- **Decreased costs of juvenile corrections.** Applying the appropriate graduated sanctions and developing the required community-based resources should reduce significantly the need for high-cost beds in training schools. Savings from the high costs of operating these facilities could be used to provide treatment in community-based programs and facilities.

- **Increased responsibility of the juvenile justice system.** Many juvenile offenders currently waived or transferred to the criminal justice system could be provided for intensive services in secure community-based settings or in long-term treatment in juvenile training schools, camps, and ranches.

- **Increased program effectiveness.** As the statistical information presented herein indicates, credible knowledge exists about who the chronic, serious, and violent offenders are, that is, their characteristics. Some knowledge also exists about what can effectively be done regarding their treatment and rehabilitation. However, more must be learned about what works best for whom under what circumstances to intervene successfully in the potential criminal careers of serious, violent, and chronic juvenile offenders. Follow-up research and rigorous evaluation of programs implemented as part of this strategy should produce valuable information.

- **Crime reduction.** The combined efforts of delinquency prevention and increased juvenile justice system effectiveness in intervening immediately and effectively in the lives of delinquent offenders should result in measurable decreases in delinquency in sites where the above concepts are demonstrated. In addition, long-term reduction in crime should result from fewer serious, violent, and chronic delinquents becoming adult criminal offenders.

NEXT STEPS

Implementing this comprehensive strategy for serious, violent, and chronic juveniles is a major program priority for OJJDP. Awards were made to two jurisdictions last year for community-wide assessment and planning toward implementing the strategy. The Office anticipates awarding competitive grants to two more jurisdictions in fiscal year 1994 to carry out the assessment, planning, and implementation process. Training and technical assistance will be provided to participating communities. Additional resources are expected to be available in fiscal year 1995 to support further implementation of the Comprehensive Strategy.

NOTES

1. OJJDP has developed the following definitions of serious, violent, and chronic juvenile offenders for purposes of this program. *Serious juvenile offenders* are those adjudicated delinquent for committing any felony offense, including larceny or theft, burglary or breaking and entering, extortion, arson, and drug trafficking or other controlled dangerous substance violations. *Violent juvenile offenders* are those serious juvenile offenders adjudicated delinquent for one of the following felony offenses—homicide, rape or other felony sex offenses, mayhem, kidnapping, robbery, or aggravated assault. *Chronic juvenile offenders* are juveniles adjudicated delinquent for committing three or more delinquent offenses. These definitions include juveniles convicted in criminal court for particular offense types.

REFERENCES

FEDERAL BUREAU OF INVESTIGATION. (1993). *Uniform Crime Reports: 1993.* Washington, D.C.: U.S. Department of Justice.

HAWKINS, DAVID, AND RICHARD CATALANO, JR. (1992). *Communities That Care.* San Francisco: Jossey-Bass.

HUIZINGA, DAVID, ROLF LOEBER, AND TERENCE THORNBERRY. (1993). *Urban Delinquency and Substance Abuse: Initial Findings Report.* Washington, D.C.: OJJDP.

KRISBERG, BARRY, ET AL. (1992) *National Juvenile Custody Trends 1978–1989.* Washington, D.C.: OJJDP.

LIPSEY, MARK W. "What Do We Learn From 400 Research Studies on the Effectiveness of Treatment with Juvenile Delinquents?" Presented at the 1992 What Works Conference, University of Salford, Great Britain, September 1992.

NATIONAL COUNCIL OF JUVENILE AND FAMILY COURT JUDGES. (1984). *Children and Families First, A Mandate for Change.* Reno, Nevada. NCJFCJ.

———(1984). "The Juvenile Court and Serious Offenders: 38 Recommendations." *Juvenile and Family Court Journal.*

OFFICE OF JUVENILE JUSTICE AND DELINQUENCY PREVENTION. *Juveniles Taken Into Custody: Fiscal Year 1990 Report.* Washington, D.C.: OJJDP, September 1991.

———(1994). *Juveniles Taken Into Custody: Fiscal Year 1992 Report.* Washington, D.C.: OJJDP.

PARENT, DALE, ET AL. *Conditions of Confinement: A Study to Evaluate Conditions in Juvenile Detention and Corrections Facilities.* Final report submitted to the OJJDP. April 1993.

SNYDER, HOWARD. (1988). *Court Careers of Juvenile Offenders.* Washington, D.C.: OJJDP.

———. et al. (1993). *Juvenile Court Statistics: 1990.* Washington, D.C.: OJJDP.

———. (1994). *Are Juveniles Driving the Violence Trends?* OJJDP Fact Sheet.

———. et al. (1993). *Arrests of Juveniles 1991.* Washington, D.C.: OJJDP.

SPERGEL, IRVING, ET AL. (1991). *Youth Gangs: Problems and Response.* Final Report submitted to OJJDP. See the "Executive Summary," Stage 1: Assessment.

WILSON, JOHN J. AND JAMES C. HOWELL (1993). *A Comprehensive Strategy for Serious, Violent, and Chronic Juvenile Offenders.* Washington, D,C.: OJJDP.

QUESTIONS FOR DISCUSSION

1. There are six indicators, presented by the authors, that juvenile crime has increased significantly in frequency and seriousness. List and discuss these indicators.

2. Five general principles are presented as a framework to guide efforts at preventing and reducing juvenile delinquency. List and discuss these principles.

3. According to the authors, juvenile delinquency, substance abuse, school dropout, and teen pregnancy share a common set of four risk factors. List and discuss these risk factors.

4. List and discuss several programs that may be effective when addressing each of the four identified risk factors.

5. What are the expected benefits of OJJDP's Comprehensive Strategy? In your opinion, will this approach be effective?

APPLICATIONS

1. It is important for juvenile delinquency prevention programs to integrate with law enforcement, social services, child welfare, schools, and the family. You have been asked, as an expert, to make fifteen recommendations for the prevention of juvenile delinquency. List and explain these recommendations.

2. What steps can be taken to curtail the continuing disintegration of the family? Discuss with other class members what steps each of you might take in your own families.

KEY TERMS

ameliorate   to make better or to improve.

mediation   intervention; the attempt to bring about a peaceful solution between people involved in a dispute.

multisystemic   refers to several systems or variables impacting a particular occurrence or event.

surrogate   a person or thing that is substituted for another person or thing.

31

Emerging Trends and Issues in Juvenile Justice

Michael F. Aloisi

The juvenile justice system is experiencing a period of uncertainty and has been for some time now. Since about the middle 1960s, when juvenile arrests went soaring, there have been attacks on the system's ineffectiveness and its failure in meeting the goals of its *parens patriae* philosophy—protecting children. Many states have modified their juvenile justice codes since the 1970s in response to perceived shortcomings of the system. These changes reflect competing visions of what the system should look like and the interests and purposes it ought to serve. While states struggle to achieve the reforms pronounced in the late 1960s, many feel constrained by a need to deal more effectively with violent and chronic juvenile offenders. The future direction of the juvenile justice system, in short, remains unclear.

One unwelcome result of recent (and conflicting) trends has been a bifurcated response to juveniles centered in legislative change. Policymakers in most states have been reluctant

From Correctional Theory and Practice, Edited by Clayton A. Hartjen and Edward E. Rhine 1992:235–252. Reprinted by Permission of Nelson-Hall Publishing.

to give up the *parens patriae* vision and rehabilitative focus toward minor offenders and nonoffenders. At the same time, there is a clear trend toward viewing the serious and chronic offender as a willing perpetrator rather than as a youthful victim of circumstance (Shireman & Reamer, 1986, pp. 1–30). Consequently, policymakers increasingly view juvenile justice system "clients" in two very different ways—children to be helped and protected versus offenders to be punished or from whom the community must be protected. Responses are shaped accordingly. I will argue that this situation has had a negative impact on the system.

RECENT DELINQUENCY TRENDS

Juvenile justice policy decisions and the day-to-day decisions of system actors are shaped by broader contexts. Economic, political, organizational, and philosophical considerations play an important role in these deliberations (Mahoney, 1987; McGarrell, 1988). Changing perceptions of the extent of juvenile involvement in crime, especially violent crime (and, more recently, drug violations), have had a clear impact on legislation and policy reform. The fear of crime among the public (sometimes more, sometimes less realistic) remains high.

Juvenile arrests soared in the 1960s and continued to increase well into the 1970s, fueled in part by a growing youth population. A look at the fifteen-year period from 1960 to 1974 reflects the enormity of the rise (U.S. Department of Justice, 1975). Juvenile arrests rose nearly 140 percent. The increase was slightly greater for the generally more serious index offenses. For violent index offenses alone (murder, manslaughter, rape, robbery, and aggravated assault) arrests rose by a staggering 254 percent. Then, as now, serious violent crime accounted for a small portion of all juvenile arrests, not more than 5 percent. Such serious offending was and continues to be troubling, nonetheless.

The steep rise in juvenile arrests leveled off and began to decline in the mid-1970s. More recently, juvenile arrests continued to decline during the ten year period of 1979 through 1988. This included a 17 percent drop in arrests for index offenses, with a 7 percent decline for serious violent offenses (U.S. Department of Justice, 1989, p. 172). However, arrests increased somewhat between 1984 and 1988. During that five year period, total juvenile arrests rose 6 percent, while arrests for index offenses increased 5 percent (with a 9 percent rise for violent index offenses).

Juvenile populations began to decline in the mid-1970s and have continued to decline (Cook & Laub, 1987, p. 124). Taking population change into account, juvenile arrest *rates* peaked in 1974 and have declined more recently (Cook & Laub, 1987, pp. 114–118; Strasburg, 1984, pp. 8–12). The pattern for violent index rates, however, has generally persisted at, or near, the relatively high level of 1974.

A NATIONAL FOCUS ON JUVENILE JUSTICE

Widespread dissatisfaction with the discrepancy between juvenile justice goals (foremost, the rehabilitative ideal) and the actual operation of the system led to what some have called a revolution in juvenile justice that has spanned over twenty years. The federal government has taken an active role throughout this period in the revolution and "counterrevolution" we have experienced.

The year 1967 was a focal point for change. This was the year of the highly-influential President's Commission Report. Later that year came the landmark Gault decision extending due process rights in juvenile court proceedings (President's Commission on Law Enforcement and the Administration of Justice, 1967).[1]

Central to the reform agenda of the President's Commission Report were four reforms that have come to be known as the 4Ds: diversion from formal system handling, decriminalization of status offenses (e.g., running away from home), deinstitutionalization (development of noninstitutional alternatives to training schools), and extension of due process rights. These four strategies continue to inform public policy today, although in modified form. Each of these reforms reflected a growing skepticism about the fairness and effectiveness of the juvenile justice system's attempt to deal with troubled youths. In large part, they reflected a belief that involvement in the system might do more harm than good.

While the report viewed the process of formal delinquency adjudication as a last resort and sought community-based responses where possible, it also suggested that the juvenile court should not have an "exclusive preoccupation" with rehabilitation (1967, p. 81). Instead, it called for the "frank recognition" of society's claim to protection and the condemnation of unacceptable behavior, in cases reaching this formal stage. This recognition of a punitive response, in turn, provides a rationale for mandating the extension of basic principles of due process in juvenile court.

The President's Commission Report, along with the Gault decision (and the recommendations of a series of government and private commission reports that have followed), precipitated a wave of national and state legislative reform. The reform goals were fundamental to the Juvenile Justice and Delinquency

Prevention Act of 1974. Its passage reflected the federal government's resolve to encourage states' implementation of the ideas of the reform movement. Among other things, the JJDP Act tied federal grants to state compliance with its call to deinstitutionalize status offenders and non-offenders (i.e., dependent and neglected youths) and to remove juveniles from adult jails and institutions.

There has been substantial but uneven movement toward achieving these reform goals, with some modification in recent amendments to the JJDP Act. Almost all state legislatures have moved to create a nondelinquent status offender designation (e.g., juveniles or children in need of supervision, "JINS" or "CHINS") for juveniles who commit acts that would not be considered criminal if committed by adults (e.g., incorrigibility, truancy, running away) (King, 1987, pp. 14–20; Rubin, 1986, p. 26). There has, as a result, been a significant decline in the national rate of status offense dispositions in juvenile court (Miller, 1986, p. 113). Incarceration of status offenders has also dropped markedly, with a large majority of states now considered to be in full compliance with the JJDP Act's deinstitutionalization mandate. The call for deinstitutionalization in *delinquency* cases, however, has met with more mixed results with great variation from state to state in their continued utilization of large training schools.

Also, there has been extensive development of diversion programs nationwide for less serious offenses, at both the police and the court levels, to avoid potential stigmatization of formal court involvement and to focus resources on more serious offenders. A number of formal programs, however, initiated with federal funds in the early 1970s, notably youth service bureaus, began to disappear after federal funding ceased. Finally, states have widely extended due process rights in juvenile court, a few even allowing jury trials.

Despite the gains, some argue that this reform movement has had its "down side." For example, diversion critics feel that diversion, while it may help juveniles avoid stigmatization that can be associated with court involvement,

often leads to a "widening of the net" of social control (Austin & Krisberg, 1981). That is, diversion programs are likely to handle (or refer for further services) juveniles who otherwise would have been simply released from the formal system.

The decriminalization of status offenders has come under increasing criticism. Although status offenders are much less likely to be found in detention centers or training schools today, there is evidence that the reform movement resulted in the relabeling and placement of many youths in private mental health and other child care institutions. (Lerman, 1980; Shireman & Reamer, 1986, pp. 136–139). Thus, Weithorn suggests, the result has been, not deinstitutionalization, but "transinstitutionalization," substituting often unnecessary hospital stays for commitments to training schools (Weithorn, 1988).

A separate critique is that the deinstitutionalization of status offenders has left a void in the care of troubled juveniles, especially where alternative services have been slow to develop, following the lead of the earlier deinstitutionalization movement in mental health (McCorkell, 1987, pp. 22–30). The well-publicized exodus of mentally ill patients from state mental institutions in the 1960s and 1970s is judged by many to have contributed to the ranks of the homeless in many urban areas. This is because cities failed to respond by developing the hoped for network of community-based mental health services.

A major focus has been the difficulty in providing adequate care for runaways within the present policy environment (Regnery, 1984). Going beyond the issue of deinstitutionalization of status offenders, several highly regarded national groups have recommended that status offense cases be totally removed from the juvenile court's jurisdiction. Only a few states (e.g., Washington, Pennsylvania) have actually abolished or seriously curtailed court jurisdiction over these cases, leaving responsibility for care in the hands of private or government human service agencies. Critics argue that the loss of the court's threat of coercion, even if largely symbolic in status offense cases, is a serious mistake. They argue, further, that in this policy void juveniles have been left to the exigencies of the streets—often leading to sexual victimization and other serious threats to health and safety of chronic runaways (Kearon, 1989). Certainly, the human service community has been slow to fill the void. The issue continues to be hotly debated (Bea rrows, 1987).

A SHIFT IN FOCUS: "GETTING TOUGH"

The main focus of the nationwide reform movement in juvenile justice in the mid-1960s and early 1970s was on first-time and minor offenders, status offenders, and nonoffenders. These federal efforts at reform largely failed to directly address a rising concern throughout the nation—what to do with serious, violent and repetitive juvenile offenders.[2] Beginning in the late 1970s and continuing in recent years, widespread state legislative reform has rushed to fill the void. By 1979, at least six states (California, Florida, New York, Colorado, Delaware and Washington) had legislated a more punitive response to the serious juvenile offender (Smith, Alexander, Kemp, & Lemert, 1980). With adoption of its Juvenile Offender Law in 1978, New York became perhaps the most dramatic example at that time of the rejection of the *parens patriae* approach. Among its provisions were:

> automatic placement in criminal court, long sentences, mandated secure confinement, low age jurisdiction, and overall community protection emphasis. (McGarrell, 1988, p. 178)

Since that time, many other states have either adopted or introduced various "get tough" policies for serious juvenile offenders (Miller, 1986, pp. 106–110). While the concept of rehabilitation and concern for the juvenile's welfare remains central to the juvenile system in the great ma-jority of states, many now see it as only one of several legitimate purposes to be served by the juvenile justice system (e.g., protection of the community, punishment or accountability).

The *new* reform agenda was spurred on by several catalysts: continuing high rates of violent crime; continuing reports that rehabilitative efforts were, largely, failing; and research that, for the first time, revealed the extent of the chronic offender problem. The influential cohort study of Philadelphia youths conducted by Wolfgang and his colleagues found that 6 percent of the cohort had five or more contacts with the police. These "chronic delinquents" were responsible for 52 percent of the cohort's police contacts and 63 percent of the contacts for UCR index offenses (Wolfgang, Figlio, & Sellin, 1972). Research following cohorts into adulthood reveals that many of them go on to commit offenses as adults (U.S. Department of Justice, 1985a, p. 20; Wolfgang, Thornberry, & Figlio, 1987, p. 33).[3]

States' "get tough" strategies have taken several forms with two main goals: removing certain categories of juveniles from the jurisdiction of the juvenile court and decreasing the broad discretion of judges and other juvenile justice personnel. All states have some provision through which specified juveniles can be transferred to adult criminal court. Juvenile offenders are transferred to criminal courts primarily through statutes that mandate exclusion of certain offenses from the juvenile court's jurisdiction and through judicial waiver of serious and/or repetitive offenders.

Over the past fifteen years or so, almost every state has either made it easier to waive cases, lowered the age of judicial waiver, or excluded additional offenses from jurisdiction (Hamparian, 1987, p. 134). As of 1987, eighteen states excluded certain serious offenses from juvenile court jurisdiction; 48 states have judicial waiver provisions tied to particular offenses and prior offense history (US. Department of Justice, 1988a, p. 79). It should be pointed out, though, that handling serious and repetitive (including violent) offenders through waiver and other transfer provisions continues to be the exception and not the rule.

Since the late 1970s, a number of states have initiated mandatory minimum terms of incarceration or minimum lengths of stay, or developed presumptive sentencing guidelines (Krisberg, Schwartz, Litsky, & Austin, 1986, p. 9; U.S.

Department of Justice, 1988a, p. 95). Finally, several states (most notably, Washington) have modified the purpose clause of their juvenile codes to reflect increased concern for the goal of holding juveniles accountable for their offenses (Hamparian, 1987, p. 135). The clear emphasis of the recently issued "Model Code," developed under OJJDP funding, is accountability (Rossum, Koller, & Manfredi, 1987).

SOME APPARENT CONSEQUENCES OF "GETTING TOUGH"

The "get tough" policies emerging in recent years appear to have contributed to two trends: rising public custody rates for juveniles and the increasingly disproportionate number of minorities held in public institutions.

National youth populations have been declining since the early 1970s. More recently, there was a drop of over 1.5 million juveniles "at risk" between 1983 and 1987 (U.S. Department of Justice, 1986a, 1988b). In addition as we saw earlier, juvenile arrest rates for serious offenses have dropped or stabilized (for serious violent offenses) since the mid-1970s. Yet, there were 53,503 juveniles held across the country in public juvenile facilities on the day of OJJDPs 1987 Children in Custody Census. This is a 10 percent increase over 1983 (and a 24 percent increase over 1979). The figure represents the highest population in juvenile public facilities since the census began in 1971. The juvenile custody rate (208 per 100,000 juveniles) was up 18 percent.

If we focus on long-term institutional settings only (including training schools), the increase over 1983 was just over 8 percent. In addition, the volume of juvenile admissions to public facilities was up approximately 13 percent, the highest since 1977.

There is some indication that increasing numbers of juveniles in custody are there on less serious offenses. The number held for serious, violent offenses dropped 8 percent between 1985 and 1987; the number for serious property offenses was down by 2 percent. The number held for alcohol or drug law violations, however, increased significantly.

A second apparent consequence of the "get tough" policies, the increasingly disproportionate incarceration of minorities, is of special concern. According to the latest OJJDP Children in Custody report, the 1987 one-day count showed minorities comprising 56 percent of the training school and detention center populations. While the nonminority population remained practically unchanged from 1985 to 1987, the number of minorities in custody increased by 17 percent. Further, since 1979 the minority population in custody has increased by more than half, alongside a slight increase for nonminorities. Krisberg and his colleagues estimated that blacks, in 1982, were more than four times as likely to be incarcerated as white non-Hispanics; Hispanics were nearly three times as likely. This disparity had grown in the 1980s (Krisberg et al., 1987, pp. 183–187).

"WATERSHEDS" AND "BELLWETHERS"

The current period in juvenile justice has been described as a "watershed" with much at stake concerning its future direction (Krisberg et al., 1986). The national trend seems to be toward greater punitiveness, departing from much of the reform agenda of the 1960s and early, 1970s. Certainly, the federal government's focus has moved on to how to more effectively identify and handle the serious and chronic juvenile offender. Many states, as we have seen, have facilitated transfers of the most serious juvenile cases to adult court and provide for determinate or, at least, more punitive dispositions.

In addition, there are isolated calls for abolishing the juvenile court. More common are efforts to narrow the jurisdiction of the court (i.e., remove the most serious cases, as well as status offenders, and abuse and neglect cases) and limit judicial discretion. Washington State's 1977 Juvenile Justice Code most closely embodies this "criminalized" model of the juvenile court (Moore, 1987, pp. 53–55).

Finally, the principle of using the "least restrictive alternative" in delinquency dispositions (a reflection of the earlier reform movement) is considered by some to be dead, replaced by the new call words of just deserts and accountability (Hurst, 1982, p. 62; Moore, 1987, pp. 117–121).

The current juvenile justice scene, however, is far from one dimensional, with no clear "winner" in a battle between advocates of the earlier reform movement and the more recent reform agenda of the 1980s. While some call for a court almost indistinguishable from adult criminal court, others call for the development of a comprehensive family court with expansive authority or influence over juveniles, families, and community institutions (Moore, 1987).

Although more punitive legislation has increased the use of incarceration, overall, states vary greatly in their incarceration practices. For example, among the fifty states and the District of Columbia, the highest rates of commitment to juvenile public facilities in 1987 (based on one-day counts) were found in Washington, D.C. (330 per 100,000), Nevada (288), and California (284). Among the lowest were Massachusetts (16), Utah (21), West Virginia (47), and Pennsylvania (55).[4]

A number of other states have moved to follow the lead of Massachusetts and Utah in either closing or drastically reducing the use of large state institutions, favoring development of a network of community-based programming for juveniles. Blackmore and colleagues describe the "decarceration" process under way in several "bellwether" states that have taken a lead role in what is considered a crucial and progressive direction for change (Blackmore, Brown, & Krisberg, 1988). These states include Colorado, Louisiana, Oklahoma, Oregon, and Pennsylvania. Pennsylvania, for example, (like Massachusetts and Utah) relies heavily on a network of private agencies to provide community-based residential and nonresidential services for juveniles. It provides fiscal incentives for counties by providing a state reimbursement to counties of 75 percent for a range of community-based dispositional services and detention alternatives (up to a set county appropriation cap) (Juvenile Delinquency Commission, 1990b).

Other states have, likewise, taken this route.

Delaware has, in a short period of time, reduced its institutional male population from 250 to 70, with further reductions expected (Juvenile Delinquency Commission, 1990b). Correctional placements have been replaced by a comprehensive network of community-based programs that include group homes, specialized foster care, tracking, and intensive supervision programs.

A BIFURCATED RESPONSE TO JUVENILES IN TROUBLE

In addition to juvenile justice policies that vary from state to state, many states maintain an uneasy mix of policies side by side, with no unifying rationale for how they view juveniles in trouble with the law or for how they structure their responses. Rather than choose one set of goals or strategies over the other, it appears that states have attempted to incorporate these competing visions in their juvenile codes and to implement them in their court practices. A bifurcated (or divided) approach to different categories of court-involved youth is, unfortunately, the result.

Minor delinquent offenders and status offenders tend to be looked upon, largely, as victims of circumstances beyond their control, along the lines of the turn of the century juvenile court philosophy. Therefore, the court attempts to understand the social context leading to the juvenile's problem behavior (increasingly viewed in terms of family dysfunction). The court, finally, seeks a community response to remediate the problems through diversion, or it maintains the case under minimal supervision in the community, sometimes providing or ordering the delivery of services.

At the same time, the serious offender (e.g., having committed a violent or property "felony" offense) or the repetitive offender is seen not as a victim but as a willing victimizer in need of punishment or of being held accountable for breaking the law. Ironically, although many chronic offenders are more likely to have been the "victims" of an array of undesirable circumstances or to experience greater skills deficits than many minor offenders, the court is less prone to acknowledge limited "blame-worthiness" for them. The vision of the most serious offenders is not conducive to seeking truly rehabilitative interventions. Rather, the focus is on transfer to adult court, mandatory sanctions, or longer training school sentences.

As we saw, earlier, however, states vary greatly in their espousal of the "get tough" movement and in the degree to which they entertain this split image of delinquent behavior.[5] Nevertheless, there is often a clear distinction between the family and community, focus for minor offenders and the image of the serious and chronic wrongdoer in need of punishment. The split image is reflected in the way the recently revised Pennsylvania juvenile code distinguishes between the "delinquent child" and the "dangerous juvenile offender" (Juvenile Court Judges' Commission, 1988).

The split in how juvenile justice systems see juveniles in trouble with the law has some, it would appear, undesirable consequences. By focusing formal court proceedings on "willing perpetrators" of crime, the court has been "criminalized." Taken in concert with the extension of many due process rights to juveniles, this approach potentially facilitates the demise of a separate juvenile justice system. At the least, the bifurcated approach paves the way for increasingly punitive responses and increases the likelihood that more serious offenders will be incarcerated (McGarrell, 1988, pp. 180–181). In addition, despite an escalation in response for serious offenders, it is likely that many minor offenders never get the message, early on, that what they have done is wrong and unacceptable to the community or the system fails to identify and address real needs. In either case, their chances of returning to court have certainly not been diminished (Barnum, 1987).

In place of a bifurcated approach, a more integrated vision of the delinquent youth along with a more integrated system response is required. One such approach would both hold juveniles across the range of offending responsible for their actions *and* commit the system to contributing to juveniles' future growth into healthy and productive adults. Delinquent (and related problem) behavior would be under-

stood in terms of individual decisions that are both, in some sense, freely made and influenced by a wide range of factors—internal to the individual, part of the individual's immediate environment (e.g., family, school, and peers), and the results of broader societal forces (Aloisi, 1984; Gottfredson, 1982).

In essence, this is a call to see delinquent youths as both children and offenders, simultaneously. This means that accountability has an important place across the range of offending. One important potential payoff is a rehabilitative one—if punishment is fairly administered. Barnum suggests that while punishment may not instill a sense of guilt,

> it may still inform the offender of the wrongfulness of his actions and underscore his responsibility for it…The right solution to the confusion about punishment and treatment is to use both (1987, pp. 74–75, 77).

What this integrated approach also means is tempering the court's coercive response with the goal of serving the special helping purpose of the juvenile justice system, that is, rehabilitation. Zimring suggests two rationales for the more lenient handling of juveniles within a, primarily, accountability context (1978, pp. 71–81). First, regardless of the seriousness of the offense, the court needs to take into account the relative "immaturity" of adolescent decision making. An additional and even more fundamental point is that the court's response should take into account that adolescence is a crucial period of growth:

> One purpose of mitigating the harshness of punishment for young offenders is to enhance the opportunity to survive adolescence without a major sacrifice in life chances…Social policy toward the young offender should be designed, as much as practical, not to diminish the individual's chances to make that transition successfully (Zimring, 1978, pp. 88–89.)[6]

Consistent with this approach, Maloney, Romig, & Armstrong (1988) advance what they call "the balanced approach" to juvenile justice. This approach attempts to reconcile the seemingly incompatible values that have caused the "pendulum swings" in federal government and state legislative initiatives and system response in recent decades. The approach would require a balancing of the following, objectives: community protection, accountability, and rehabilitation, specifically in the form of competency life skills) development (1988, pp. 5–8). It would pull the juvenile justice pendulum more to the center away from both a single-minded "get tough" approach and a one-sided rehabilitative bias.

A CONTINUUM OF CARE AND ACCOUNTABILITY

For this integrated vision to have an impact on juvenile justice practice, there needs to be in place a more comprehensive continuum of dispositional options than is currently available in most jurisdictions. This wide range of response must integrate concerns for both care and accountability to allow the juvenile court to truly provide for the most appropriate response for each case. A wide range of dispositional options is already allowed by law in many states (National Conference of State Legislatures, 1988). Yet, while it may exist statutorily, many jurisdictions are still faced with the limited choice of "traditional supervision or training school" in practice.

An adequate continuum of response would provide "alternatives to incarceration" for at least some of the more serious and even violent juvenile offenders. In abandoning its use of large training schools, Massachusetts has replaced them with a diverse network of highly individualized options—very small secure treatment programs for the more violent and serious juvenile offenders and a large number of highly structured community-based programs. These community-based programs include group homes, foster homes, a forestry camp, and, for those not requiring residential placements, day treatment programs (providing daily structure and supervision) and outreach and tracking programs providing intensive supervision for juveniles in the community (Krisberg, Austin, & Steele, 1989, pp. 3–6).

A number of other "alternatives to incarceration" have been suggested for juvenile offenders (and utilized in various jurisdictions) including restitution, intensive probation supervision, electronic monitoring, and intermittent or short-term confinement. For example, restitution (financial restitution to the victim or unpaid community service or service to the victim) has been offered as a viable alternative that can both serve accountability purposes and rehabilitate (U.S. Department of Justice, 1985b). According to one researcher, restitution shows promise in reducing recidivism (Schneider, 1986).

While many speak in terms of "alternatives to incarceration," an adequate continuum of care and accountability might better be conceptualized in terms of the development of an array of "intermediate responses."[7] While some alternatives may be appropriate for more serious or chronic offenders, other options are needed at the "lower end of the spectrum," in terms of the type of juvenile offender and his or her needs as well as the degree of restrictiveness of control or intensity of treatment services required.

It is becoming clear that implementing a network of community-based options is one of the most difficult chores facing the juvenile justice system. For example, despite the strong commitment of the "bellwether" states mentioned earlier to avoid the use of large state training schools and develop community-based options, these states have had varying degrees of difficulty (once they have begun to "decarcerate") putting into place the desired array of community-based programs (Blackmore, Brown, & Krisberg, 1988). The difficulties are largely fiscal, although political and competing philosophical visions also impede development.

EXPERIENCES IN ONE STATE— NEW JERSEY'S BIFURCATED APPROACH

New Jersey substantially revised its juvenile justice code at the end of 1983. Along with the new code, a Family Court was created through constitutional amendment. The amendment consolidated jurisdiction over a diverse collection of family matters under one court, making possible a more unified approach to all family law matters (Juvenile Delinquency Commission, 1986, pp. 38–39).

An important thrust of the legislation, was a new emphasis on the family and its contributing role in delinquency and other juvenile problem behavior. A major reform reflecting this focus involved how status offenses were to be viewed and handled. No longer was this type of behavior to be seen as an offense. Rather, "status offenses" were to be treated as "juvenile-family crisis" situations. In addition, in lieu of being handled by the court (except as a last resort), newly created family crisis intervention units (FCIUs) in each county were to provide crisis intervention counseling for the juvenile and family, with referral to community service agencies where appropriate. The large majority of cases handled by FCIUs concern family conflict, truancy, or running away (although they also handle other types of cases such as those involving a threat to a child's safety or minor delinquency charges).

Since their inception, FCIUs have been a successful diversion mechanism. The state's Administrative Office of the Courts recently reported that FCIUs are petitioning only about 11 percent of their cases for a family court hearing (Administrative Office of the Courts, 1989).

The increased family focus was, however, only part of a dual reform agenda. The code's bifurcated approach is reflected in the following statement:

> This bill recognizes that the public welfare and the best interests of juveniles can be served most effectively through an approach which provides for harsher penalties for juveniles who commit serious acts or who are repetitive offenders, while broadening family responsibility and the use of alternative dispositions for juveniles committing less serious offenses. (Juvenile Delinquency Commission, 1986, p. 14).[8]

"Get tough" measures of the code included provisions to facilitate "waiver" or transfer to adult court. The code expanded the range of offenses and circumstances that can lead to waiver. It also shifted the burden of proof of amenability to treatment to the defense: the defense attorney must now show that rehabilitation is feasible before the age of nineteen.

In addition to revisions concerning waivers, the code provided extended incarceration terms for juveniles meeting certain criteria. For example, the court can sentence a juvenile to an extended term beyond the maximum provided by the code (the maximum for murder is twenty years) if he or she had been adjudicated on two separate occasions for first or second degree offenses and was previously committed to a state correctional facility. The maximum extended term is an additional five years in the case of murder. (Despite code provisions, use of waiver and extended terms continues to be very limited.)

An additional reform involved the expansion of a range of dispositional options open to judges (to 20) along, with a call for an increased local role in providing community-based dispositional responses. Not unlike many other states, New Jersey has seen only limited progress in putting into place the local programs and services that would implement the broad range of options allowed by law, despite the creation of local planning and coordinating agencies to establish need and foster program development (Juvenile Delinquency Commission, 1988, pp. 59–61). One major impediment has been that state government has provided limited funding to push the process ahead. To date, county or municipal governments have been provided little incentive to take over responsibility of dispositional options that have largely fallen to state government in the past.

To partially fill the void, the Department of Corrections (DOC) has created a broad network of state-run community-based group homes and day treatment centers for juvenile offenders, serving more than seven hundred juveniles. Despite these new programs, training school populations have not declined. In fact, despite a decline in juvenile arrests in the 1980s, the average number of juveniles under the jurisdiction of the department rose by more than half (Juvenile Delinquency Commission, 1990a).[9]

CONCLUSION

Incarceration of juveniles has increased in recent years despite the fact that serious juvenile crime has apparently stayed somewhat stable. The broad development and acceptance of a wide range of community-based alternatives to incarceration (both residential and non-residential) seems unlikely within the context of what was described as a bifurcated approach.

This seems more likely to occur within the context of a more integrated vision of juvenile crime and juvenile justice that attempts to accommodate accountability concerns along with the traditional (and pragmatic) concern to contribute to juveniles' growth into healthy and productive adults. By maintaining a clear link between minor and serious/chronic juvenile offenders, a more coherent rationale can be offered to eschew or minimize responses to the more troubling juvenile offenders that, in many cases, may be inappropriate. Such inappropriate responses include giving up on the rehabilitative goal and transferring to the adult system, or incarcerating when some other response will adequately hold a particular juvenile accountable, protect the community, and not unduly interfere with future opportunities for growth.

NOTES

1. Dissatisfaction with the operation of the juvenile system predated these national initiatives. For example, revision of juvenile codes to provide many of the procedural safeguards later to be guaranteed in Supreme Court cases had already appeared in California (1961) and New York (1962) (McGarrell, 1988, p. 7).

2. A policy shift, however, is evident on the federal level in recent years. This includes both a call for the federal government to take a lead role in developing policies focusing on serious, violent, and chronic offenders, and to modify, earlier JJDP Act initiatives (see Krisberg, 1986, pp. 7–10).

3. According to Hamparian and her colleagues, three quarters of the violent and chronic offenders became adult offenders. Tracy, Wolfgang, & Figlio (1985), found that 45 percent of the chronic juvenile offenders went on to become chronic offenders as adults.

4. Commitment rates have been compiled utilizing 1987 information provided by OJJDP. A more discrete breakout of data is provided in their October 1988

Bulletin (U.S. Department of Justice, 1988b). The custody rates above include commitments only, for training schools, ranches, camps, farms and halfway houses/group homes.

5. Armstrong and Altschuler (1982) note the divergent strategies apparent in the handling of serious and violent juvenile offenders across the country.

6. As a result, Zimring argues for a juvenile dispositional policy that includes a presumption against secure confinement for juveniles adjudicated delinquent on property offenses (including most first- and second-time offenders) (1978, pp. 88–89).

7. One emphasis has been on providing a range of intermediate sanctions or punishments between "ordinary" probation and incarceration (see Morris & Tonry, 1990). Yet, broadening the concept to include clearly rehabilitative responses for juveniles seems appropriate. As was alluded to earlier, while we sometimes "overrespond" by incarcerating youths inappropriately (at times because we cannot provide an adequate treatment setting, e.g., intensive mental health services), we also "underrespond" in less serious cases by not taking the opportunity to show juveniles that there are consequences to their behavior. In addition, and perhaps more important, at times we wait too long to respond with "treatment," whether that means counseling, drug treatment or providing for much-needed job skills or other life skills development.

8. This is a quote of a Senate Judiciary Committee statement in February 1982.

9. Juvenile arrests in New Jersey dropped 26 percent from 1980 to 1989. Arrests for index offenses declined, as well (–35 percent), although there was a small increase of 5 percent for violent index offenses (murder, rape, robbery, and aggravated assault) (Juvenile Delinquency Commission, 1990c). Arrests for these serious violent offenses, however, had risen a substantial 73 percent from 1977 to 1983 (the year New Jersey's revised code legislation was passed). This may have contributed to concerns "get tough" in the early 1980s. In the most recent period (1985-1989), however, even arrests for violent index offenses have dropped (–16 percent).

REFERENCES

ADMINISTRATIVE OFFICE OF THE COURTS. (1989). *Report on Juvenile-Family Crisis Intervention Units*, Trenton, NJ: Administrative Office of the Courts.

ALOISI, MICHAEL. (1984). *Chronological age and the differential impact of social and personality factors in adolescent delinquency.* Unpublished doctoral dissertation, Rutgers University, New Brunswick, New Jersey.

ARMSTRONG, TROY, & ALTSCHULER, DAVID. (1982). Conflicting trends in juvenile justice sanctioning: Divergent strategies in the handling of the serious juvenile offender. *Juvenile and Family Court Journal, 33(4),* 15–30.

AUSTIN, JAMES, & KRISBERG, BARRY. (1981). Wider, stronger and different nets: The dialectic of criminal justice reform. *Journal of Research in Crime and Delinquency, 18* 165–196.

BARNUM, RICHARD. (1987). The development of responsibility: Implications for juvenile justice. In Francis X. Hartmann (ed.), *From children to citizens, Vol. 2: The role of the juvenile court.* New York: Springer-Verlag.

BEARROWS, THOMAS. (1987). Status offenders and the juvenile court: Past practices, future prospects. In Francis X. Hartmann (Ed.), *From children to citizens, Vol. 2: The role of the juvenile court.* New York: Springer-Verlag.

BLACKMORE, JOHN, BROWN, MARCI, & KRISBERG, BARRY. (1988). *Juvenile justice reform: The bellwether states.* Ann Arbor, MI: Center for the Study of Youth Policy.

COOK, PHILIP, & LAUB, JOHN. (1987). Trends in child abuse and juvenile delinquency. In Francis X. Hartmann (Ed.), *From children to citizens, Vol. 2: The role of the juvenile court.* New York: Springer-Verlag.

GOTTFREDSON, MICHAEL. (1982). The social scientist and rehabilitative crime policy. *Criminology, 20,* 29–42.

HAMPARIAN, DONNA. (1987). Violent juvenile offenders. In Francis X. Hartmann ED., *From children to citizens, Vol. 2: The role of the juvenile court.* New York: Springer-Verlag.

HURST, HUNTER. (1982). Issues for resolution in the eighties: Family courts and retribution. *Today's Delinquent, 1* 57–68.

JUVENILE COURT JUDGES' COMMISSION. (1988) *The juvenile act.* Harrisburg, PA: Juvenile Court judges' Commission.

JUVENILE DELINQUENCY COMMISSION. (1986). *The impact of the New Jersey Code of Juvenile Justice.* Trenton, NJ: Juvenile Delinquency Commission.

JUVENILE DELINQUENCY COMMISSION. (1988) *Juvenile justice—Toward completing the unfinished agenda.* Trenton, NJ: Juvenile Delinquency Commission.

JUVENILE DELINQUENCY COMMISSION. (1990a, February 16). Juvenile correctional populations: Looking back at the eighties. *JDC Clearinghouse* Trenton, NJ: Juvenile Delinquency Commission.

Juvenile Delinquency Commission. (1990b, April 6). A backyard dialogue. *JDC Clearinghouse.* Trenton, NJ: Juvenile Delinquency Commission.

JUVENILE DELINQUENCY COMMISSION. (1990c, June 1). Looking back—Juvenile crime in the '80s. *JDC Clearinghouse.* Trenton, NJ: Juvenile Delinquency Commission.

KEARON, WILLIAM. (1989). Deinstitutionalization and abuse of children on our streets. *Juvenile and Family Court Journal, 40(1),* 21–26.

KING, JANET. (1987). *A comparative analysis of juvenile codes.* Champaign, IL: Community Research Associates.

KRISBERG, BARRY, AUSTIN, JAMES, & STEELE, PATRICIA. (1989).

Unlocking juvenile corrections: Evaluating the Massachusetts Department of Youth Services. San Francisco: National Council on Crime and Delinquency.

KRISBERG, BARRY, SCHWARTZ, IRA, FISHMAN, GIDEON, EISIKOVITS, ZVI, GUTTMAN, EDNA, & JOE, KAREN. (1987). The incarceration of minority youth. *Crime and Delinquency, 33,* 173–205.

LERMAN, PAUL. (1980). Trends and issues in the deinstitutionalization of youths in trouble. *Crime and Delinquency, 26,* 81–298.

MAHONEY, ANNE RANKIN. (1987) *Juvenile justice in context.* Boston: Northeastern University Press.

MALONEY, DENNIS, ROMIG, DENNIS & ARMSTRONG, TROY. (1988). Juvenile probation: The balanced approach. *Juvenile & Family Court Journal, 39,* 1–63.

MCCORKELL, JOHN. (1987). The politics of juvenile justice in America. In Francis X. Hartmann (Ed.), *From children to citizens, Vol. 2: The role of the juvenile court.* New York: Springer-Verlag.

MCGARRELL, EDMUND. (1988). *Juvenile Correctional reform: Two decades of policy and procedural change.* Albany: State University of New York Press.

MILLER, MARC. (1986). Changing legal paradigms in juvenile justice. In Peter W. Greenwood (Ed.), *Intervention strategies for chronic juvenile offenders.* New York: Greenwood Press.

MOORE, MARK HARRISON. (1987). *From children to citizens, Vol. 1: The mandate for juvenile justice.* New York: Springer-Verlag.

MORRIS, NORVAL, & TONRY, MICHAEL.(1990, January/February). Between prison and probation—Intermediate punishments in a rational sentencing system. *NIJ Reports* pp. 8–10.

NATIONAL CONFERENCE OF STATE LEGISLATURES (CRIMINAL JUSTICE PROGRAM). (1988, July). Legal dispositions and confinement policies for delinquent youth. *State Legislative Report,* p 13.

PRESIDENT'S COMMISSION ON LAW ENFORCEMENT AND ADMINISTRATION OF JUSTICE. (1967). *The challenge of crime in a free society.* Washington DC: U.S. Government Printing Office.

REGNERY, ALFRED. (1984) *Runaway children and the juvenile justice and delinquency prevention act: What is the impact? (Introduction).* Washington DC: U.S. Government Printing Office.

ROSSUM, RALPH, KOLLER, BENEDICT, & MANFREDI, CHRISTOPHER. (1987) *Juvenile justice reform: A model for the states.* The Rose Institute of State and Local Government; The American Legislative Exchange Council. Claremont McKenna College.

RUBIN, SOL. (1986) *Juvenile offenders and the juvenile justice system.* New York: Oceana.

SCHNEIDER, ANNE. (1986). Restitution and recidivism rates of juvenile offenders: Results from four experimental studies. *Criminology, 24,* 533–552.

SHIREMAN, CHARLES, & REAMER, FREDERIC. (1986). *Rehabili-*

tating juvenile justice. New York: Columbia University Press.

SMITH, CHARLES, ALEXANDER, PAUL, KEMP, GARRY, & LEMERT, EDWIN. (1980). *A national assessment of serious juvenile crime and the juvenile justice system. The need for a rational response, Vol. III: Legislation, jurisdiction, program interventions, and confidentiality of juvenile records.* Washington DC: U.S. Department of Justice.

STRASBURG, PAUL. (1984). Recent national trends in serious juvenile crime. In Robert A. Mathias et al. (Eds.), *Violent juvenile offenders, An anthology.* Newark, NJ: National Council on Crime and Delinquency.

TRACY, PAUL, WOLFGANG, MARVIN, & FIGLIO, ROBERT. (1985). *Delinquency in two birth cohorts: executive summary.* Washington DC: U.S. Department of Justice.

U.S. DEPARTMENT OF JUSTICE, BUREAU OF STATISTICS. (1986a). *Children in custody, 1982–83: Census of juvenile detention and correctional facilities.* Washington DC: Government Printing Office.

U.S. DEPARTMENT OF JUSTICE, BUREAU OF STATISTICS. (1986b). *Children in custody, public juvenile facilities, 1985.* Washington DC: Government Printing Office.

U.S. DEPARTMENT OF JUSTICE, BUREAU OF STATISTICS. (1988a). *Report to the nation on crime and justice.* (2nd ed.) Washington DC: Government Printing Office.

U.S. DEPARTMENT OF JUSTICE, FEDERAL BUREAU OF INVESTIGATION. (1975). *Crime in the United States: Uniform crime reports.* Washington DC: Government Printing Office.

U.S. DEPARTMENT OF JUSTICE, FEDERAL BUREAU OF INVESTIGATION. (1989). *Crime in the United States: Uniform crime reports.* Washington DC: Government Printing Office.

U.S. DEPARTMENT OF JUSTICE, OFFICE OF JUVENILE JUSTICE AND DELINQUENCY PREVENTION. (1985a). *The young criminal years of the violent few.* Washington, DC: Government Printing Office.

U.S. DEPARTMENT OF JUSTICE, OFFICE OF JUVENILE JUSTICE AND DELINQUENCY PREVENTION. (1985b). *Guide to juvenile restitution.* Washington, DC: Government Printing Office.

U.S. DEPARTMENT OF JUSTICE, OFFICE OF JUVENILE JUSTICE AND DELINQUENCY PREVENTION. (1988b). *Children in custody: Public juvenile facilities, 1987* Washington, DC: U.S. Government Printing Office.

WEITHORN, LOIS. (1988). Mental hospitalization of troublesome youth: An analysis of skyrocketing admission rates. *Stanford Law Review, 40,* 773–838.

WOLFGANG, MARVIN, FIGLIO, ROBERT, & SELLIN, THORSTEN. (1972). *Delinquency in a birth cohort.* Chicago: University of Chicago Press.

WOLFGANG, MARVIN, THORNBERRY, TERENCE, & FIGLIO, ROBERT. (1987). *From boy to man, from delinquency to crime.* Chicago: University of Chicago Press.

ZIMRING, FRANKLIN. (1978) *Confronting youth crime: Report of the Twentieth Century Fund Task Force on sentencing policy toward young offenders (background paper).* New York: Holmes and Meier.

QUESTIONS FOR DISCUSSION

1. Because of the discrepancy between juvenile justice goals and the actual operations of the system, a revolution in juvenile justice has occurred over the past twenty years. Describe some major features of this revolution.

2. What have been the results of "getting tough" with juvenile offenders? Provide examples to support your response.

3. Many states have approached juvenile justice with a bifurcated response or an "uneasy mix of policies" that are inconsistent and irrational. What are the major problems with this type of response?

4. What are the advantages of creating policies regarding juvenile justice that are more integrated and/or balanced? Provide examples to support your answer.

APPLICATIONS

1. What other kinds of approaches might criminal justice agencies take to quell the increases in juvenile crime, particularly violent crime? Discuss with other class members.

2. Are families or criminal justice agencies responsible for curtailing juvenile crime? What may be several effective and long-term solutions to controlling juvenile crime?

KEY TERMS

amenability refers to being responsive or in agreement with a suggestion or condition.

cohort peers; those belonging to the same group.

espousal the adoption of or the taking up of a cause.

exigencies refers to pressing needs or requirements.

presumption a legal inference as to the existence or truth of a fact not certainly known, which is drawn from the known or proved existence of some other fact.

stigmatization refers to being socially disgraced; looked upon with disdain.